D1691236

WINDOW DESIGN

daab

Architects / Designers	Location	City	Page
INTRODUCTION			4
A69 – Architects (Boris Redčenkov Prokop Tomášek, Jaroslav Wertig)	House, Frantiskovy Lazne	Czech Republic	16
Miquel Adria, Isaac Broid, Michel Rojkind	National Videotheque	Mexico City	22
Aldinger & Aldinger	Bezirksärztekammer	Stuttgart	26
arge Weingart Bauer Bracke Hoffmann Architekten	Public Library Suhl	Suhl	32
Barclay & Crousse Architecture	Casa Equis	Canete	38
Bearth + Deplazes Architekten	House Meuli	Unterdorf / Fläsch	44
Behnisch & Partner	Akademie der Künste	Berlin	50
Bernardo Bader	House Salgenreuthe	Krumbach	54
Bernd Kniess Architekten Stadtplaner	Galery ads1a	Cologne	60
Bevk Perovic Architects	SB House	Ljubljana	68
Aldo Celoria	Casa Travella	Castel San Pietro	74
Central de Arquitectura	Dumas + Horacio	Mexico City	78
Moongyu Choi + ga.a architects	booksea publishing	Kyunggi	82
	taehaksa publishing	Kyunggi	88
Christoph Mäckler Architekten	dmc2	Hanau-Wolfgang	92
	Office building Eschersheimer Landstraße 6	Frankfurt am Main	98
	House Knipp	Bad Homburg	102
	Torhaus Westhafen	Frankfurt am Main	108
Rafael de la Hoz	District C of Telefónica	Las Tablas, Madrid	114
Degelo Architekten	St.-Alban-Ring	Basel	120
Dekleva Gregorič Arhitekti	House XXS	Ljubljana	124
Dellekamp Arquitectos	AR 58	Colonia Condesa, Mexico City	130
Max Dudler with Bernhard Meoller	Diocese library	Muenster	136
Max Dudler with Nina Barthélémy	Living house and atelier	Weimar	142
Enno Schneider Architekten	Police Authorities Mettmann	Mettmann	146
Feilden Clegg Bradley Architects LLP	Westfield Student Village, Queen Mary, University of London	London	152
FKL architects	Brick House	Dublin	156
Franken Architekten	Home Couture	Berlin	160
Andreas Fuhrimann, Gabrielle Hächler	Architect's and artist's house	Foot of the Üetliberg, Zurich	164
	Pavilion at Riesbach harbour	Riesbach harbour in Zurich	172
glöggler prevosti architektur	Double one-family house Almigried	Walchwil	178
	One-family house in the field	Baar	184
	One-family house Munk	Huenenberg	190
Peter Haimerl, studio für architektur	Black House	Krailling	198

Architects / Designers	Location	City	Page
Hascher Jehle Architektur	LSV Office Building	Landshut	204
HENN Architekten	Gläserne Manufaktur of Volkswagen	Dresden	212
Hofmann Keicher Ring Architekten	Weingut am Stein	Würzburg	218
Ingenhoven Architekten	Production building Gira	Radevormwald	224
Johnston Marklee & Associates	Sale House	Venice	232
Andreas Kanzian	Practice Dr. med. Wilhem Pintar	Stainach, Steiermark	238
Ken Architekten	One-family house	Möriken	244
Kengo Kuma & Associates	LVMH Omotesando	Tokyo	250
	LVMH Osaka	Chuo	254
Marcio Kogan	Du Plessis House	Paraty, Rio de Janero	258
KSP Engel und Zimmermann	1. Police Station Frankfurt	Frankfurt	262
Kuba, Pilař Architekti	Omega Department Store	Brno	266
Lab Architecture Studio	Federation Tower	Melbourne	270
Léon Wohlhage Wernik Architekten	Administrative center of social alliance Germany	Berlin	276
Mansilla Tunón	Contemporary Art Museum of Castila and León, Musac	León	282
Irie Masayuki	Hotel Andon Ryokan	Tokyo	286
Jaime Varon, Abraham Metta, Alex Metta, Migdal Arquitectos	Las Flores Corporate	Mexico City	290
Miyahara architect office	House TTN	Tokyo	296
Neil M. Denari Architects, nmda	MUFG Private Banking Office	Nagoya	300
Nike Fiedler Architekten	Speisessaal „Symposion" der Evang. Akademie Bad Boll	Bad Boll	306
oehler faigle Archkom	Office building JUWI	Bonlanden	314
Valerio Olgiati	Yellow House Museum	Flims	318
Ostoshenka Architects	Panorama House	Moscow	324
Procter:Rihl	Slice House	Porto Alegre	330
raumzeit	Youth hostel Bremen	Bremen	336
Rojkind Arquitectos	PR34 House	Mexico City	342
Sauerbruch Hutton Architekten	GSW Administrative Center	Berlin	348
	Fire and Police Station for the Government District	Berlin	352
Tham & Videgård Hansson Arkitekter	Two family house Kanoten	Danderyd	358
	House K	Stocksund	364
	House Karlsson	Västerås	370
Isay Weinfeld Arquitetura	Casa Marrom	São Paulo	376

Index 382

Imprint 384

INTRODUCTION

Windows serve as the direct interface between the interior of a building and its public environment. Visual relationships through a window offer the opportunity to establish contact with the outside world and experience the widest variety of impressions. This view can drift over the expanse of the countryside, or one can peer into the deep gorges that are the streets of a pulsating city while hearing the rush of the traffic. In Alfred Hitchcock's classic film "Rear Window", bedridden journalist Jeff uses the limited field of vision provided by his window to peer at the window across from his, and a voyeuristic tale unfolds, complete with perspectives into and from crime.

Today, windows are more than protection and a filter for light, weather and noise. They form the frame around real images, and characterize the face of buildings. The design of a window also always gives away something about the inhabitants of a building. Insights into the interior reveal what is assumed to be private or serve the extroverted staging of new product and lifeworlds. The scope ranges from the small opening with a scenographic direction of view to a complete glass skin offering total transparency.

This diversity is inseparable from the development of glass as a building material. At the beginning of our common era, windows were still simple openings in the walls that were bridged by relieving arches. It was only after the possibility of industrially manufacturing flat glass panes that windows became sources of light in previously gloomy interiors or richly-colored images in religious buildings. Yet also innovations in fittings technology as well as in the use of new and custom-made materials have enabled new types of windows.

In recent architectural history, windows emphasizing seeing and being seen have melted the border between interior and exterior and led to a new interpretation of the concept of a room. The search of humans for security and openness, for privacy and publicity, or for order and diversity, can be read in the eyes of a building. This book presents a series of remarkable solutions for this issue. It focuses on a number of selected examples from various areas that document a wide spectrum, record current trends and offer inspiration.

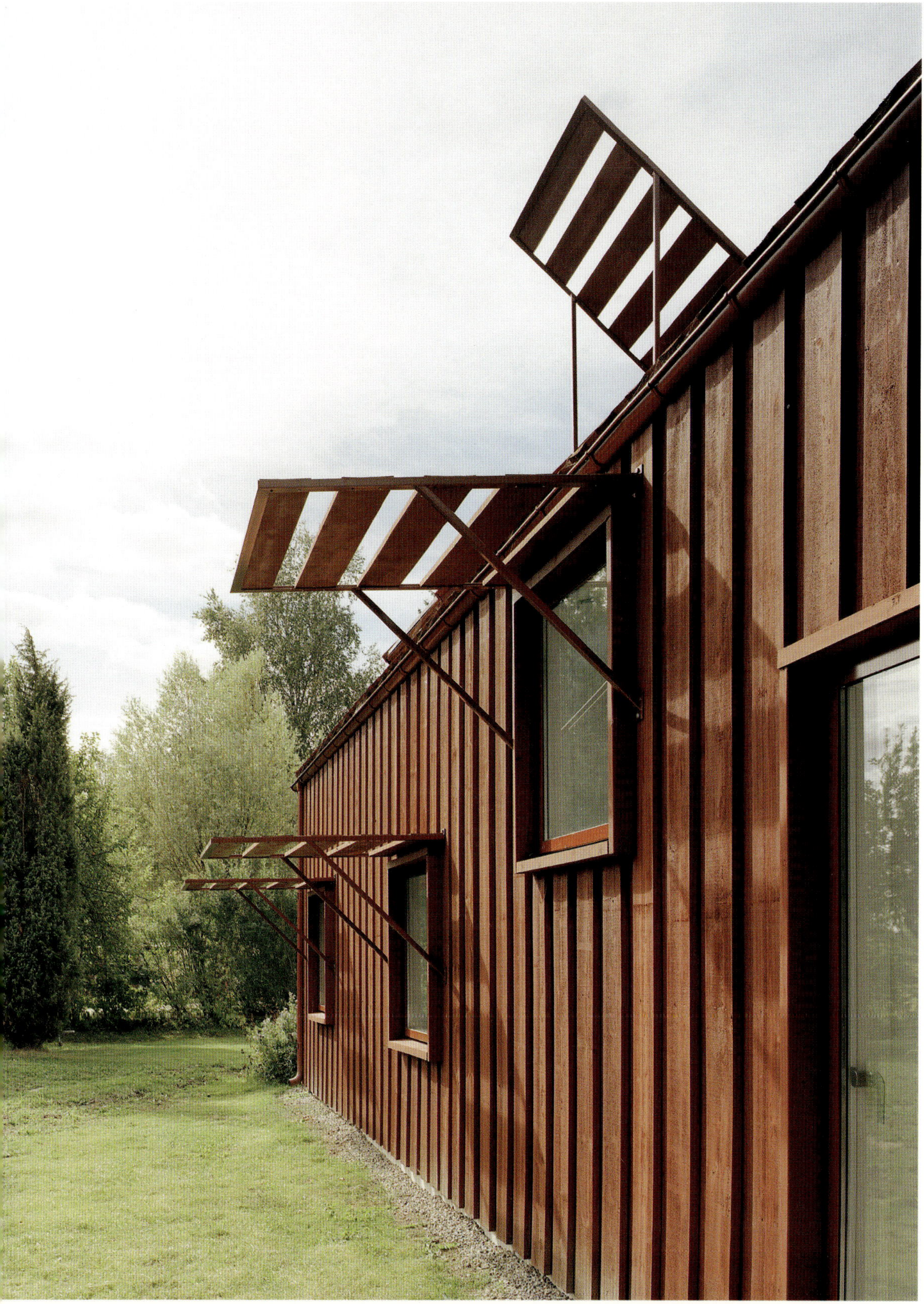

Fenster bilden die unmittelbare Schnittstelle vom Inneren eines Hauses zur öffentlichen Umgebung. Blickbeziehungen durch ein Fenster bieten die Möglichkeit, Kontakt zur Aussenwelt aufzunehmen, um verschiedenste Eindrücke zu erleben. Der Blick kann in die Weite der Landschaft schweifen oder es bietet sich der Ausblick in die tiefen Straßenschluchten einer pulsierenden Stadt und man hört den Verkehr rauschen. Der an das Bett gefesselte Journalist Jeff beobachtet in Alfred Hitchcocks Filmklassiker „Das Fenster zum Hof" durch sein eingeschränktes Blickfeld das Fenster vis á vis und es entspinnt sich eine voyeuristische Episode mit kriminalistischen Ein- und Ausblicken.

Fenster sind heute mehr als ein Schutz und Filter gegen Licht, Klima und Lärm. Sie sind der Rahmen für reale Bilder und prägen das charakteristische Gesicht von Häusern. Das Design der Fenster verrät auch immer etwas über die Bewohner eines Hauses. Einsichten in das Innere legen vermeintlich Privates offen oder dienen der extrovertierten Inszenierung von neuen Produkt- und Lebenswelten. Die Bandbreite reicht von der kleinen Öffnung mit einer szenografischen Führung des Blickes, bis hin zur kompletten Glashaut mit totaler Transparenz.

Diese Vielfalt ist untrennbar mit der Entwicklung des Baustoffes Glas verbunden. Zu Beginn unserer Zeitrechnung waren Fenster noch einfache Öffnungen im Mauerwerk, die von Entlastungsbögen überbrückt wurden. Erst mit der Möglichkeit zur handwerklichen Fertigung von flachen Glasscheiben wurden Fenster zu Lichtquellen in bislang düsteren Innenräumen und zu farbenprächtigen Bildern in Sakralbauten. Aber auch die Innovationen in der Beschlagtechnik sowie die Anwendung von neuen Materialien und custom-made Werkstoffen haben neue Fenstertypen ermöglicht.

Fenster zum Sehen und Gesehenwerden haben in der jüngeren Baugeschichte die Grenze von innen und außen verschmelzen lassen und zur Neuinterpretation des Raumbegriffes geführt. Die Suche der Menschen nach Geborgenheit und Offenheit, nach Privatheit und Öffentlichkeit oder nach Ordnung und Vielfalt lässt sich an den Augen eines Hauses ablesen. In diesem Buch wird eine Reihe bemerkenswerter Lösungsangebote zu dieser Fragestellung dokumentiert. Es handelt sich um eine Reihe von ausgewählten Beispielen aus verschiedenen Bereichen, die eine große Bandbreite dokumentieren, aktuelle Tendenzen aufzeigen und Inspiration bieten.

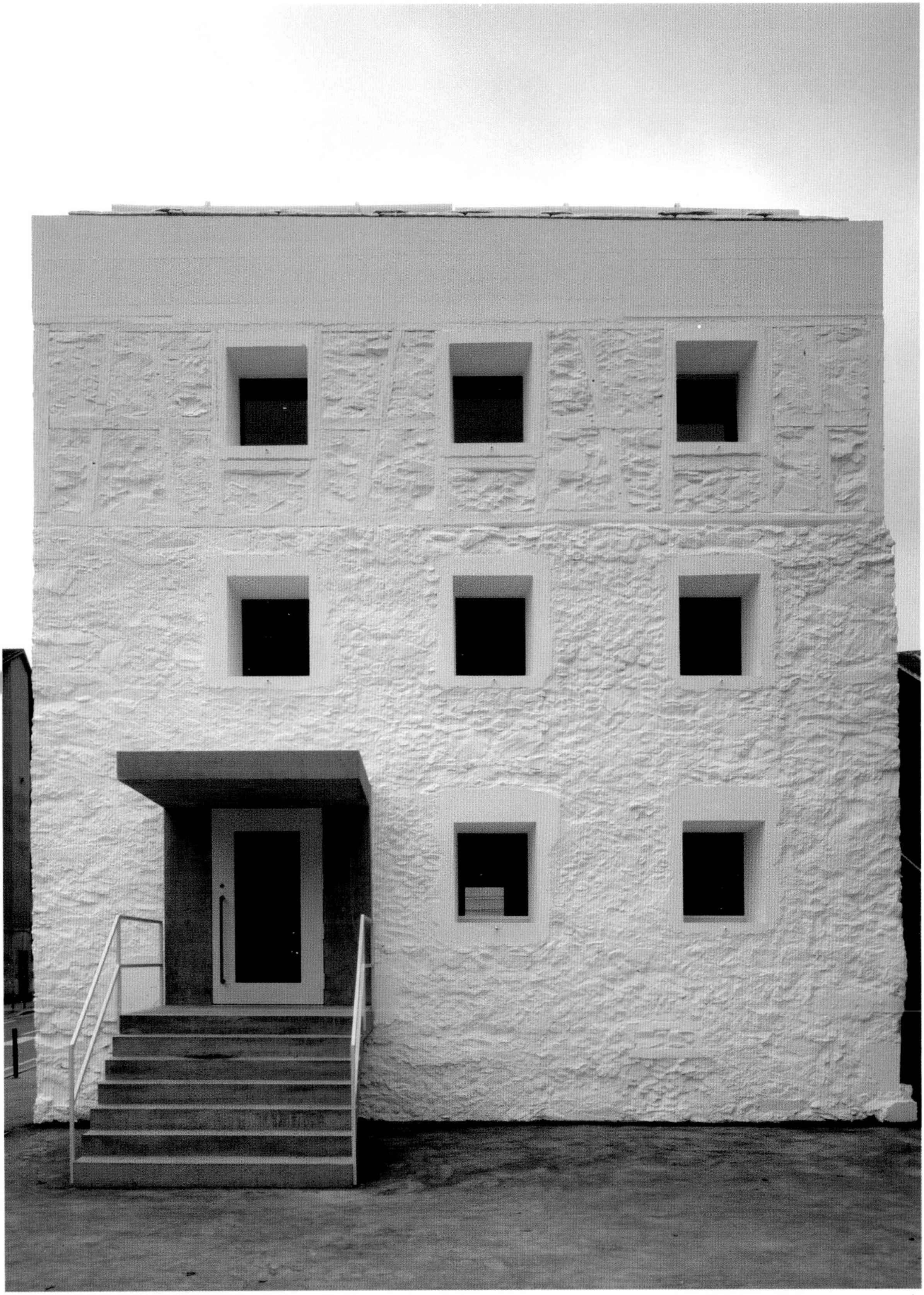

Las ventanas son la intersección inmediata entre el interior del hogar y el entorno público. Mirar por la ventana nos permite tomar contacto con el mundo exterior para experimentar impresiones diferentes. La mirada puede vagar por el paisaje hasta el horizonte o pasearse por los rincones de una ciudad vibrante mientras se oye el sordo rumor del tráfico. En el clásico de Alfred Hitchcock "La ventana indiscreta", el periodista Jeff debe guardar cama y observa el limitado campo visual que se enmarca en su ventana; así se origina una aventura voyeurista con facetas criminales.

Las ventanas son hoy más que una protección y un filtro para la luz, el clima y el ruido. Son el marco de imágenes reales y dan carácter a la fachada de los edificios. El diseño de las ventanas revela siempre algo sobre el habitante de una casa. Una mirada hacia adentro revela lo que es supuestamente privado o se deja llevar por la extrovertida puesta en escena de nuevos mundos de productos y estilos de vida. La gama va desde las pequeñas aberturas con una guía decorativa para la mirada hasta la cubierta completa de vidrio que es totalmente transparente.

Esta variedad es inseparable del desarrollo del vidrio como material de construcción. A principios de nuestra era las ventanas todavía eran simples aberturas en los muros conectados por arcos invertidos. No fue hasta que se pudieron fabricar cristales en forma artesanal que las ventanas se convirtieron en fuentes de luz para habitaciones que hasta entonces eran oscuras y en coloridas imágenes para edificios sagrados. Las innovaciones en las técnicas para empañar cristales y la aplicación de nuevos materiales y materias primas especializadas posibilitaron la creación de nuevos tipos de ventanas.

En la arquitectura moderna, las ventanas para ver y ser visto han eliminado el límite entre afuera y adentro, planteando una nueva interpretación del concepto de espacio. La búsqueda del ser humano de recogimiento y apertura, privacidad y publicidad, orden y diversidad también se puede apreciar en las ventanas de un edificio. Este libro ofrece una serie de soluciones muy particulares para esa pregunta. Se trata de una selección de ejemplos de diversos sectores que documentan una gran variedad de alternativas, reflejan las tendencias actuales y despiertan la inspiración.

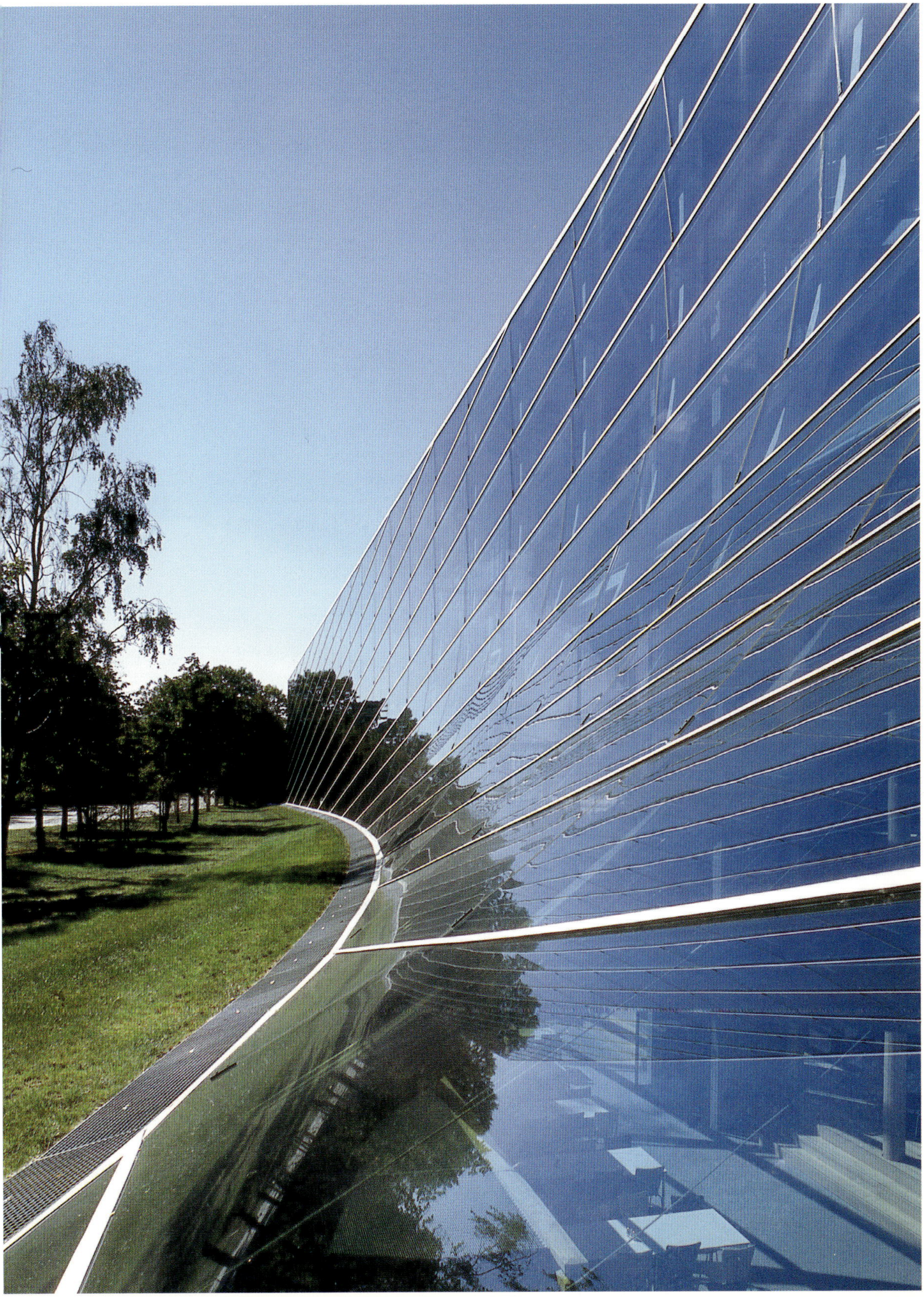

Les fenêtres constituent l'intersection immédiate entre l'intérieur d'une maison et son environnement public. Regarder par la fenêtre nous permet de prendre contact avec le monde extérieur pour ressentir les impressions les plus diverses. Le regard peut errer dans le vaste paysage ou plonger dans le profond dédale des rues d'une grande ville trépidante, pendant que l'on entend le bruid sourd de la circulation. Dans le classique d'Alfred Hitchcock, « Fenêtre sur cour », le journaliste Jeff, cloué au lit, observe à travers un champ visuel limité la fenêtre en face, ce qui débouche sur une aventure voyeuriste aux facettes criminelles.

Les fenêtres sont aujourd'hui plus qu'une protection et un filtre contre la lumière, le climat et le bruit. Elles sont le cadre d'images réelles et donnent du caractère à la façade des édifices. Le design des fenêtres révèle toujours quelque chose sur les habitants d'une maison. Un regard sur l'intérieur d'une maison dévoile des choses éventuellement privées ou permet une mise en scène extrovertie de nouveaux mondes de produits et de styles de vie. L'éventail va des petites ouvertures avec un guide décoratif pour le regard jusqu'à une couverture complète en verre d'une transparence totale.

Cette grande variété est inséparable de l'évolution du verre en tant que matériau de construction. Au début de notre ère, les fenêtres étaient encore de simples ouvertures dans les murs reliées par des cintres de soutènement. Ce n'est que lorsqu'il a été possible de fabriquer artisanalement des fenêtres en verre qu'elles sont devenues des sources de lumière dans des intérieurs jusque-là obscurs et des images multicolores pour les édifices sacrés. Les innovations aussi dans la technique de fabrication des ferrures ainsi que l'utilisation de nouveaux matériaux spécialisés ont permis la création de nouveaux types de fenêtres.

Dans l'architecture moderne, les fenêtres pour voir et être vu ont fait disparaître la frontière entre l'intérieur et l'extérieur, engendrant ainsi une nouvelle interprétation de la notion d'espace. La recherche de sécurité et d'ouverture, de vie privée et de publicité ou encore d'ordre et de diversité par l'être humain peut se lire dans les fenêtres d'un édifice. Dans cet ouvrage, vous trouverez toute une série de solutions remarquables pour répondre à ce problème. Il s'agit d'un éventail d'exemples sélectionnés de divers secteurs qui documentent une grande variété d'alternatives, présentent les tendances actuelles tout en étant une source d'inspiration.

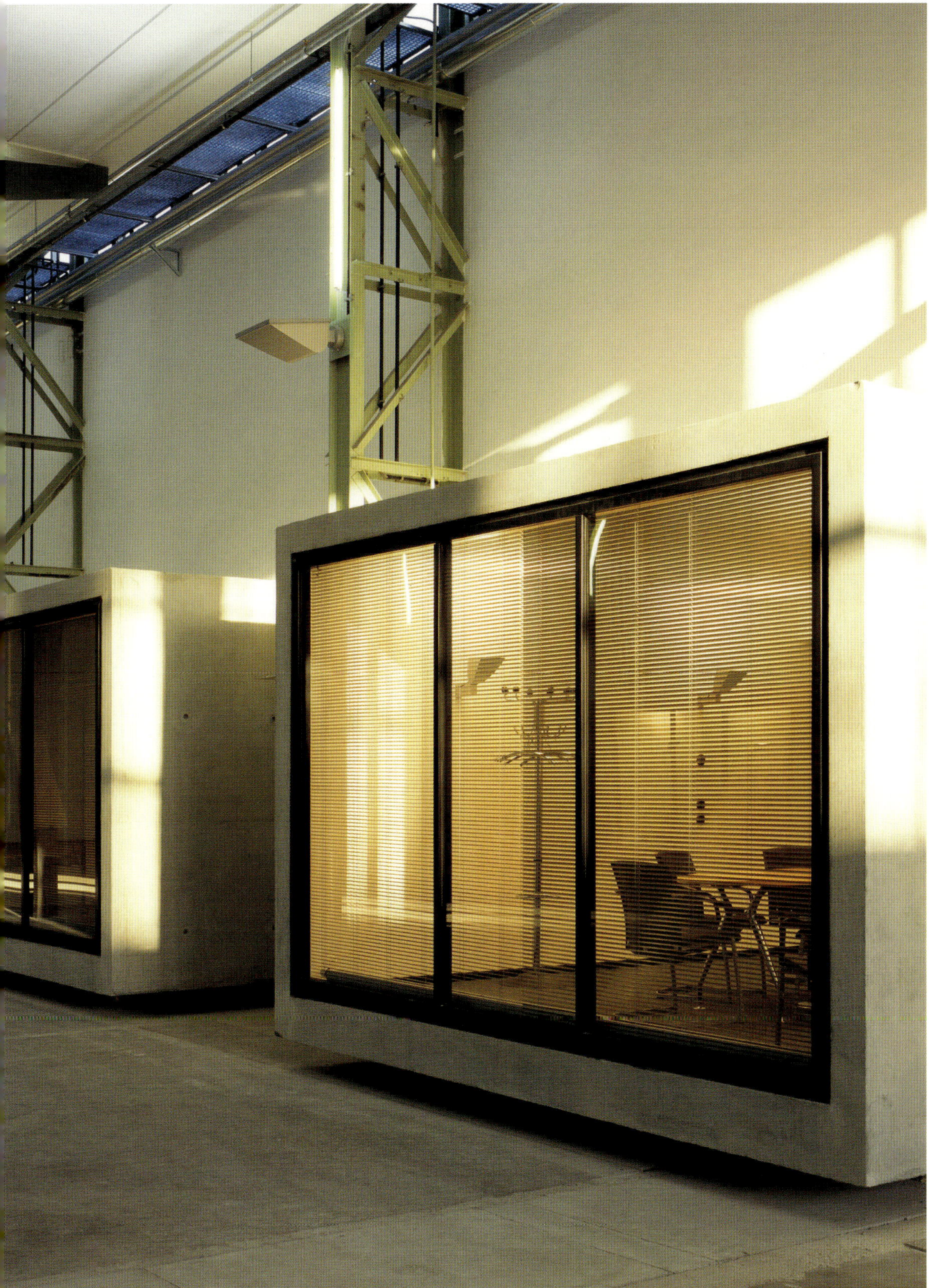

Finestre rappresentano l'immediata interfaccia tra gli interni di una casa e l'ambiente esterno e pubblico. I rapporti visivi attraverso una finestra offrono la possibilità di entrare in contatto con il mondo esterno per sperimentare le più svariate impressioni. Lo sguardo può vagare sul panorama del paesaggio oppure si apre verso le profonde gole delle strade di una pulsante città, mentre si ascolta il muggito del traffico. In un classico del cinema "La finestra sul cortile" di Alfred Hitchcock, il giornalista Jeff mentre sta inchiodato a letto, con una visuale ristretta osserva la finestra di fronte e si sviluppa un episodio di voyeurismo caratterizzato da impressioni ed espressioni della criminologia.

Oggi le finestre non soltanto proteggono e filtrano la luce, il clima e il rumore. Rappresentano anzi la cornice per immagini reali e danno il carattere all'aspetto della casa. Il design delle finestre rivela sempre anche qualcosa sugli abitanti di una casa. La vista all'interno della casa porta alla luce quanto in realtà si pensava privato oppure serve a rivolgere verso l'esterno la scenografia di nuovi mondi di prodotti e stili di vita. La vasta gamma di finestre parte dalla piccola apertura che guida lo sguardo attraverso la scenografia della casa fino alla completa pellicola in vetro che dona trasparenza assoluta.

Questa varietà è inseparabilmente legata allo sviluppo del vetro come materiale costruttivo. All'inizio dei tempi, le finestre furono semplici aperture nella muratura, colmate da traverse di sostegno. Fu soltanto con l'introduzione della produzione artigianale di vetri piatti che le finestre si trasformarono in sorgenti luminose che portarono la luce agli interni finora oscuri e che regalarono immagini dagli splendidi colori negli edifici religiosi. Tuttavia anche le innovazioni nella tecnica d'intelaiatura e nell'applicazione di nuovi materiali e materiali manufatti hanno reso possibile la costruzione di nuovi tipi di finestre.

Le finestre per vedere e per essere visti nella recente e contemporanea storia dell'edilizia, hanno fatto fondere il limite tra interno ed esterno, dando una nuova interpretazione allo spazio. La ricerca dell'uomo di trovare sicurezza ed estroversione, vita in privato ed in pubblico oppure ordine e varietà si legge negli occhi di una casa. In questo volume si trova documentata una serie di risposte a questa domanda. Si tratta di una serie d'esempi selezionati e provenienti dai più diversi settori che allo stesso momento documentano l'ampiezza della gamma, dimostrano tendenze attuali ed offrono ispirazione.

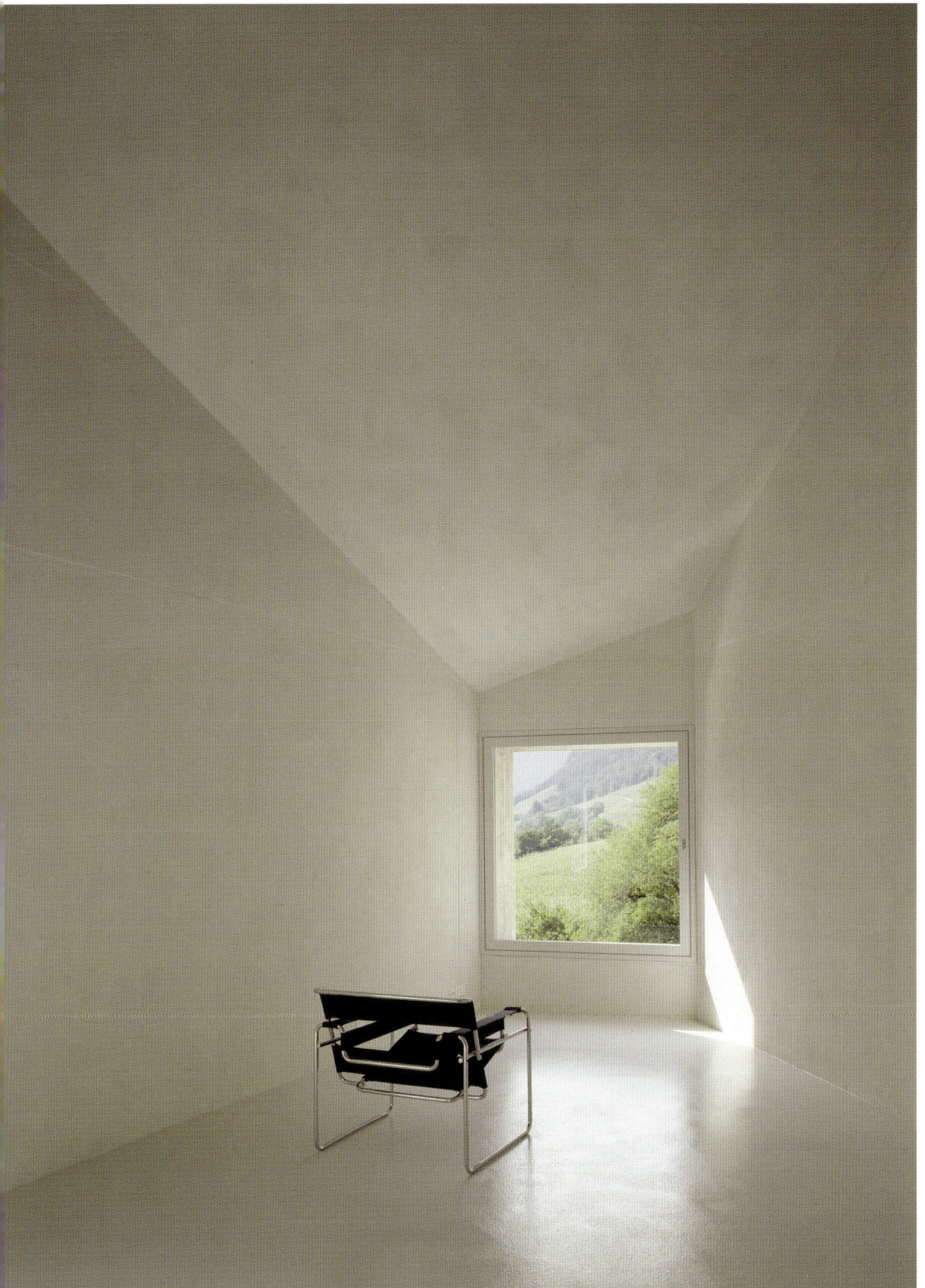

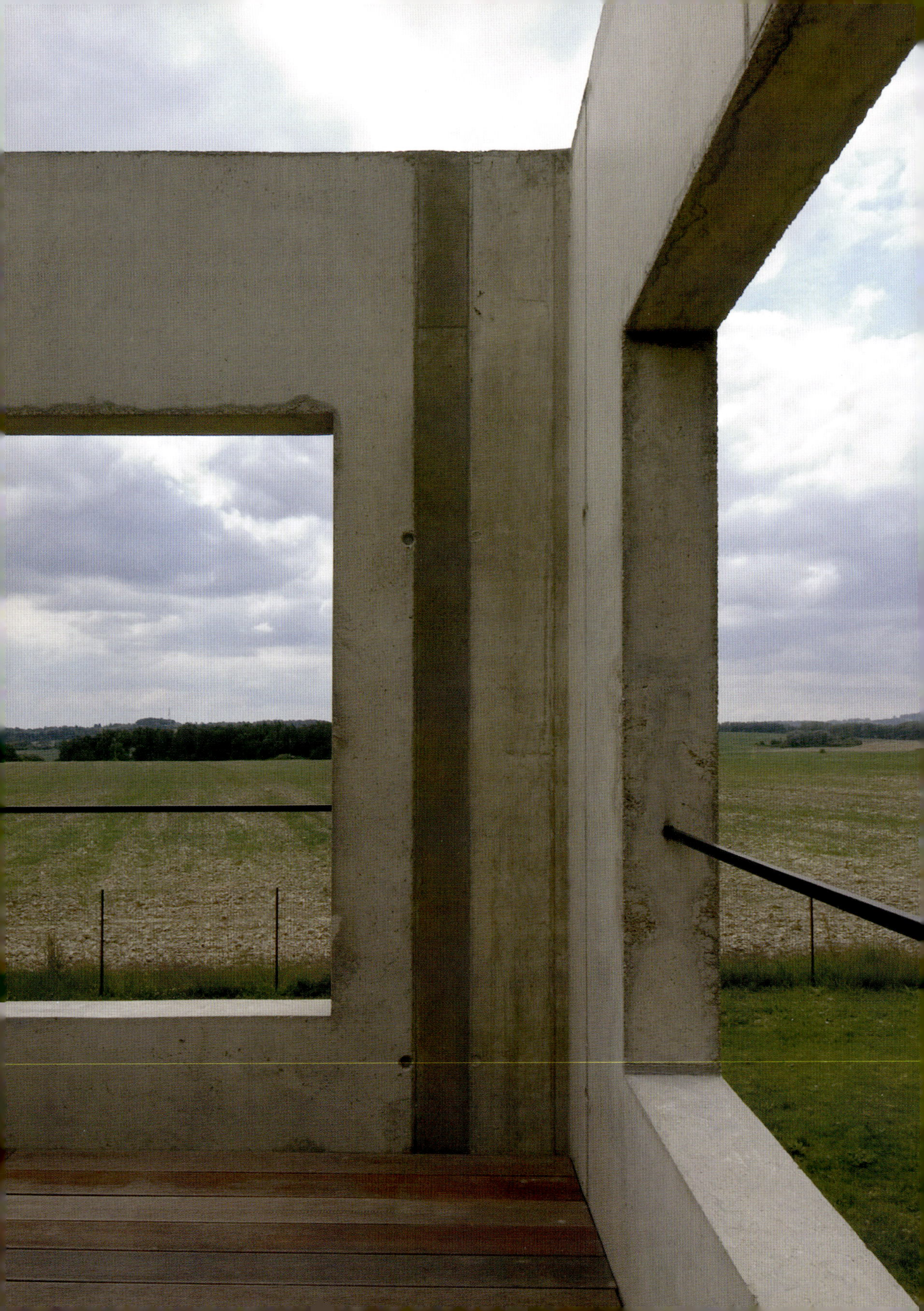

A69 - ARCHITECTS | CHEB, PRAGUE
BORIS REDČENKOV, PROKOP TOMÁŠEK, JAROSLAV WERTIG
House, Frantiskovy Lazne
Czech Republic | 2005

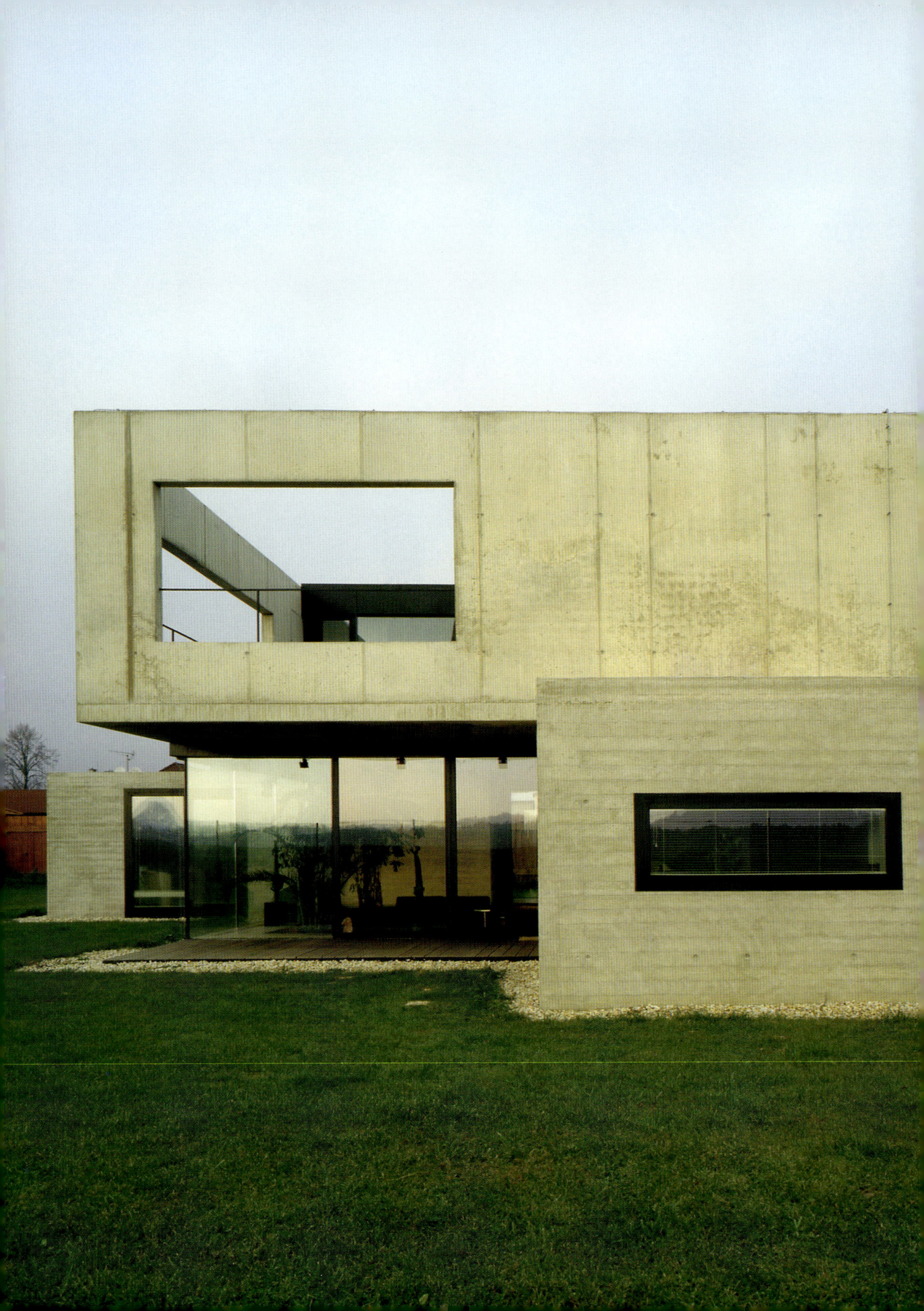

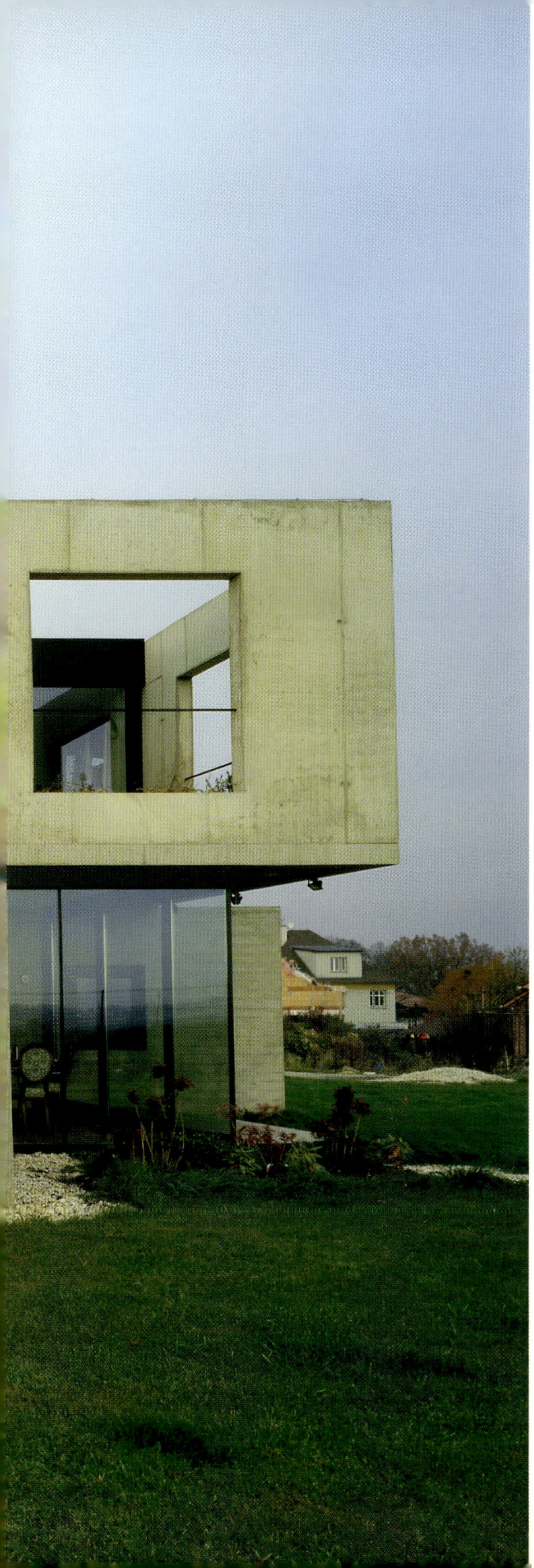

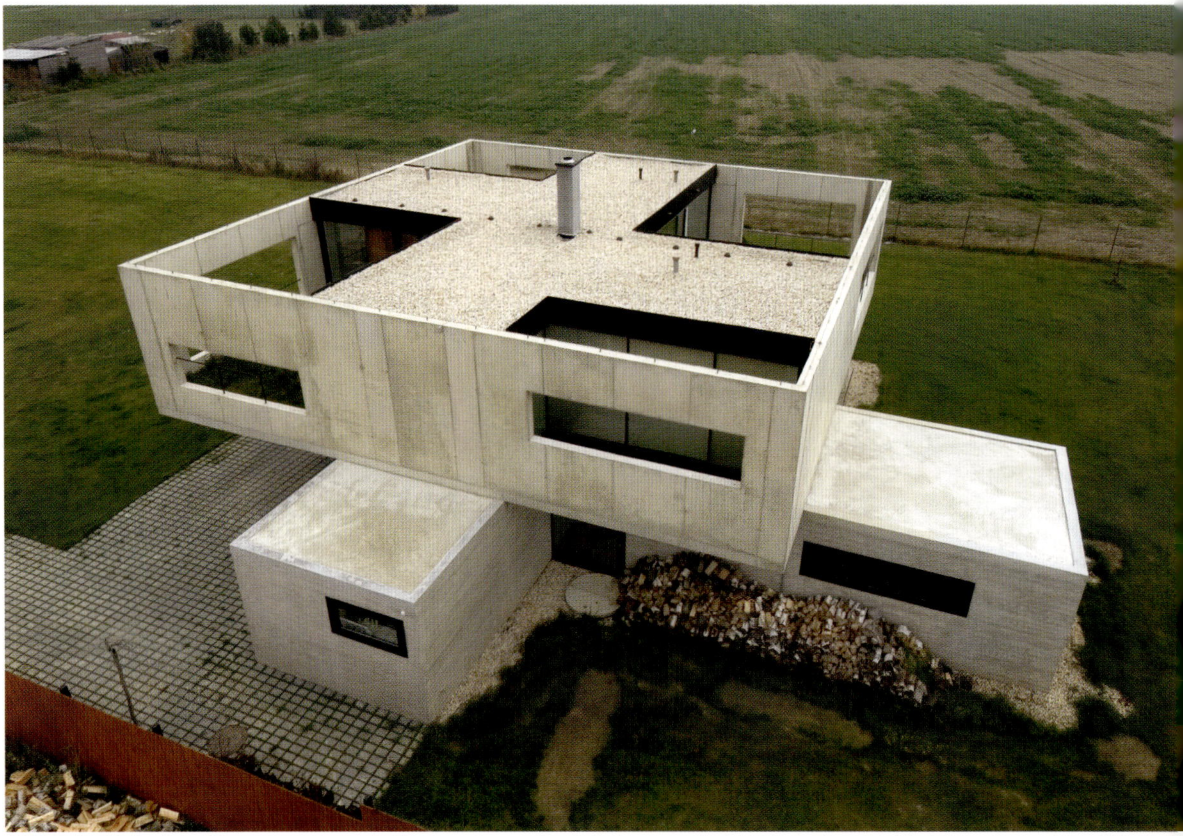

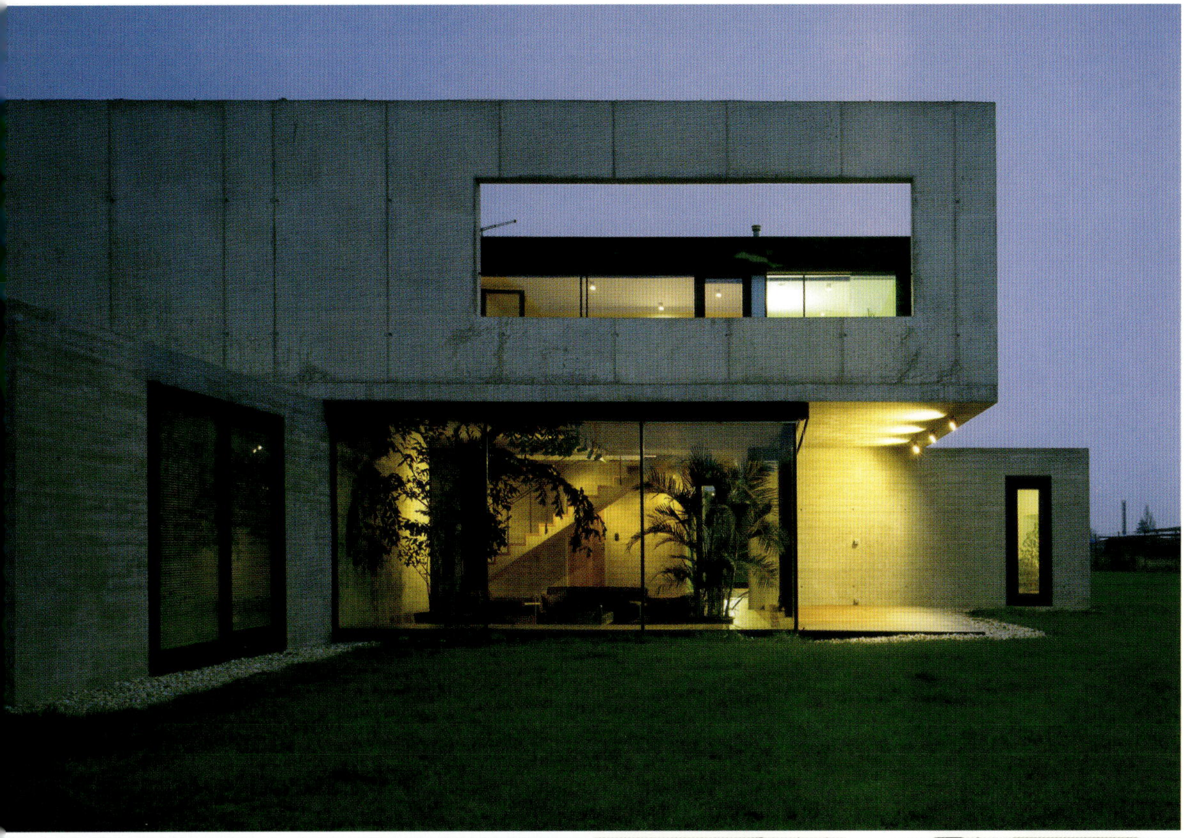
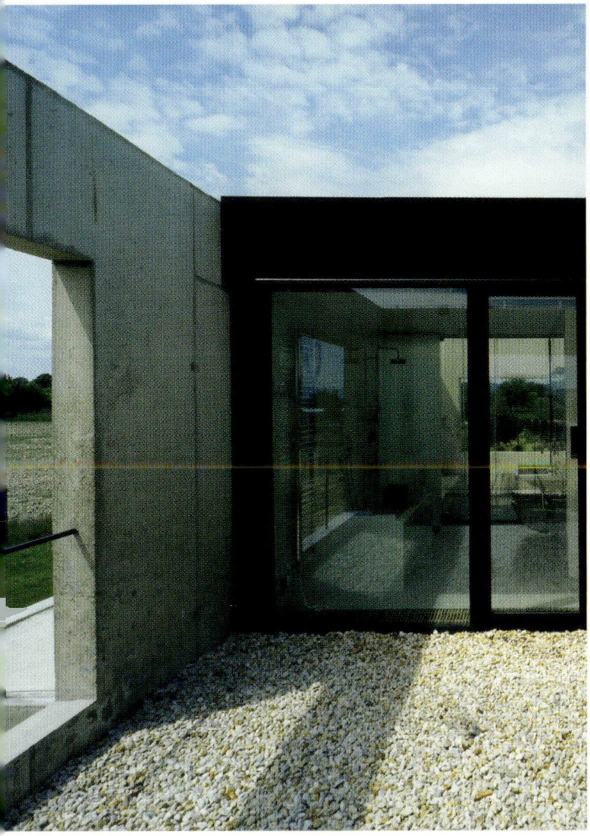
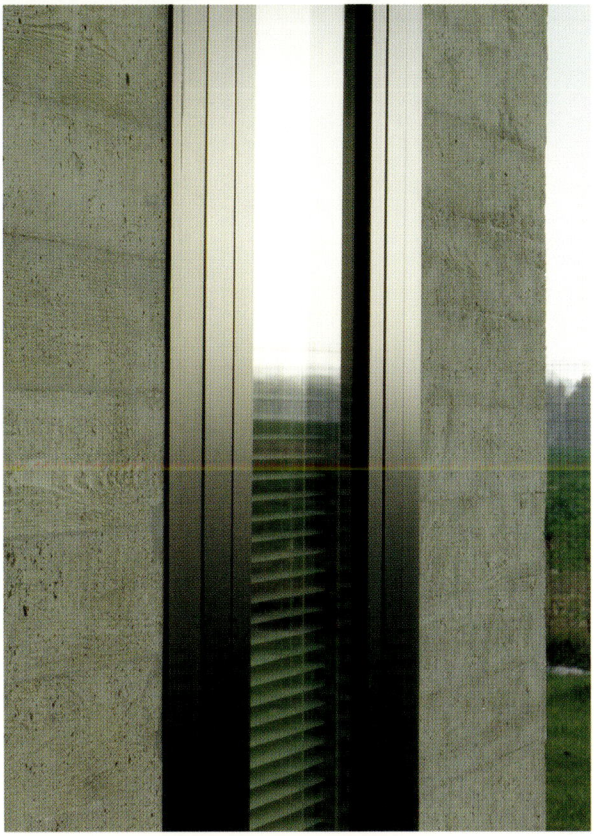

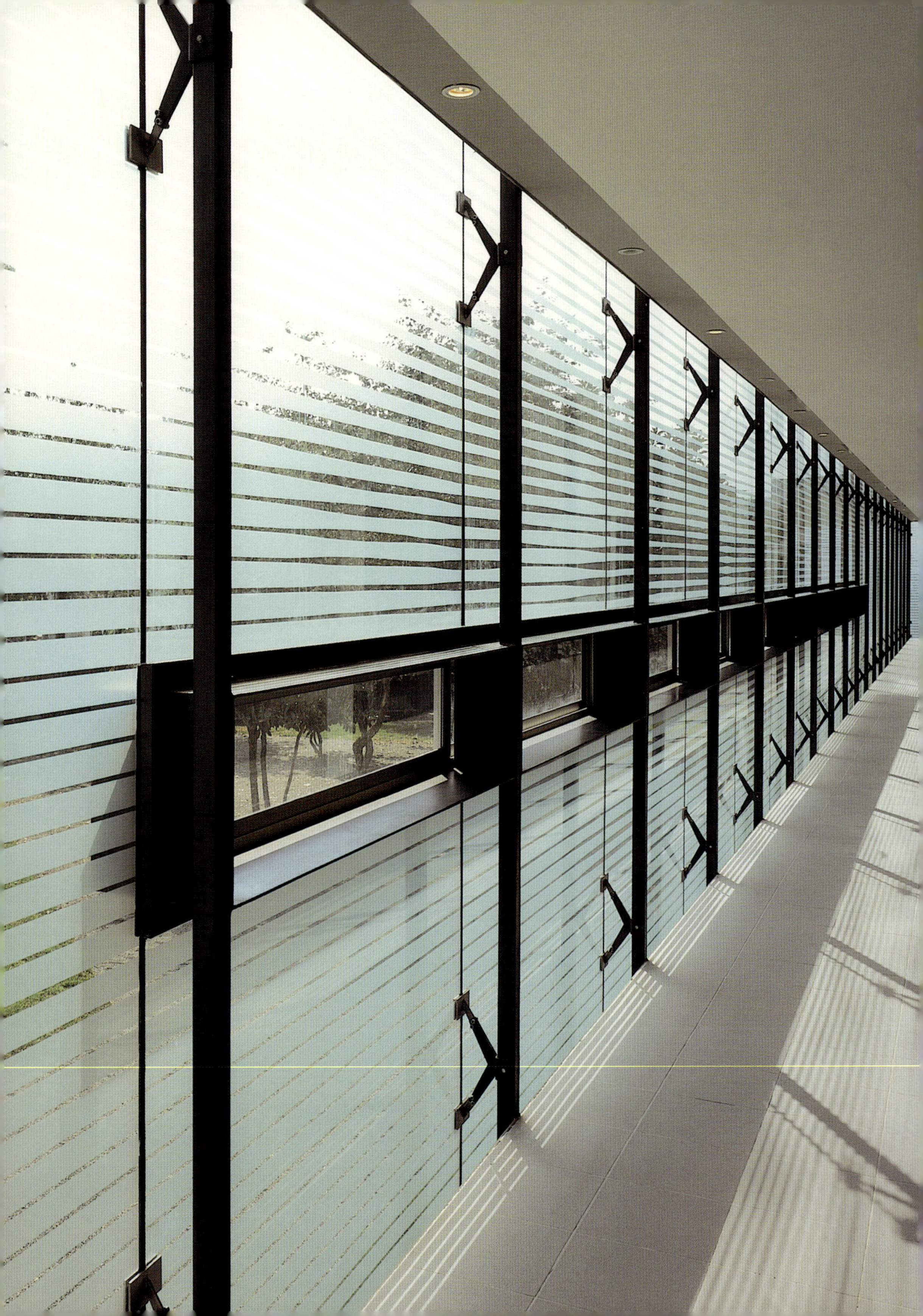

MIQUEL ADRIA, ISAAC BROID, MICHEL ROJKIND | MEXICO CITY
Mexico City National Videotheque
Mexico City, Mexico | 2000

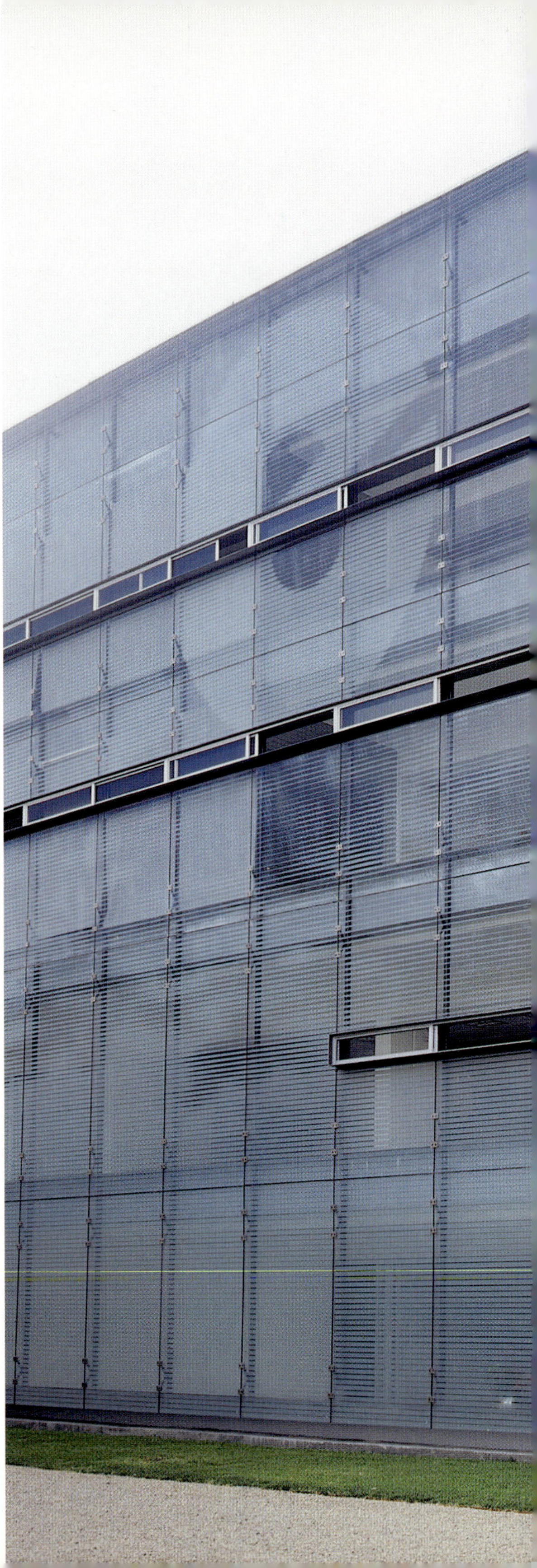

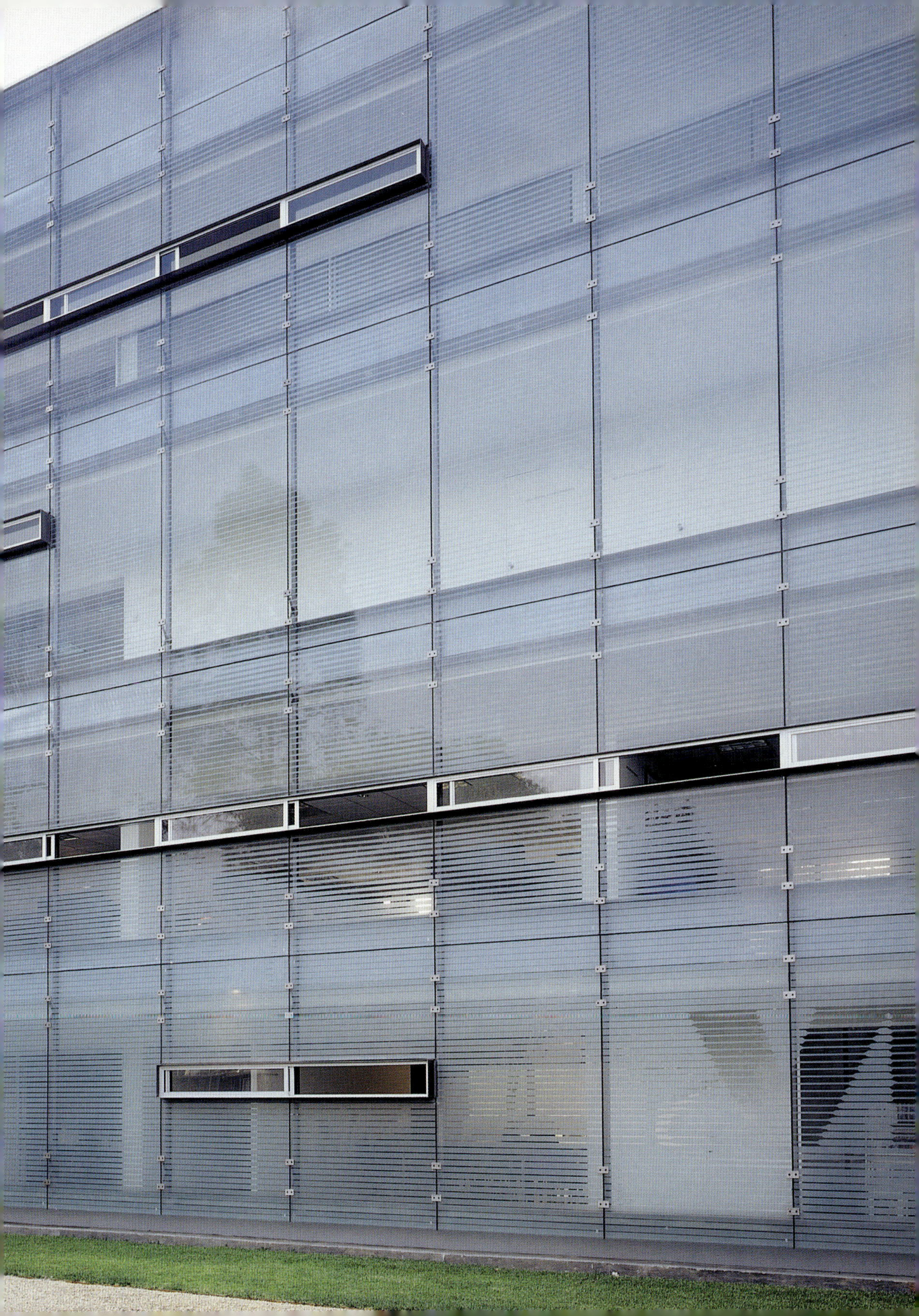

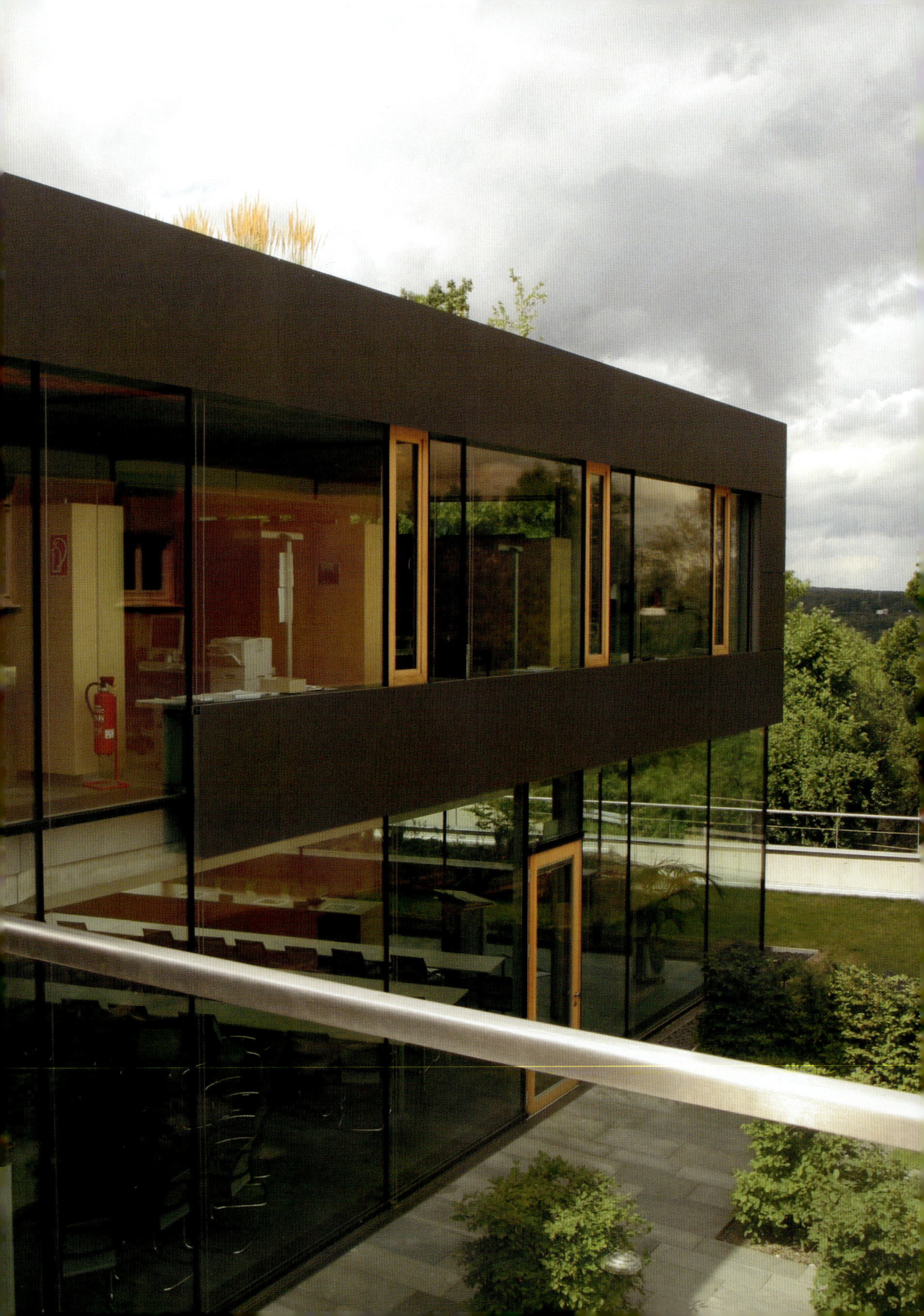

ALDINGER & ALDINGER | STUTTGART
Bezirksärztekammer
Stuttgart, Germany | 2004

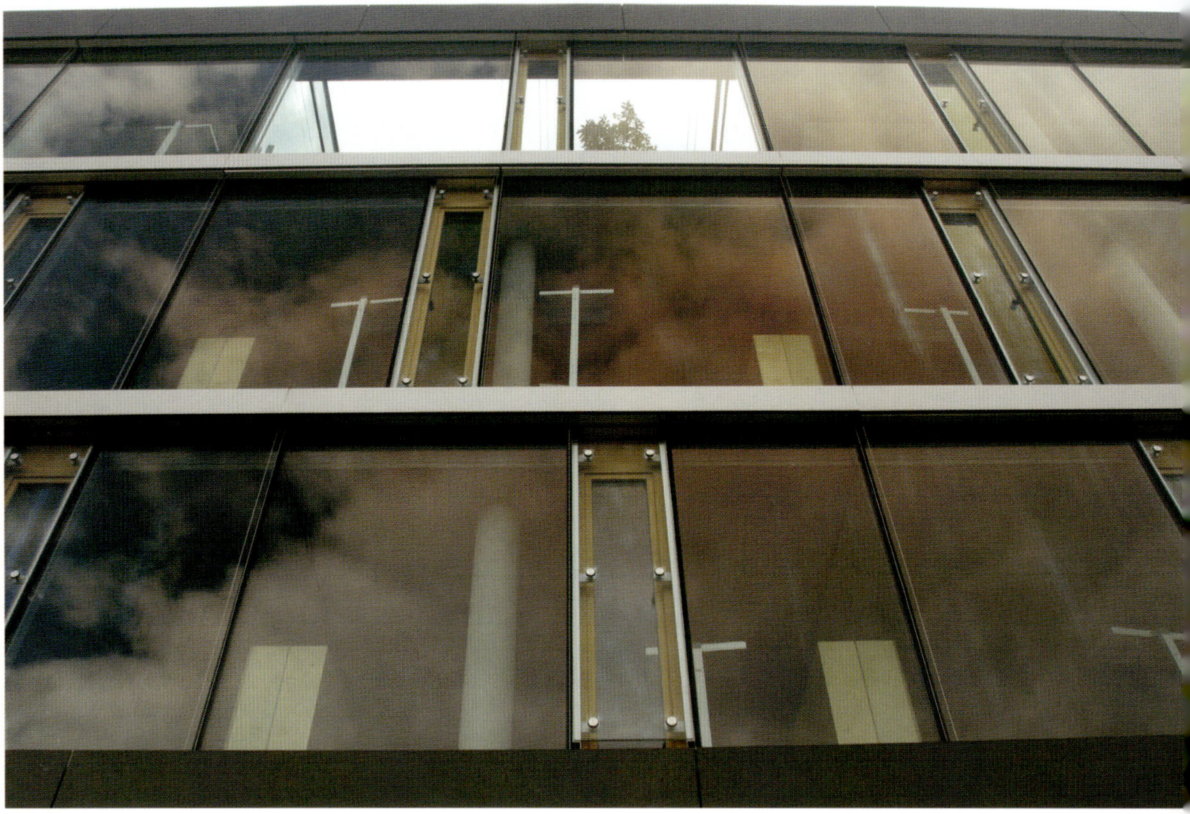

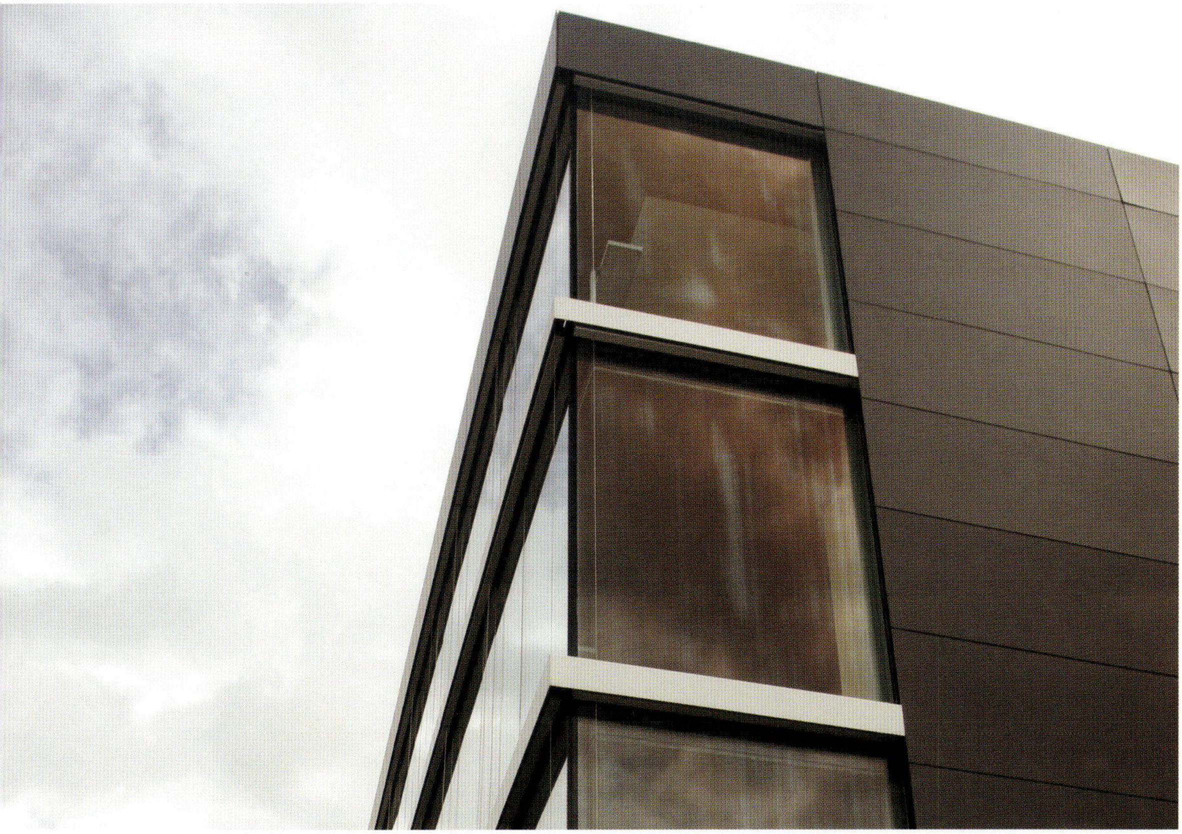

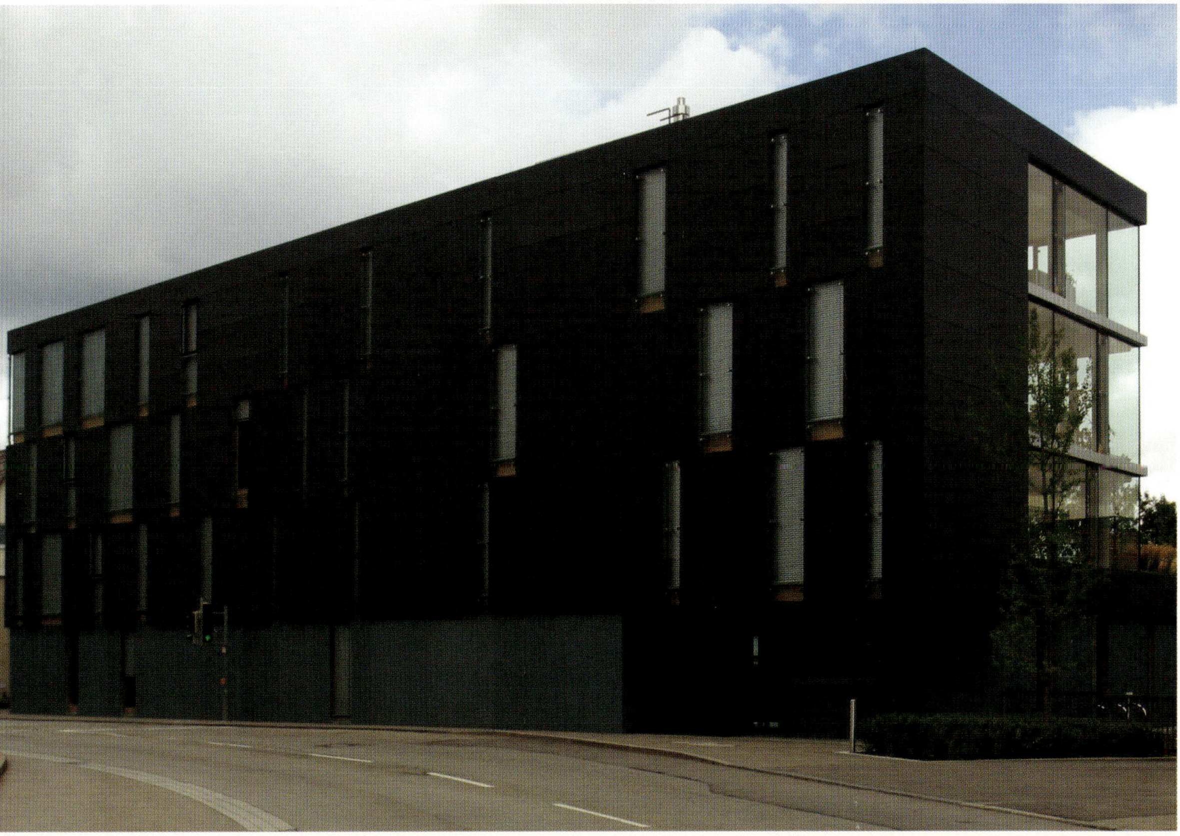

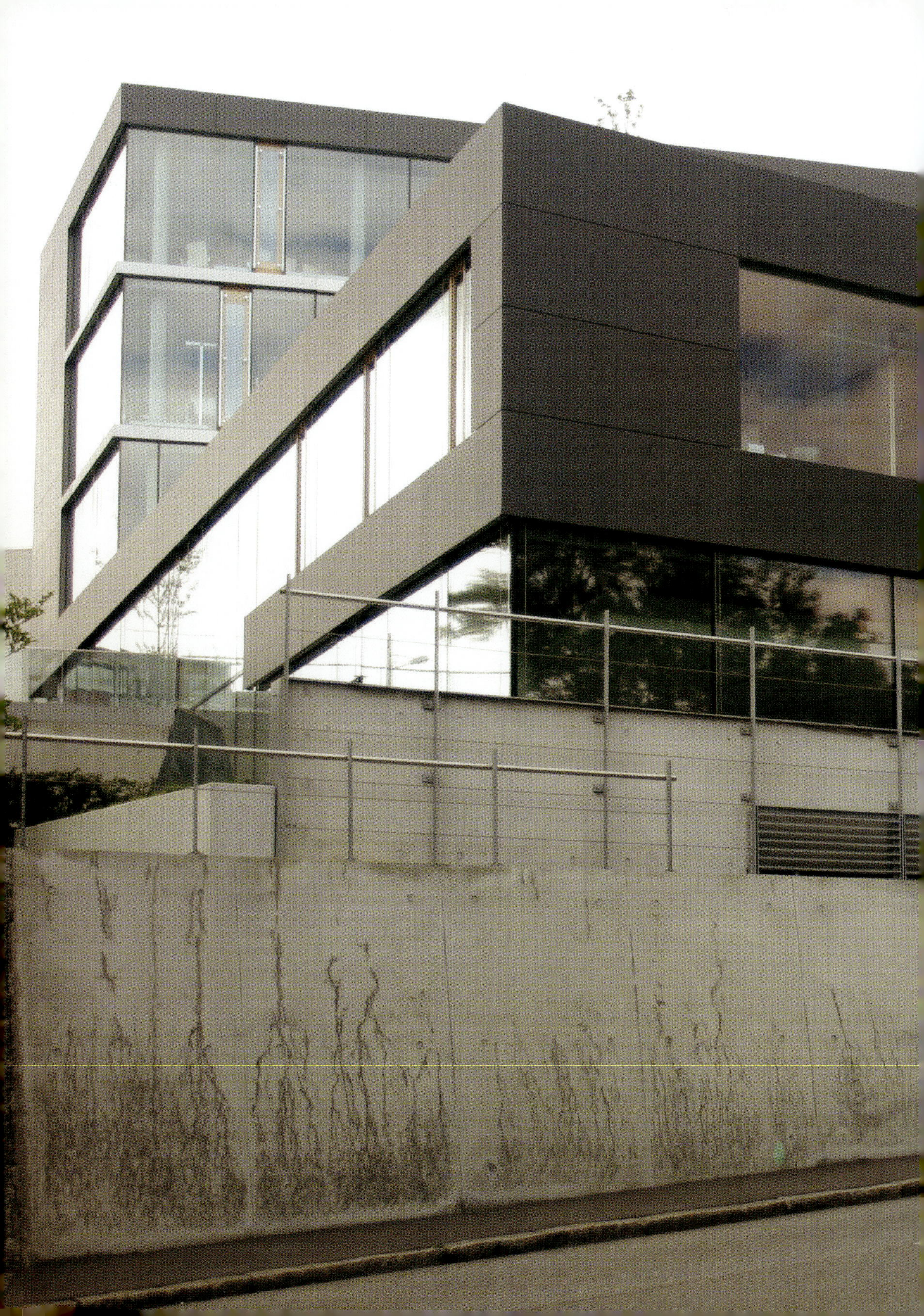

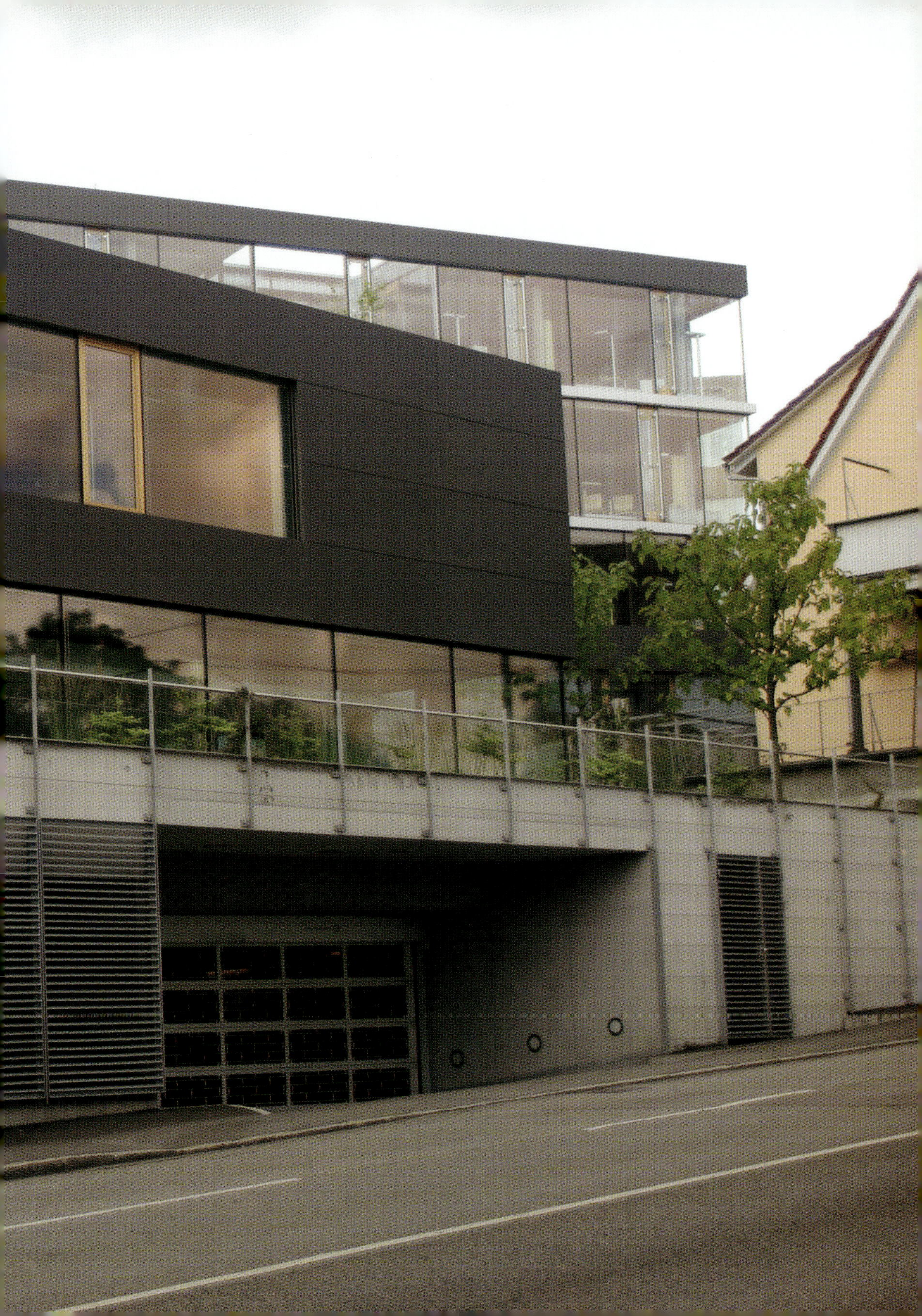

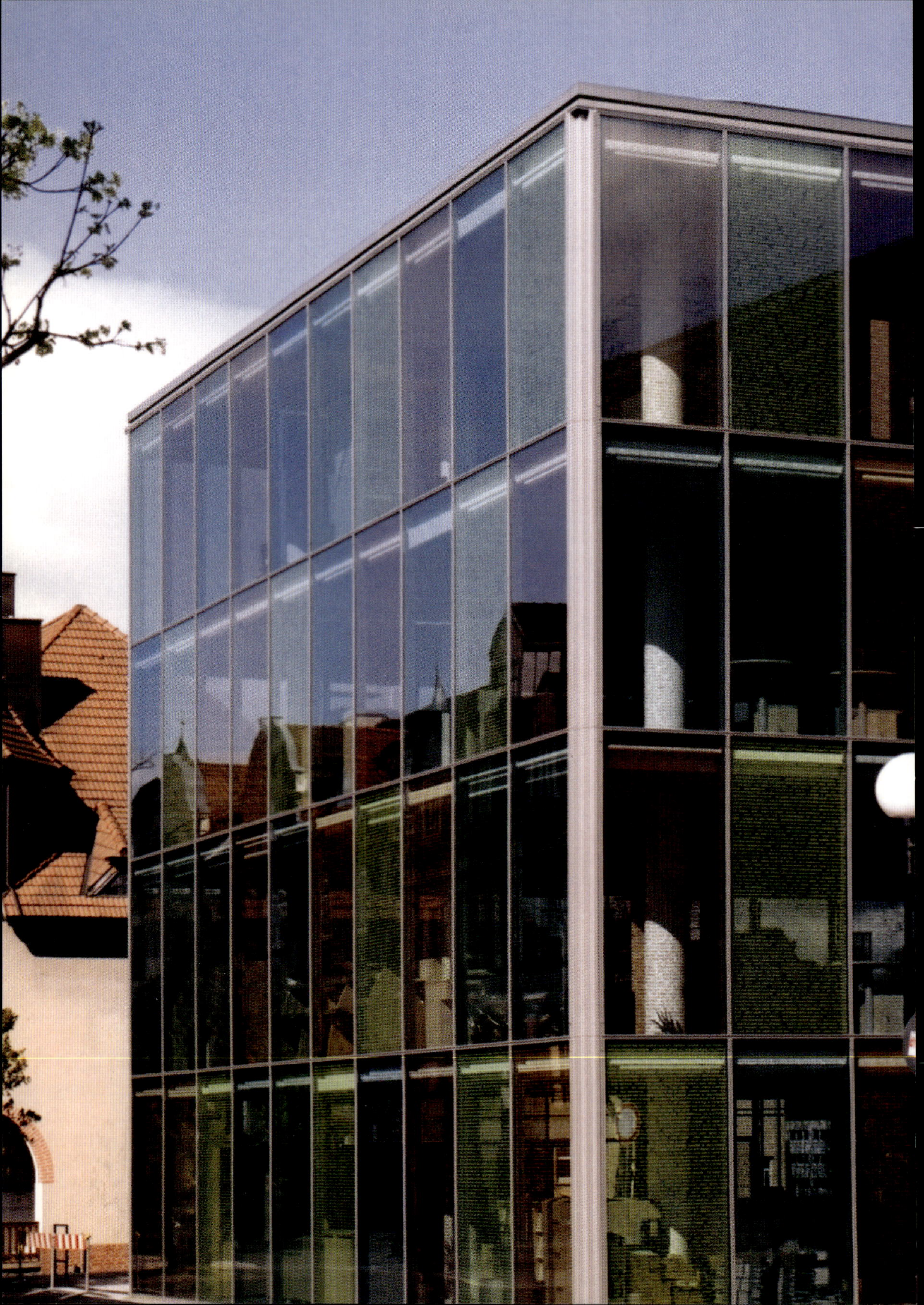

ARGE WEINGART BAUER BRACKE HOFFMANN ARCHITEKTEN | ERFURT
Public Library Suhl
Suhl, Germany | 2004

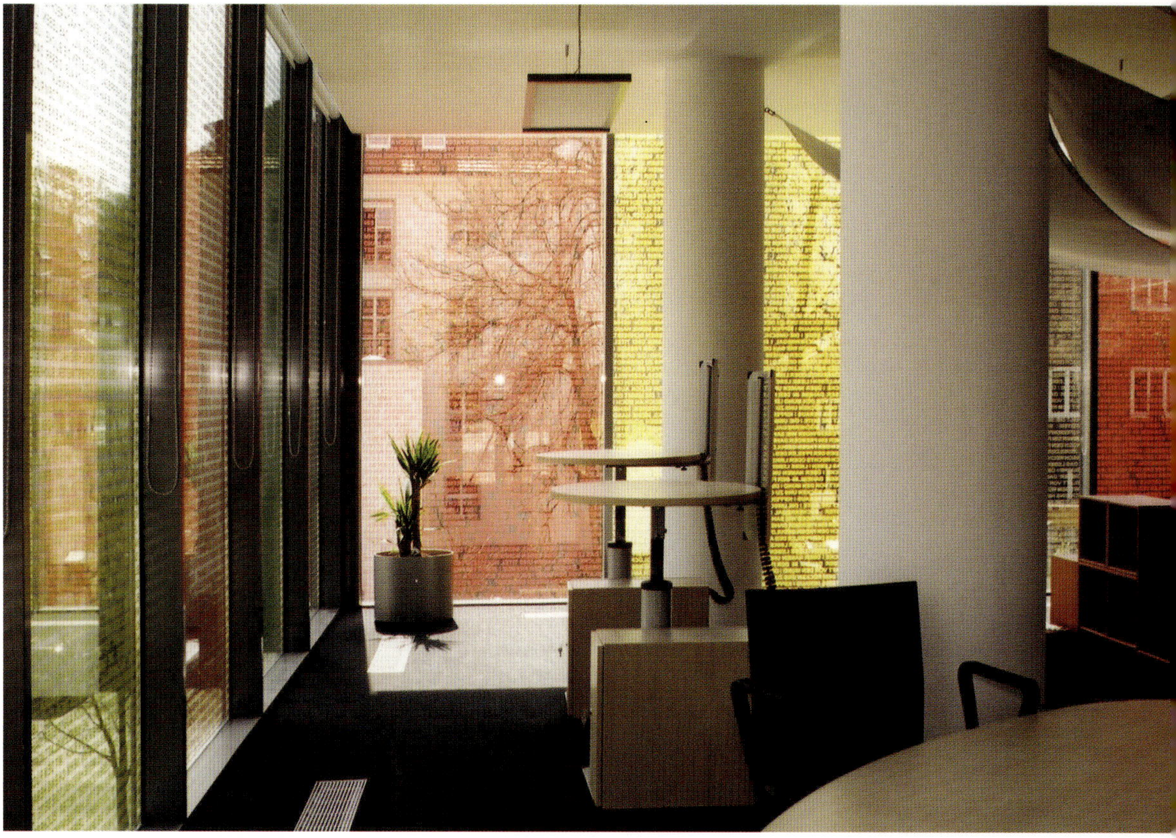

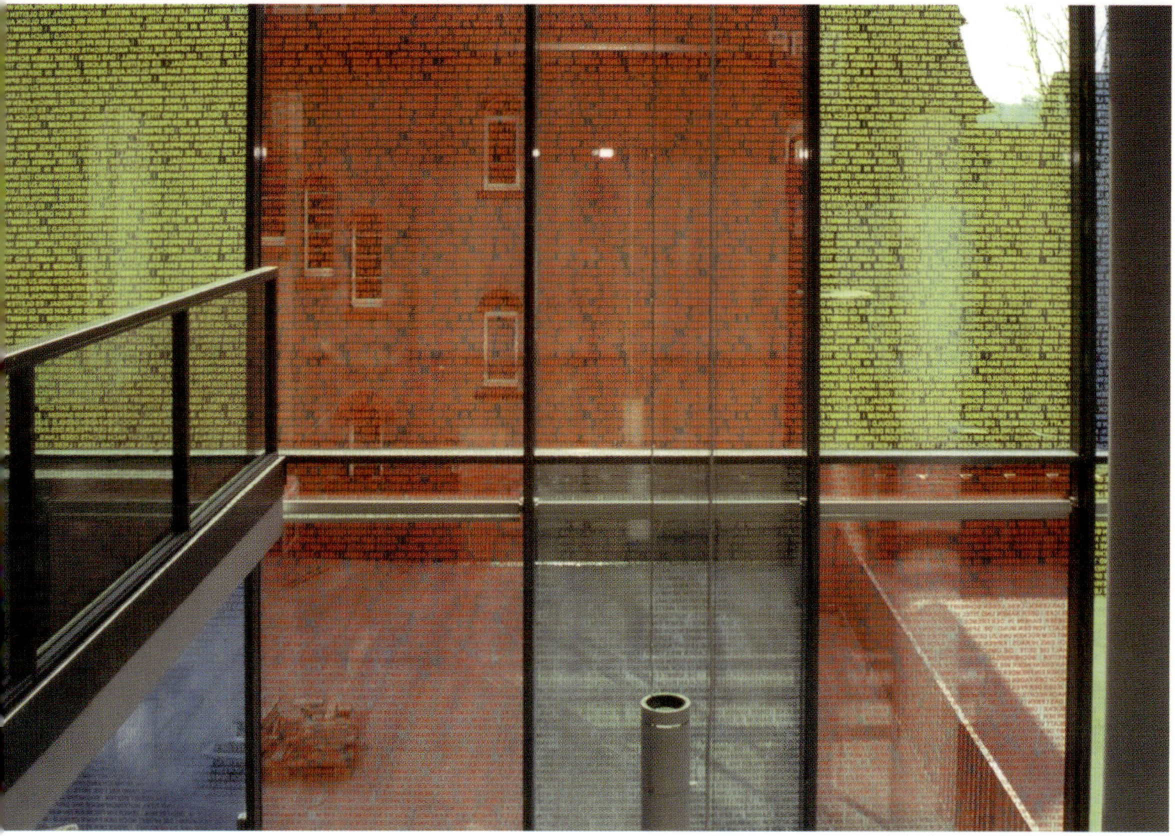

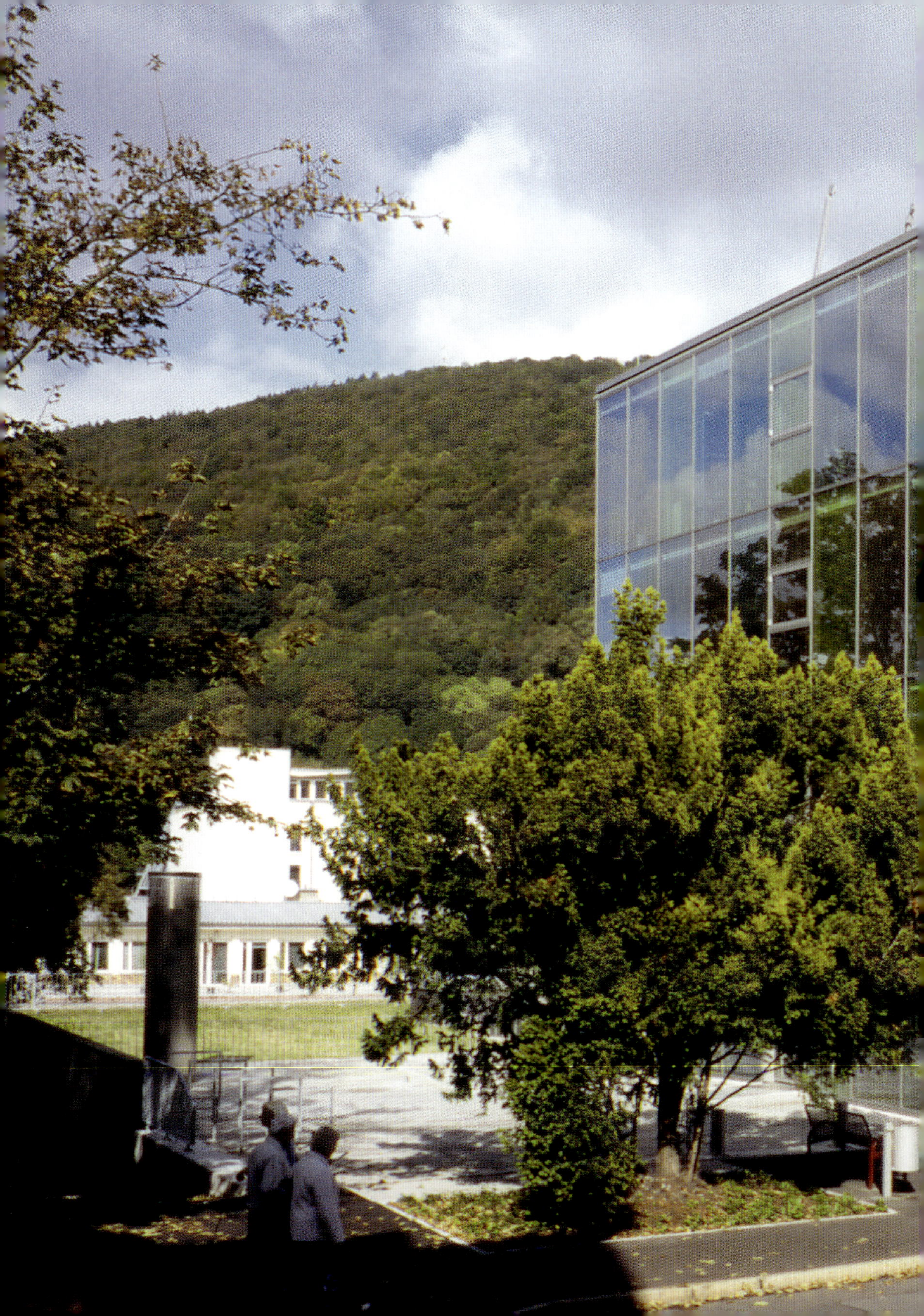

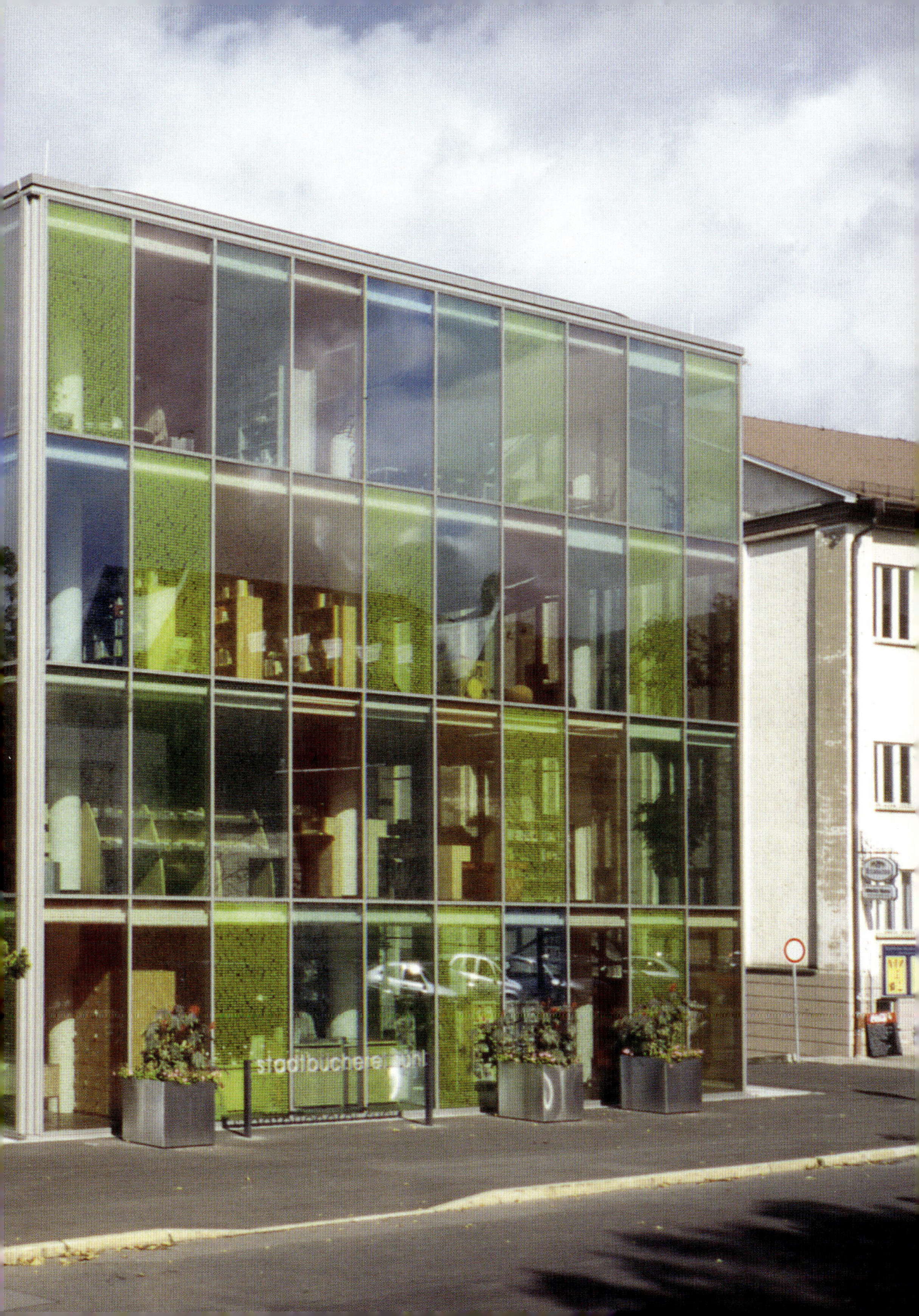

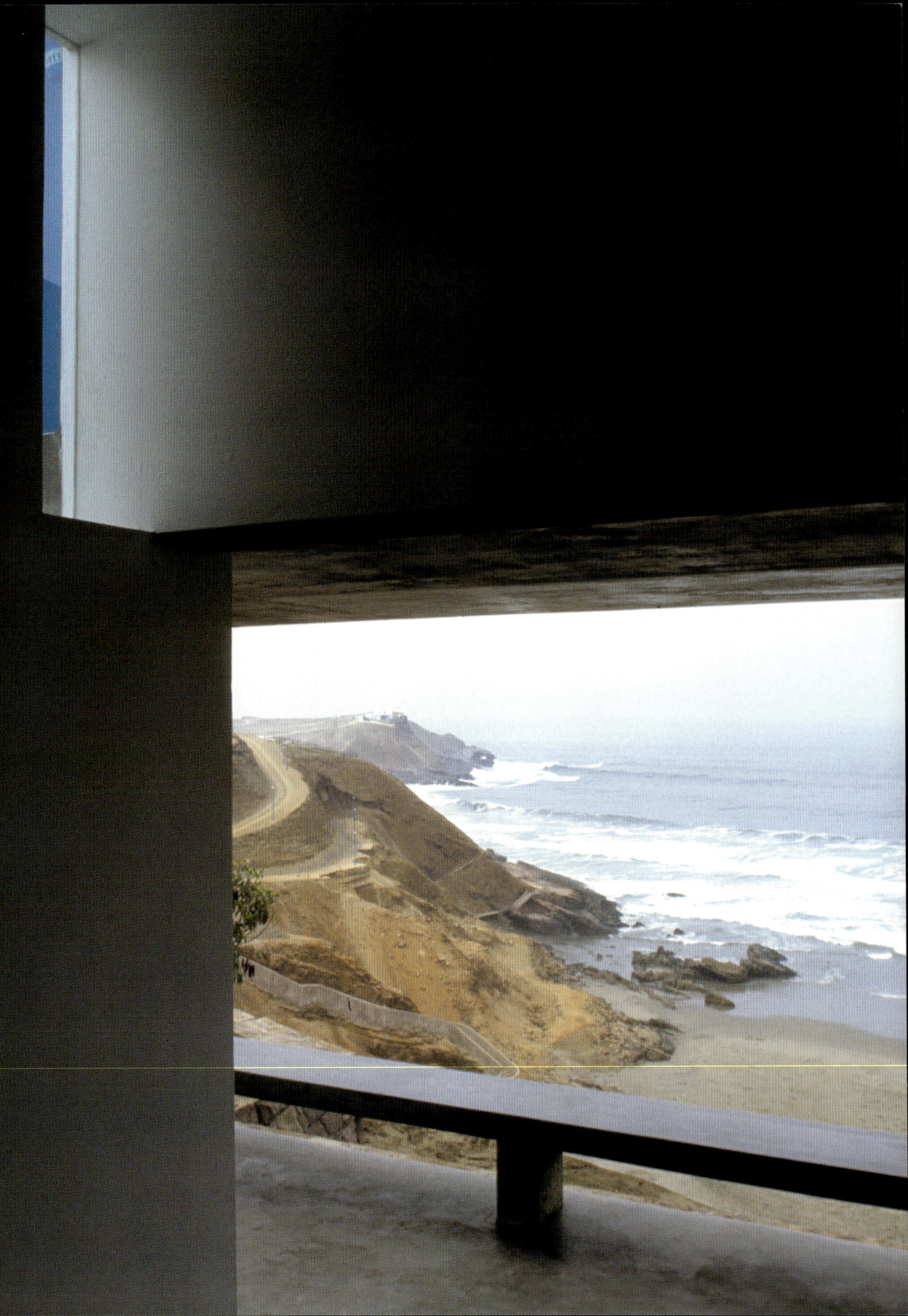

BARCLAY & CROUSSE ARCHITECTURE | PARIS
Casa Equis
Canete, Peru | 2003

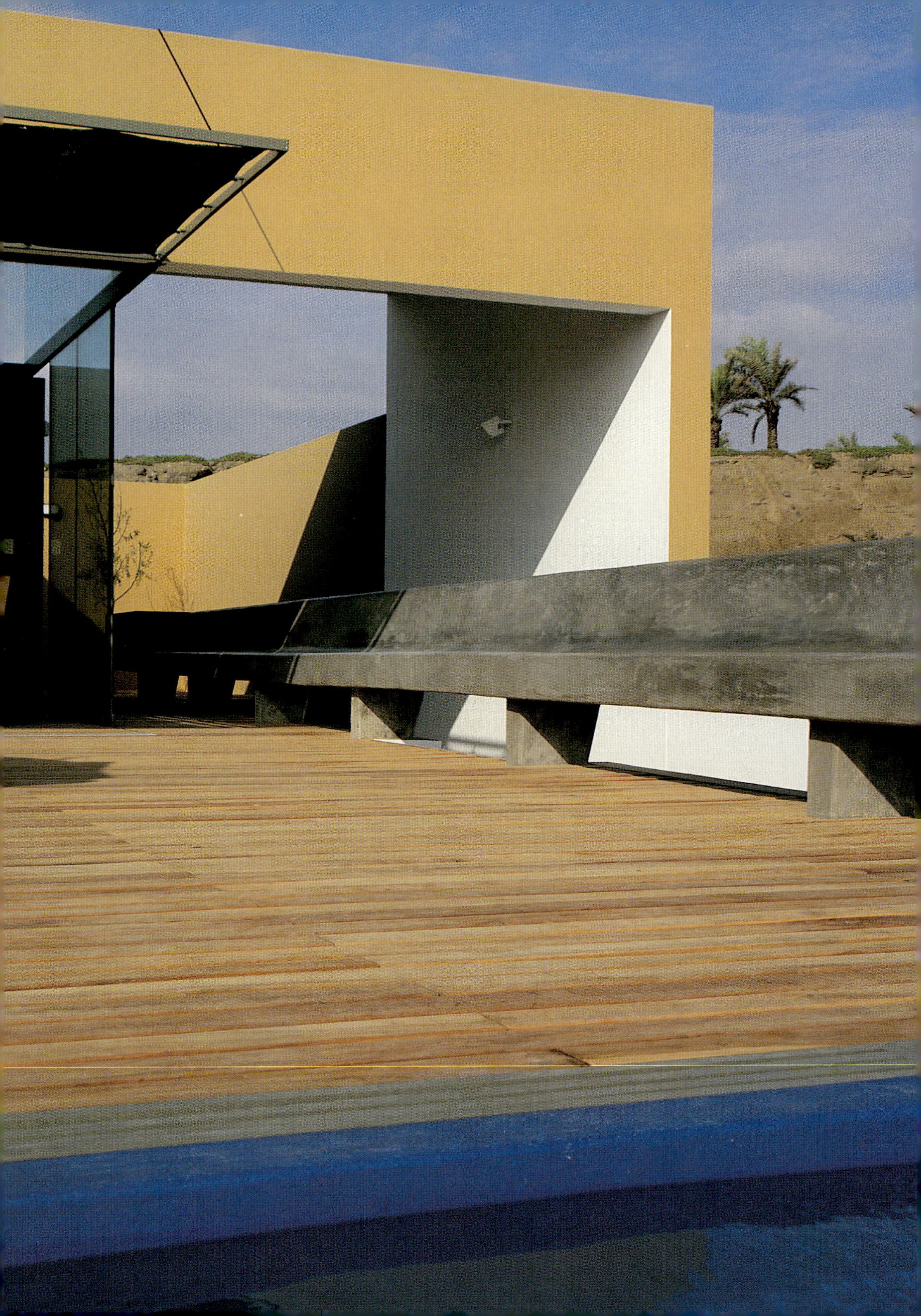

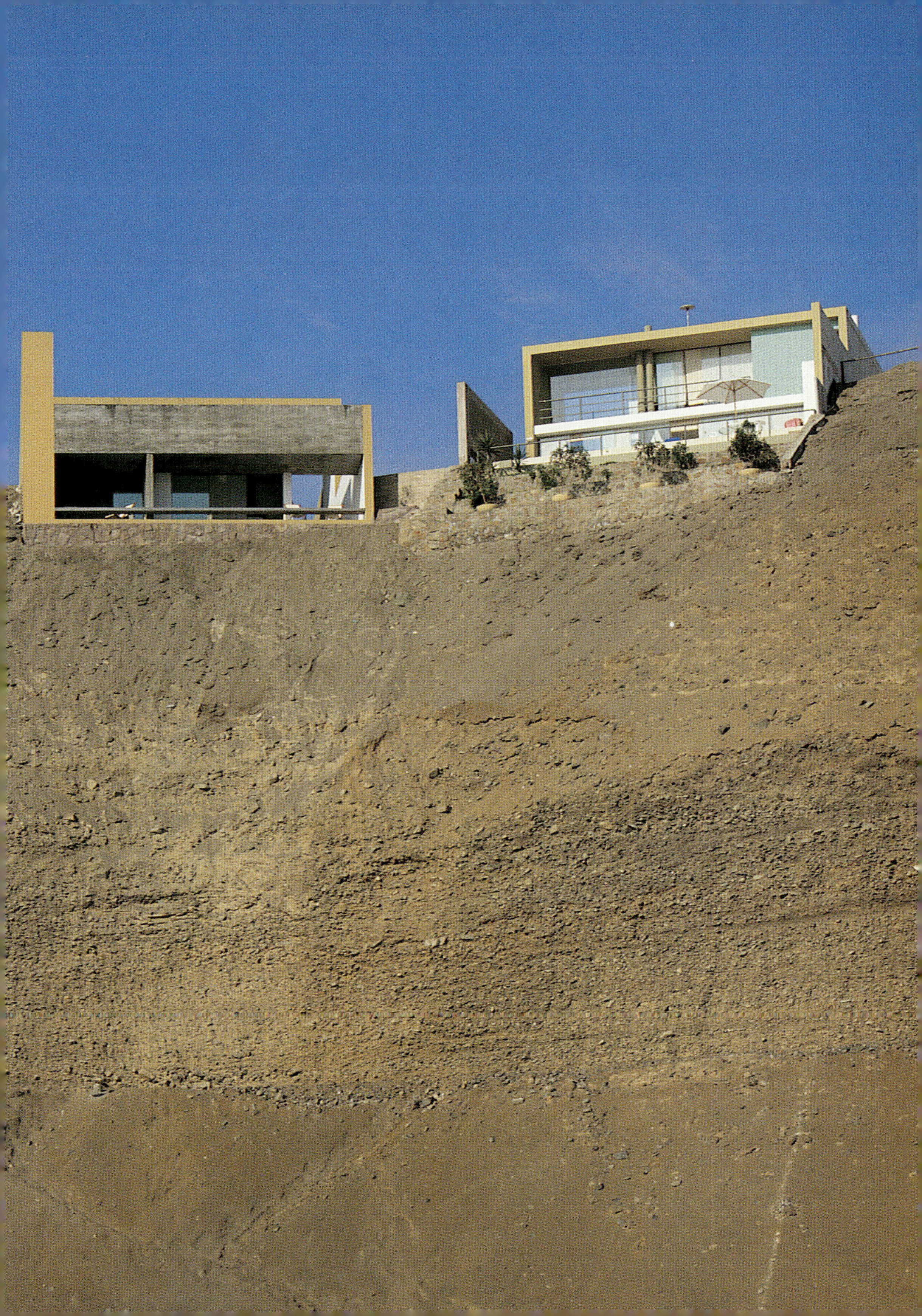

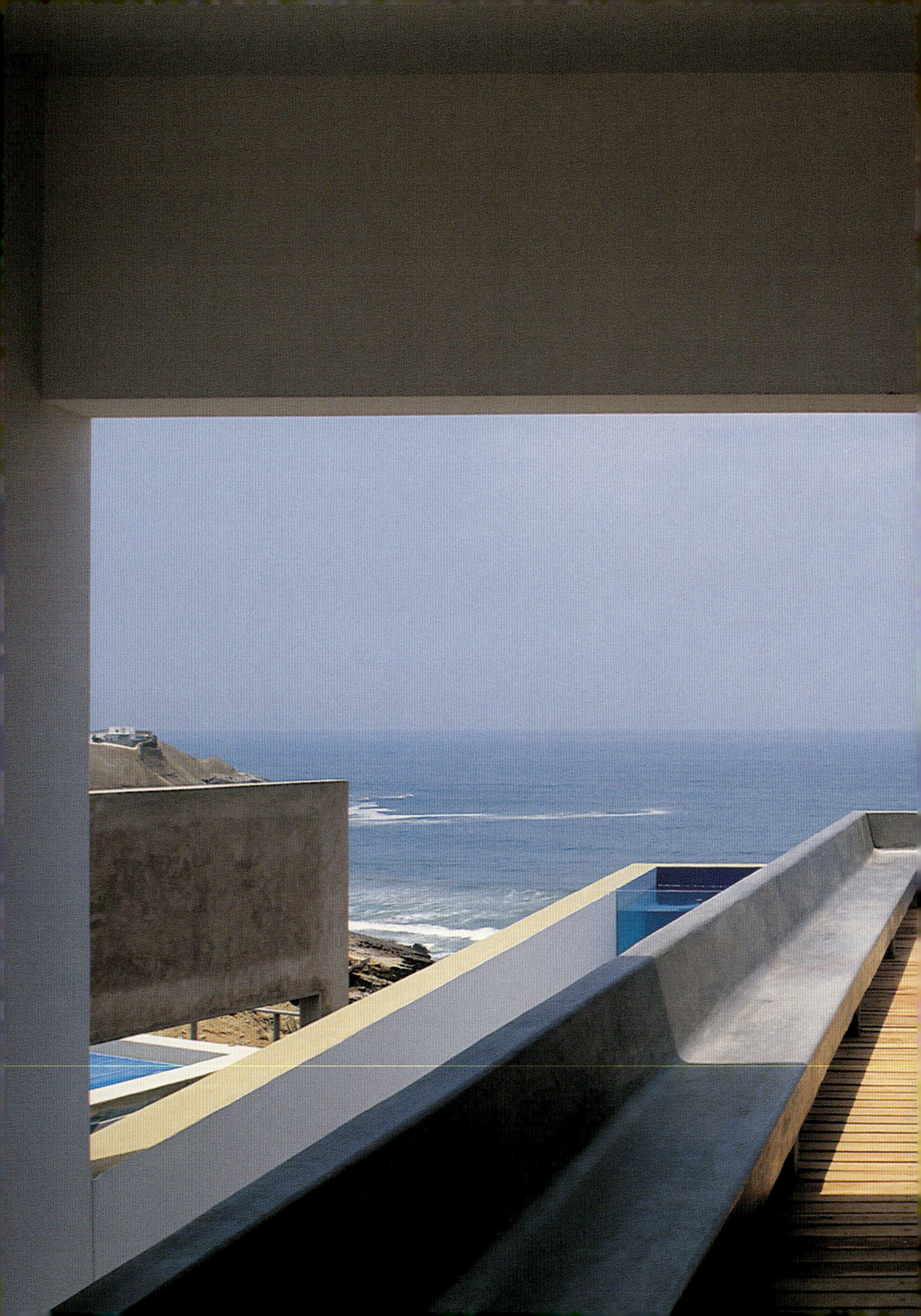

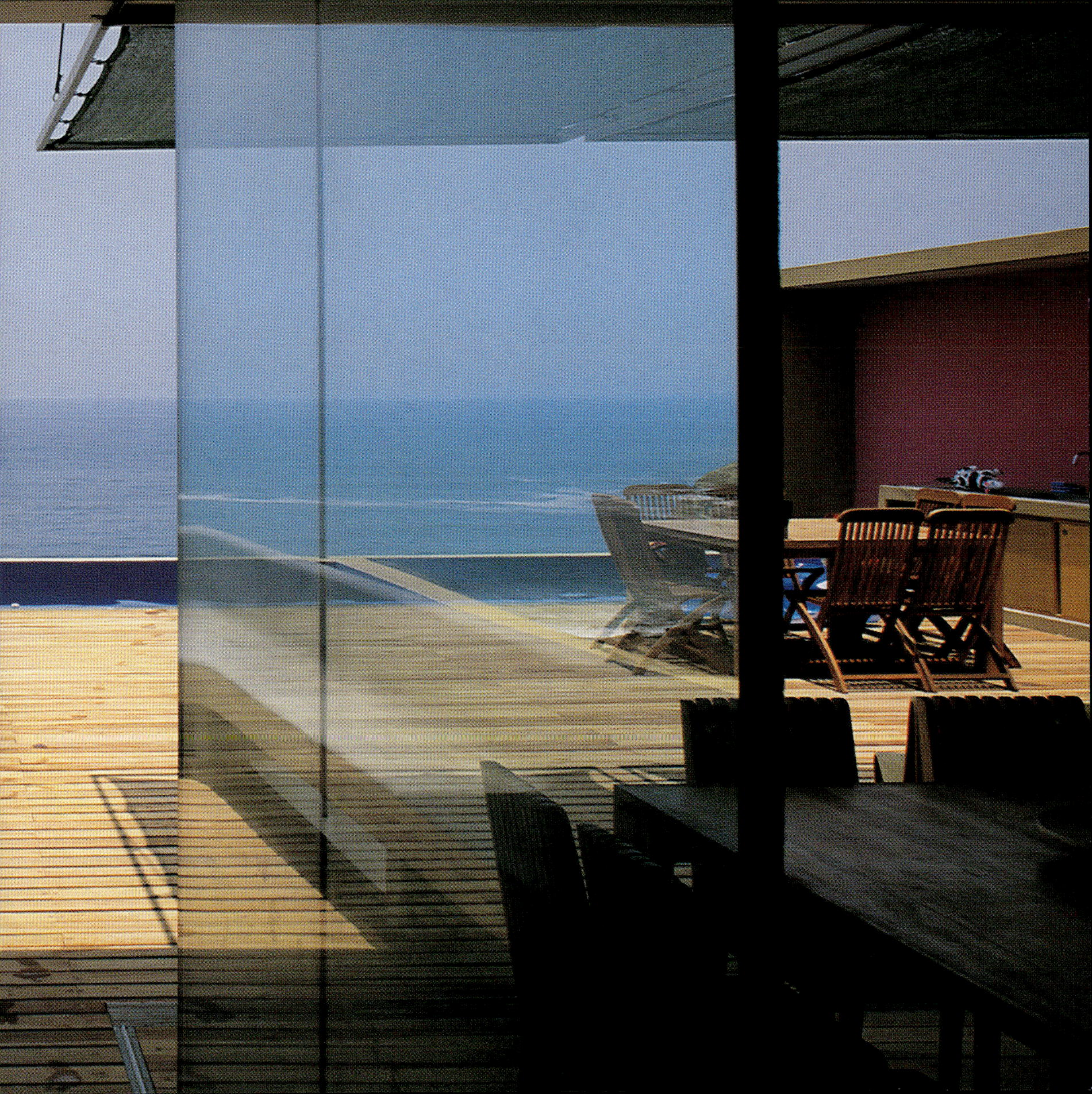

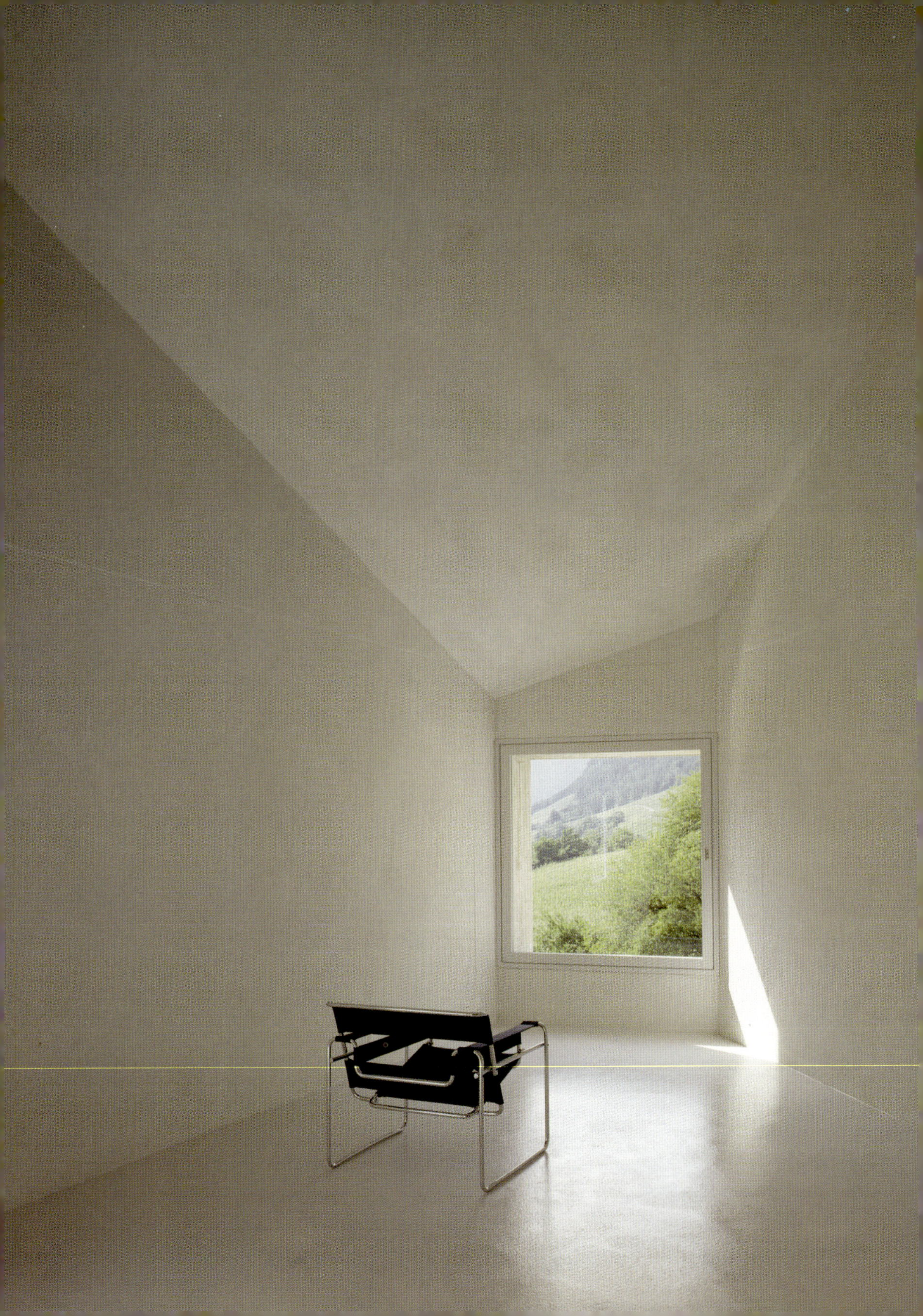

BEARTH + DEPLAZES ARCHITEKTEN | CHUR, ZURICH
House Meuli
Unterdorf/Fläsch, Switzerland | 2001

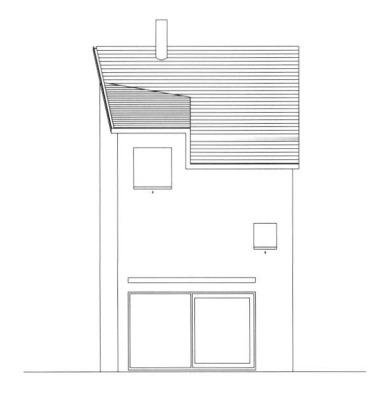

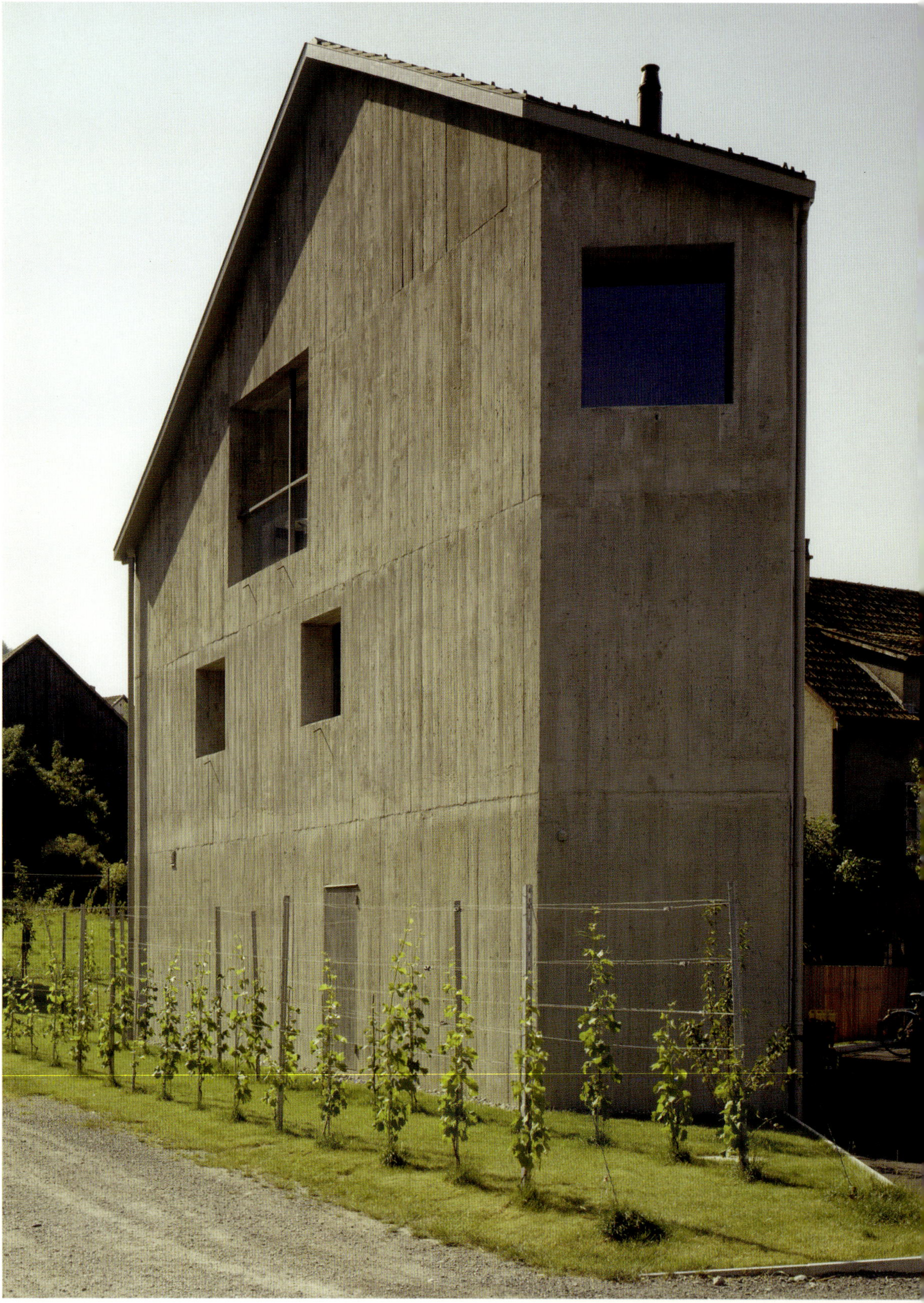

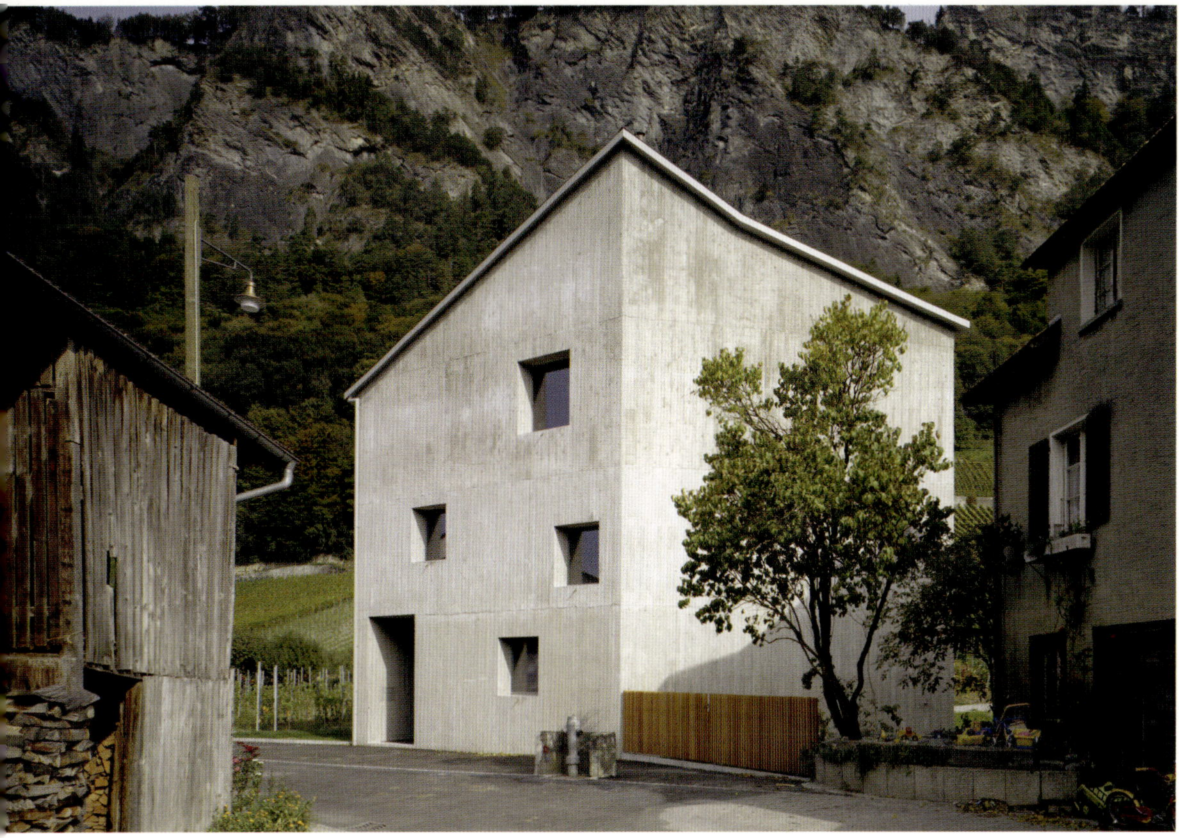

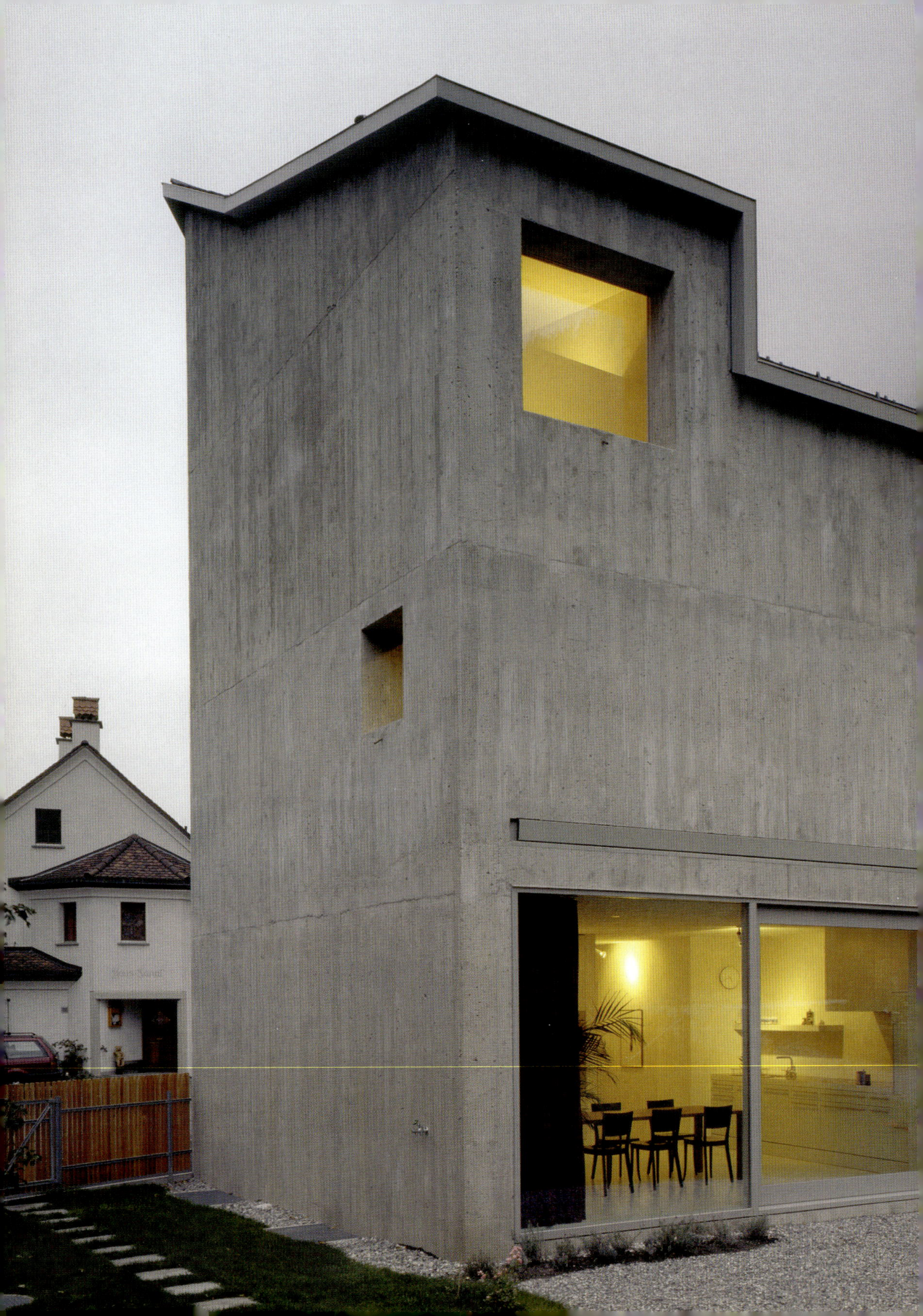

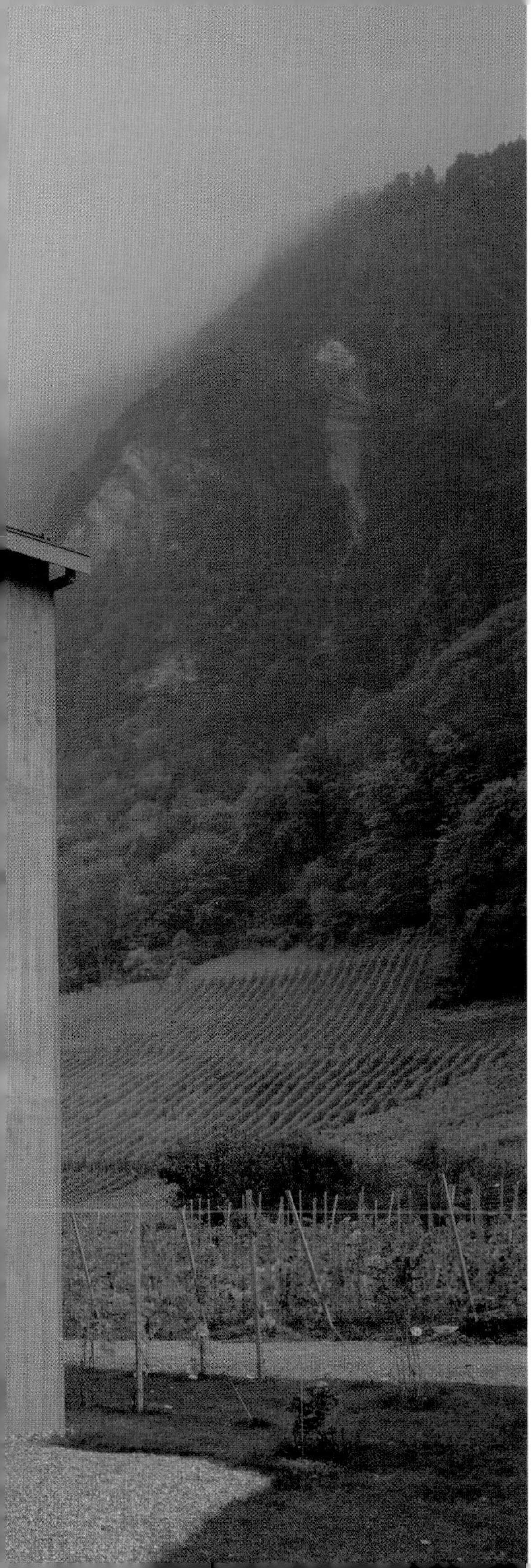

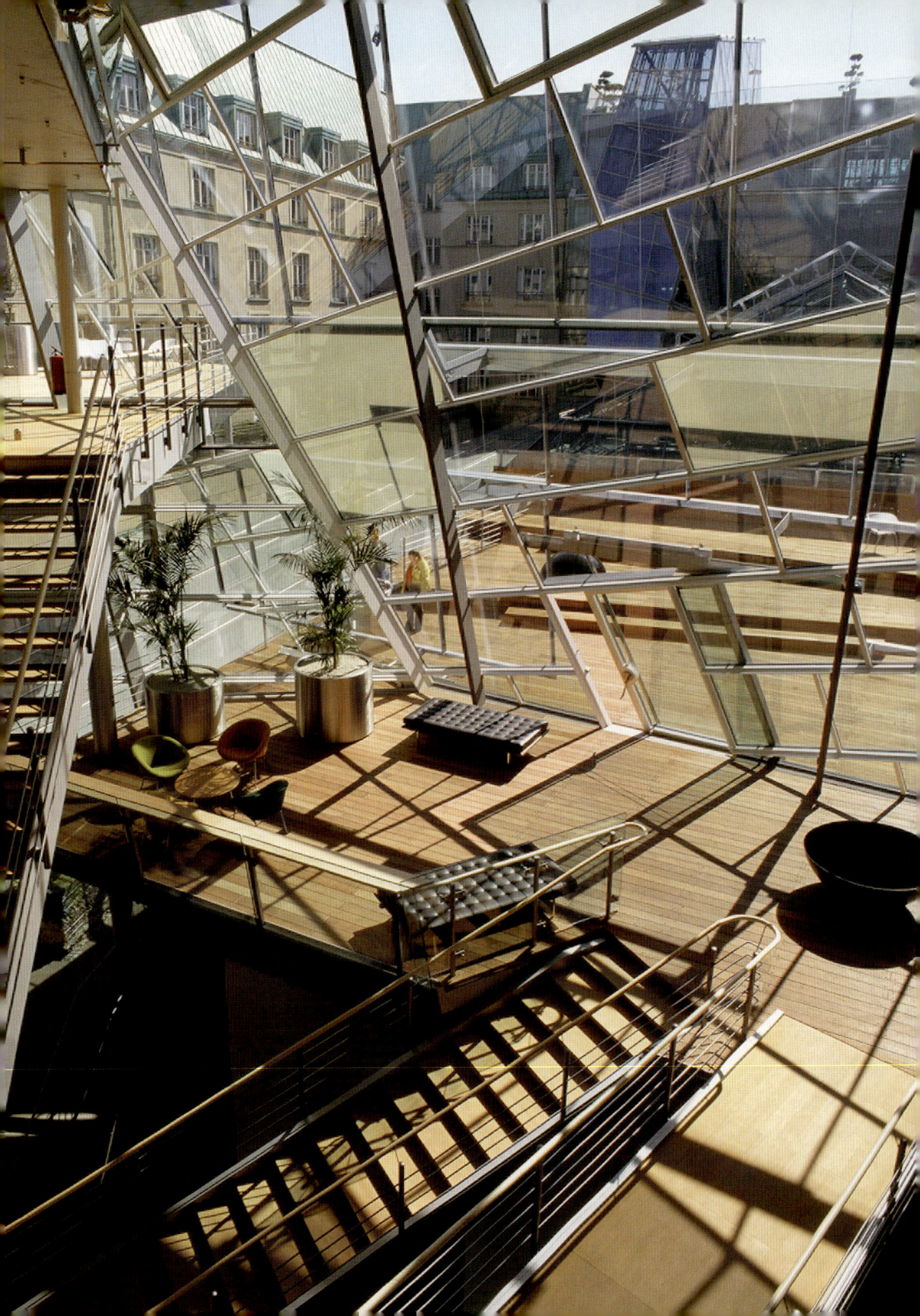

BEHNISCH & PARTNER | STUTTGART
Akademie der Künste
Berlin, Germany | 2005

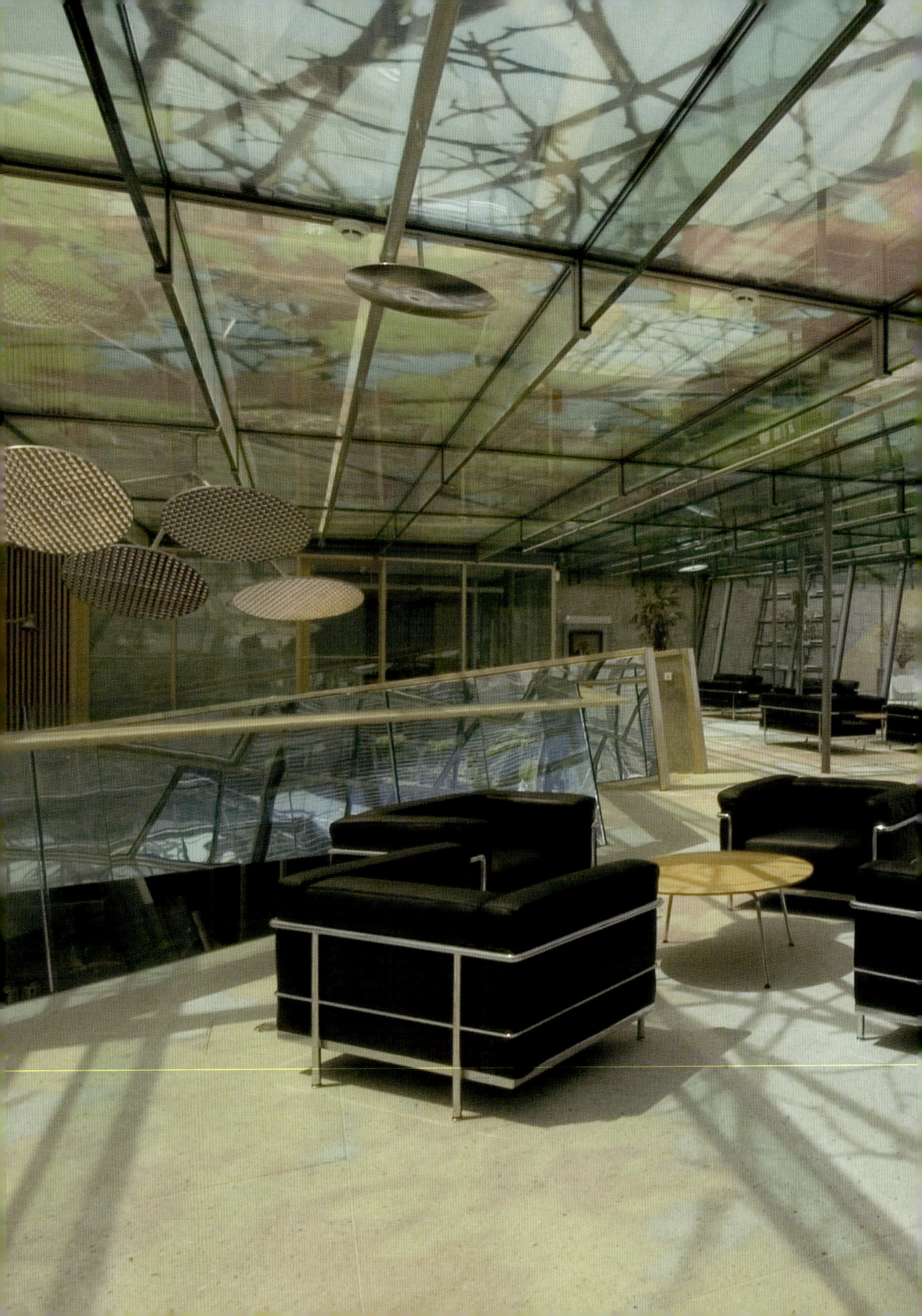

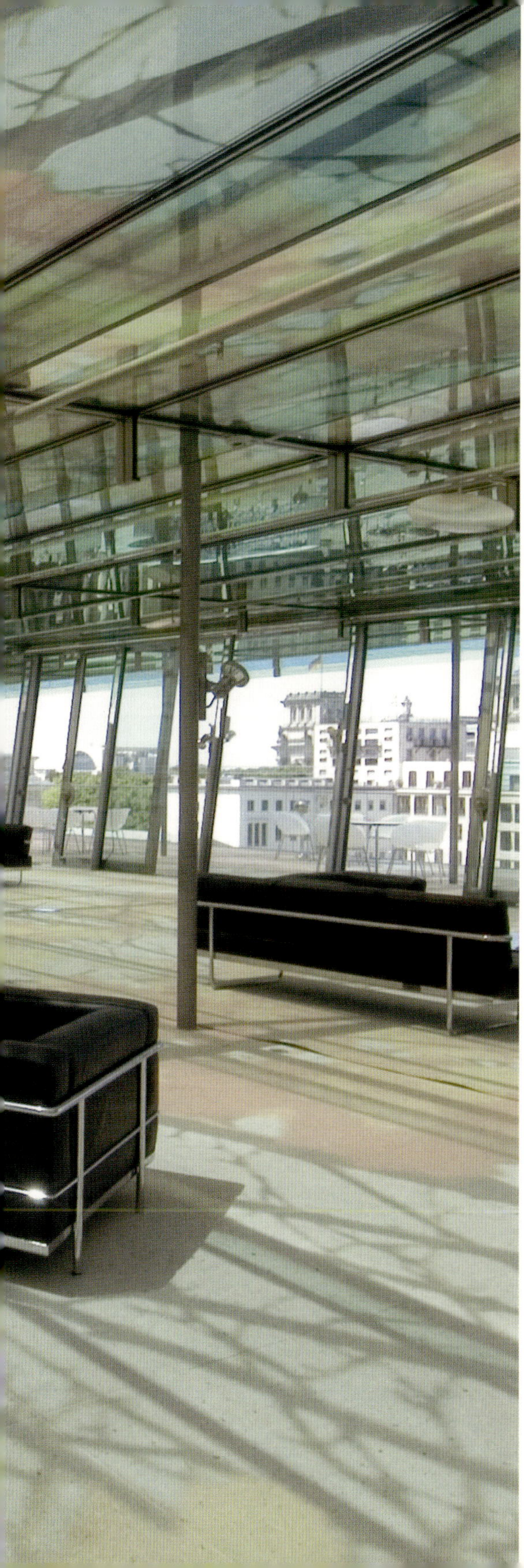

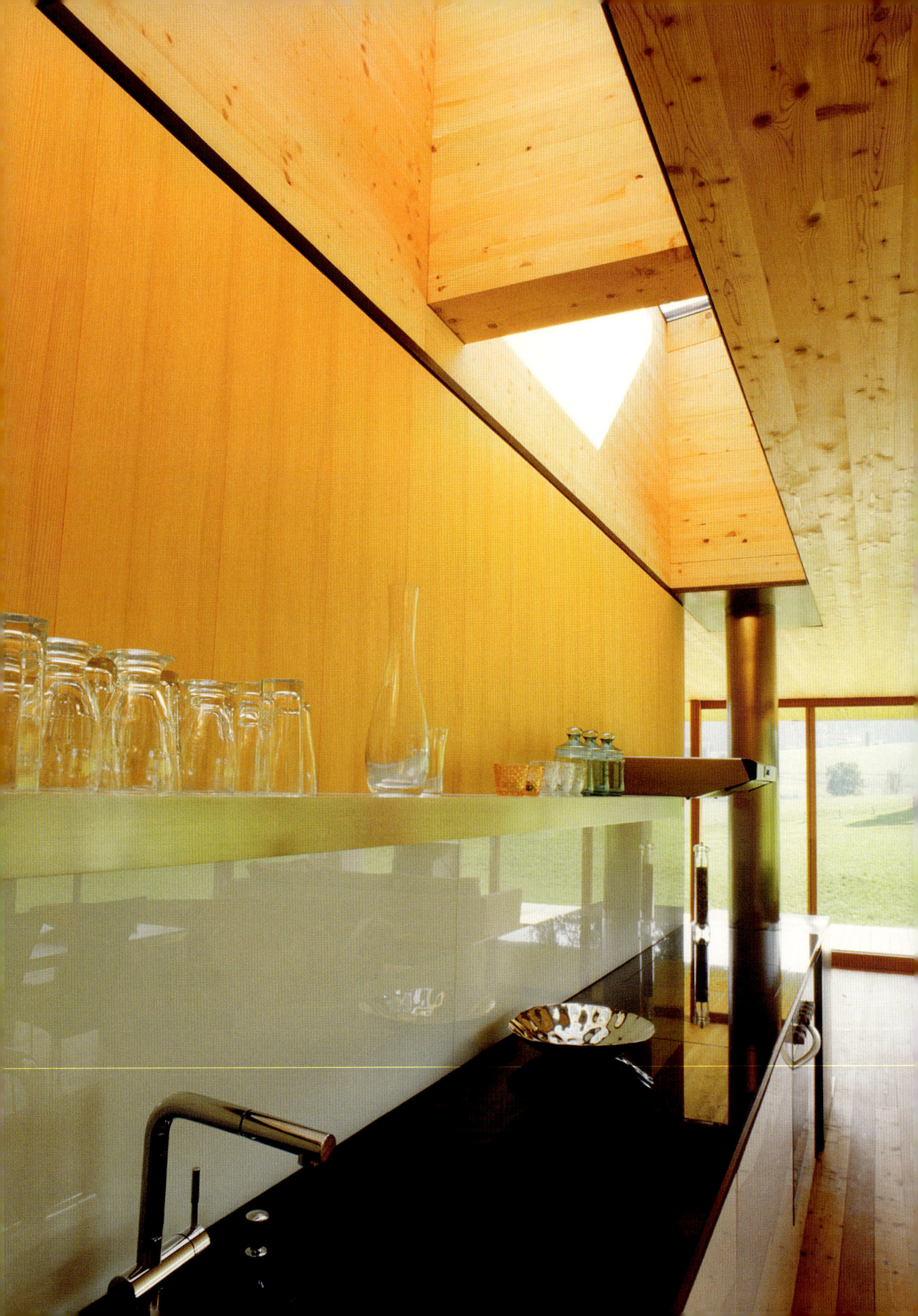

BERNARDO BADER | DORNBIRN
House Salgenreuthe
Krumbach, Austria | 2004

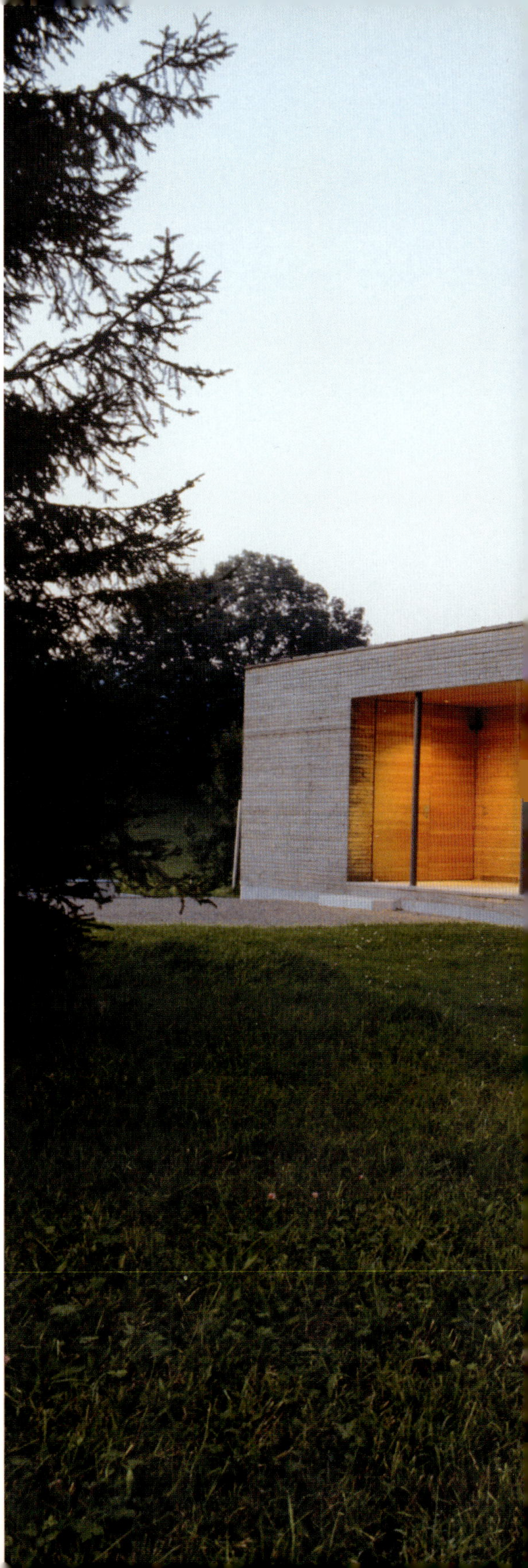

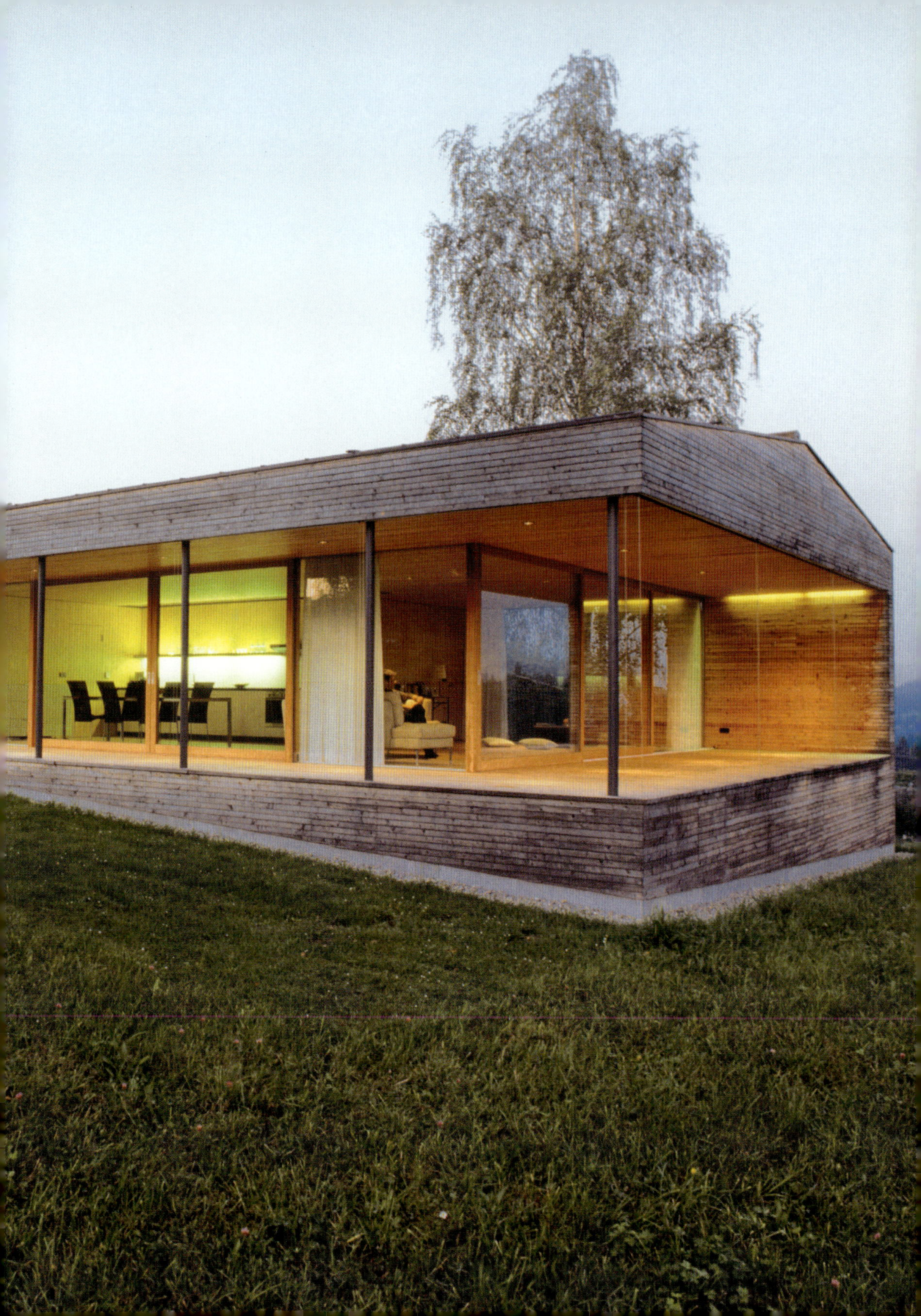

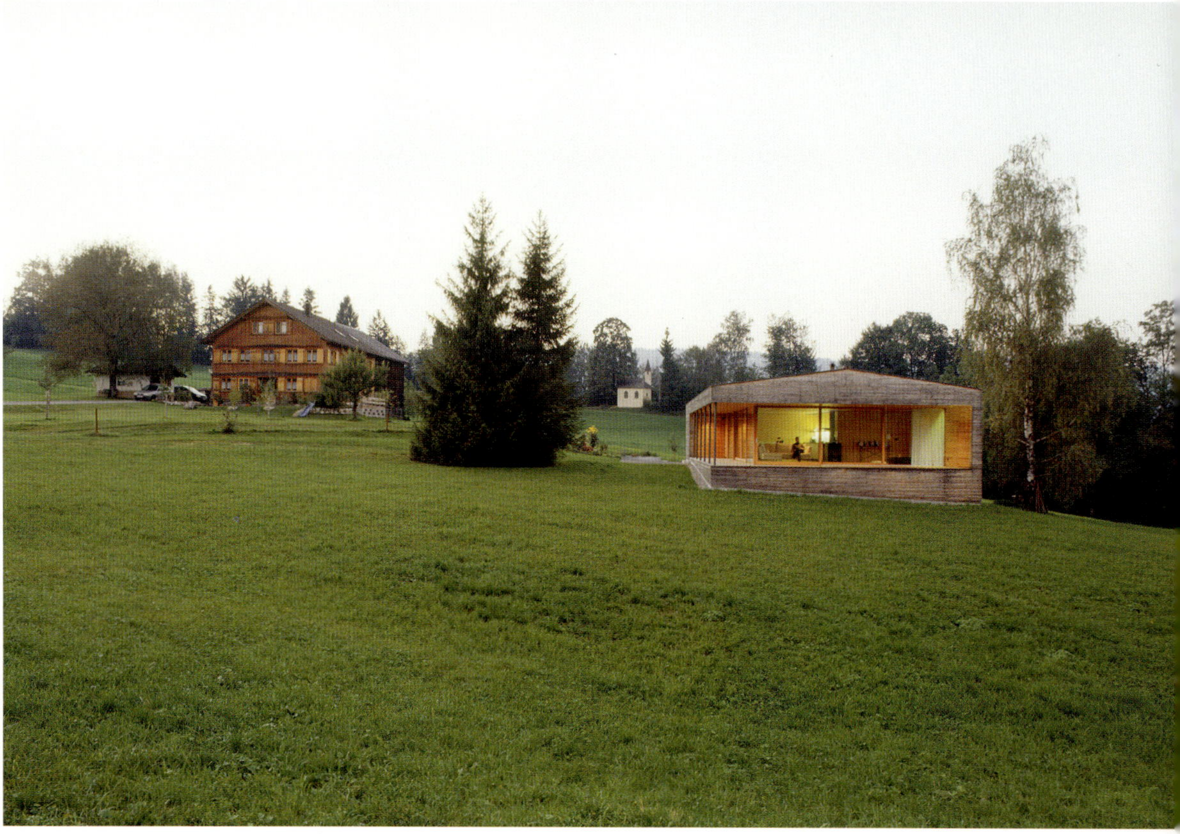

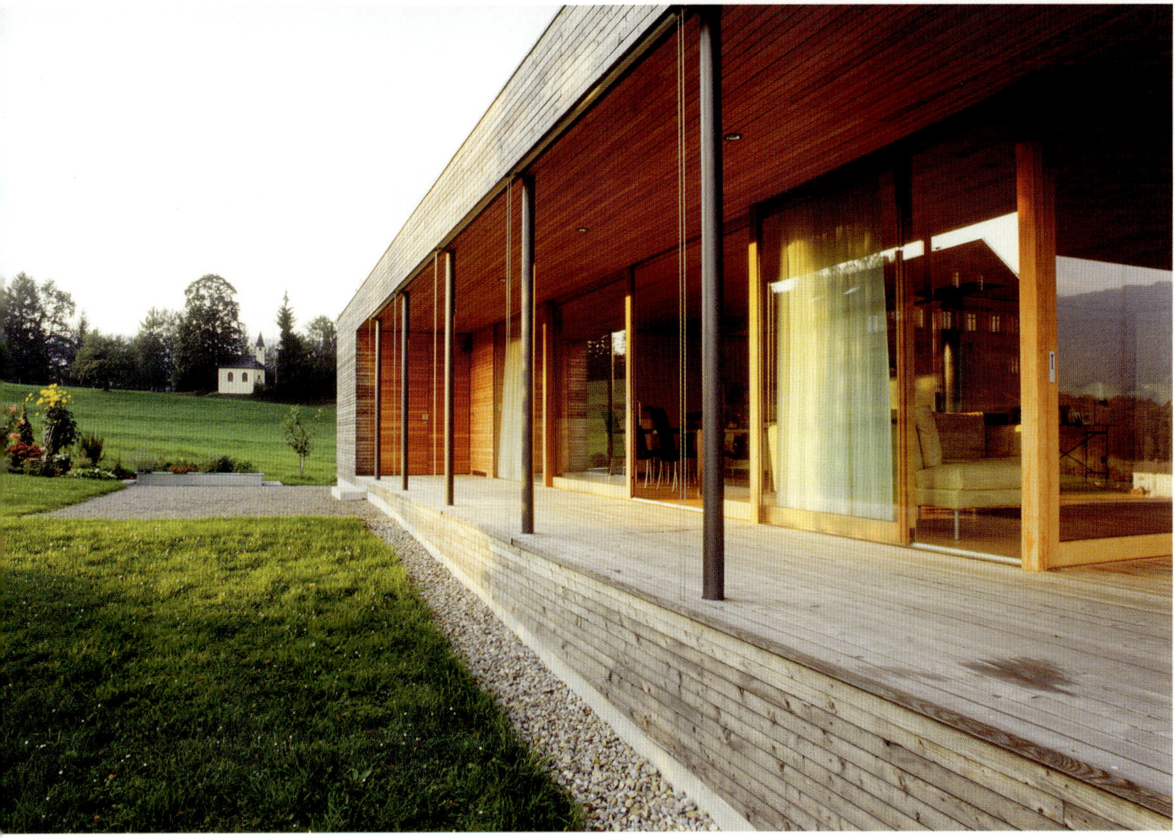

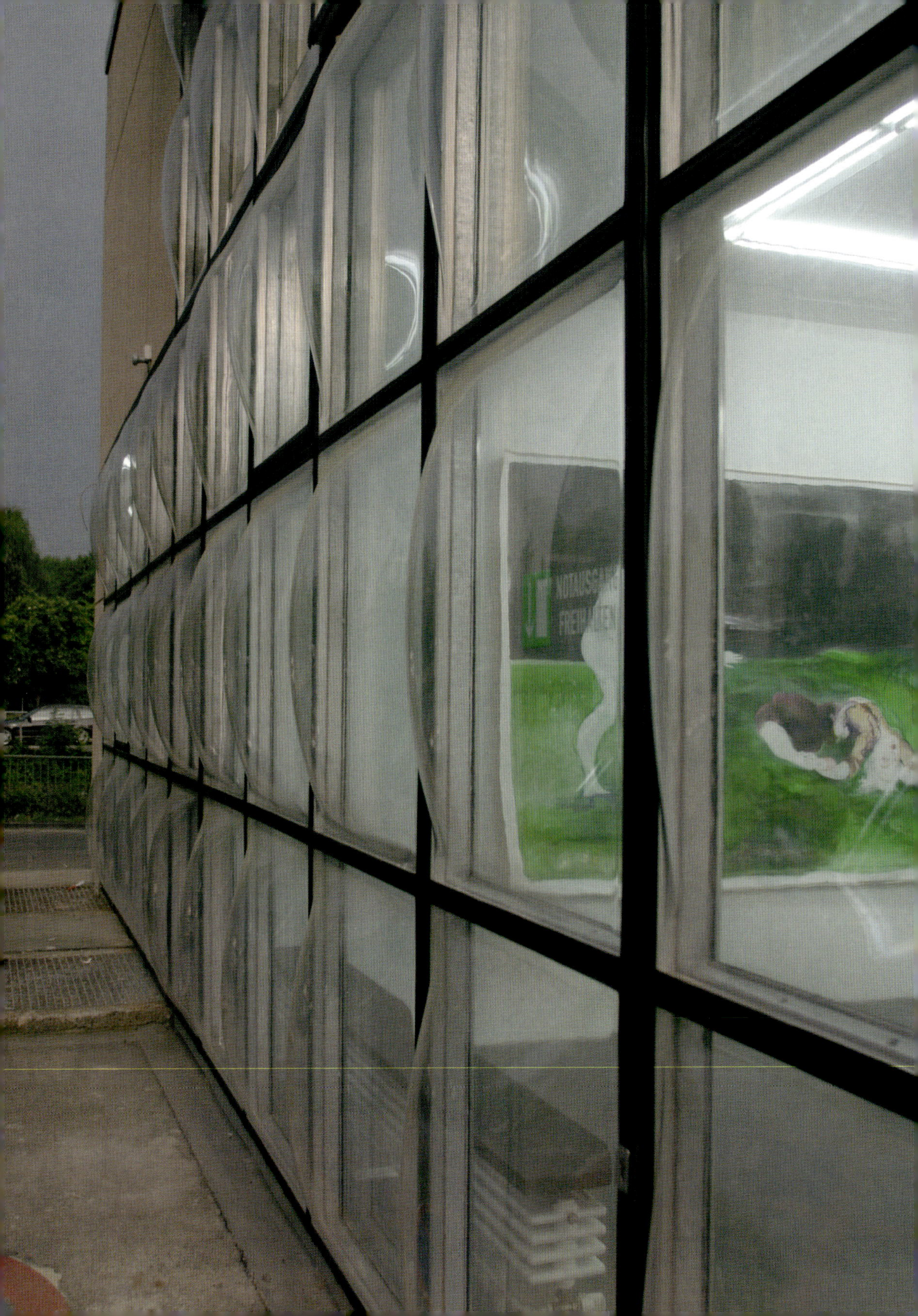

BERND KNIESS ARCHITEKTEN STADTPLANER | COLOGNE
Galery ads1a
Cologne, Germany | 2002

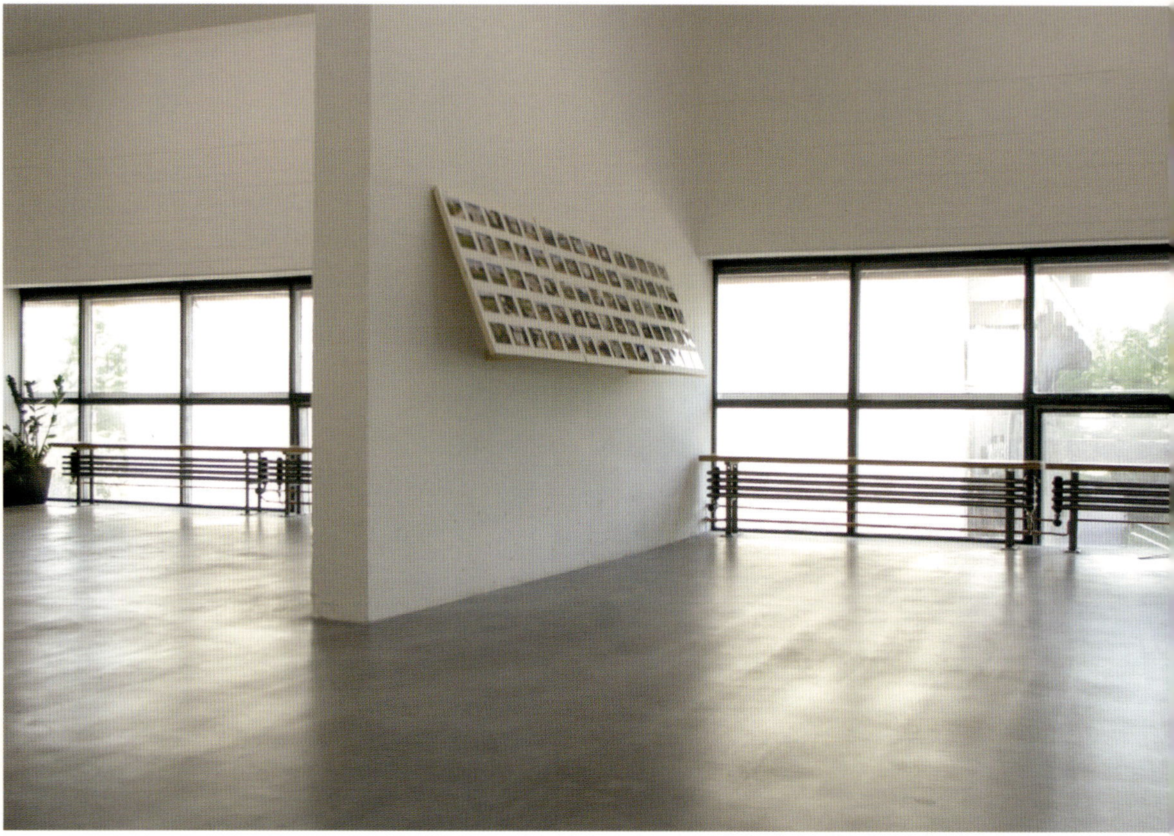

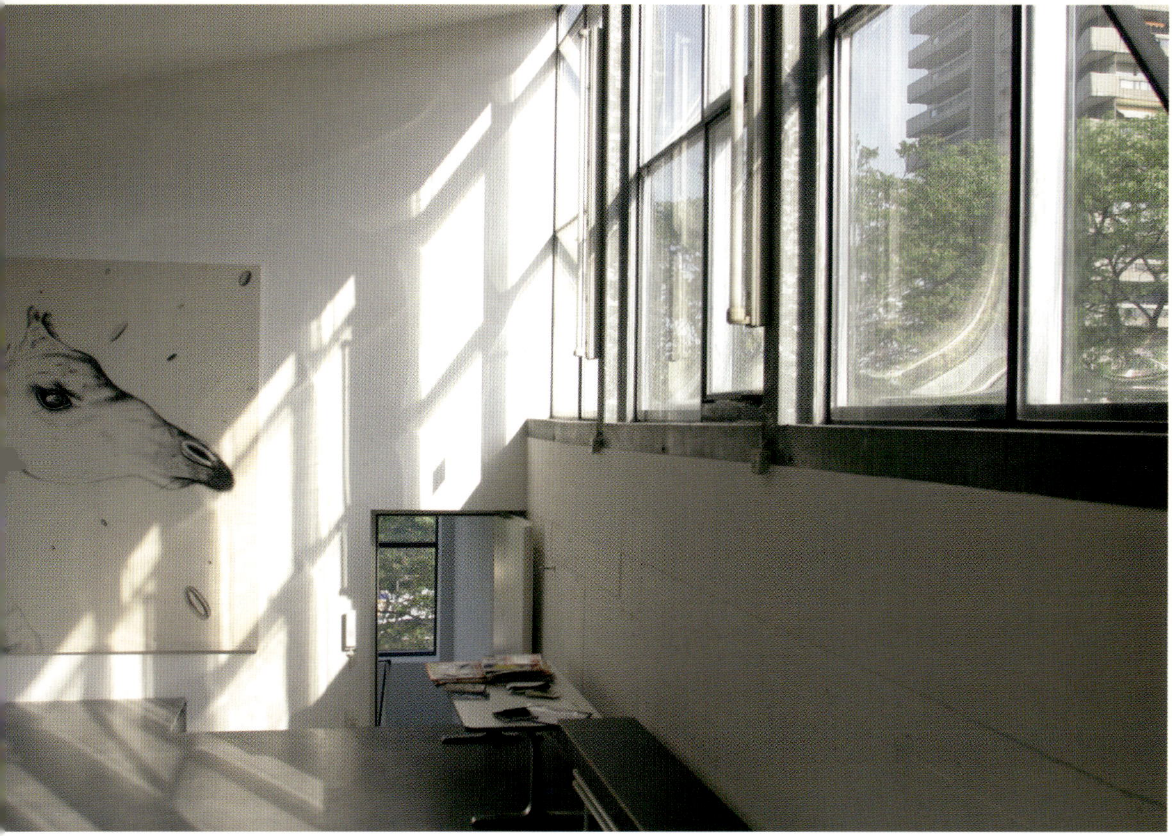

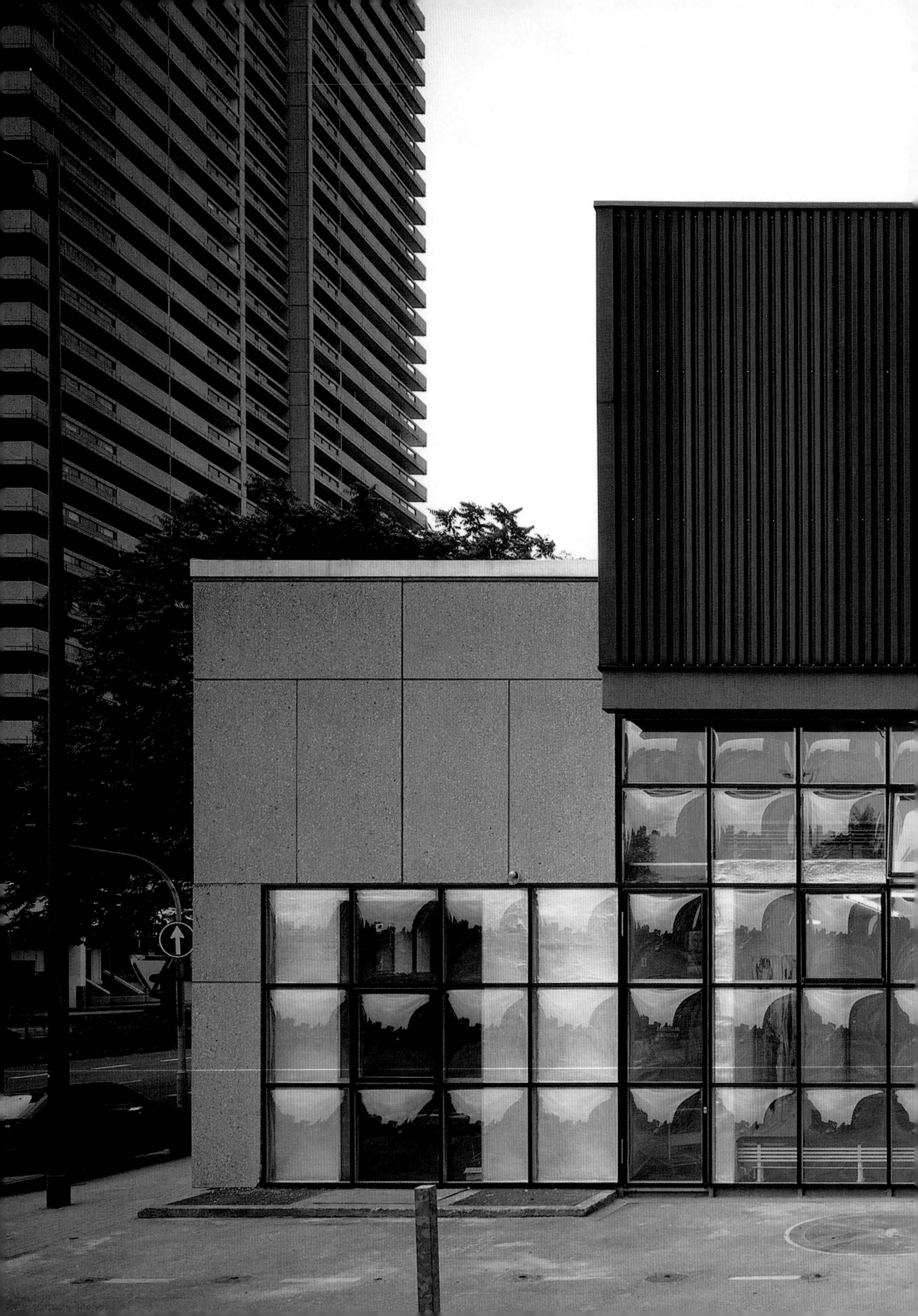

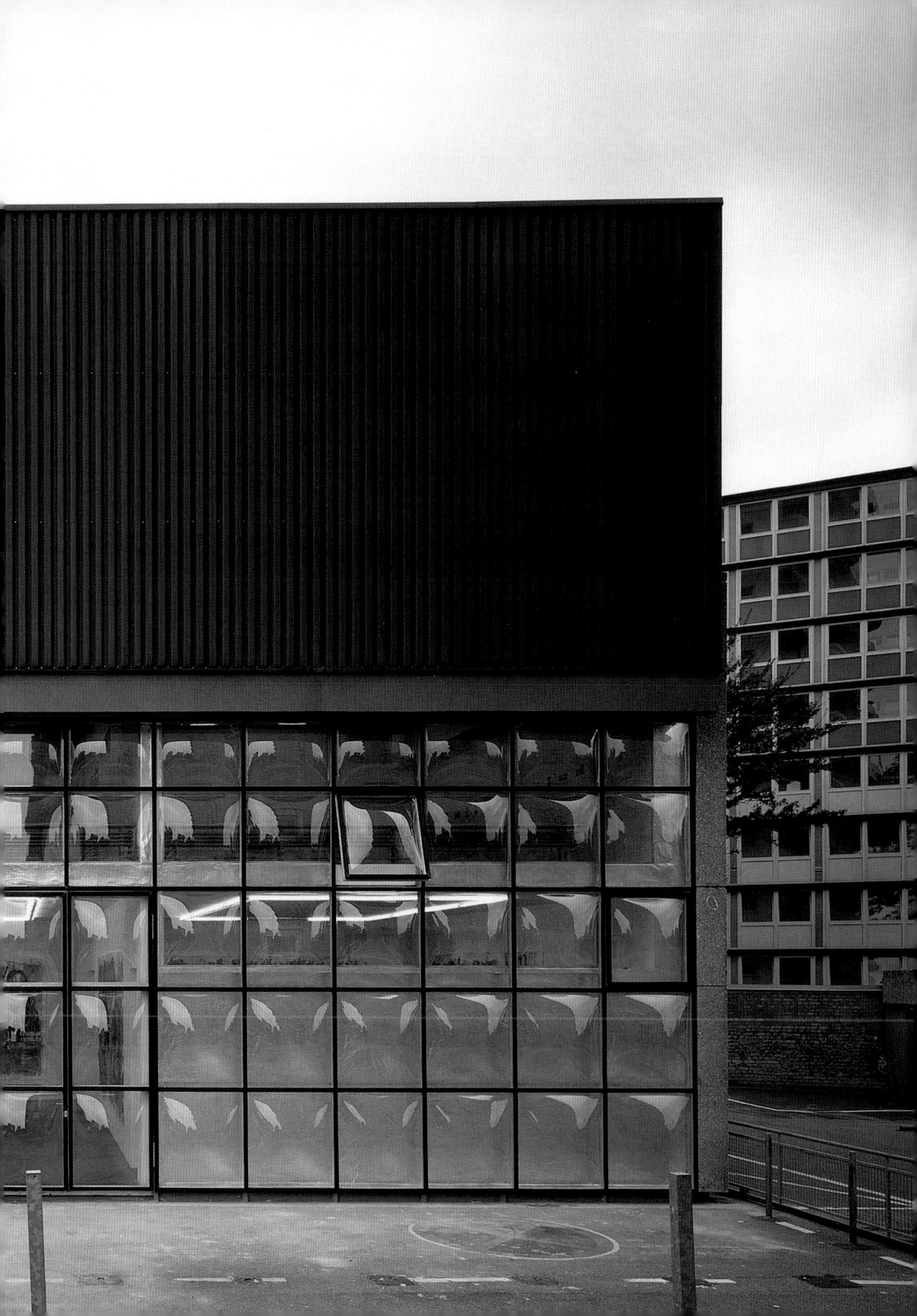

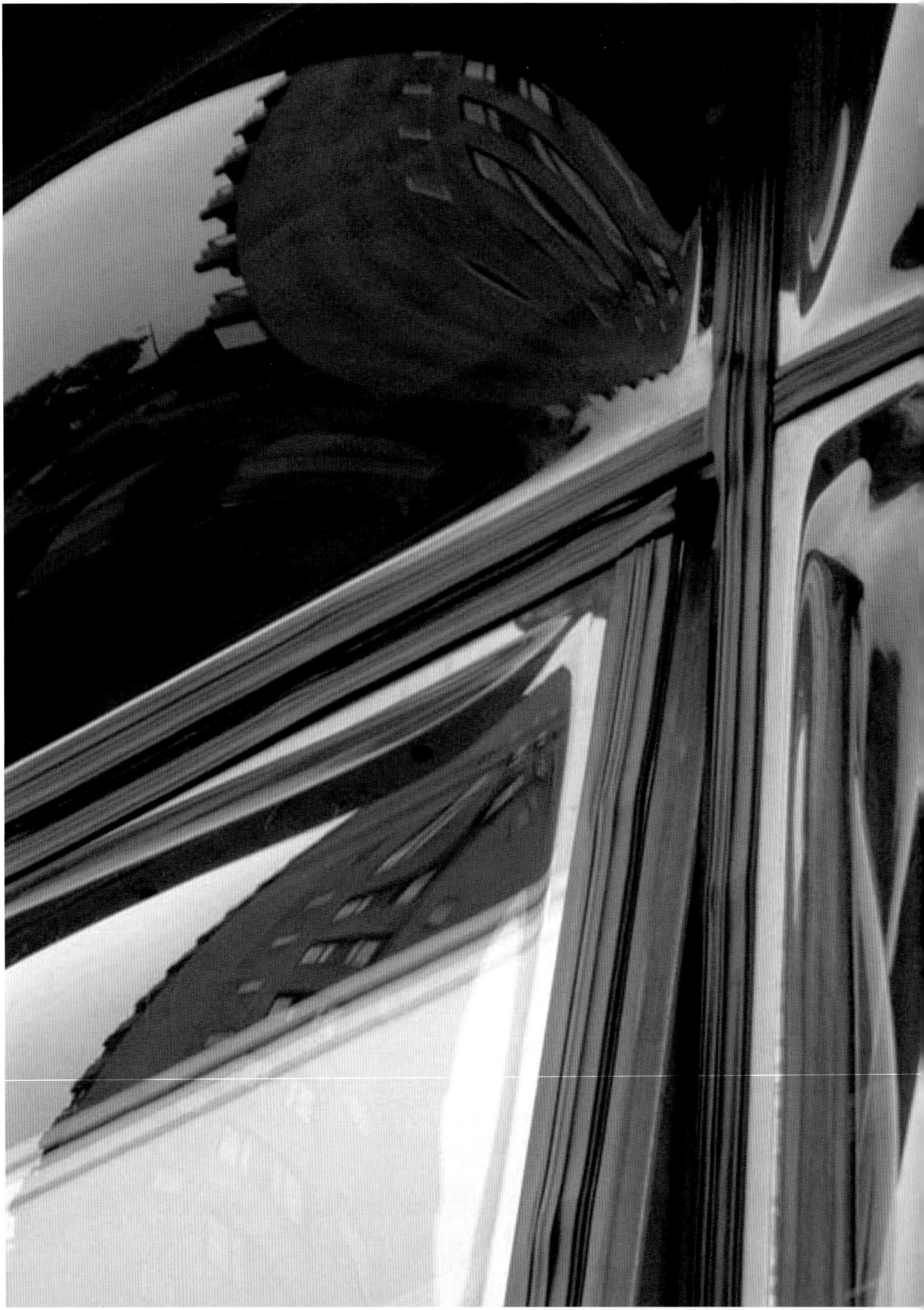

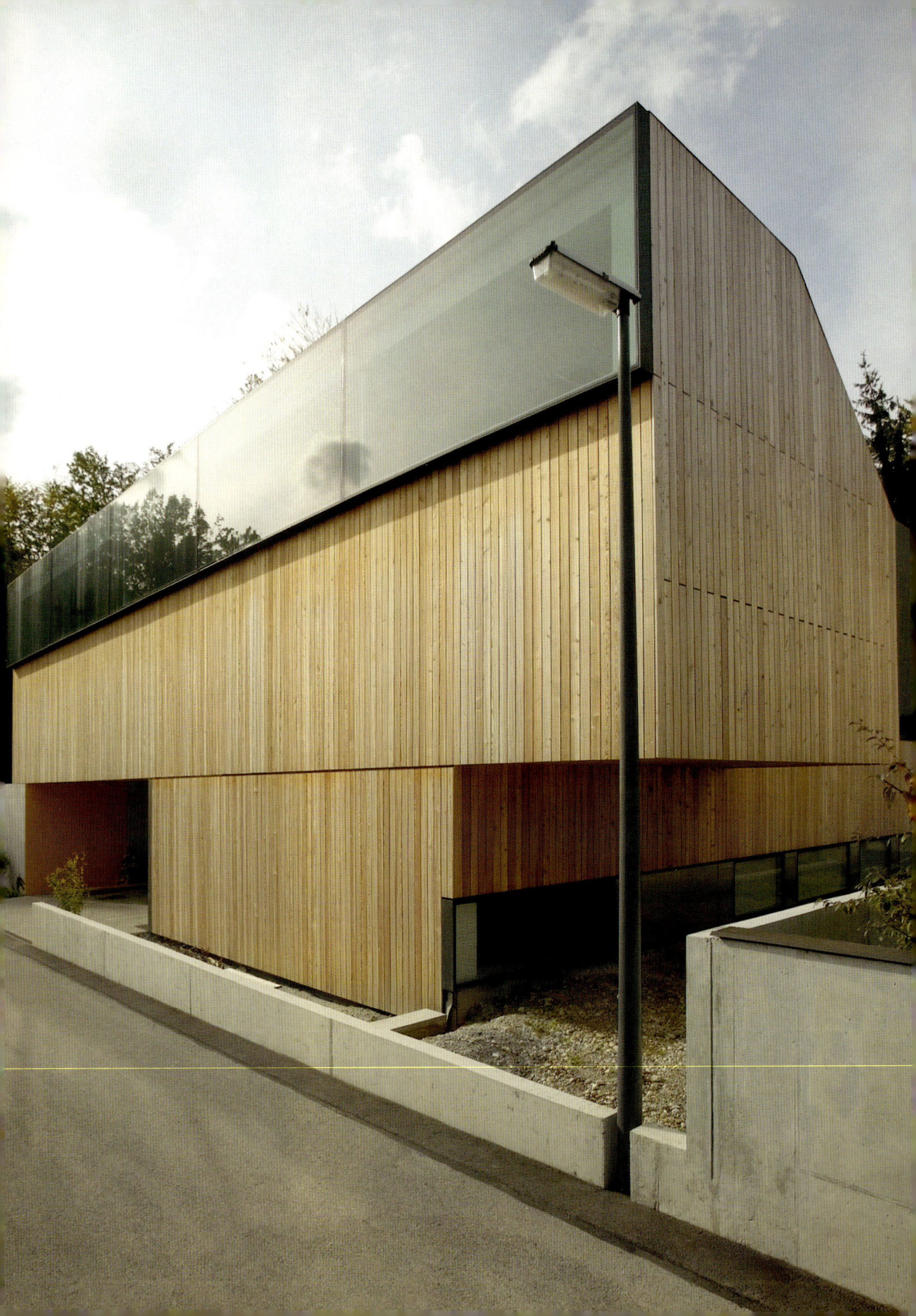

BEVK PEROVIC ARCHITECTS | LJUBLJANA
SB House
Ljubljana, Slovenia | 2004

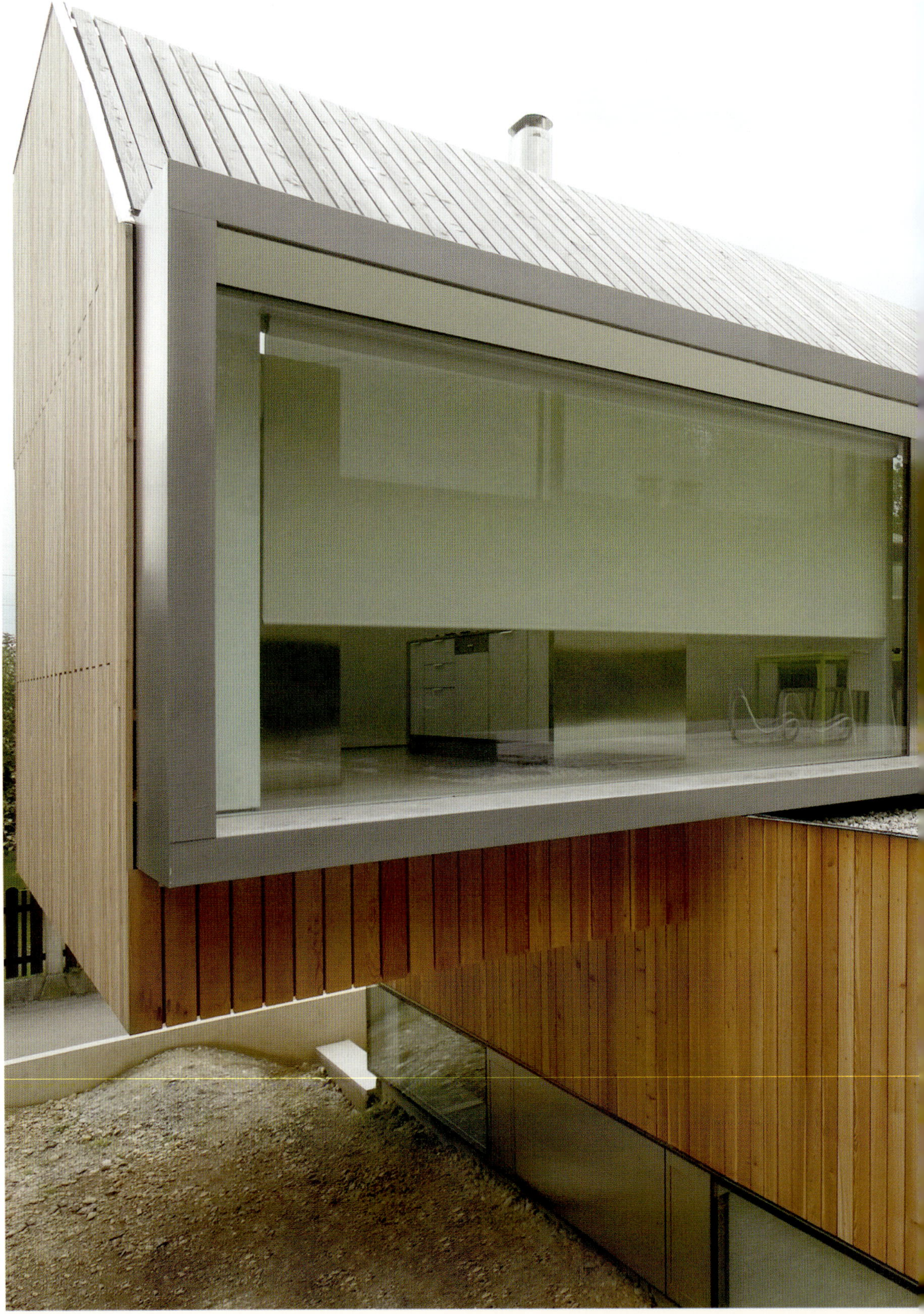

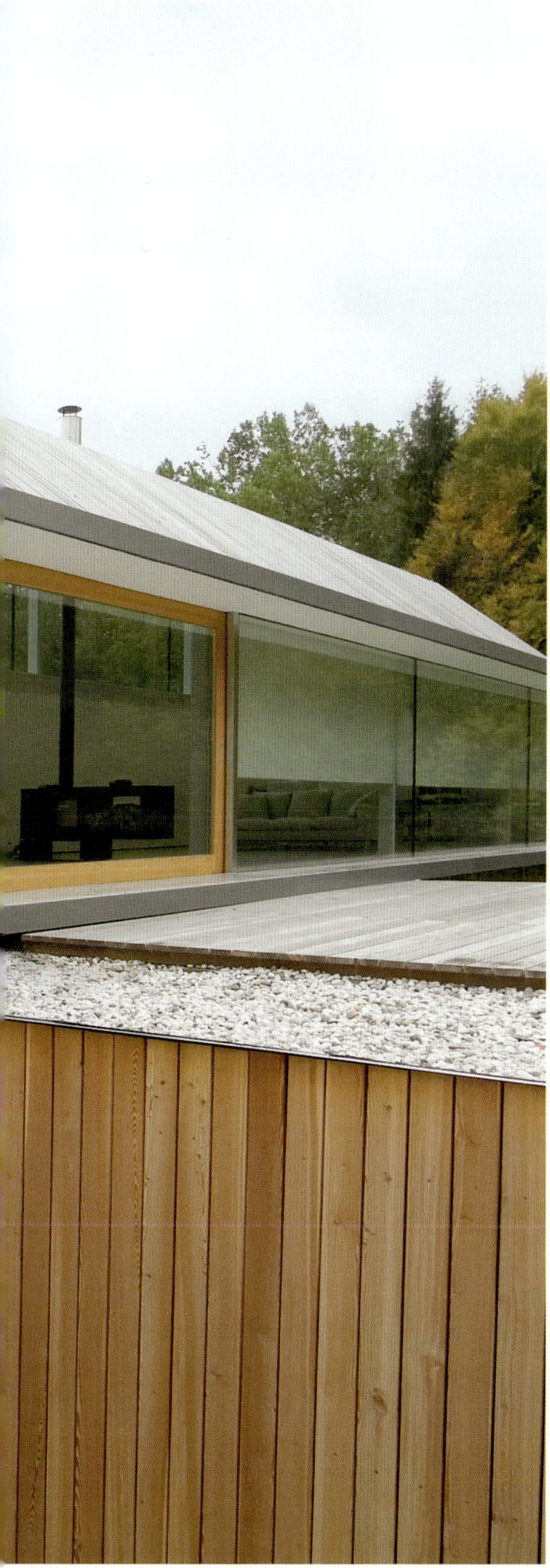

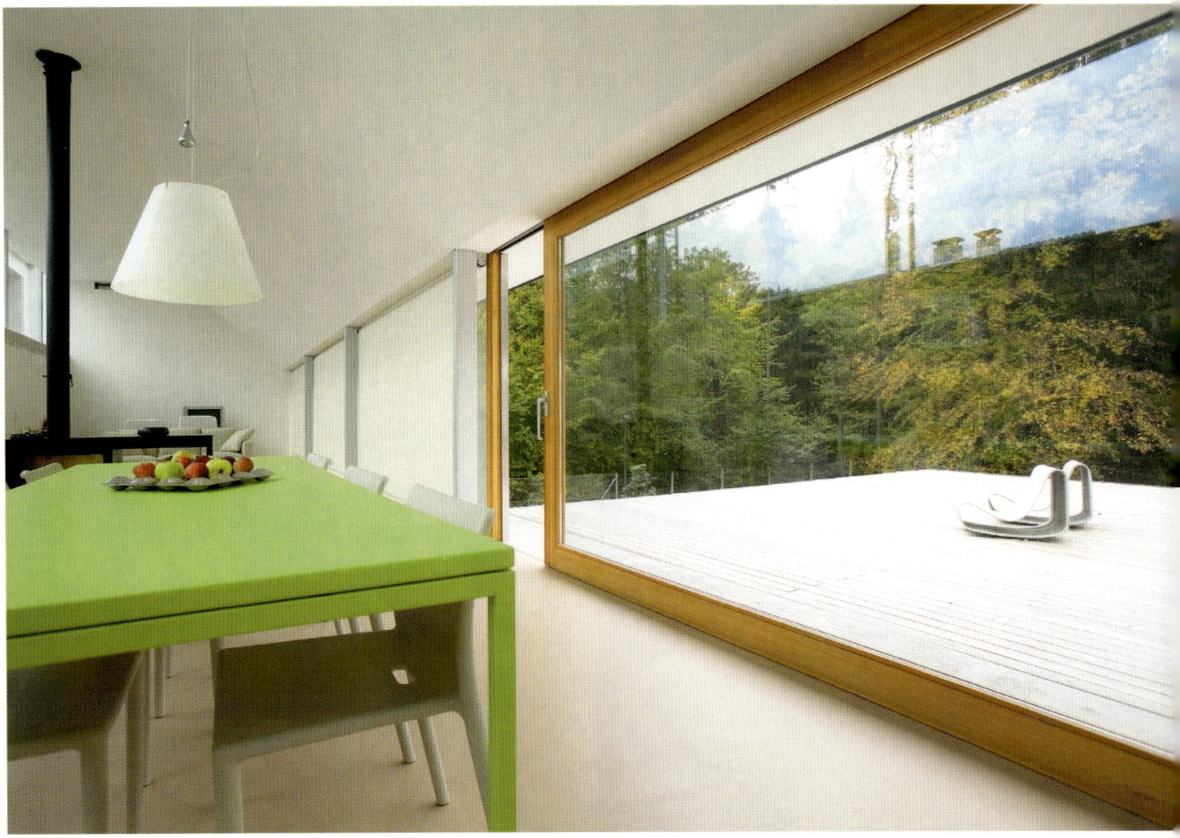

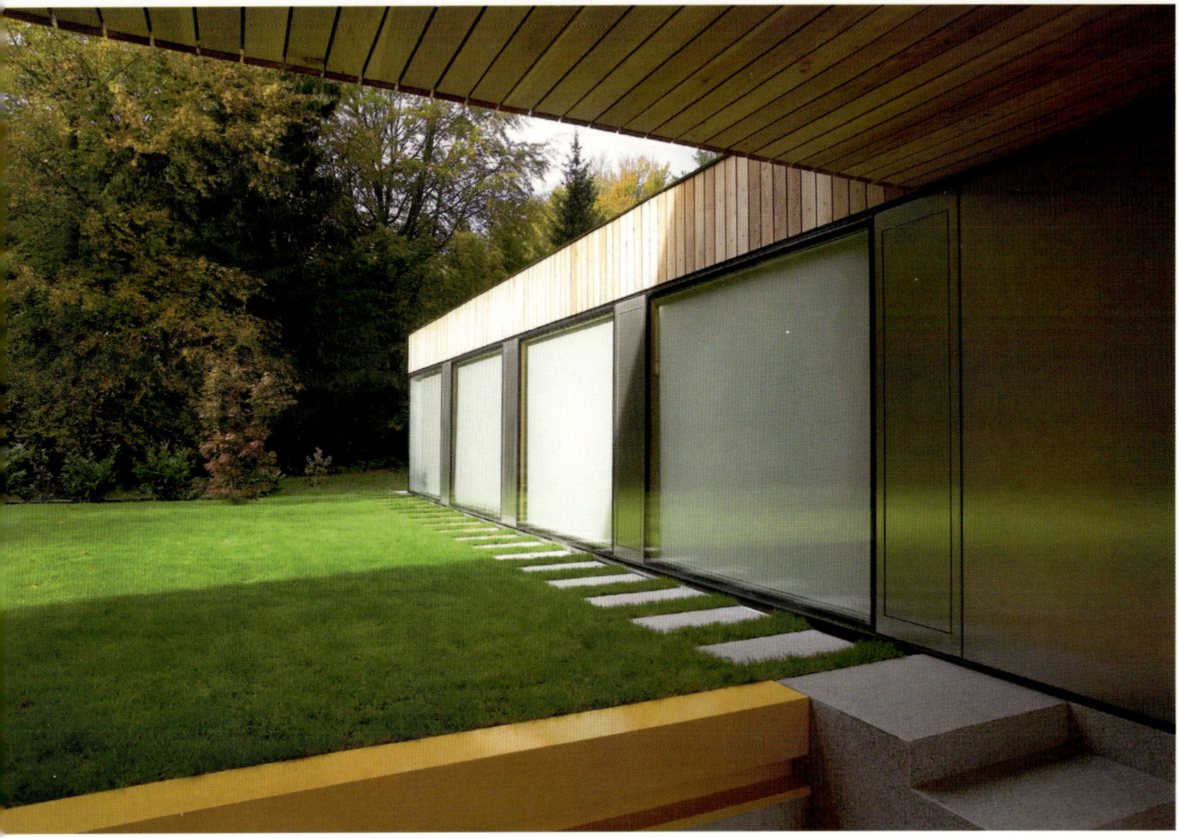

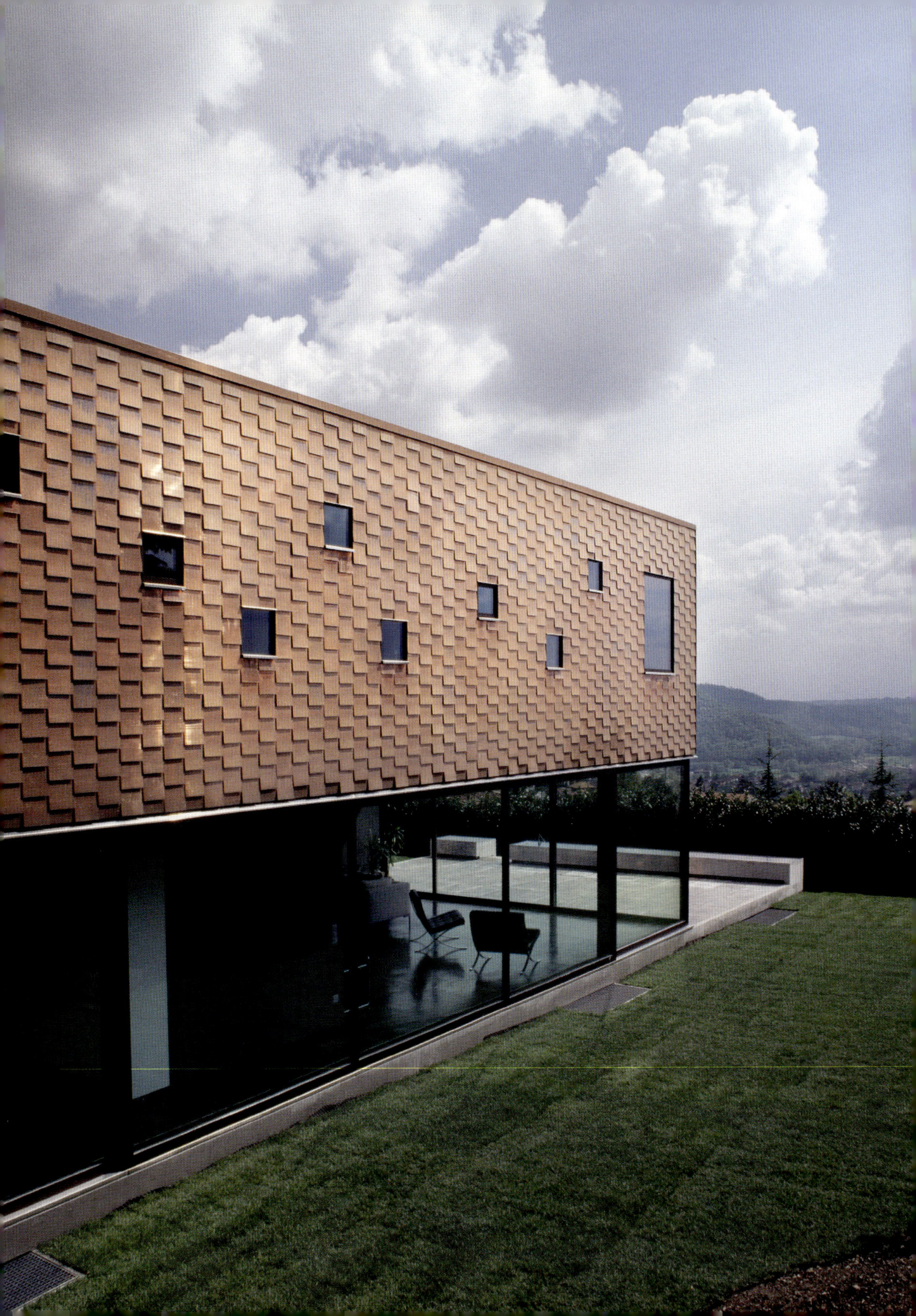

ALDO CELORIA | BALERNA
Casa Travella
Castel San Pietro, Schweiz | 2004

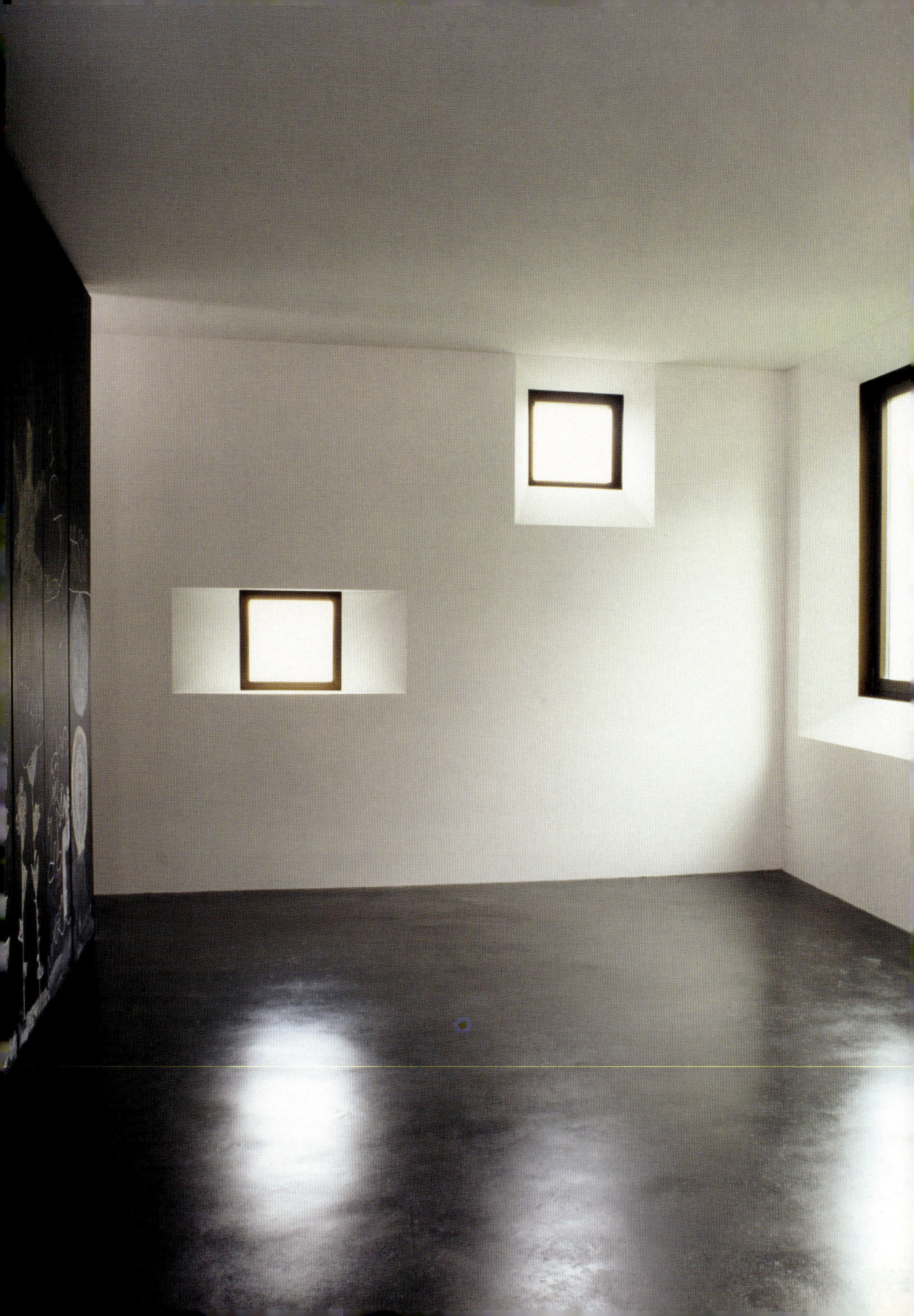

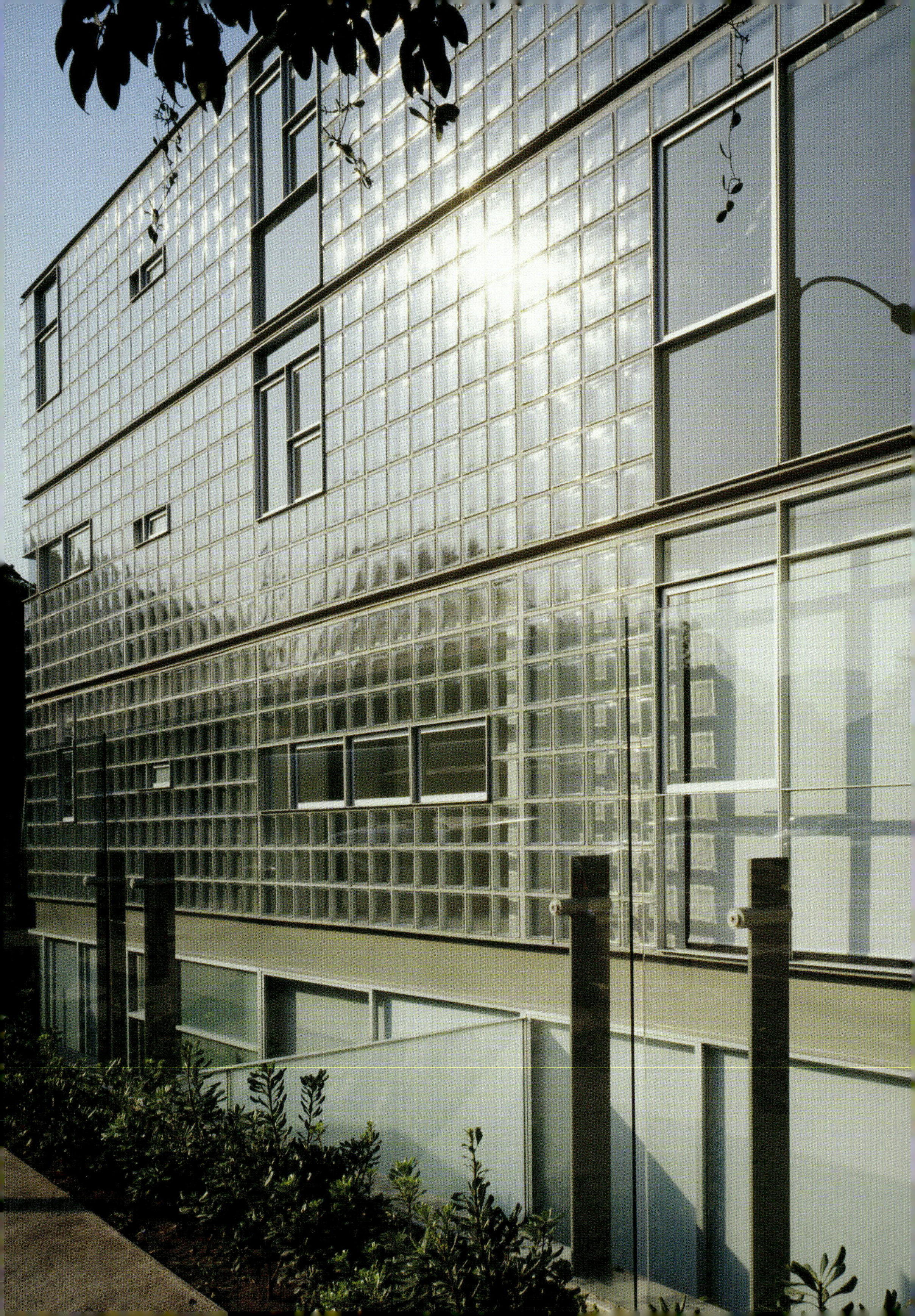

CENTRAL DE ARQUITECTURA | MEXCIO CITY
Dumas + Horacio
Mexico City, Mexico | 2005

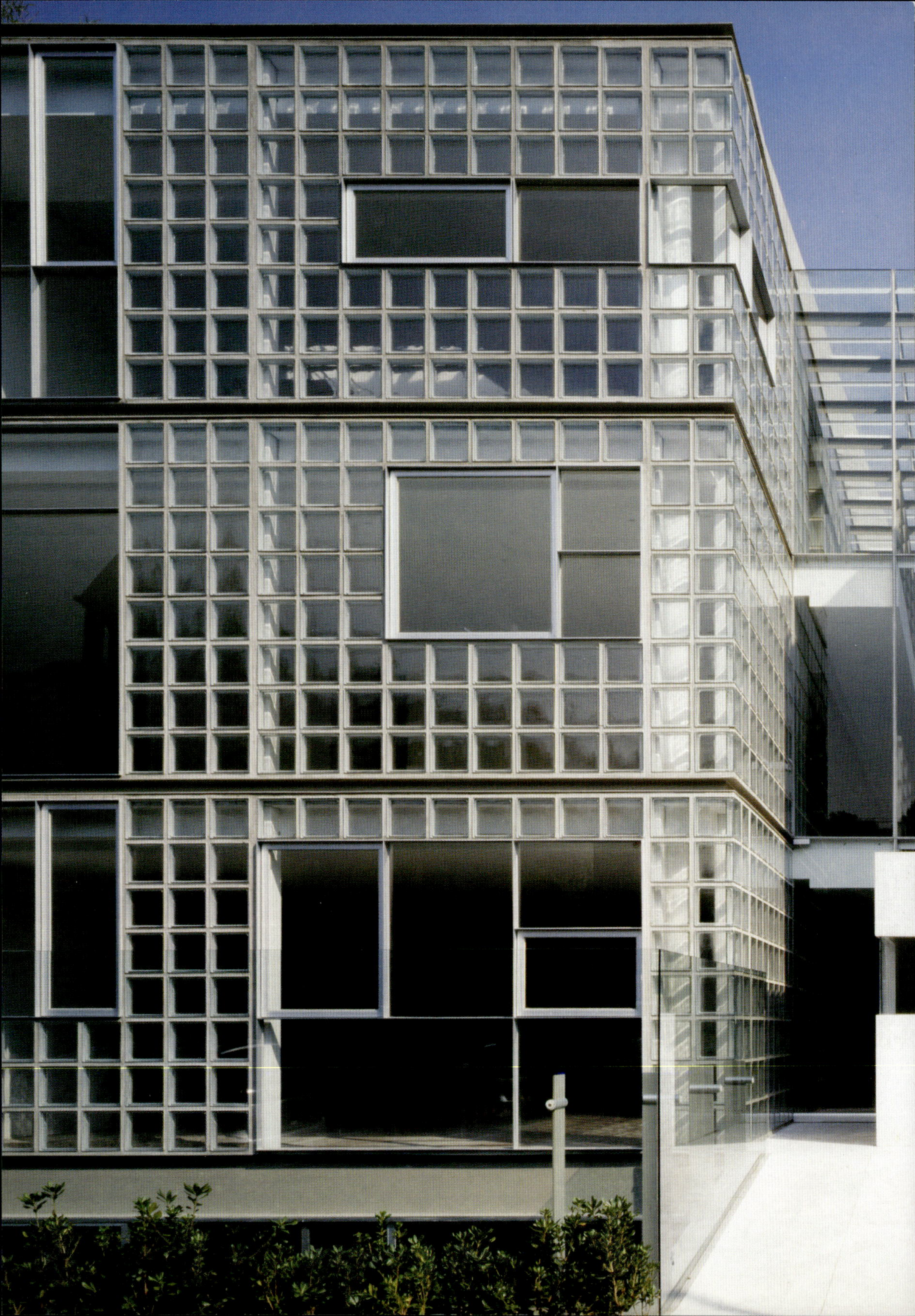

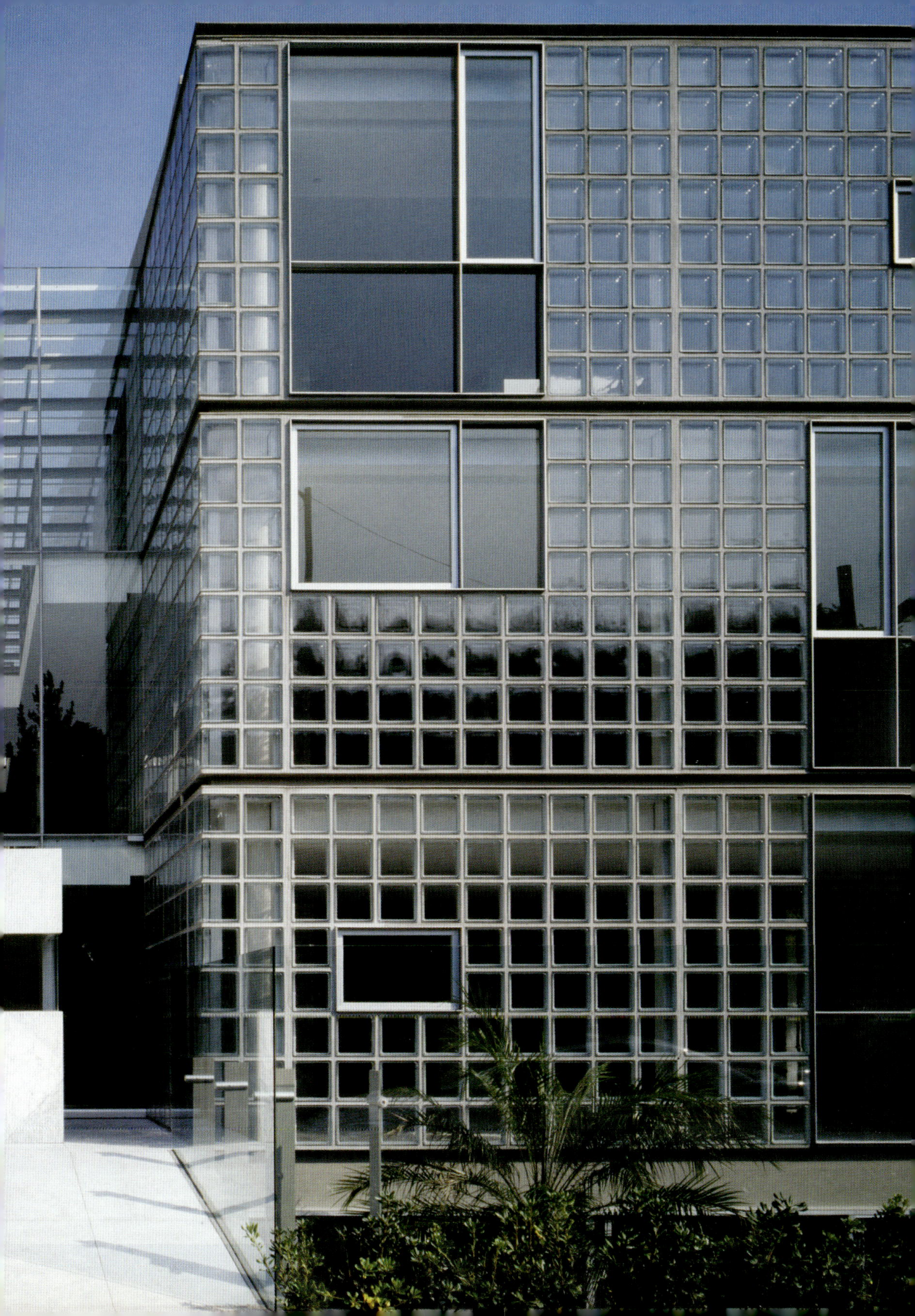

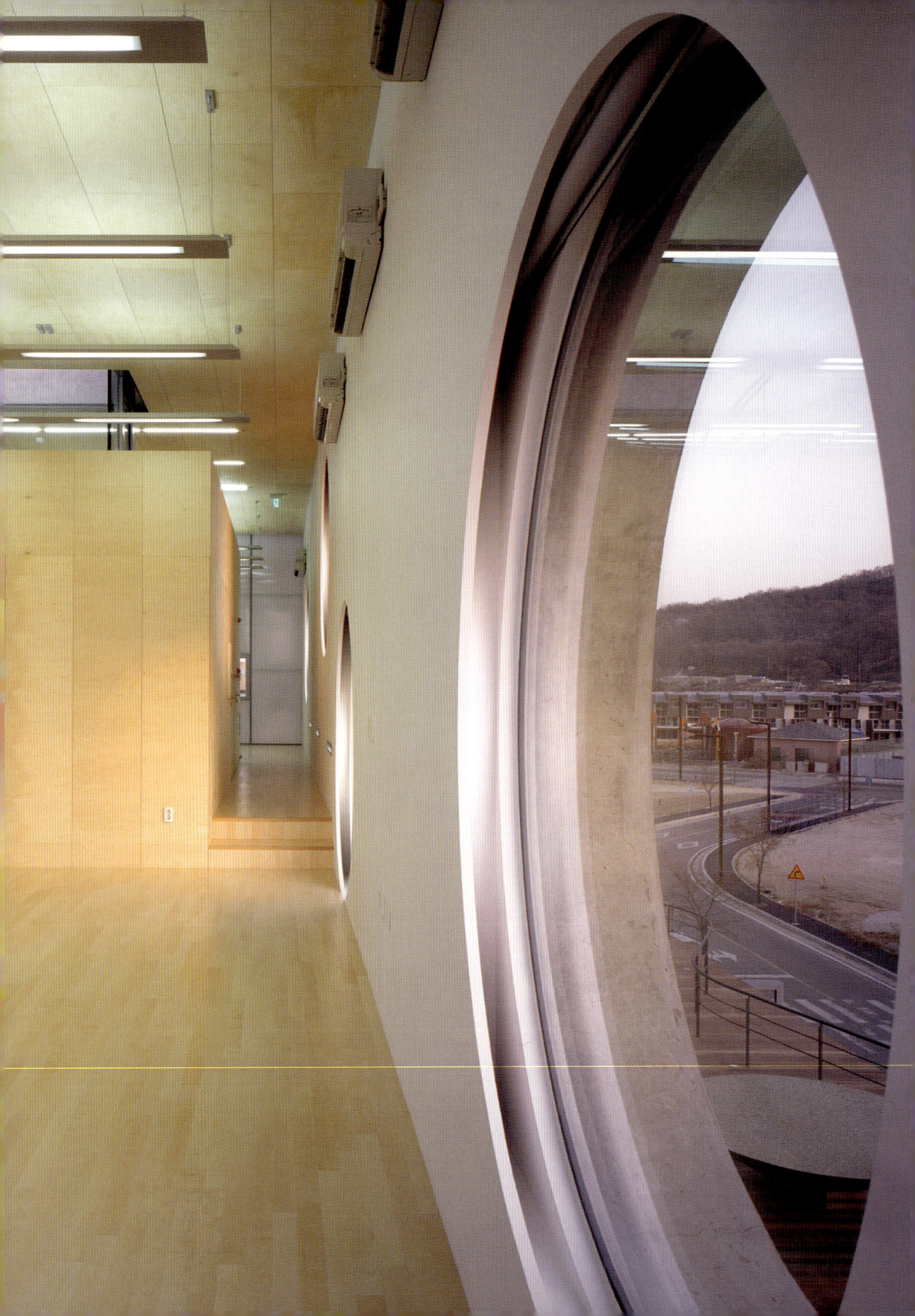

MOONGYU CHOI + GA.A ARCHITECTS | SEOUL
booksea publishing
Kyunggi, Korea | 2002

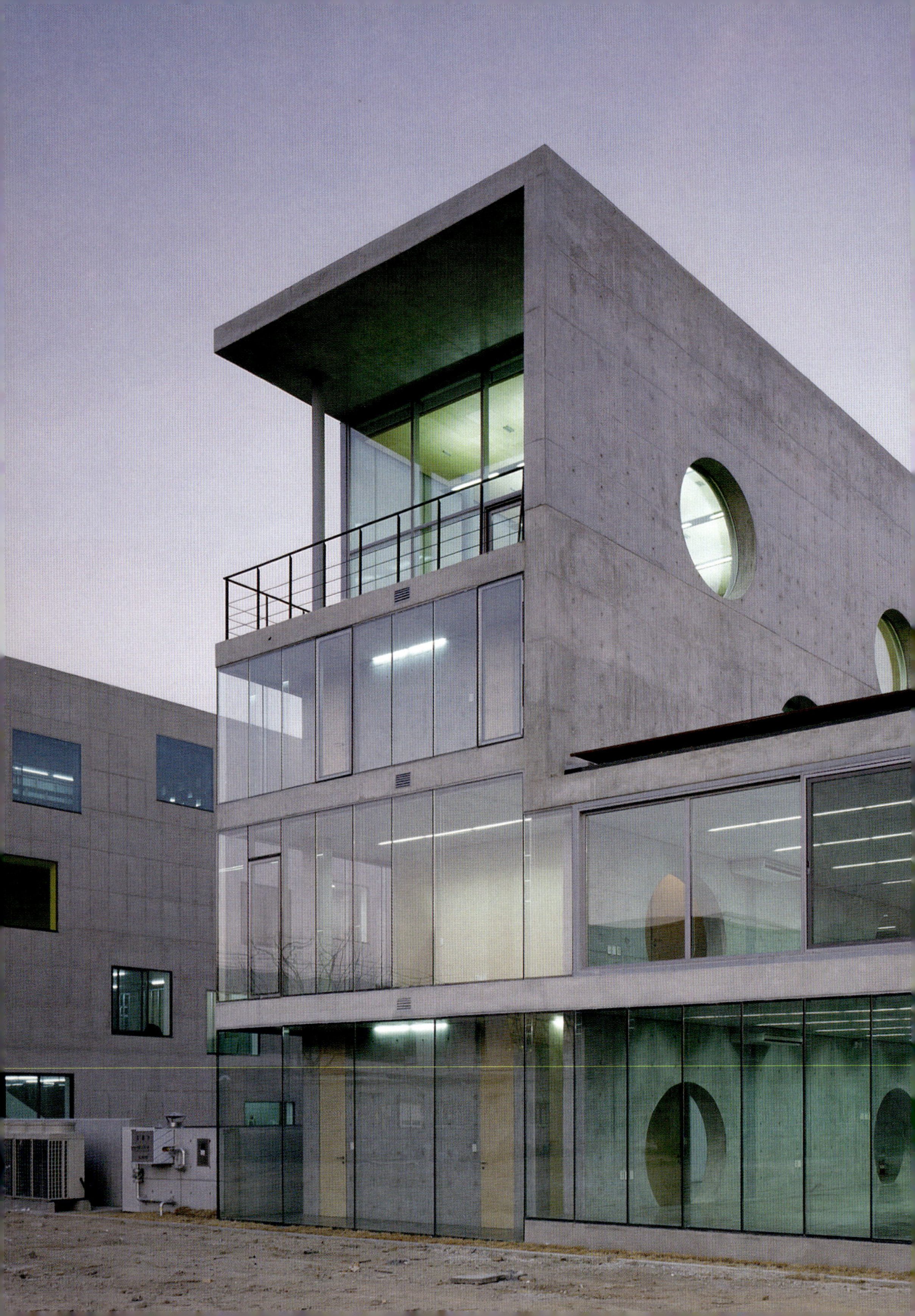

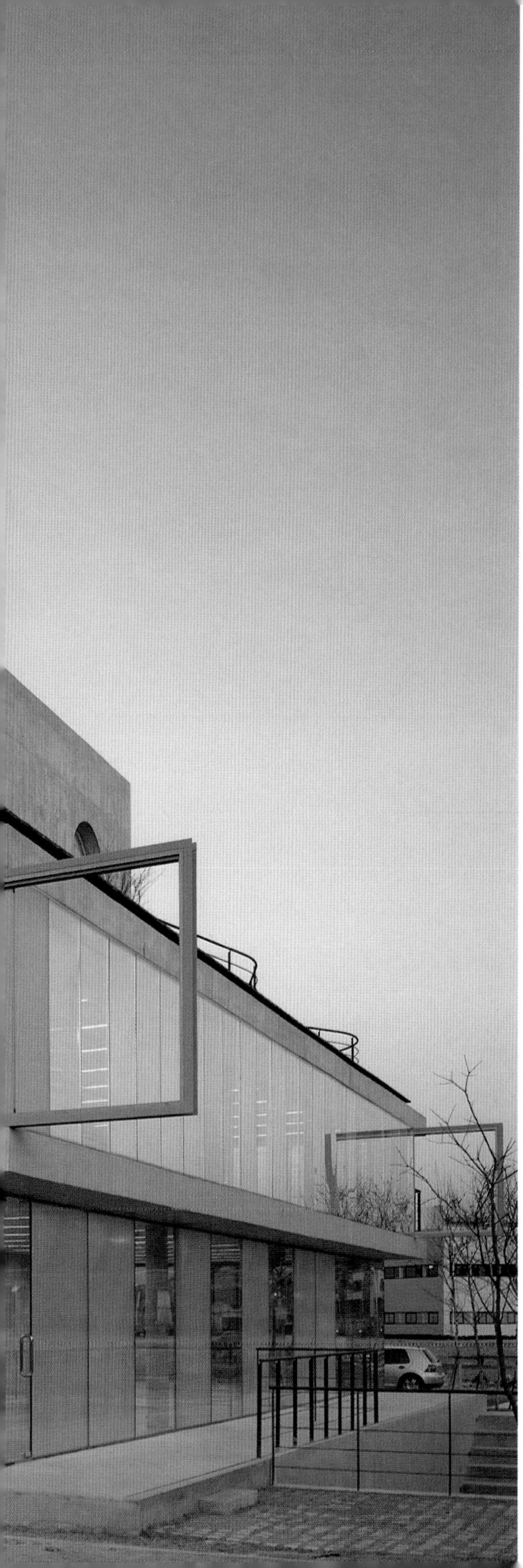

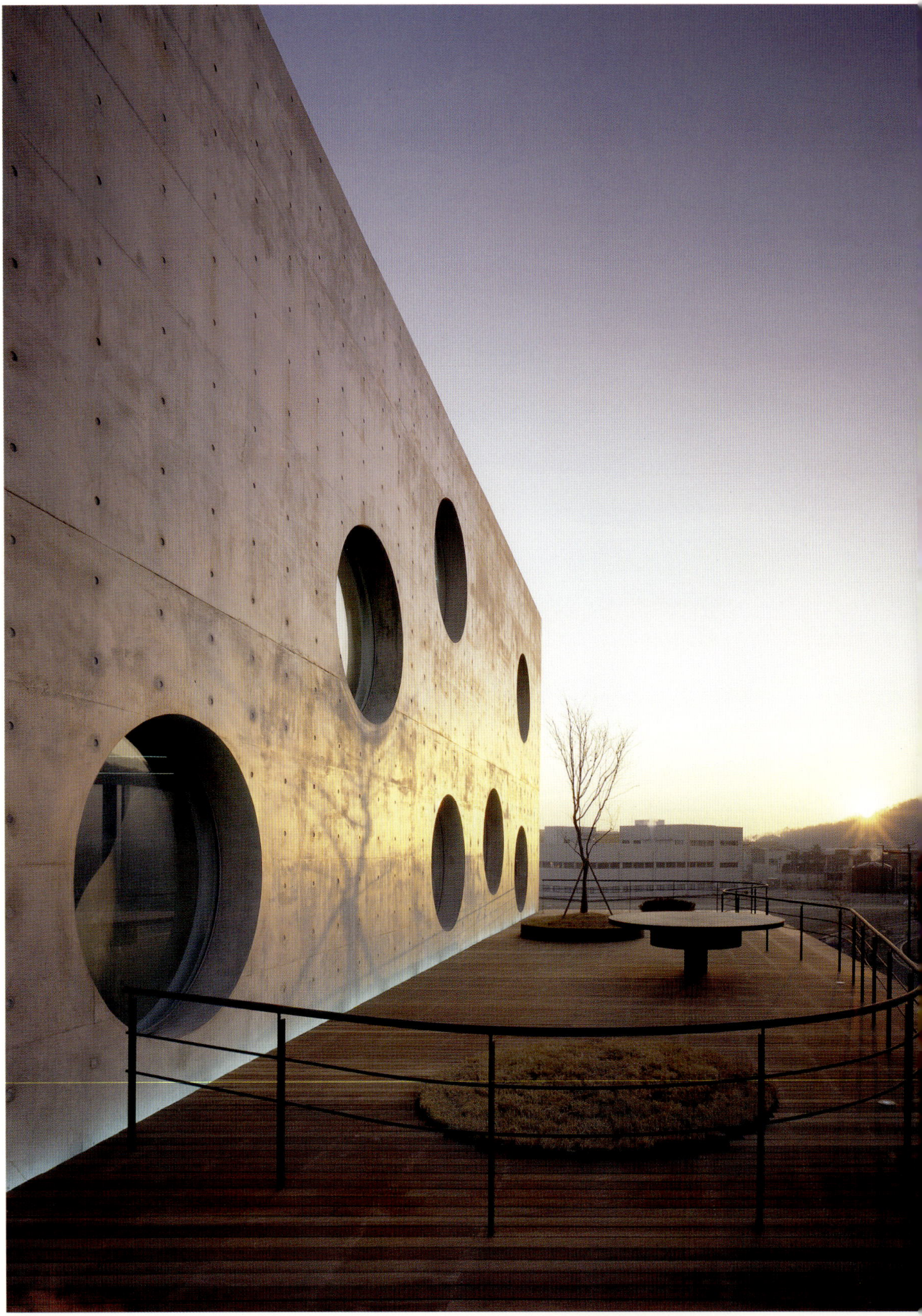

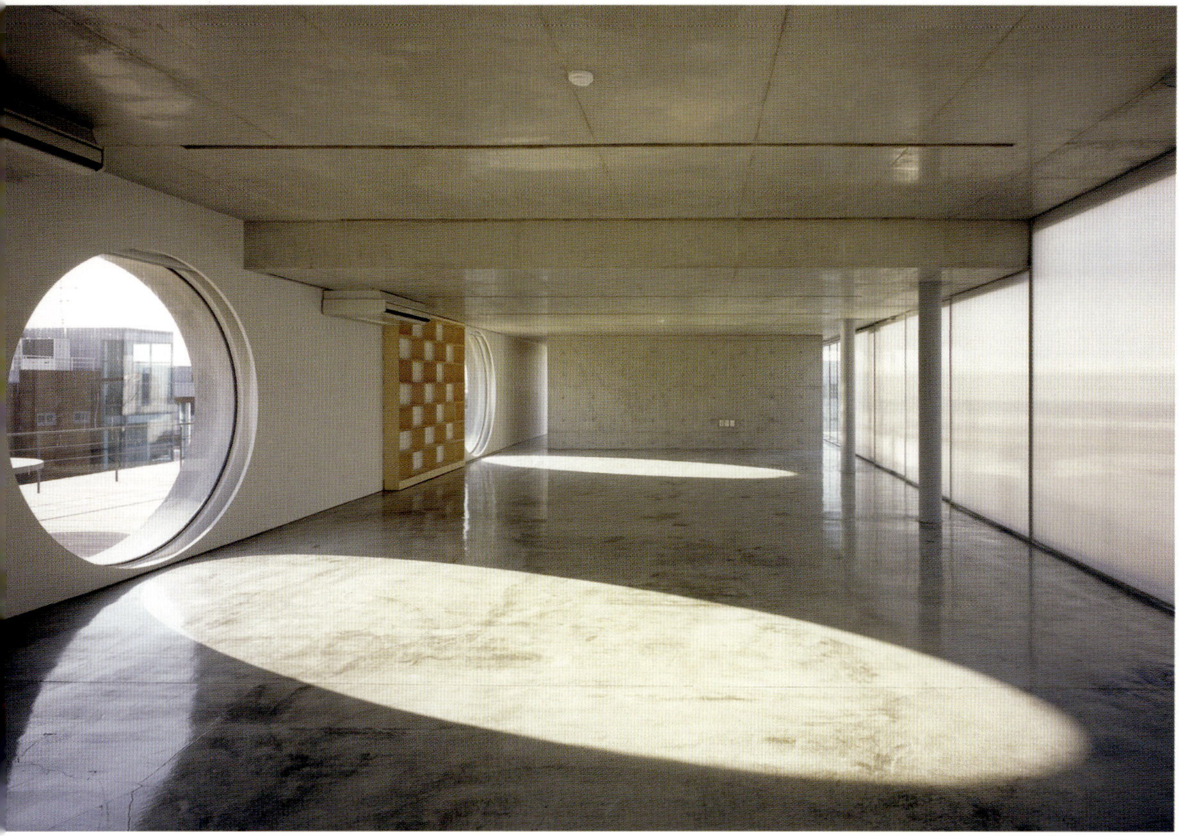

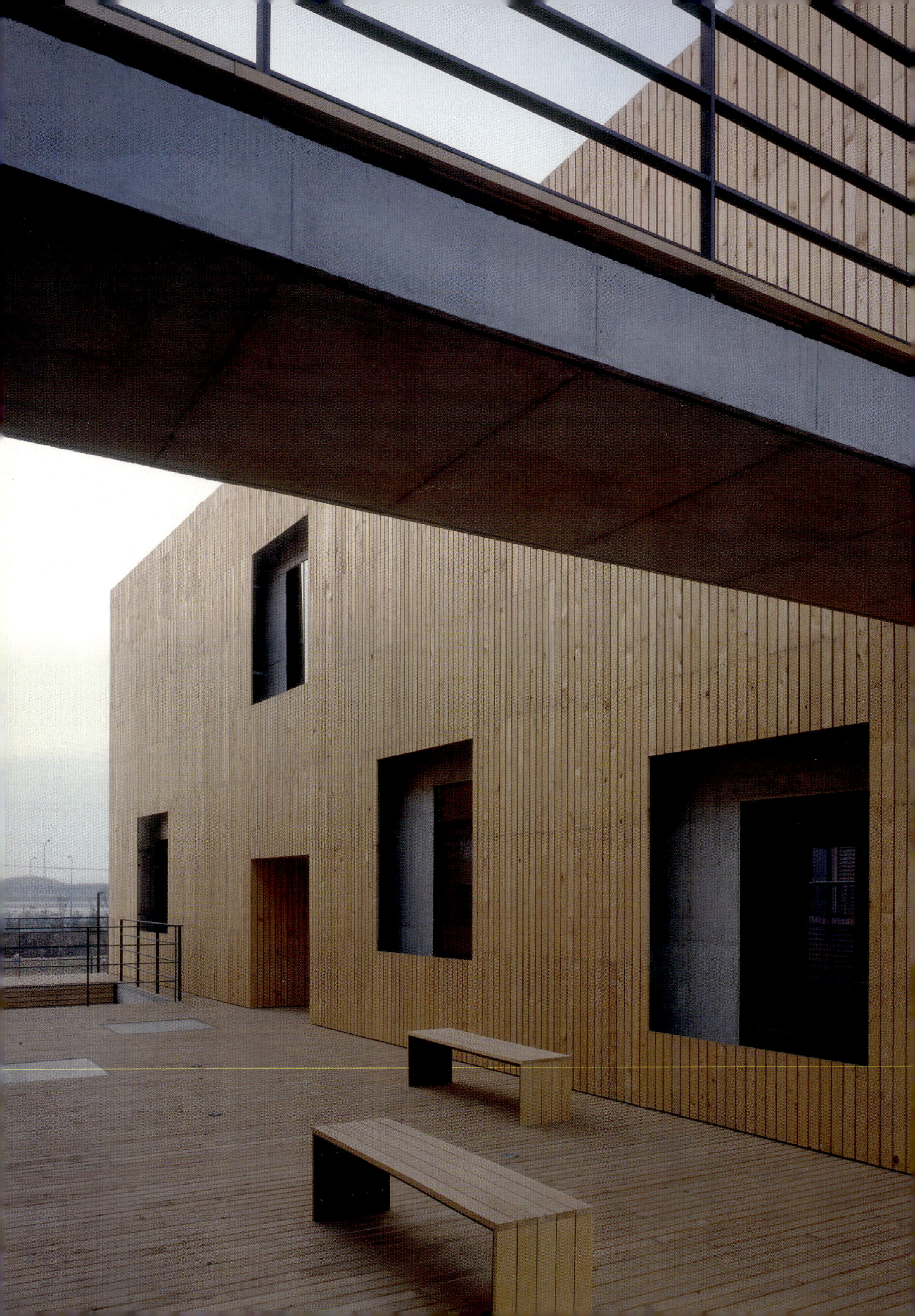

MOONGYU CHOI + GA.A ARCHITECTS | SEOUL
taehaksa publishing
Kyunggi, Korea | 2004

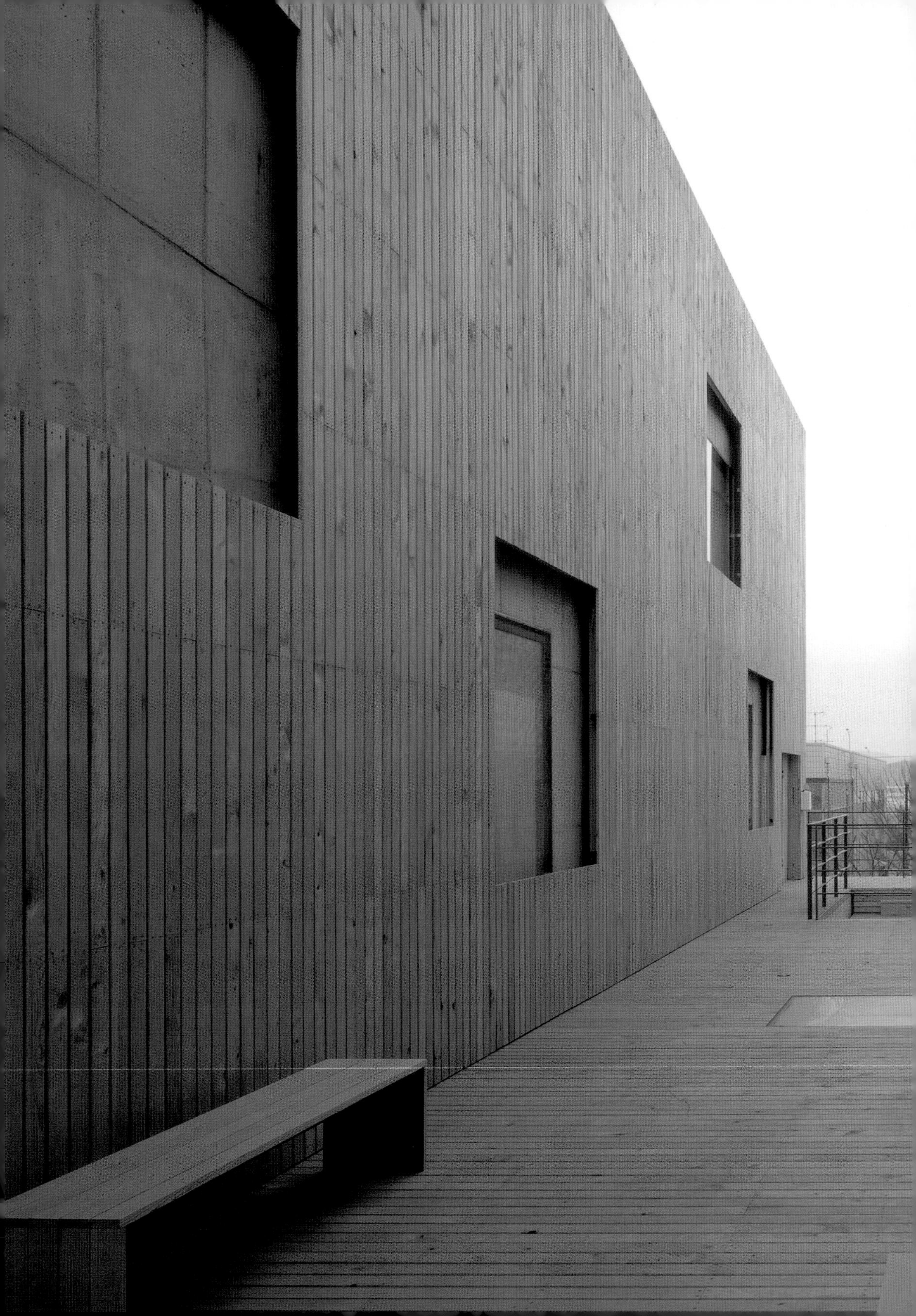

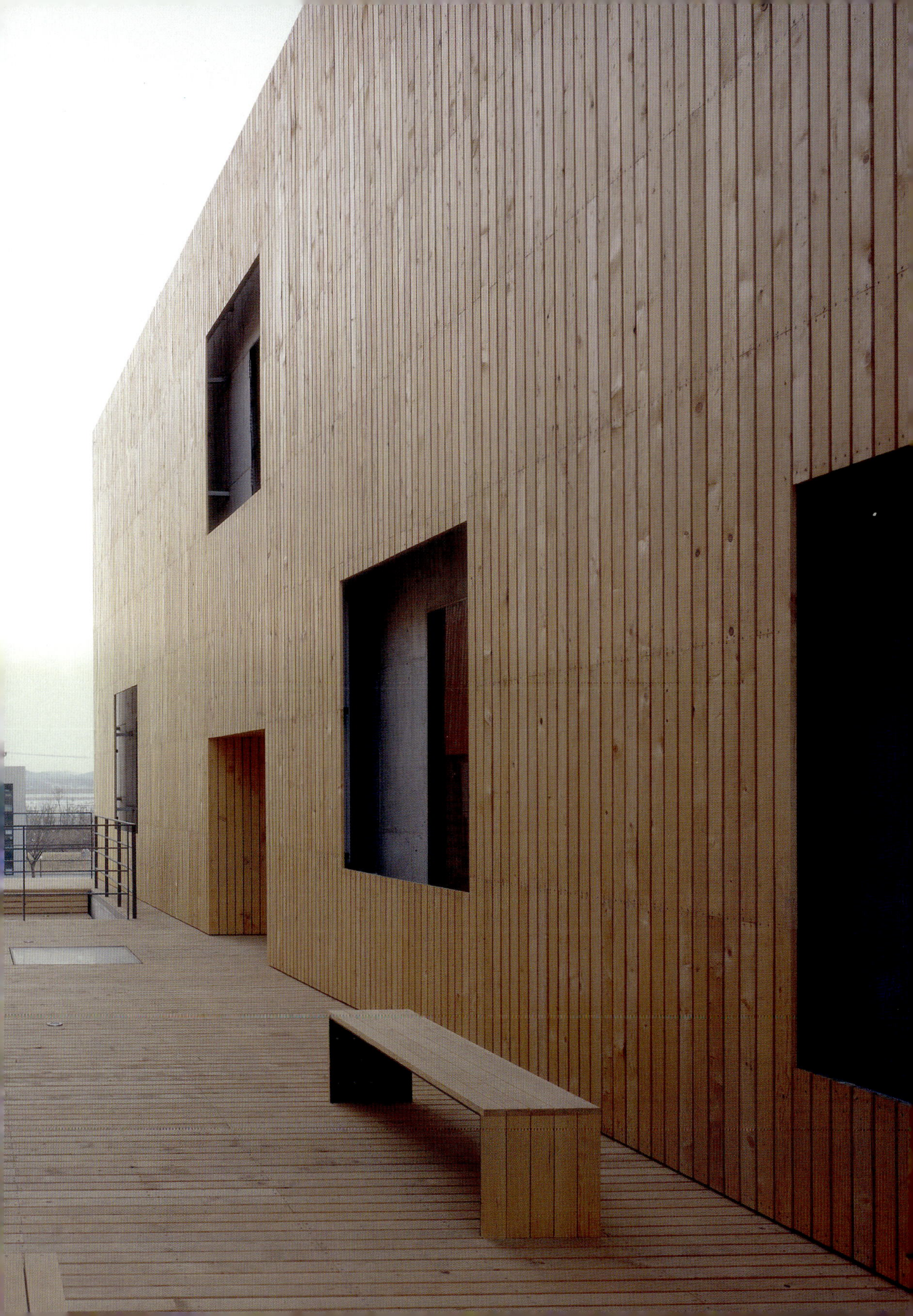

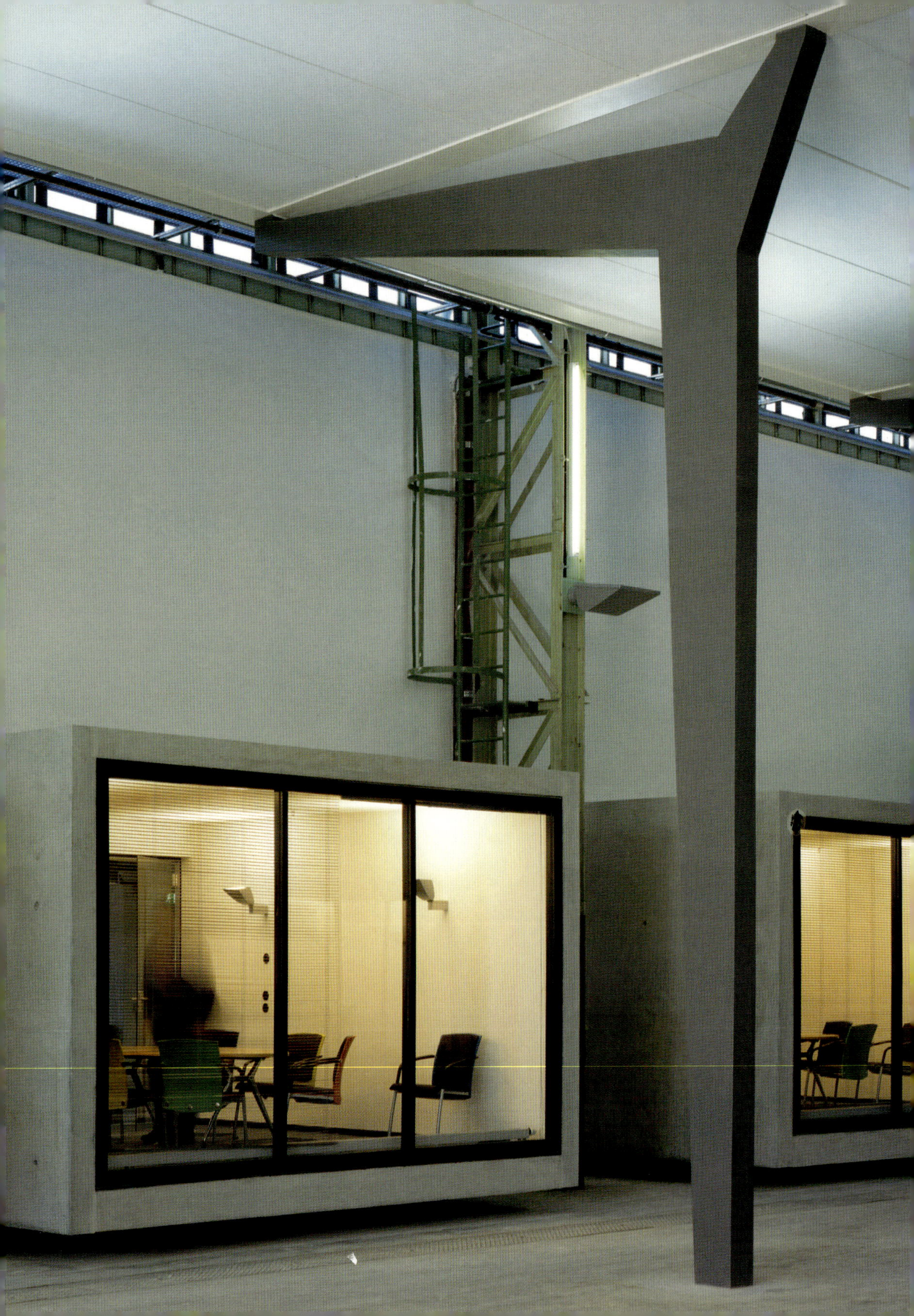

CHRISTOPH MÄCKLER ARCHITEKTEN | FRANKFURT
dmc2
Hanau-Wolfgang, Germany | 2001

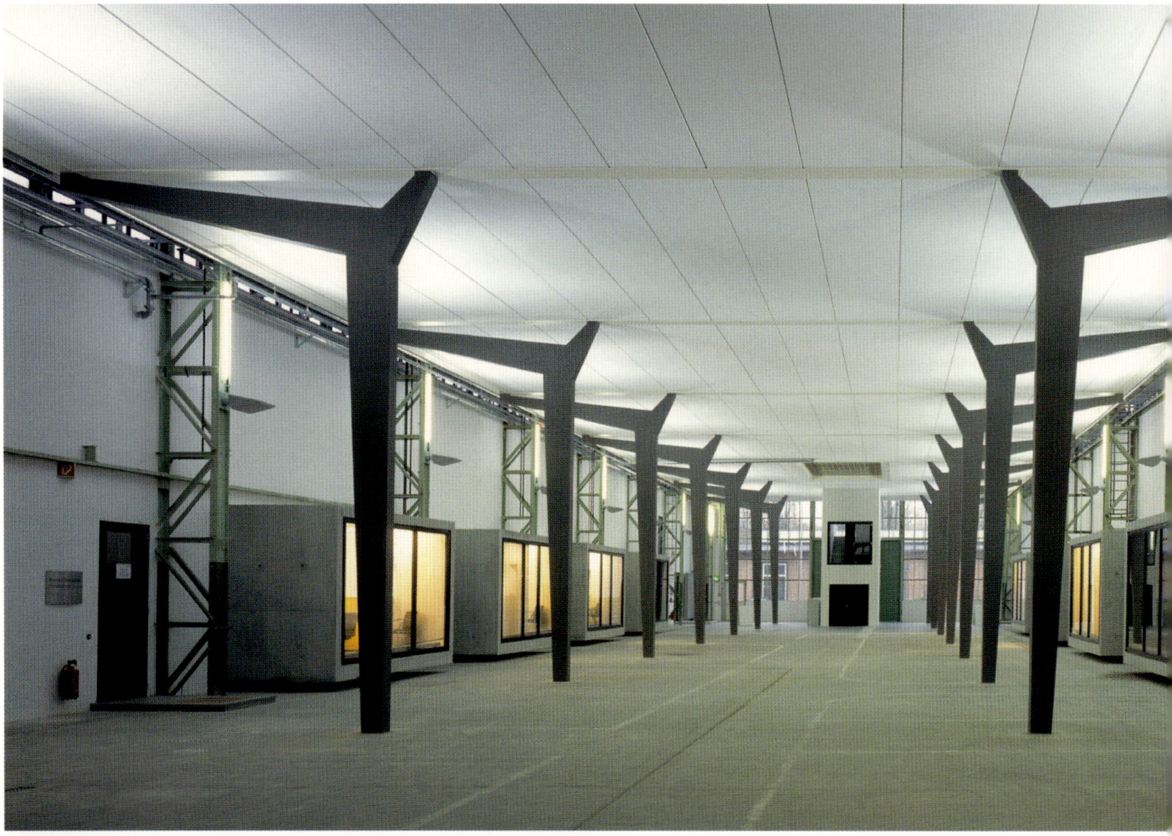

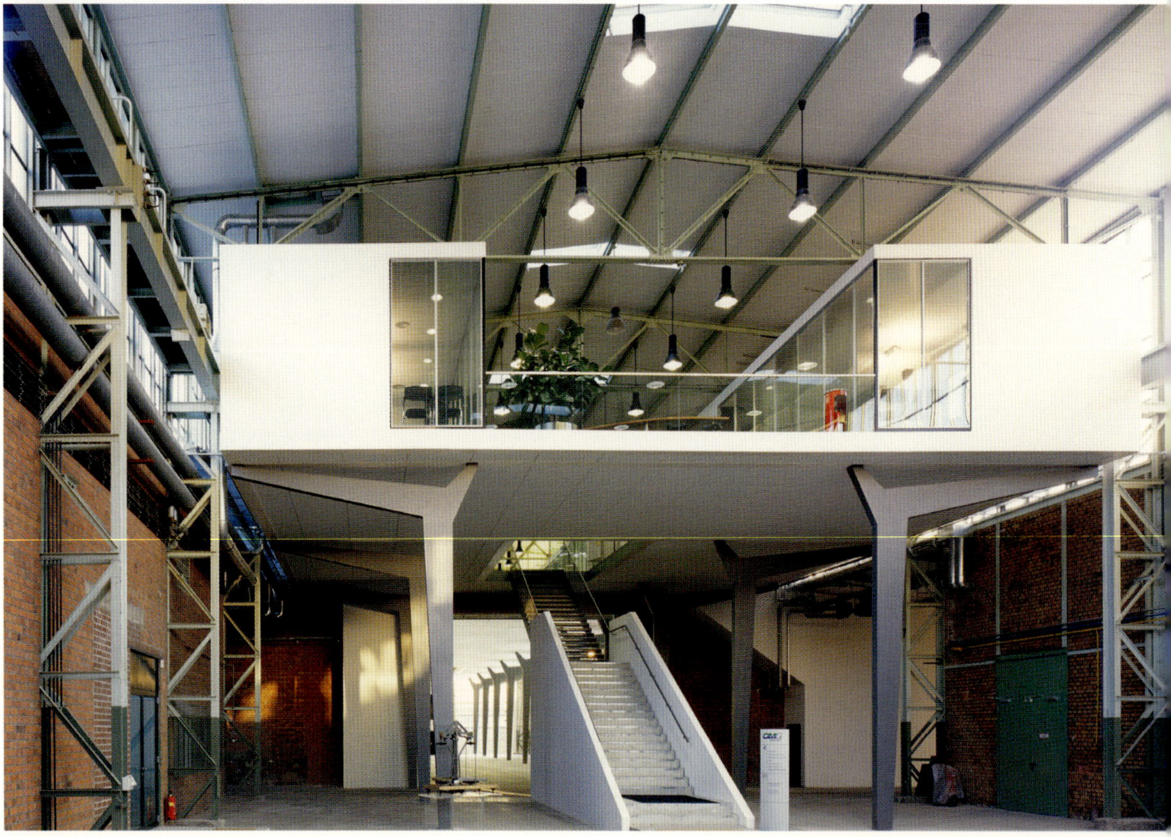

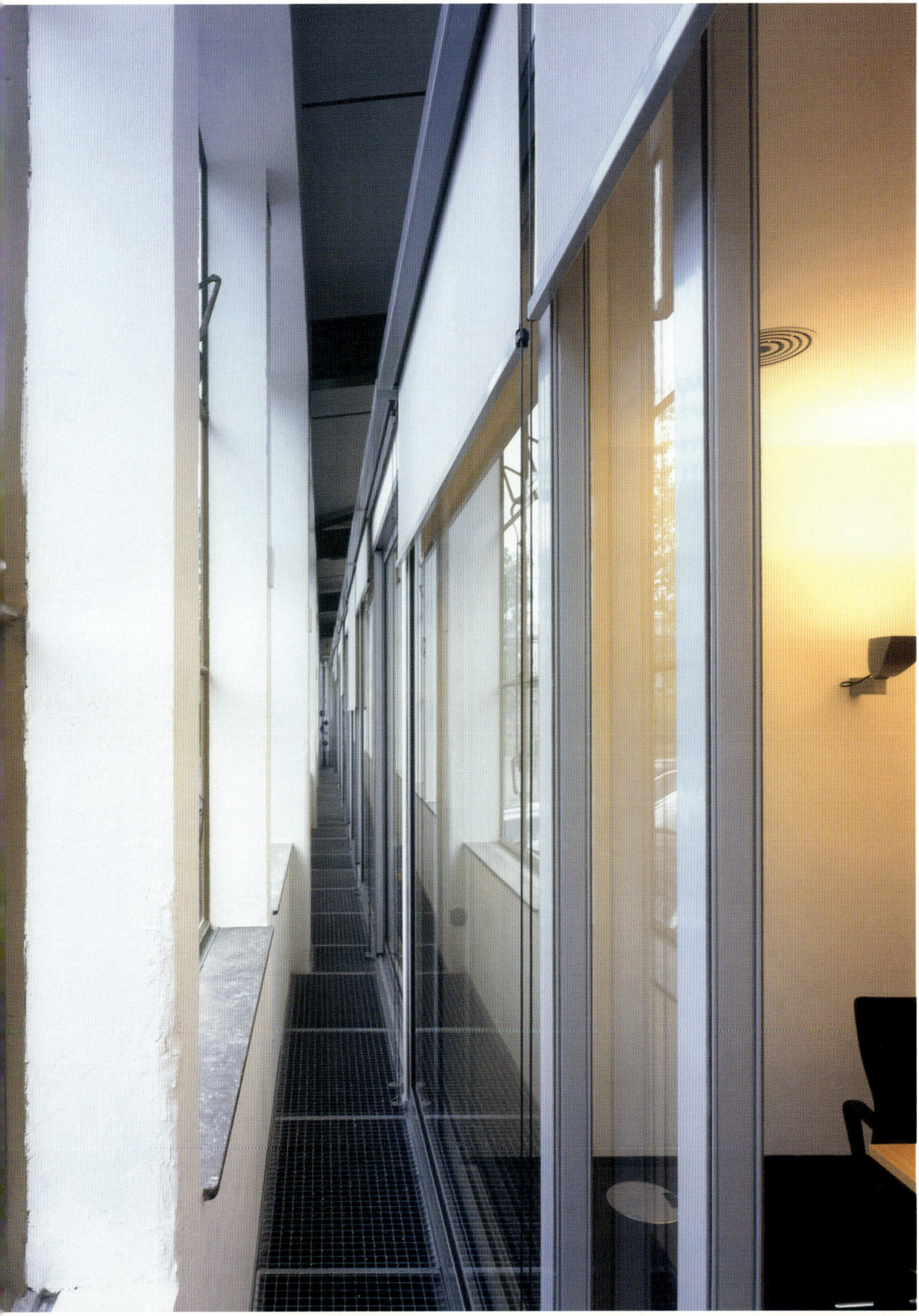

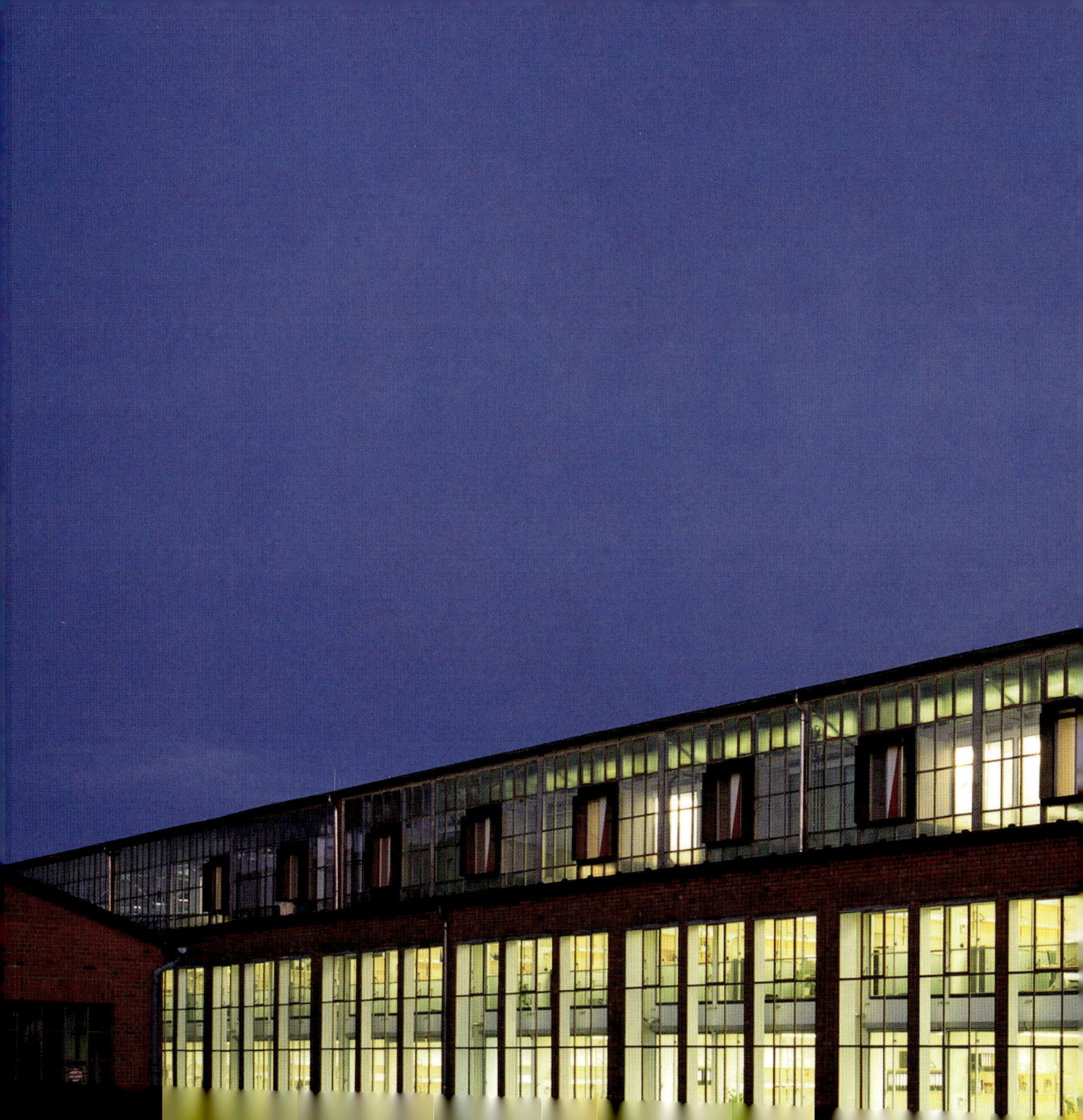

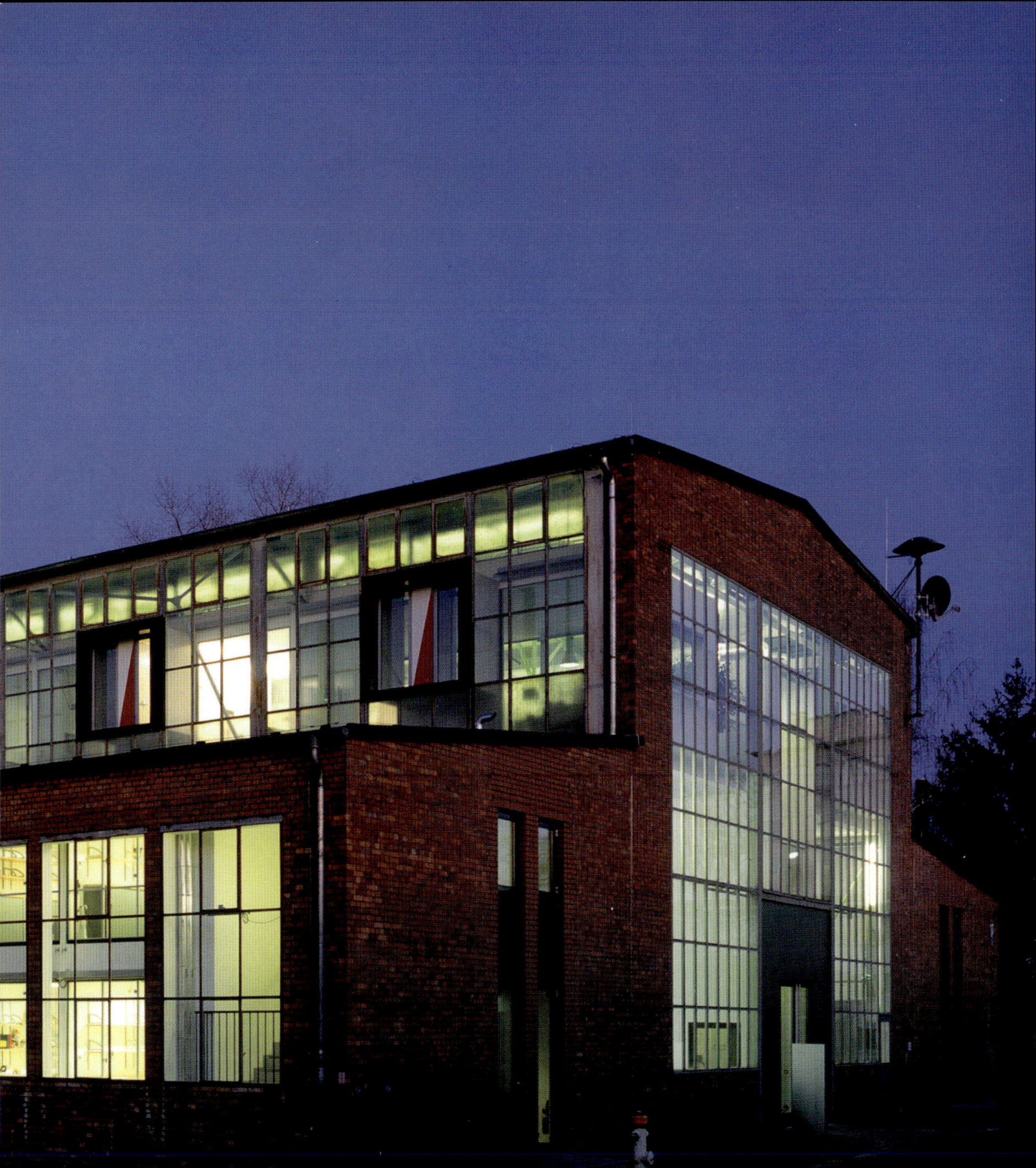

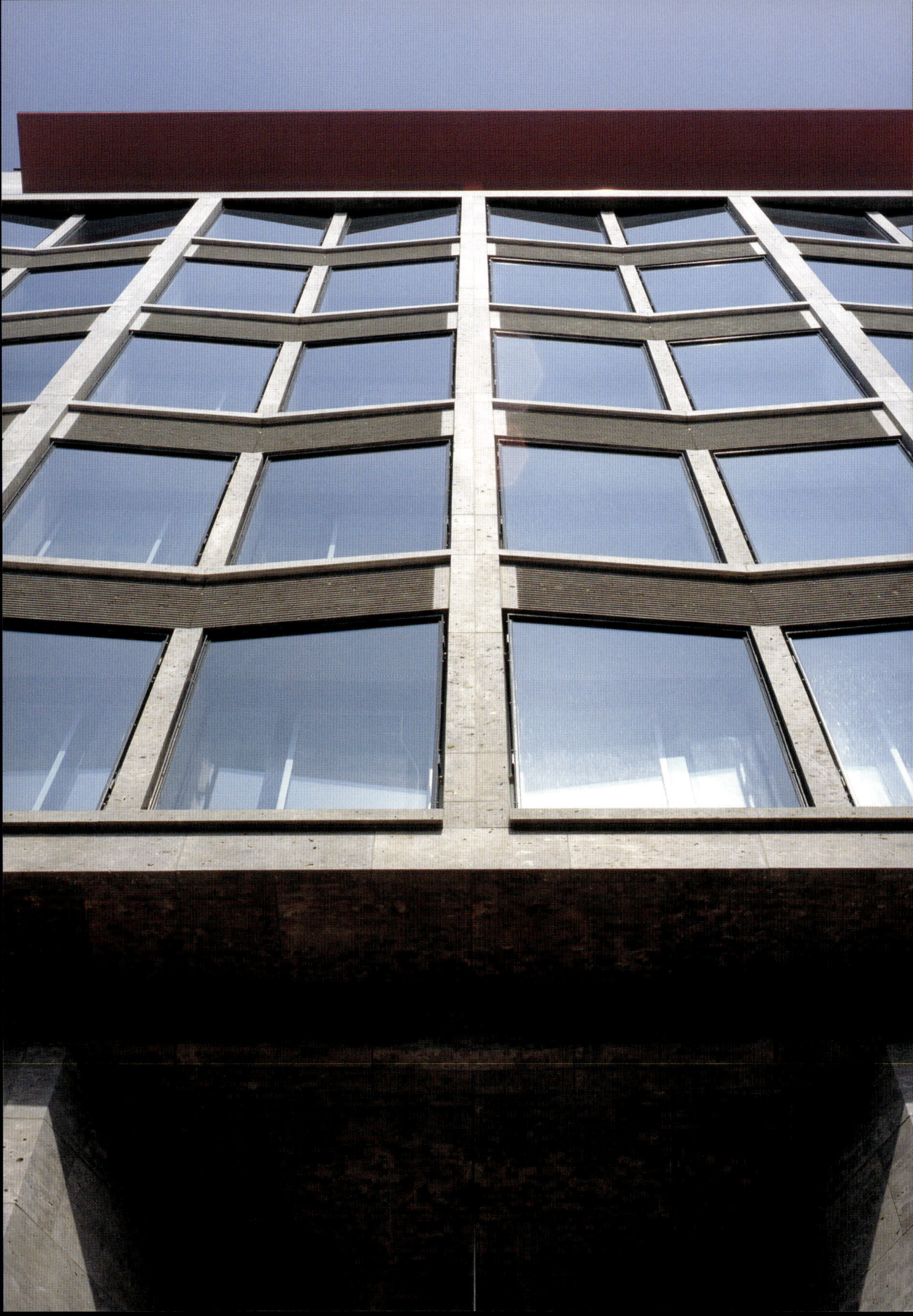

CHRISTOPH MÄCKLER ARCHITEKTEN | FRANKFURT
Office building Eschersheimer Landstraße 6
Frankfurt am Main, Germany | 2002

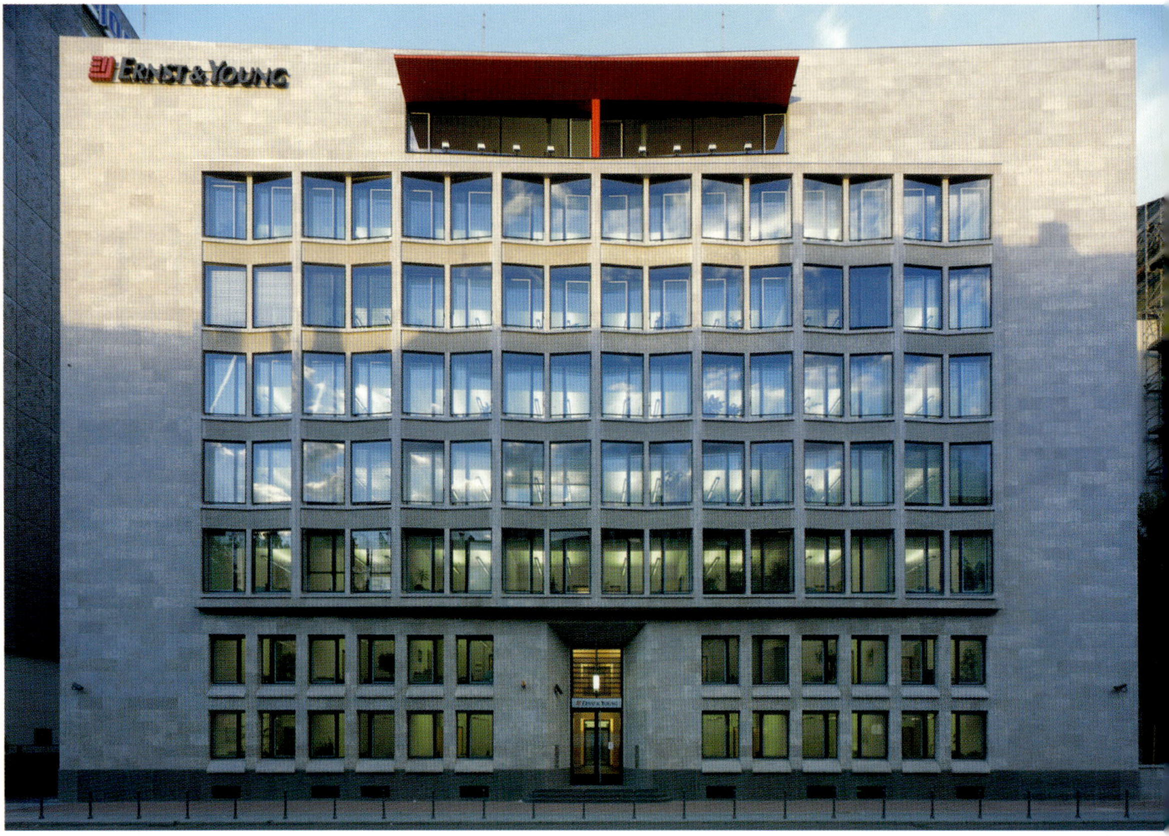
ERNST & YOUNG

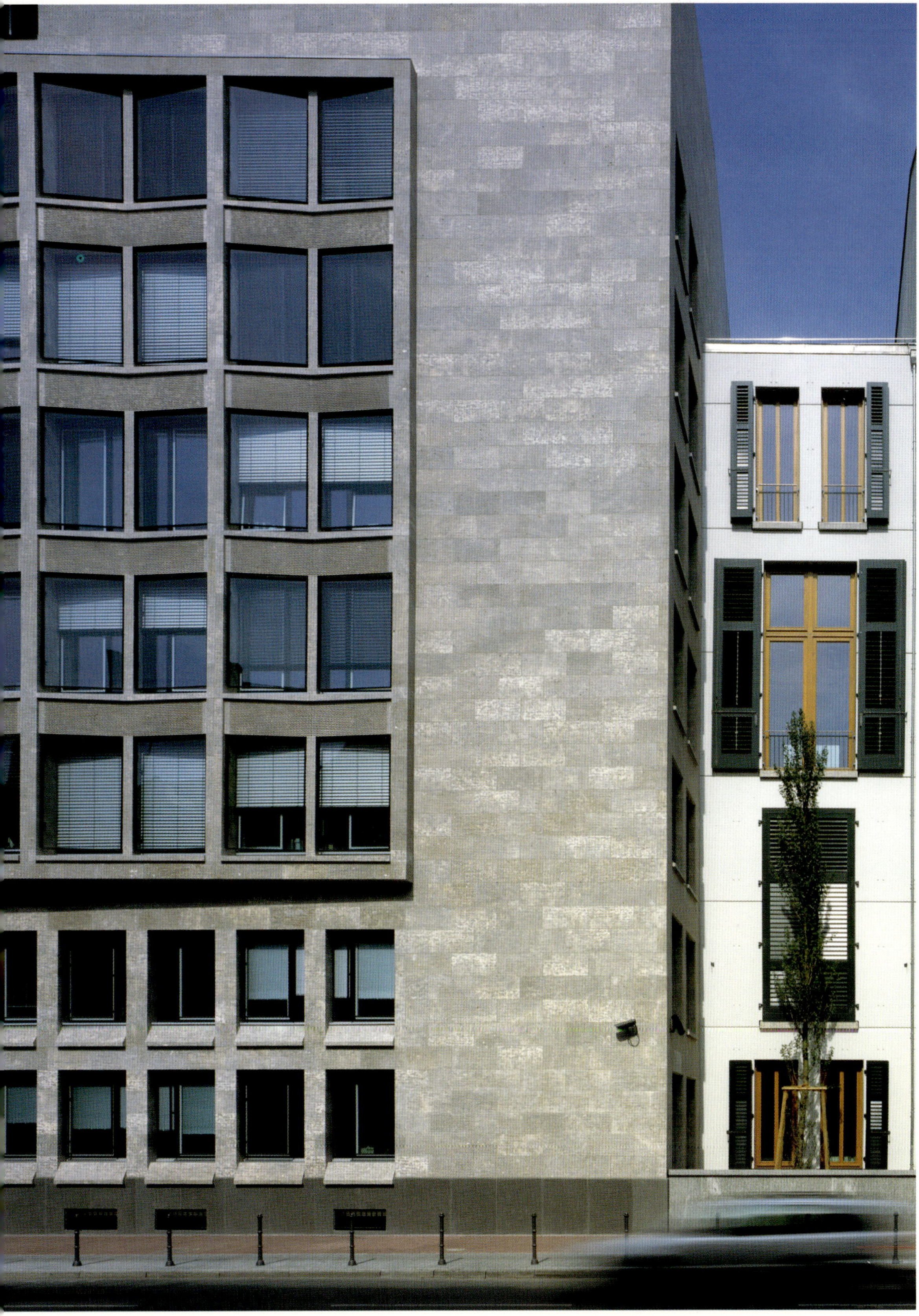

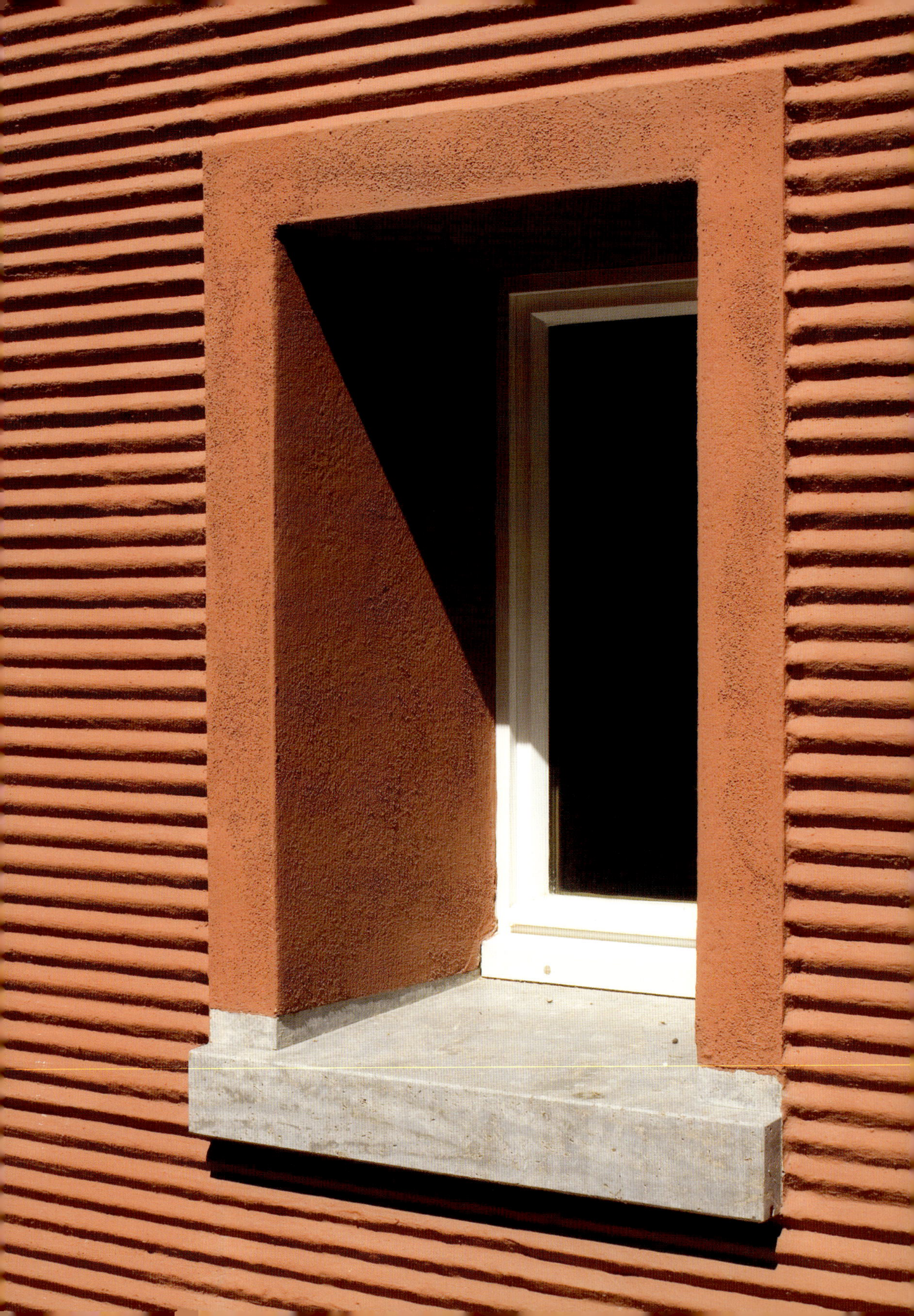

CHRISTOPH MÄCKLER ARCHITEKTEN | FRANKFURT
House Knipp
Bad Homburg, Germany | 2004

Harry Potter
Harry Potter
HARALD SCHMIDT
Der Pferdeflüsterer
HERBJØRG WASSMO
Das Buch Dina
J. M. Coetzee
SIMON
Winterabend
JAVIER MARÍAS
MEIN HERZ SO WEISS
Working Mum
Hitler
Wir sind die Wahnsinnigen
Manfred Krug
ABGEHAUEN
Boris Becker
Gerhard Schröder
Arnulf Baring Scheitert Deutschland?
Oskar Lafontaine Deutsche Wahrheiten
PIPER
MARCEL REICH-RANICKI
MEIN LEBEN
1877

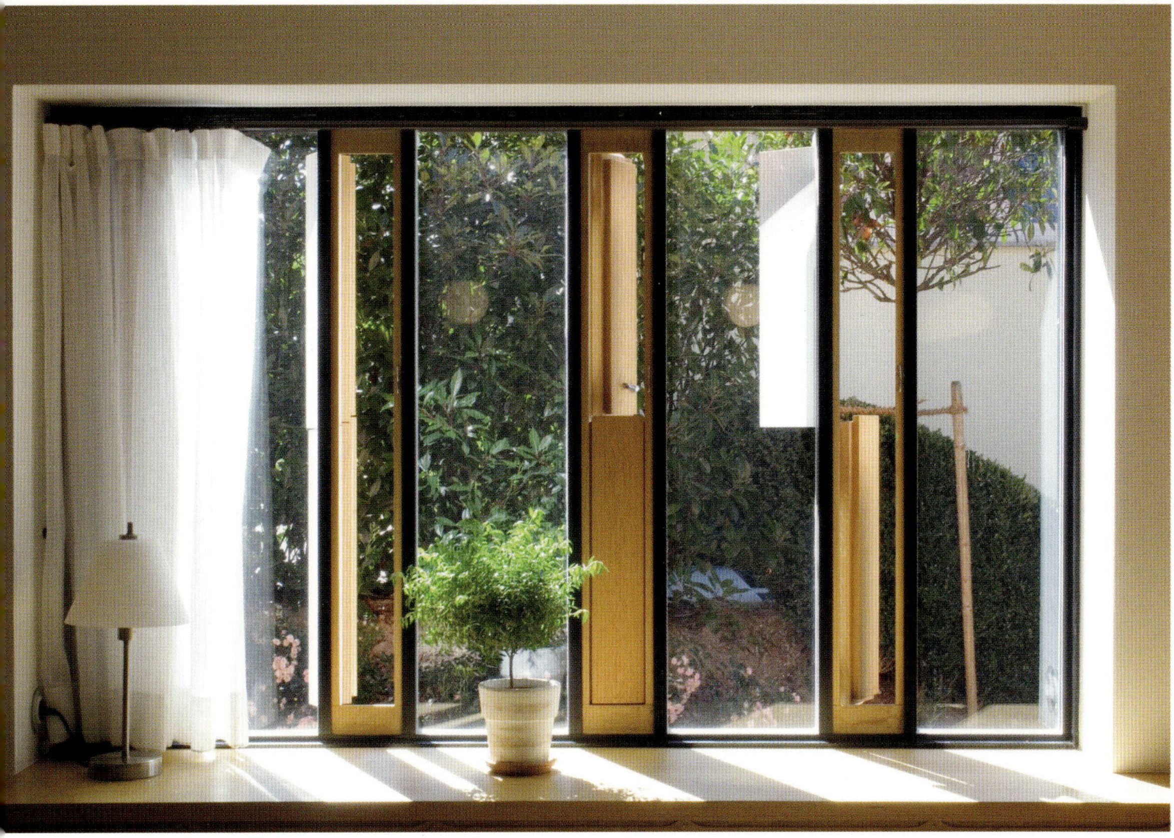

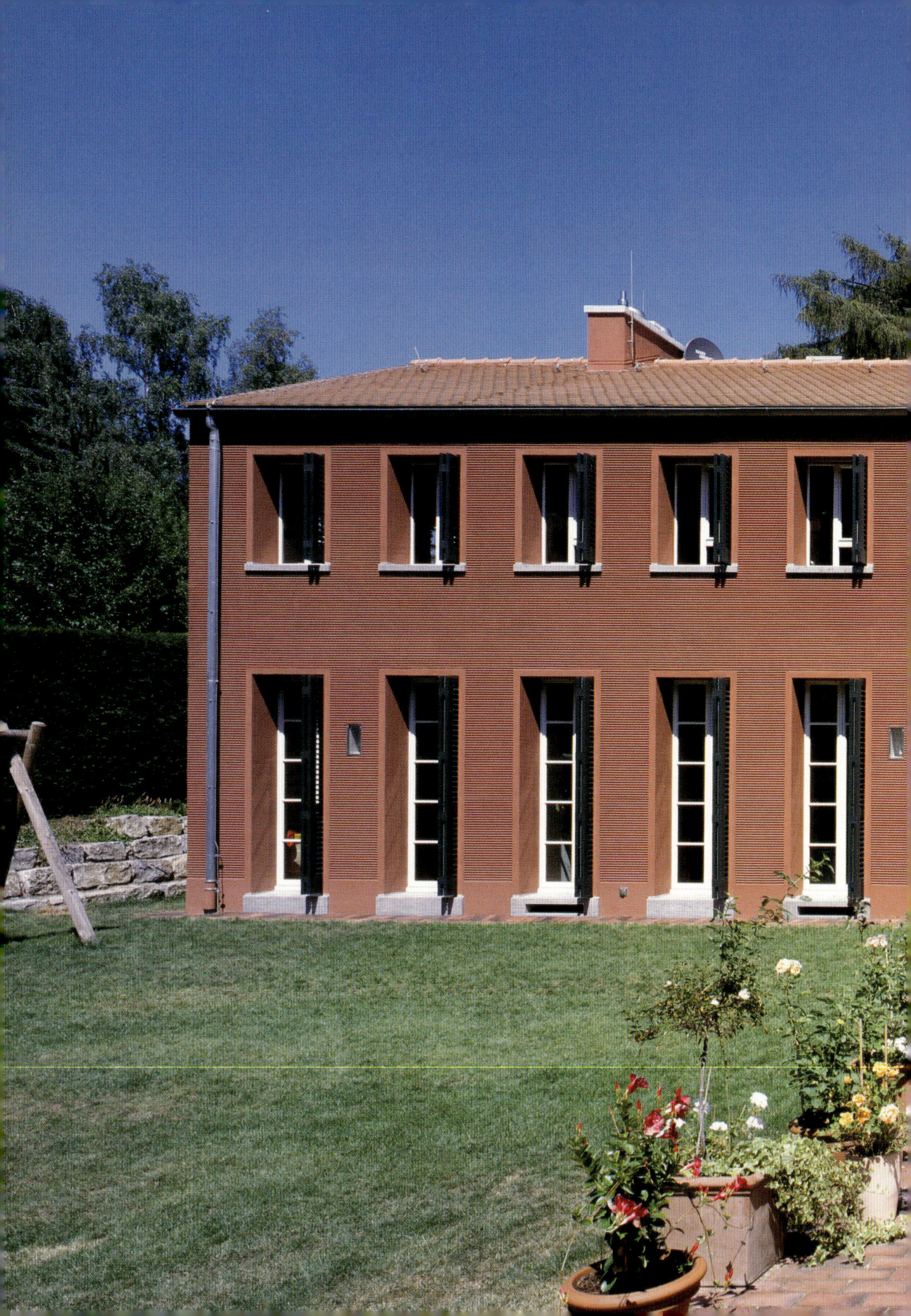

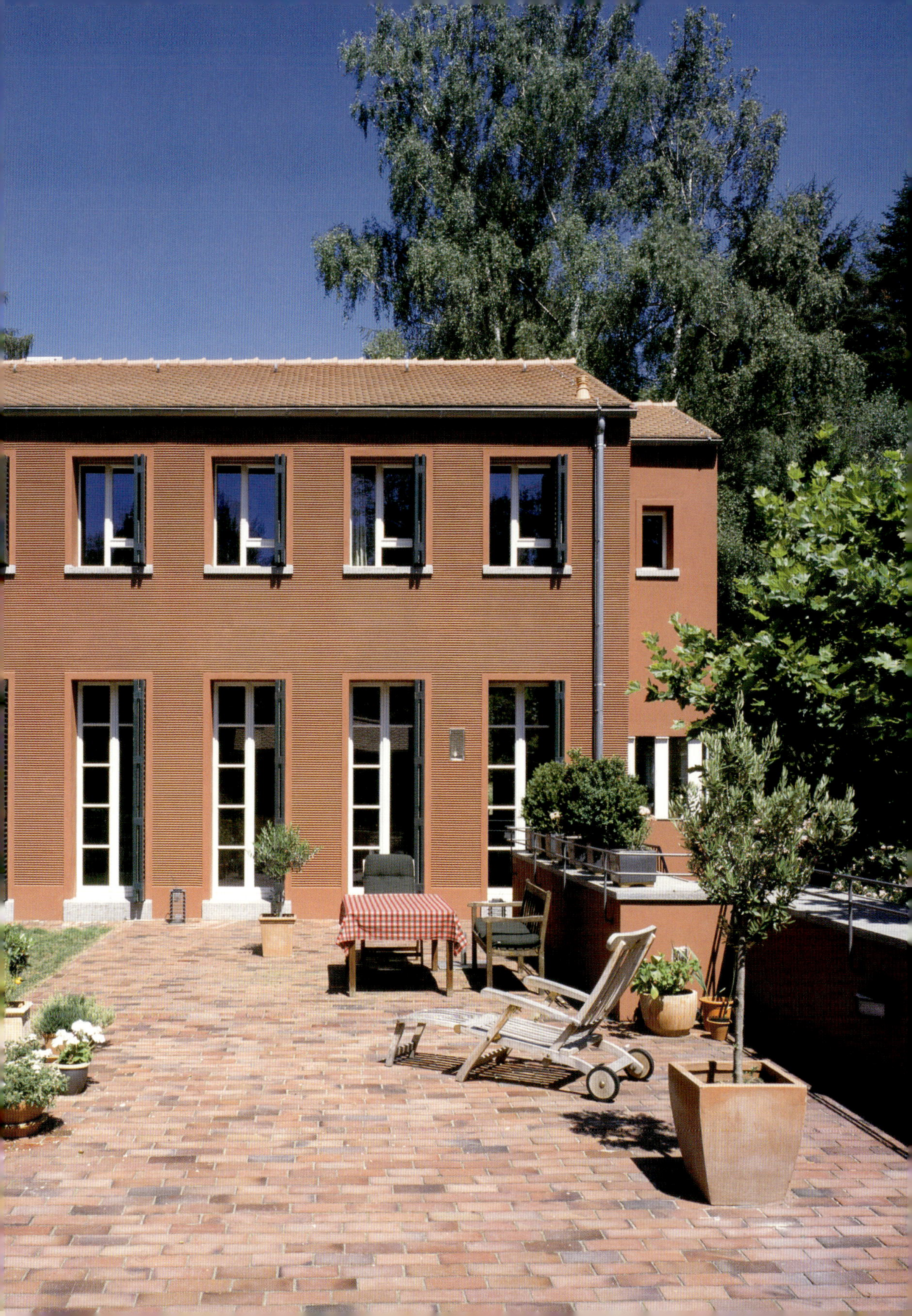

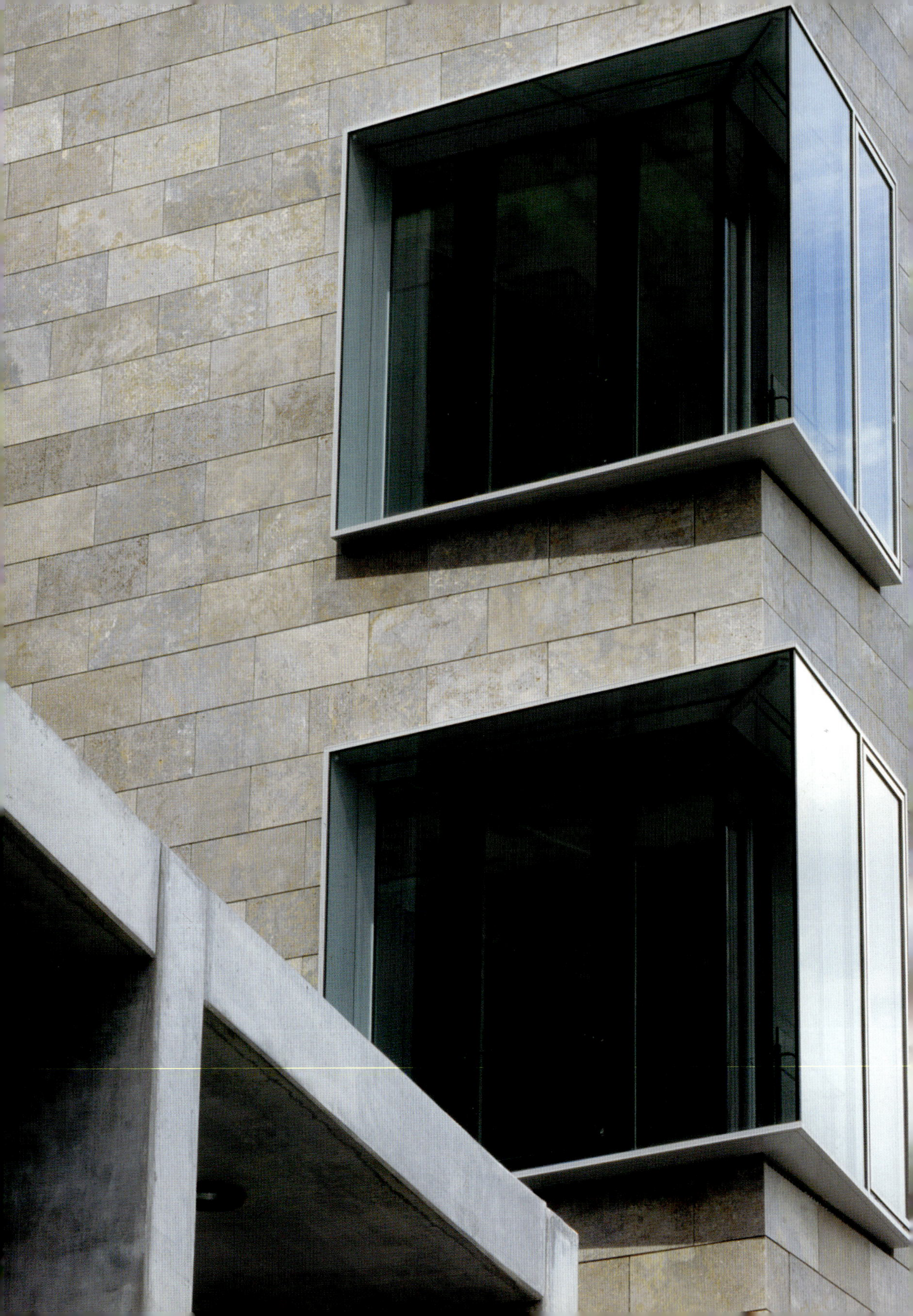

CHRISTOPH MÄCKLER ARCHITEKTEN | FRANKFURT
Torhaus Westhafen
Frankfurt am Main, Germany | 2003

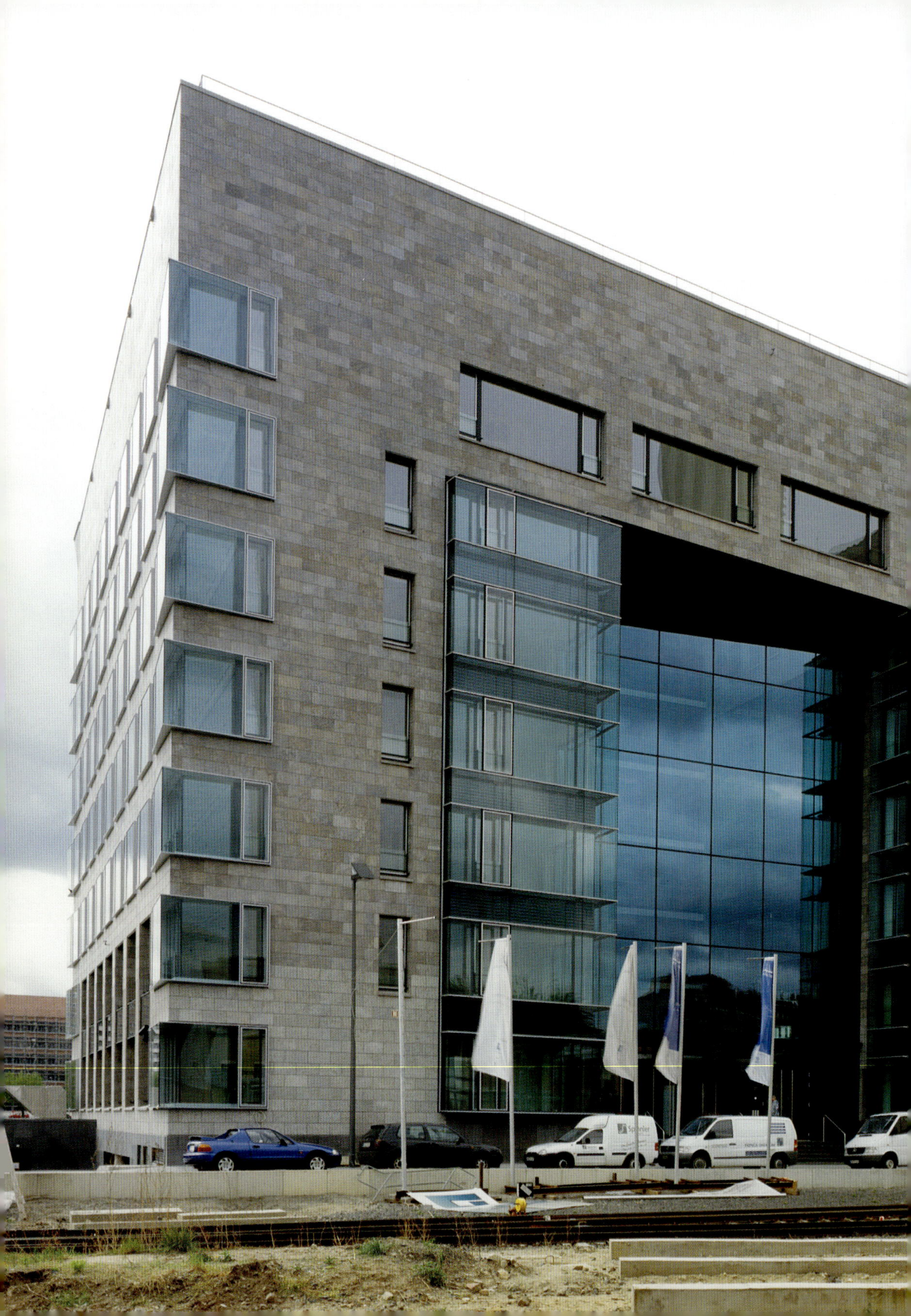

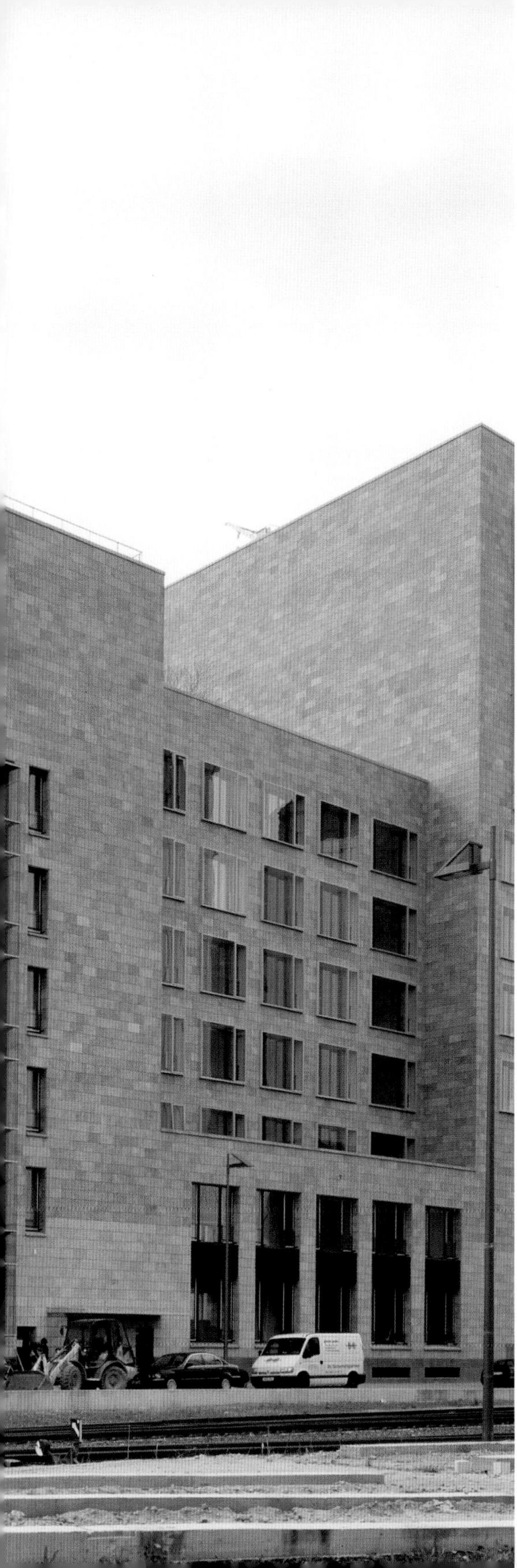

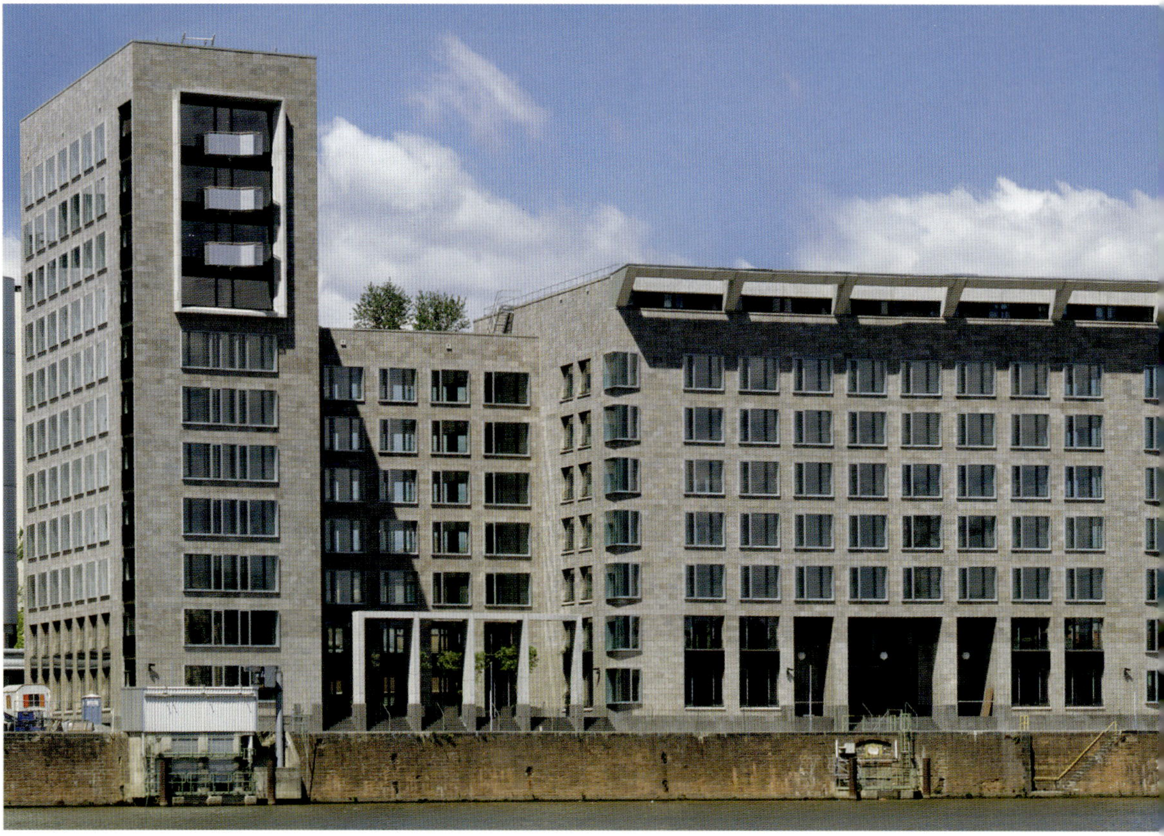

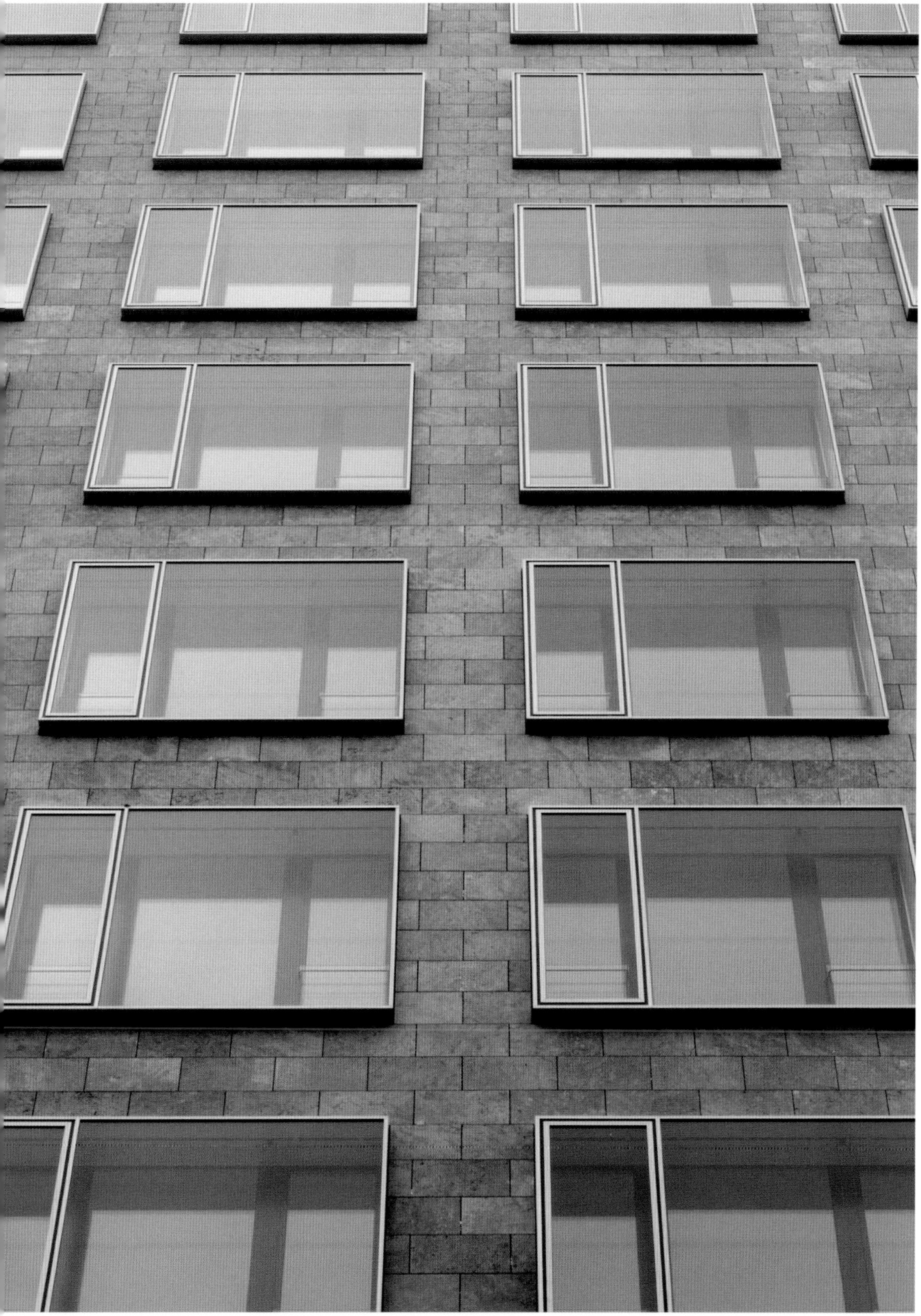

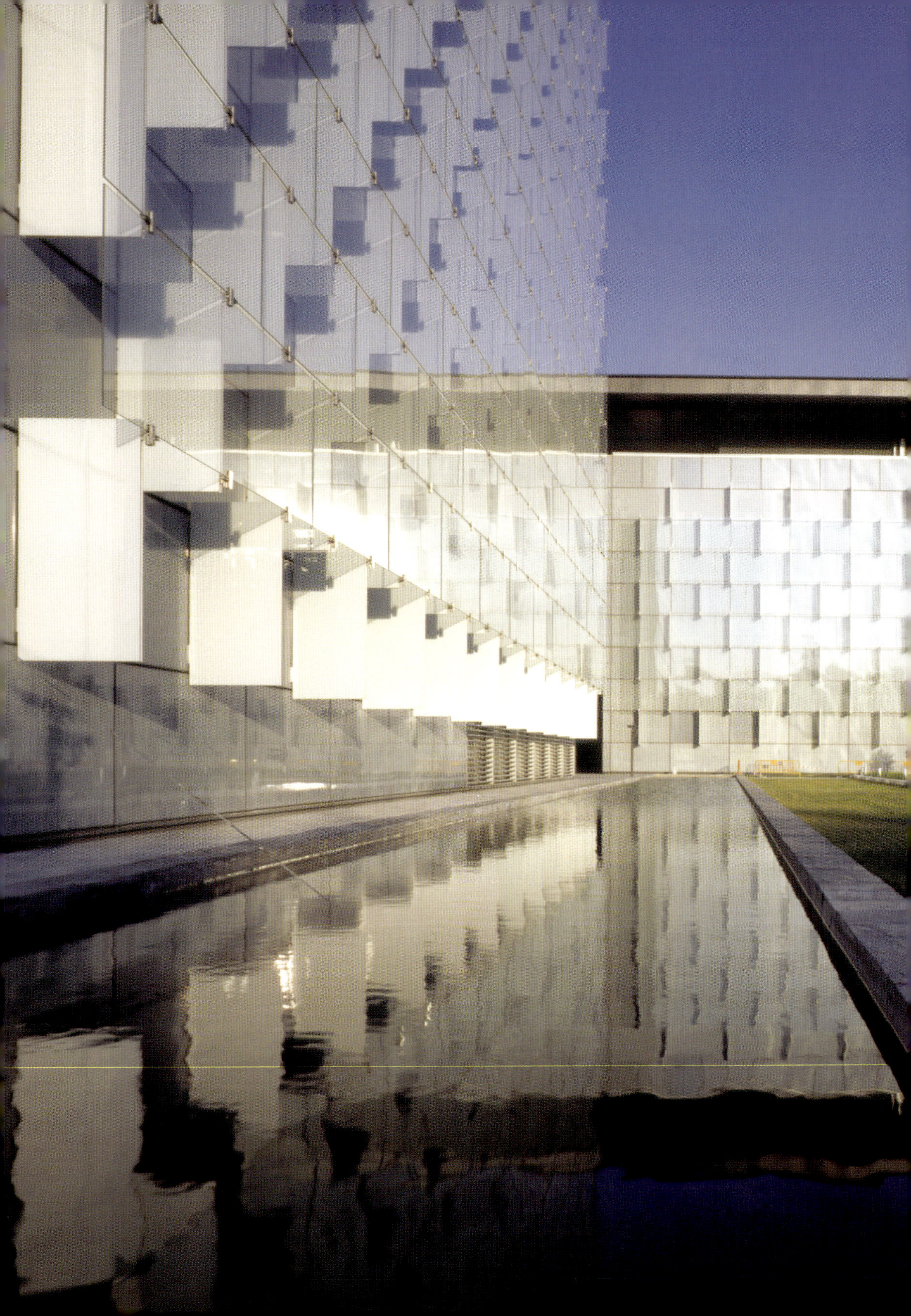

RAFAEL DE LA-HOZ | MADRID
District C of Telefónica
Las Tablas, Madrid, Spain | 2007

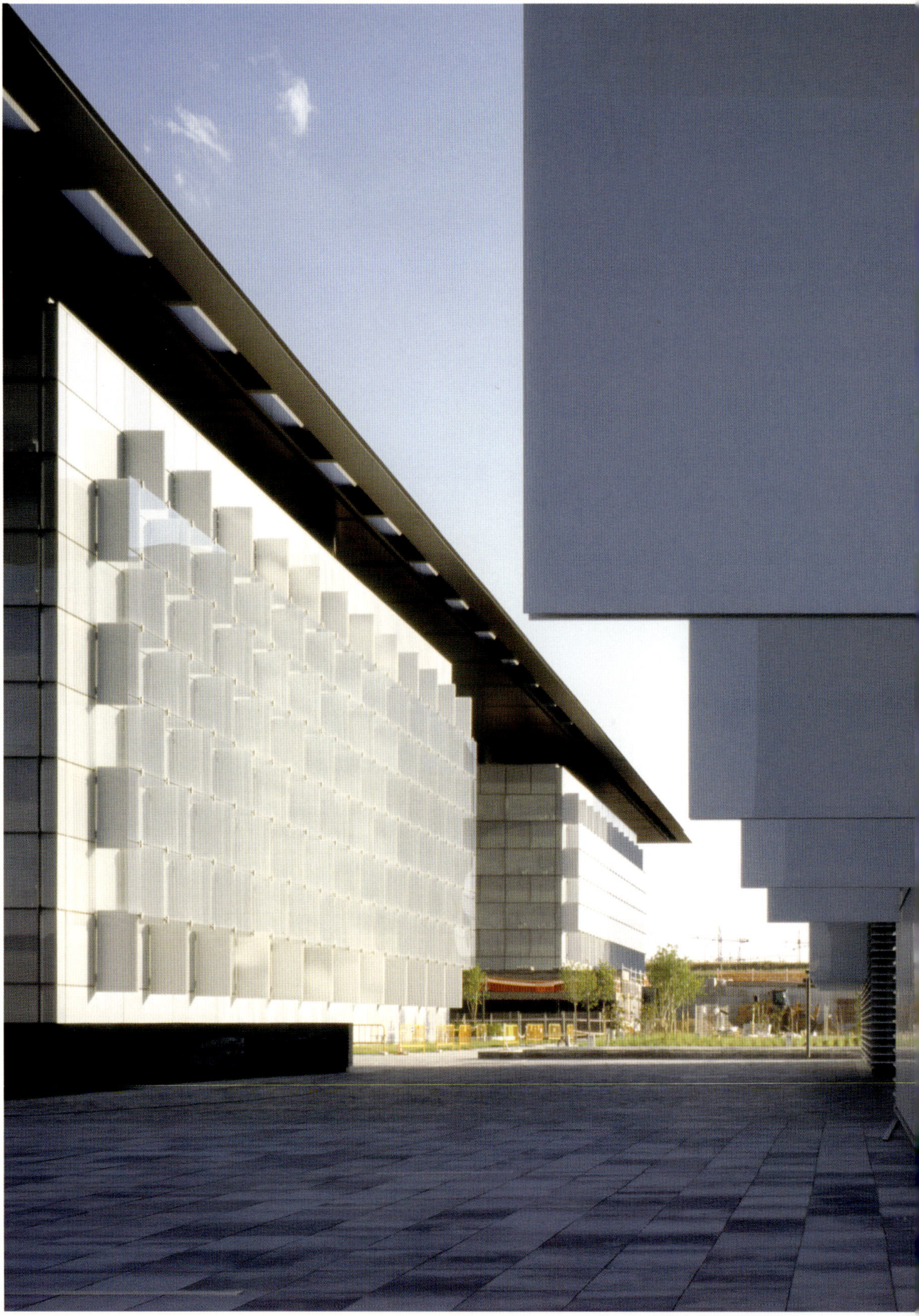

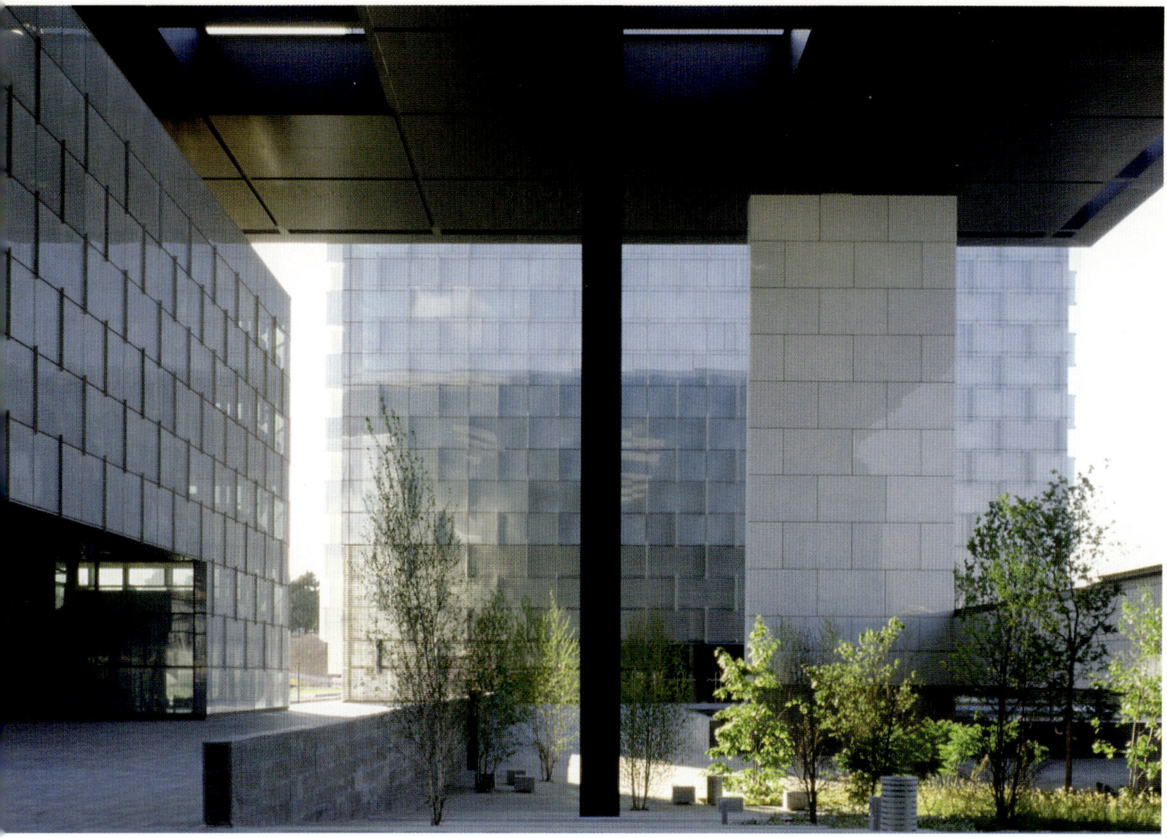

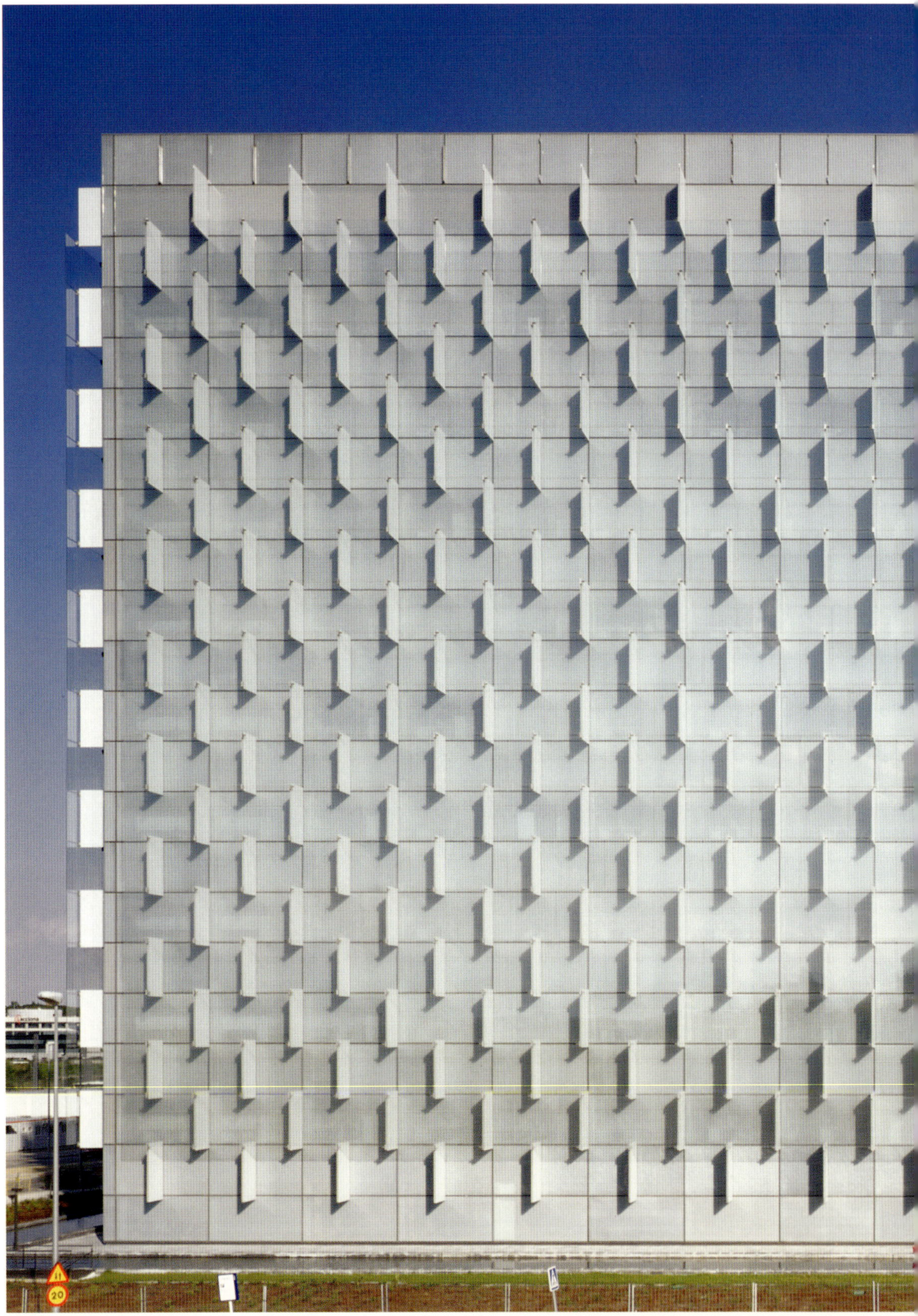

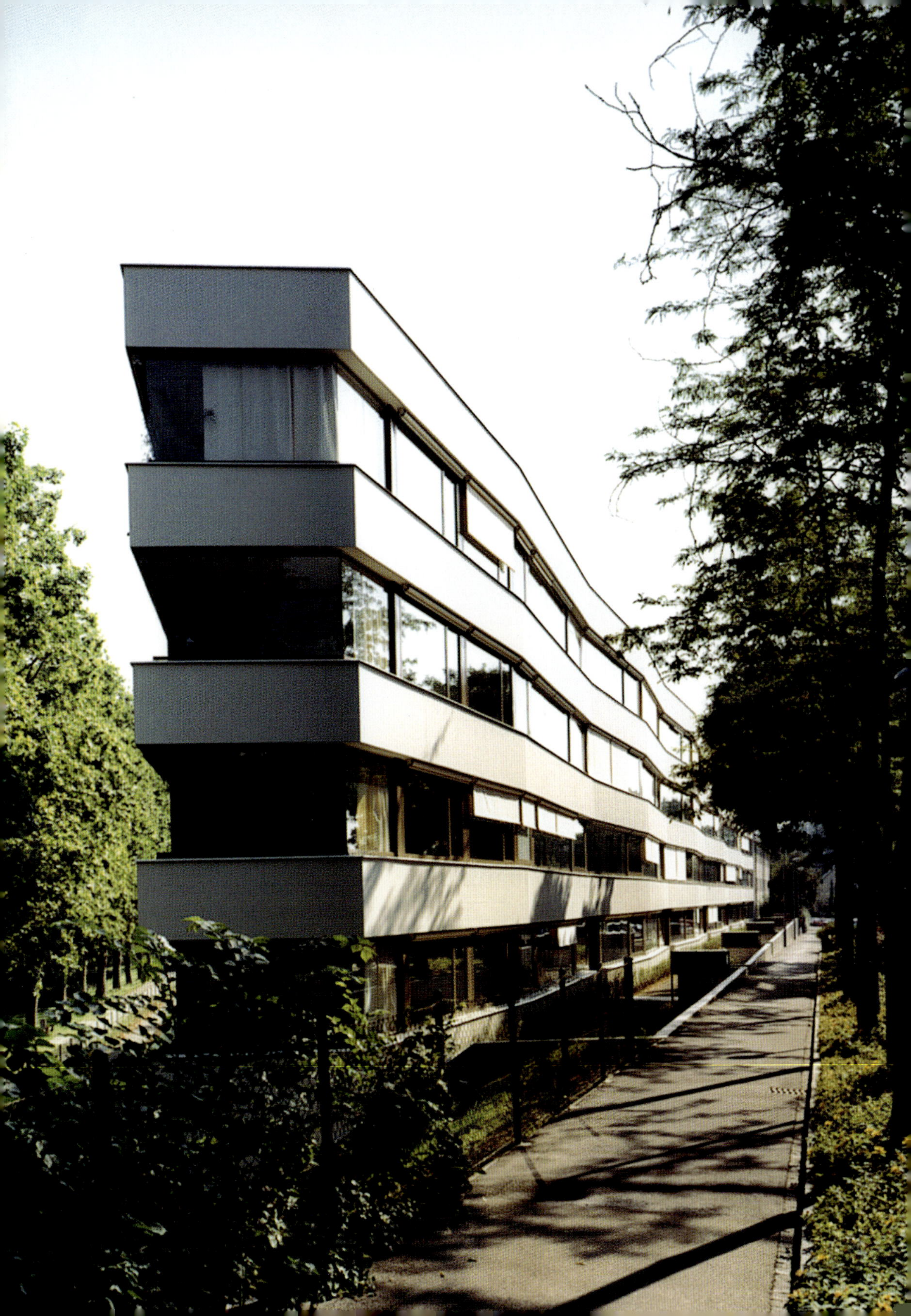

DEGELO ARCHITEKTEN | BASEL
St.-Alban-Ring
Basel, Switzerland | 2002

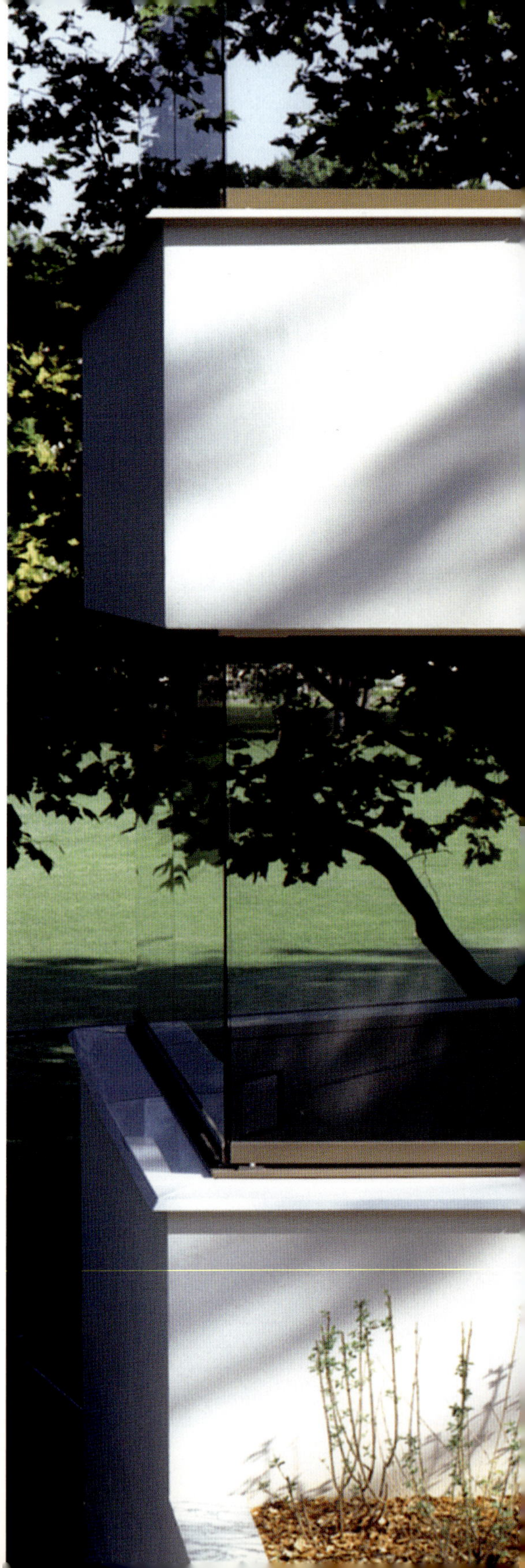

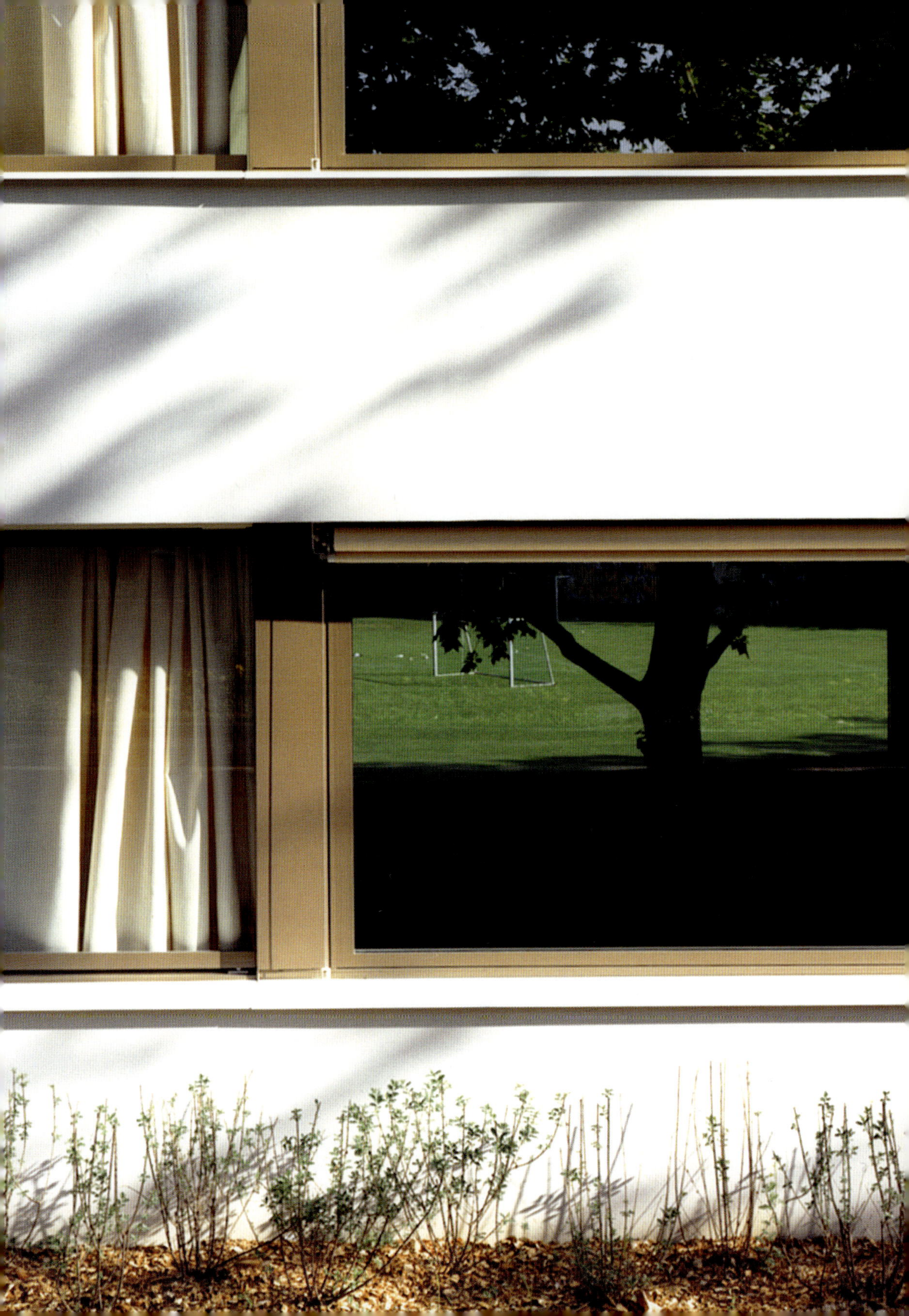

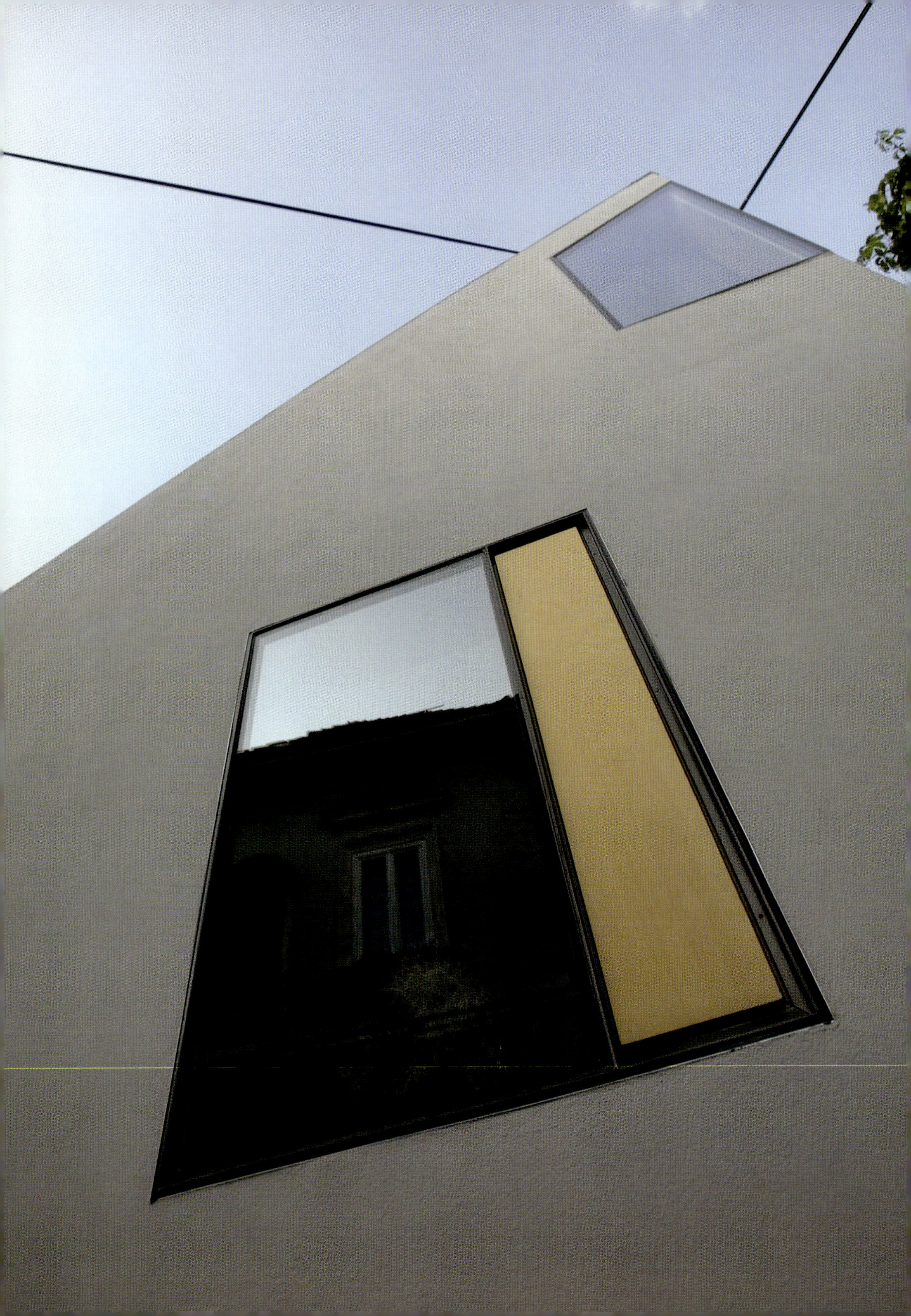

DEKLEVA GREGORIC ARHITEKTI | LJUBLJANA
House XXS
Ljubljana, Slovenia | 2004

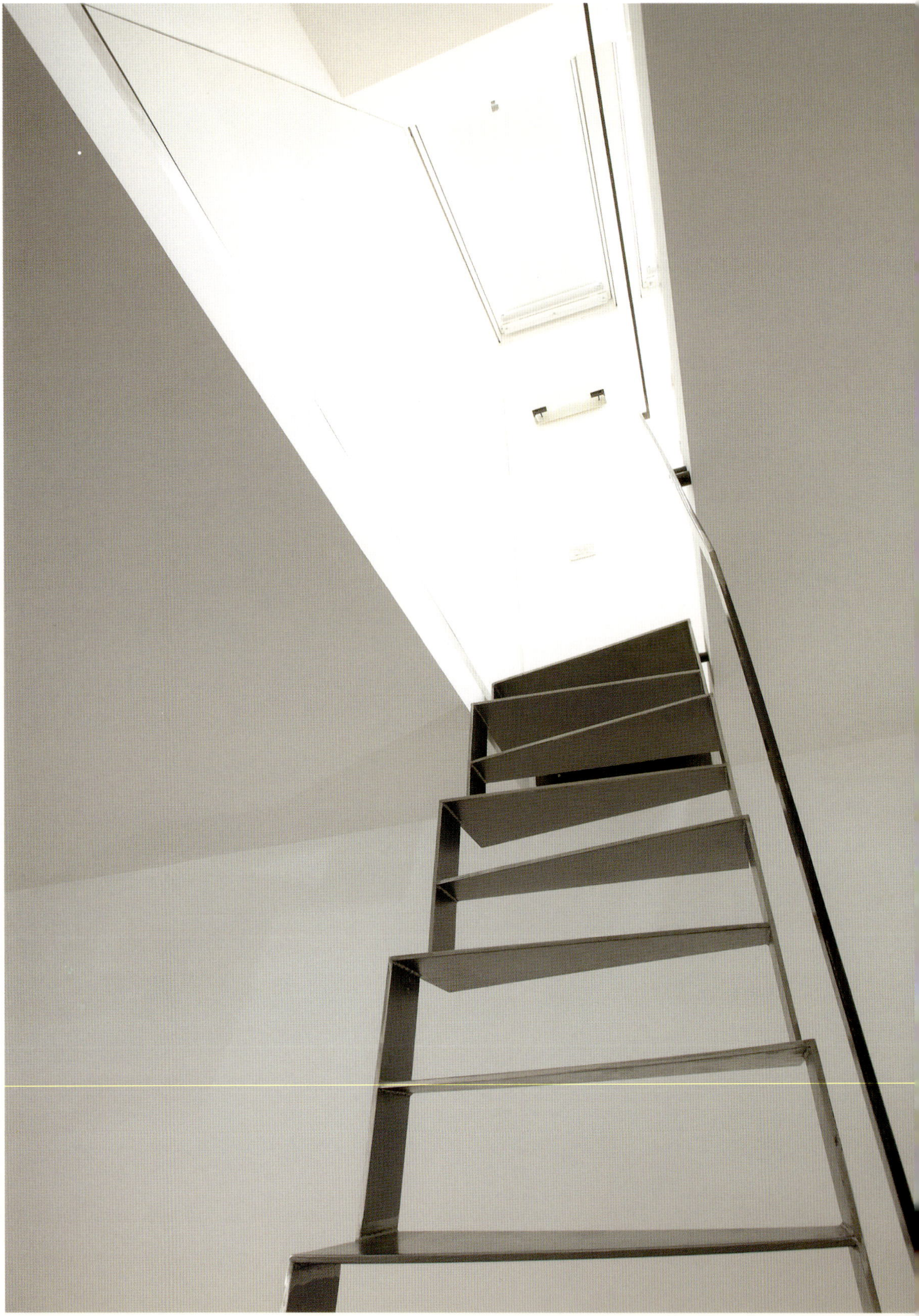

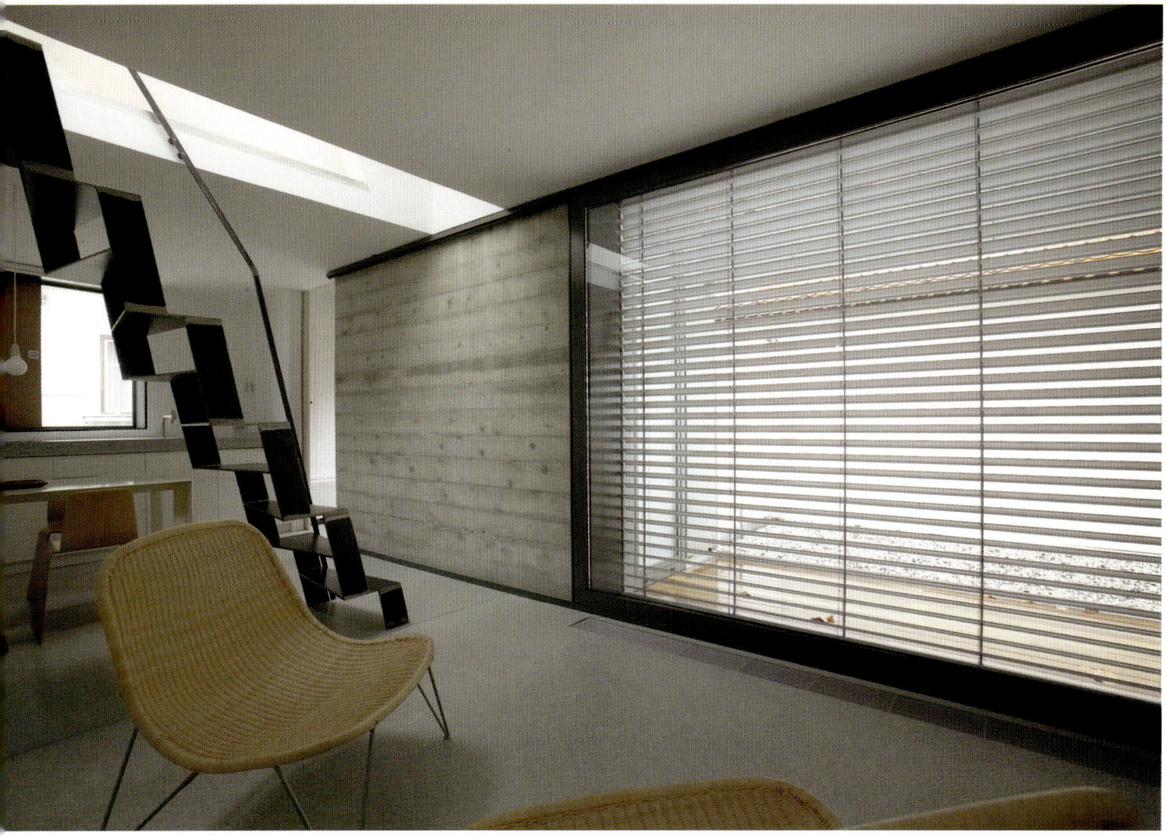

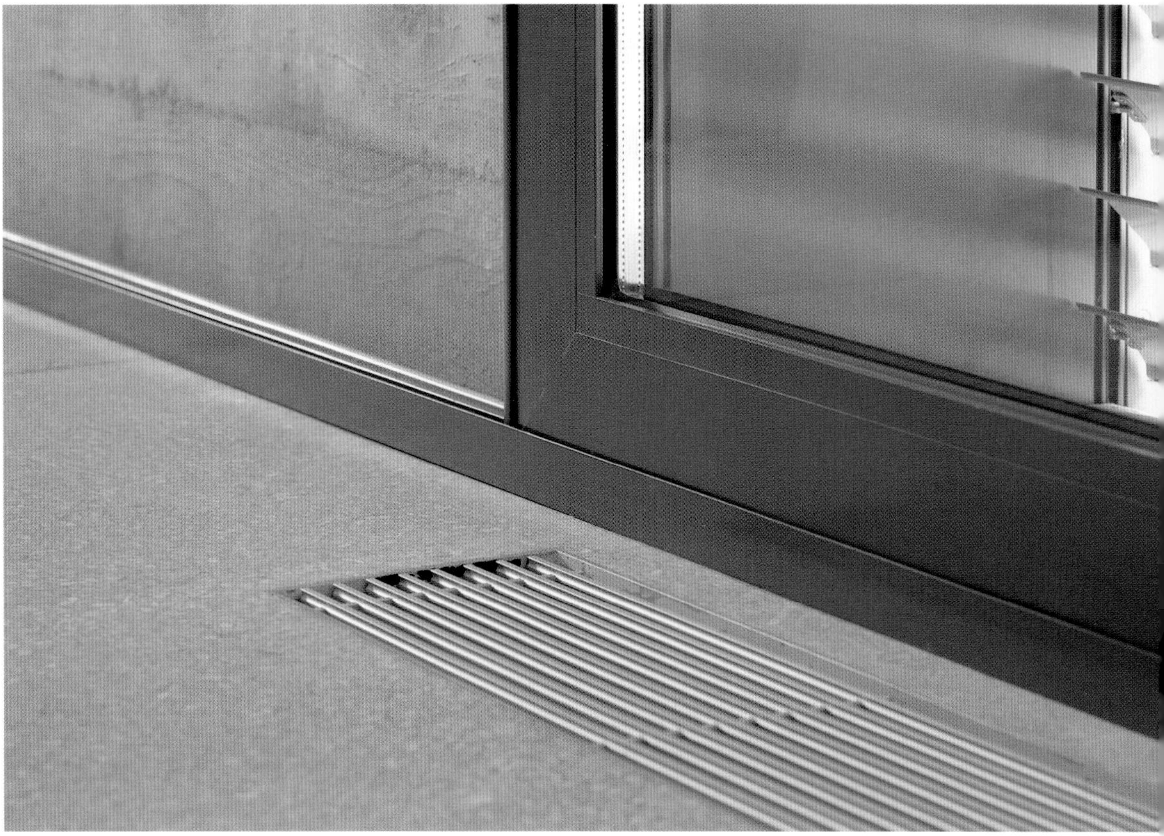

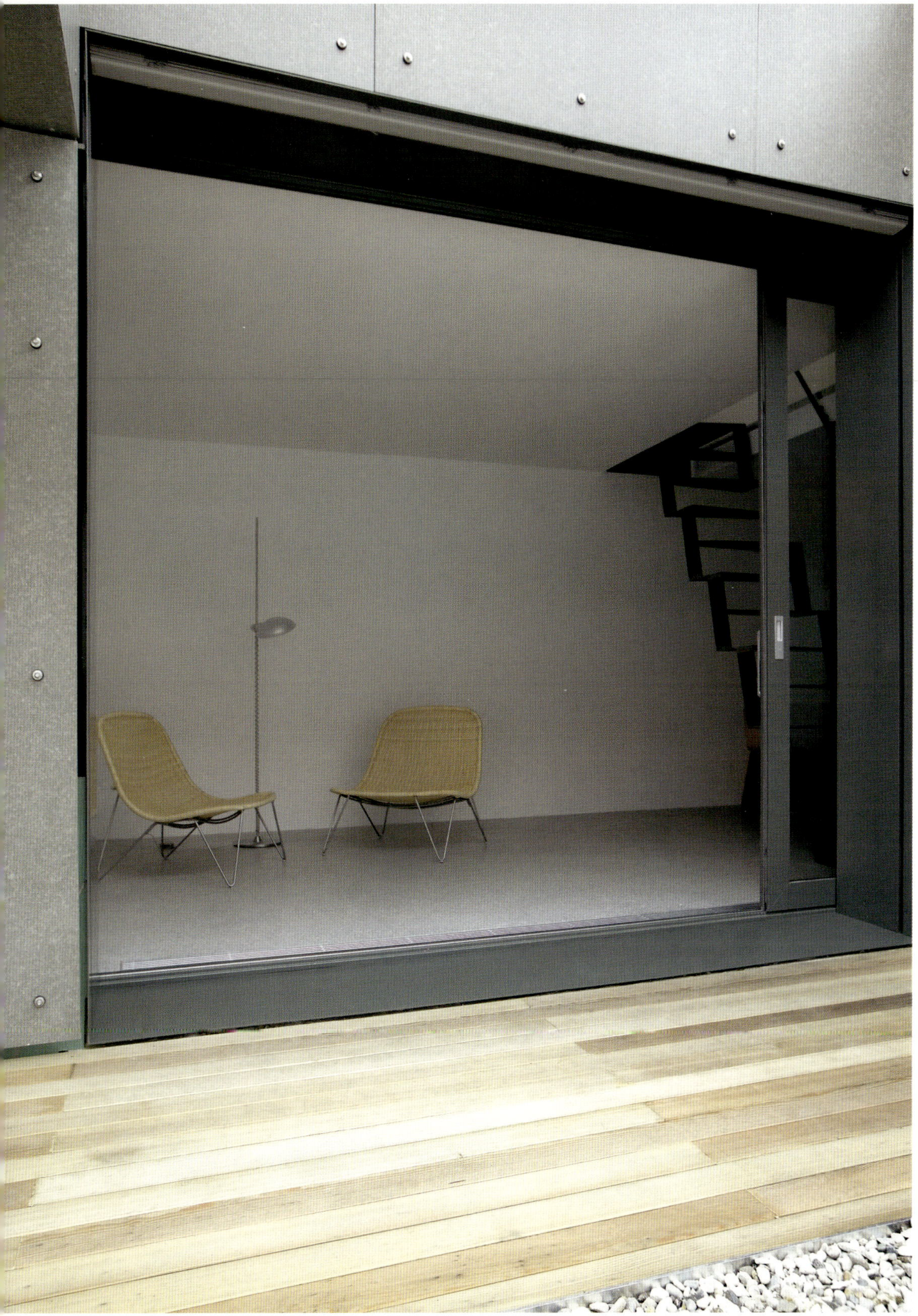

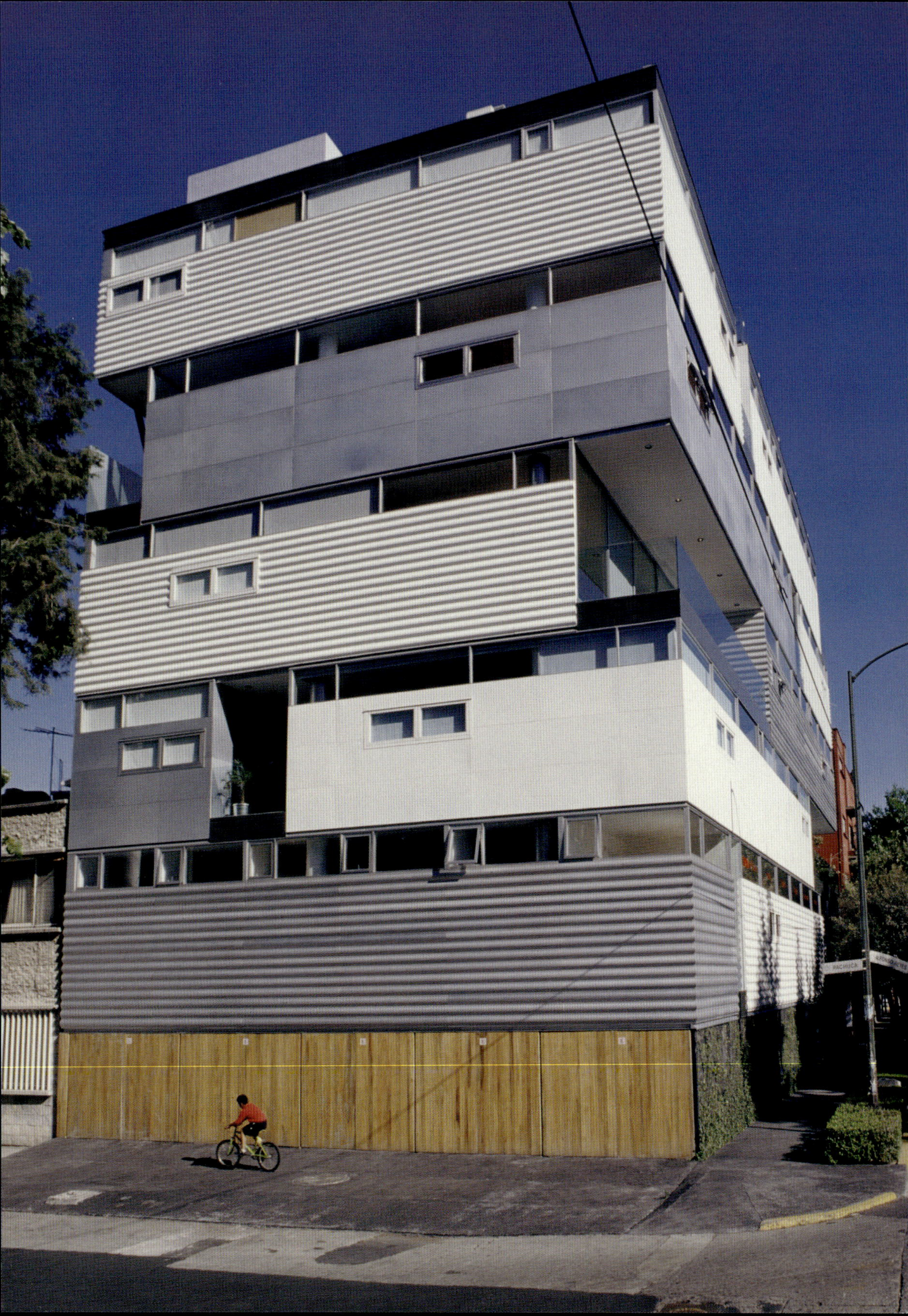

DELLEKAMP ARQUITECTOS | MEXICO CITY
AR 58
Colonia Condesa, Mexico City, Mexico | 2002

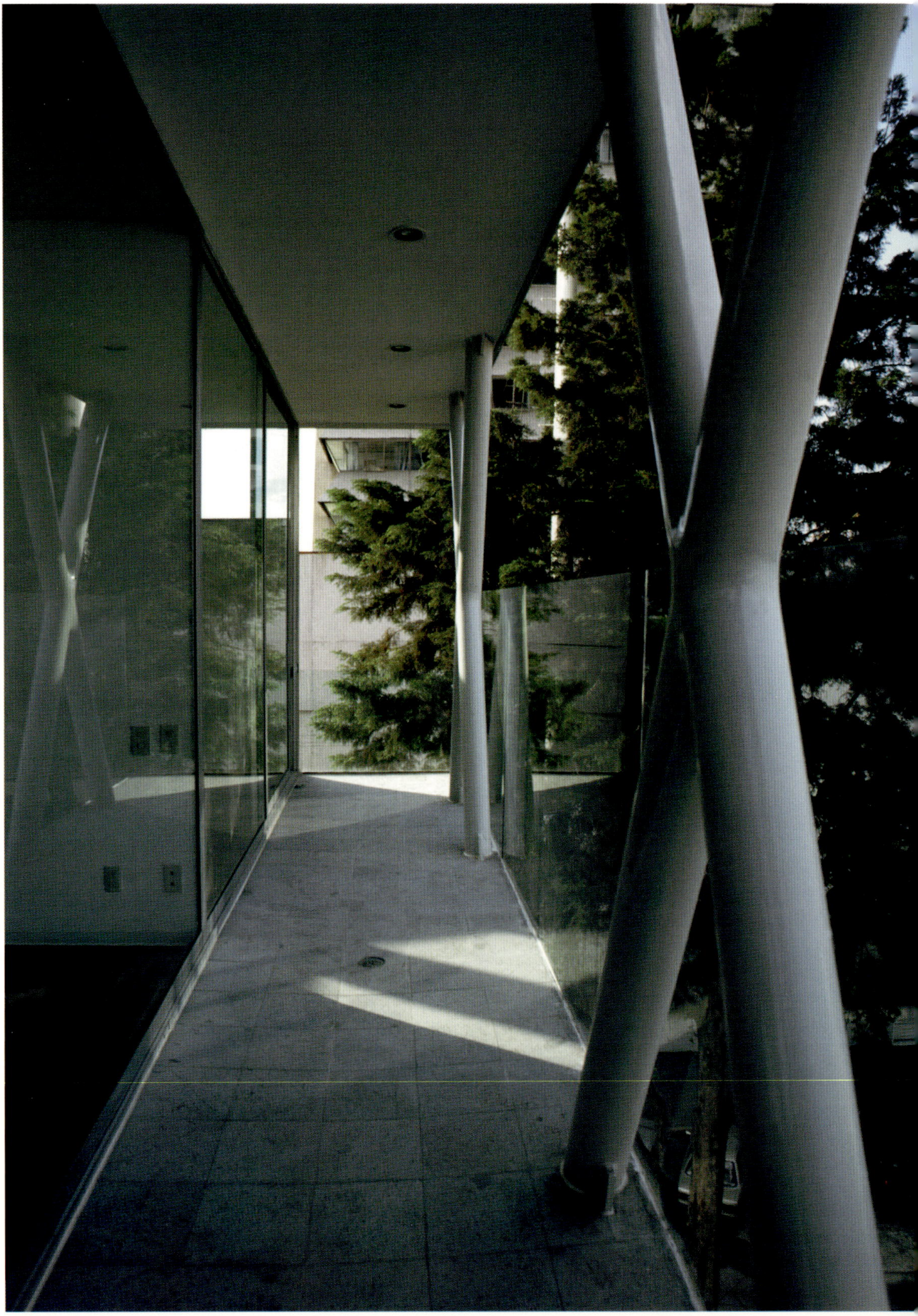

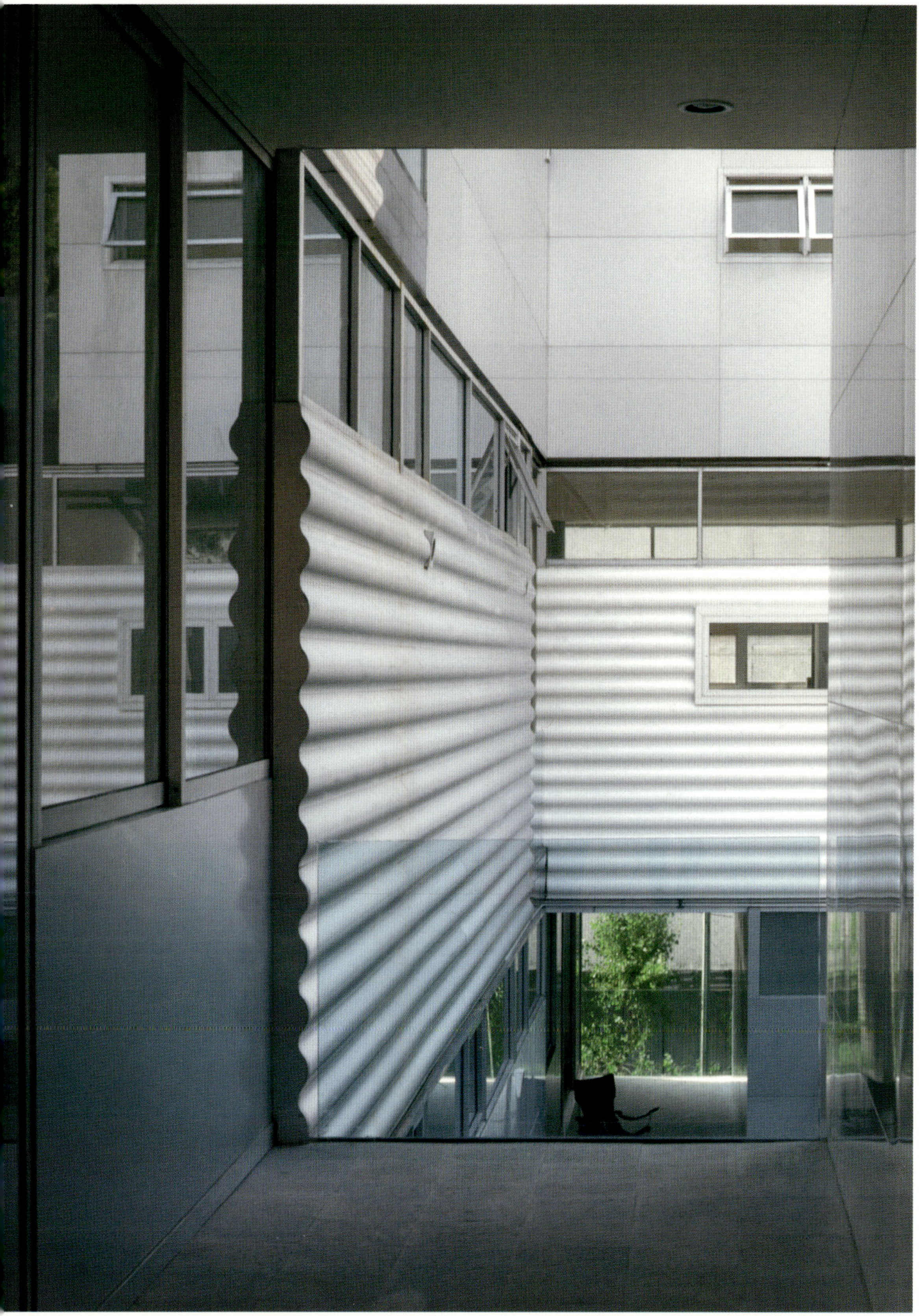

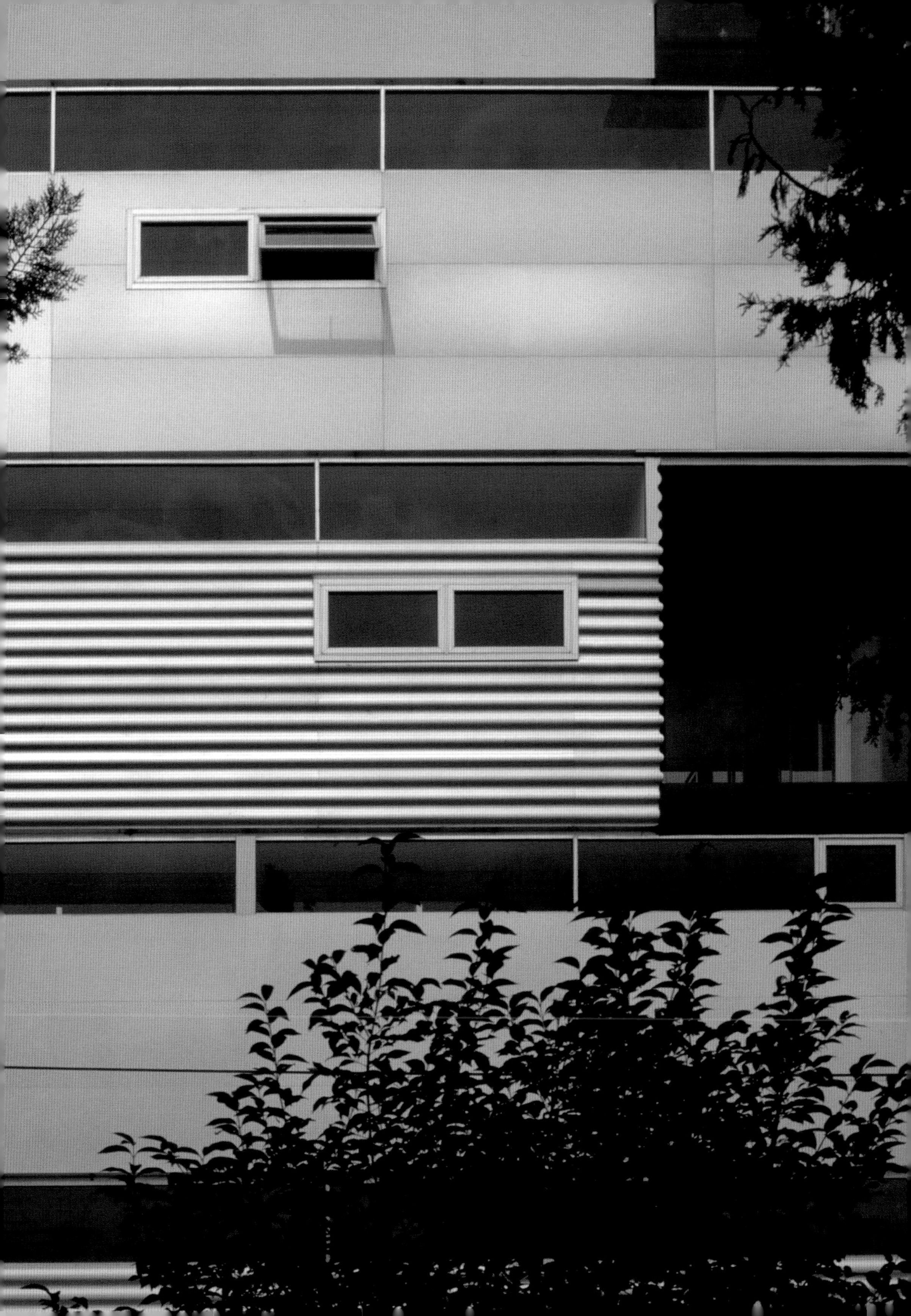

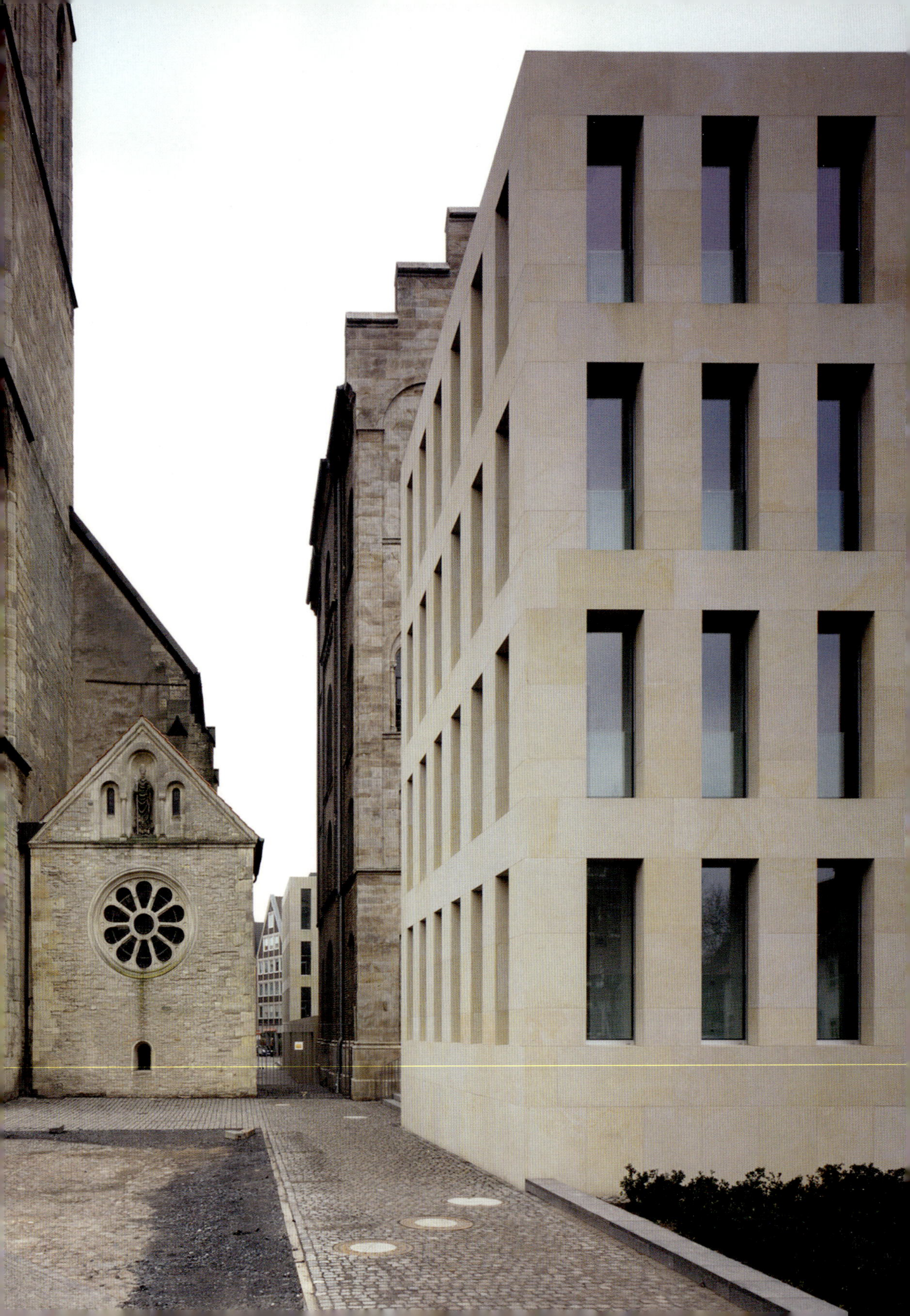

MAX DUDLER WITH BERNHARD MOELLER | BERLIN
Diocese library
Muenster, Germany | 2005

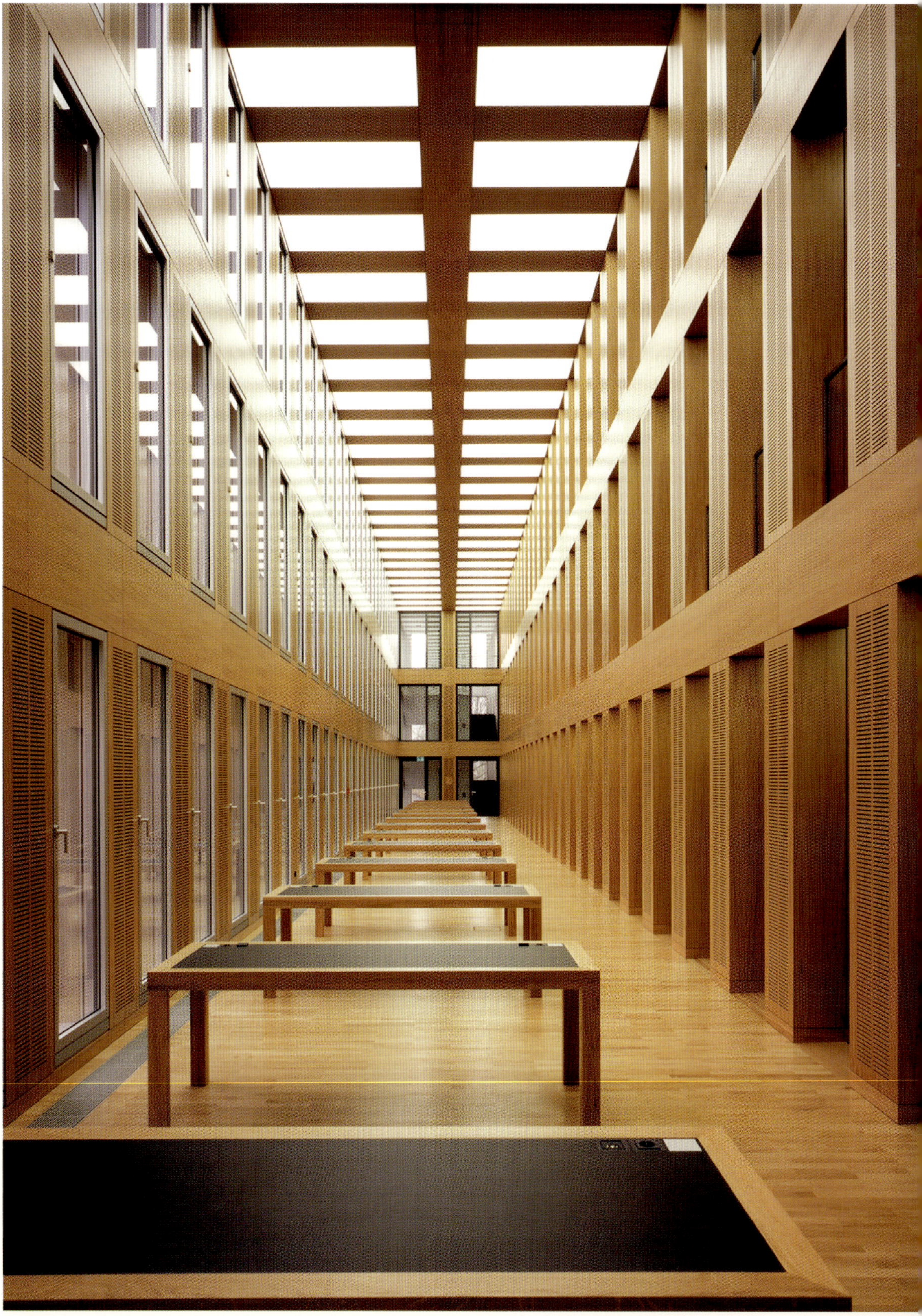

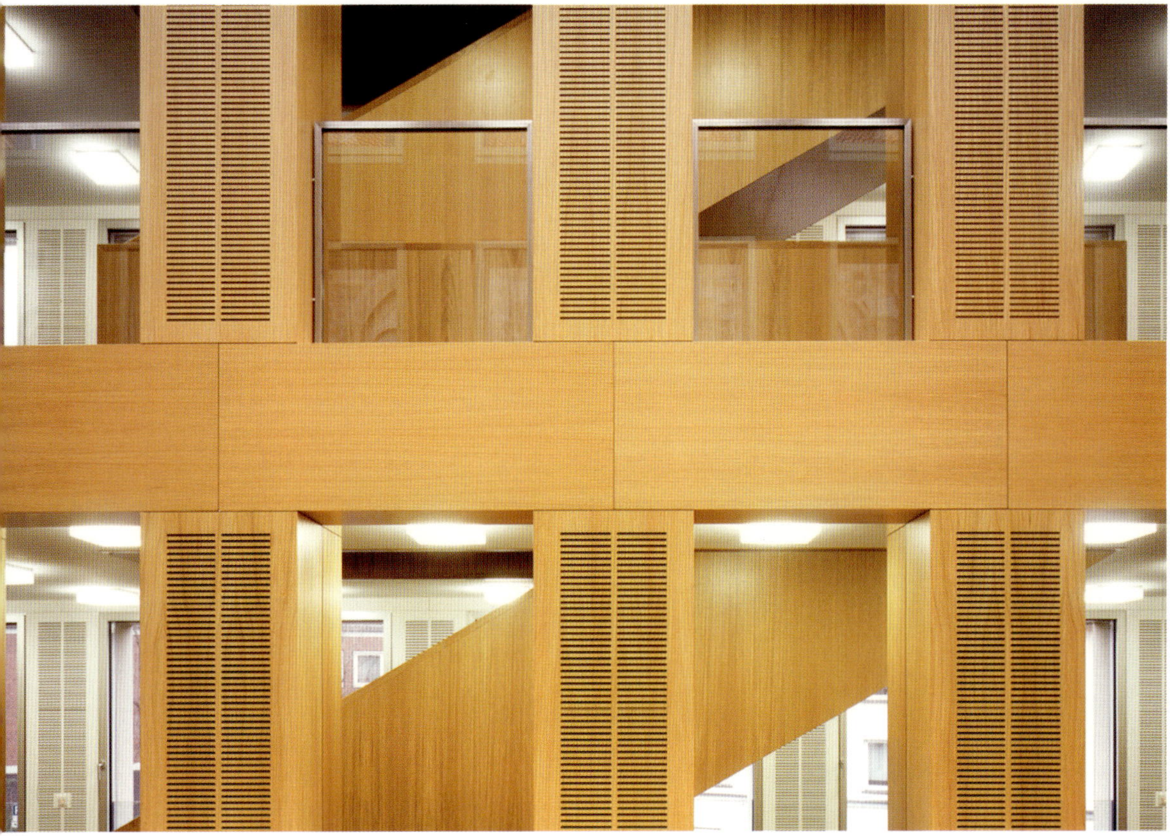

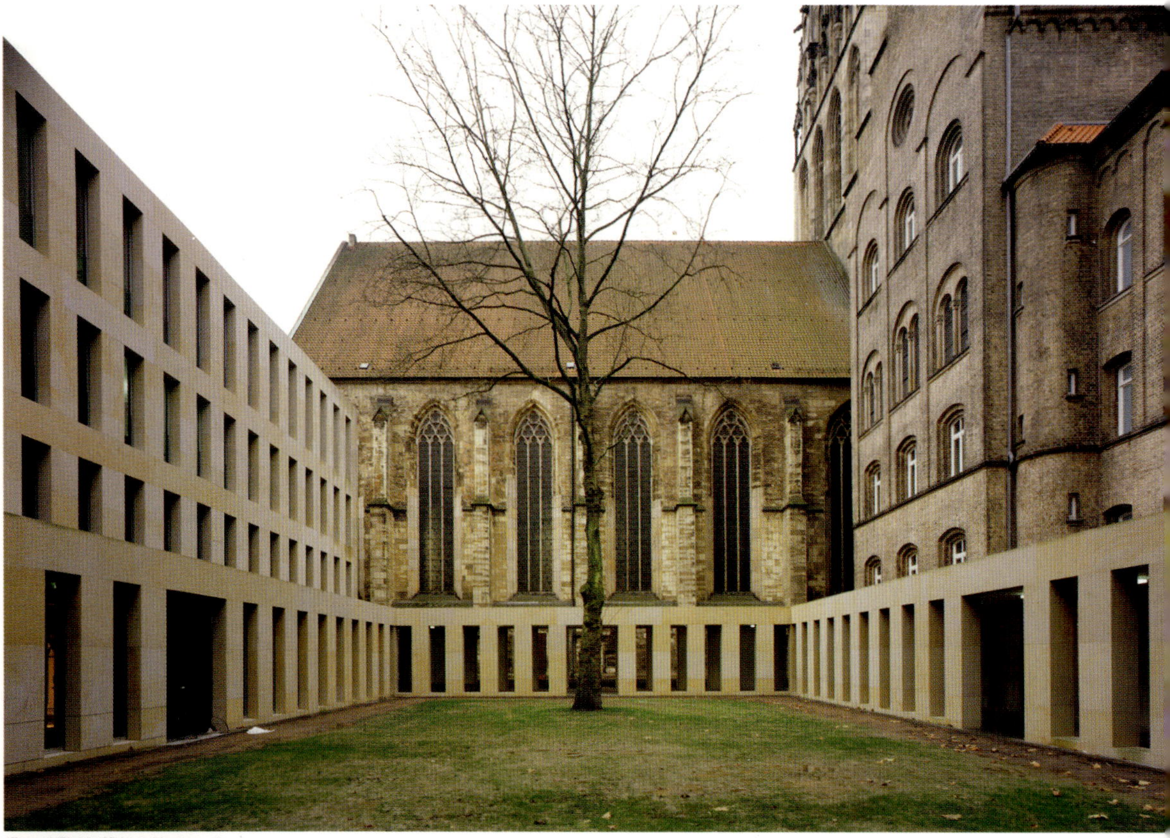

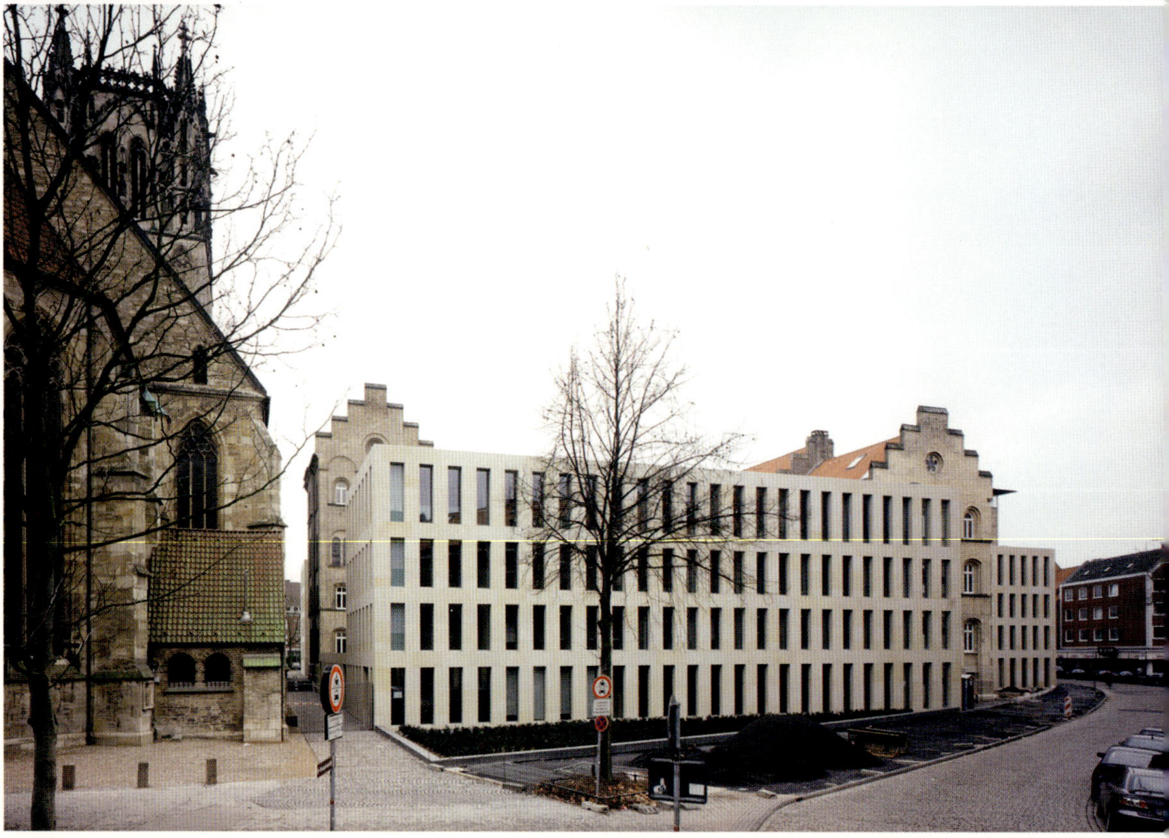

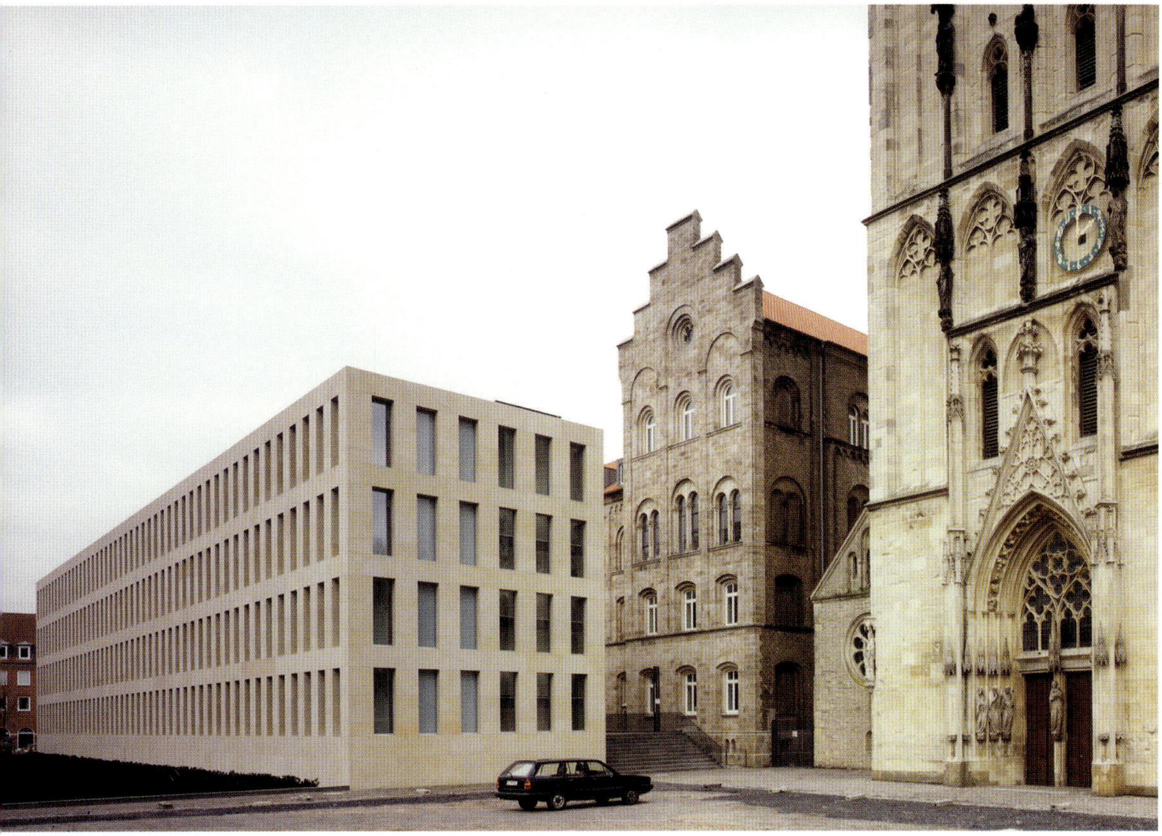

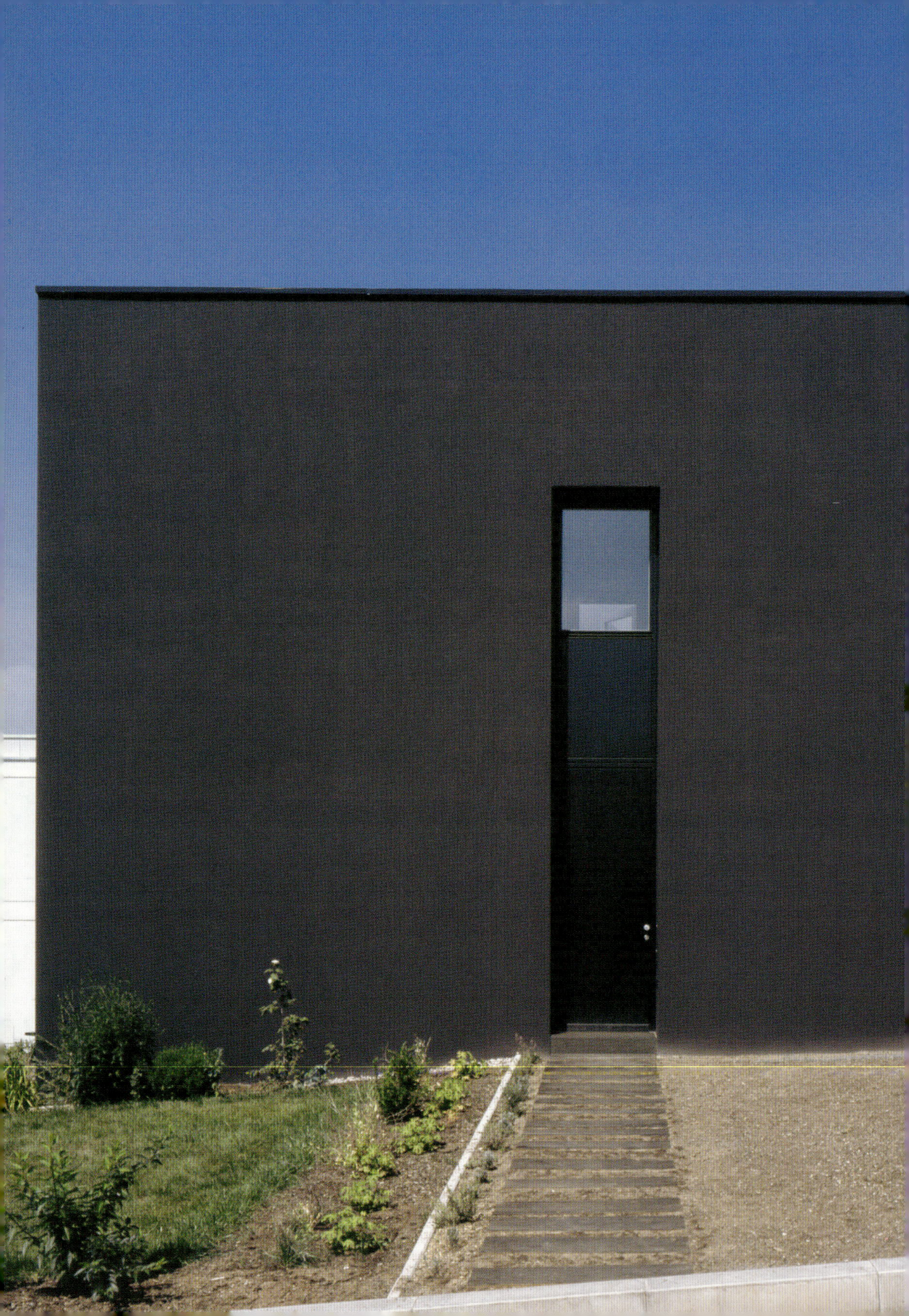

MAX DUDLER WITH NINA BARTHÉLÉMY | BERLIN
Living house and atelier
Weimar, Germany | 2003

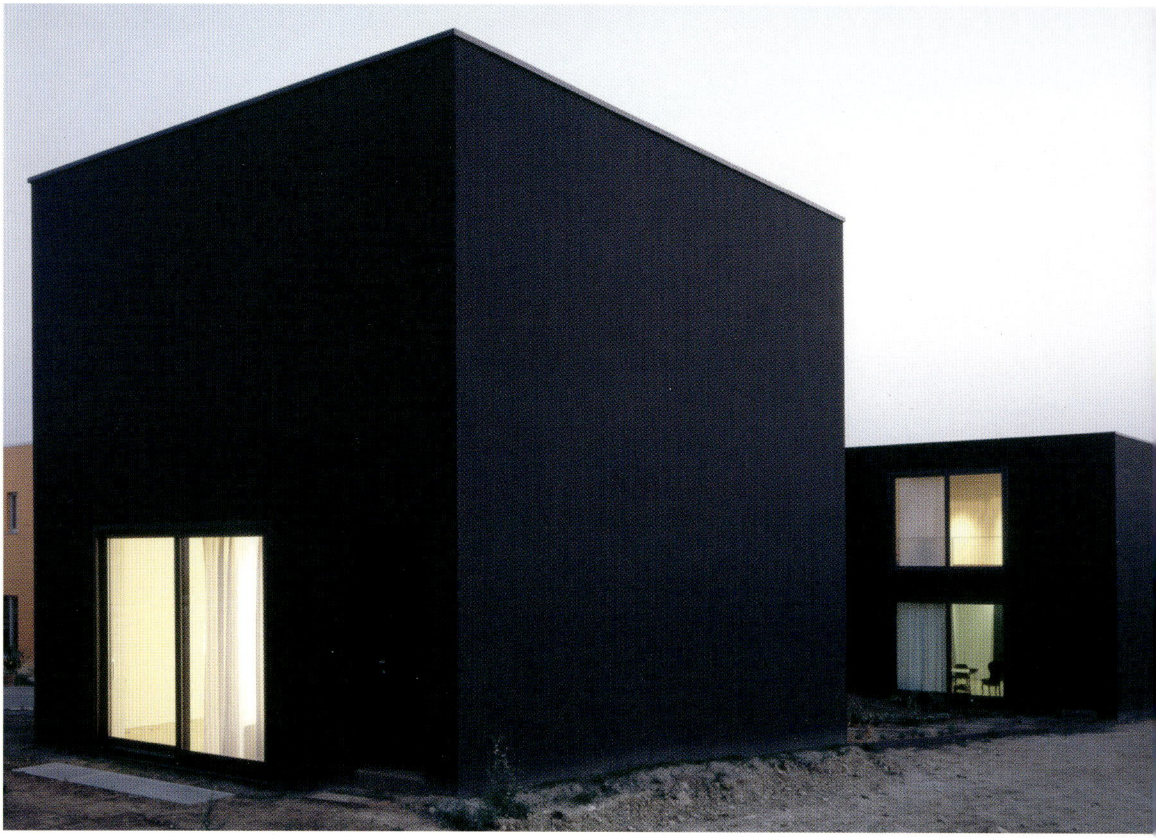

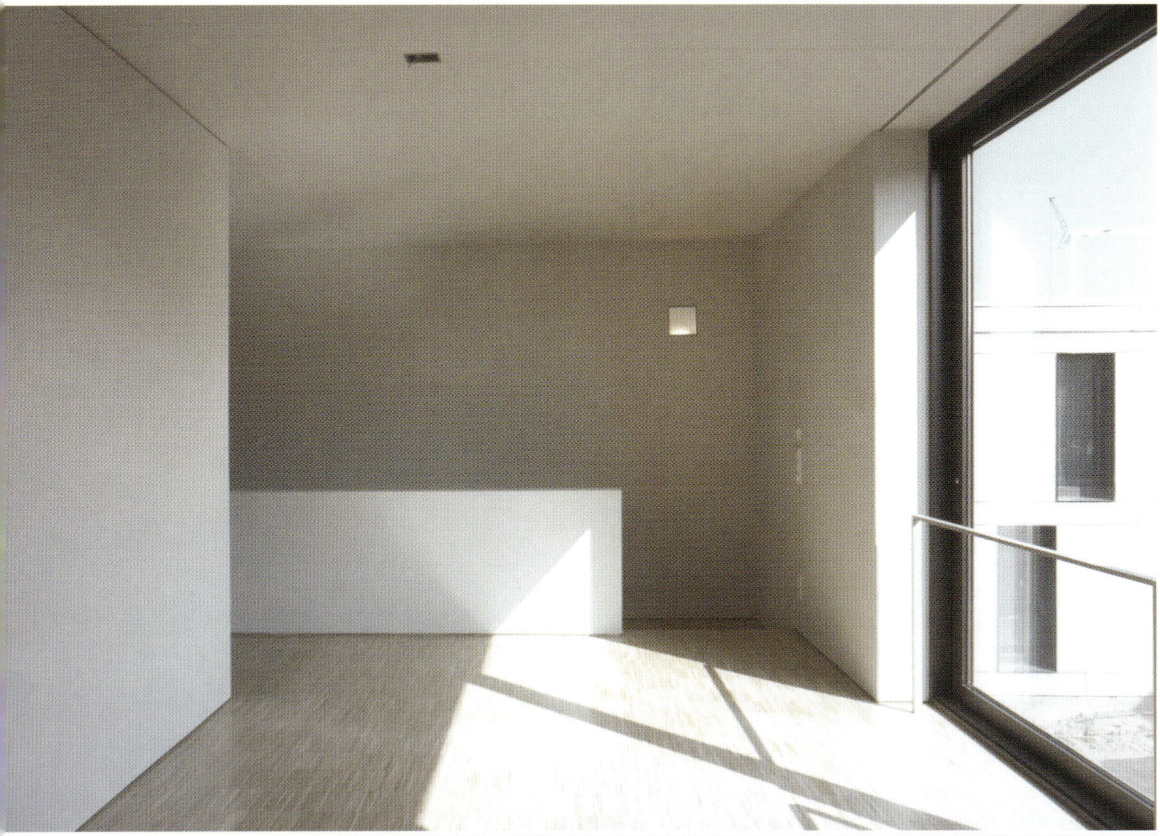

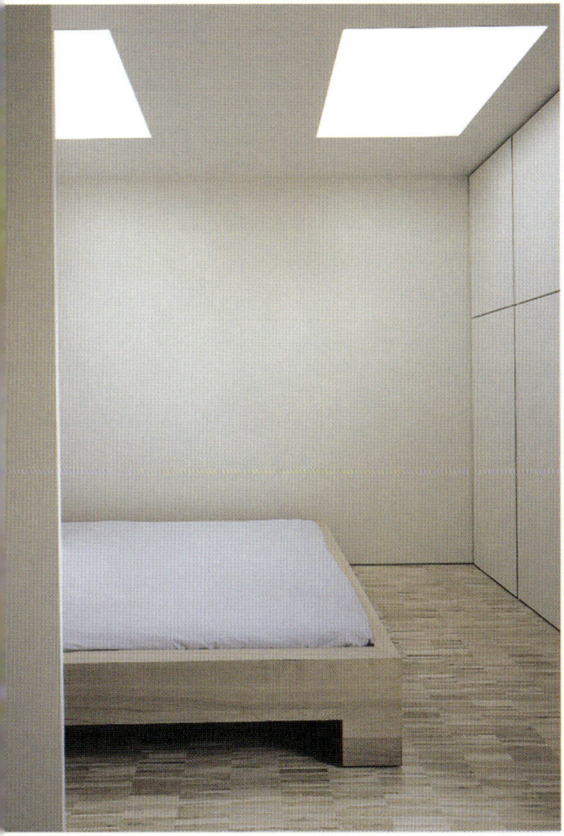

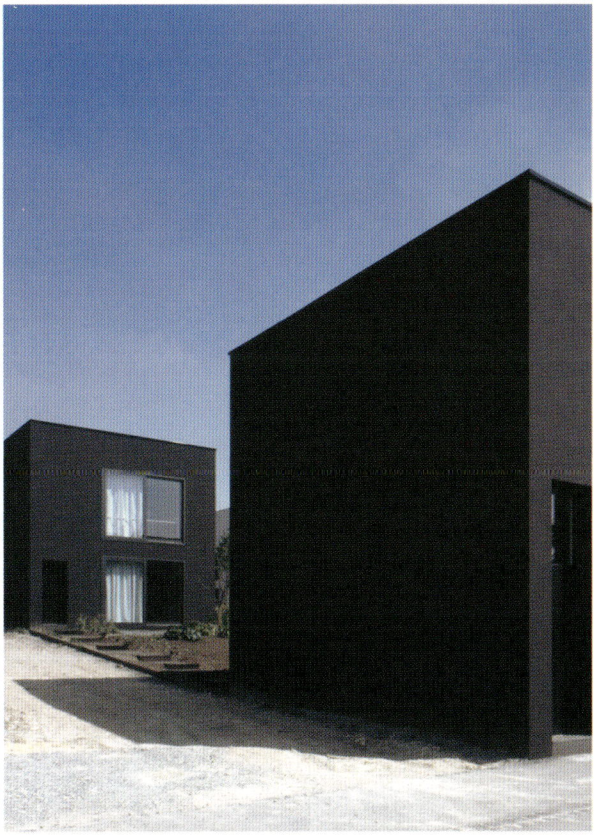

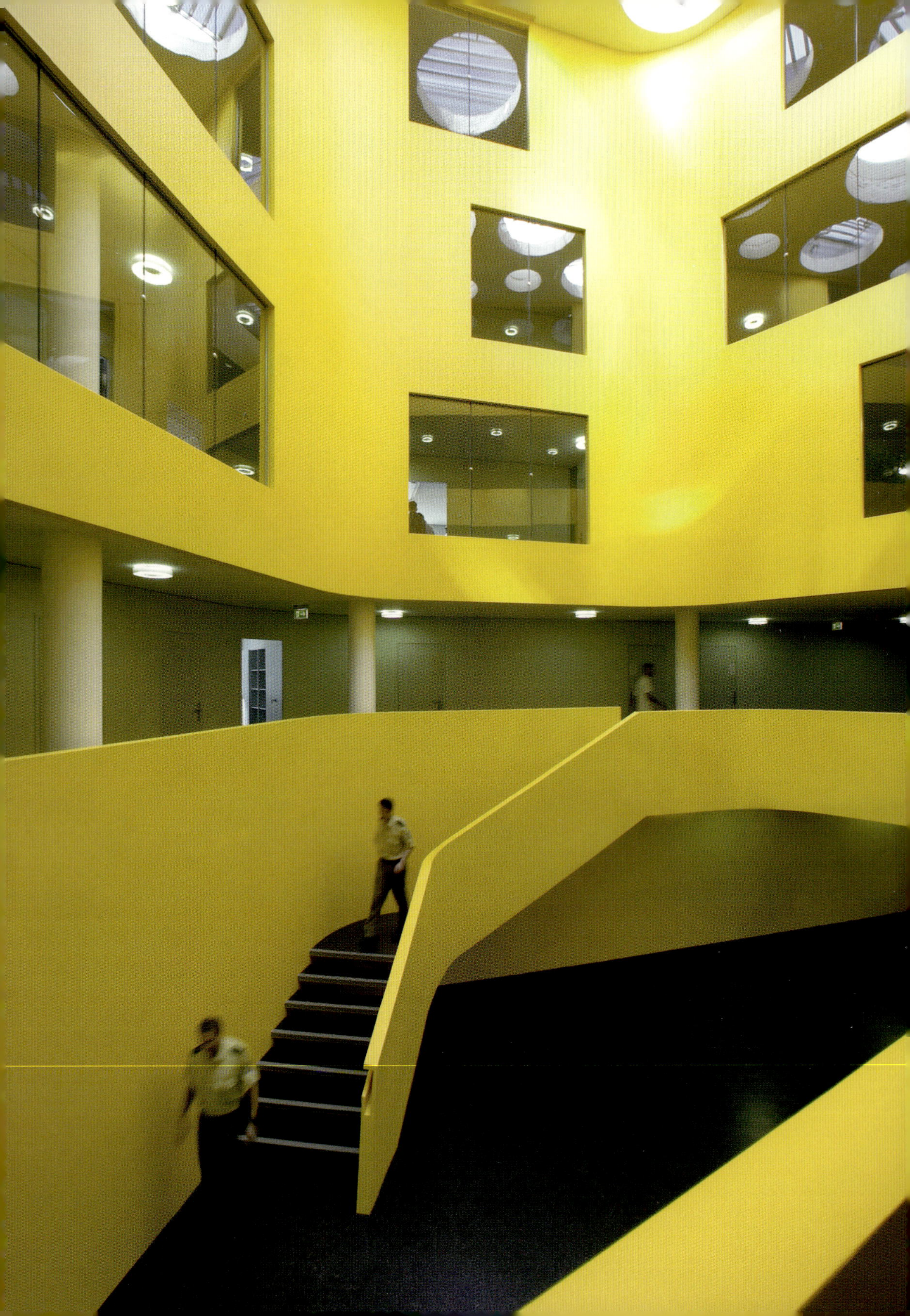

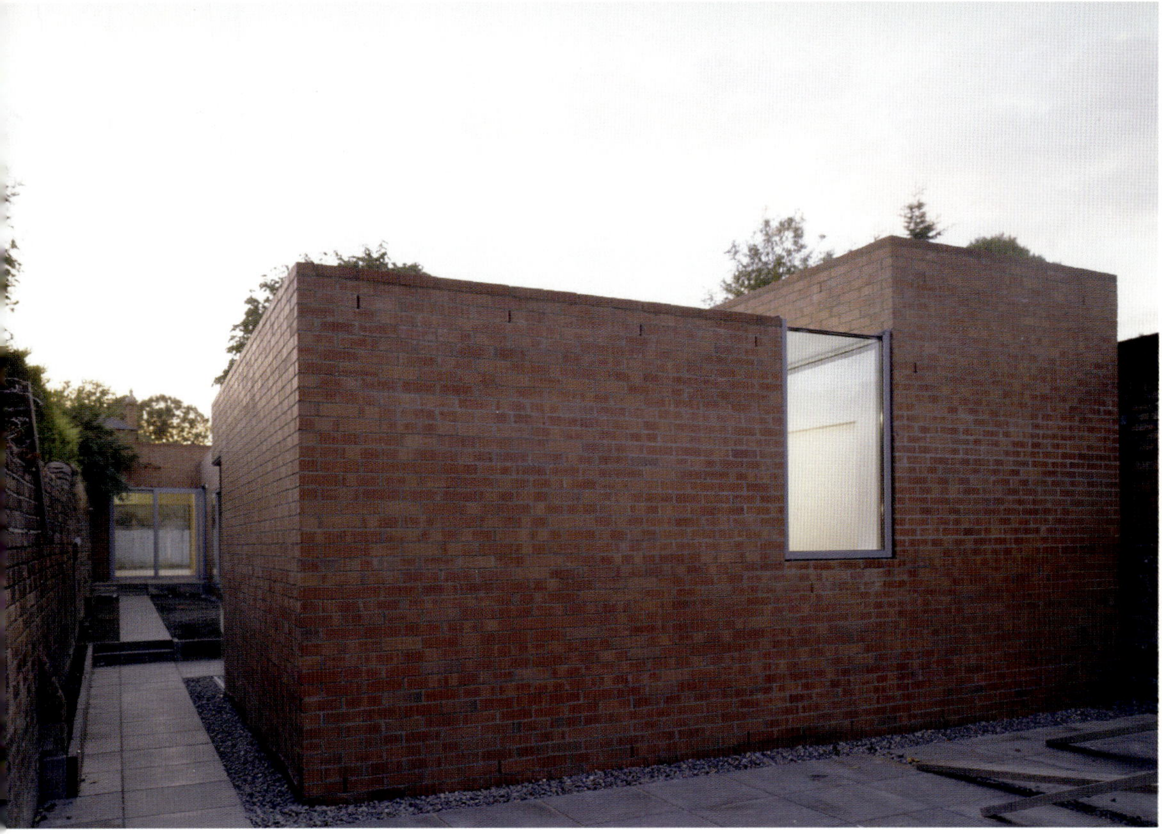

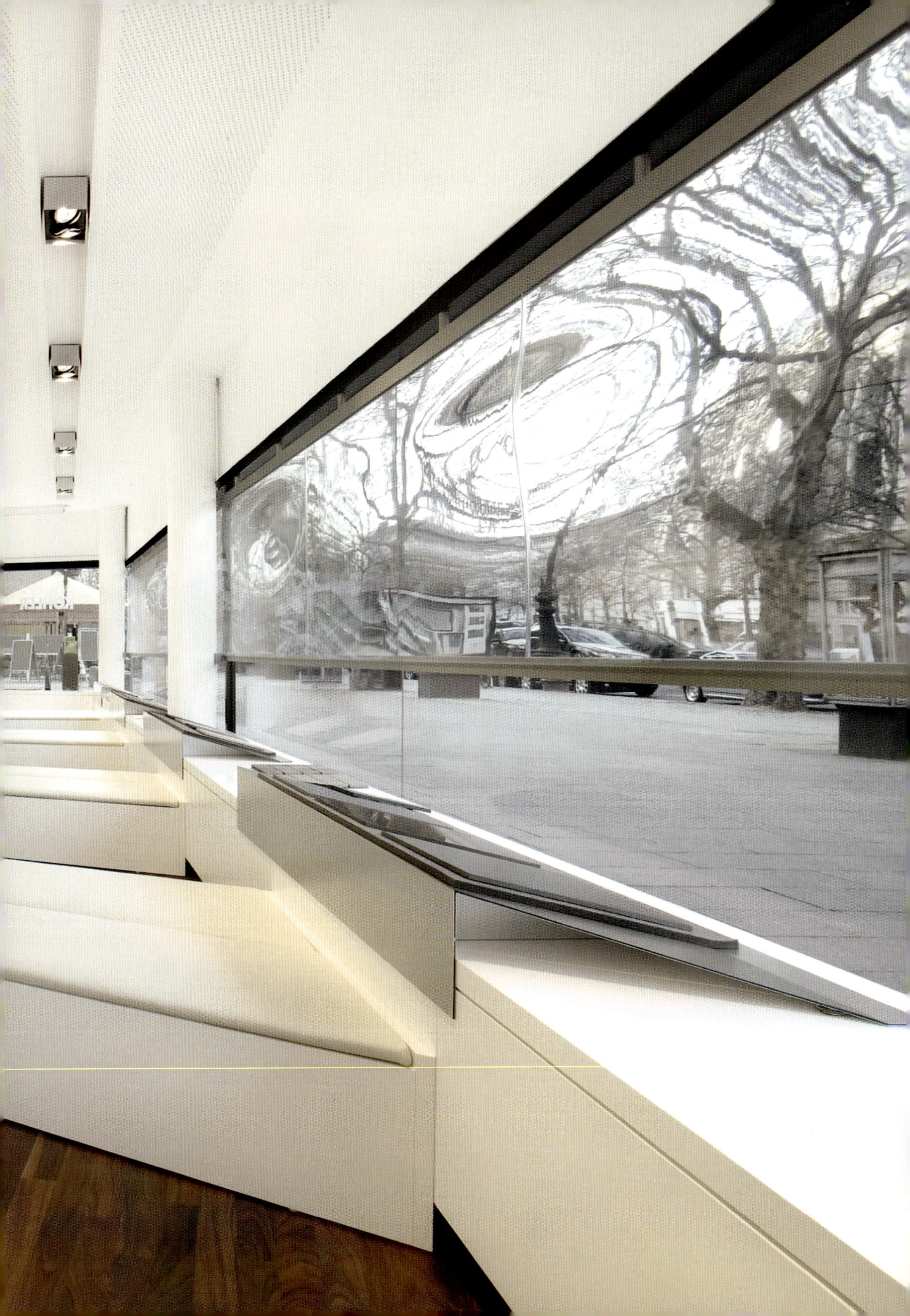

FRANKEN ARCHITEKTEN | FRANKFURT
Home Couture
Berlin, Germany | 2005

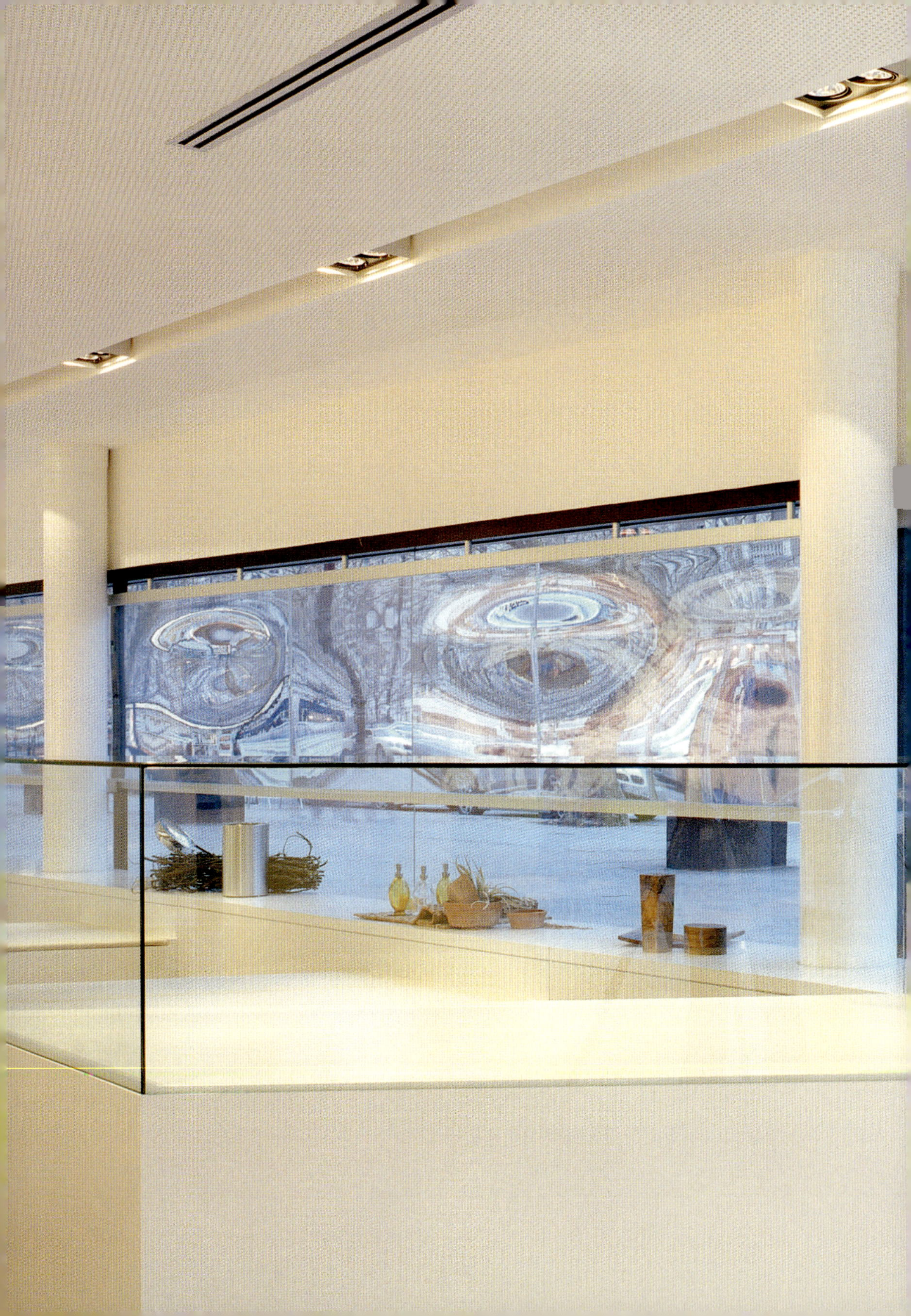

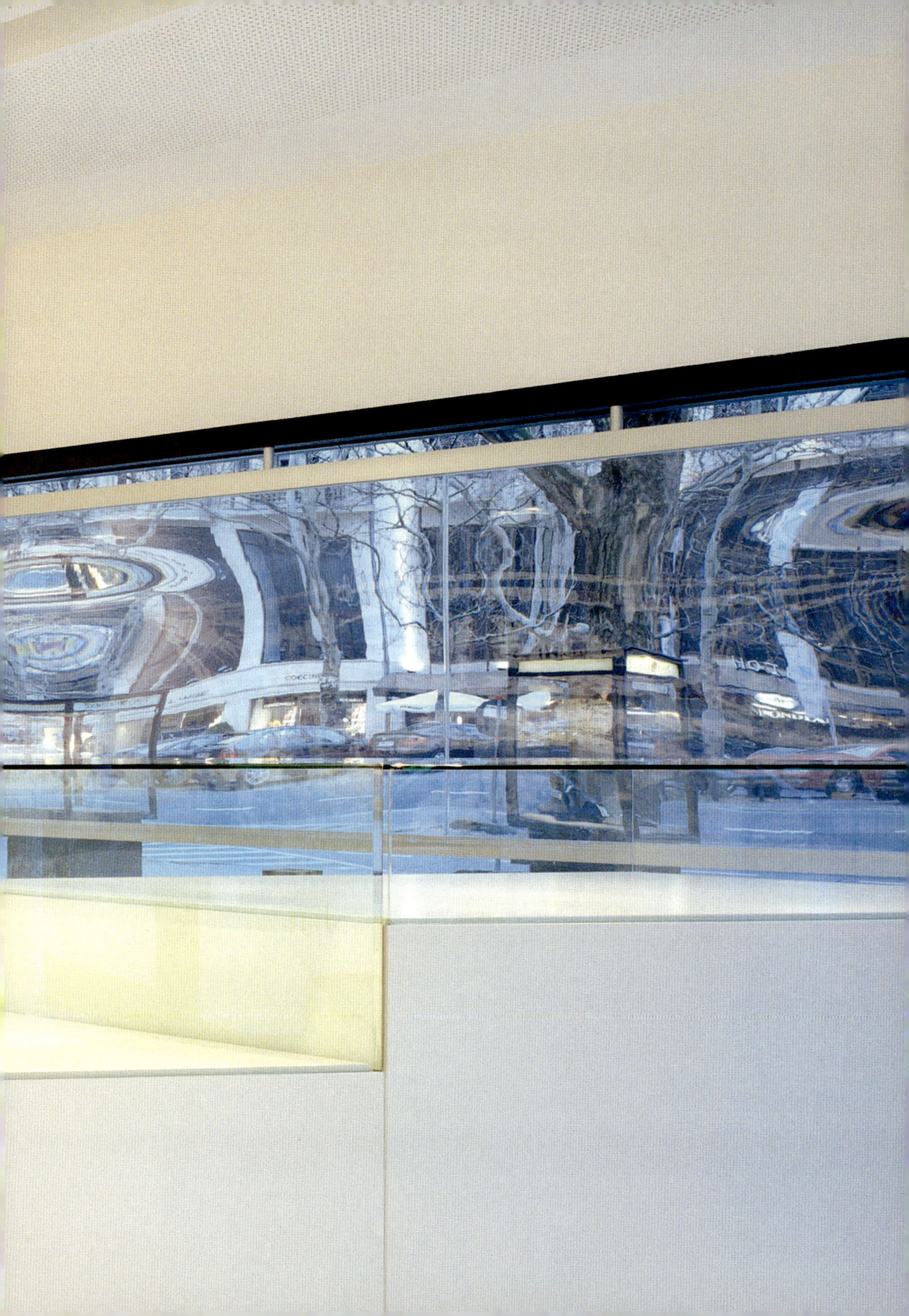

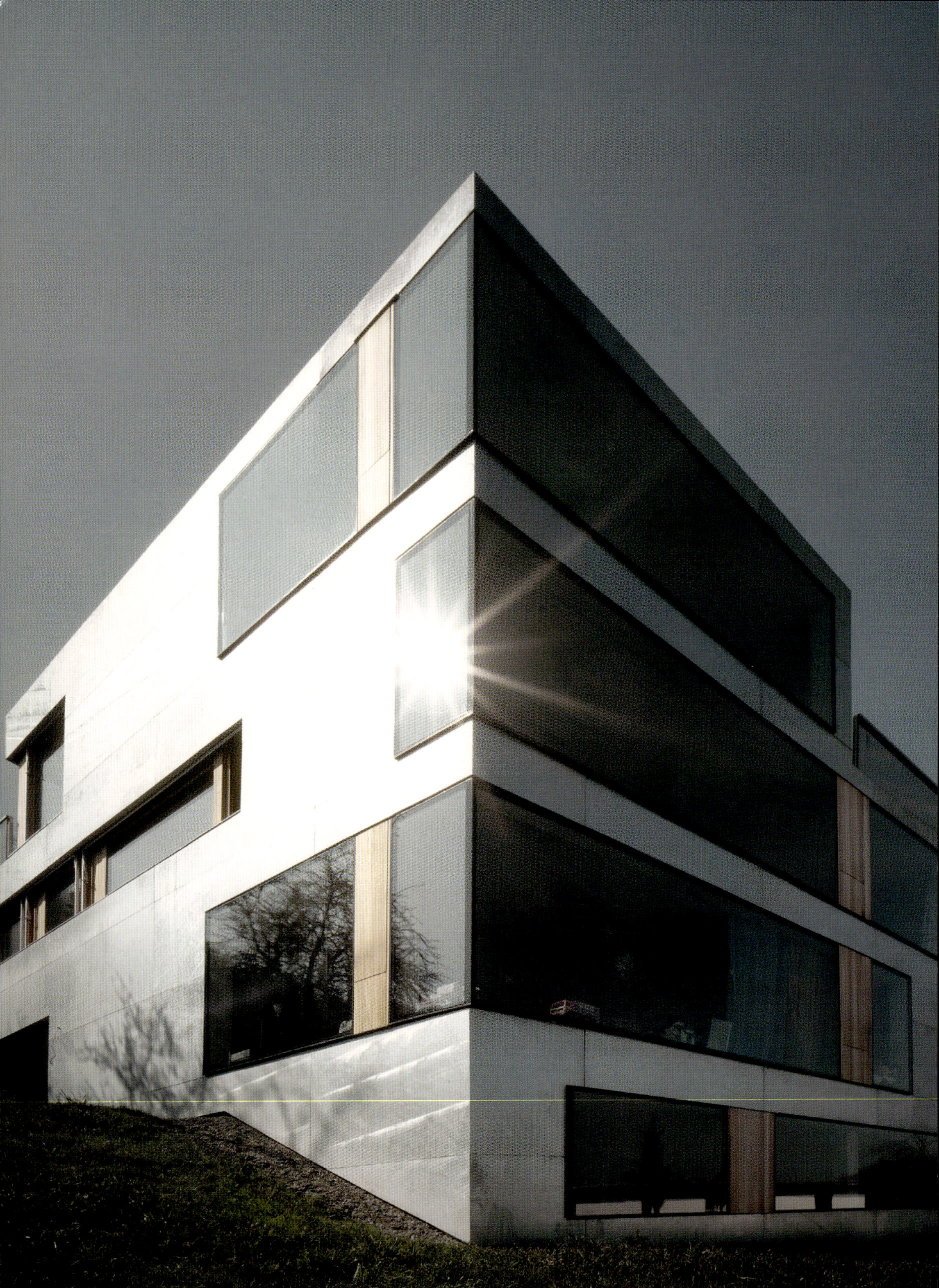

ANDREAS FUHRIMANN, GABRIELLE HÄCHLER | ZURICH
Architect's and artist's apartment house
Foot of the Üetliberg, Zurich, Switzerland | 2004

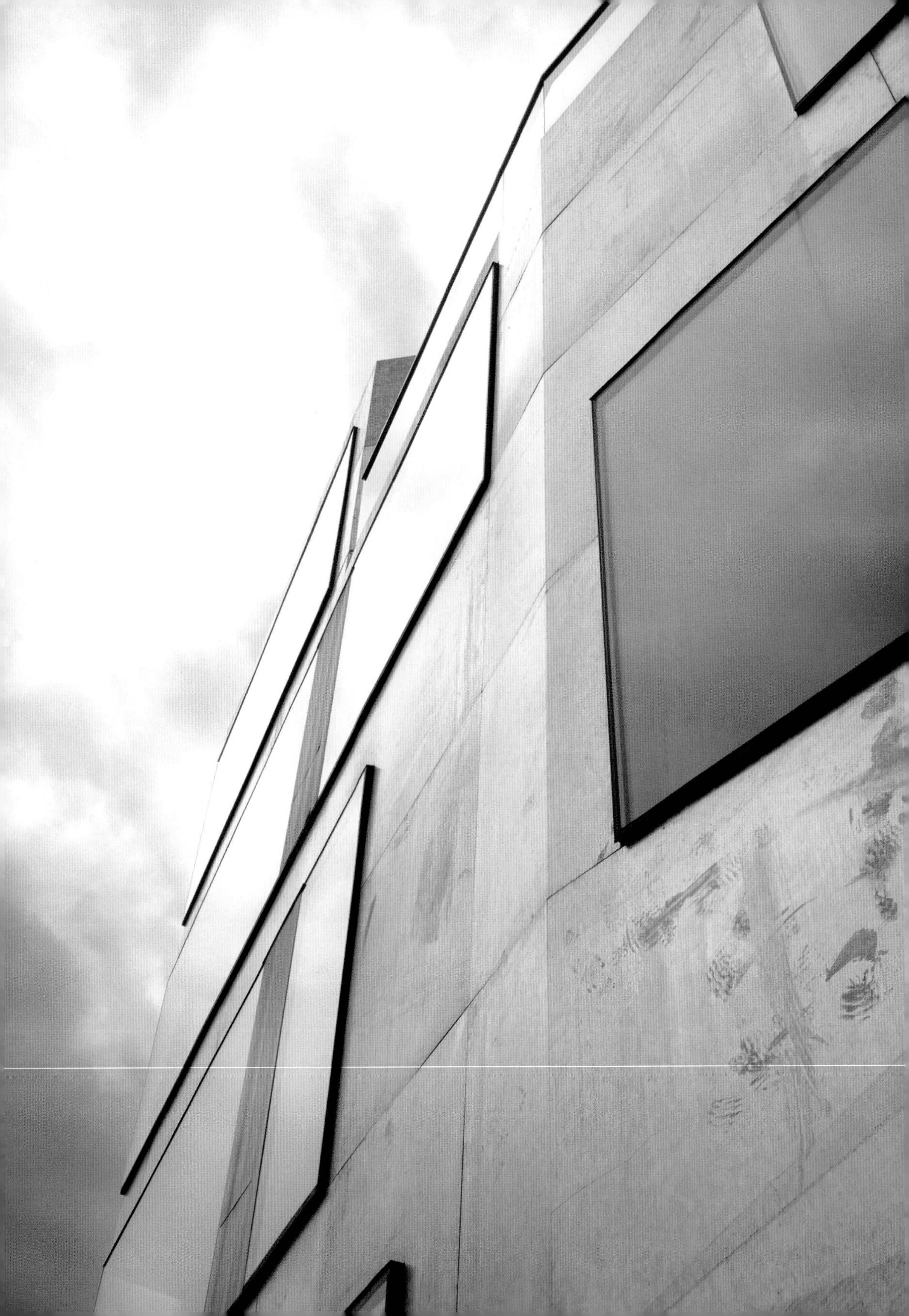

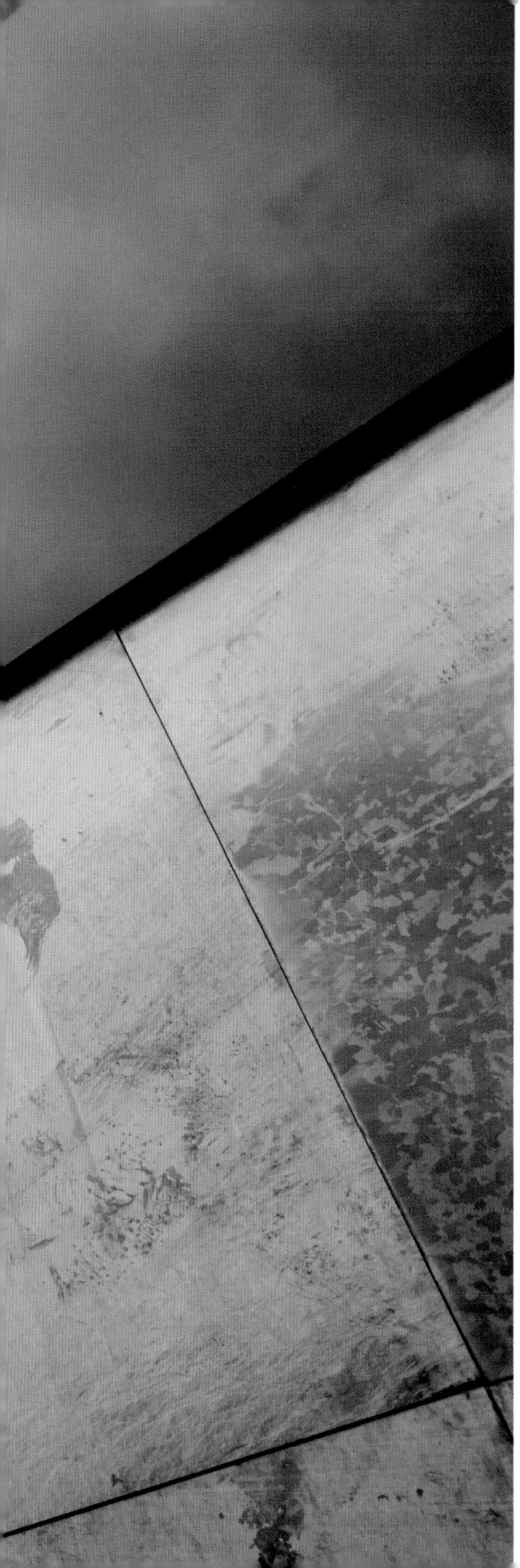

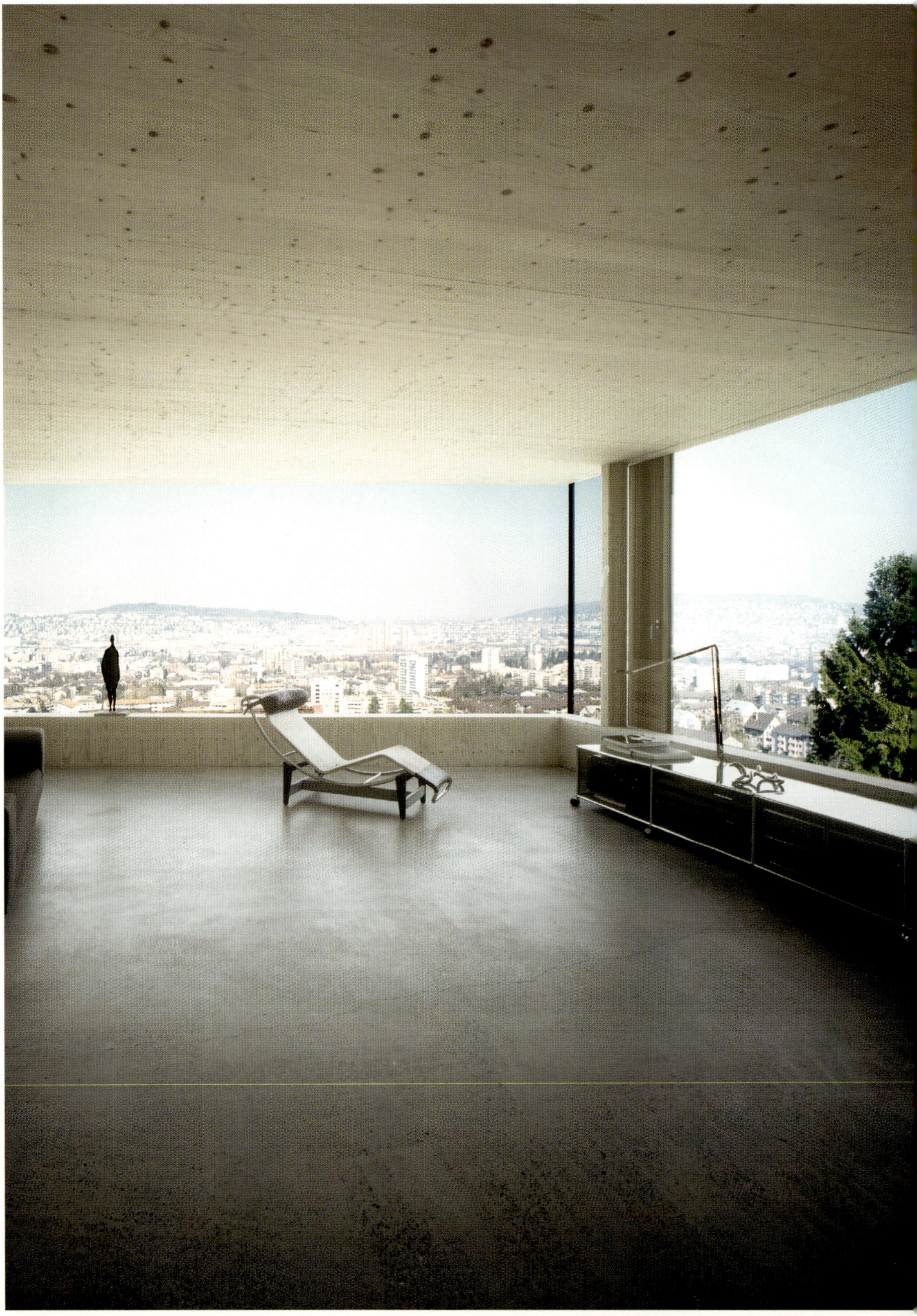

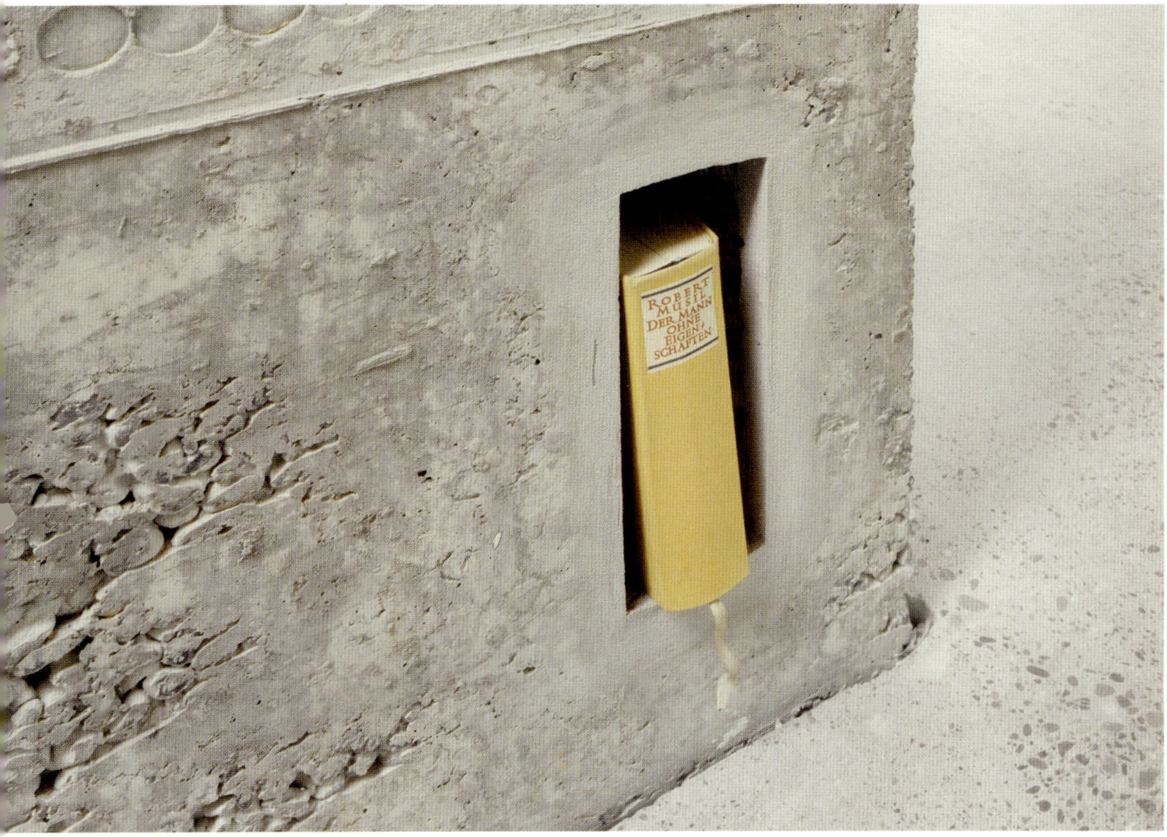
ROBERT
MUSIL
DER MANN
OHNE
EIGEN-
SCHAFTEN

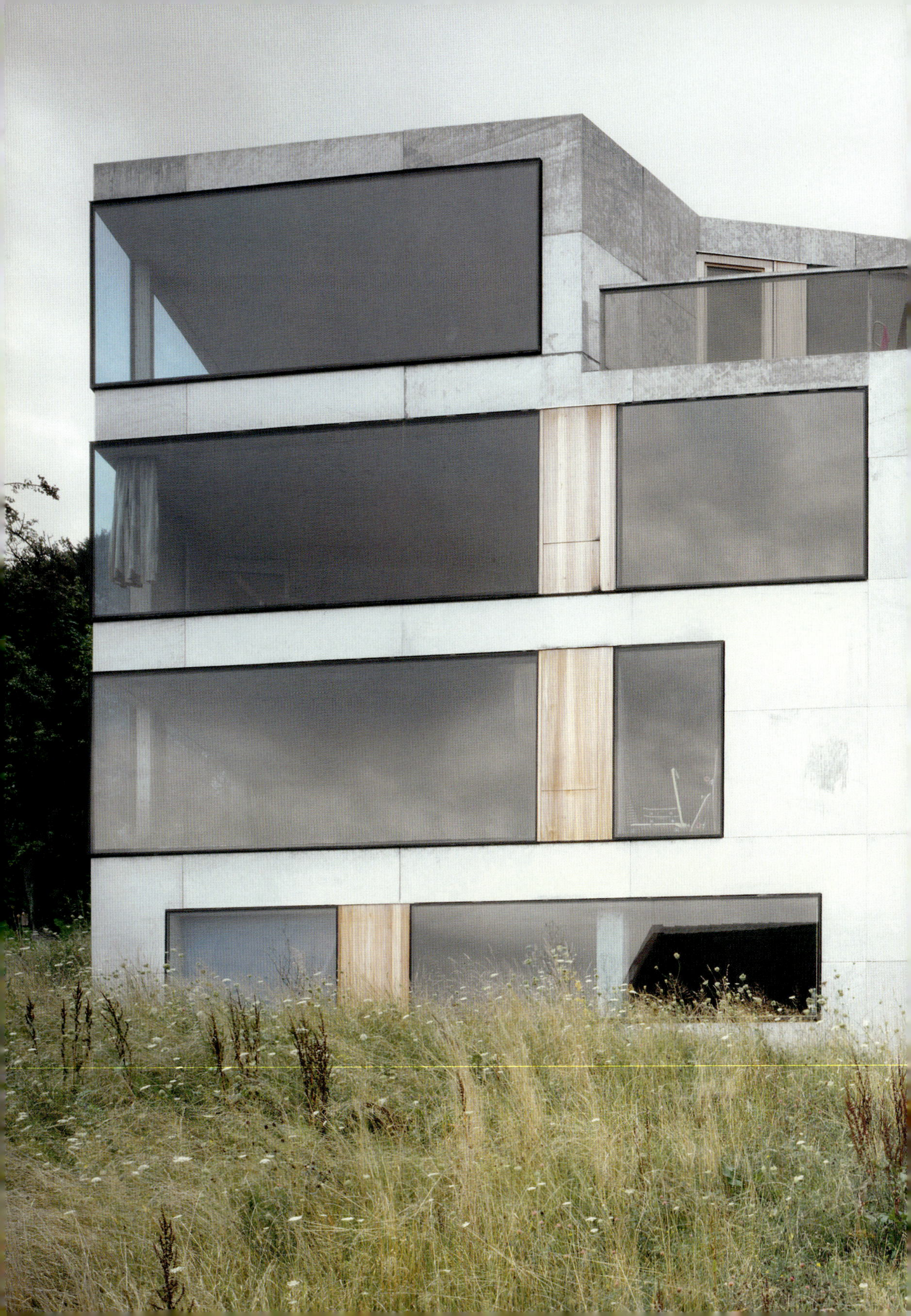

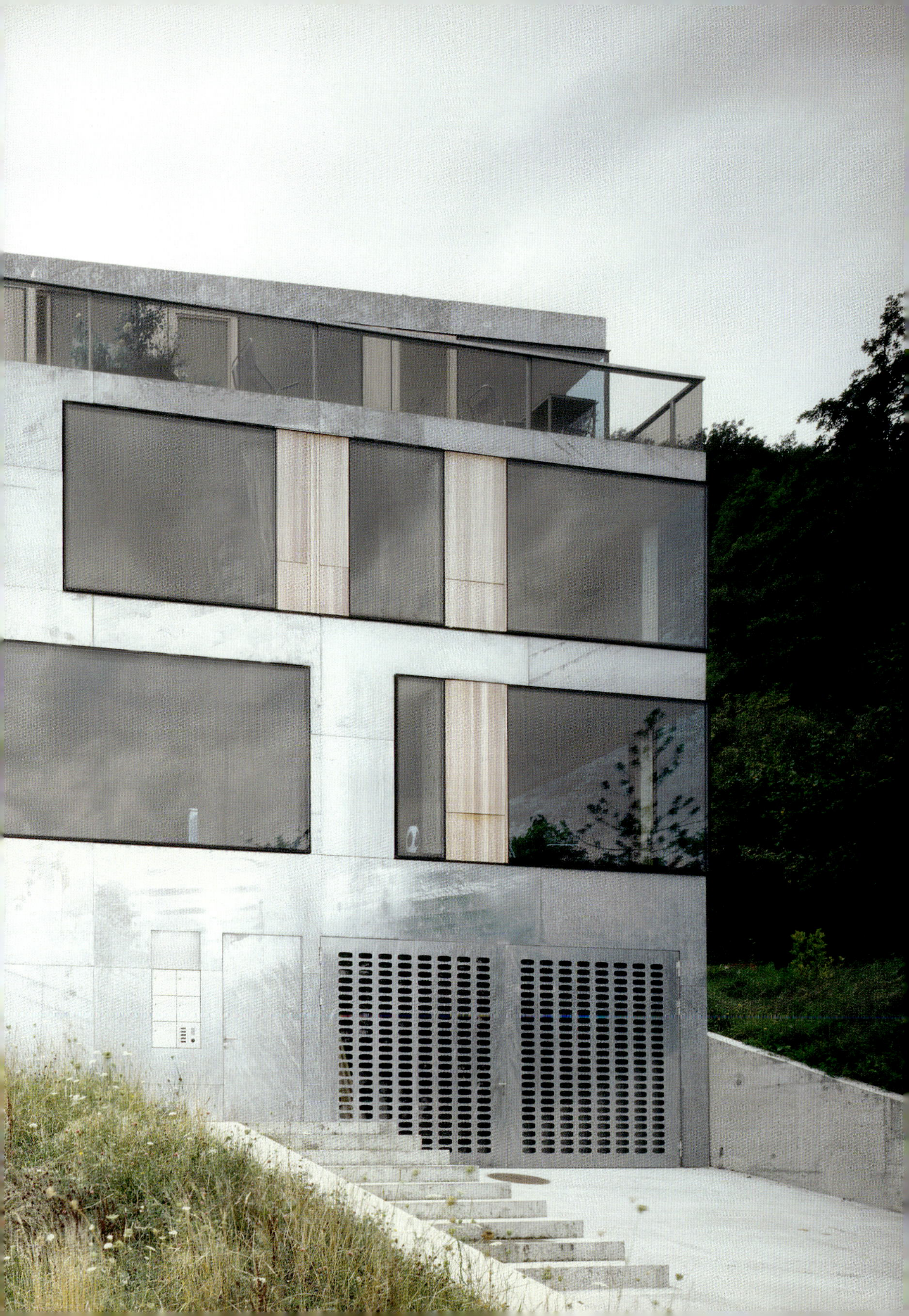

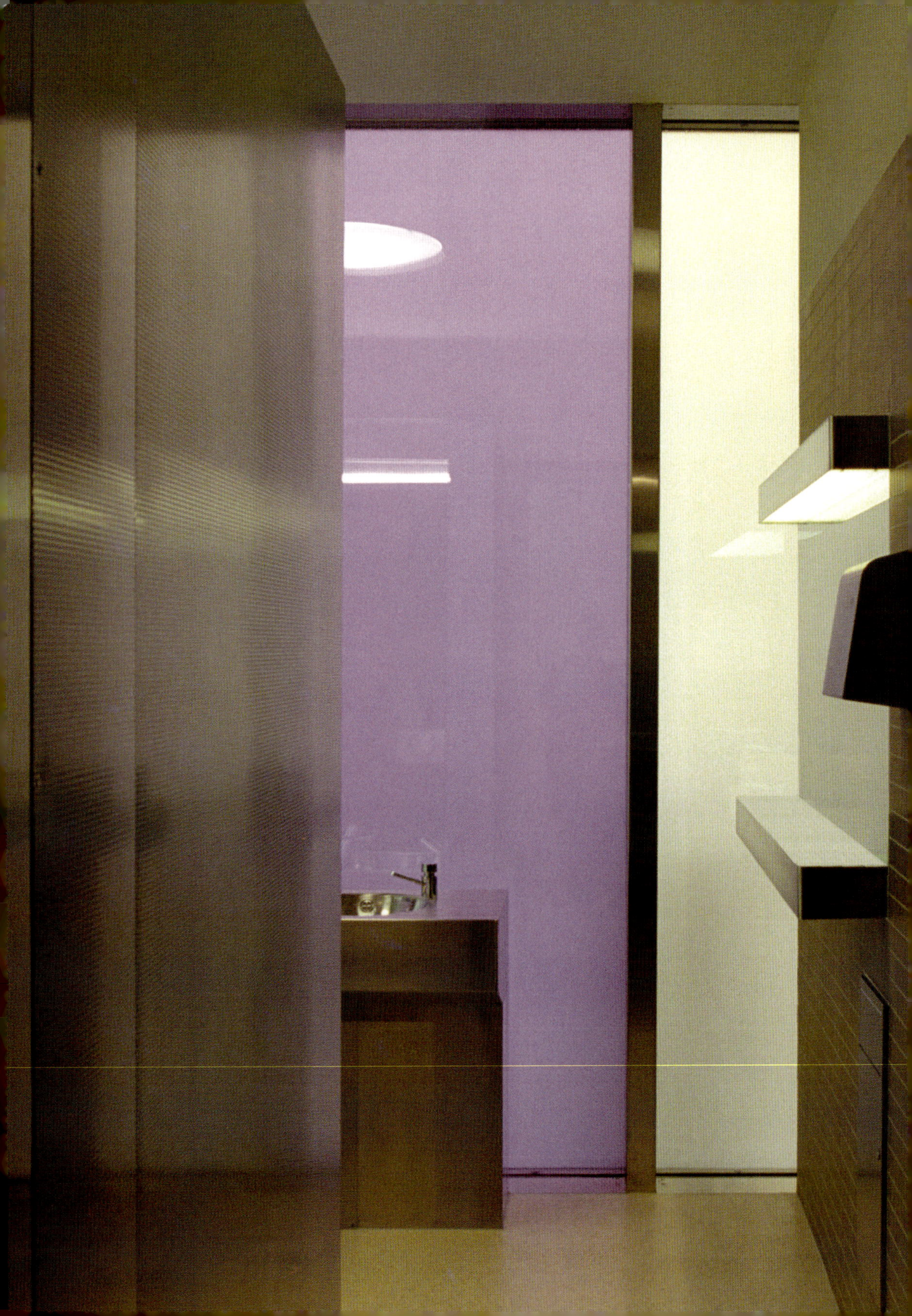

ANDREAS FUHRIMANN, GABRIELLE HÄCHLER | ZURICH
Pavilion at Riesbach harbour
Riesbach harbour in Zurich, Switzerland | 2004

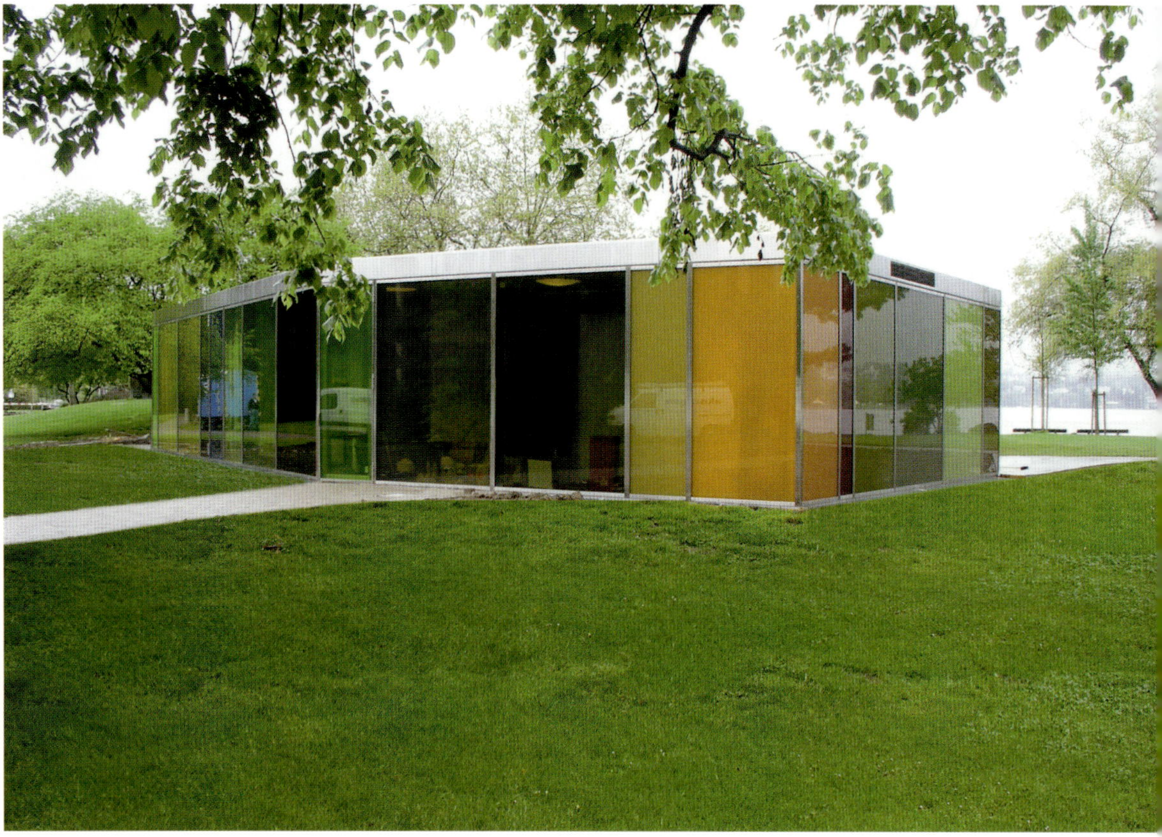

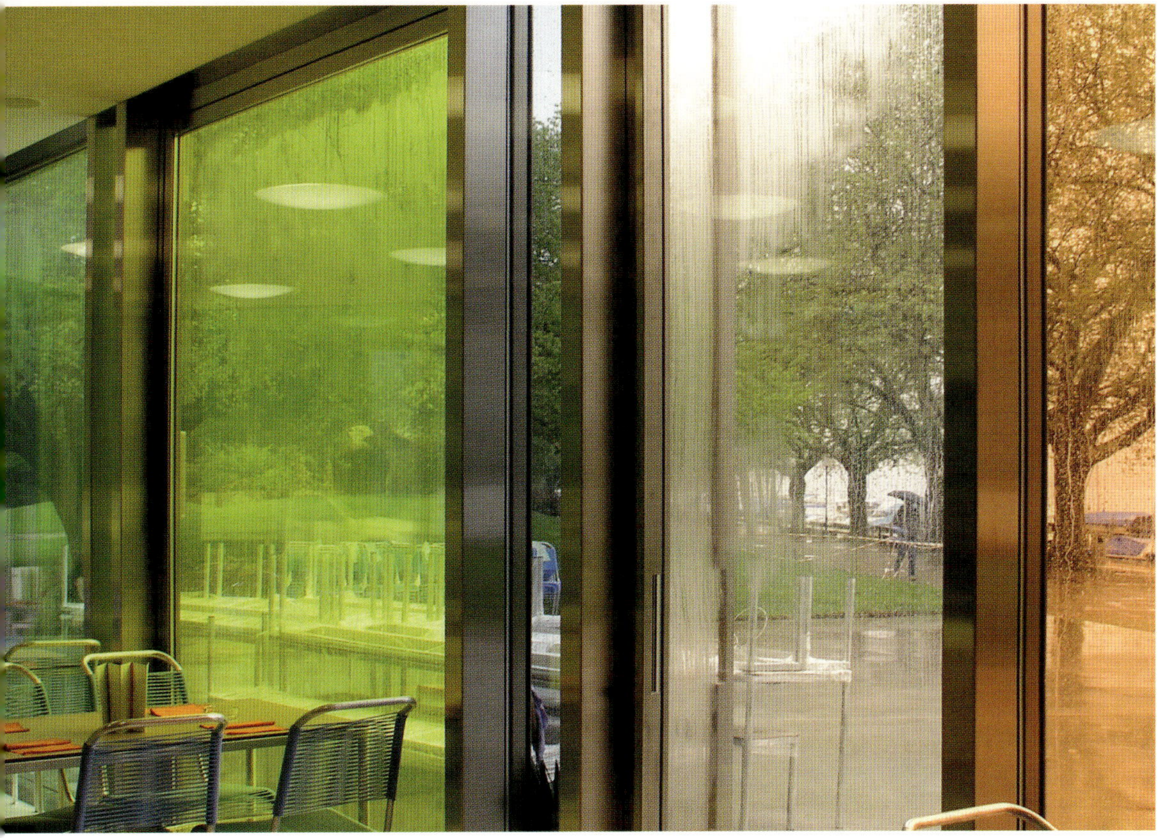

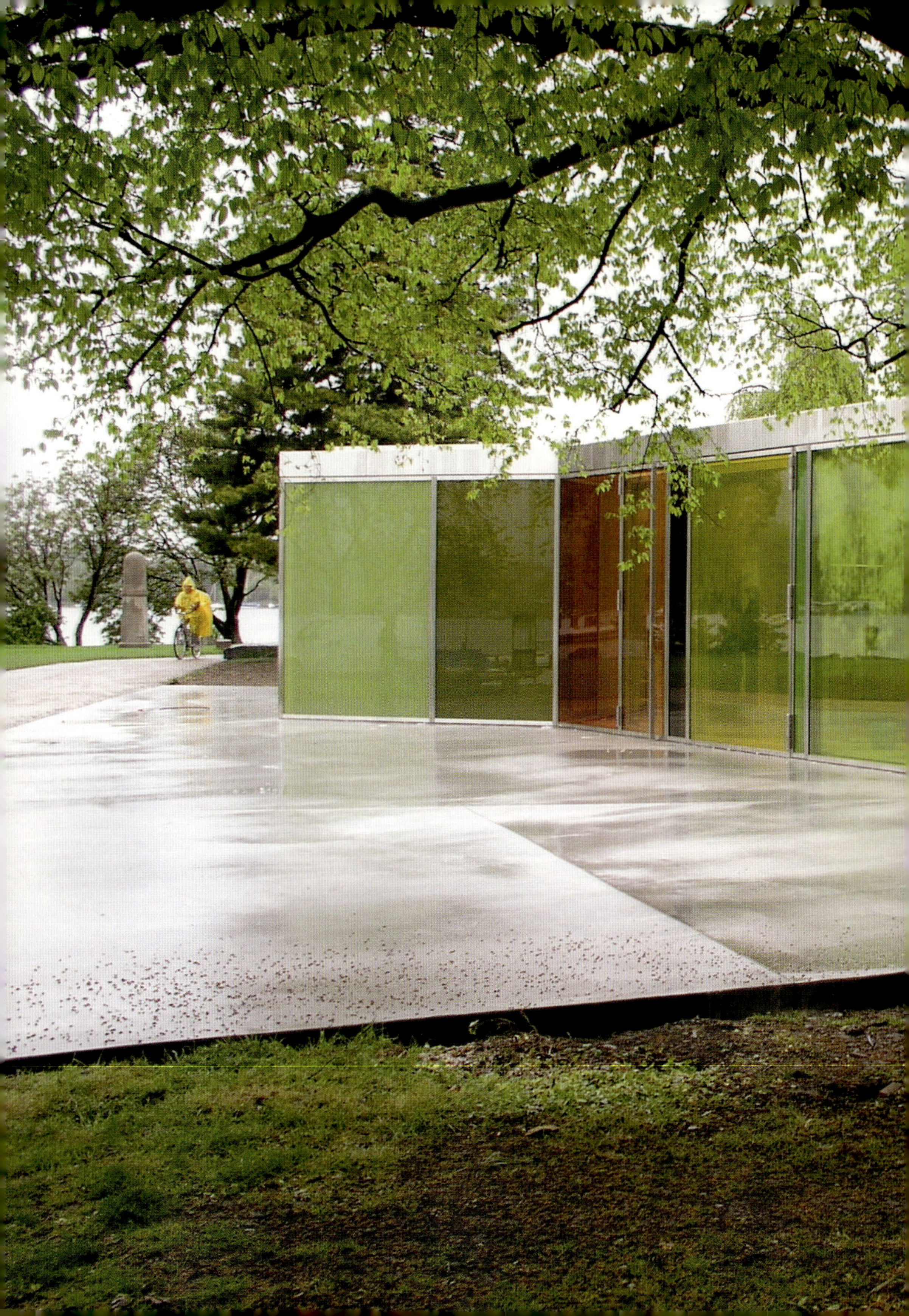

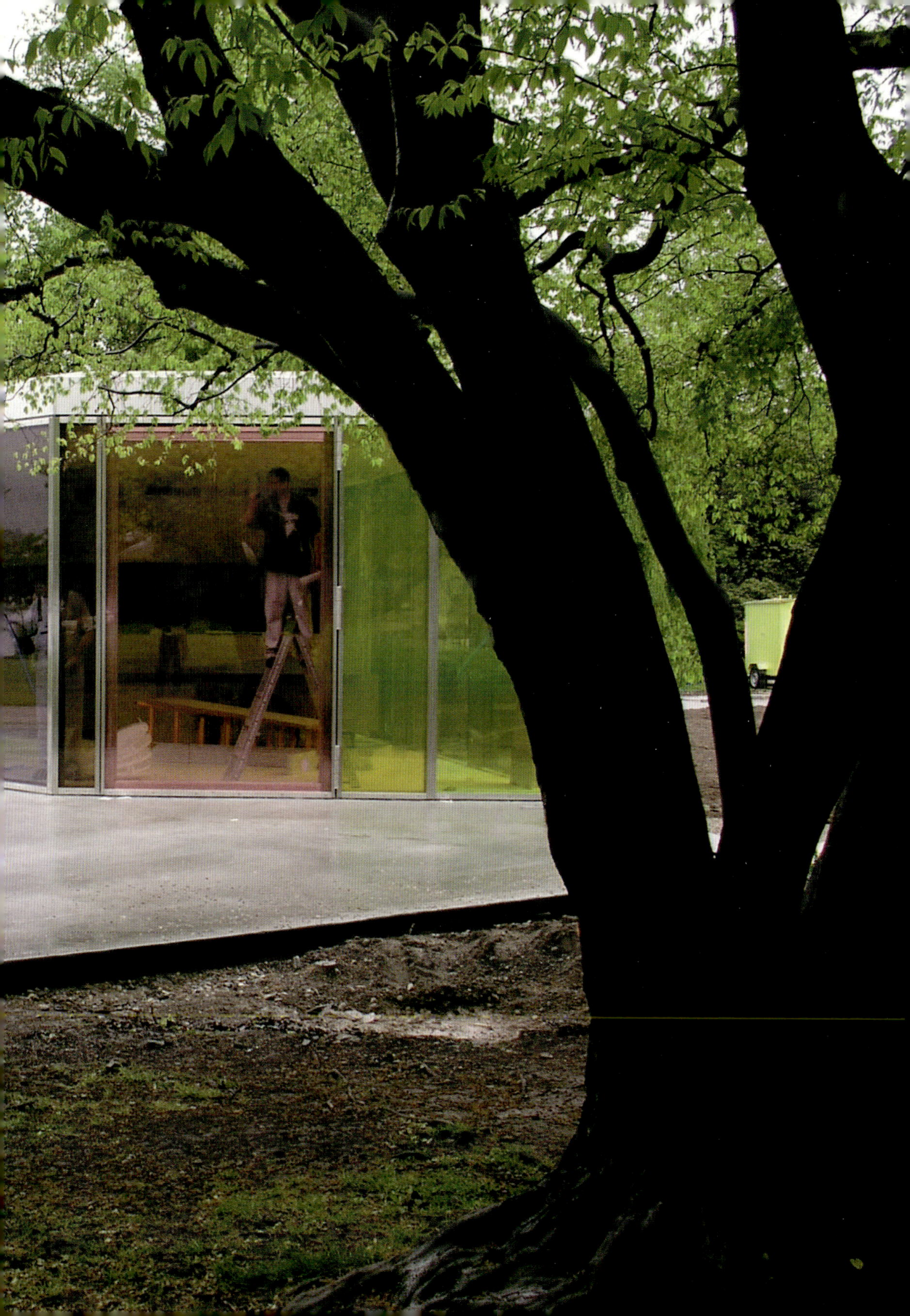

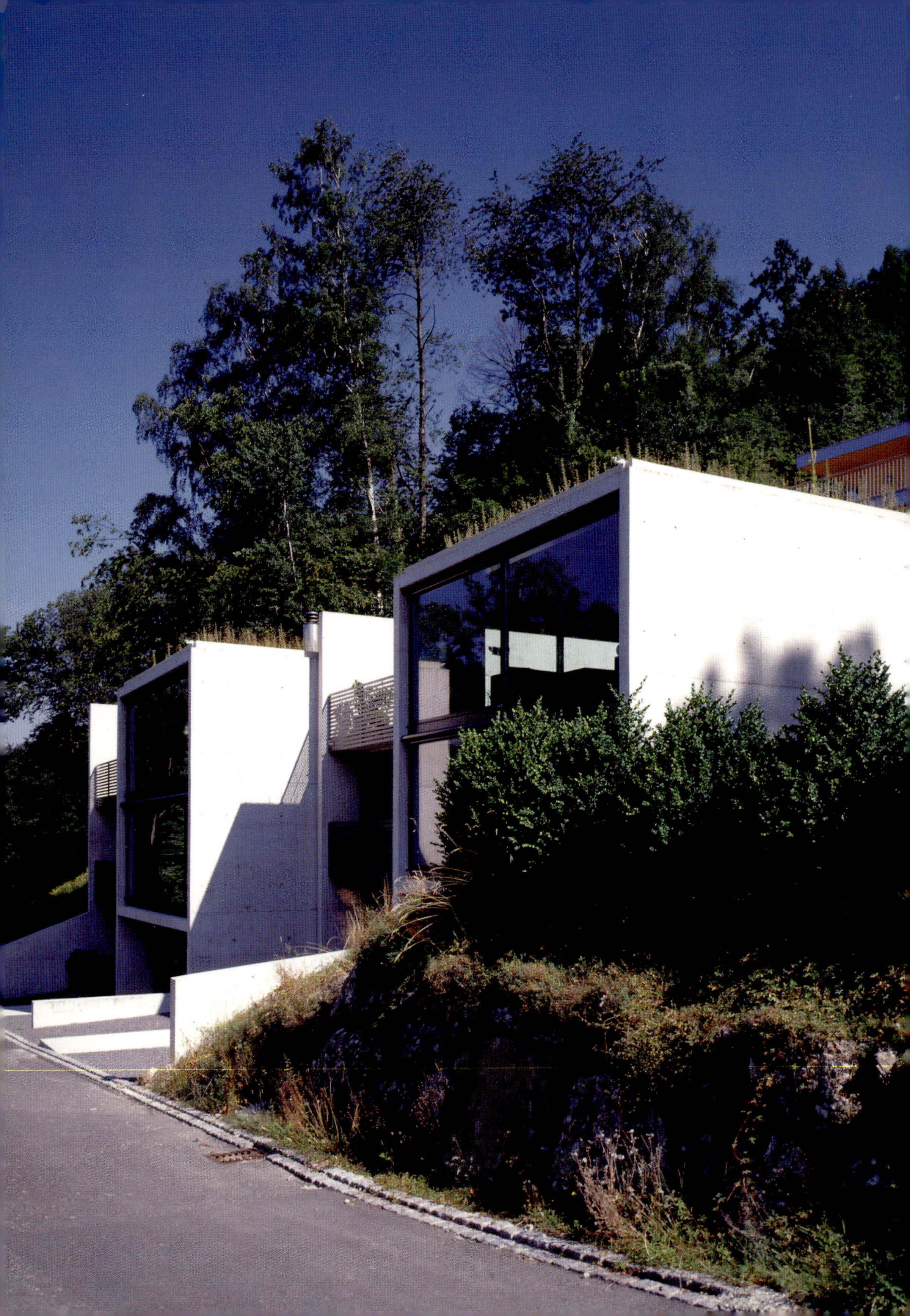

GLÖGGLER PREVOSTI ARCHITEKTUR | ZUG
Double one-family house Almigried
Walchwil, Switzerland | 2000

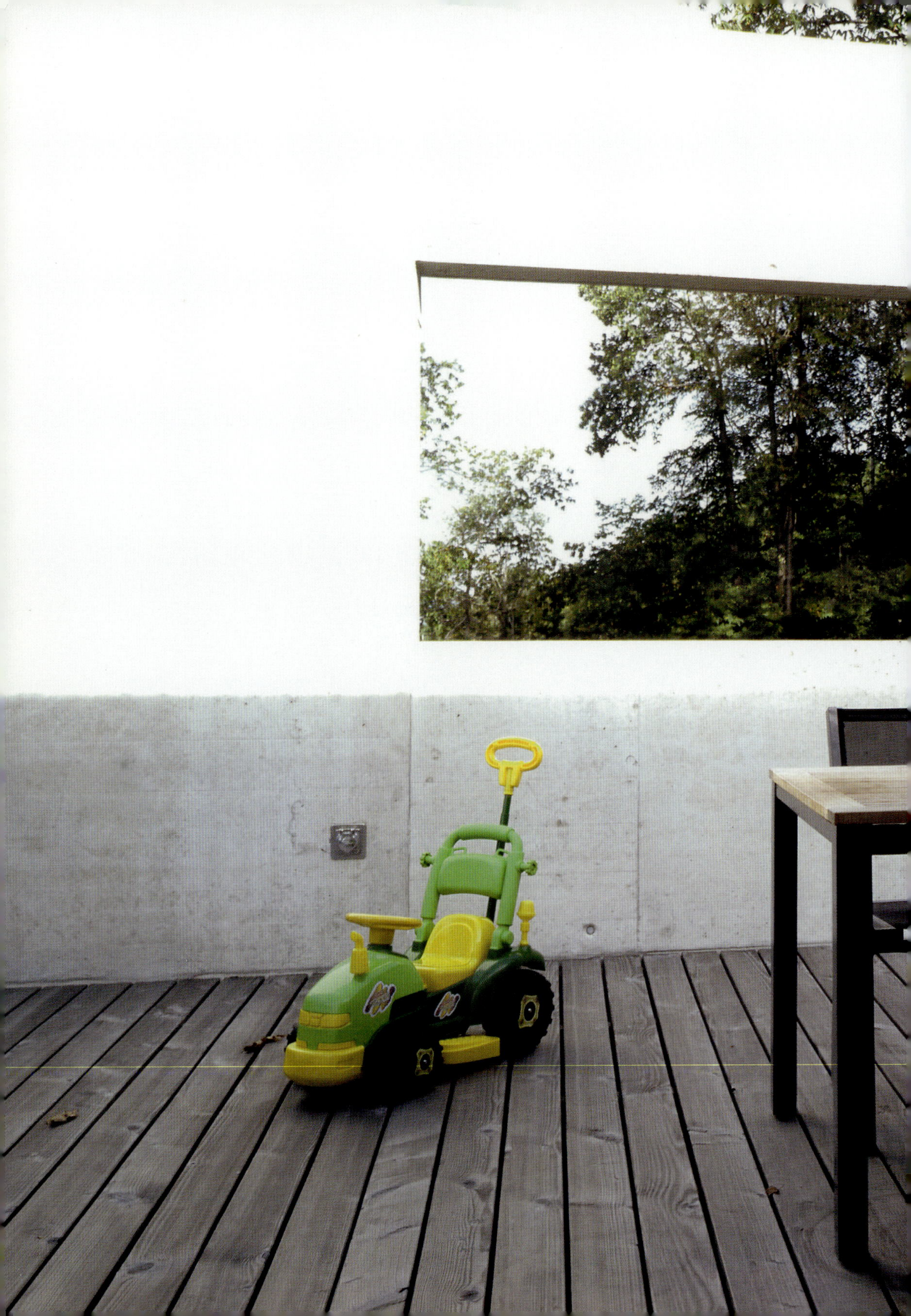

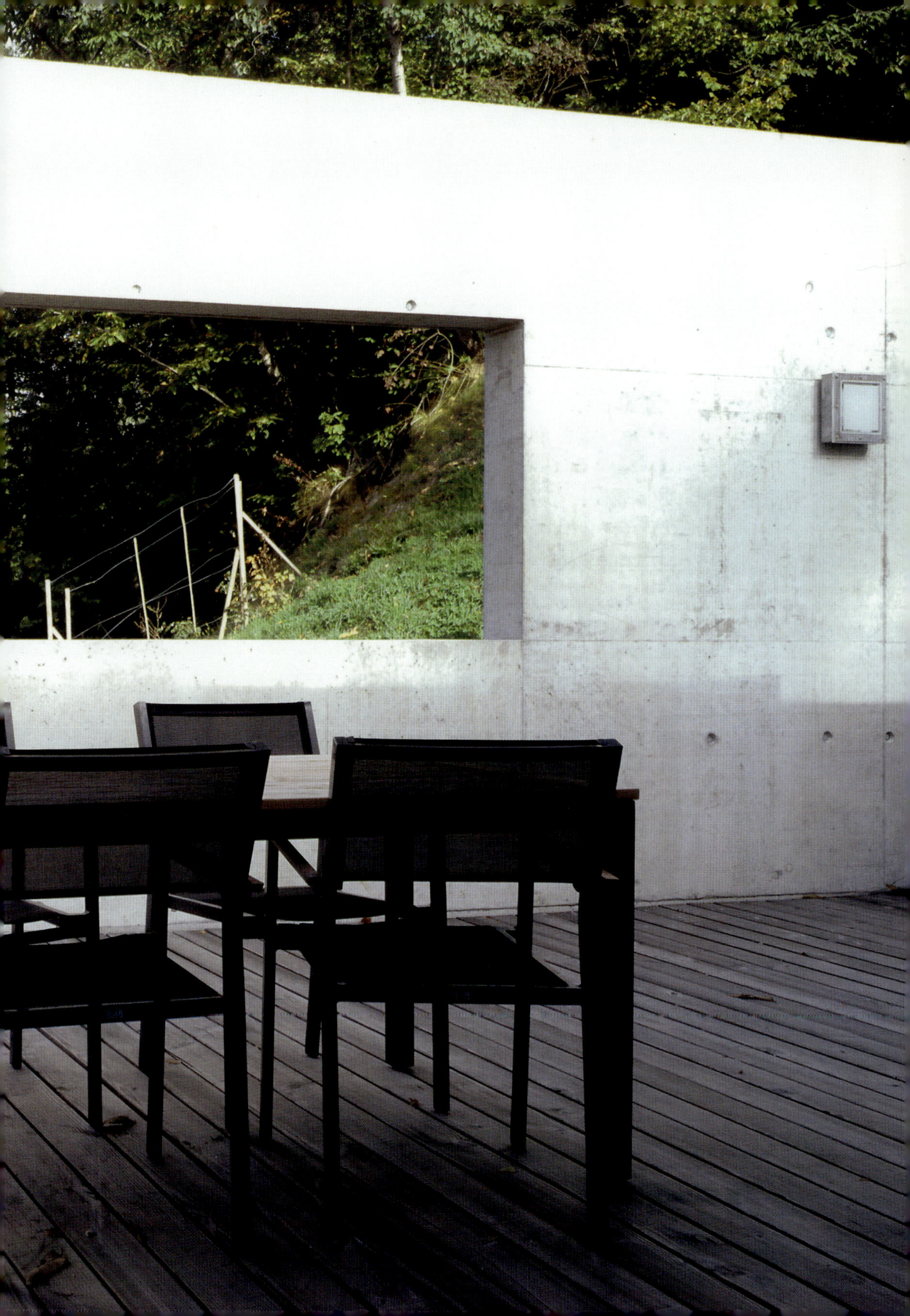

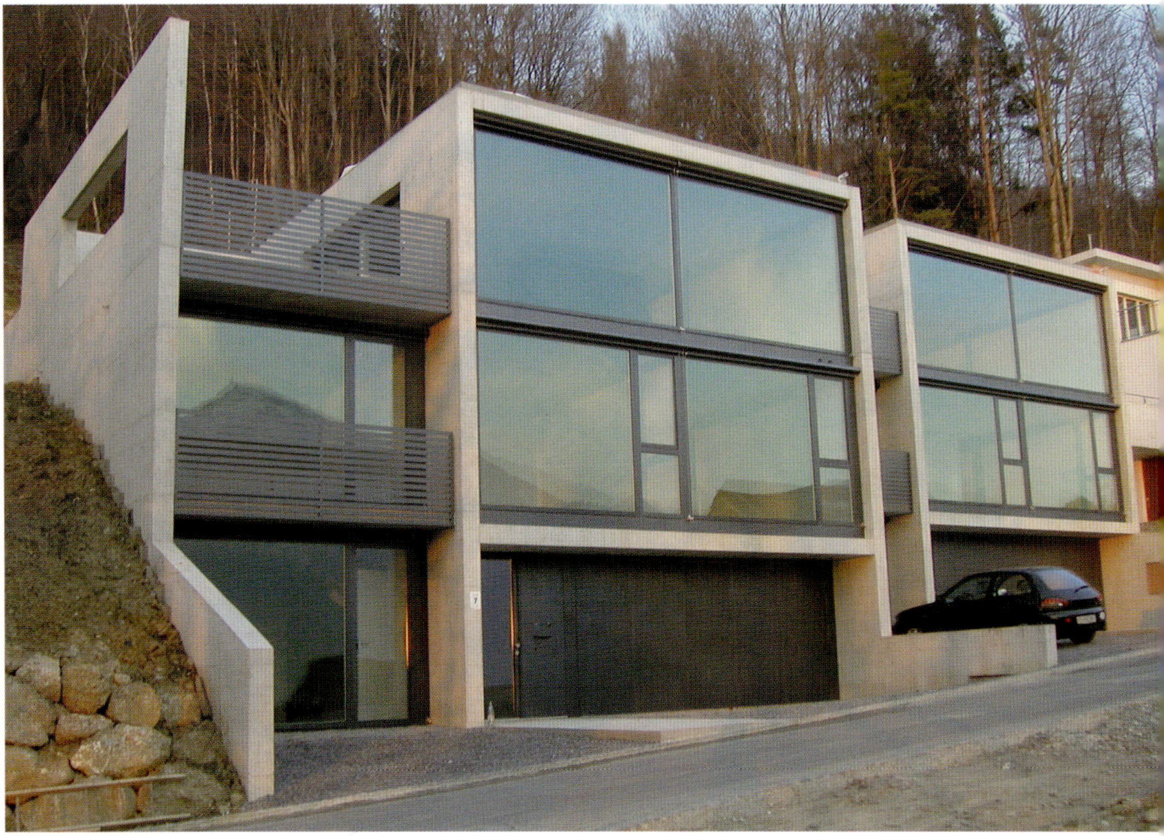

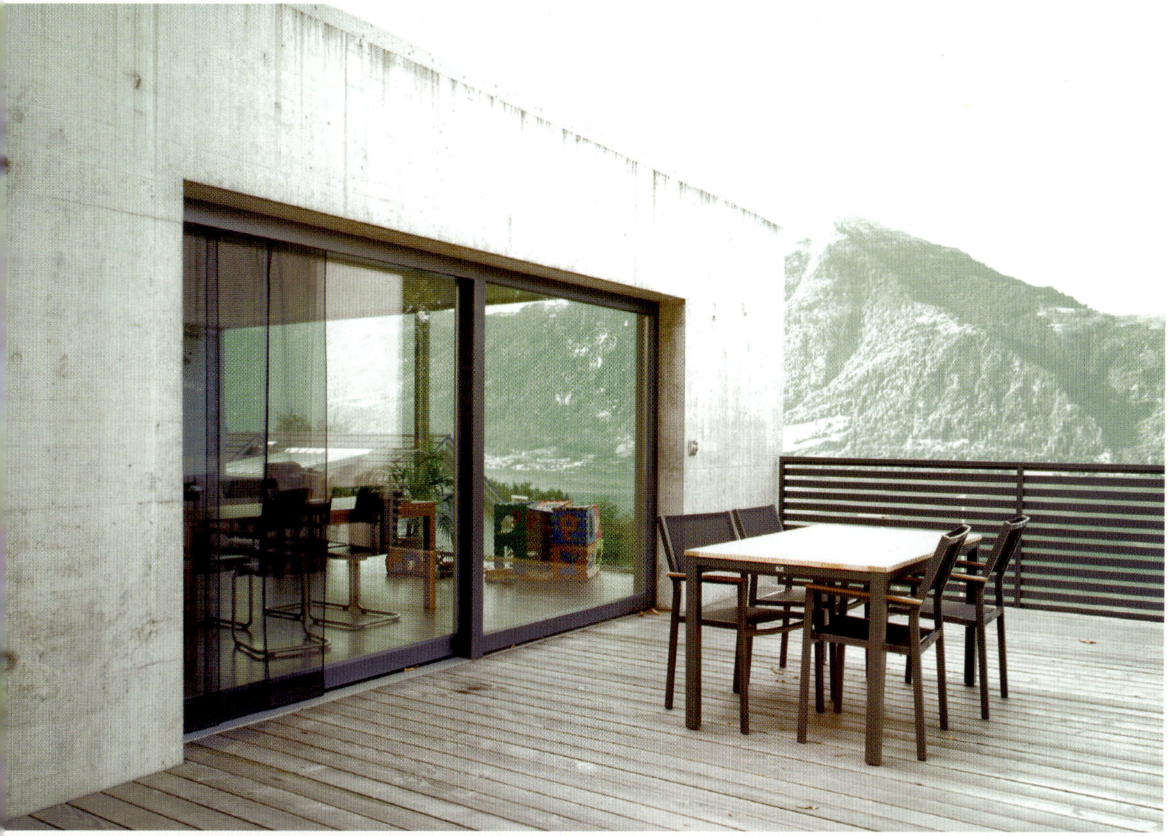

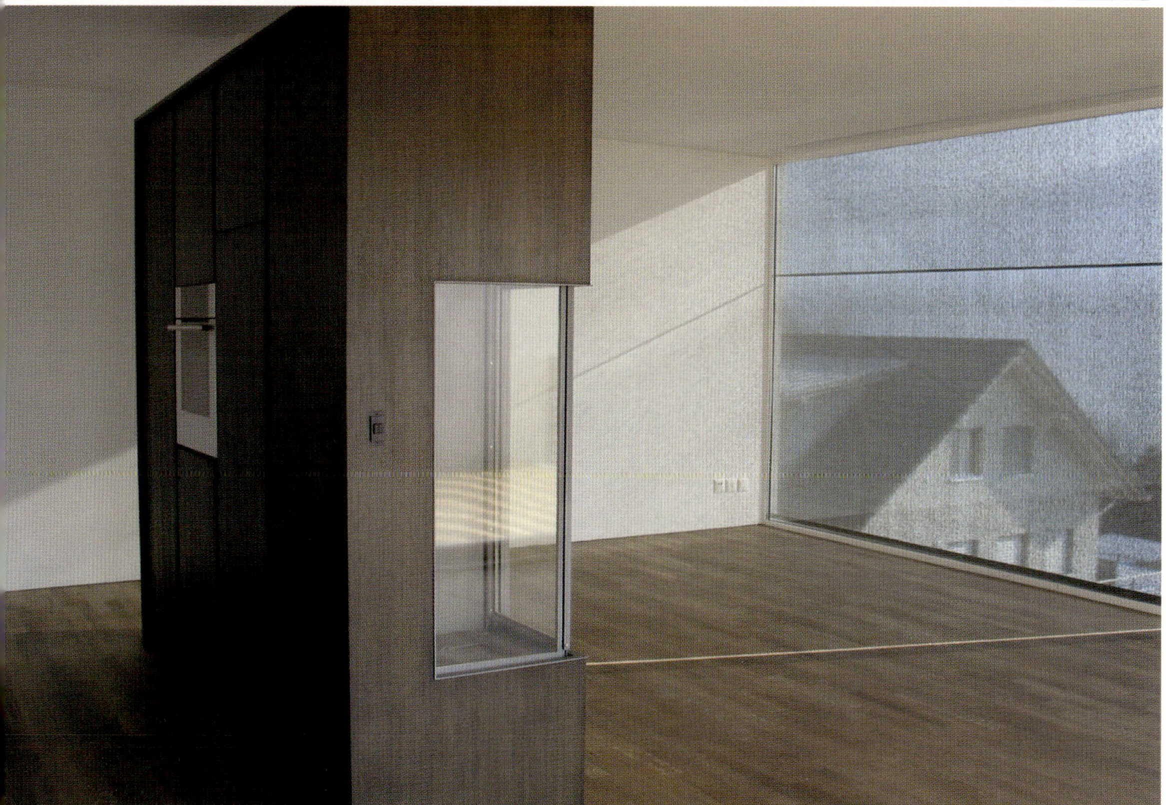

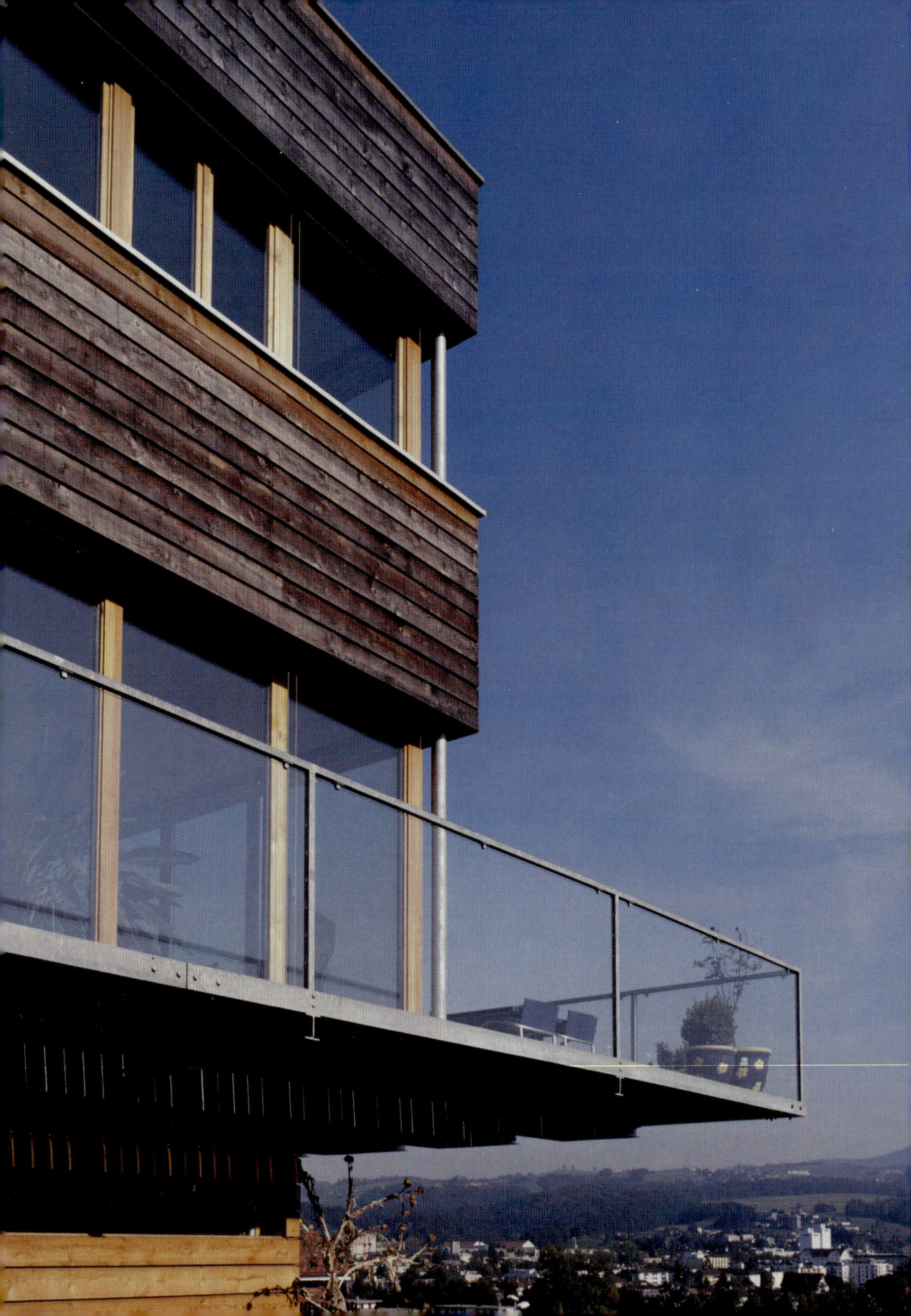

GLÖGGLER PREVOSTI ARCHITEKTUR | ZUG
One-family house in the field
Baar, Switzerland | 1998

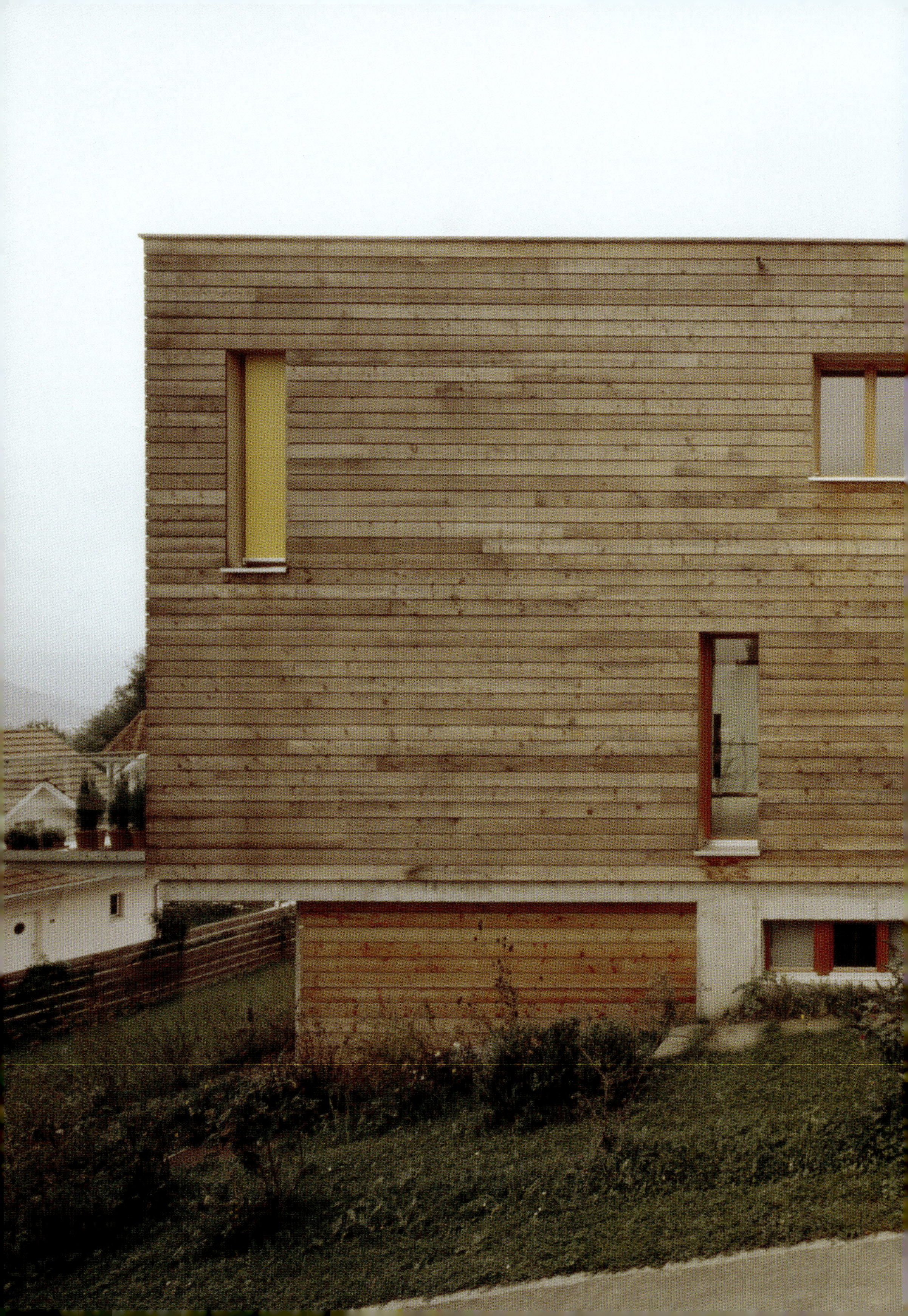

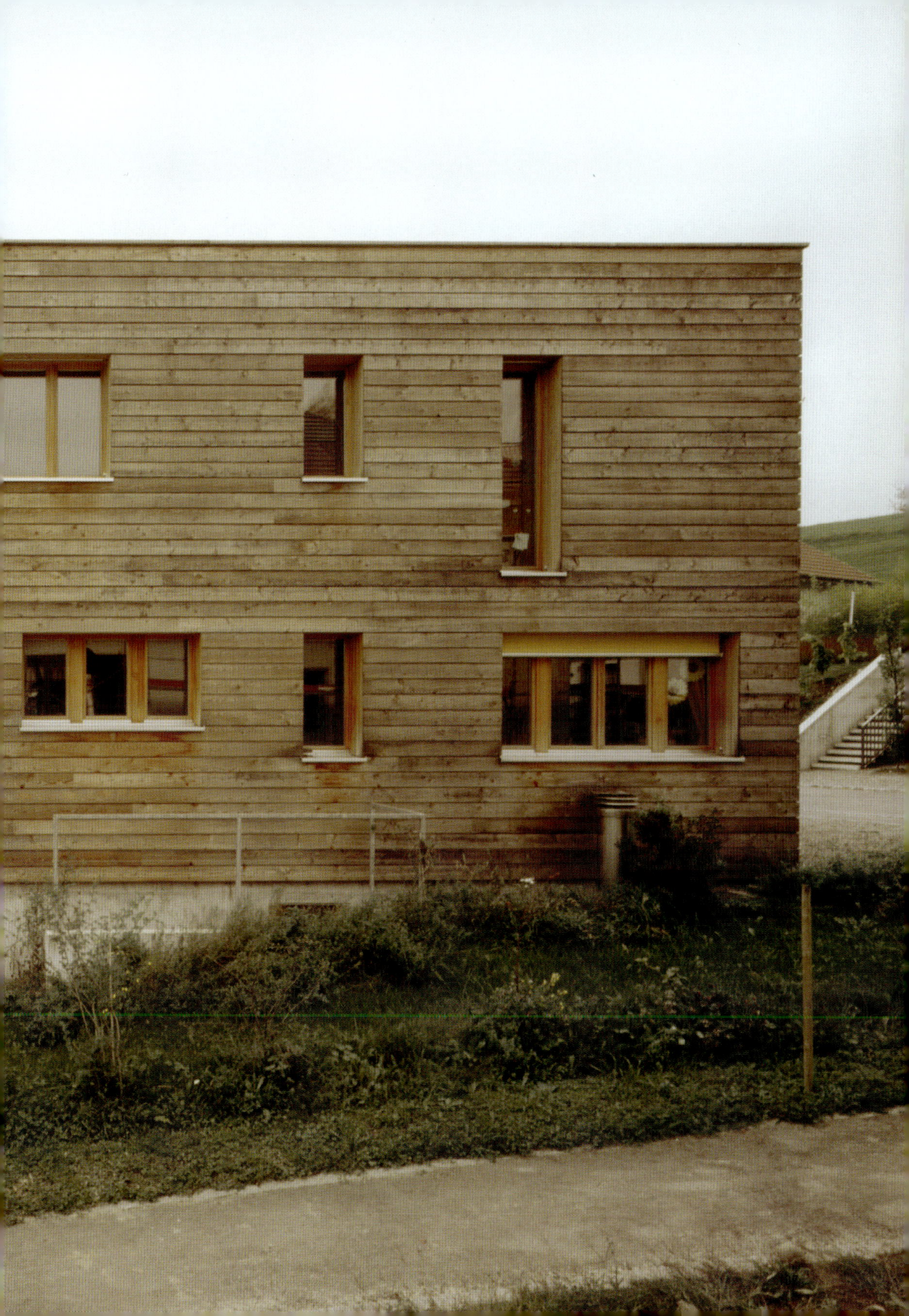

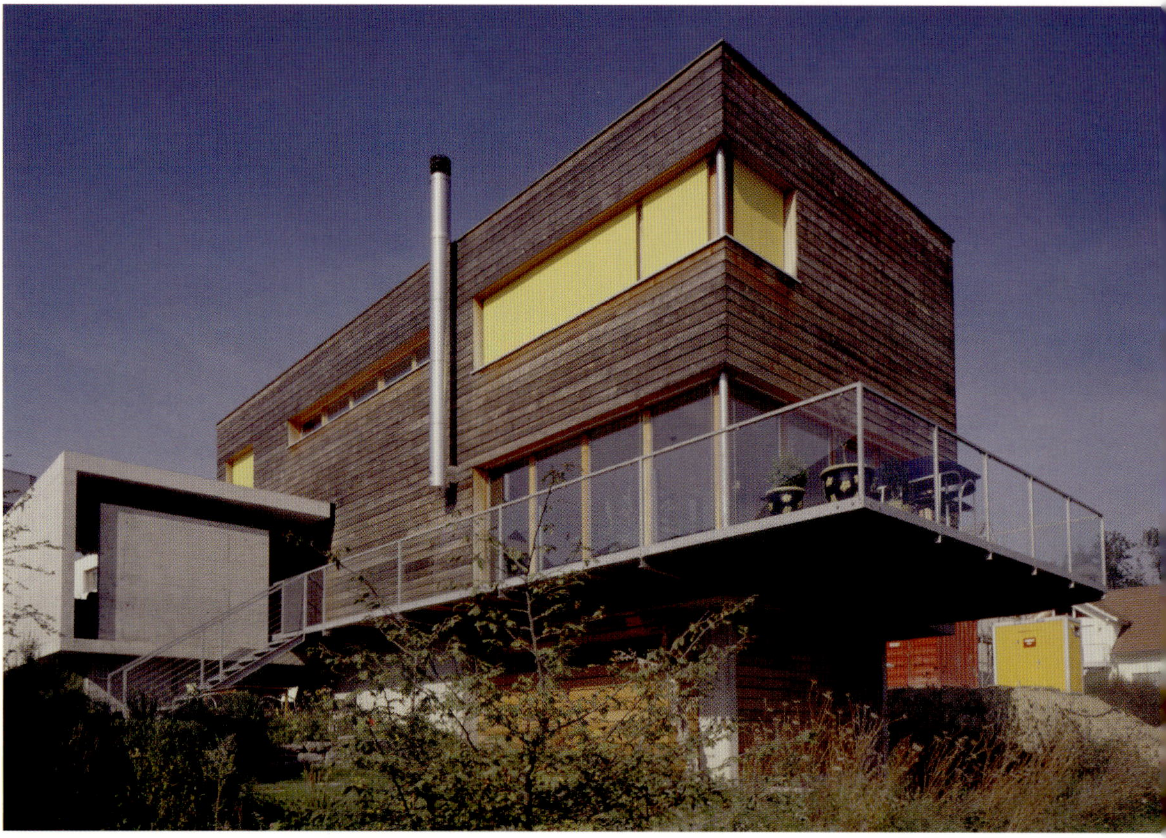

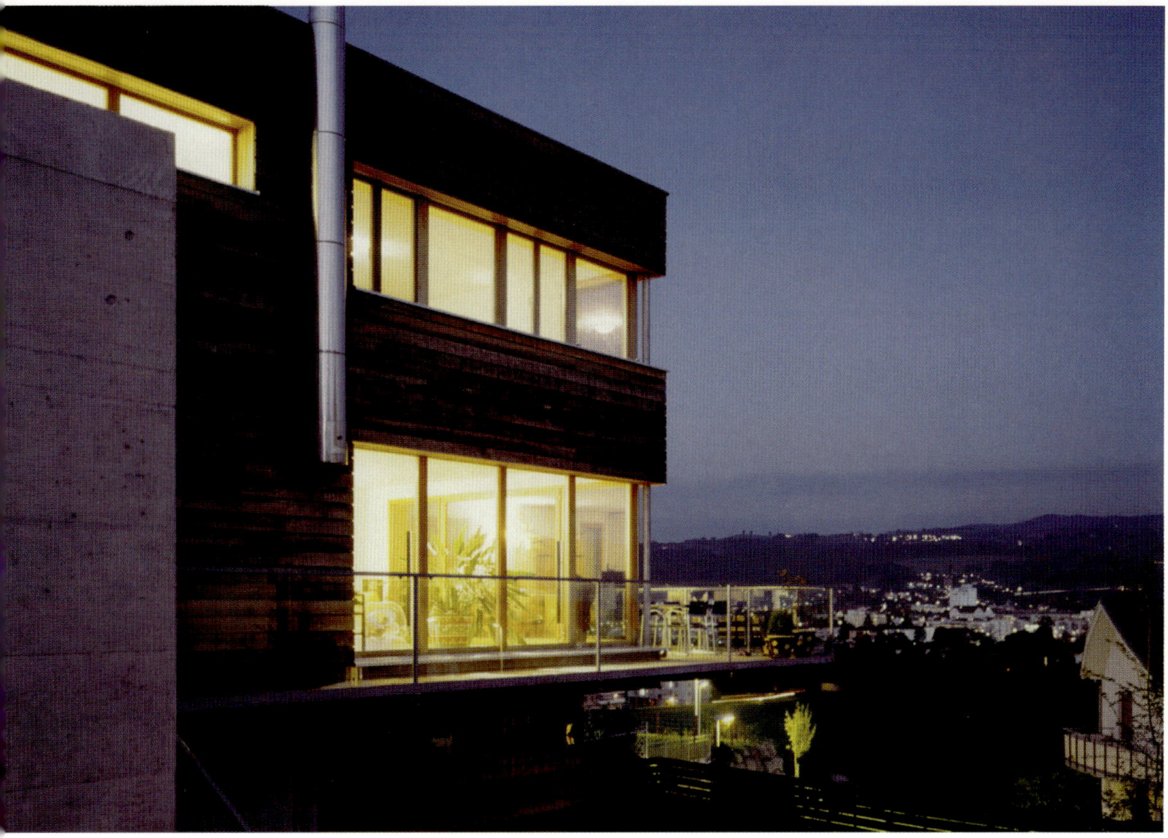

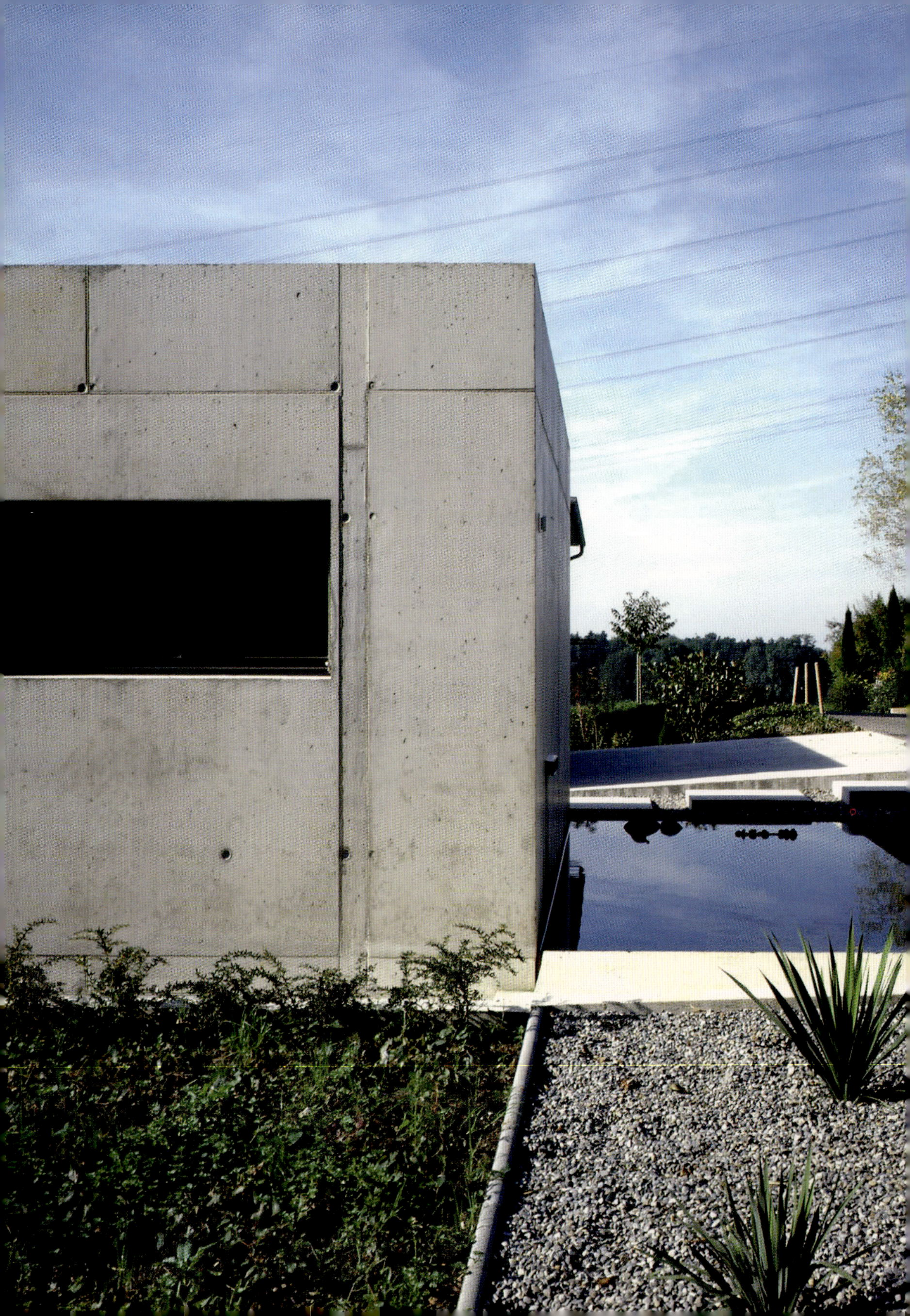

GLÖGGLER PREVOSTI ARCHITEKTUR | ZUG
One-family house Munk
Huenenberg, Switzerland | 2004

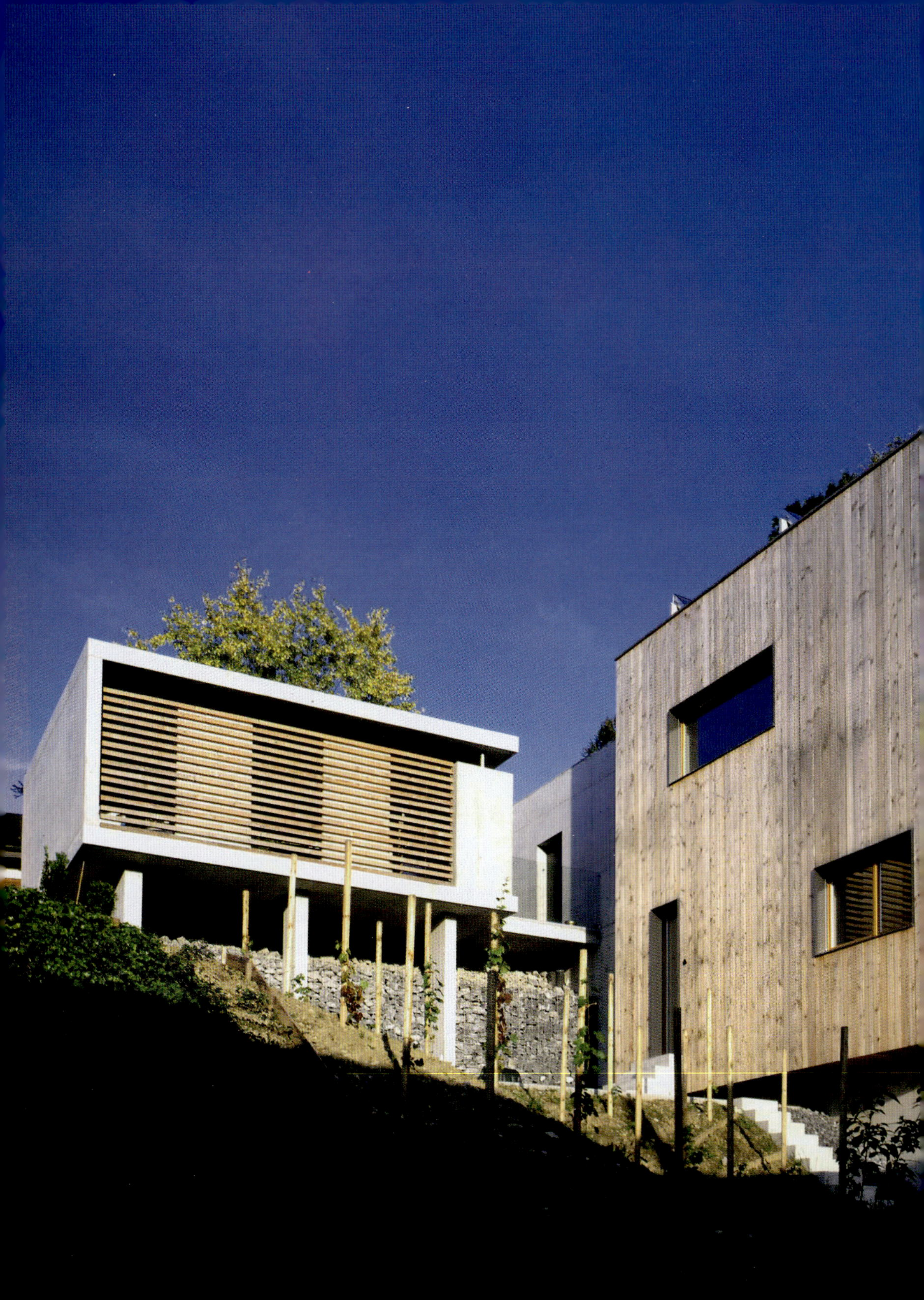

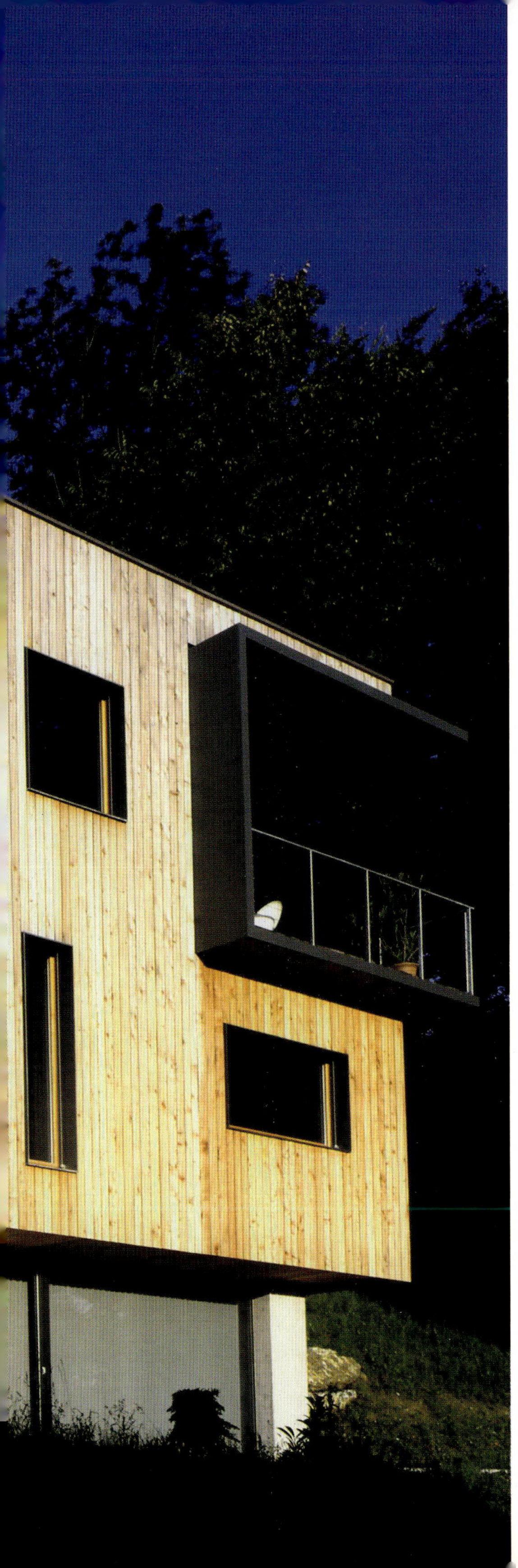

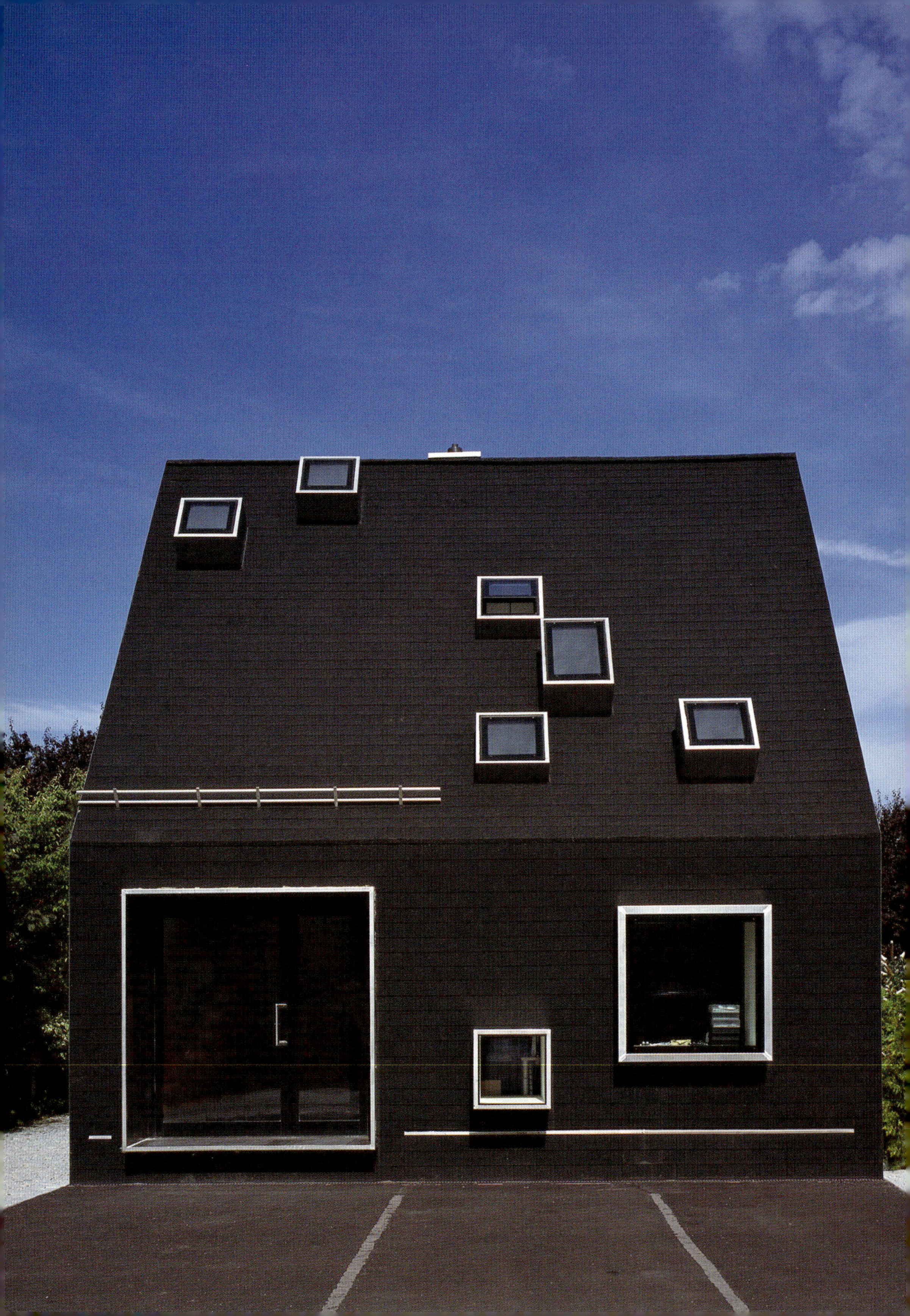

PETER HAIMERL, STUDIO FÜR ARCHITEKTUR | MUNICH
Black House
Krailling, Germany | 2006

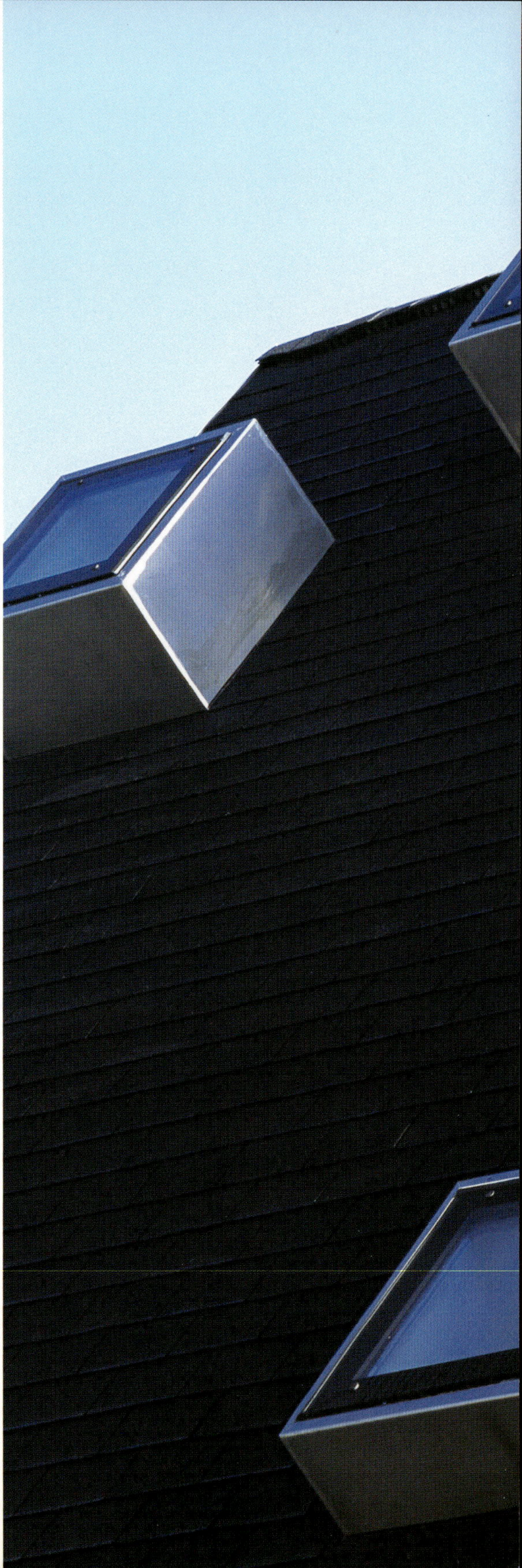

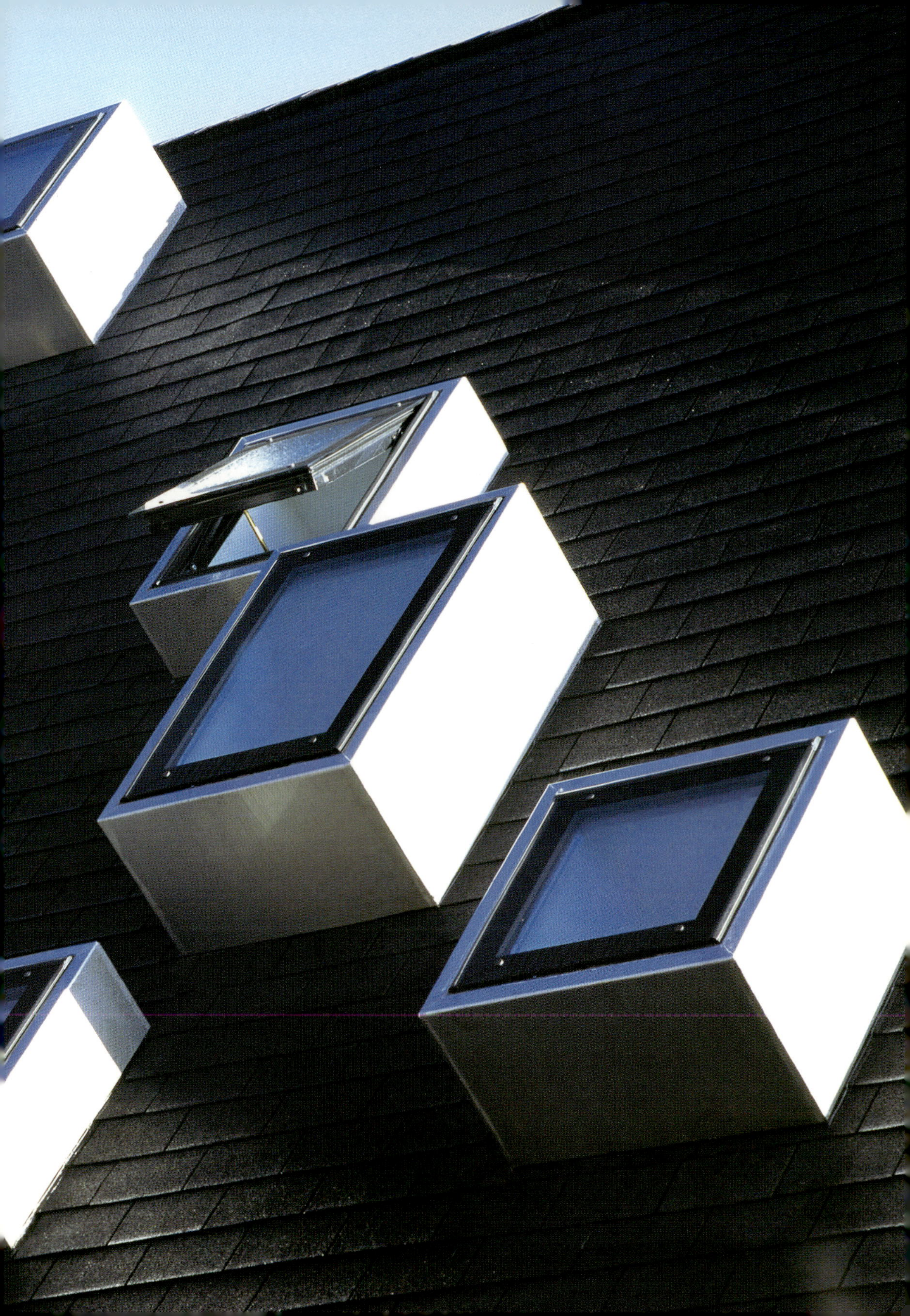

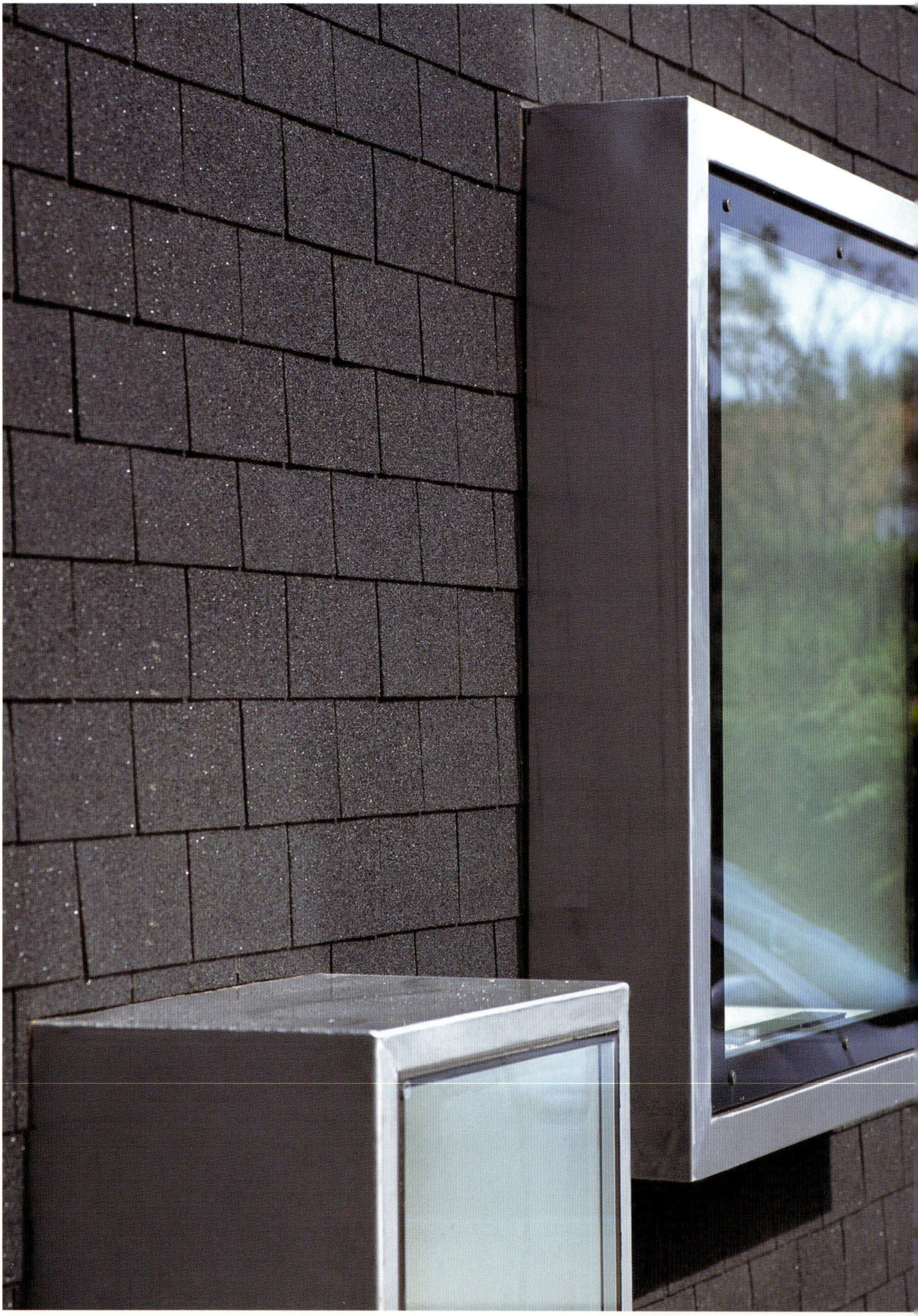

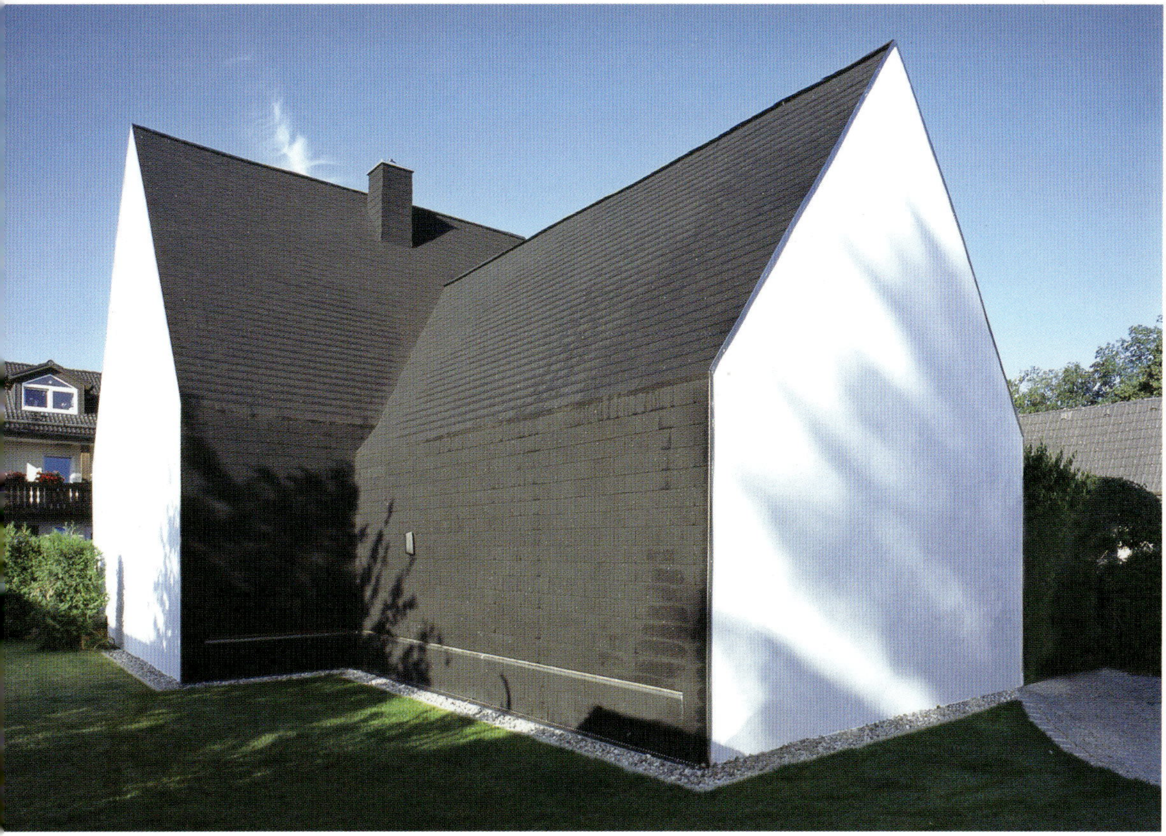

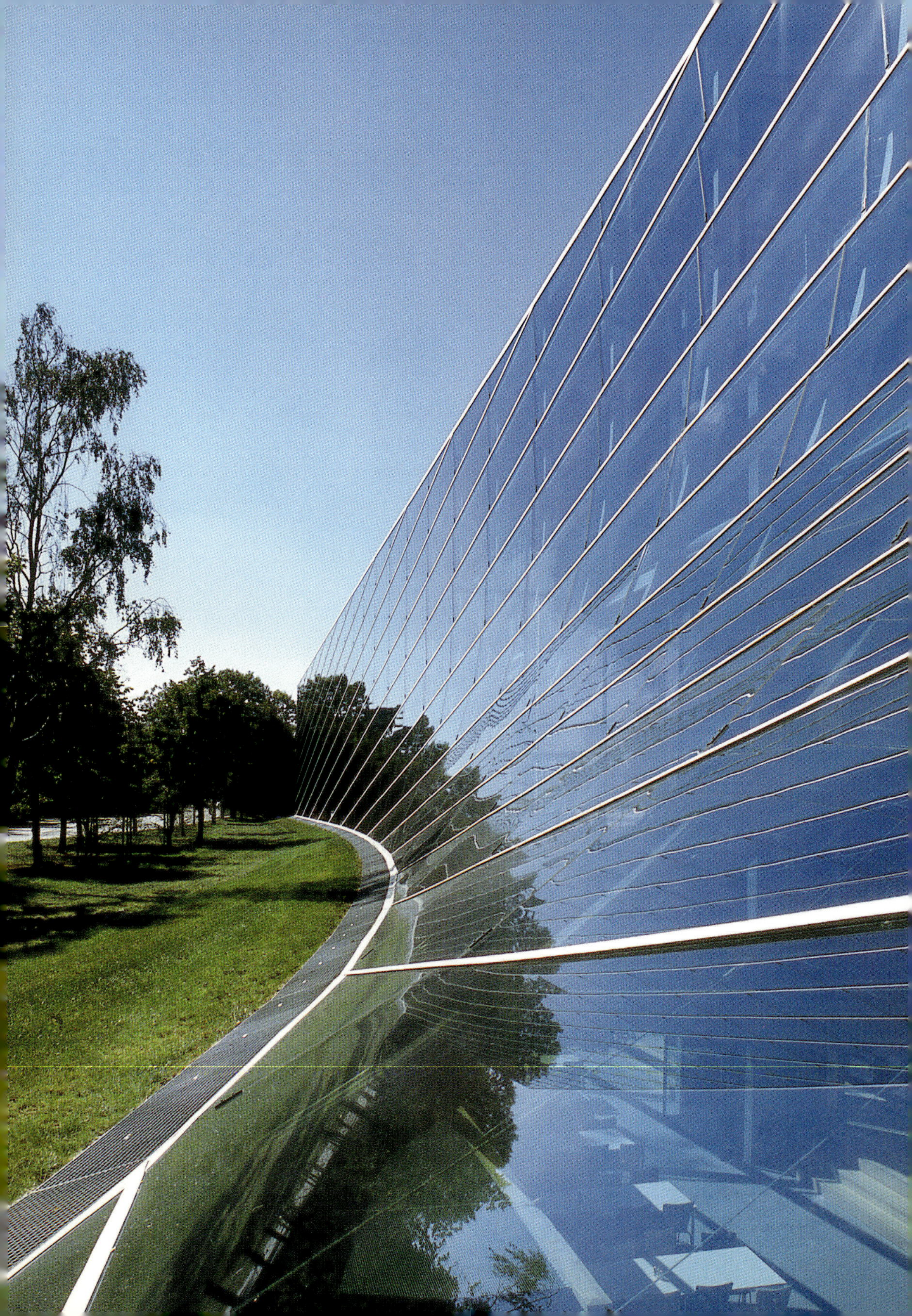

HASCHER JEHLE ARCHITEKTUR | BERLIN
LSV Office Building
Landshut, Germany | 2003

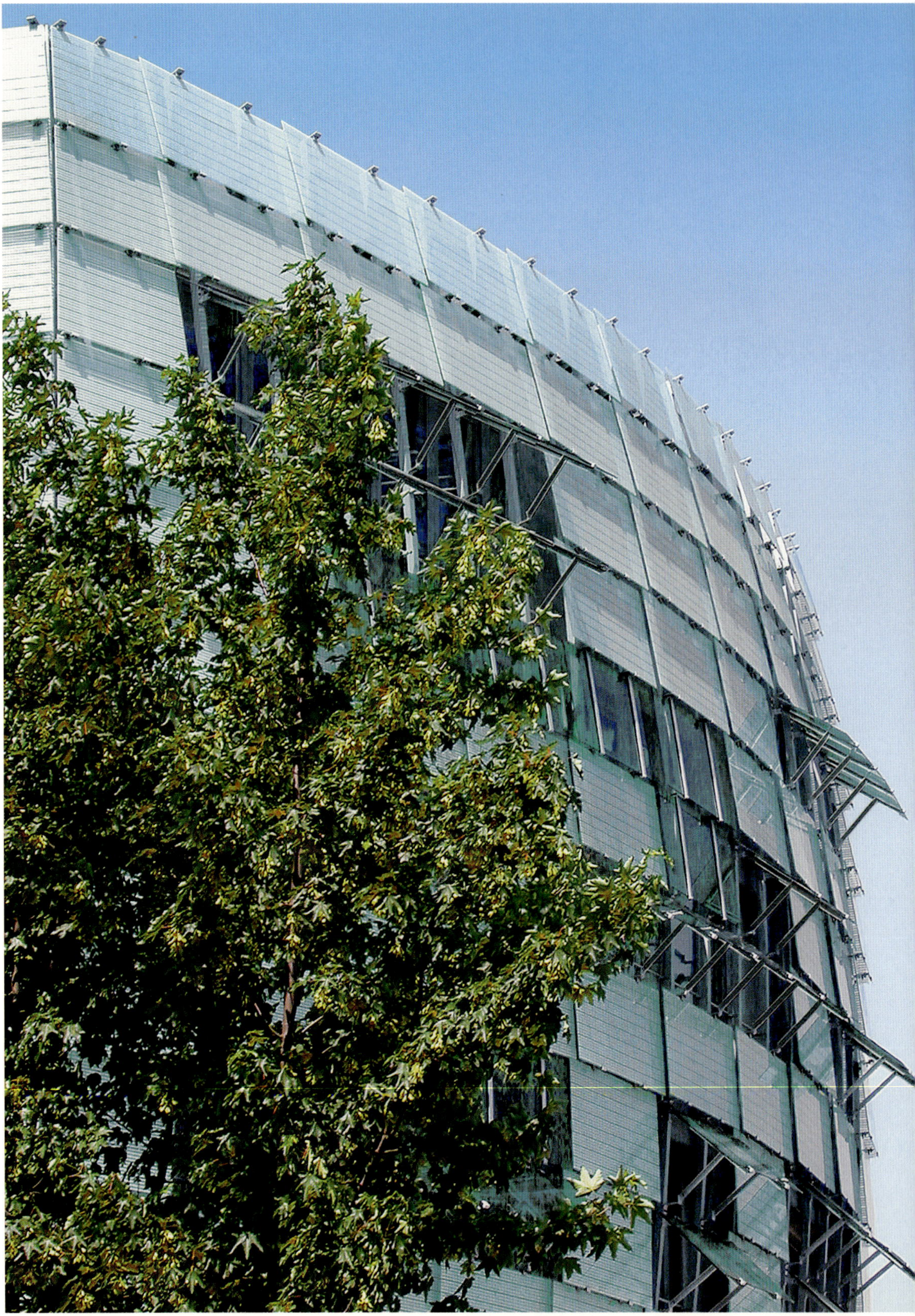

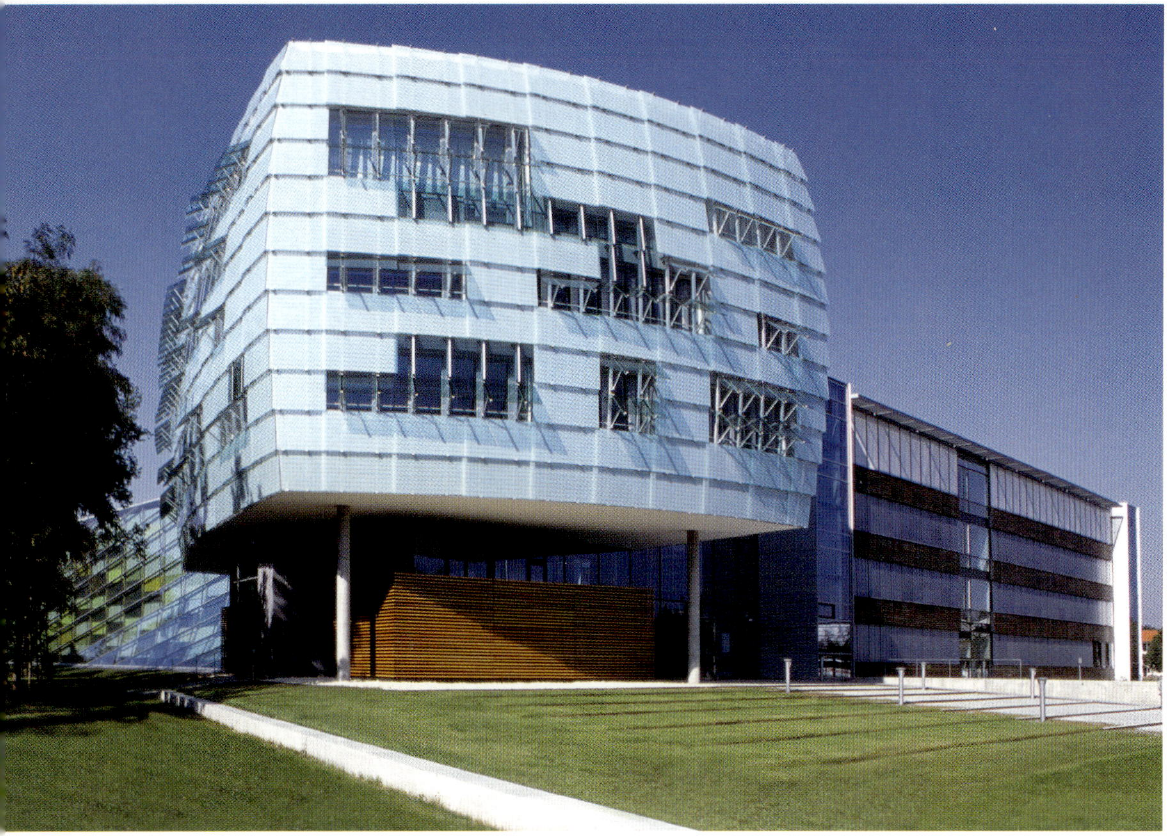

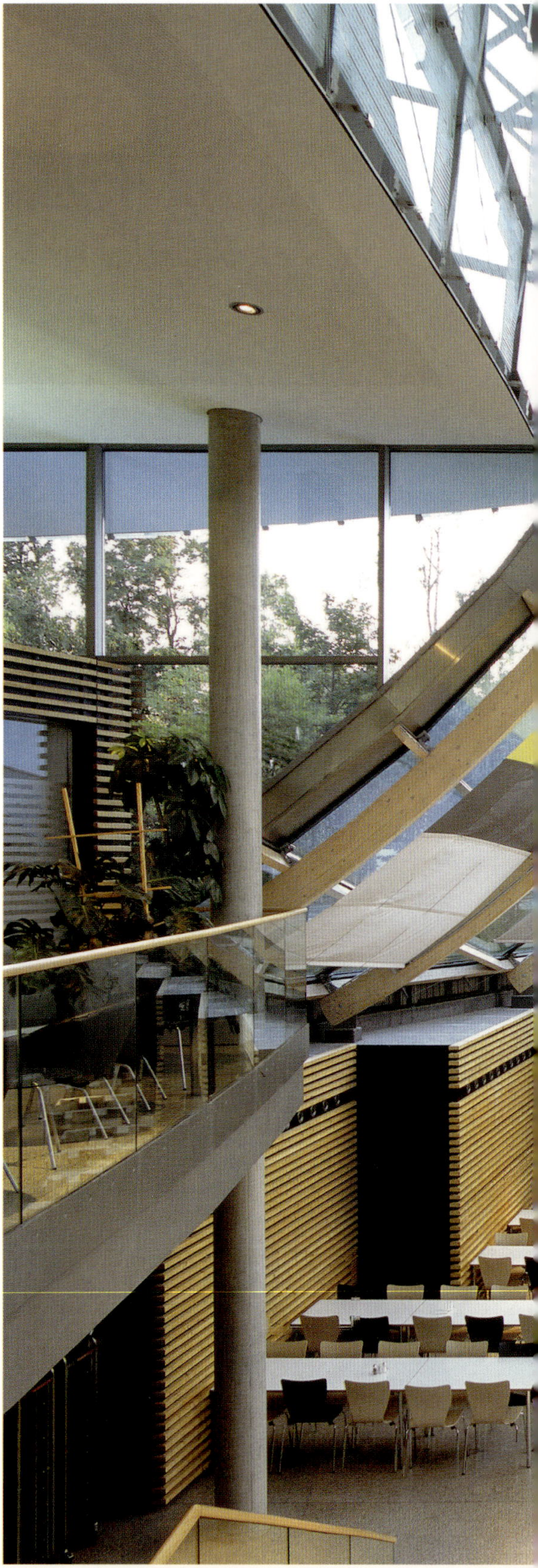

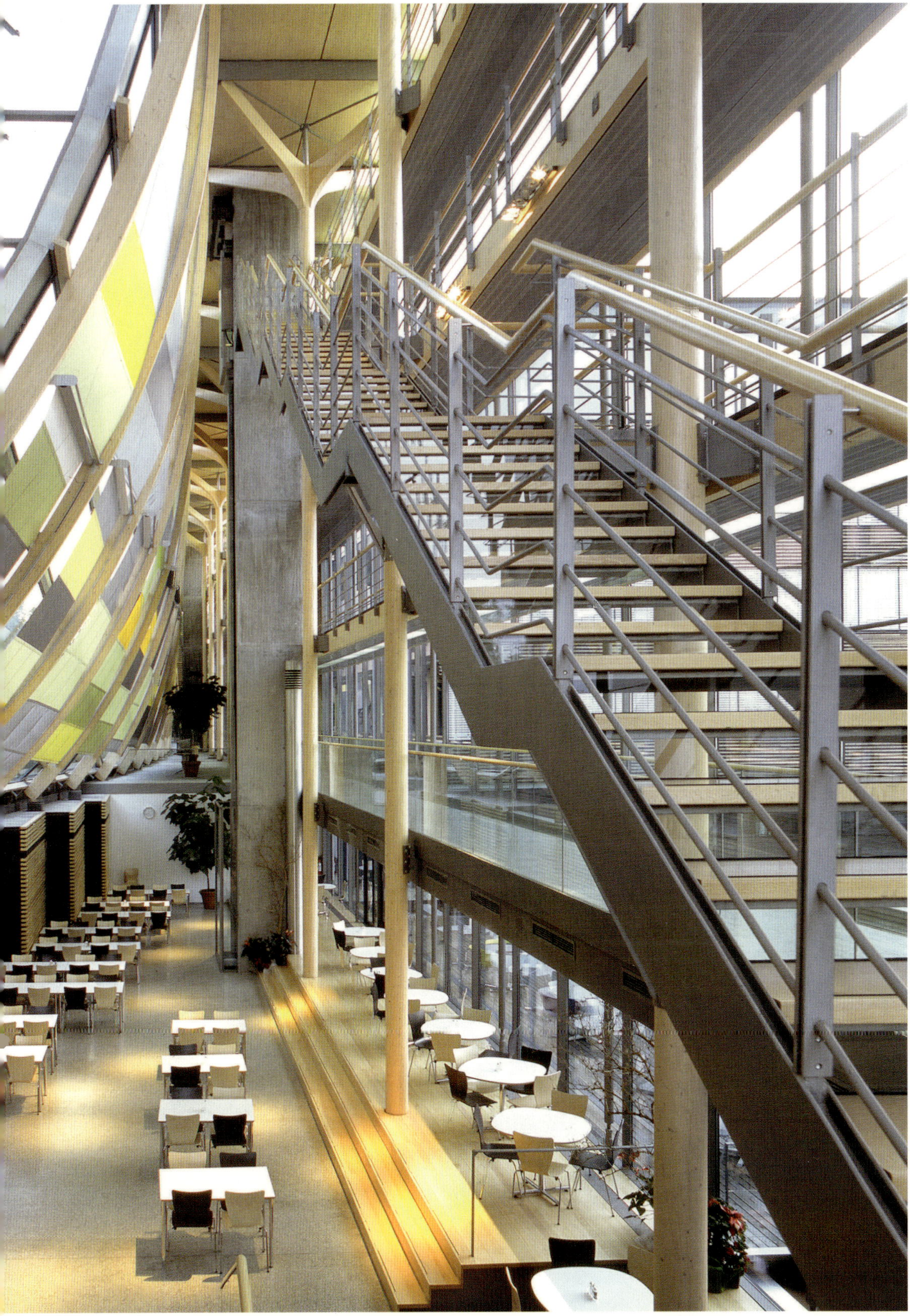

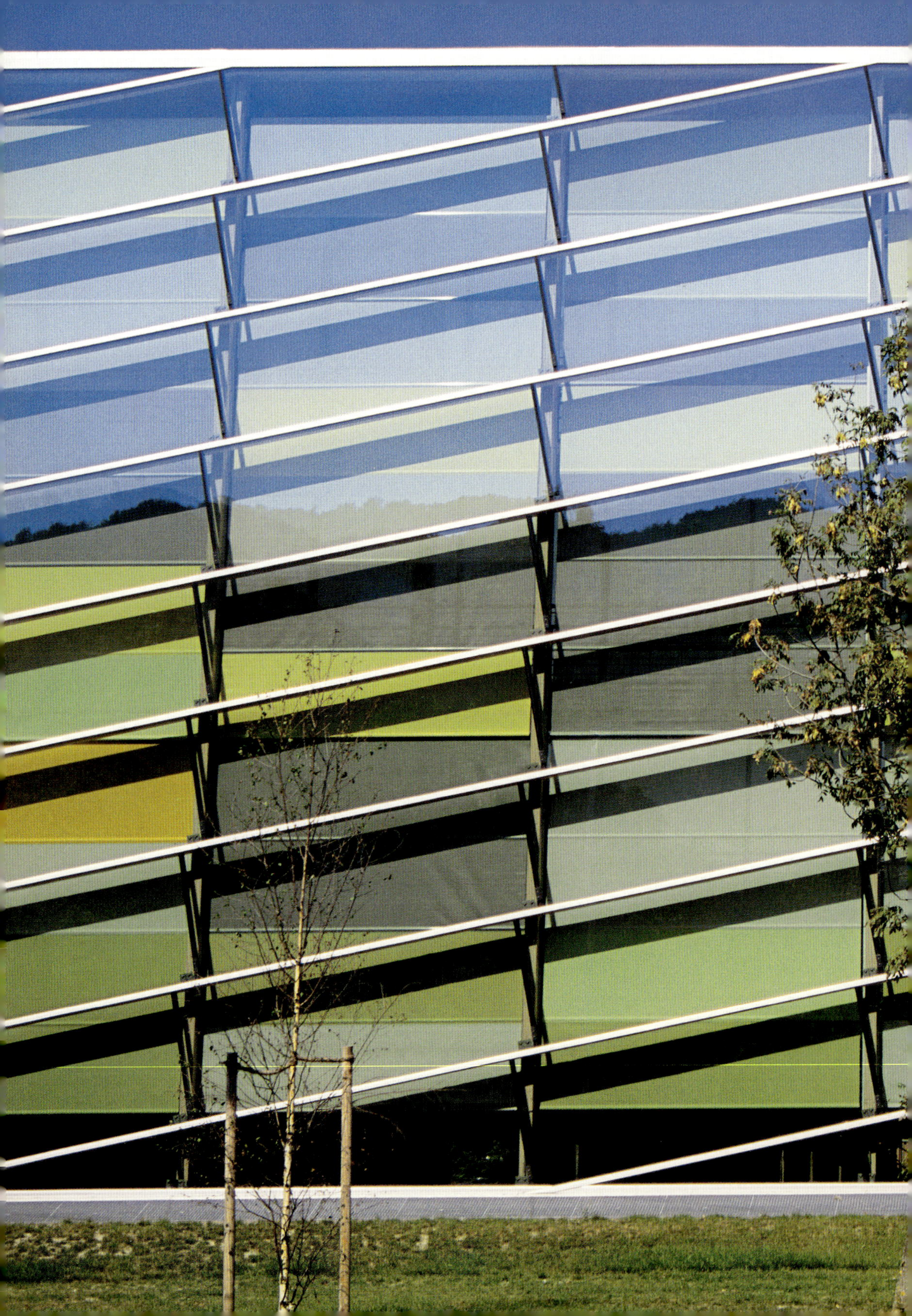

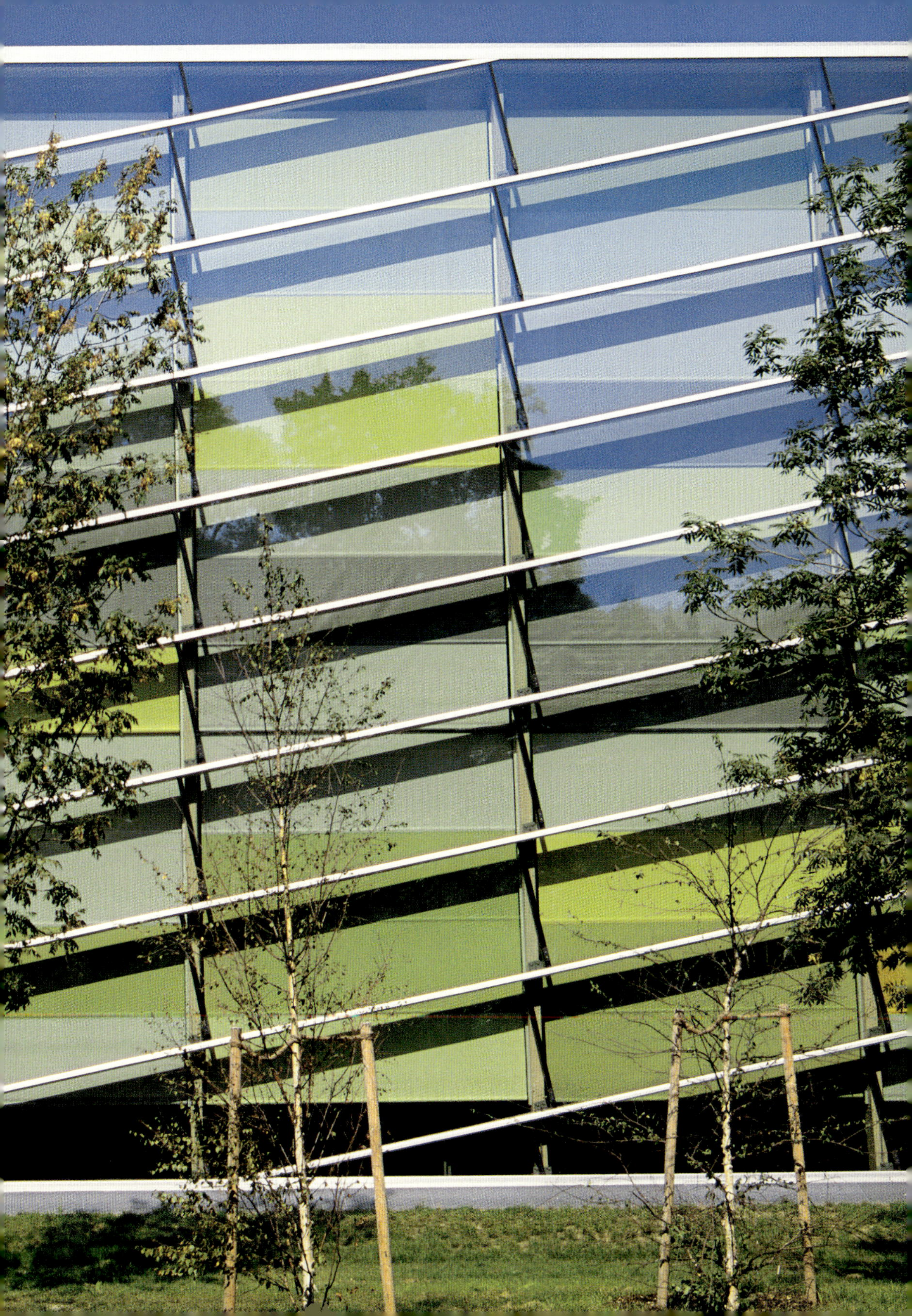

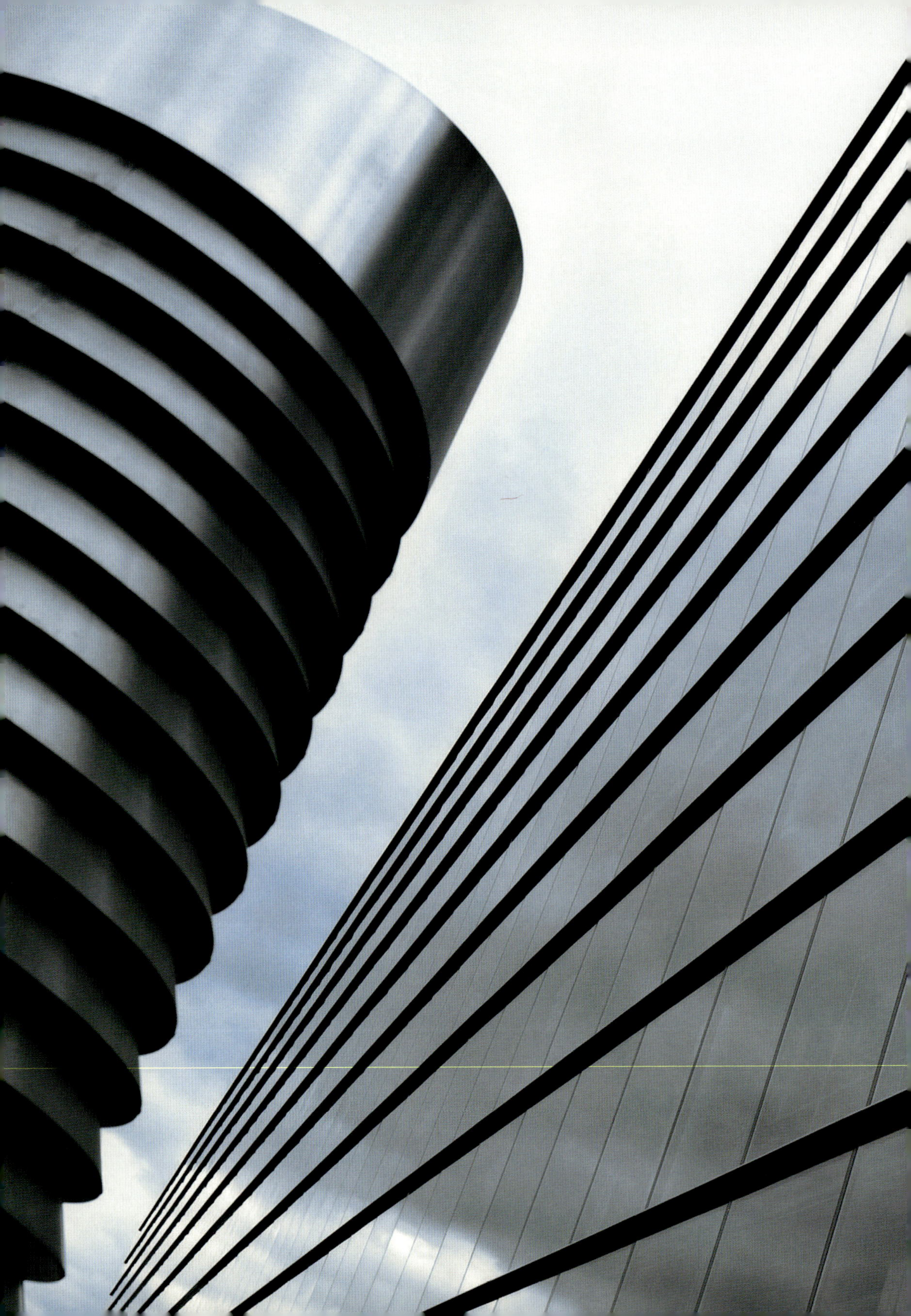

HENN ARCHITEKTEN | BERLIN, MUNICH
Gläserne Manufaktur of Volkswagen
Dresden, Germany | 2001

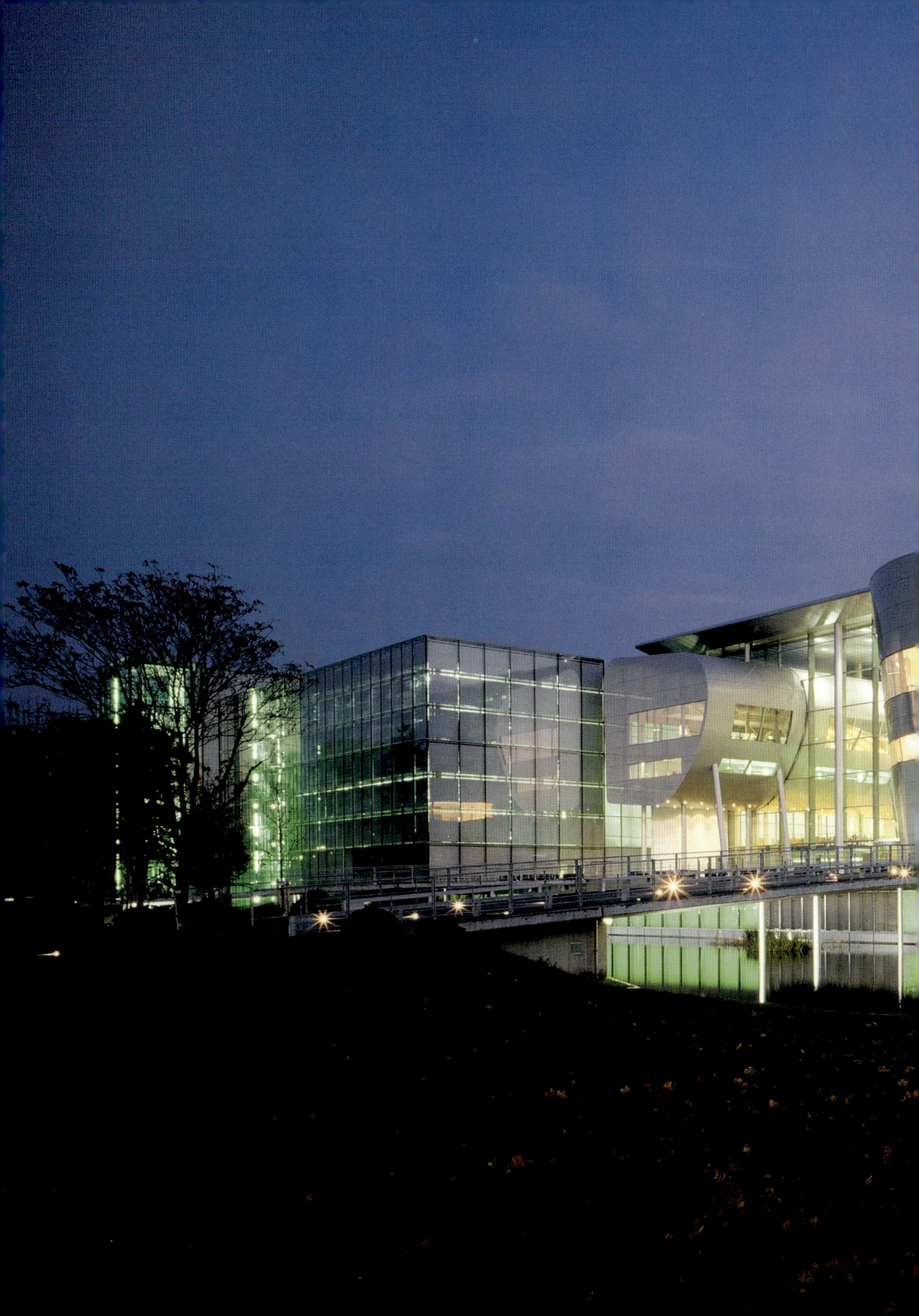

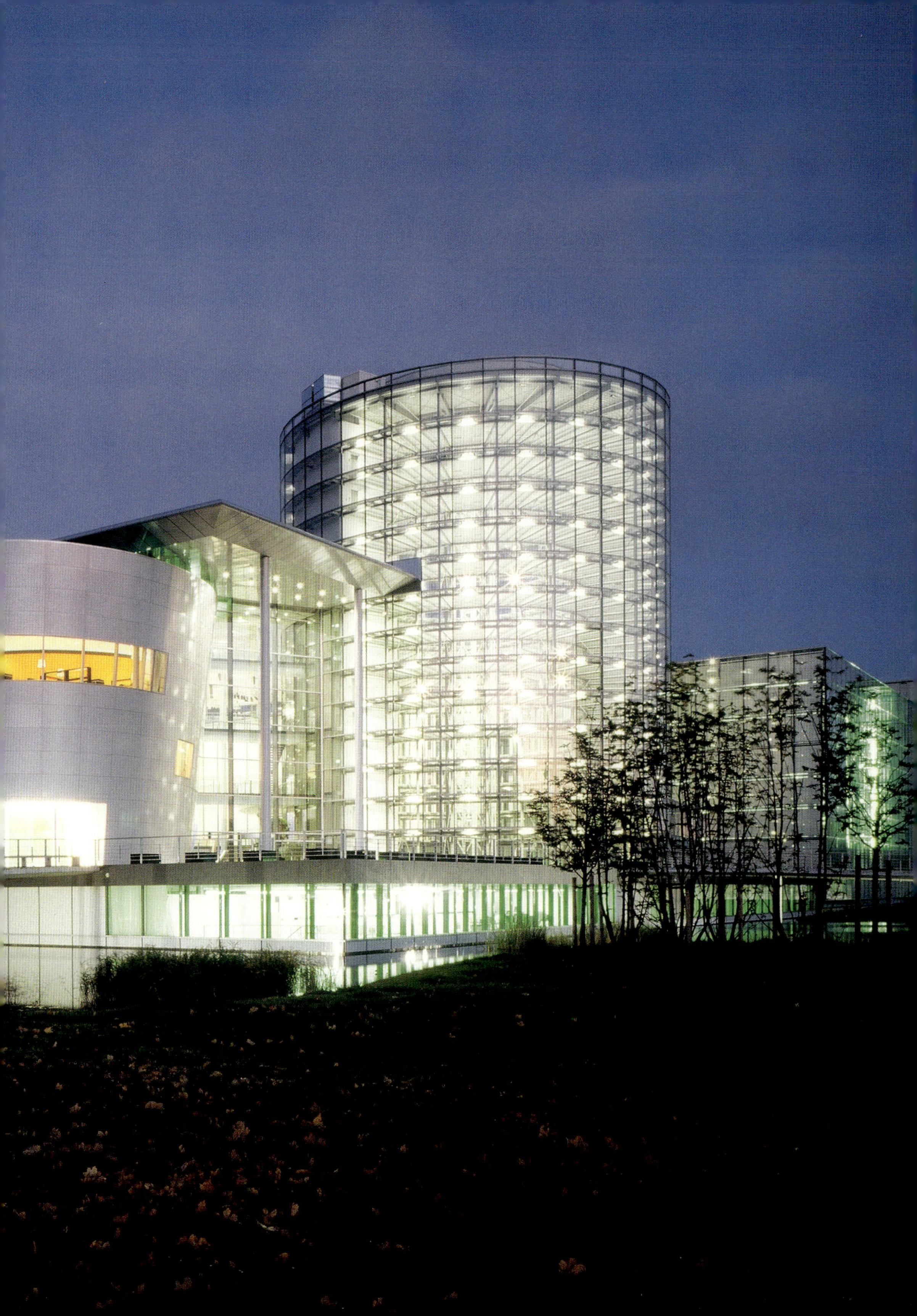

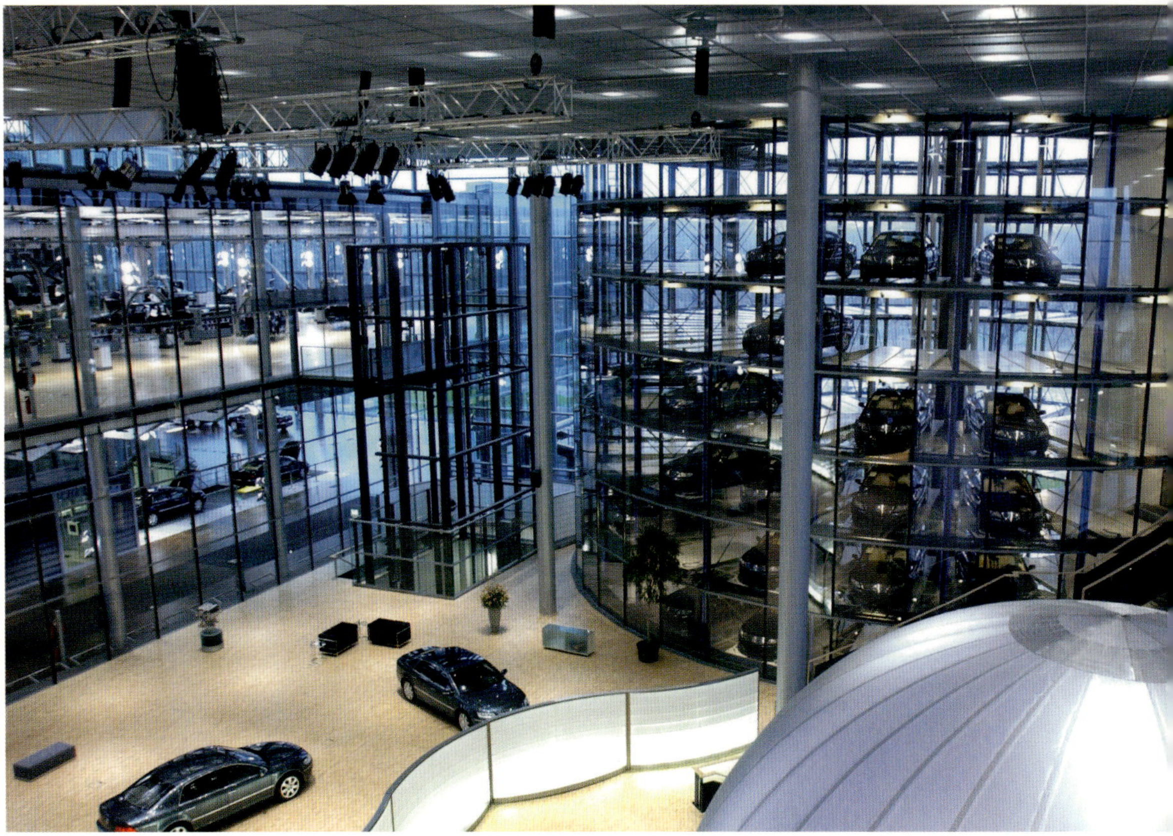

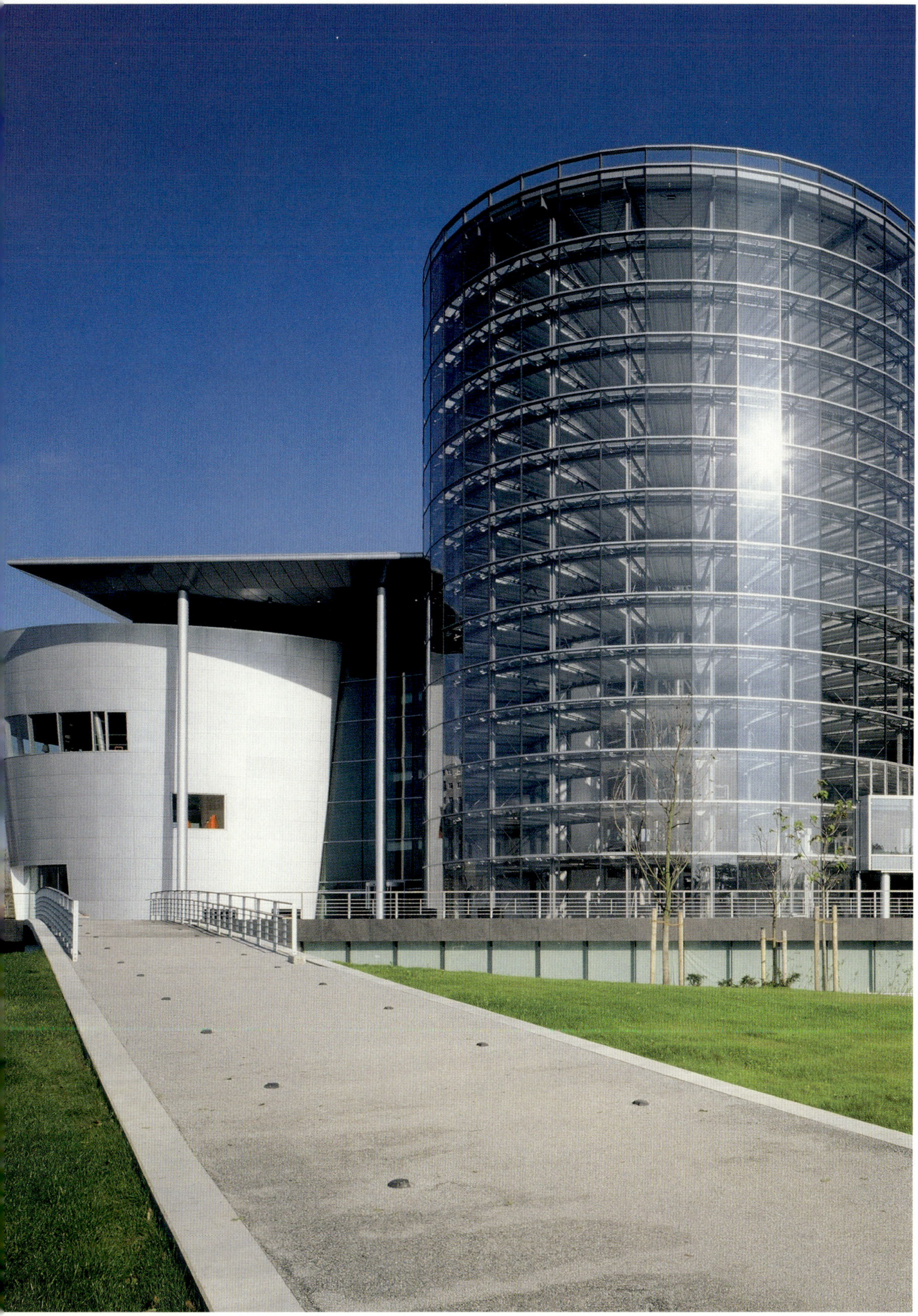

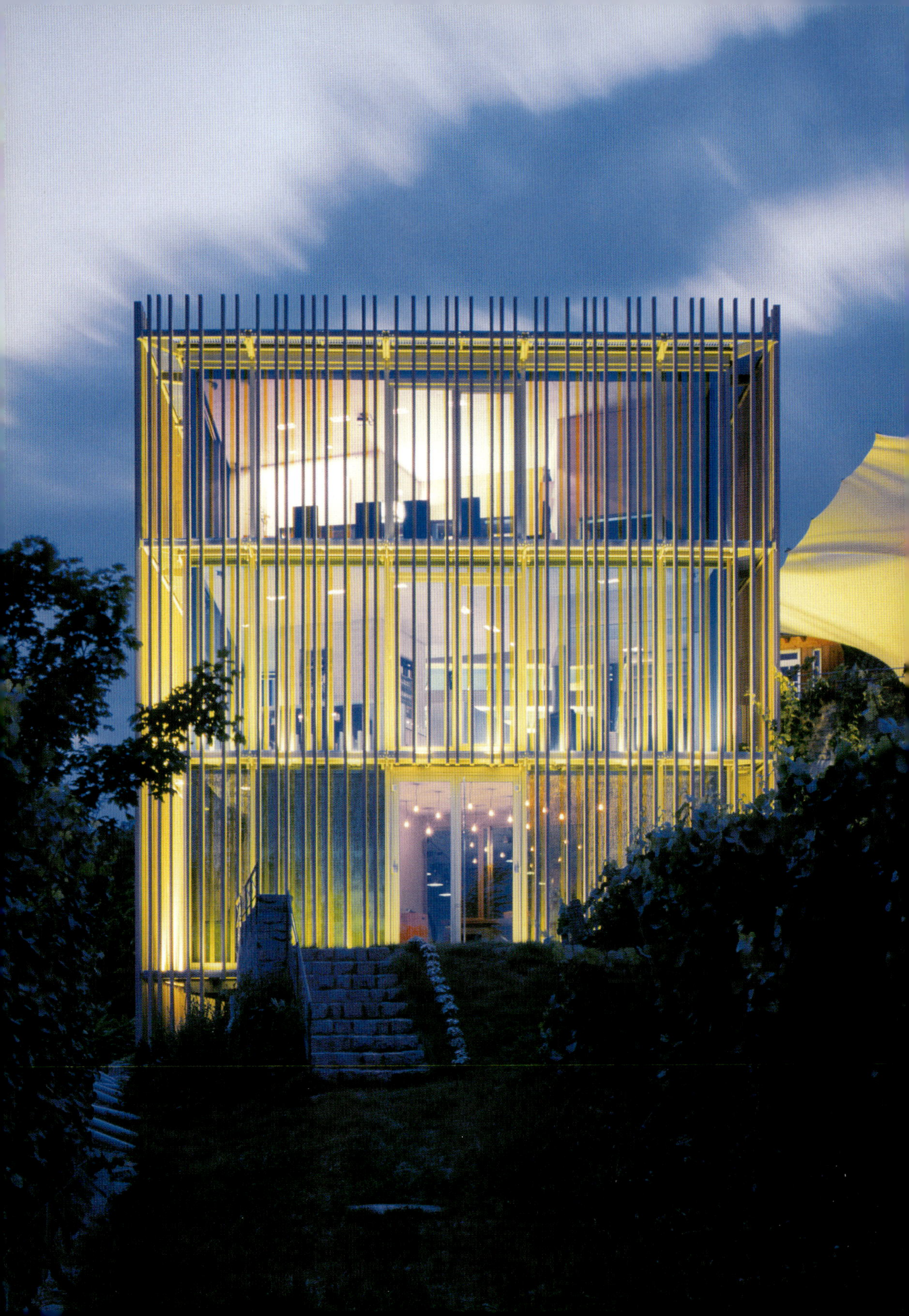

HOFMANN KEICHER RING ARCHITEKTEN + REINHARD MAY | WÜRZBURG
Weingut am Stein
Würzburg, Germany | 2005

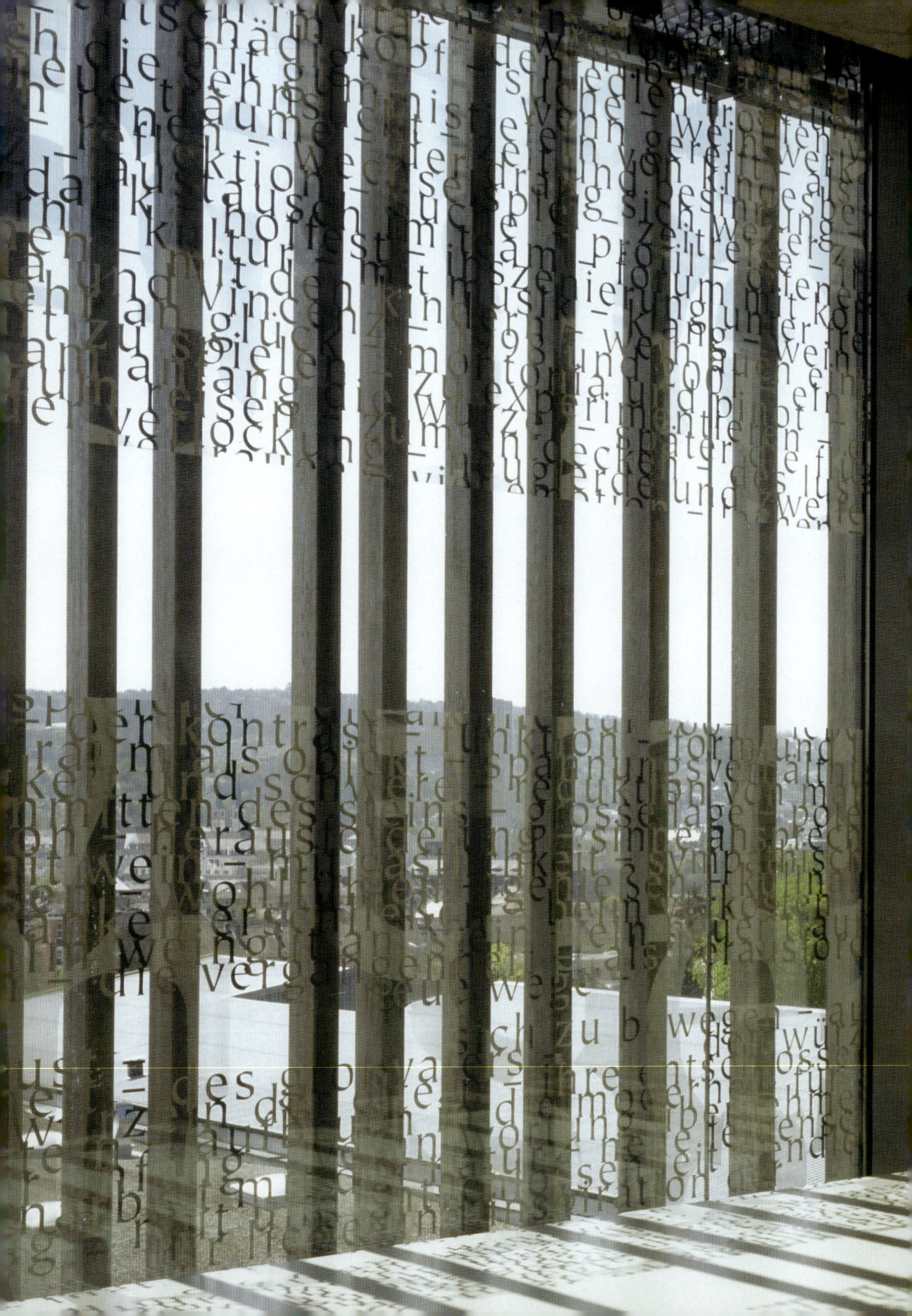

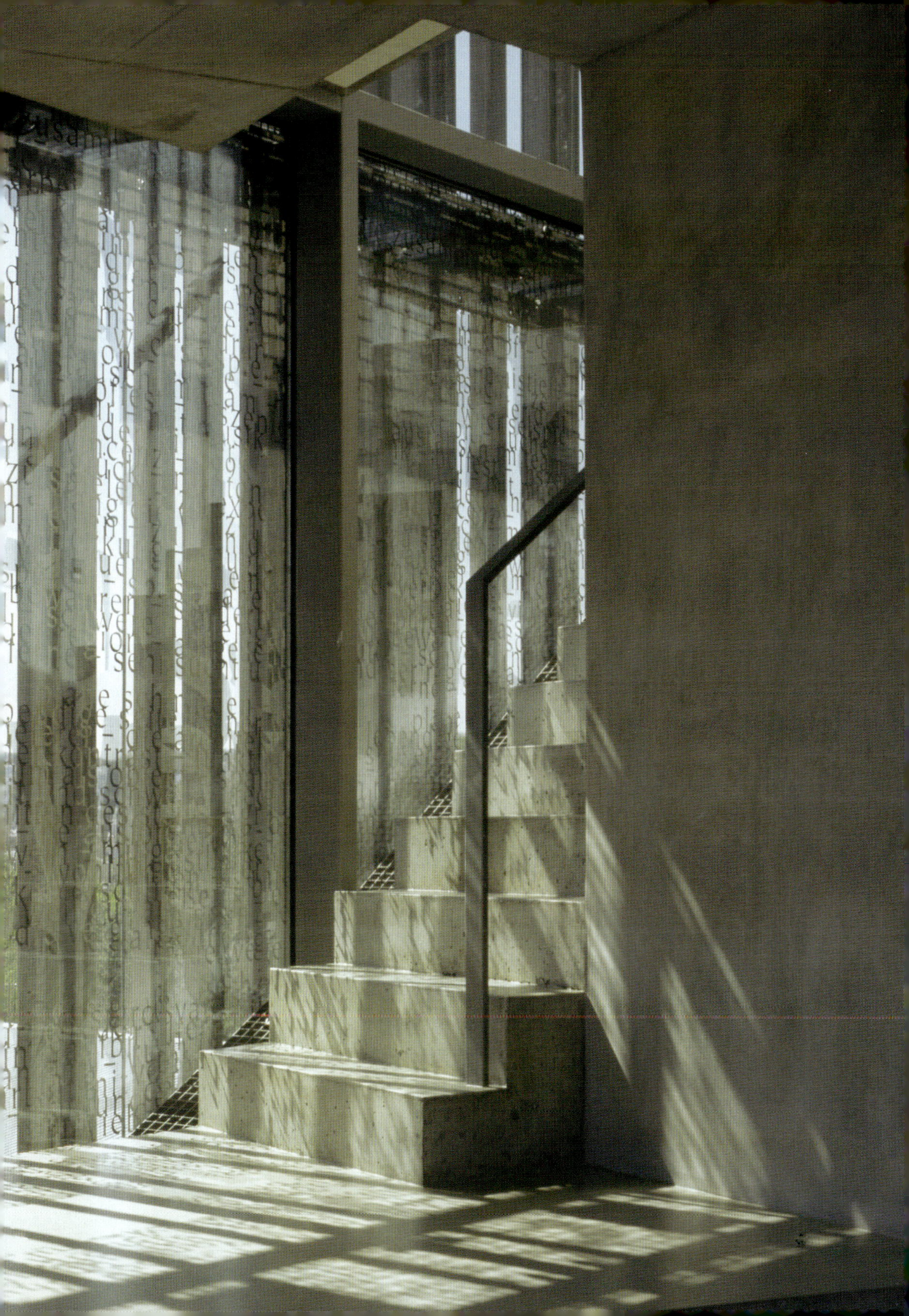

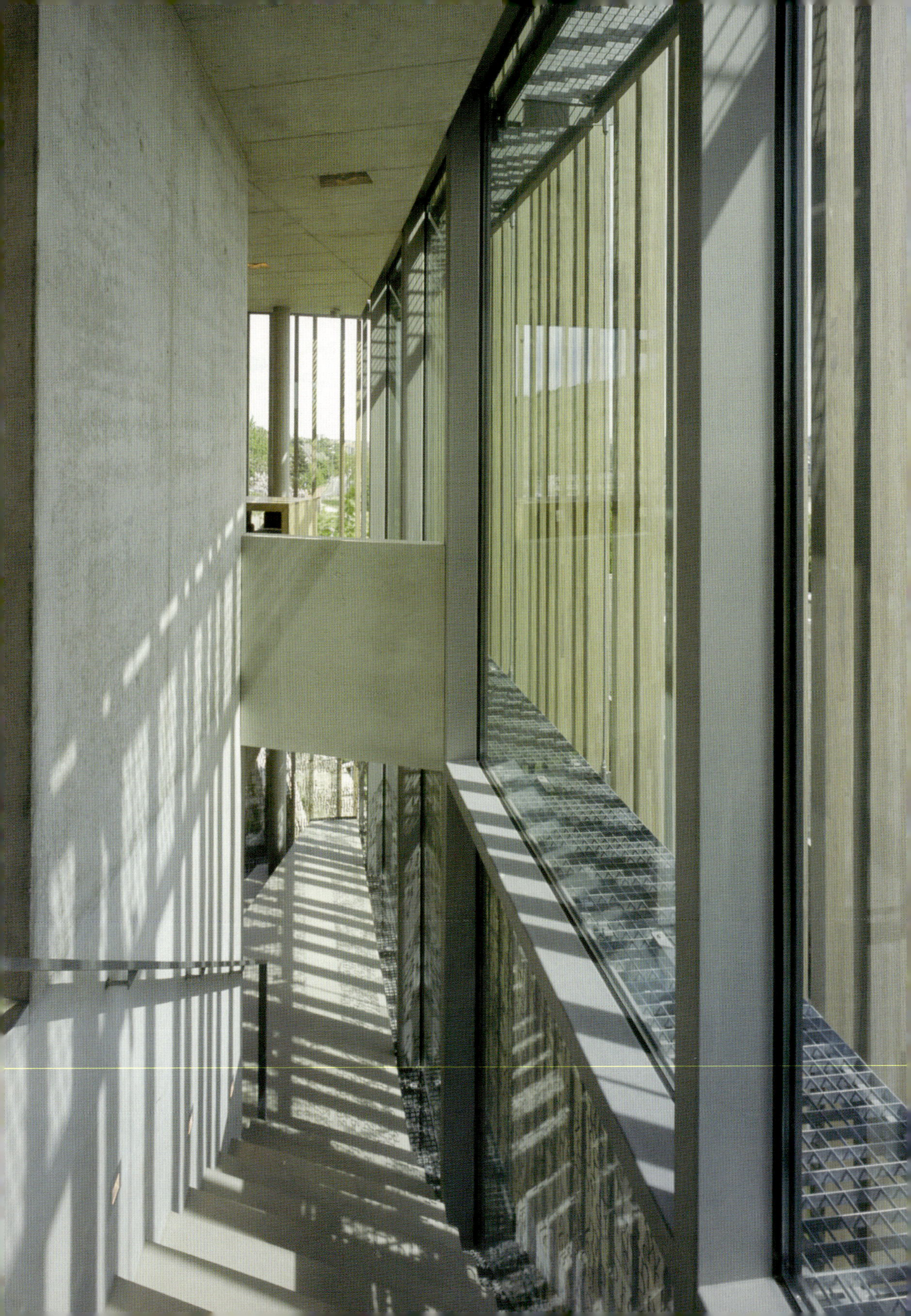

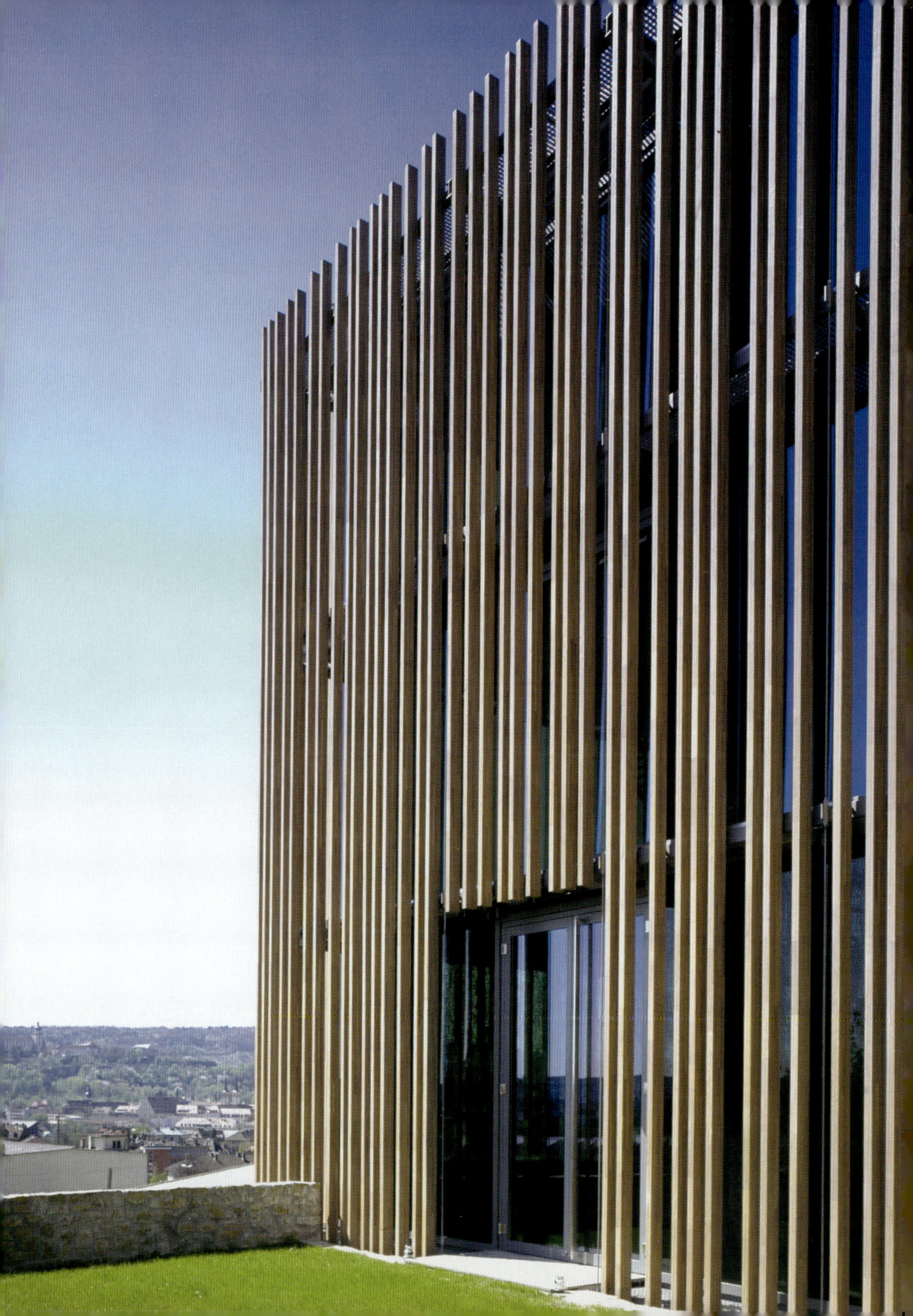

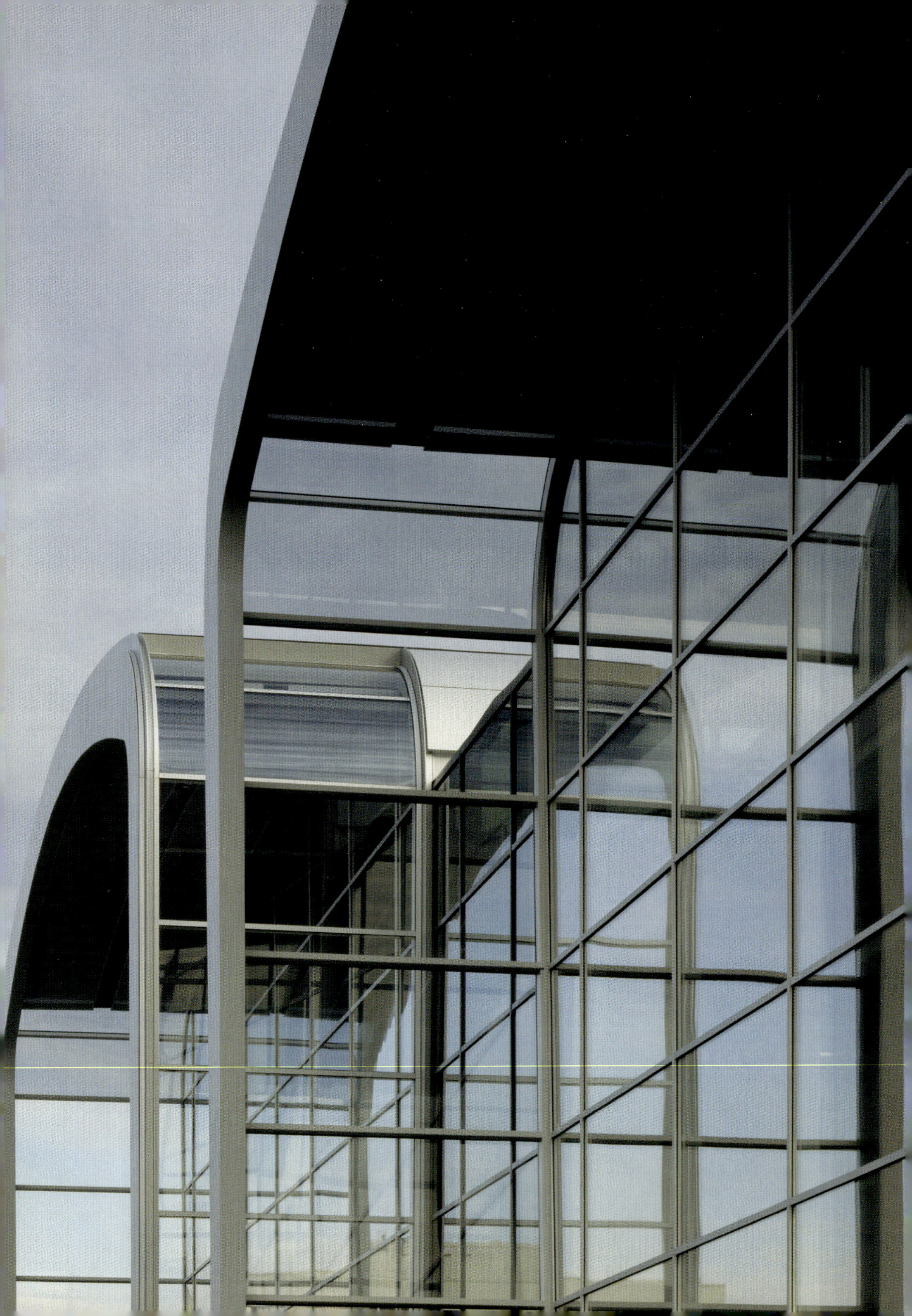

INGENHOVEN ARCHITEKTEN | DÜSSELDORF
Production building Gira
Radevormwald, Germany | 2002

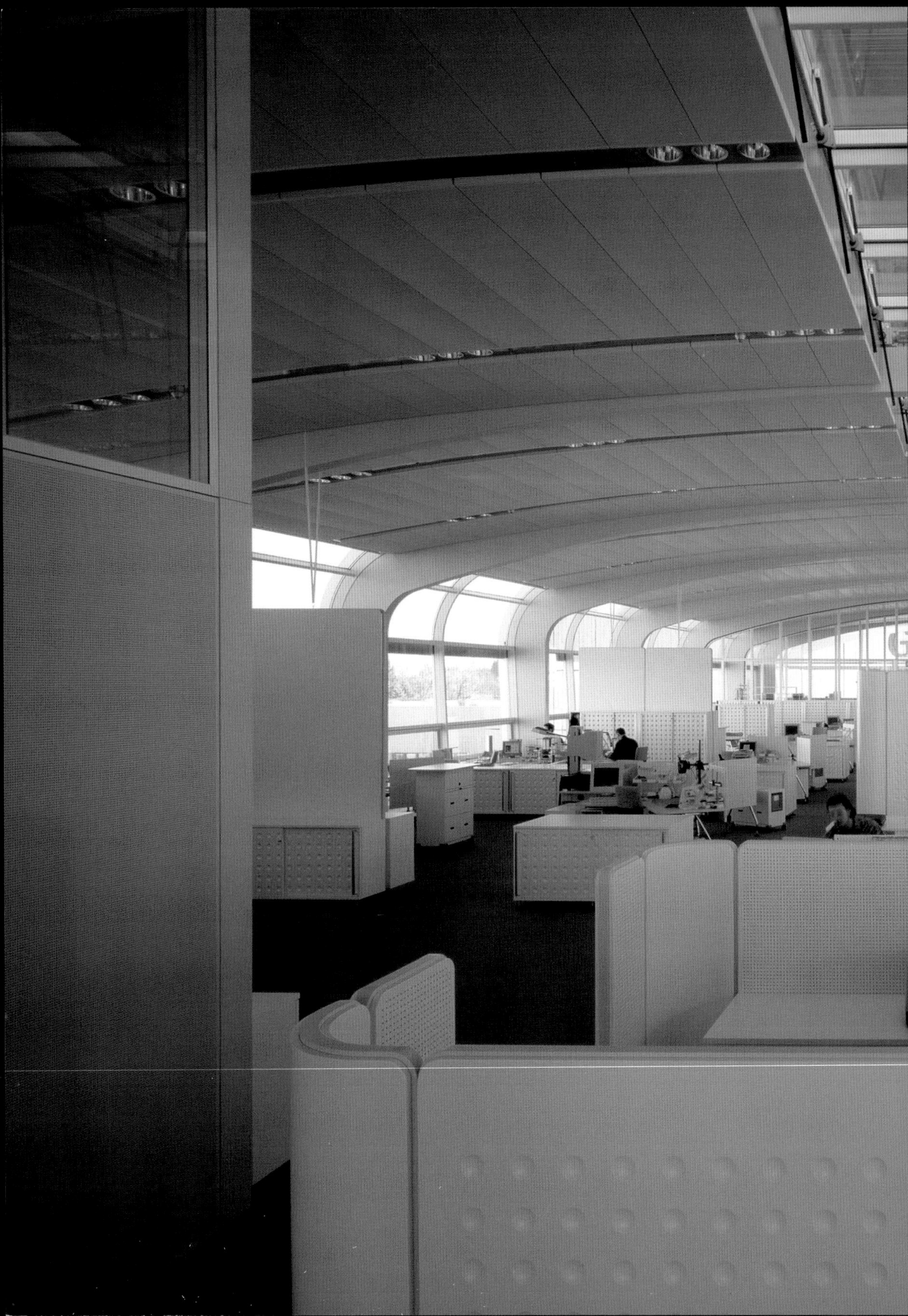

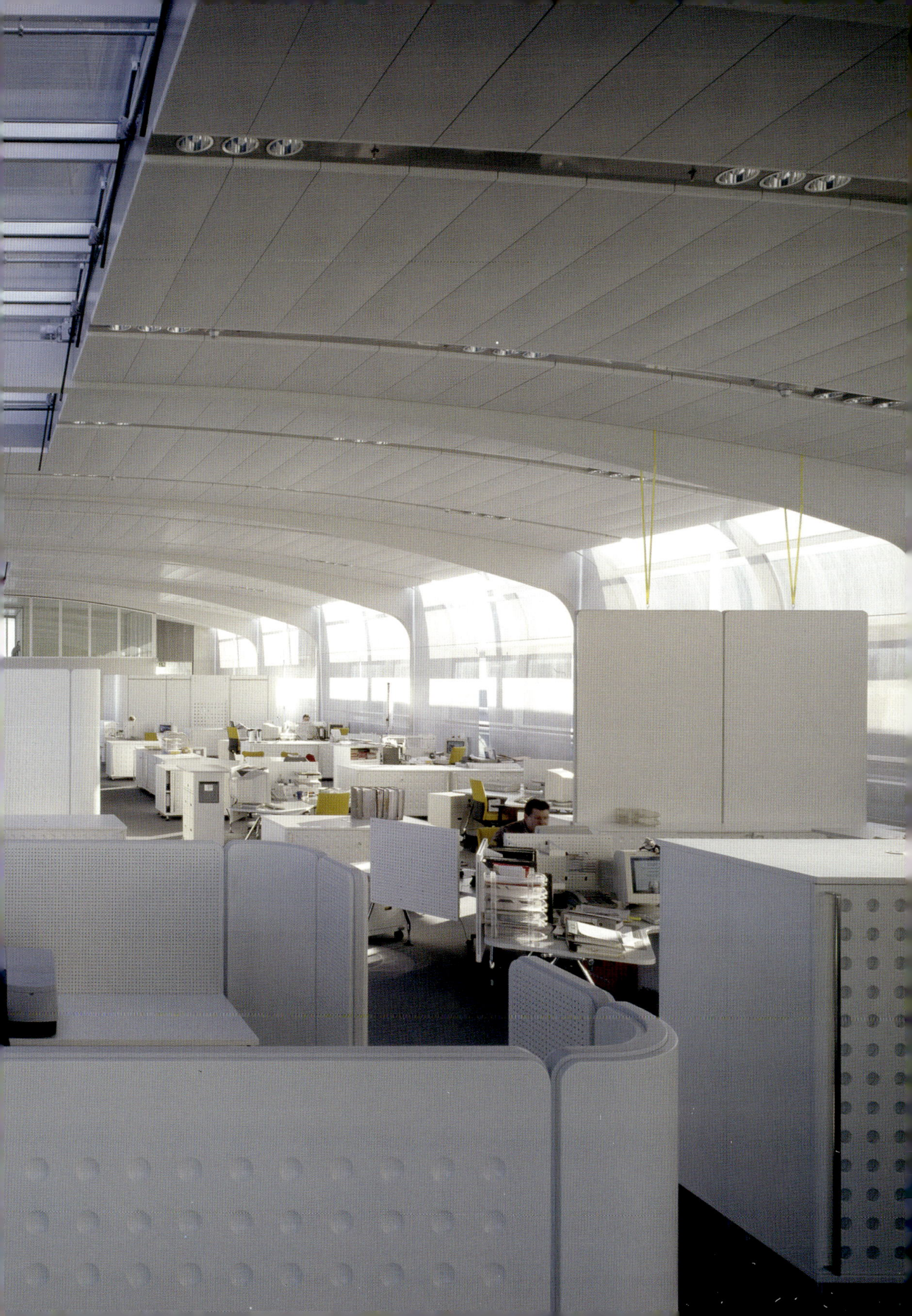

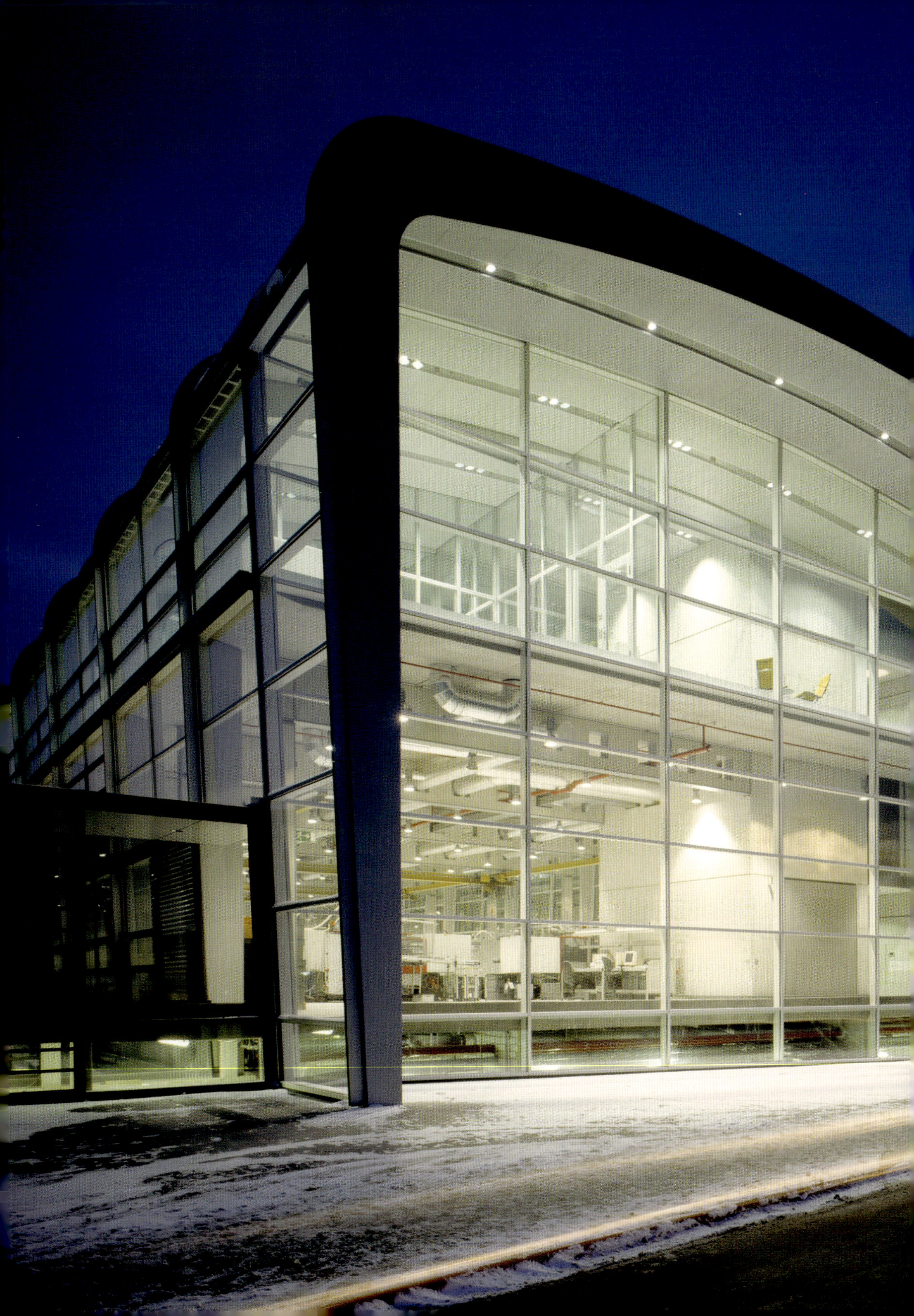

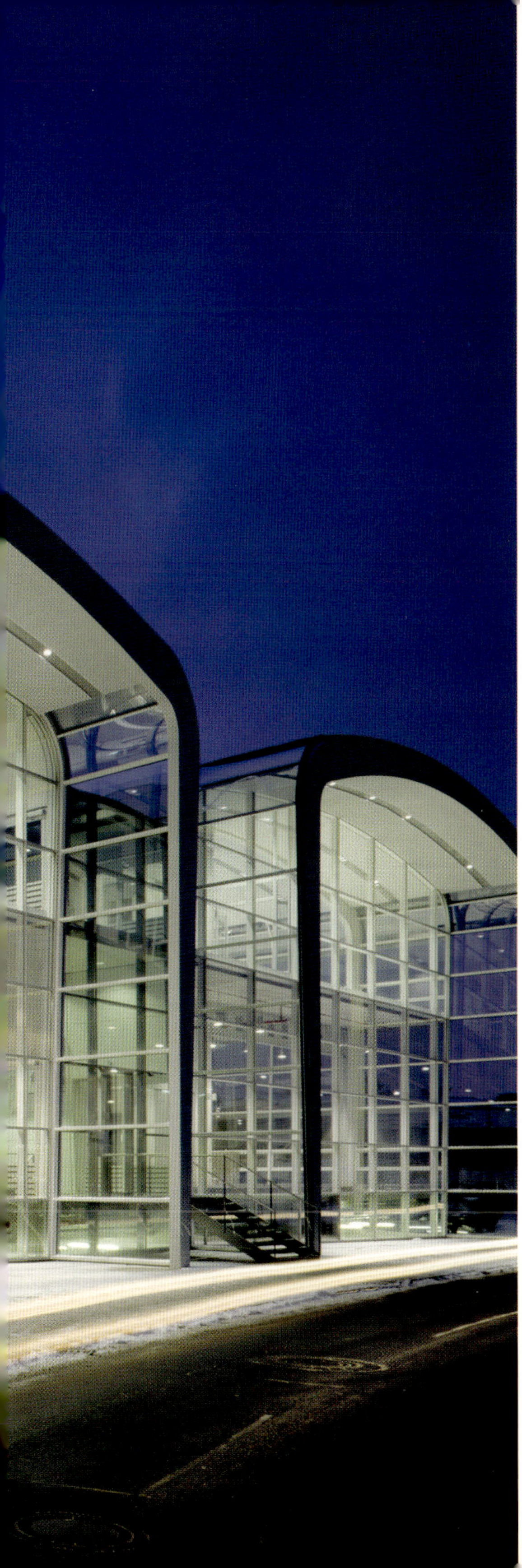

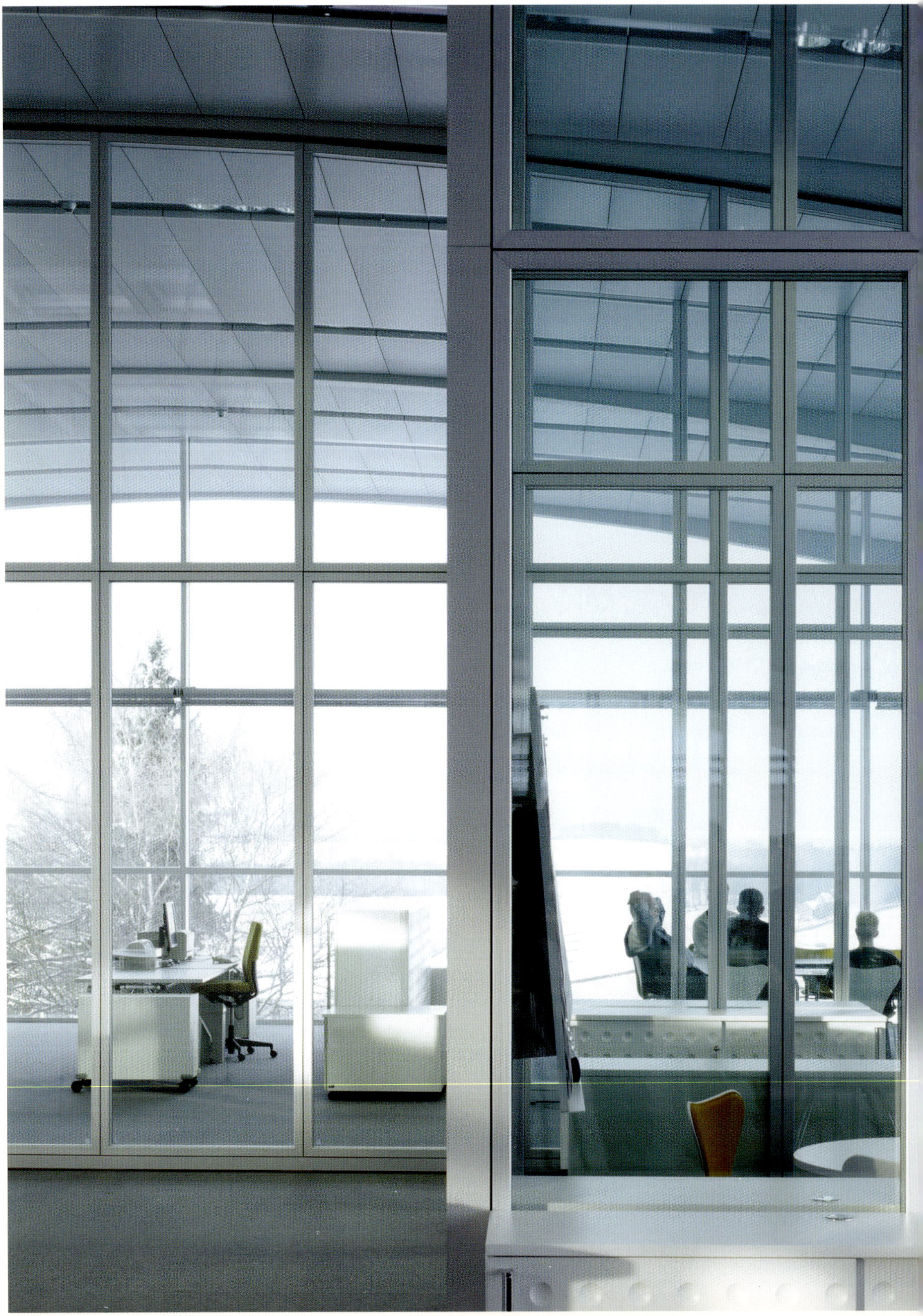

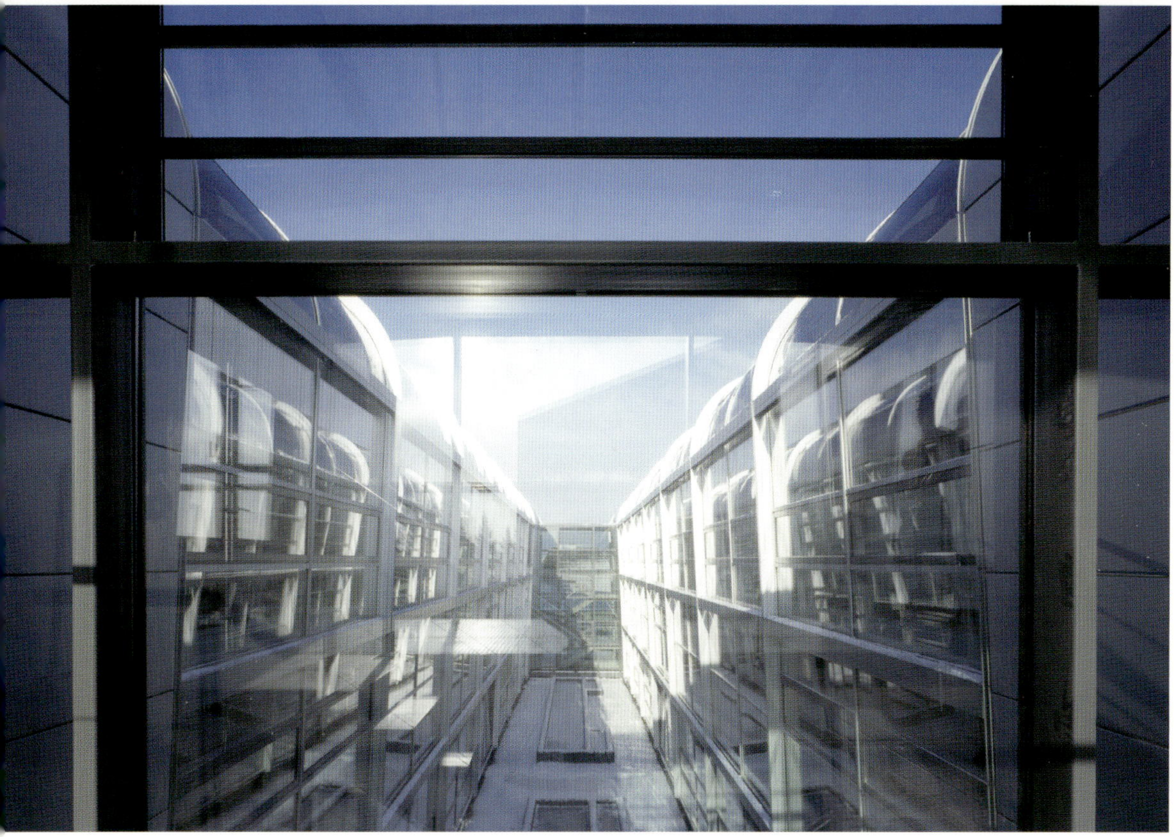

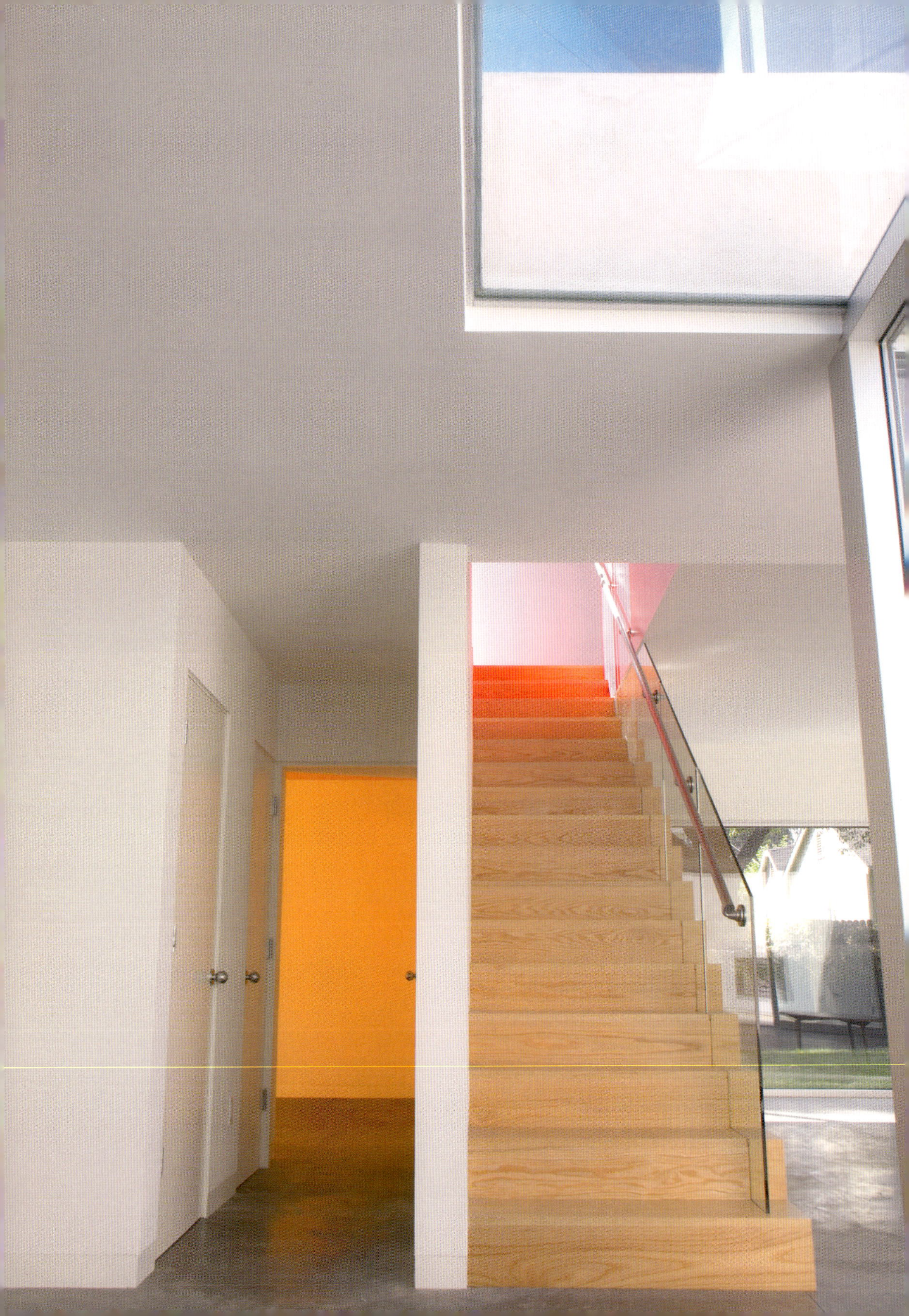

JOHNSTON MARKLEE & ASSOCIATES | VENICE
Sale House
Venice, California | 2004

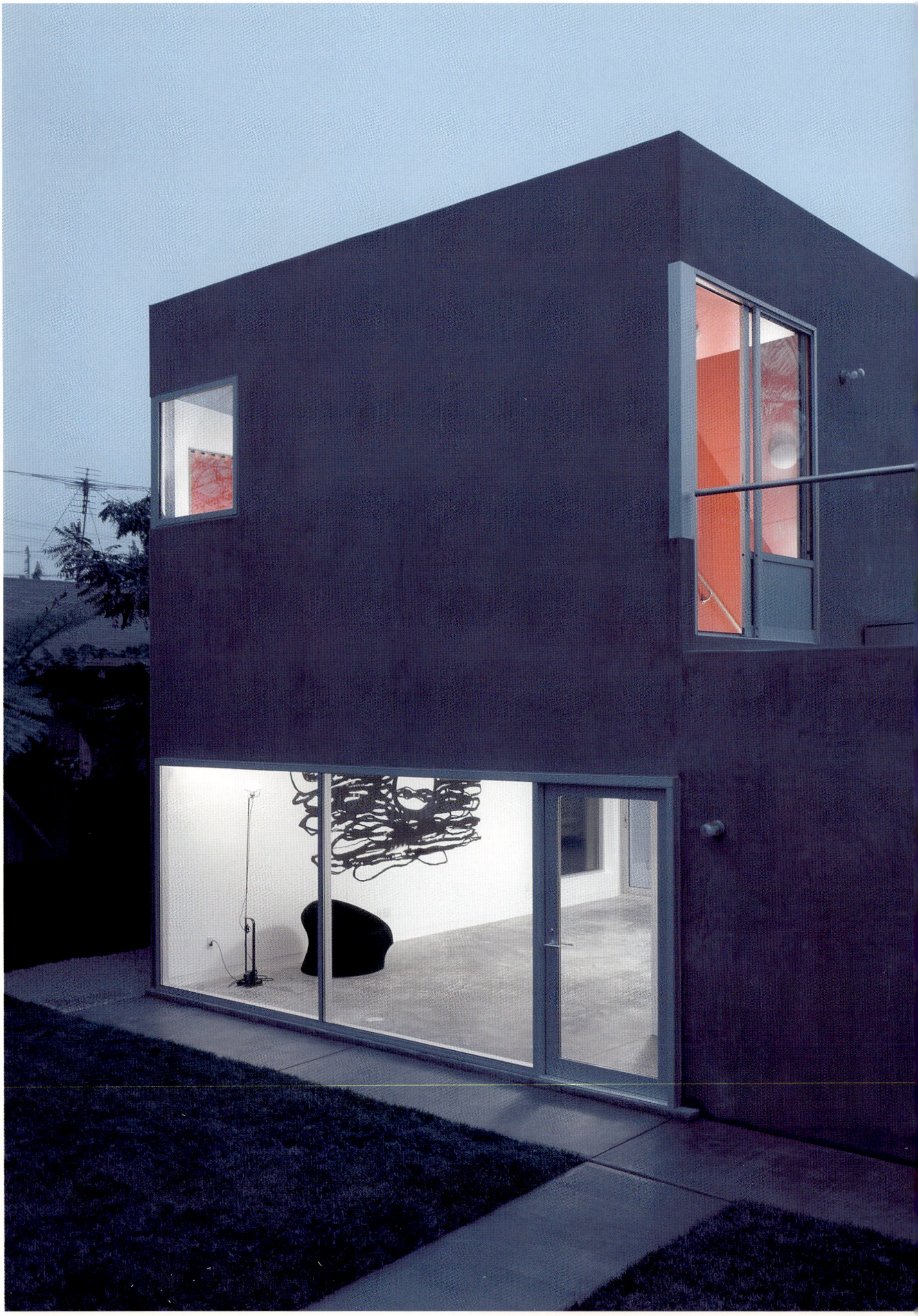

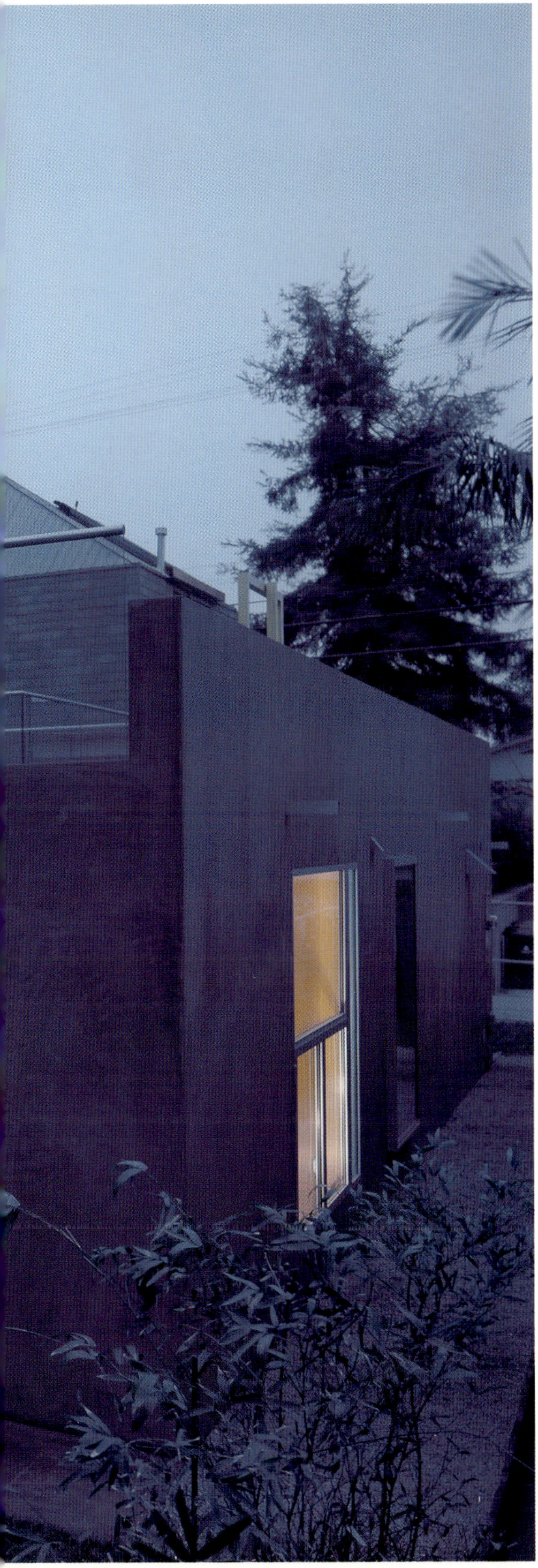

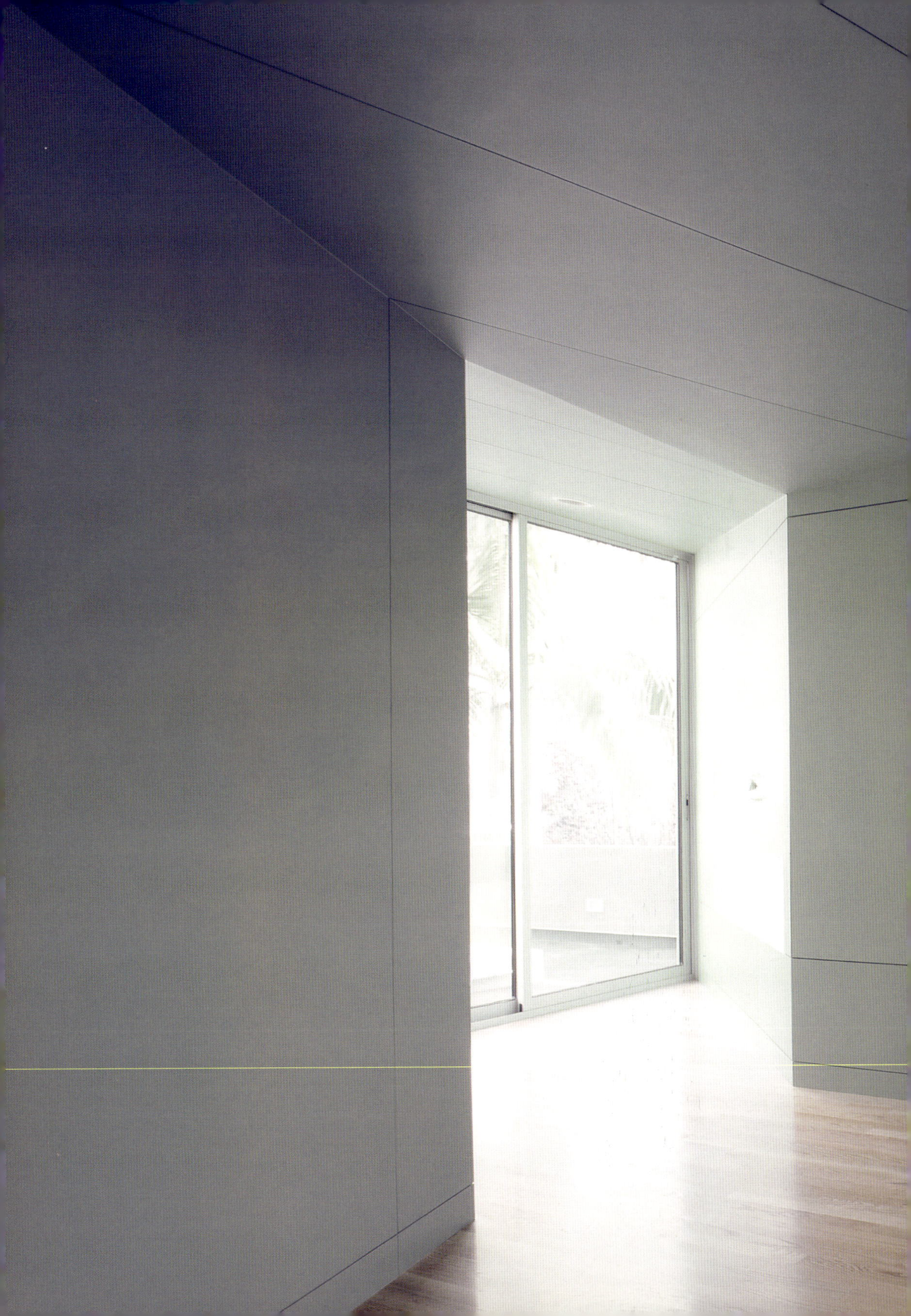

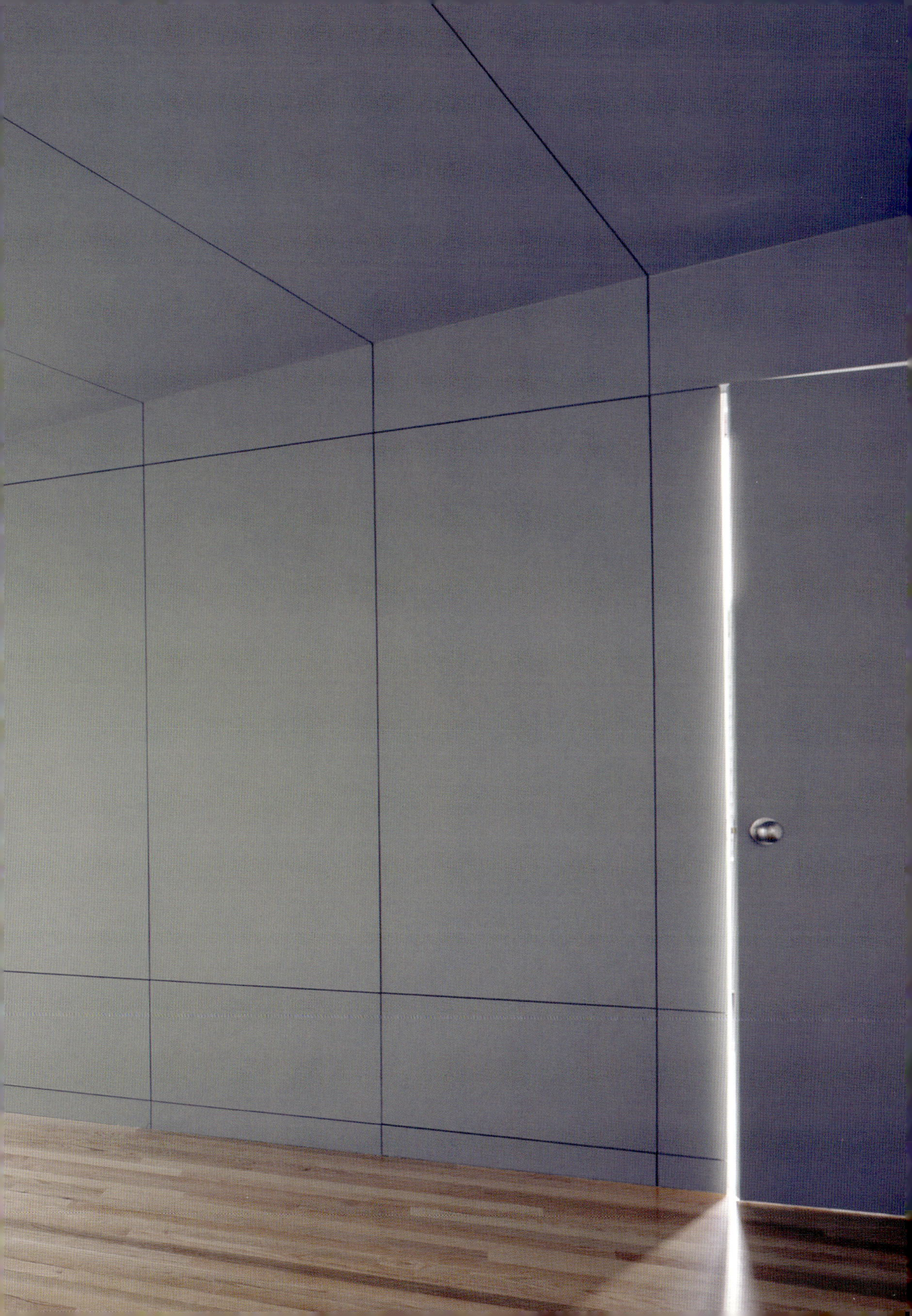

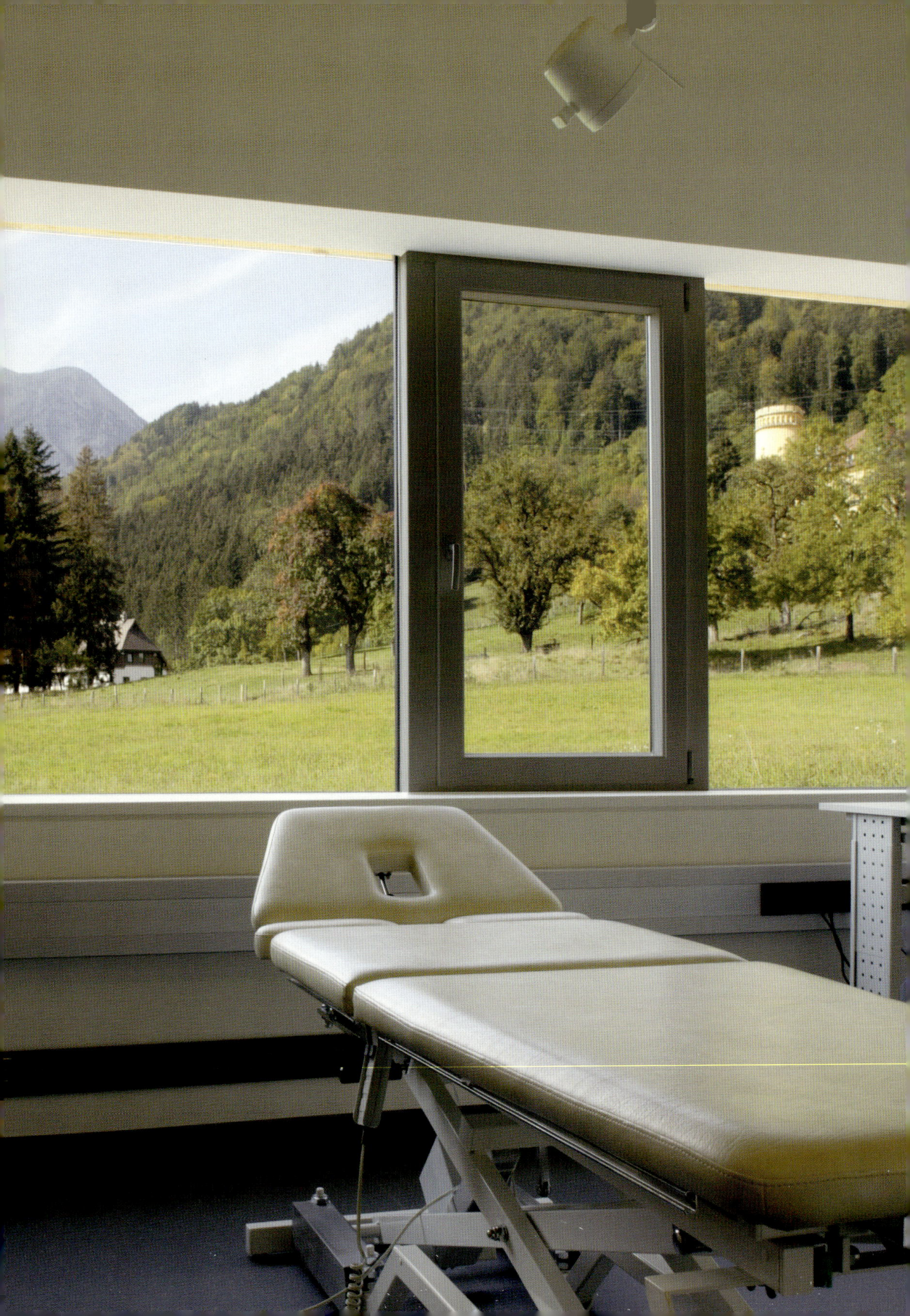

ANDREAS KANZIAN | GRAZ, BOCHUM
Practice Dr. med. Wilhelm Pintar
Stainach, Steiermark, Austria | 2003

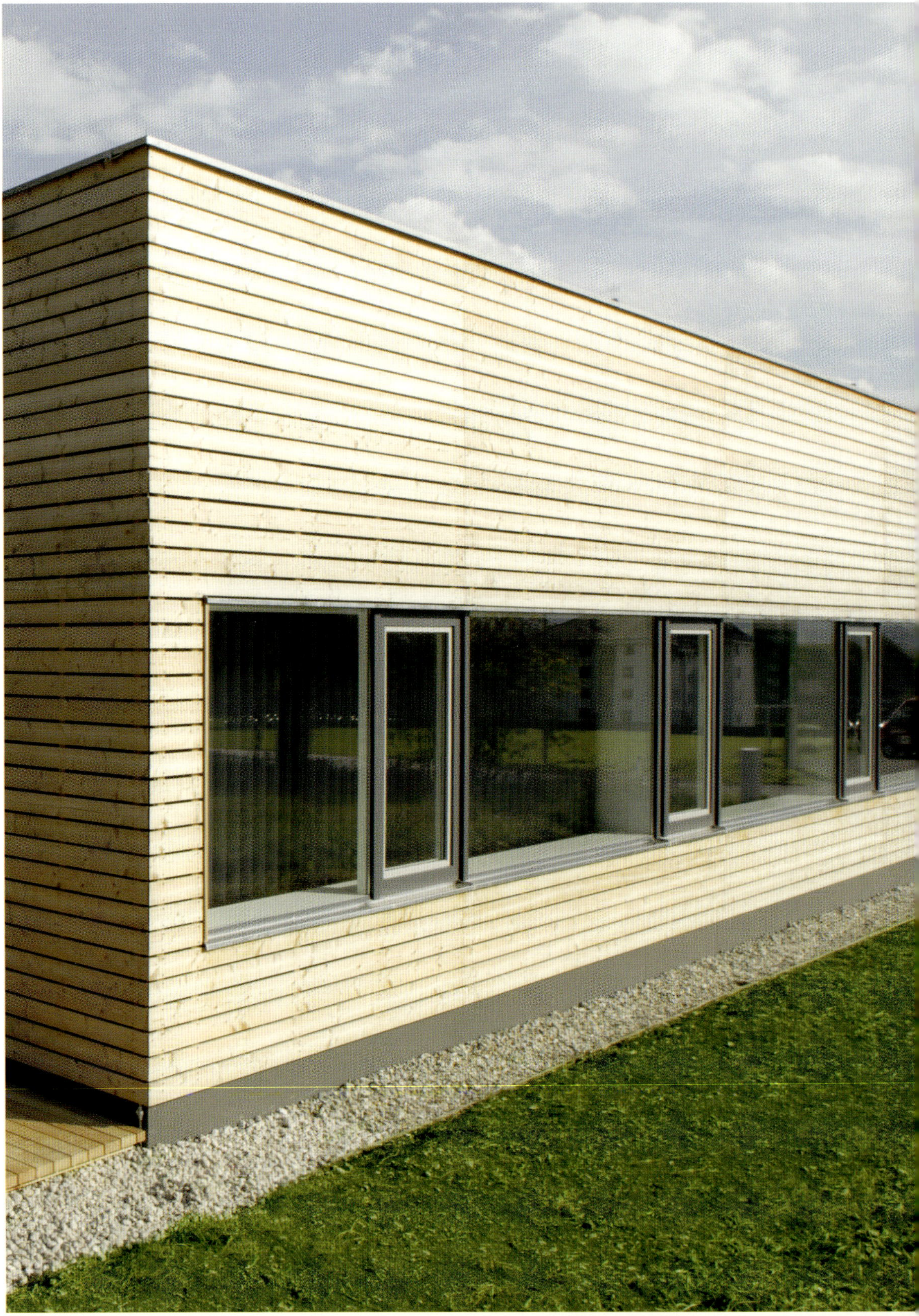

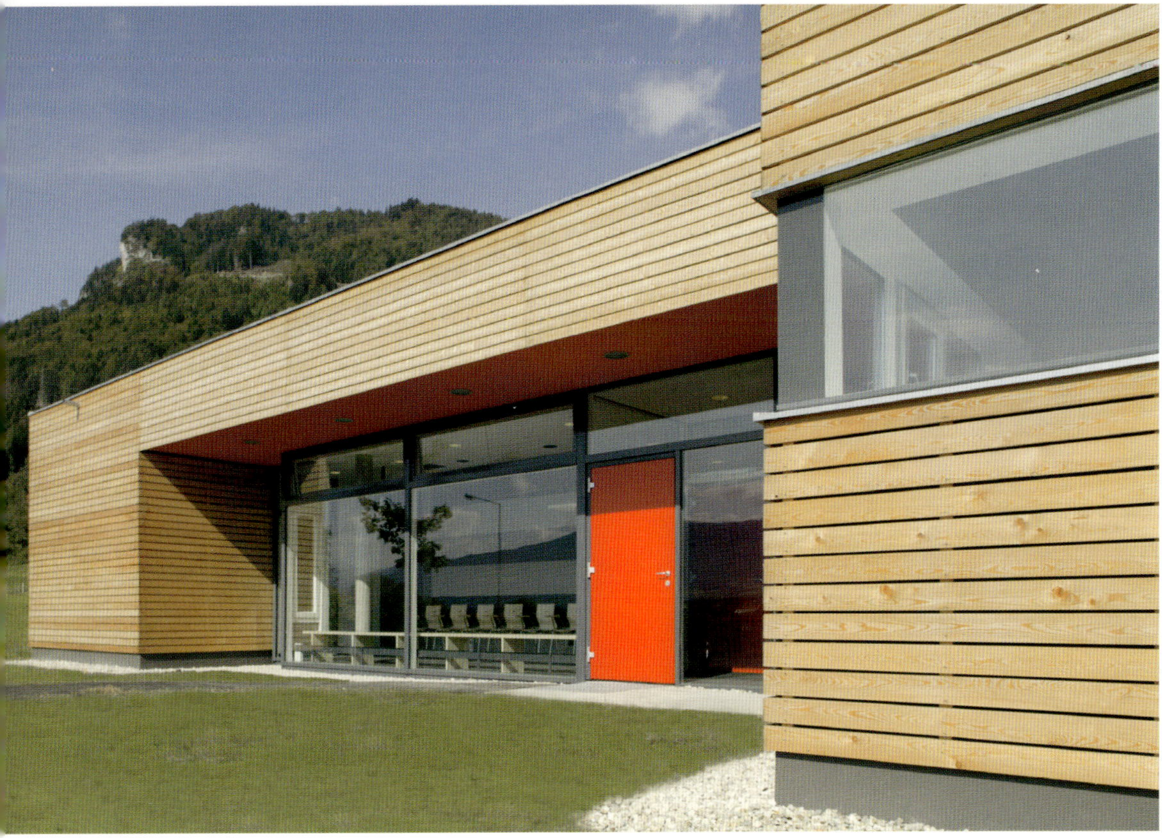

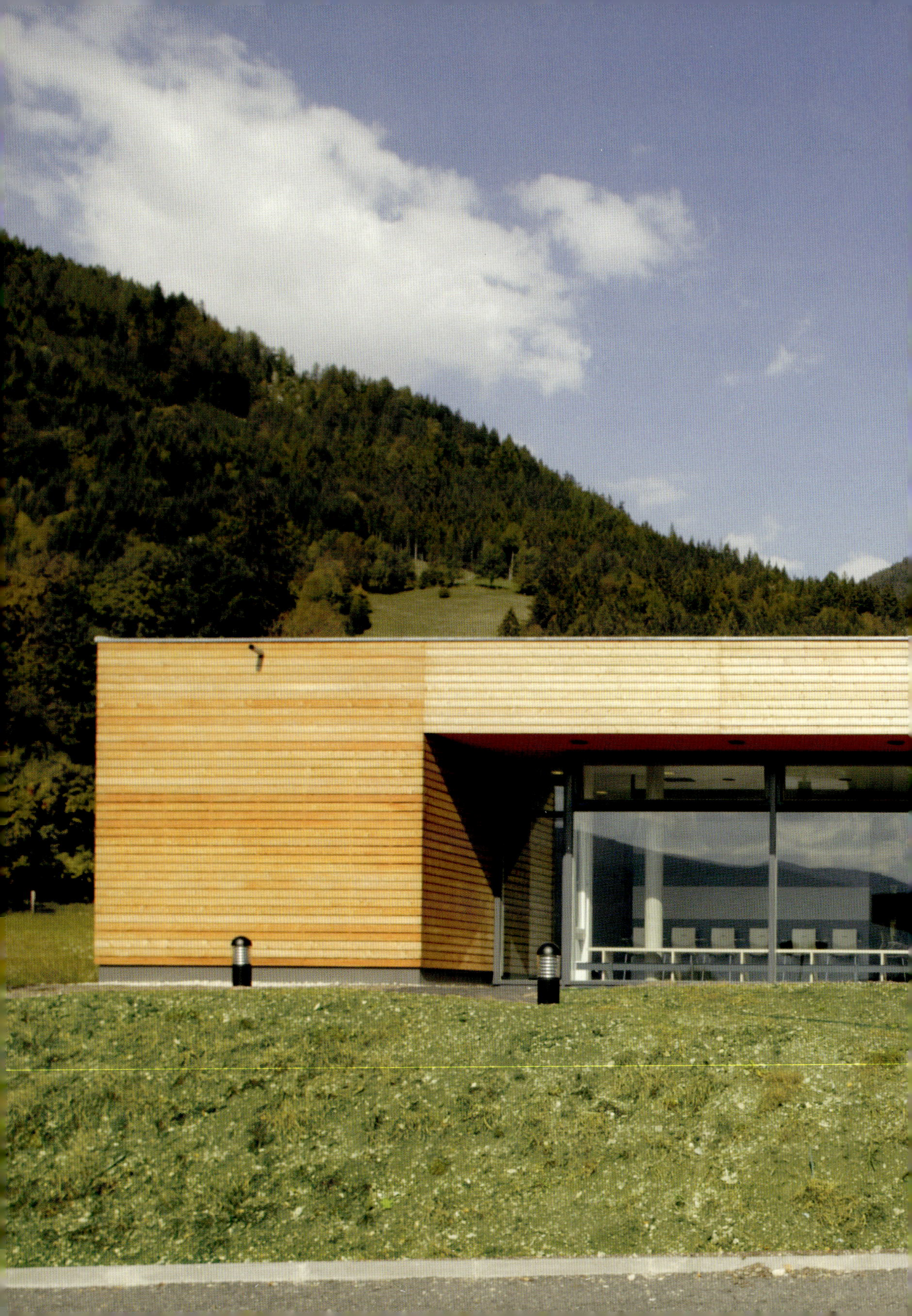

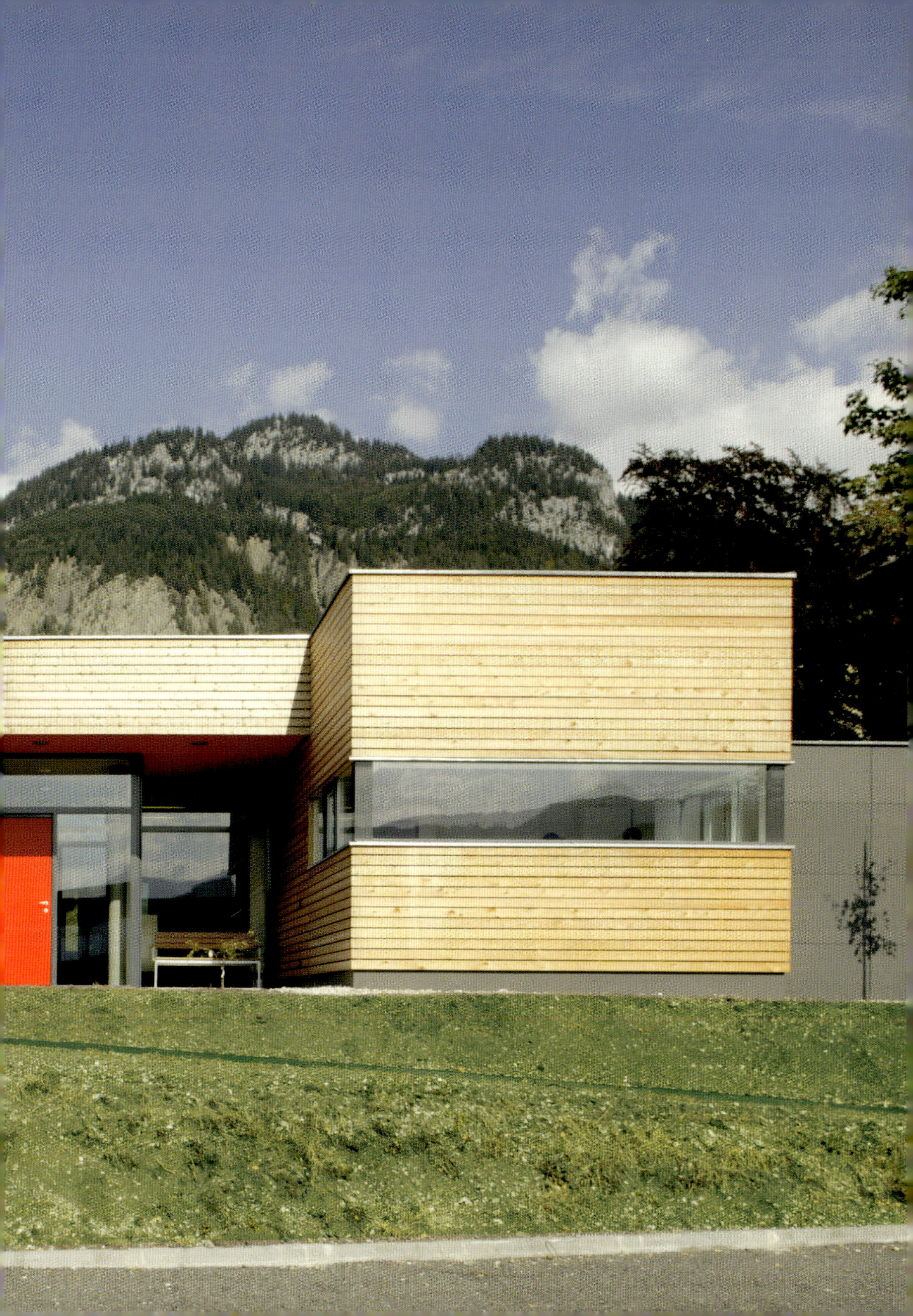

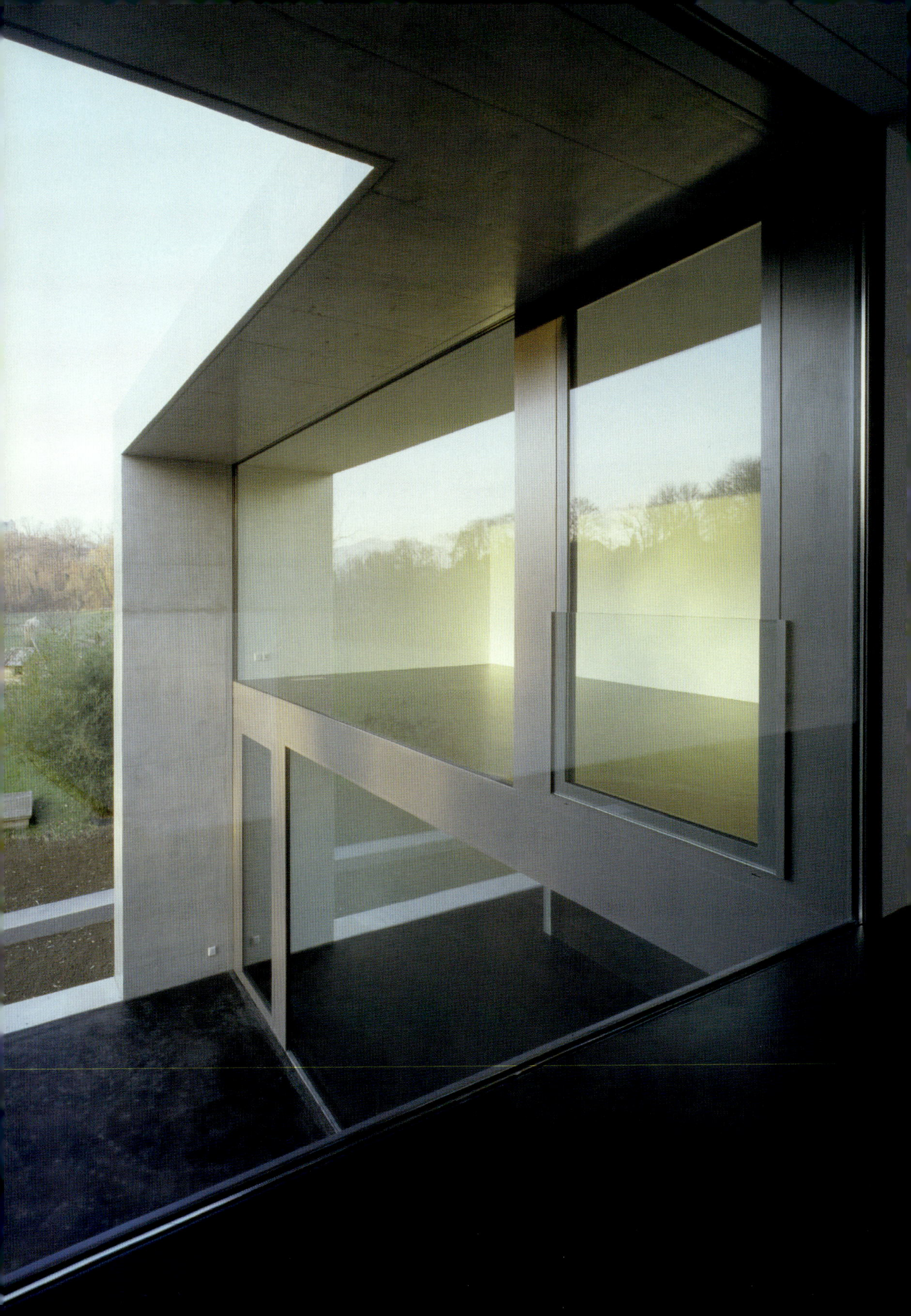

KEN ARCHITEKTEN | BADEN, ZURICH
One-family house
Möriken, Switzerland | 2005

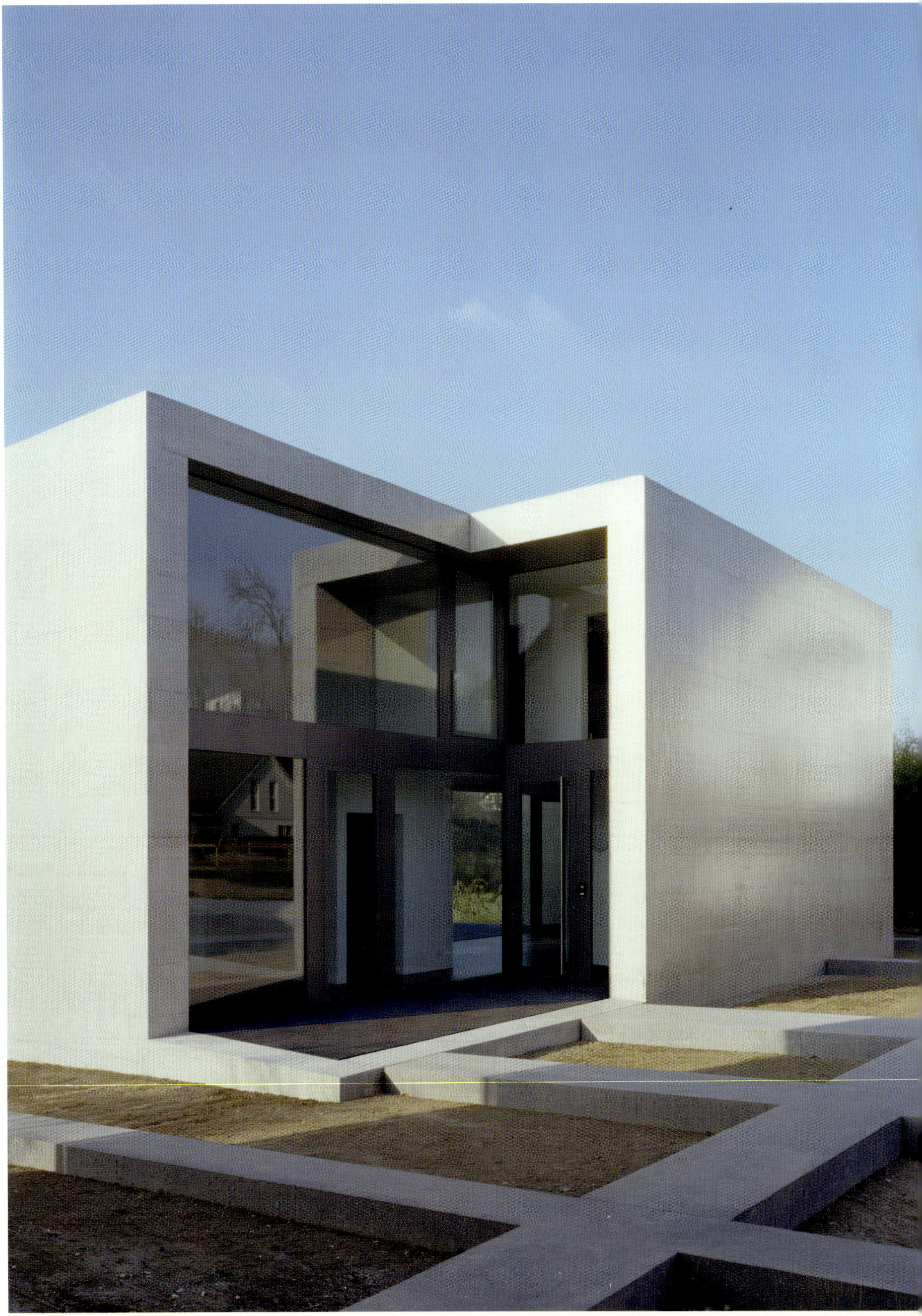

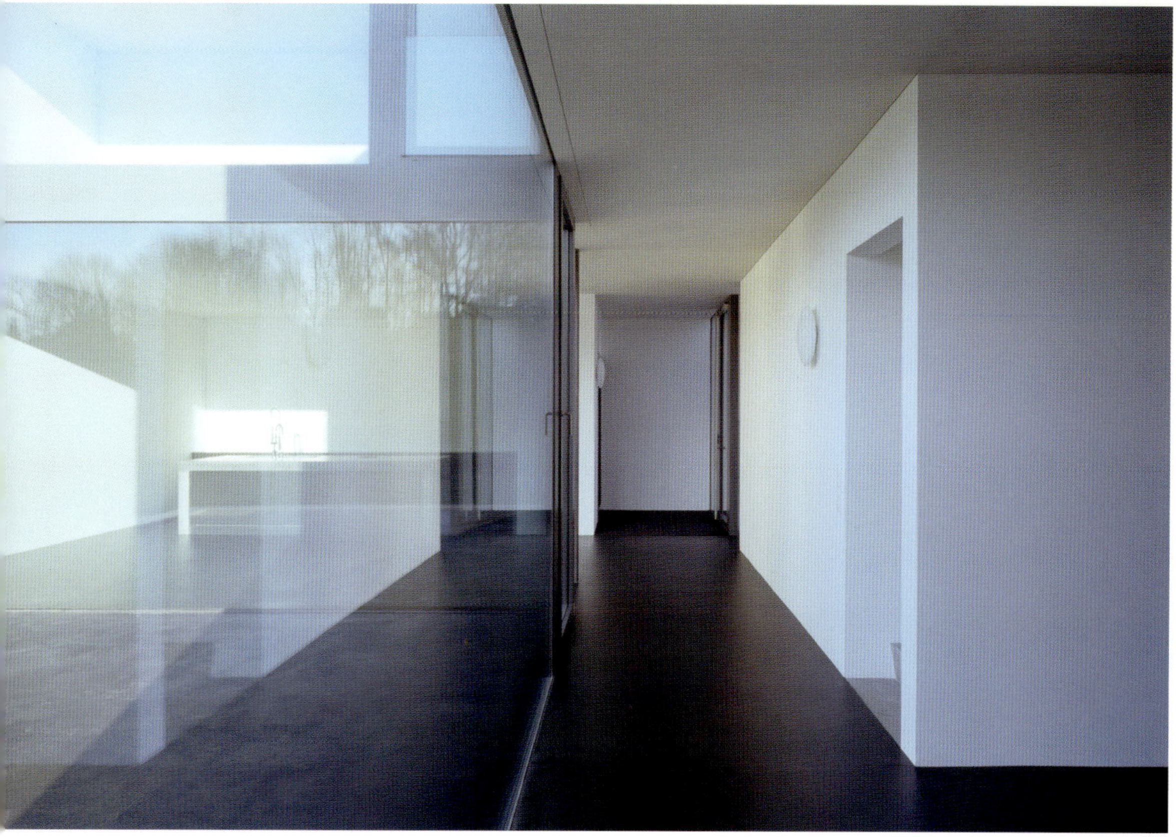

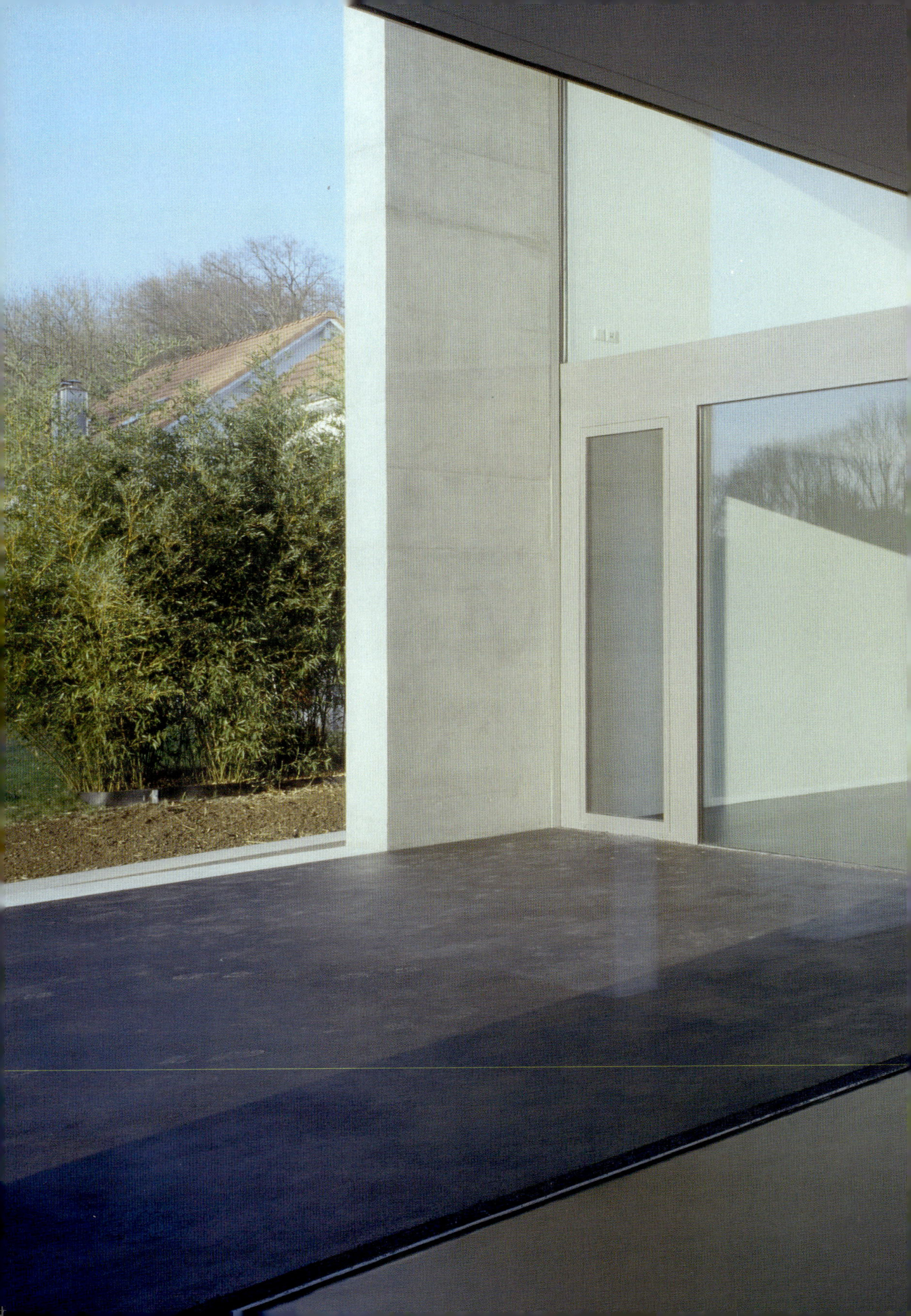

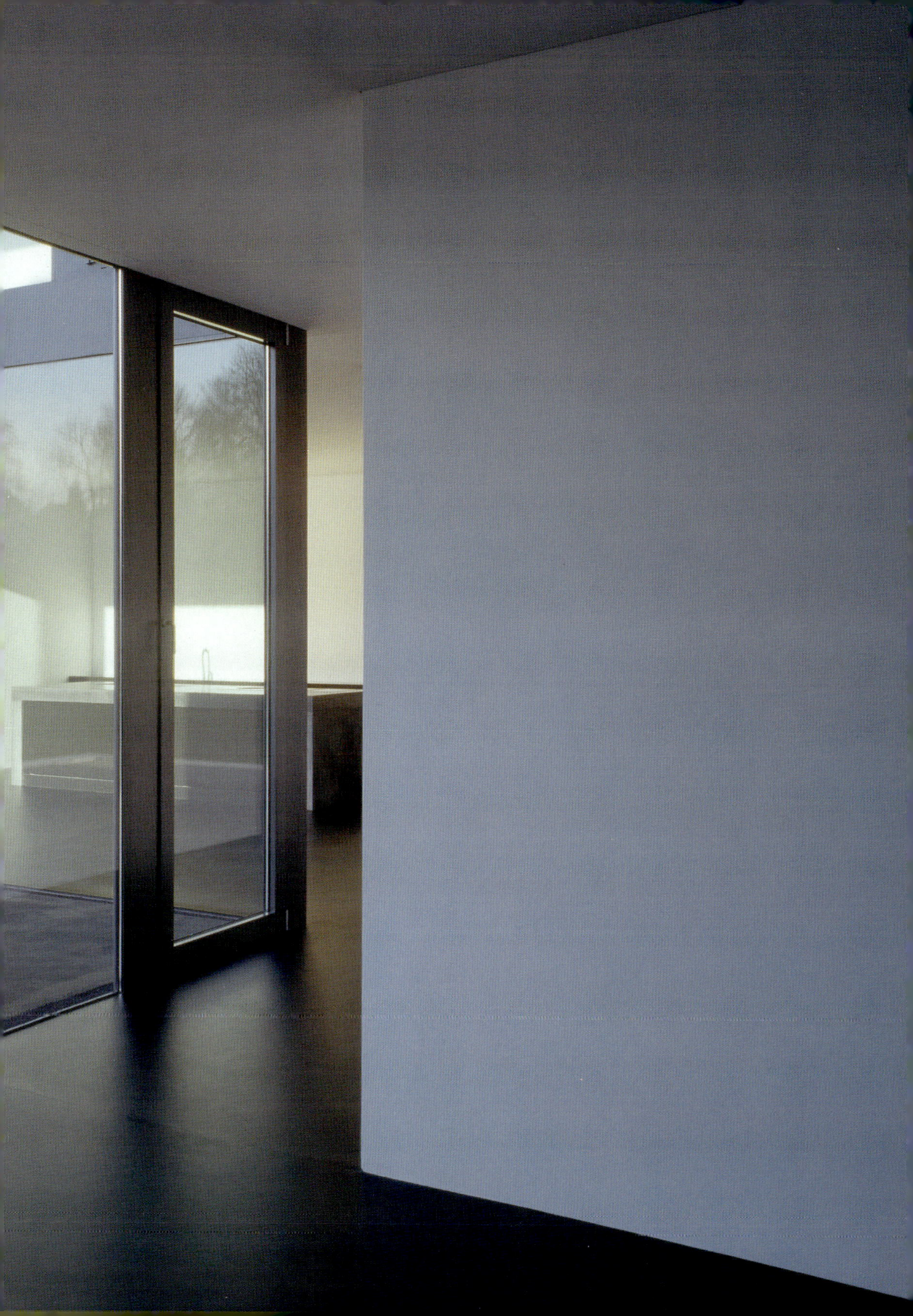

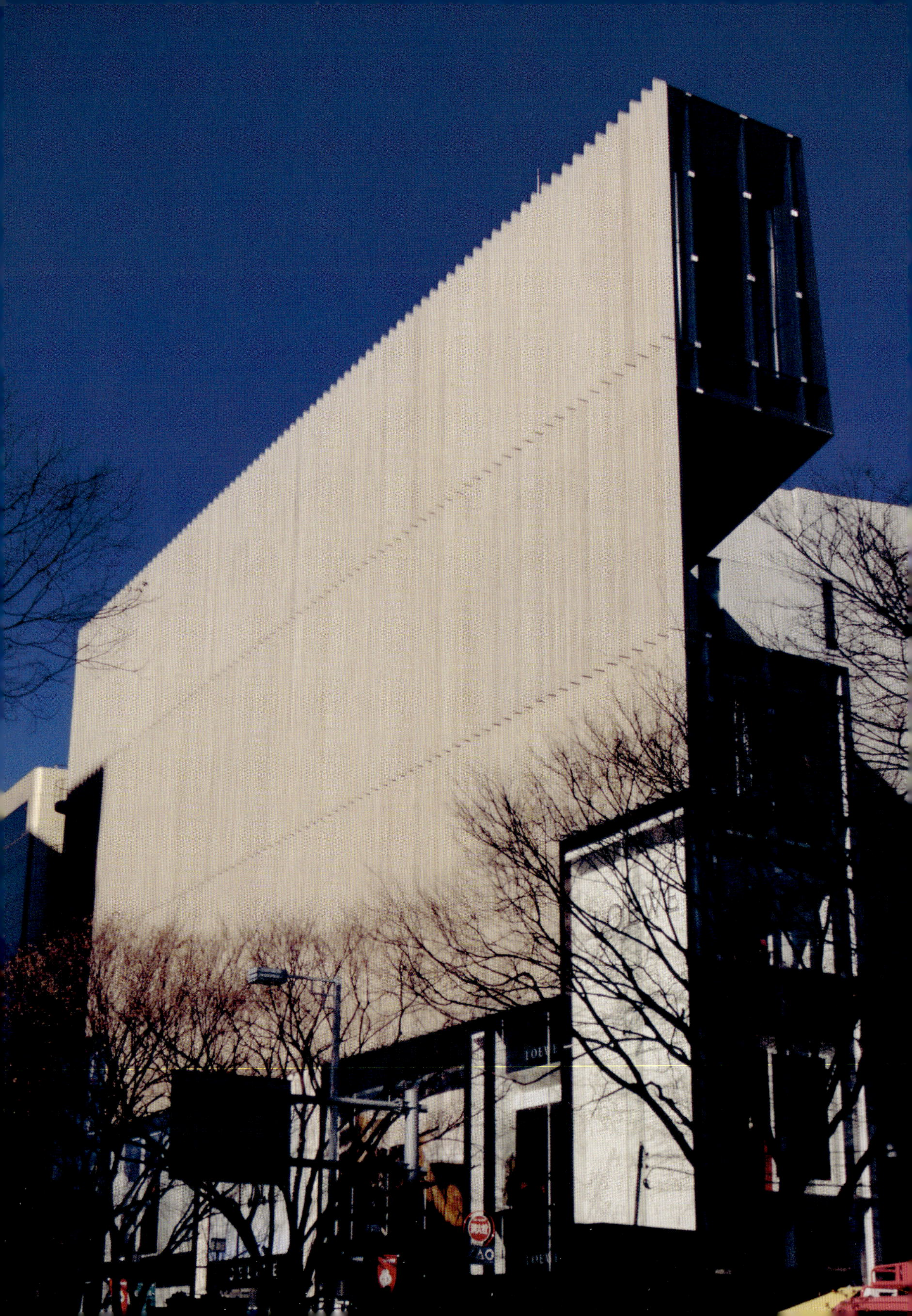
LOEWE

KENGO KUMA & ASSOCIATES | TOKYO
LVMH Omotesando
Tokyo, Japan | 2003

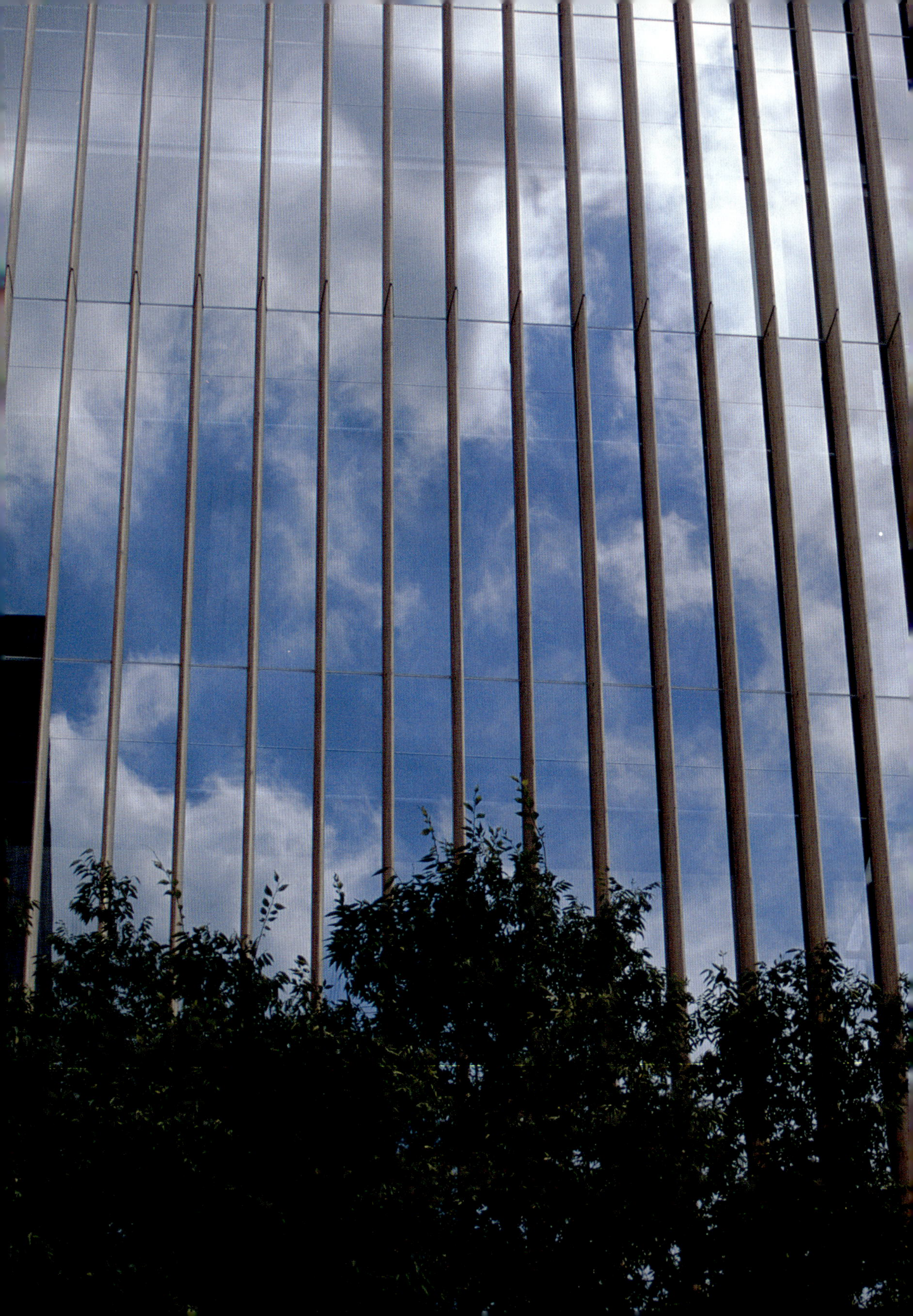

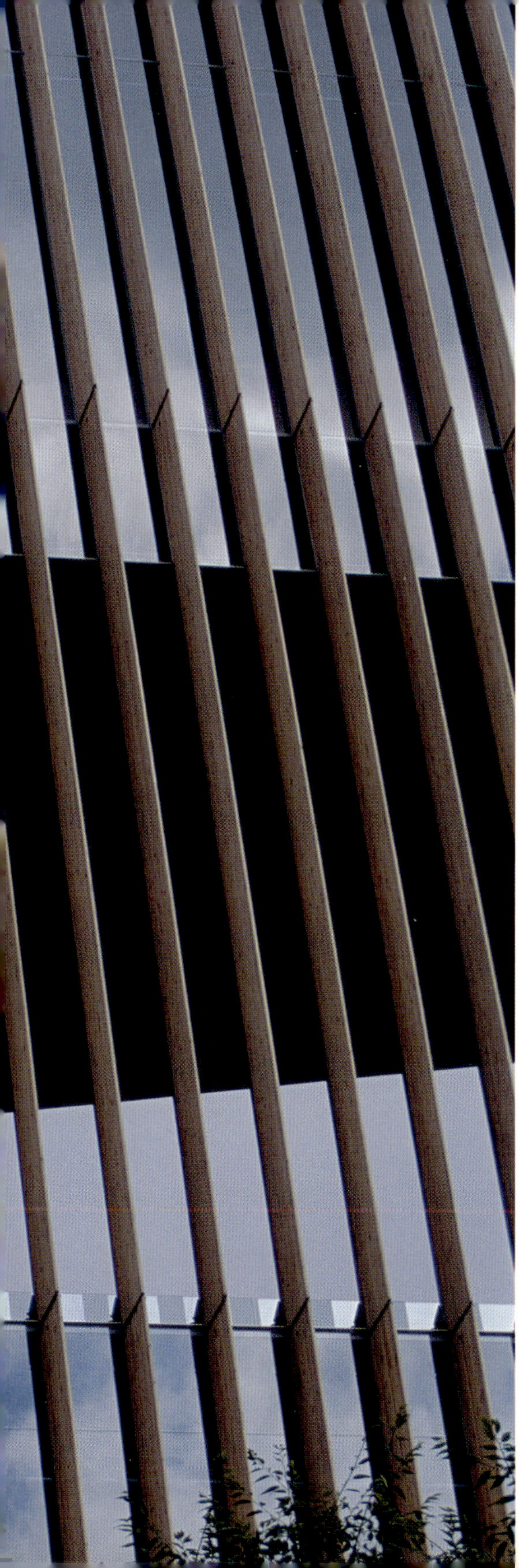

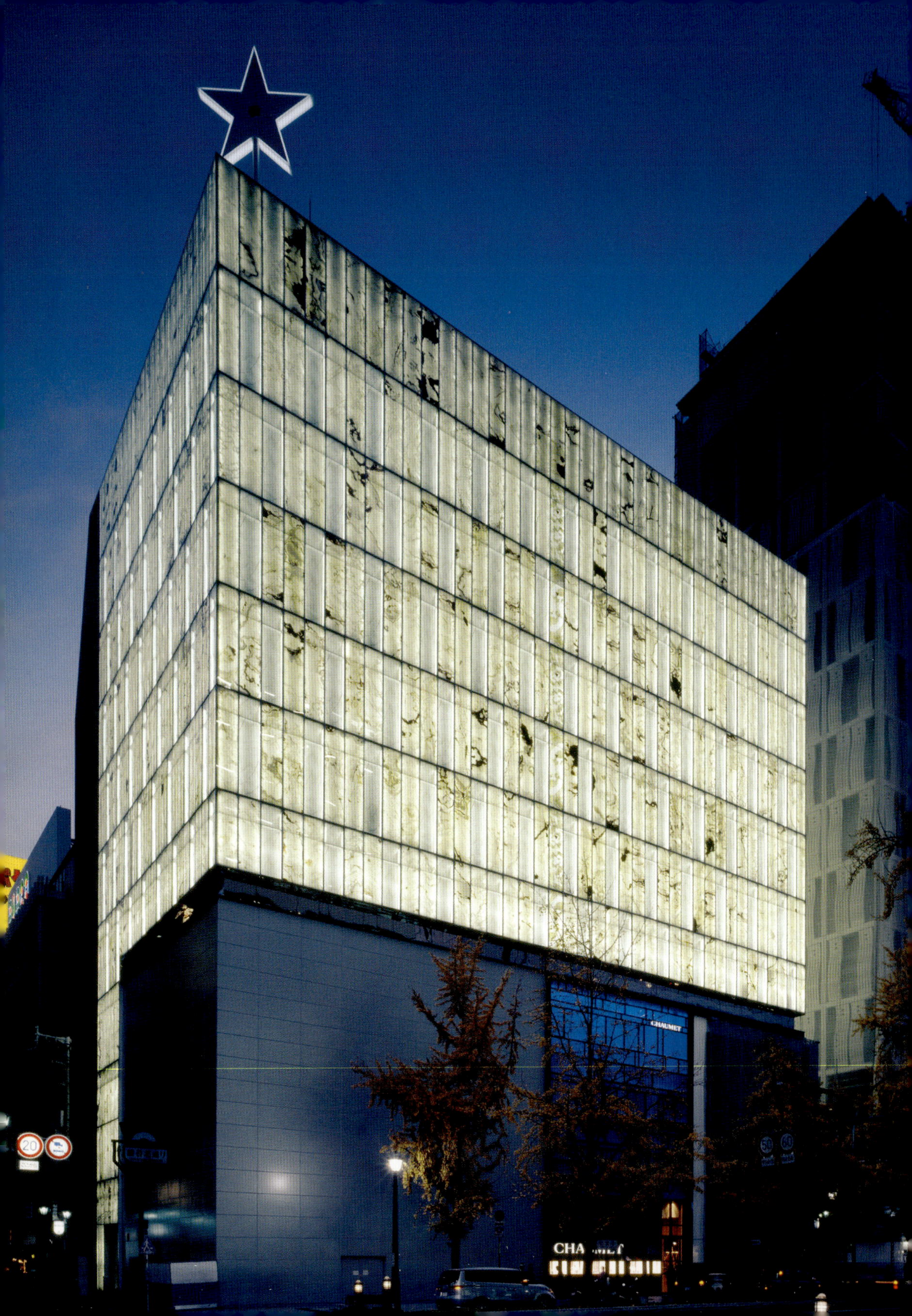
CHAUMET

KENGO KUMA & ASSOCIATES | TOKYO
LVMH Osaka
Chuo, Japan | 2004

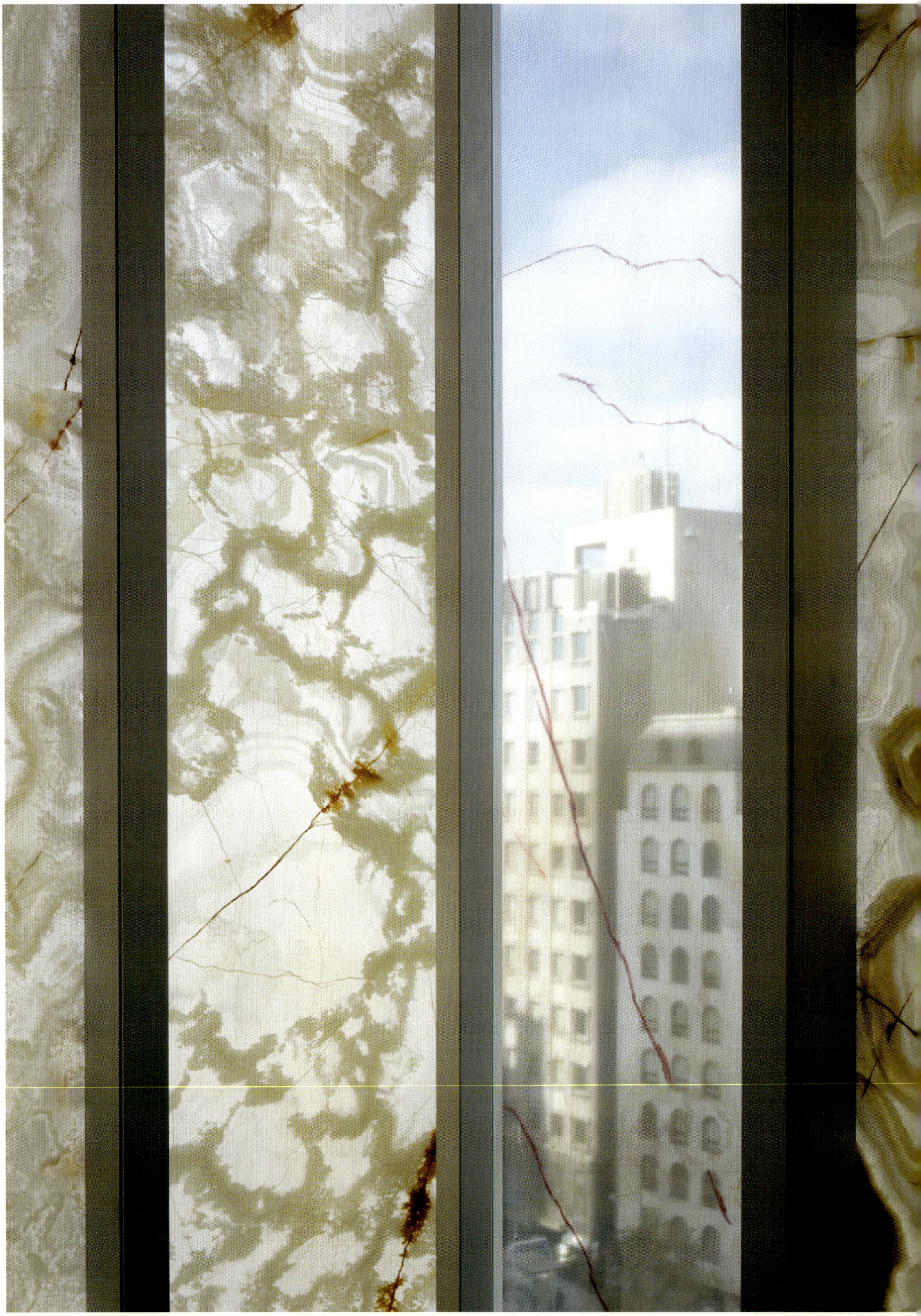

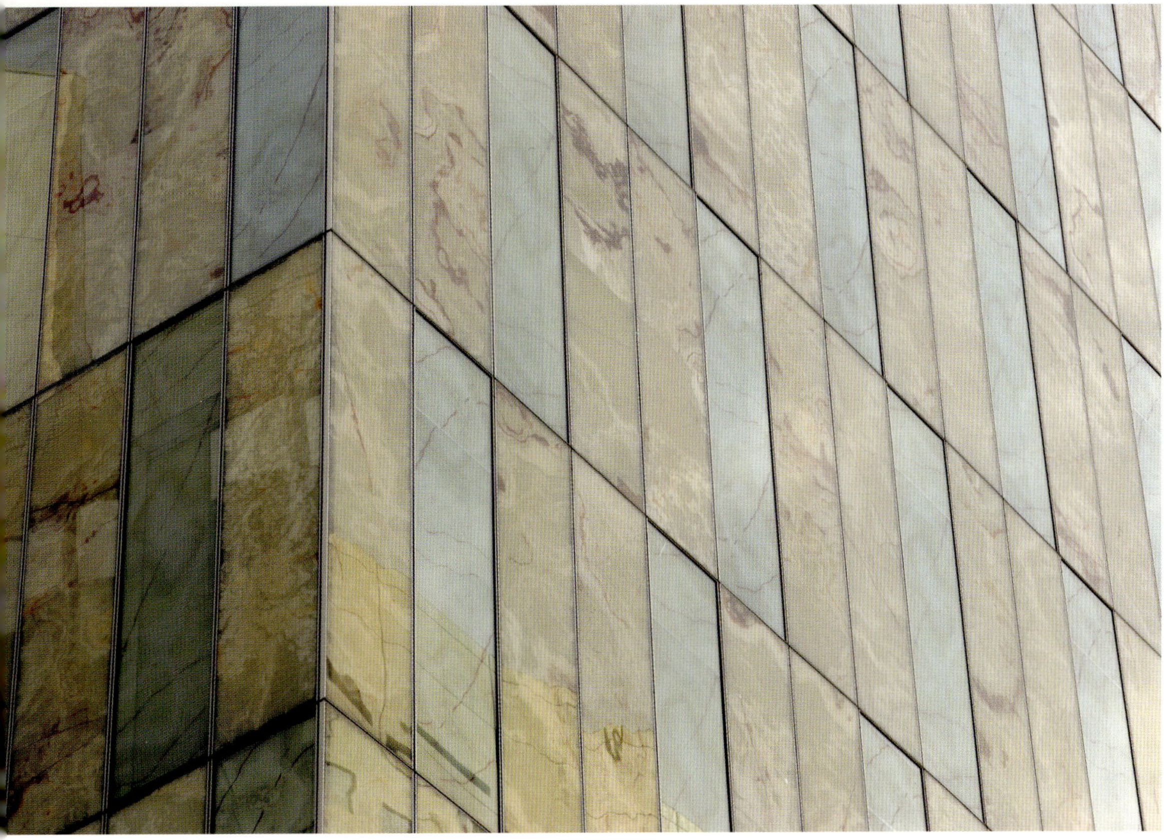

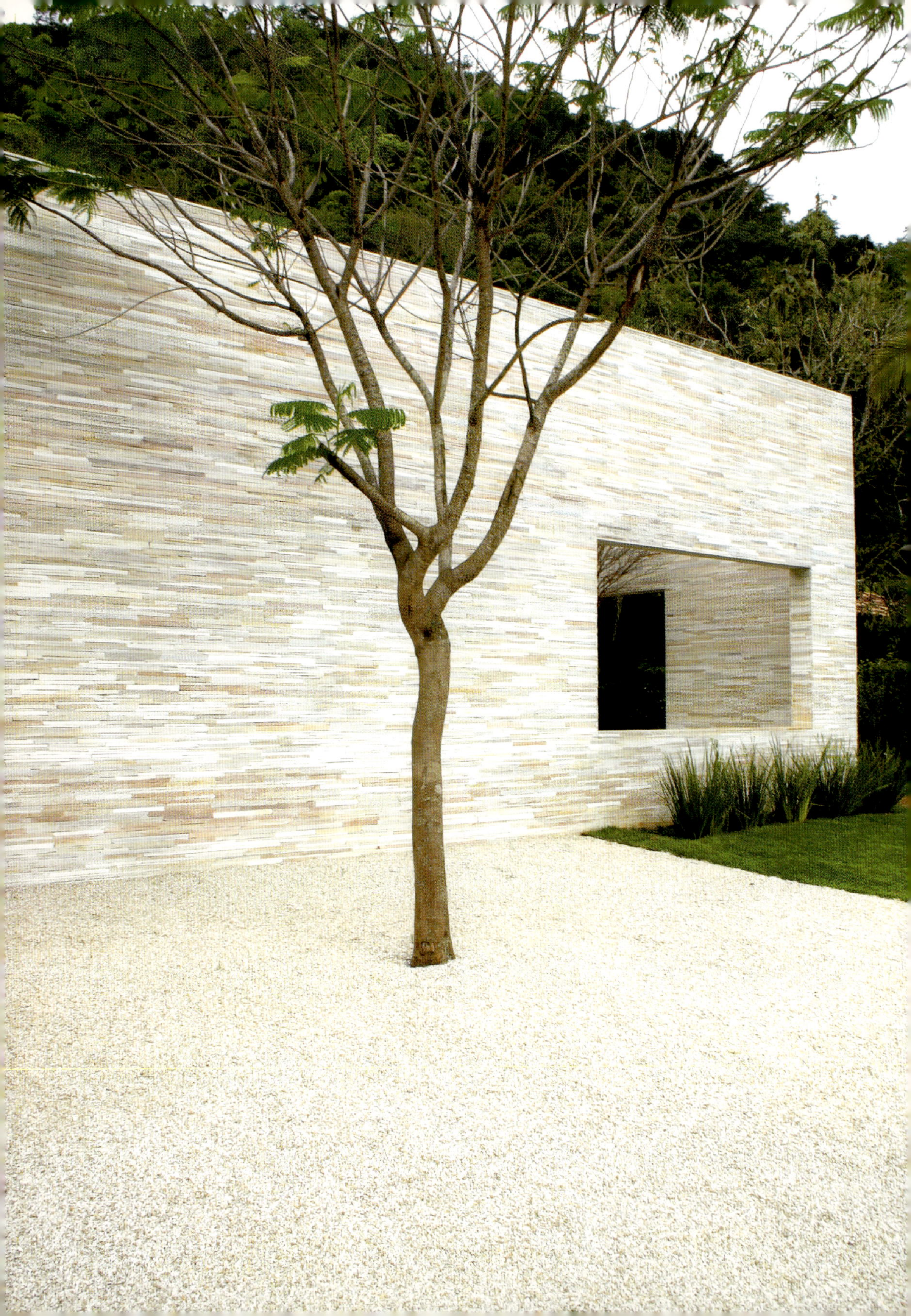

MARCIO KOGAN | SAO PAOLO
Du Plessis House
Paraty, Rio de Janero, Brasil | 2003

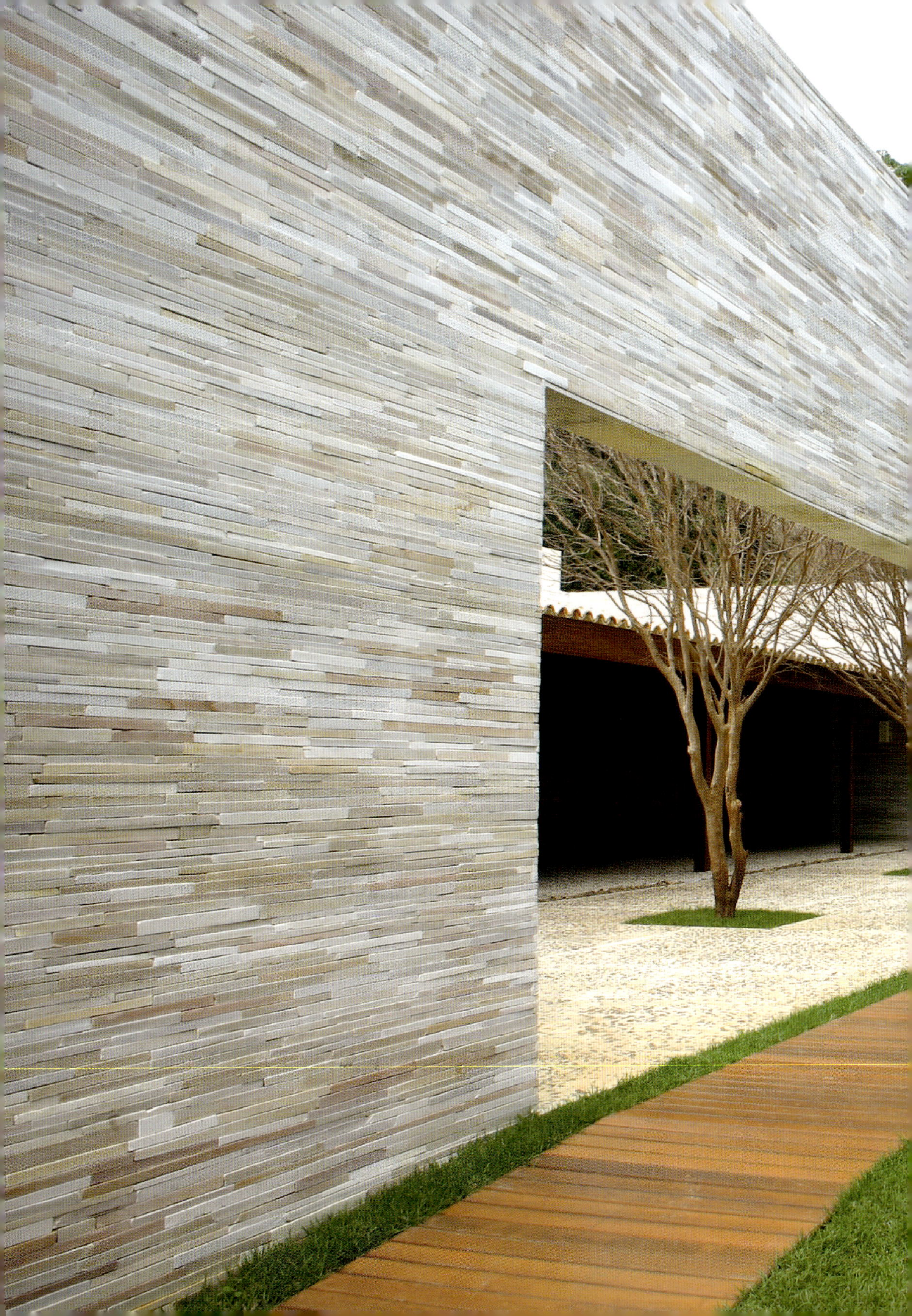

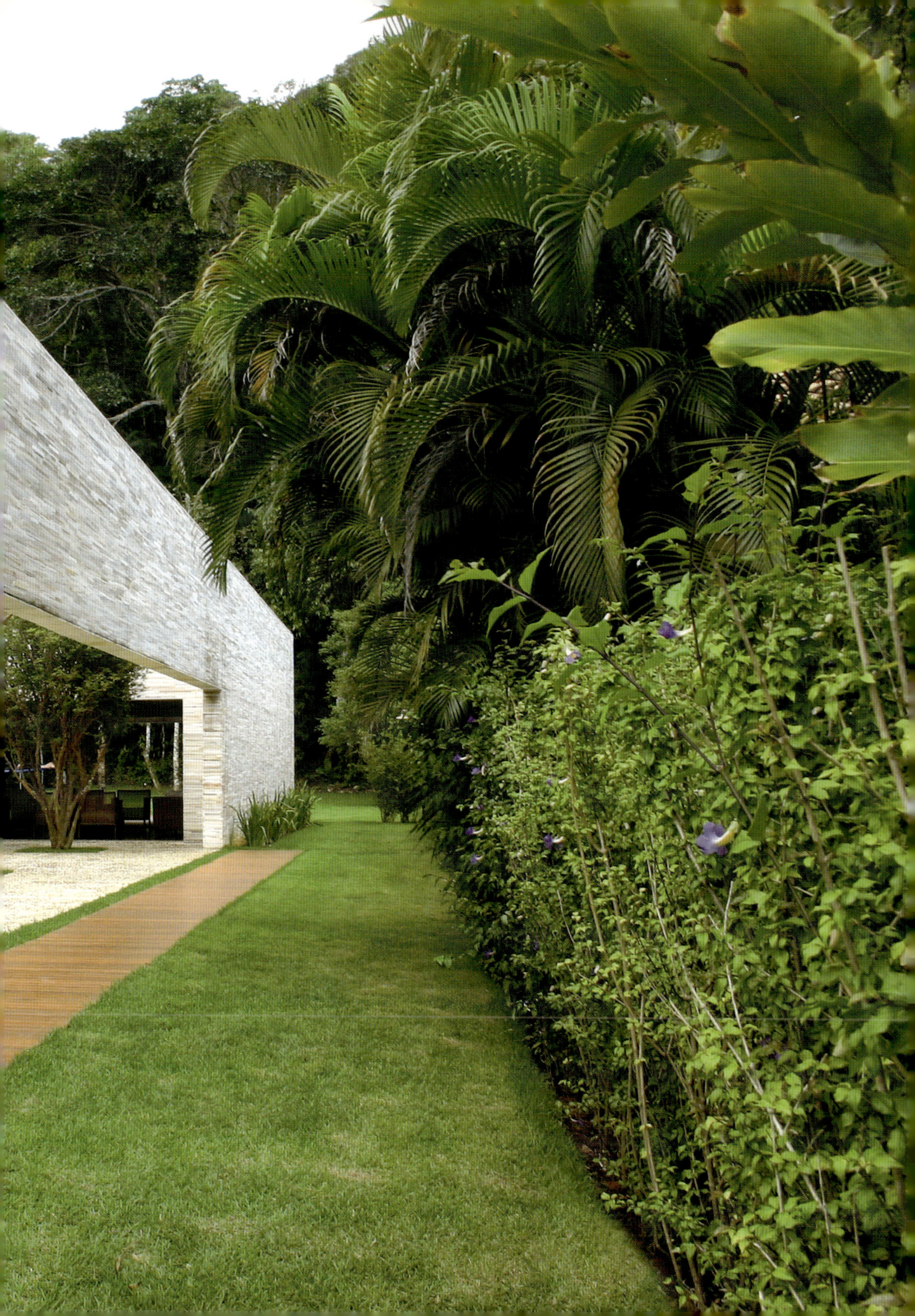

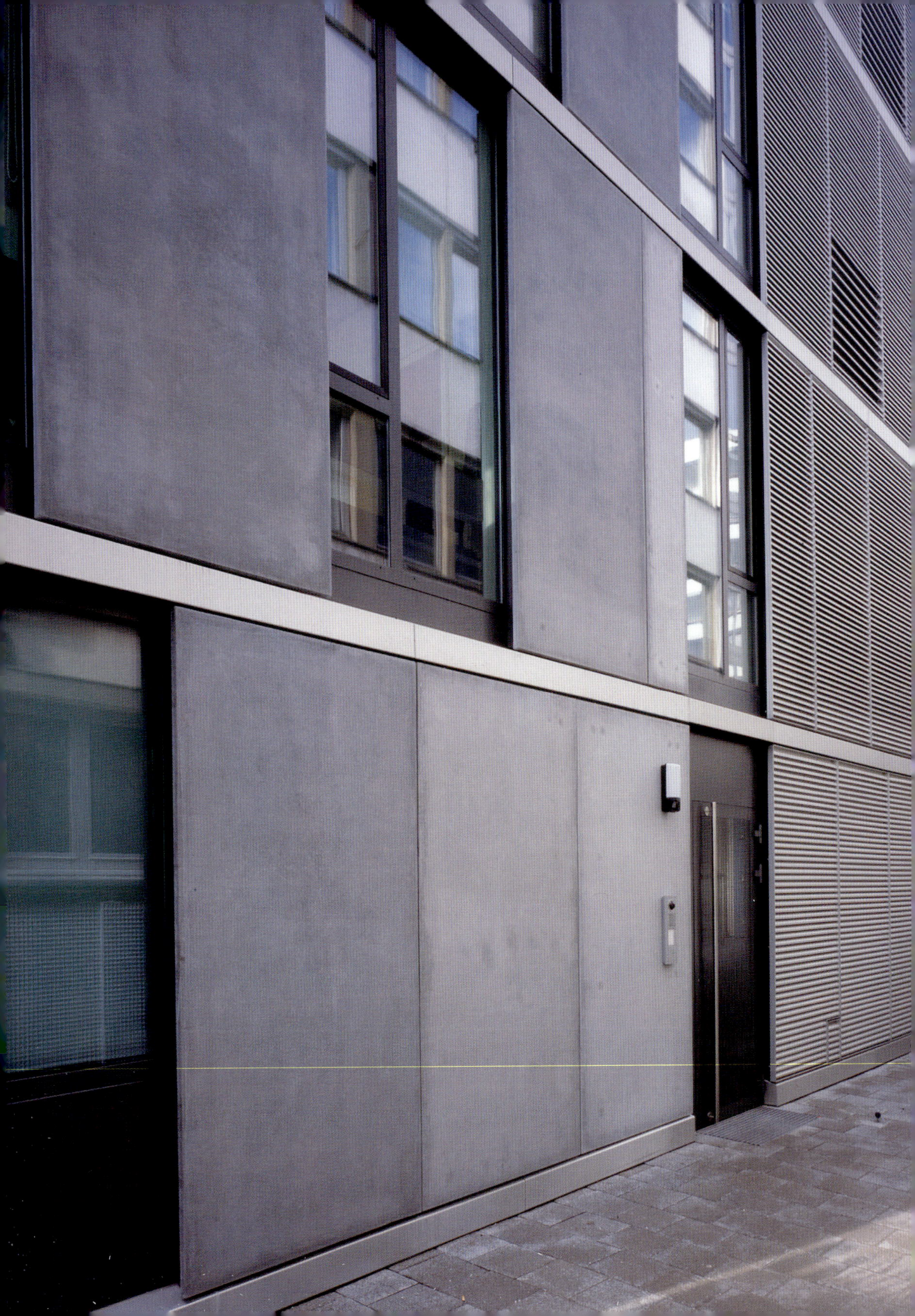

KSP ENGEL UND ZIMMERMANN | FRANKFURT
1. Police Station Frankfurt
Frankfurt, Germany | 2004

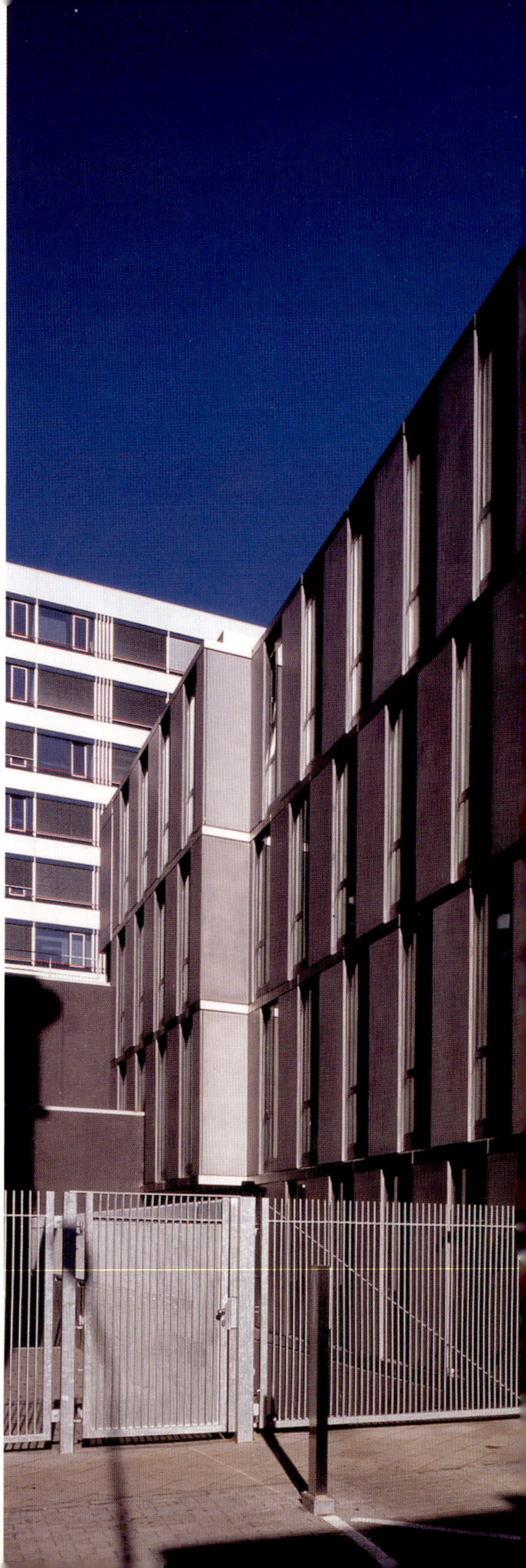

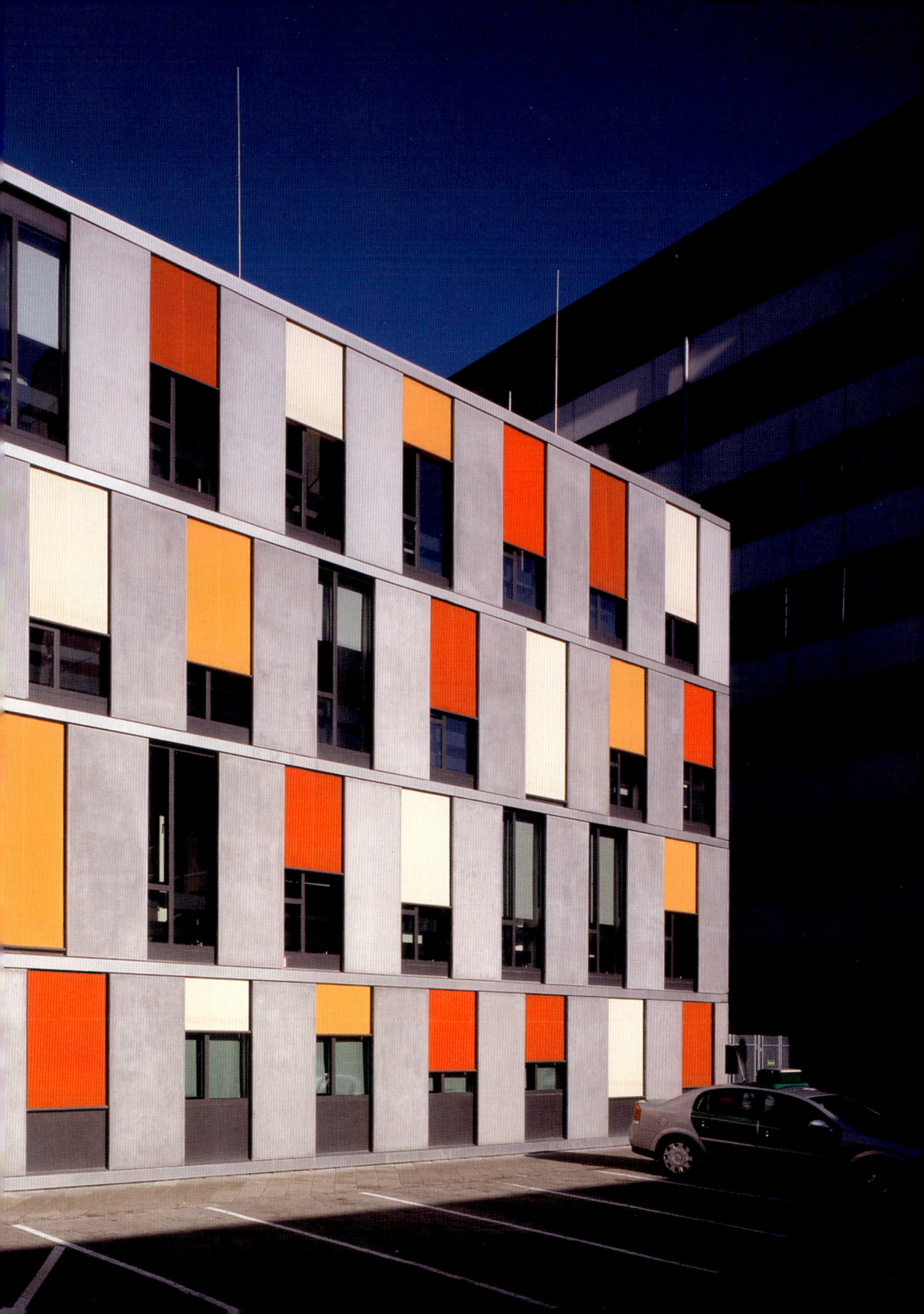

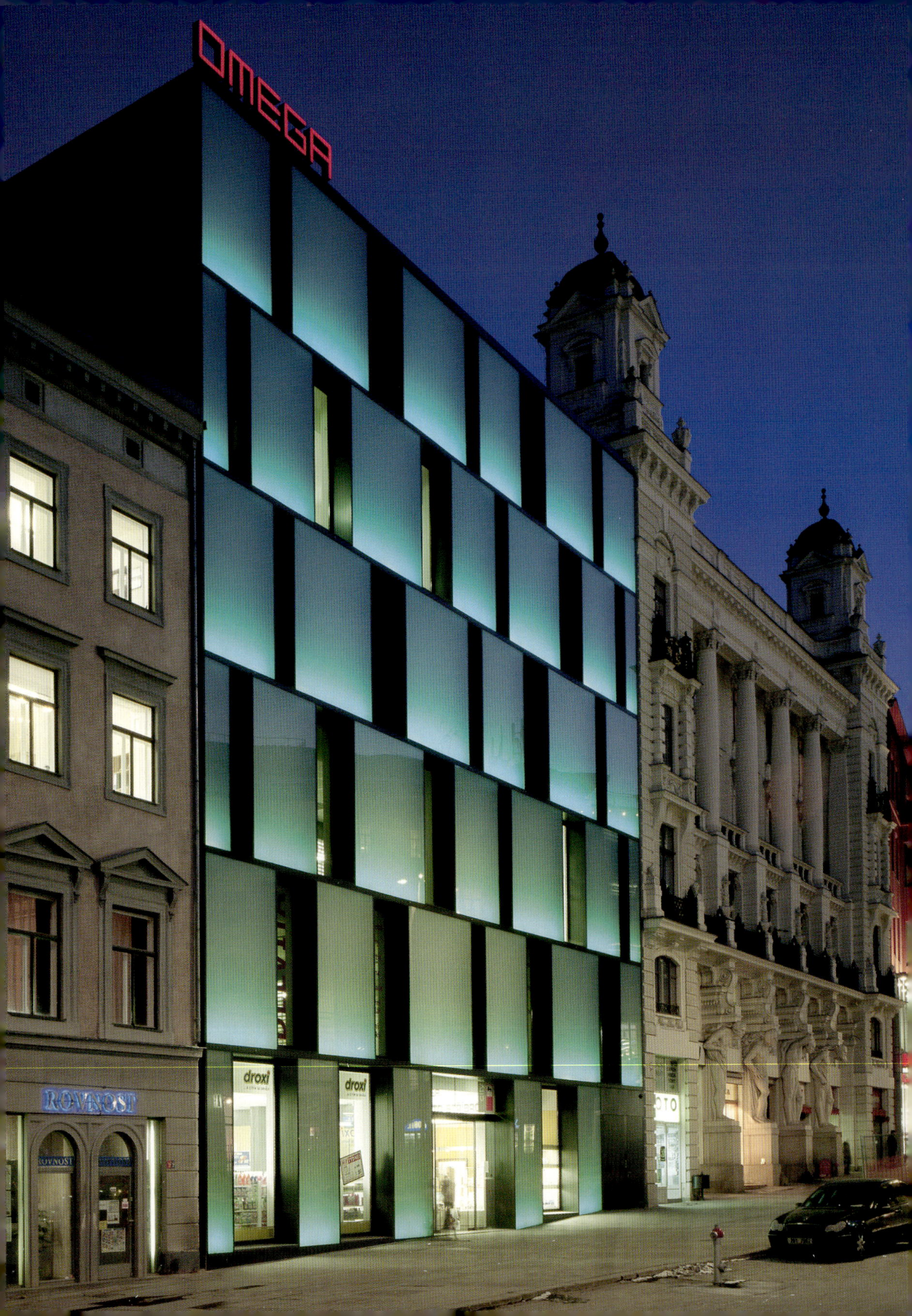
OMEGA
droxi
droxi
ROVNOST

KUBA, PILAŘ ARCHITEKTI | BRNO
Omega Department Store
Brno, Czech Republic | 2005

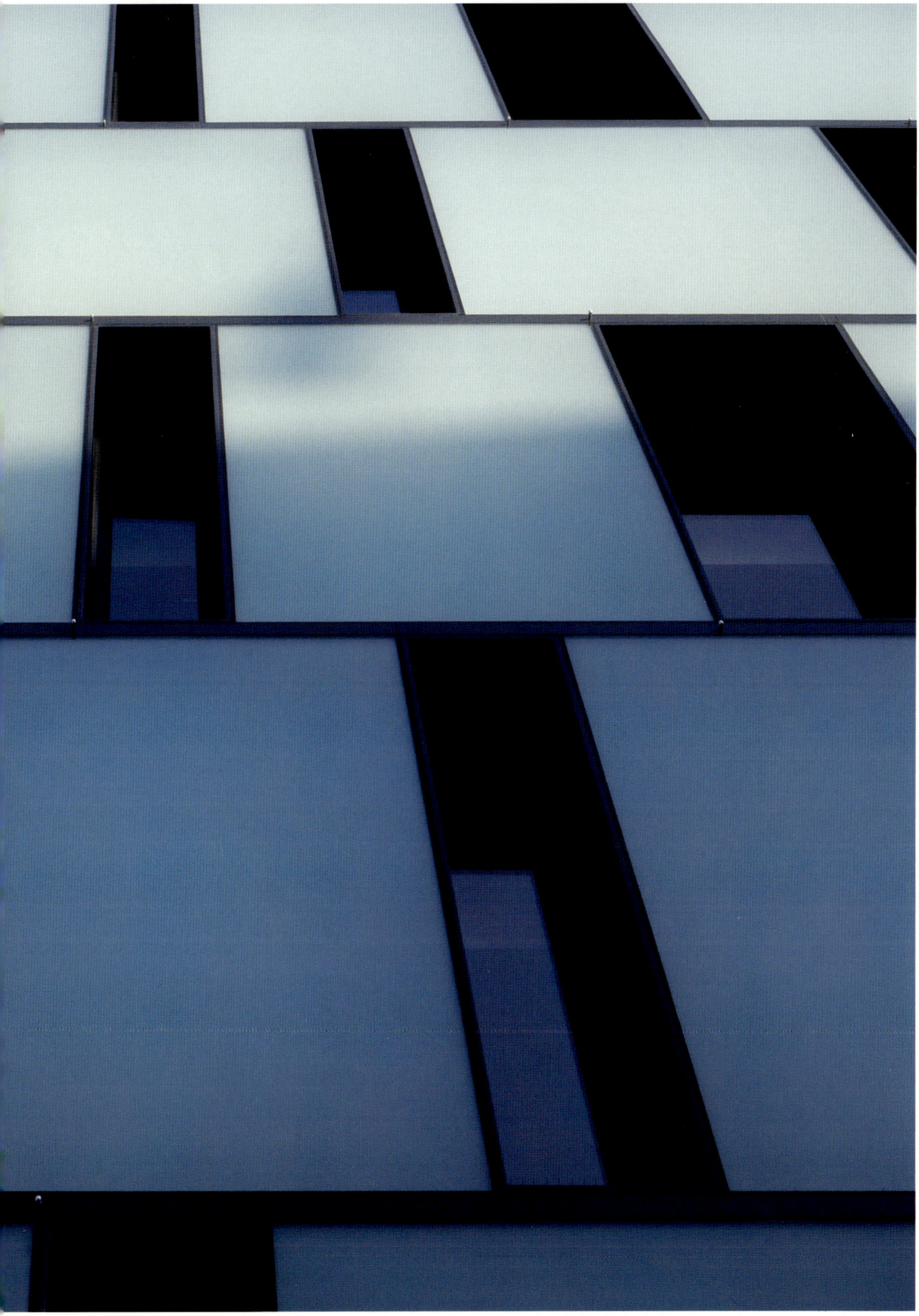

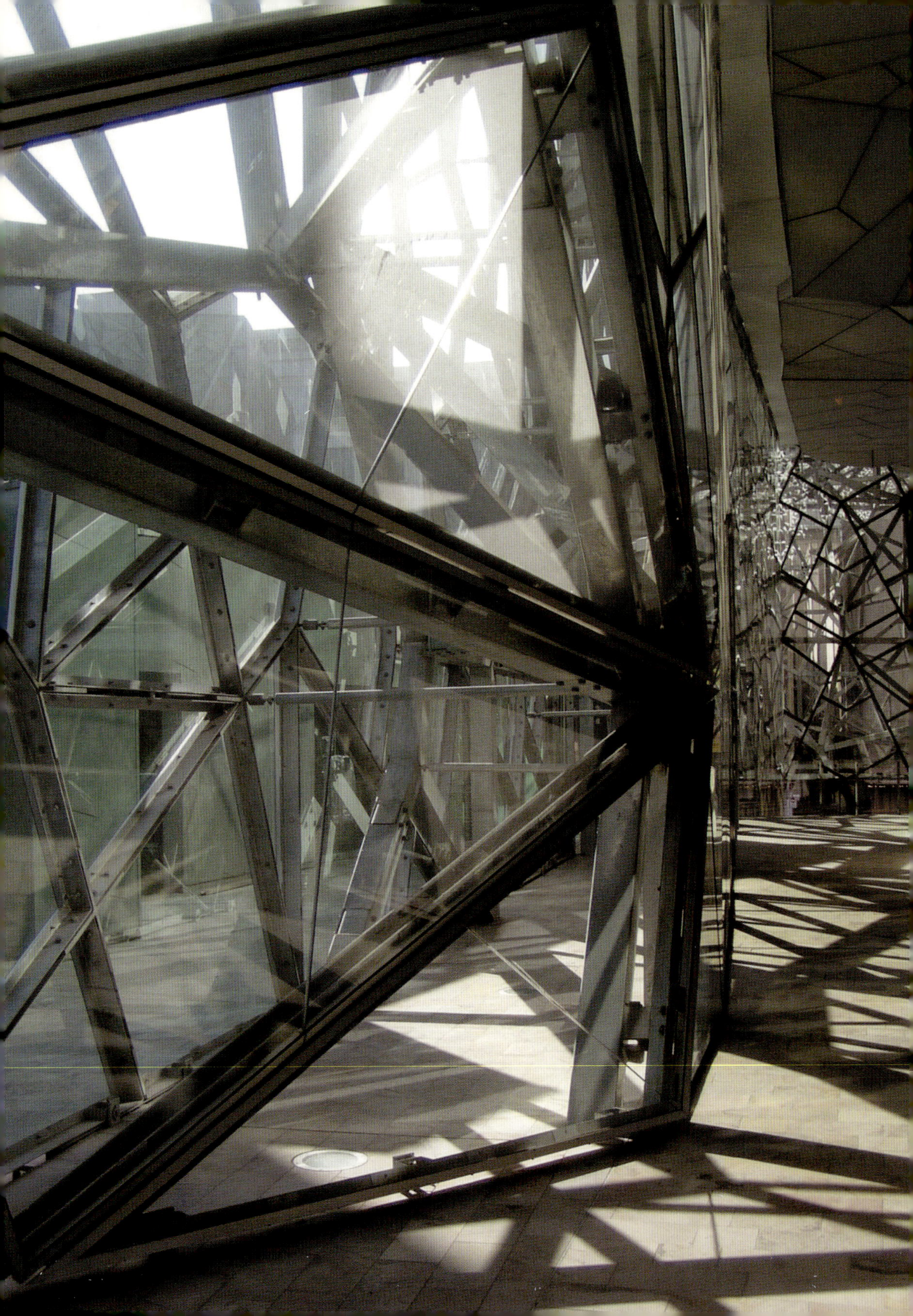

LAB ARCHITECTURE STUDIO | MELBOURNE
Federation Tower
Melbourne, Australia | 2003

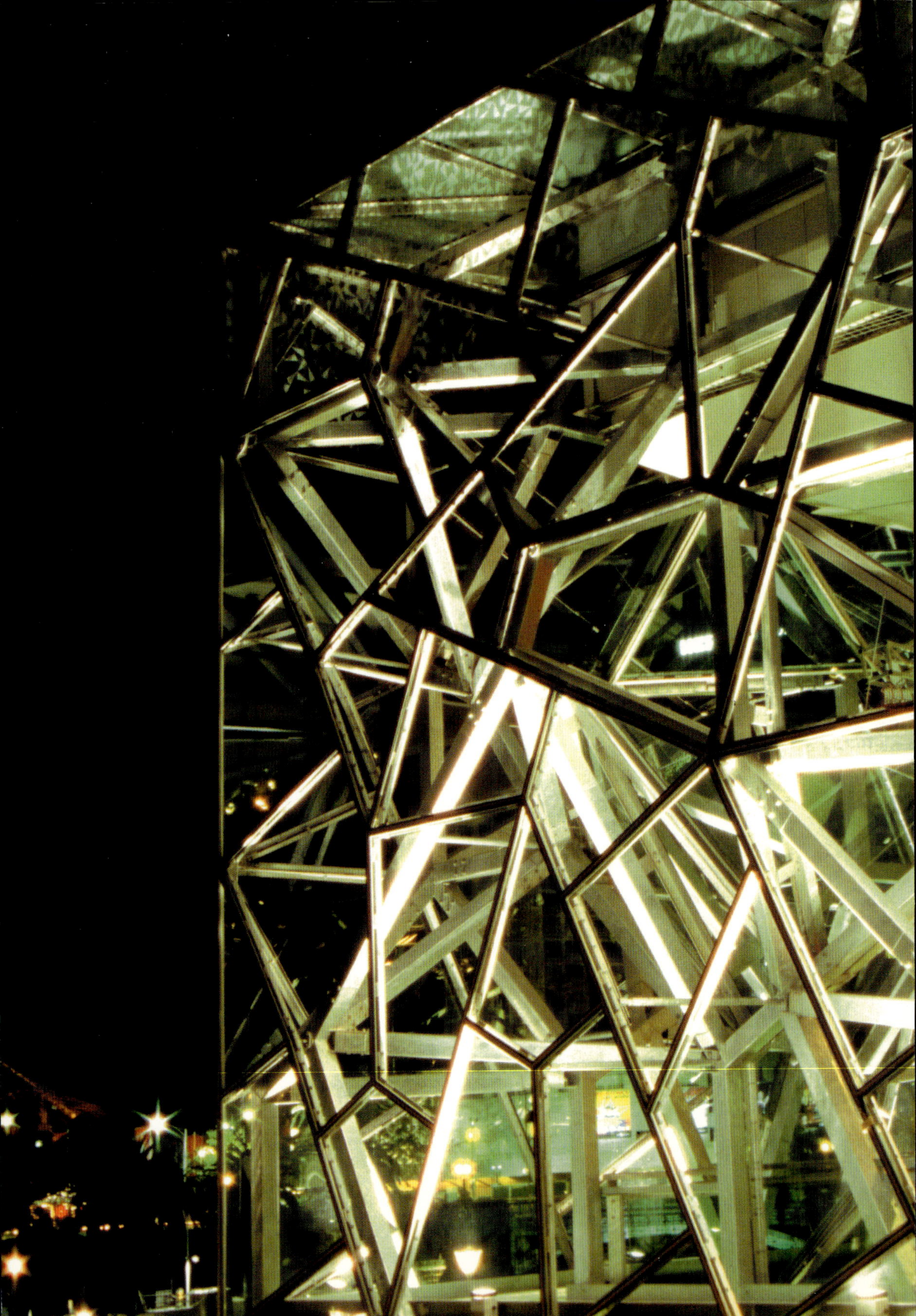

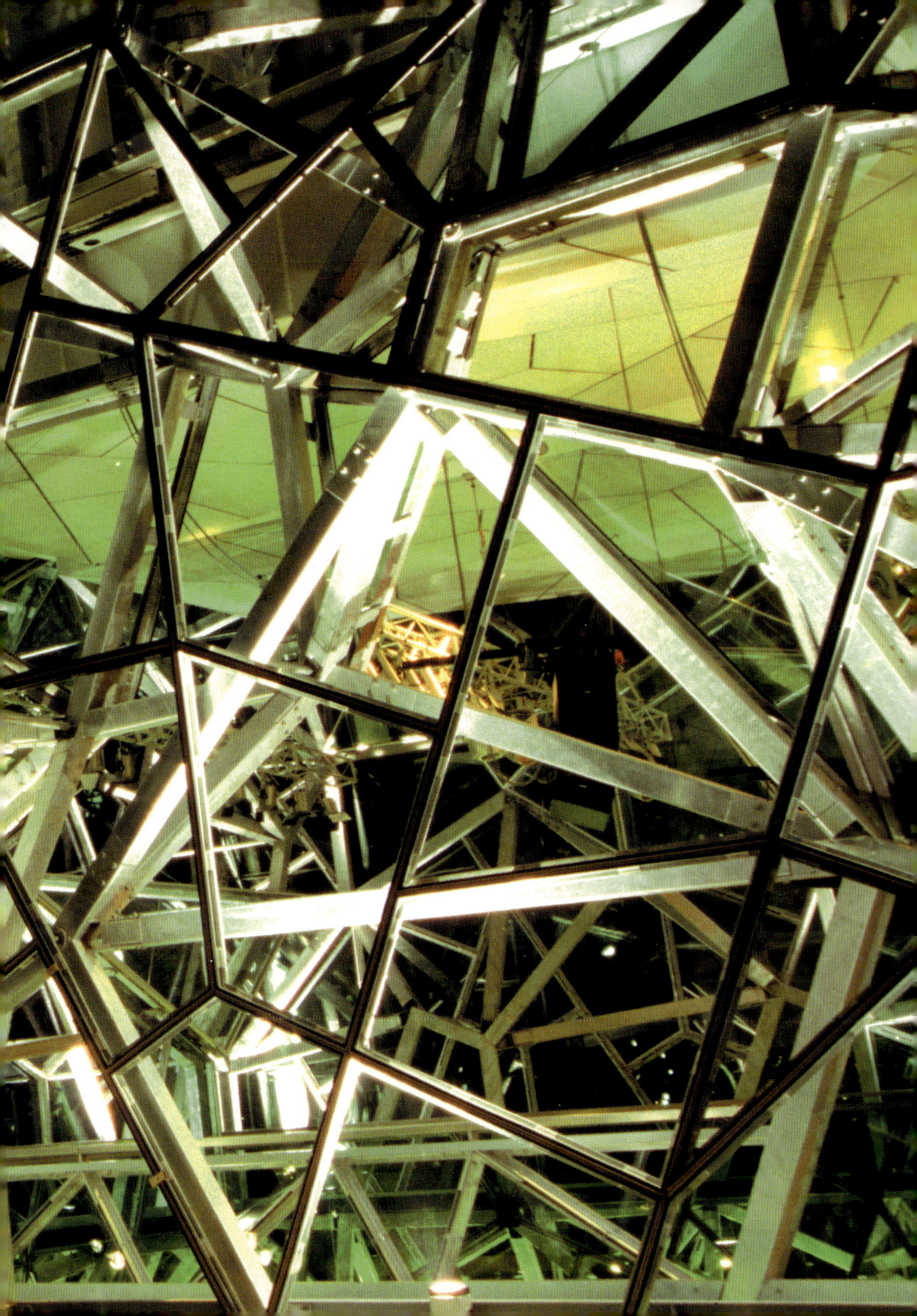

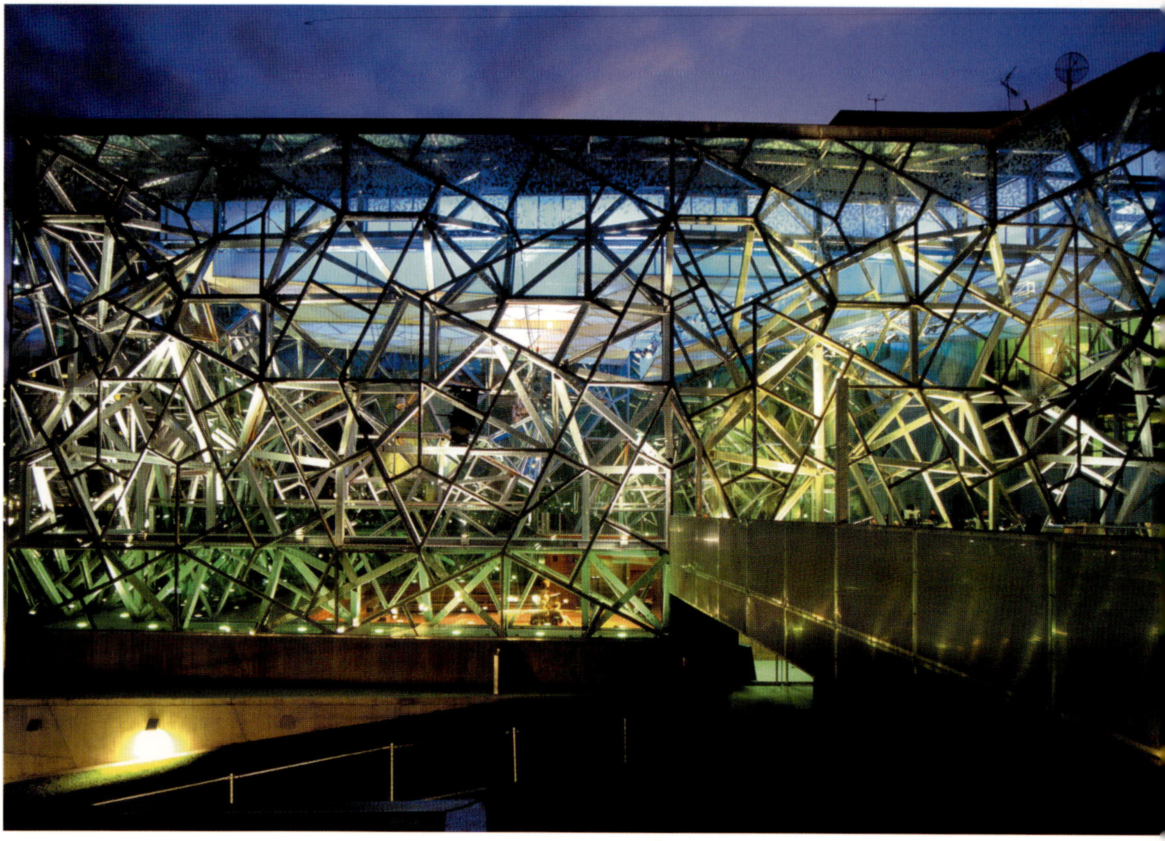

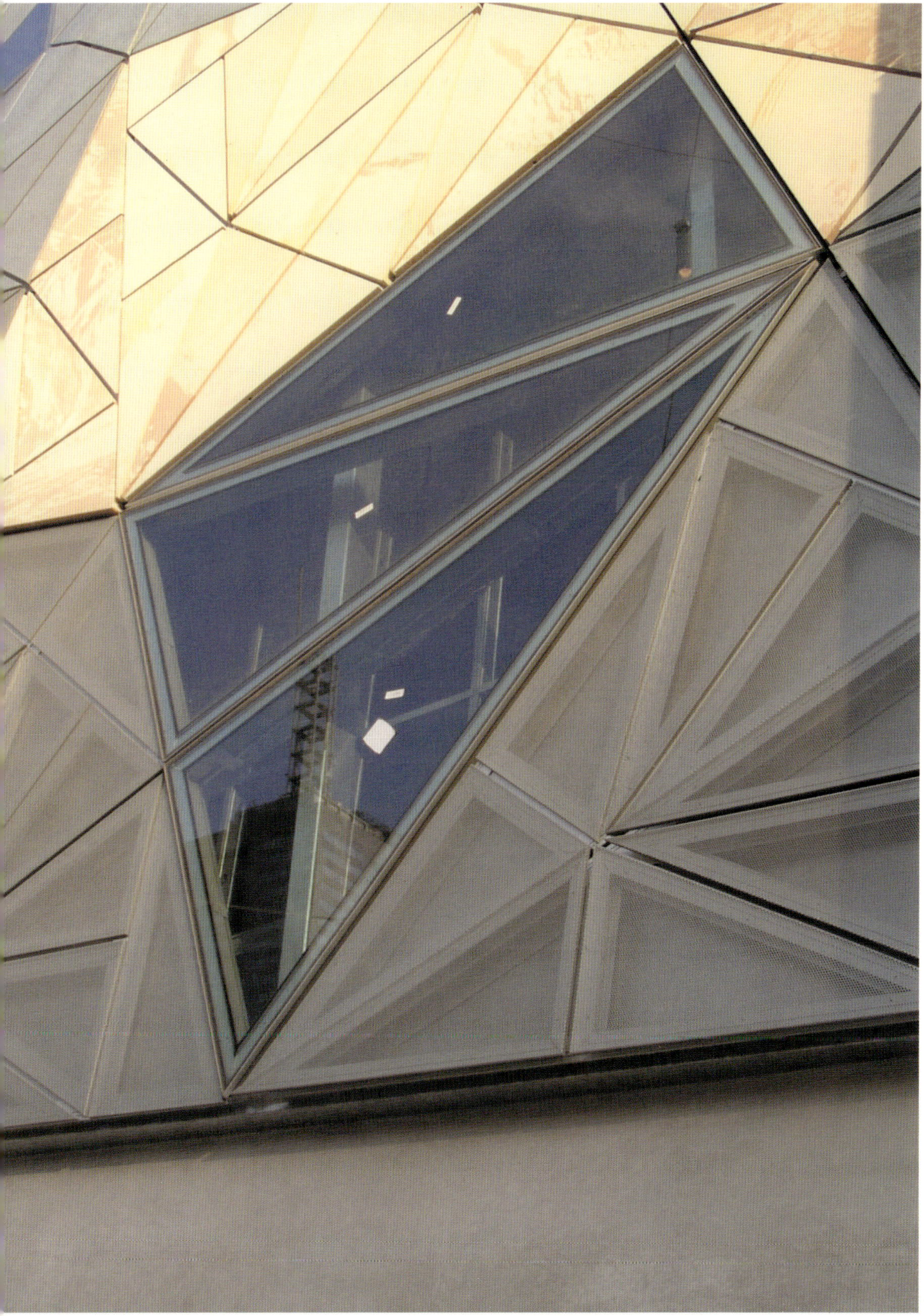

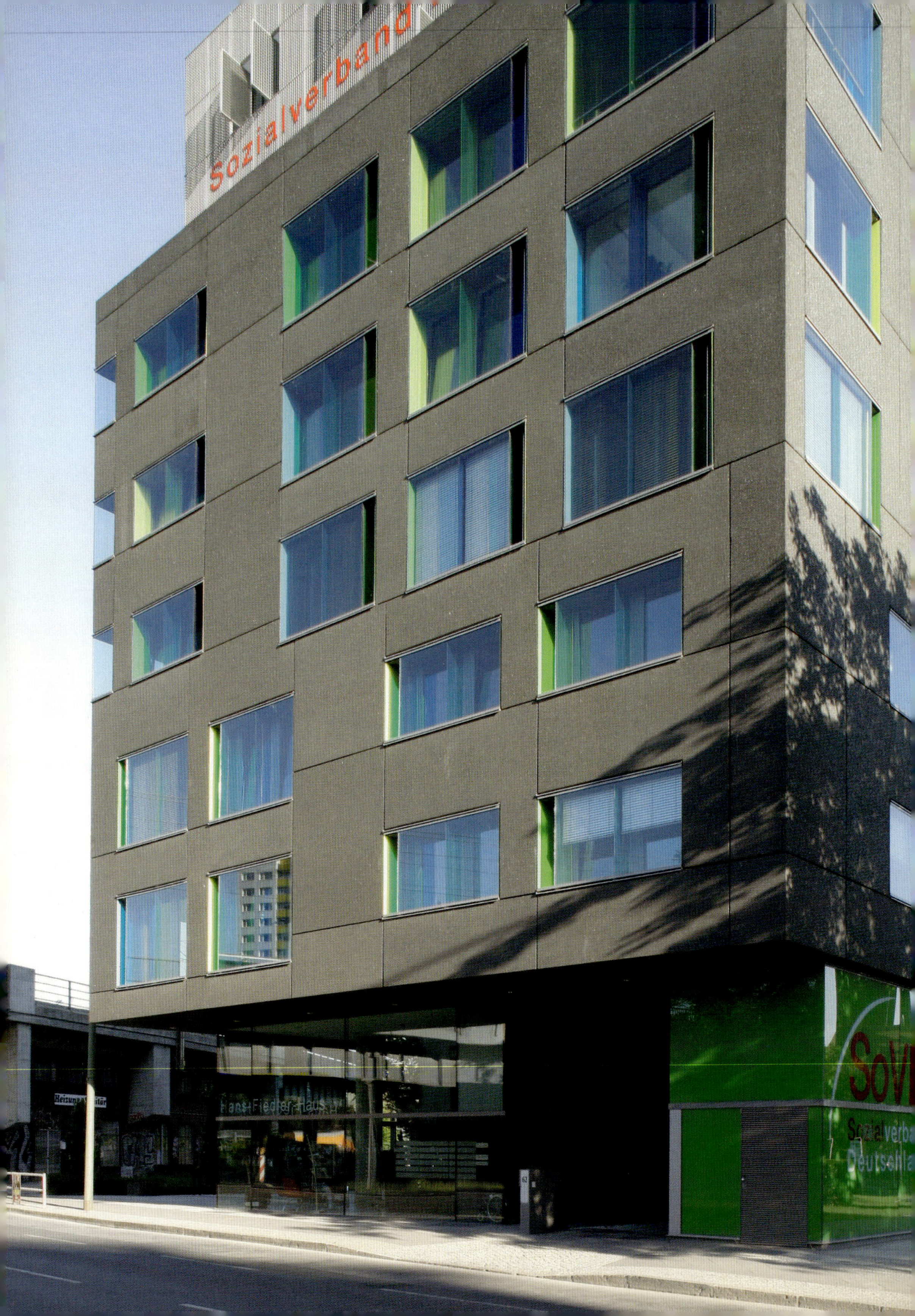
Sozialverband
Hans-Fiedler-Haus

LÉON WOHLHAGE WERNIK ARCHITEKTEN | BERLIN
Administrative center of social alliance Germany
Berlin, Germany | 2003

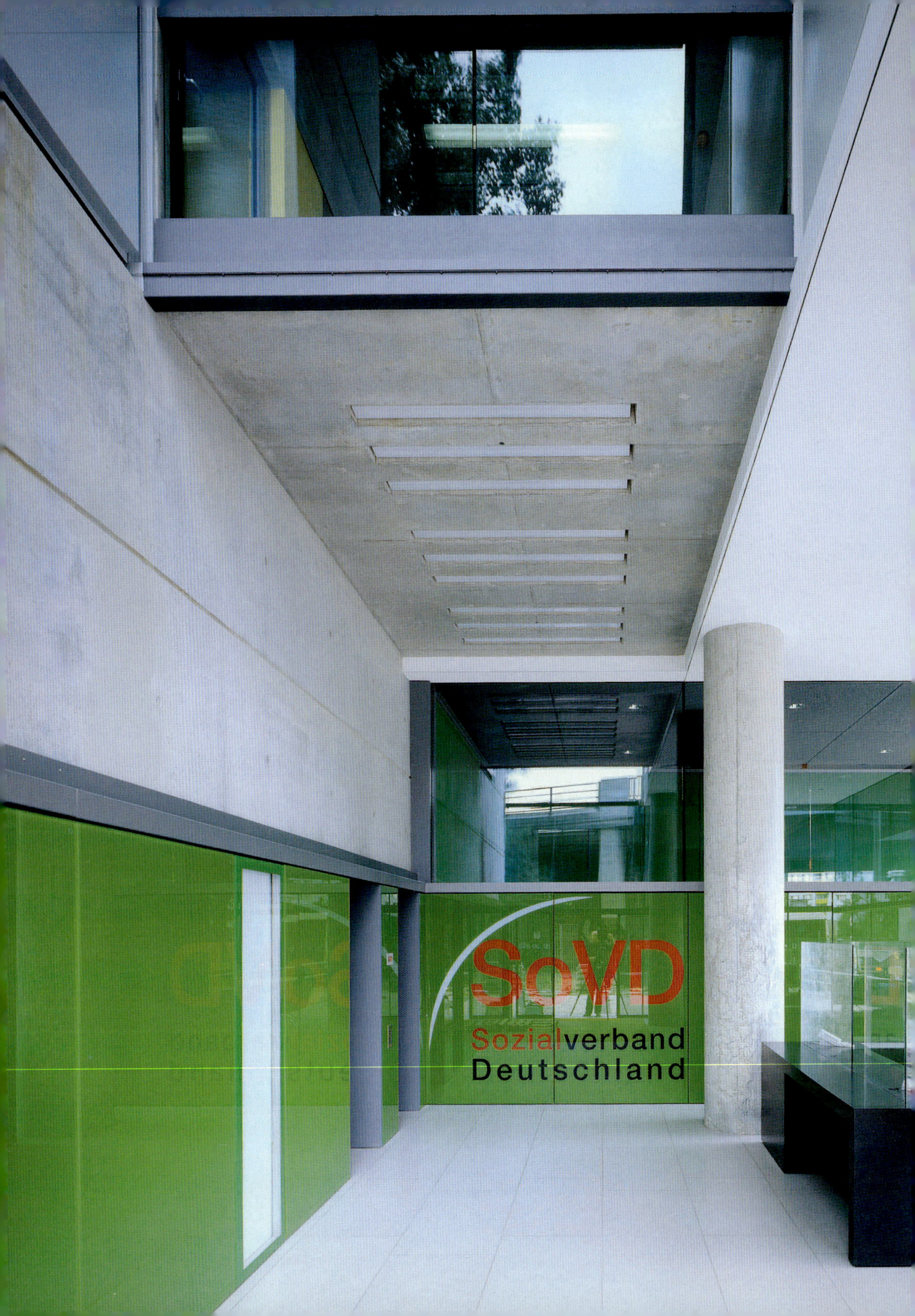
SoVD
Sozialverband
Deutschland

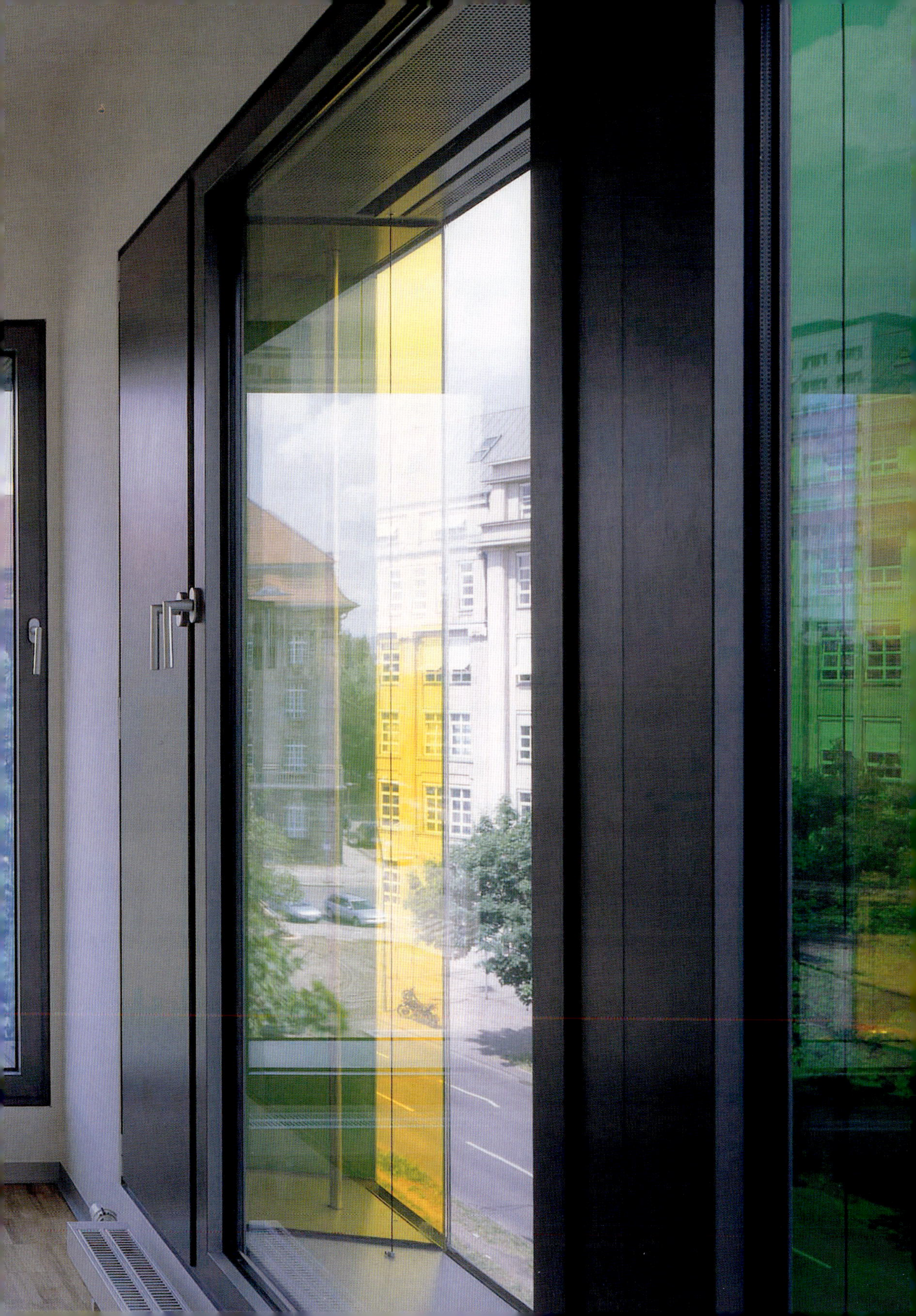

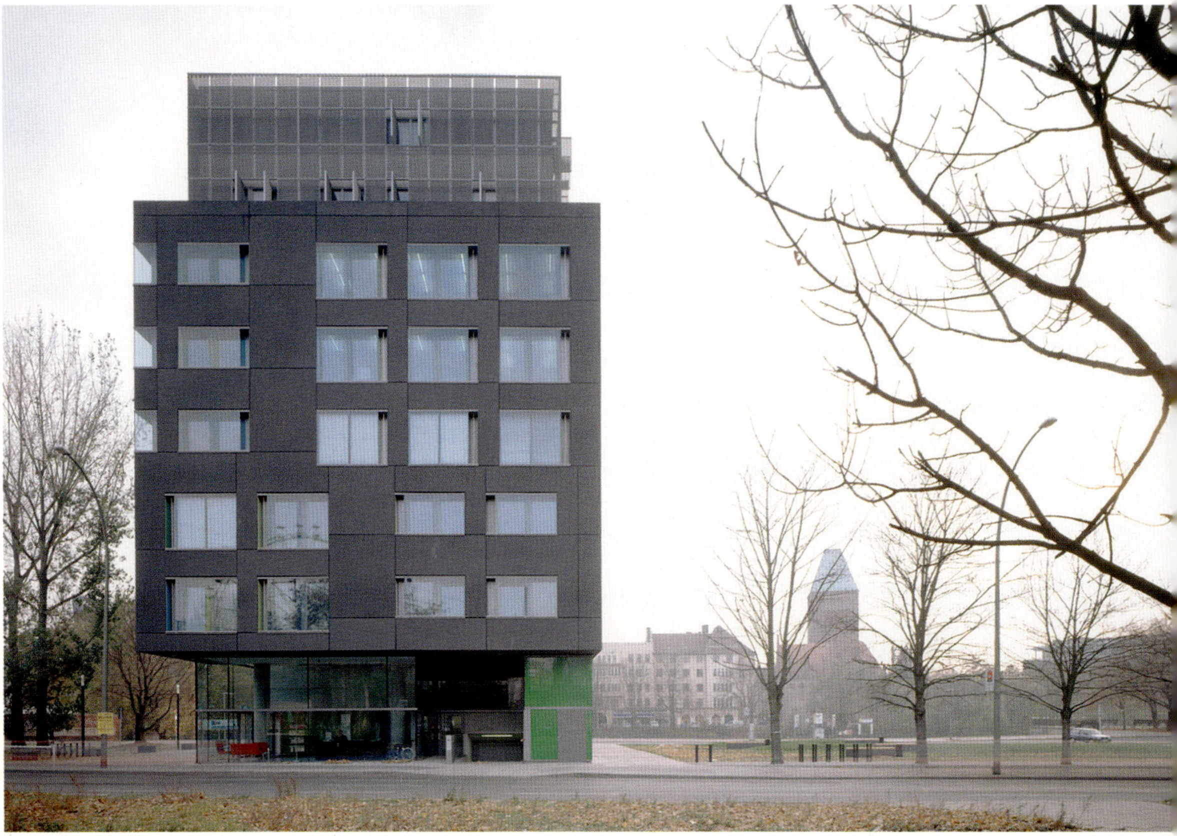

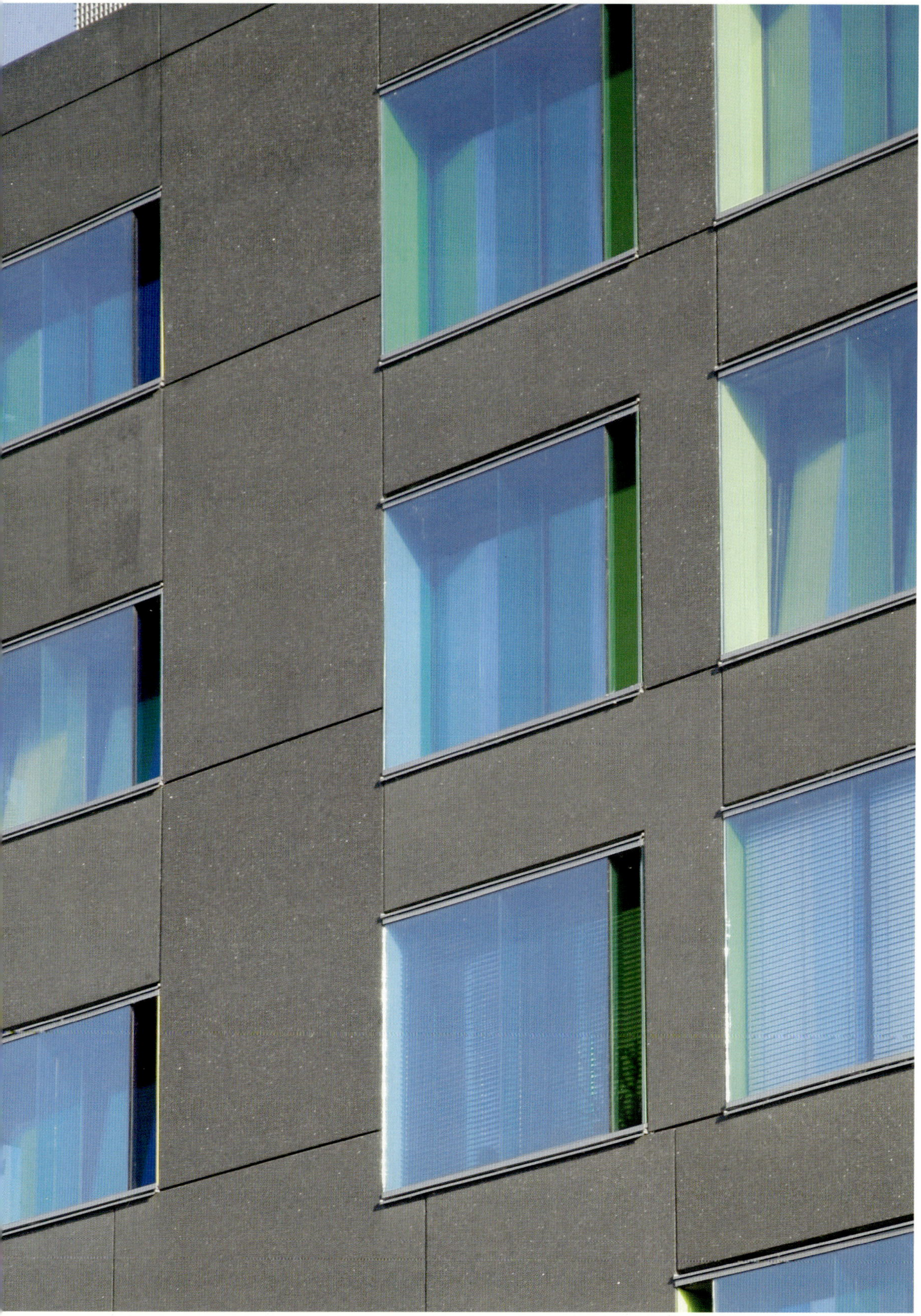

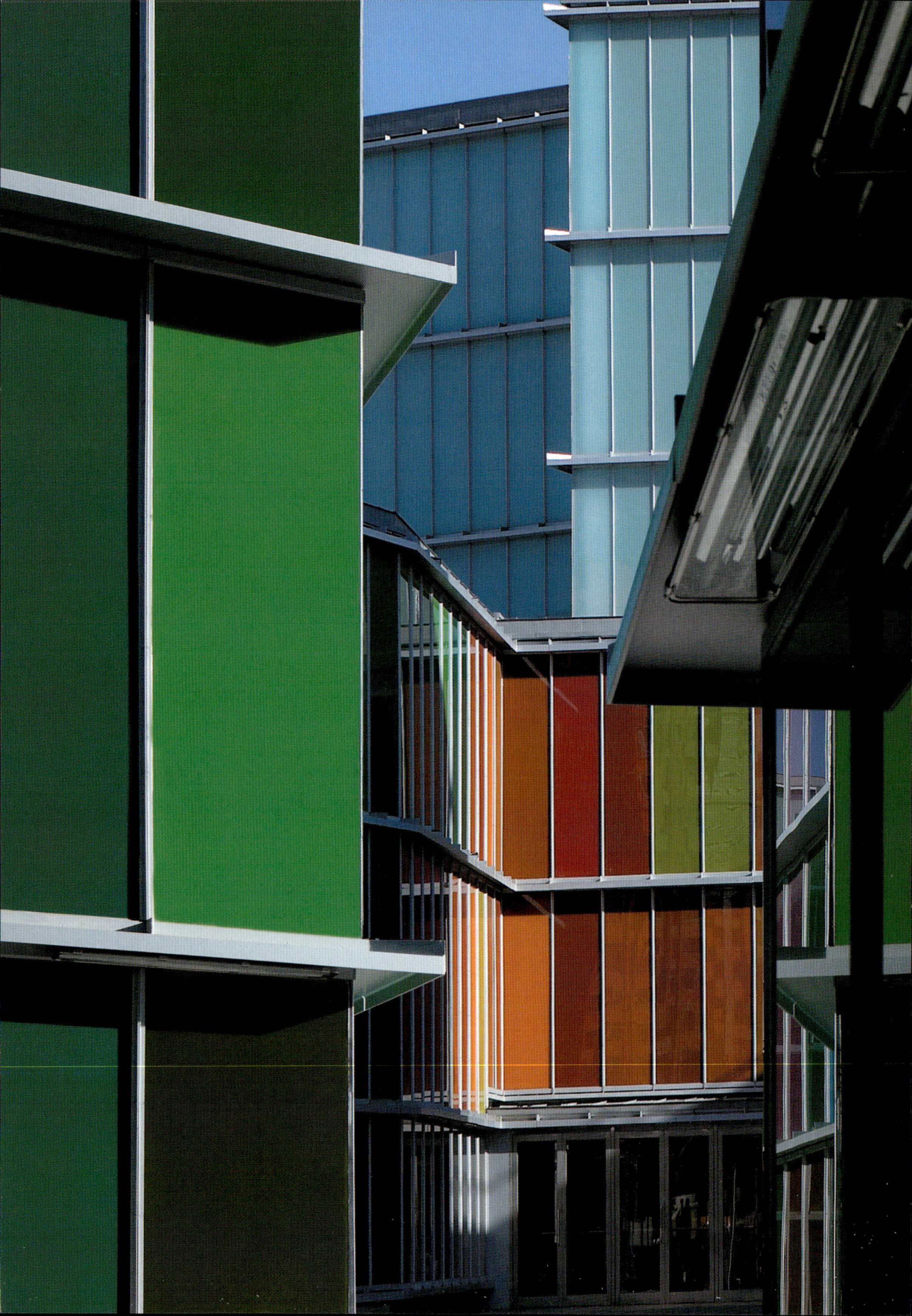

MANSILLA TUÑÓN | MADRID
Contemporary Art Museum of Castilla and León, Musac
León, Spain | 2005

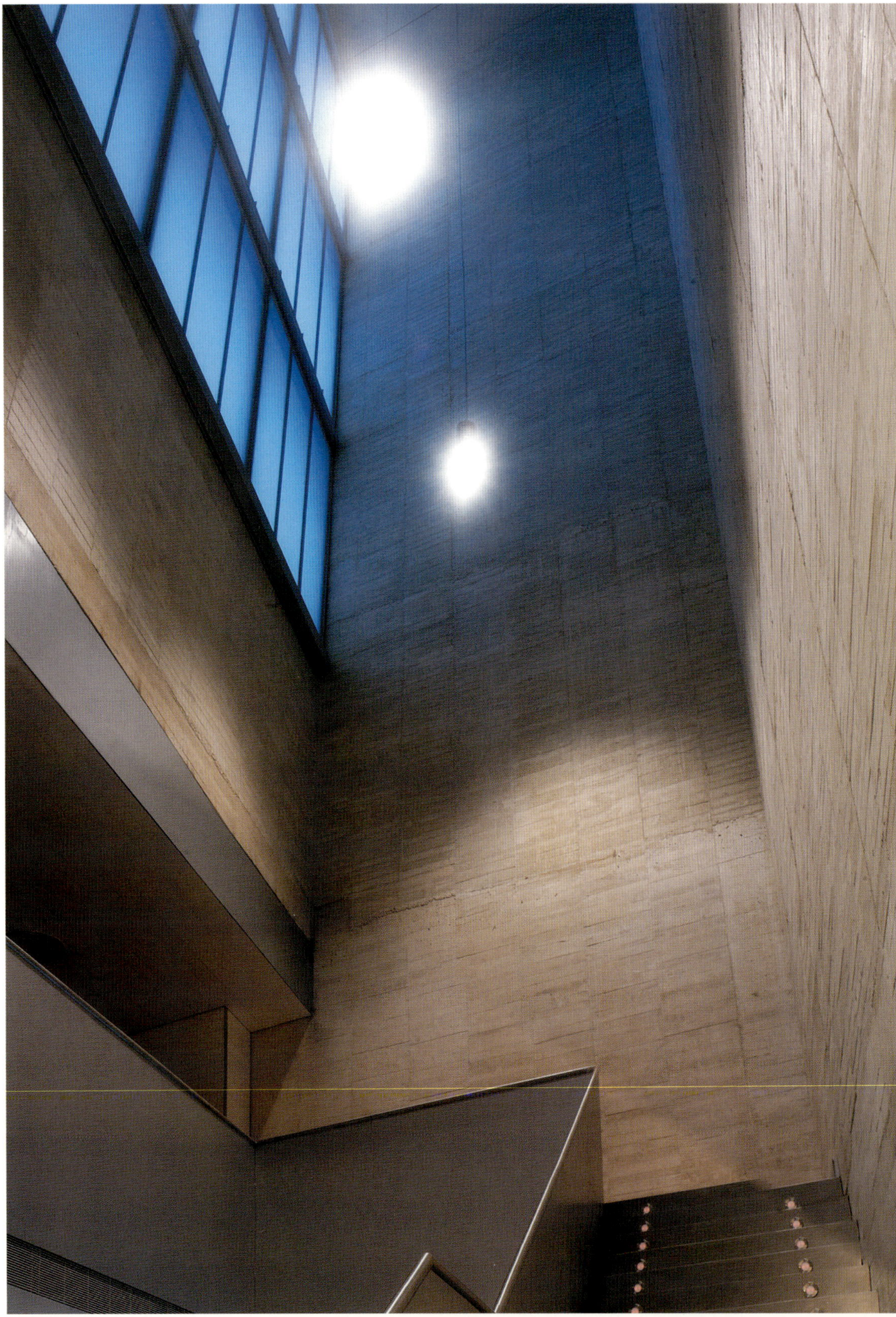

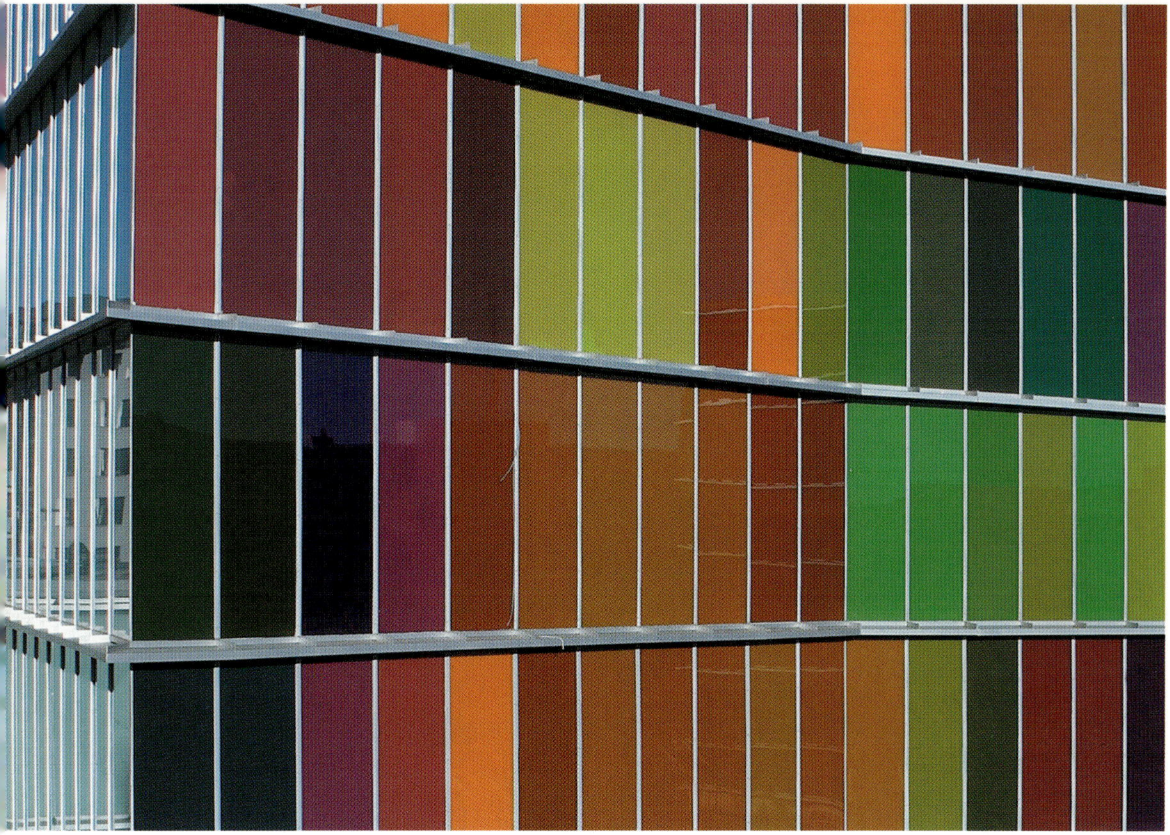

ANDON
RYOKAN
TOKYO
JAPAN

IRIE MASAYUKI | TOKYO
Hotel Andon Ryokan
Tokio, Japan | 2004

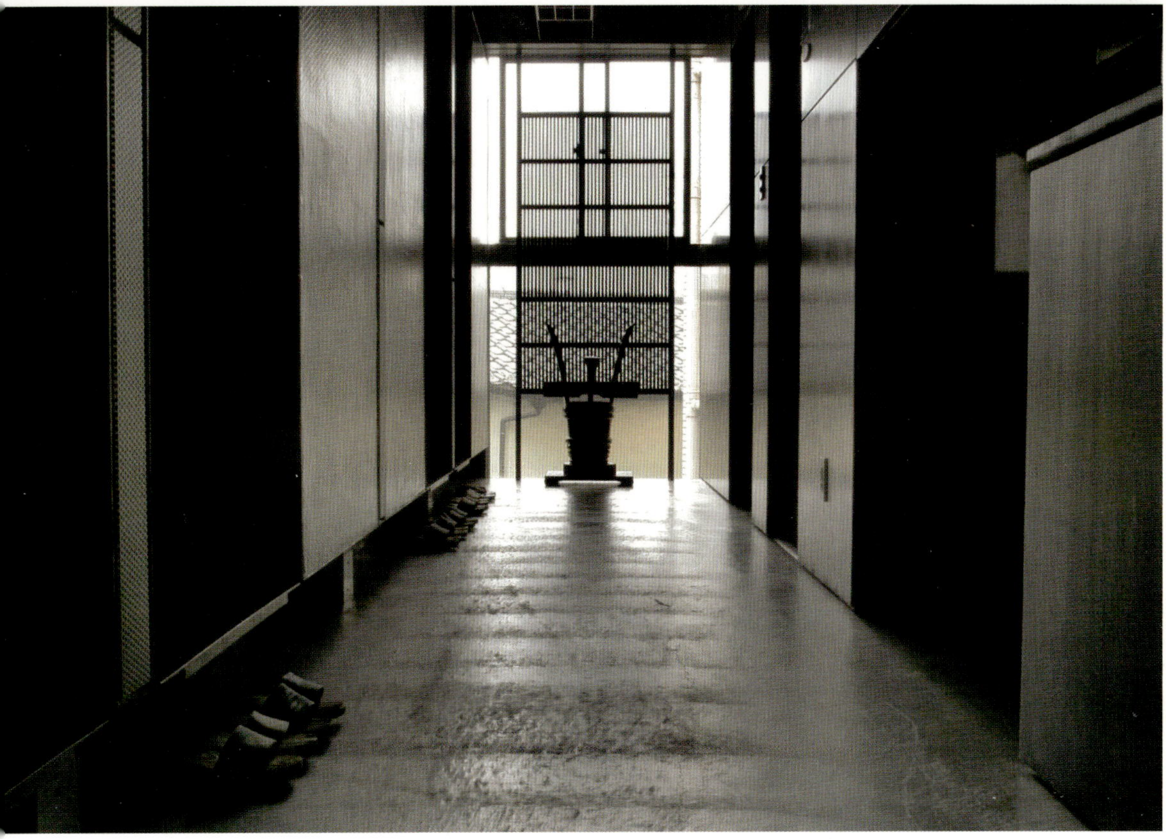

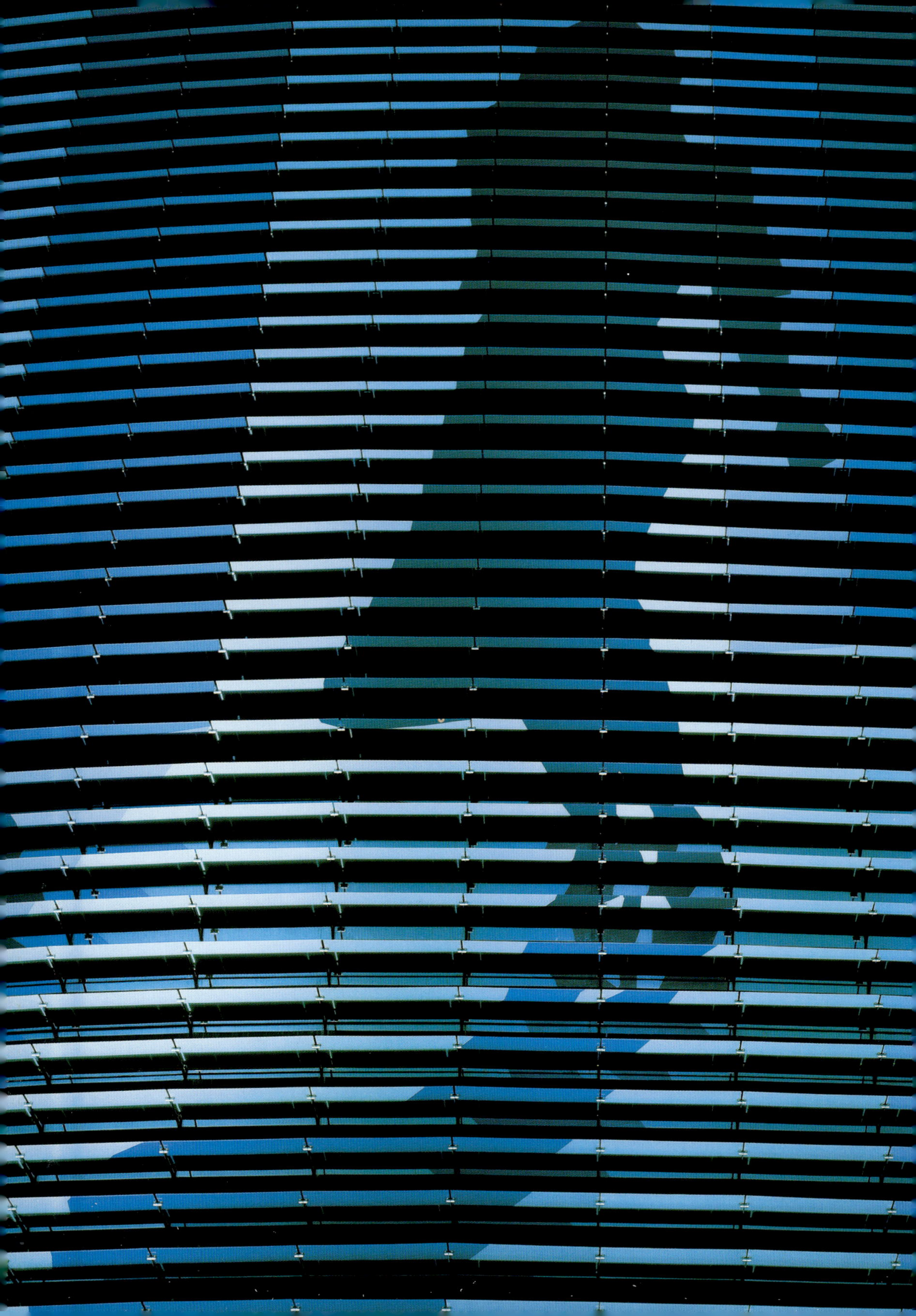

JAIME VARON, ABRAHAM METTA, ALEX METTA, MIGDAL ARQUITECTOS | MEXICO CITY
Las Flores Corporate
Mexico City, Mexico | 2003

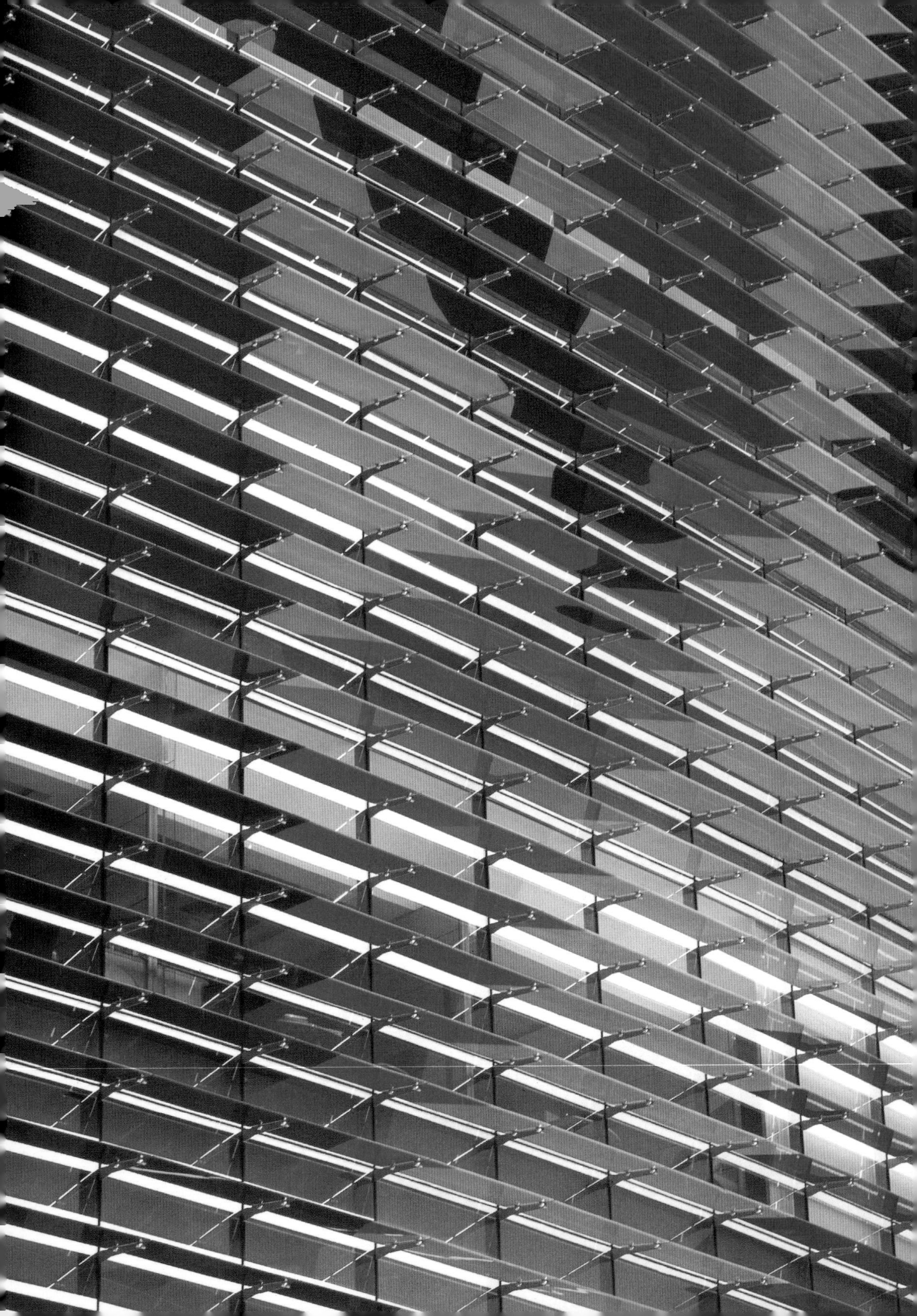

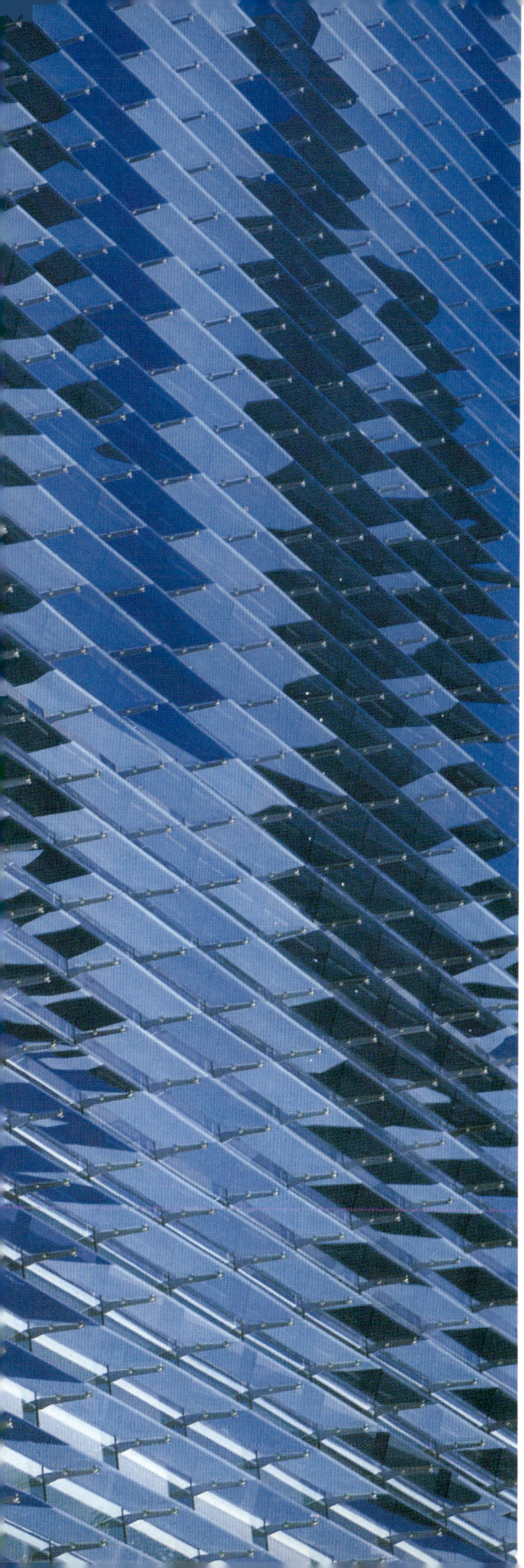

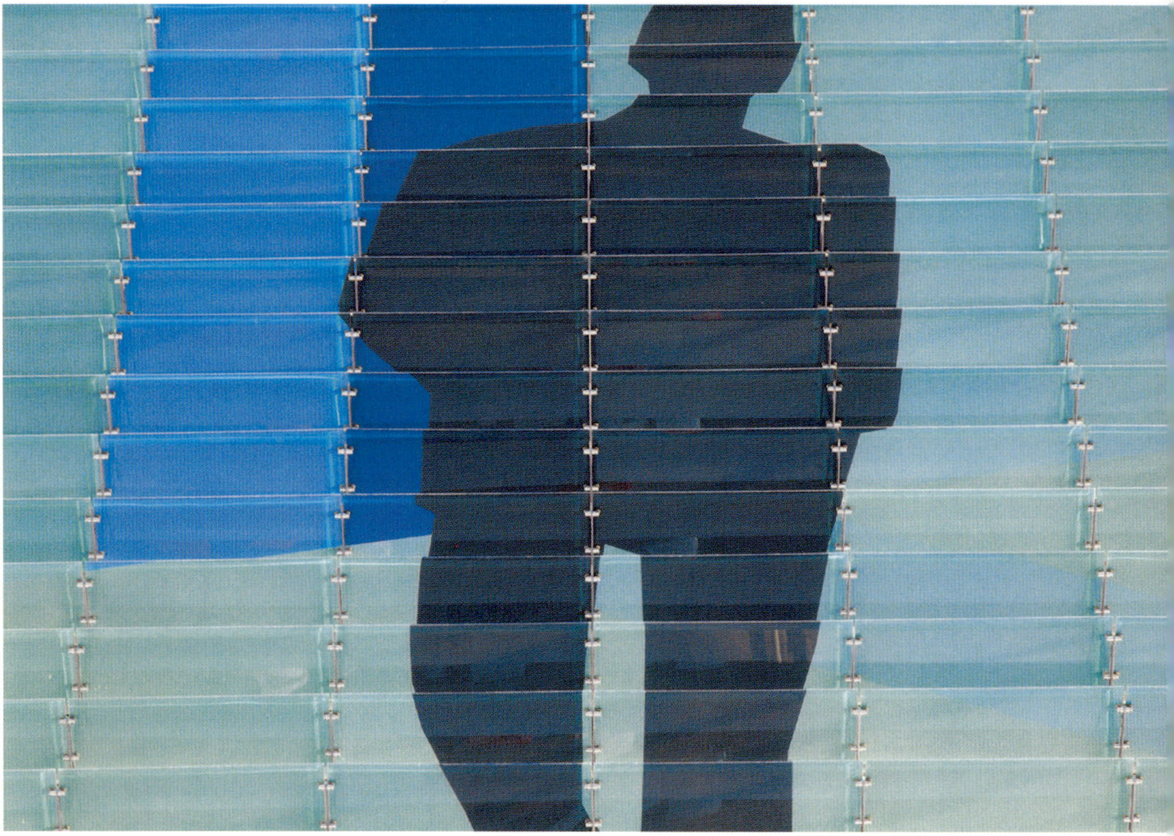

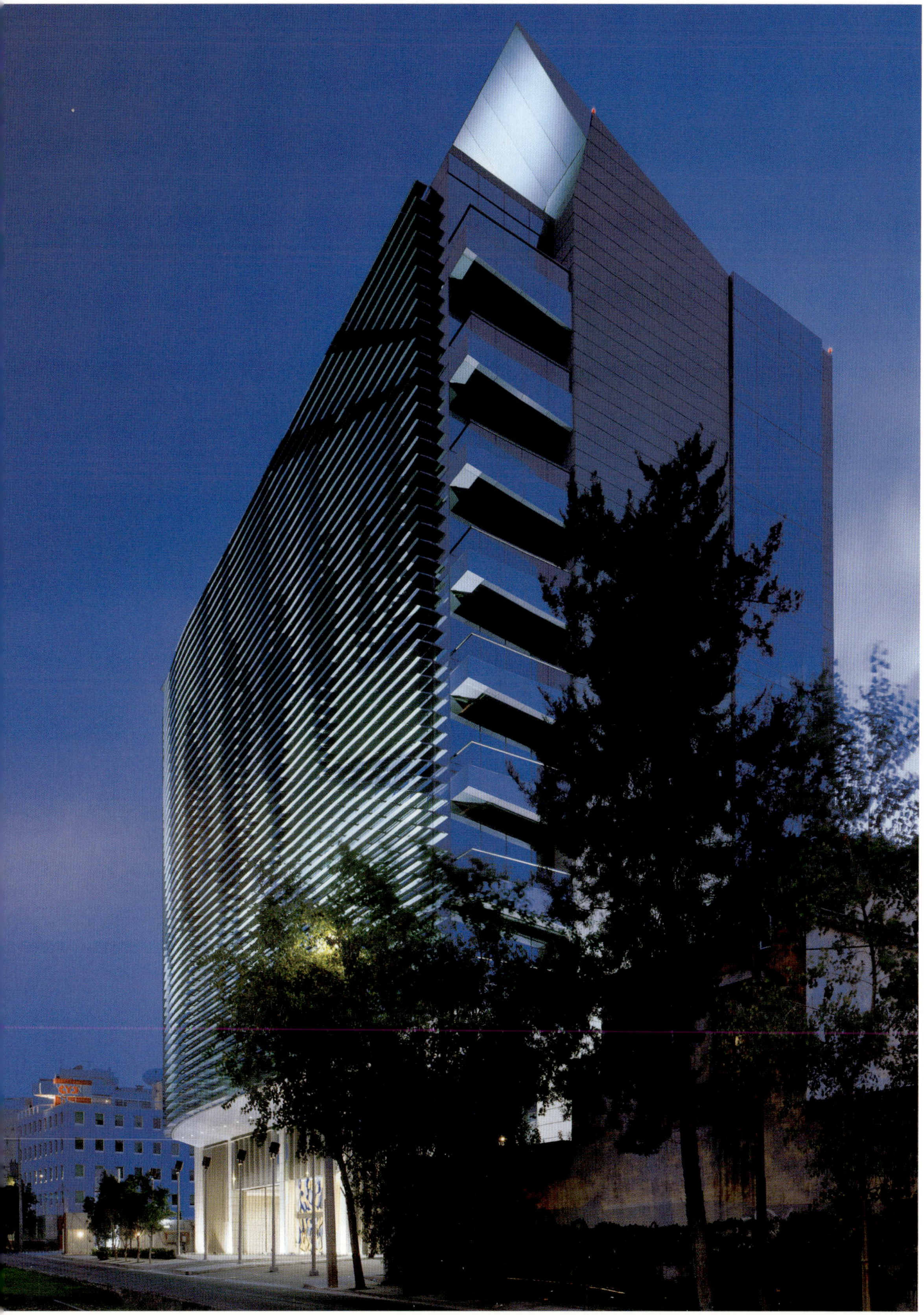

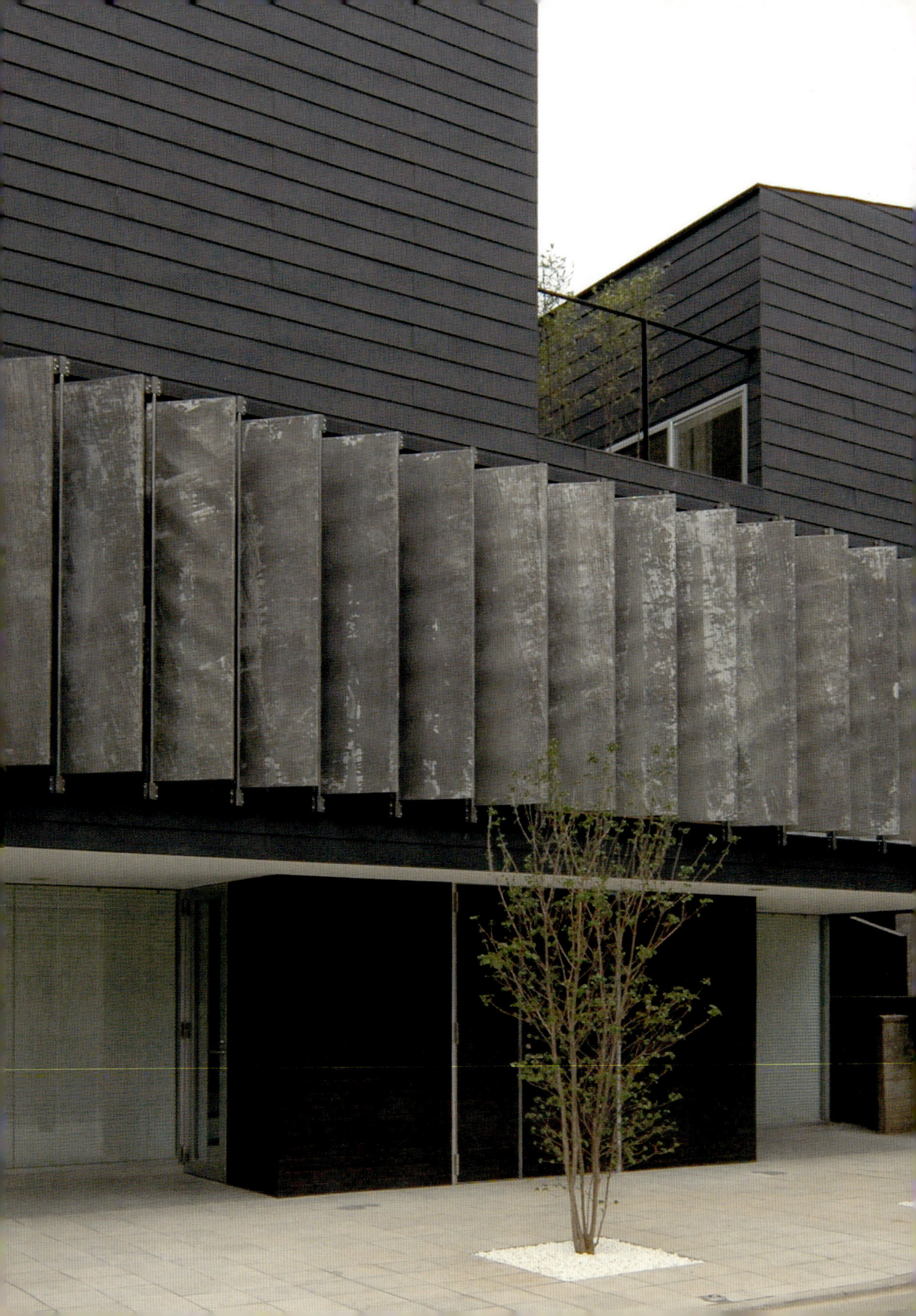

MIYAHARA ARCHITECT OFFICE | TOKYO
House TTN
Tokyo, Japan | 2005

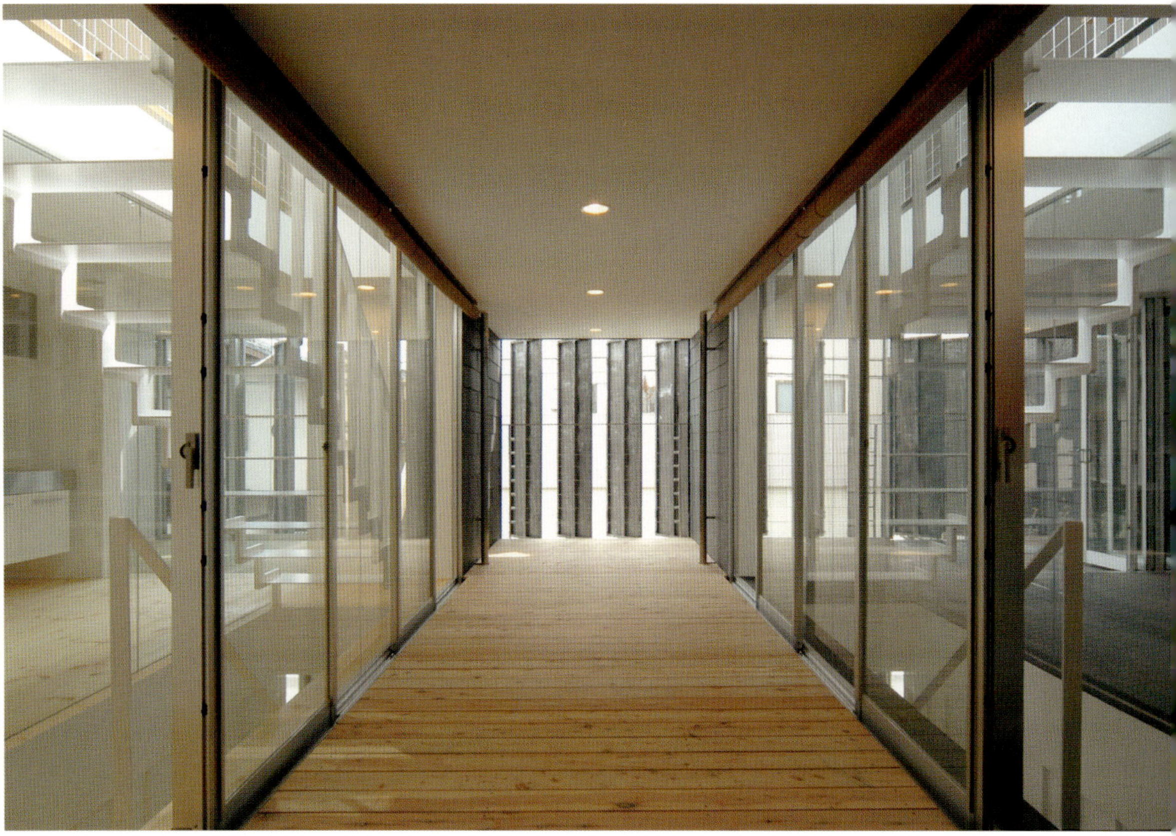

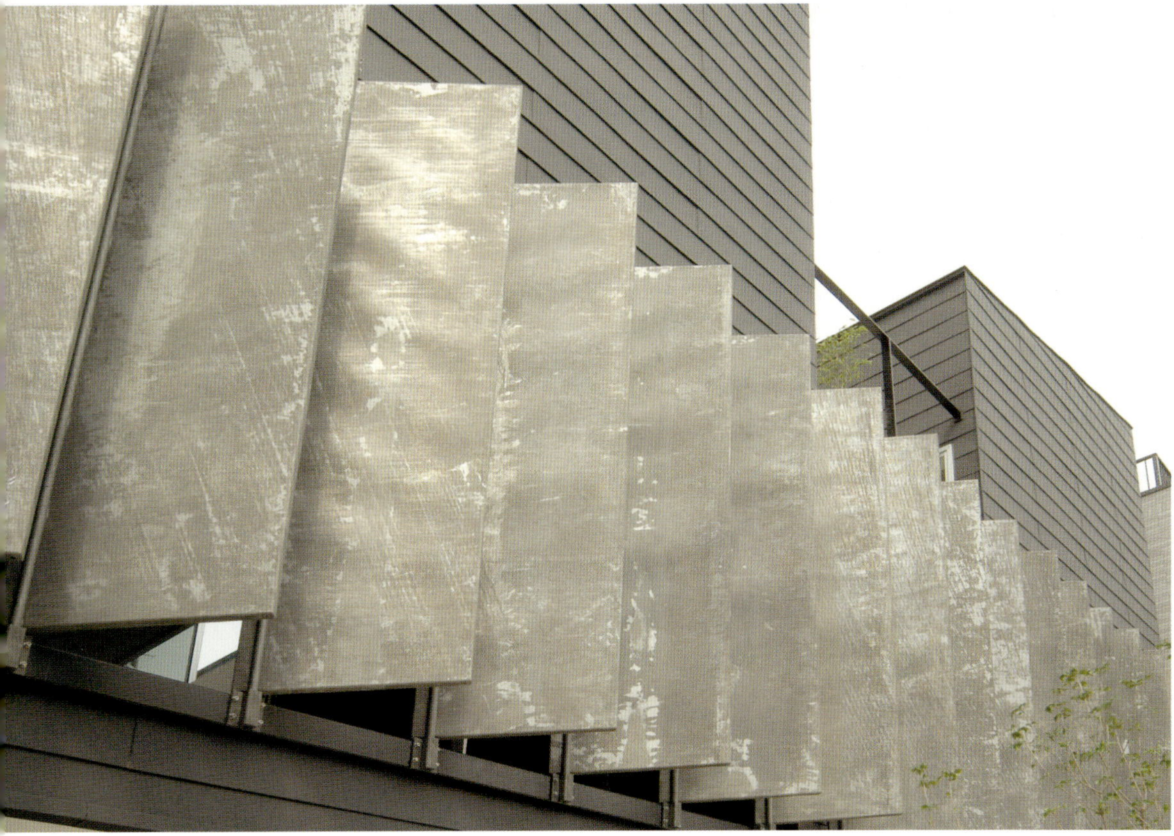

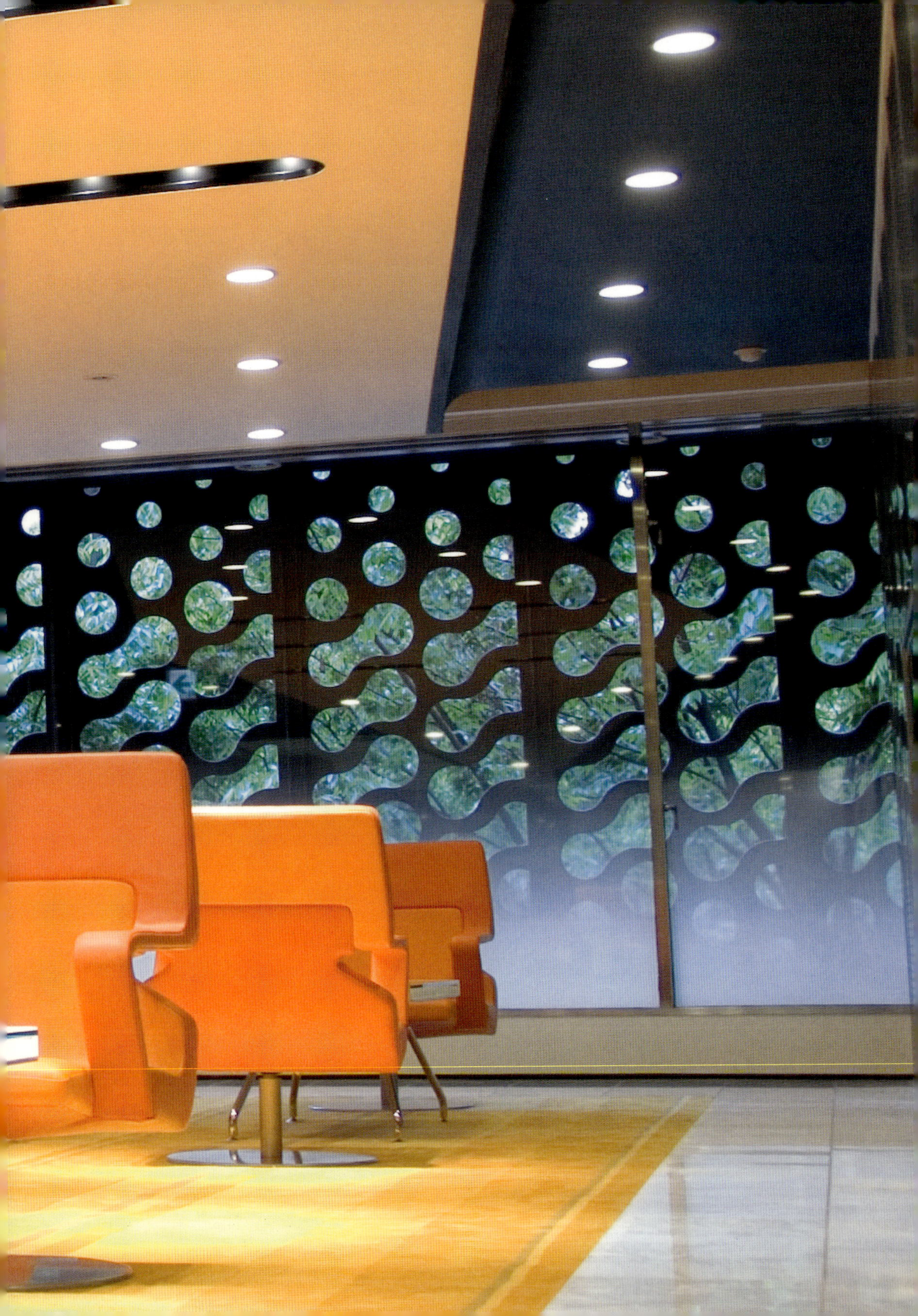

NEIL M. DENARI ARCHITECTS, NMDA | LOS ANGELES
MUFG Private Banking Office
Nagoya, Japan | 2006

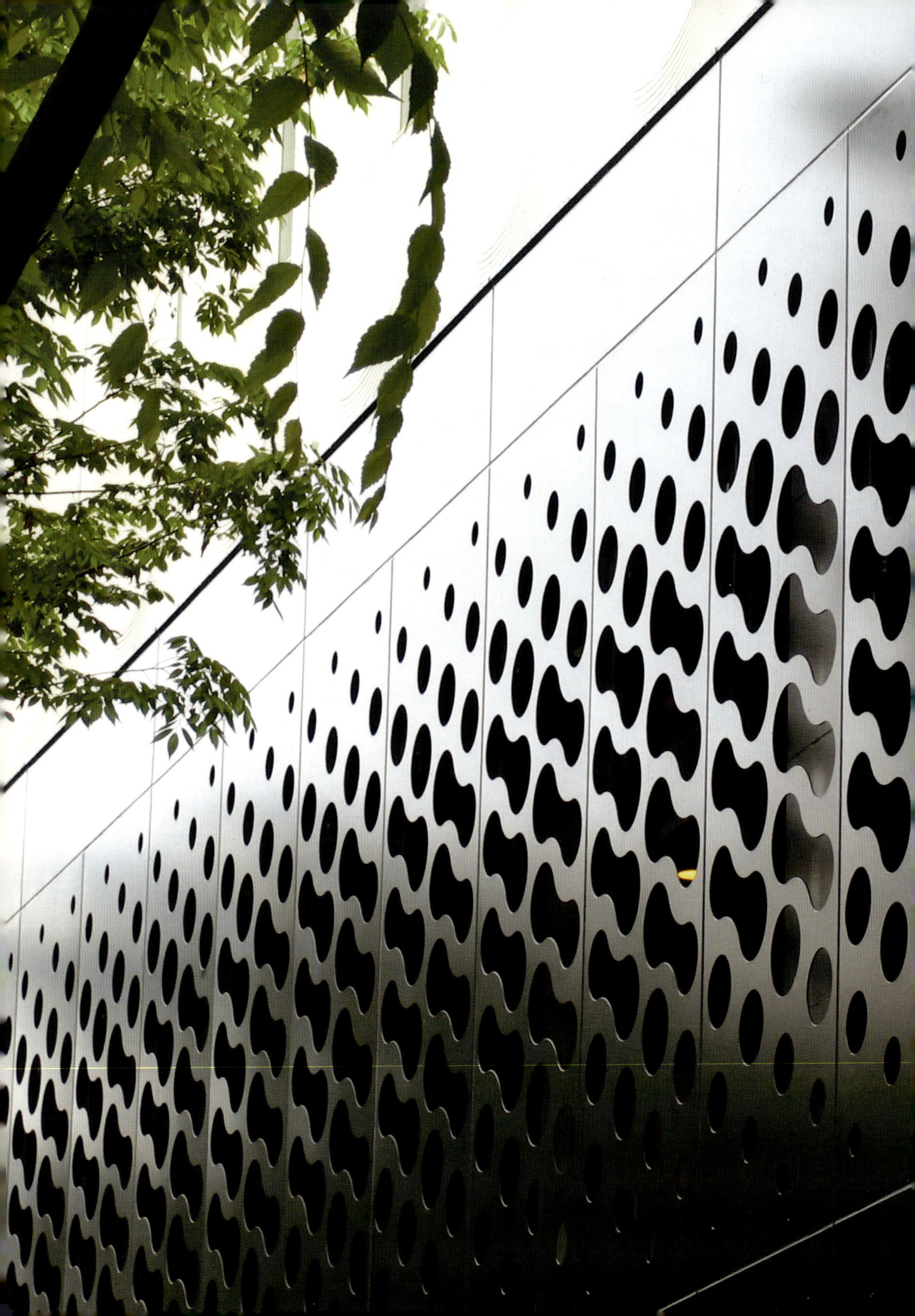

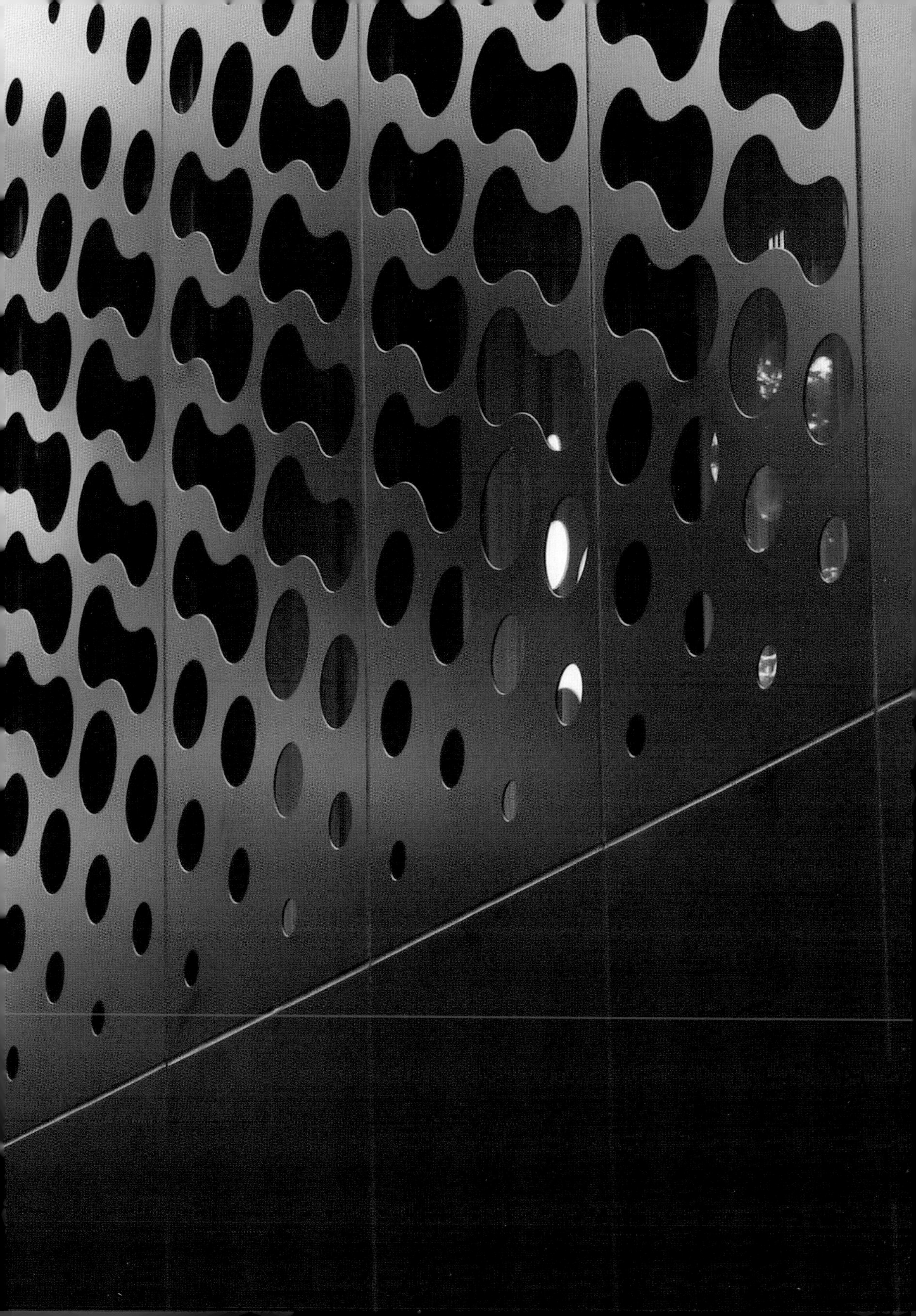

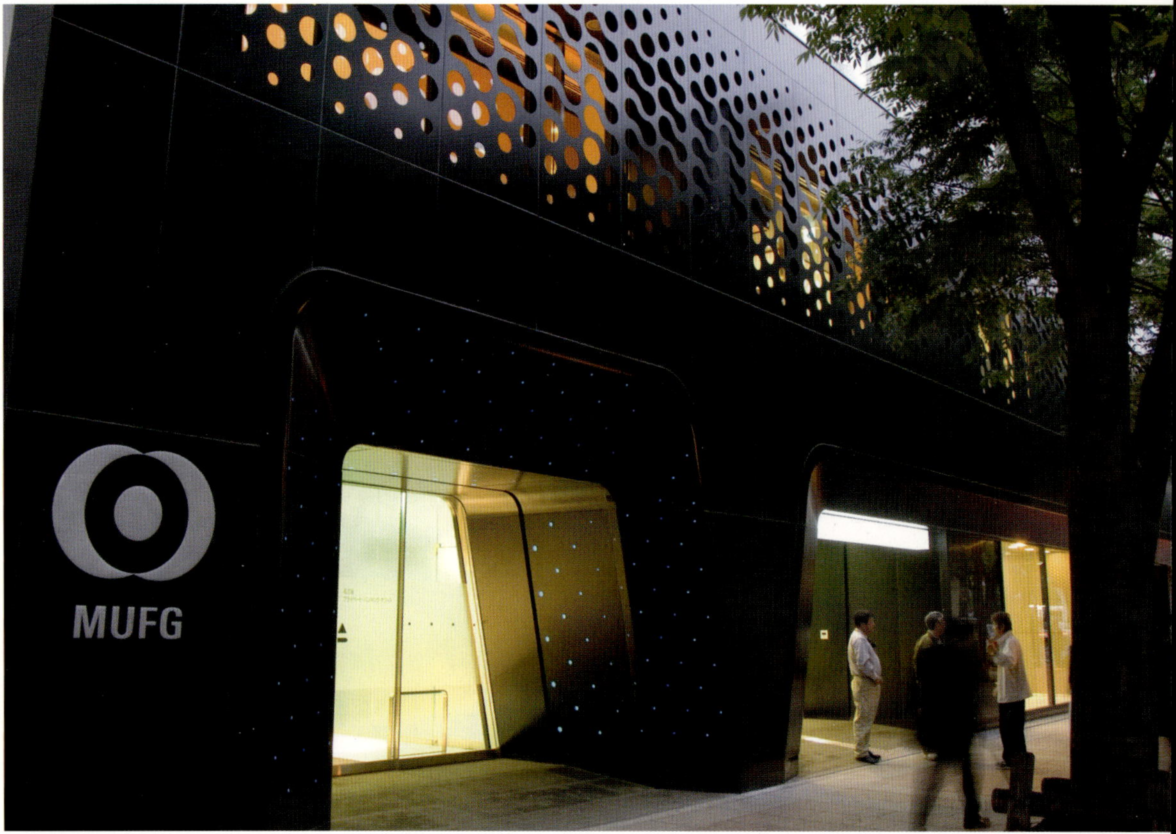
MUFG

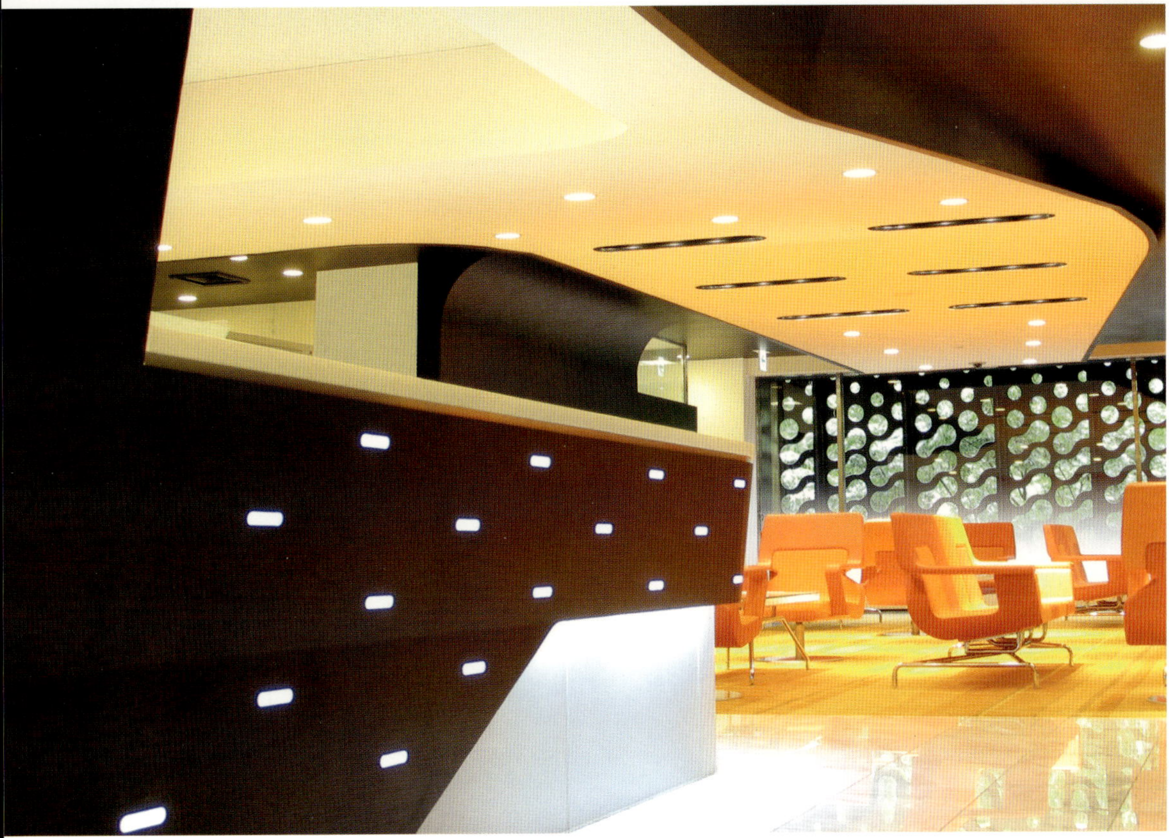

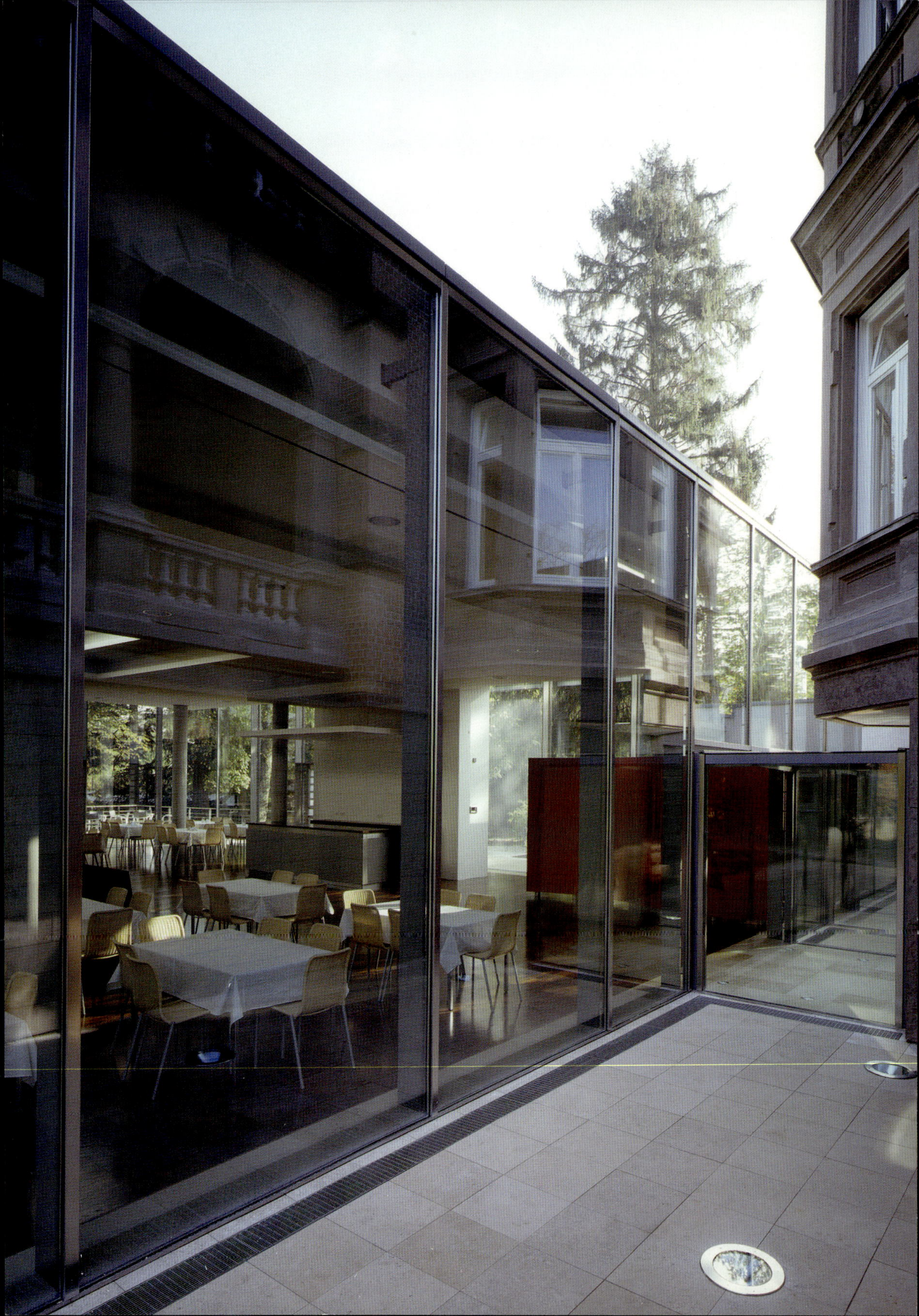

NIKE FIEDLER ARCHITEKTEN | STUTTGART
Speisesaal „Symposion" der Evang. Akademie Bad Boll
Bad Boll, Germany | 2001

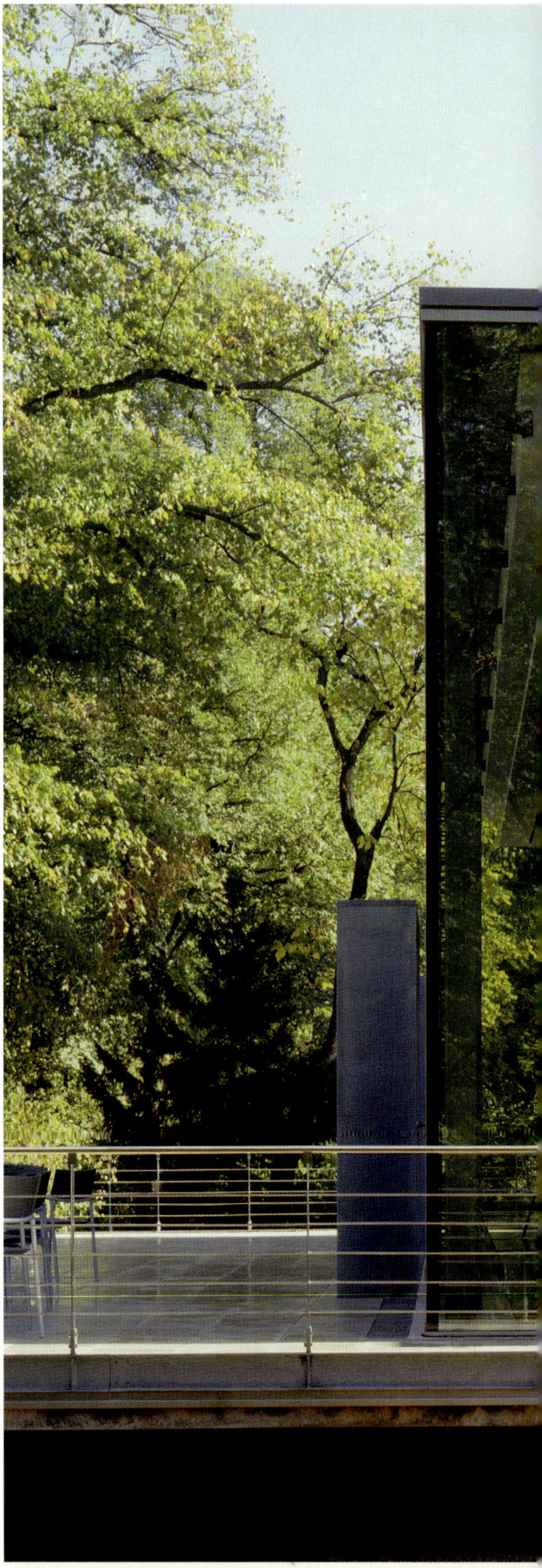

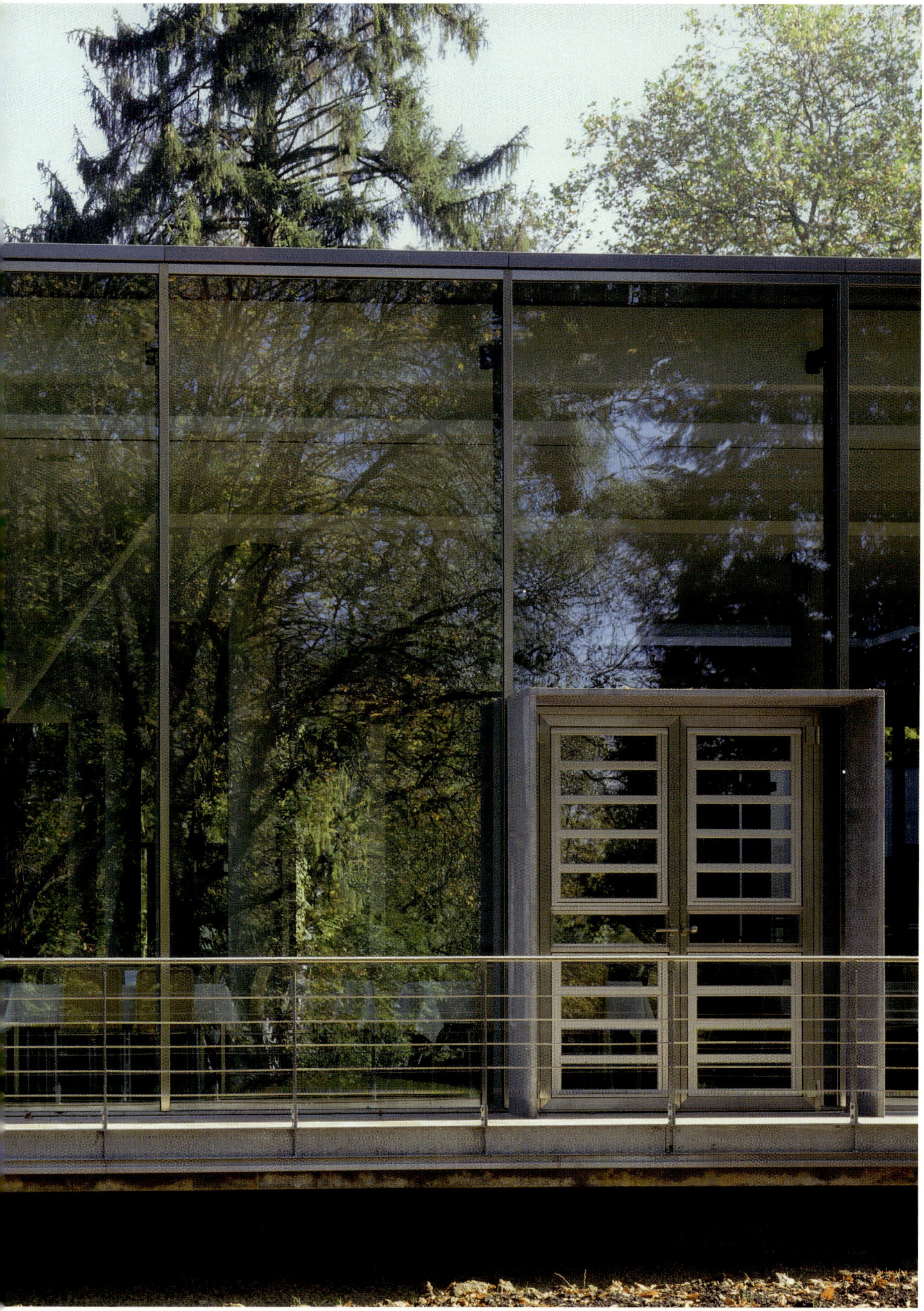

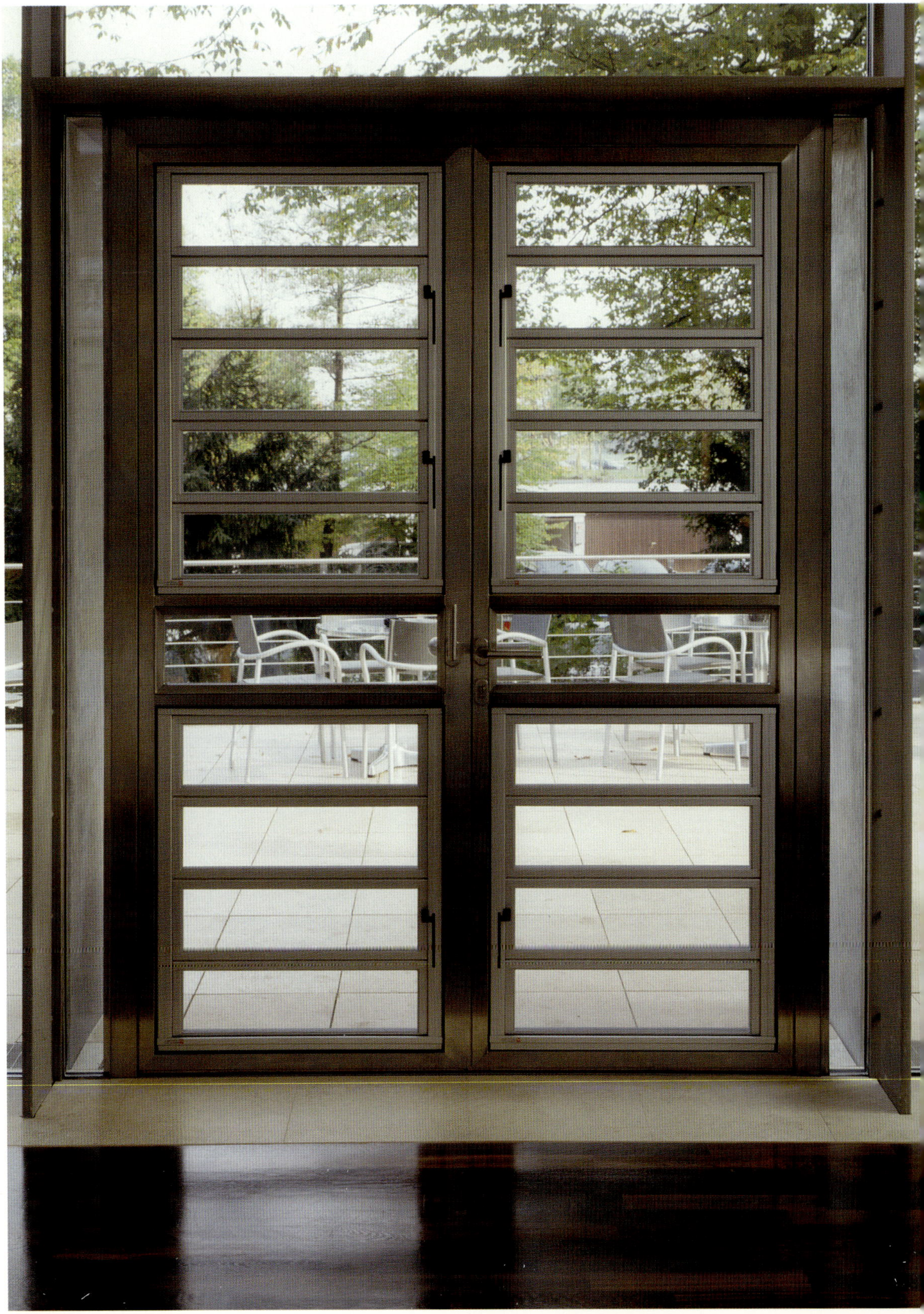

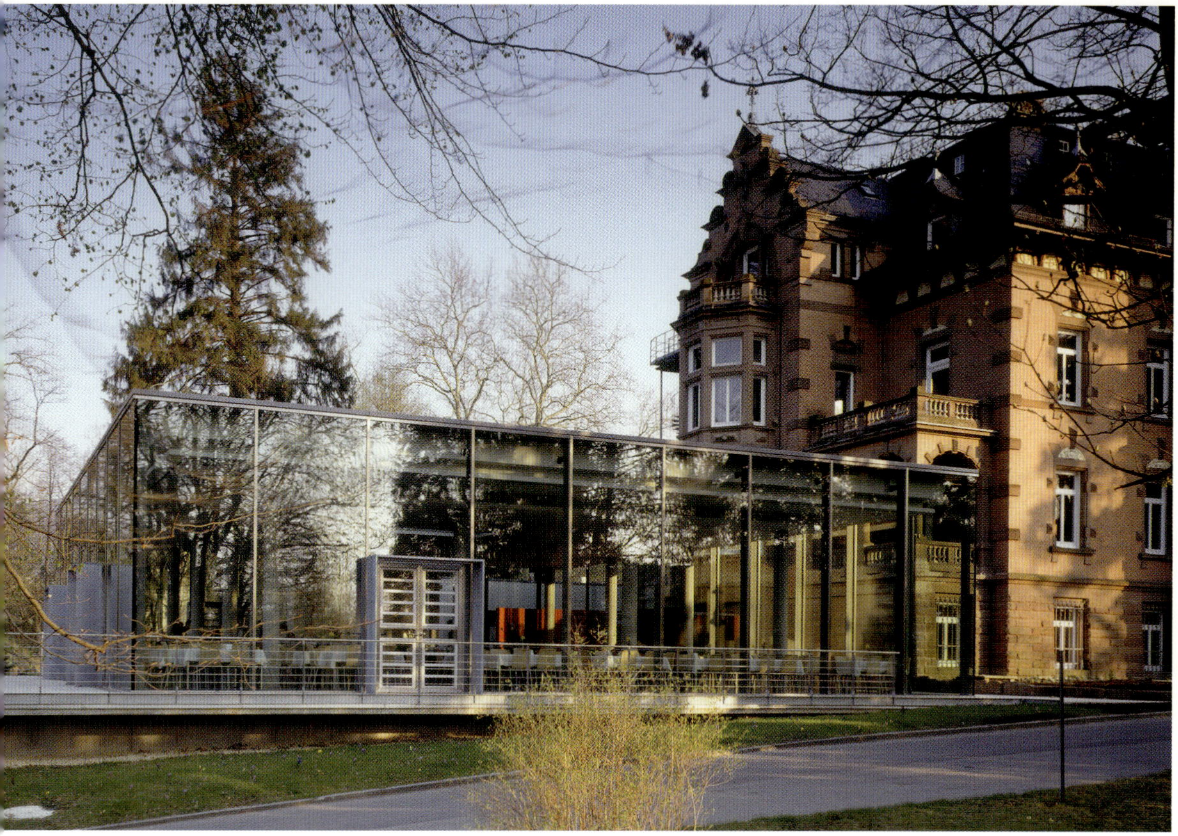

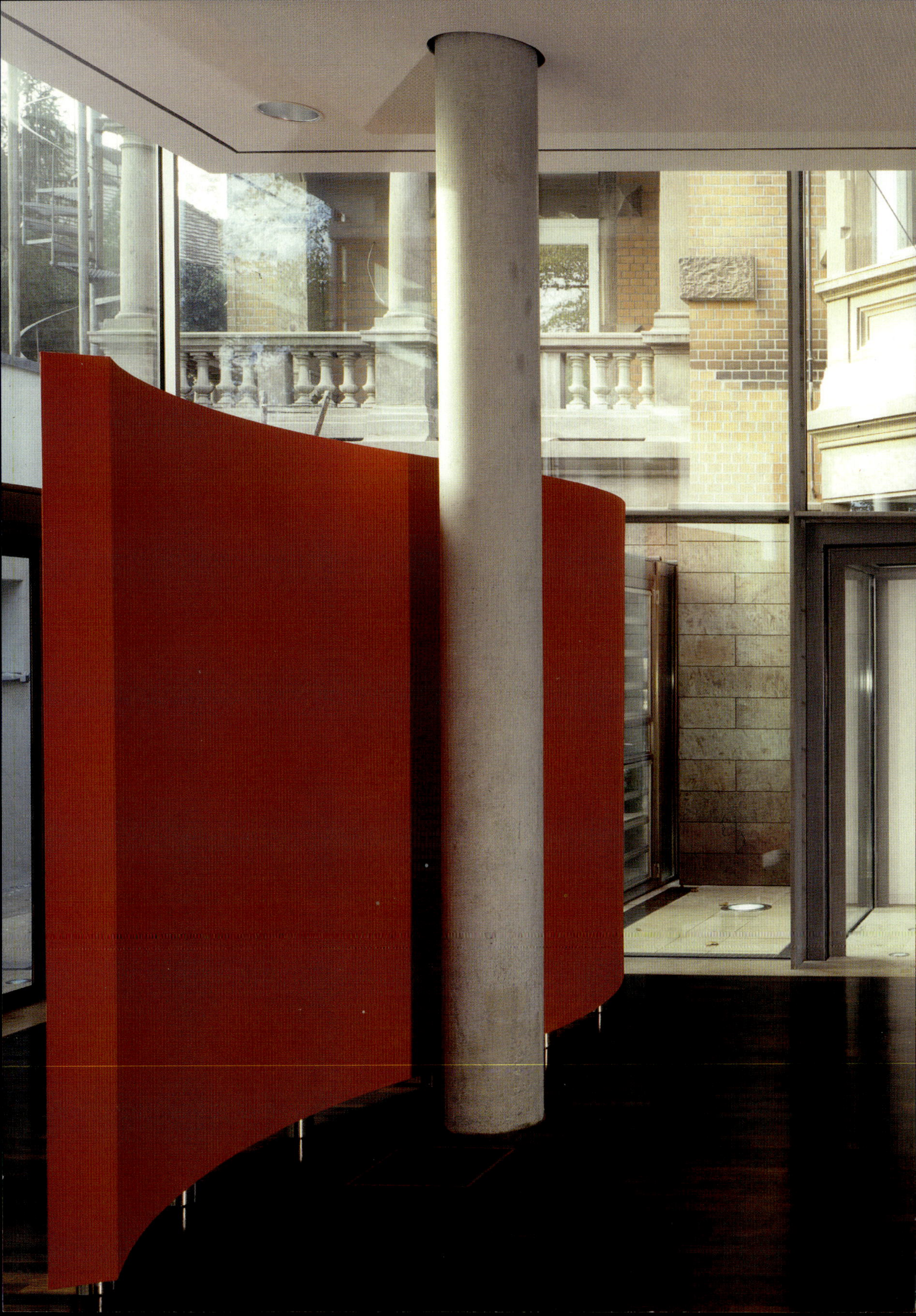

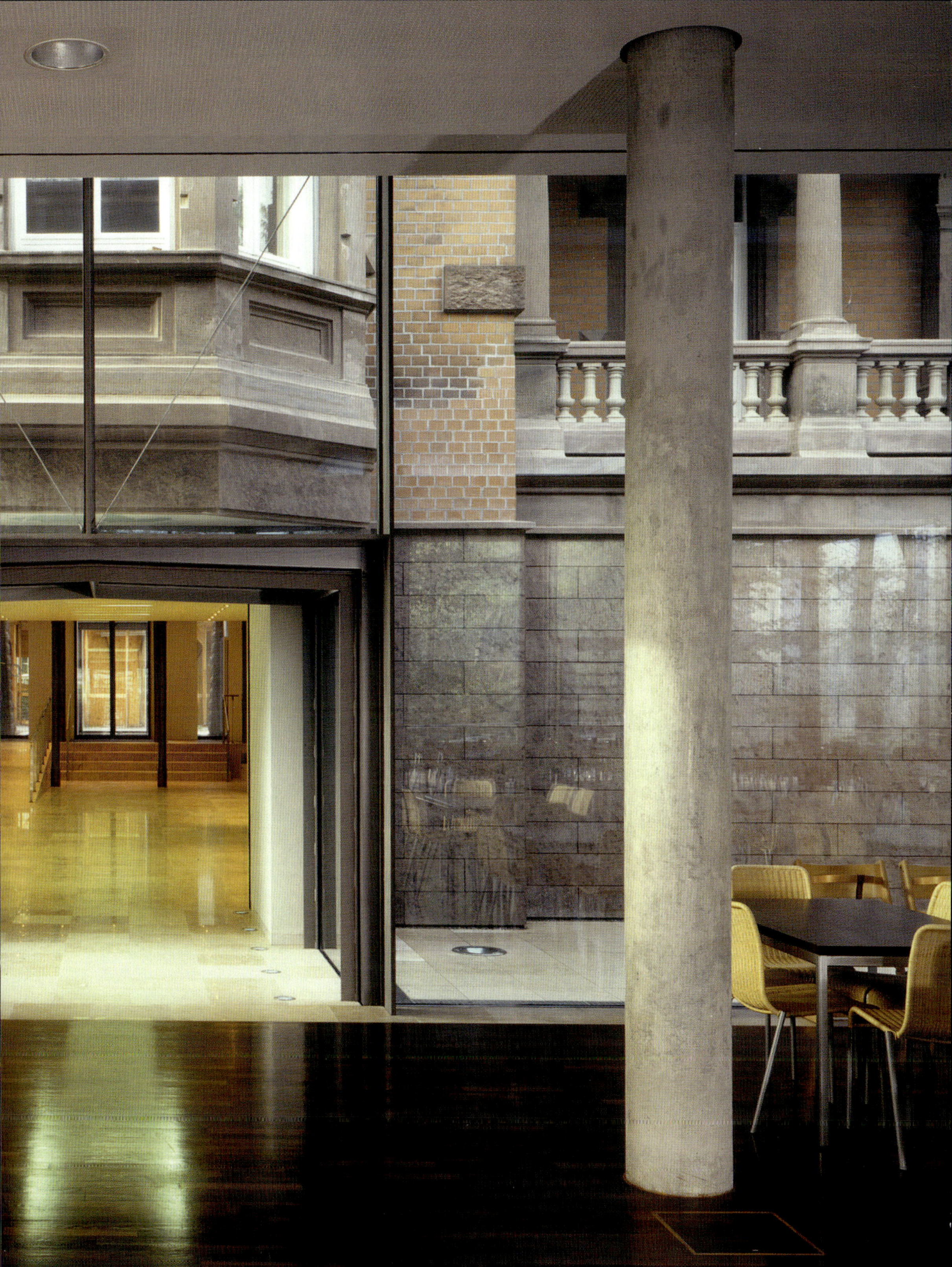

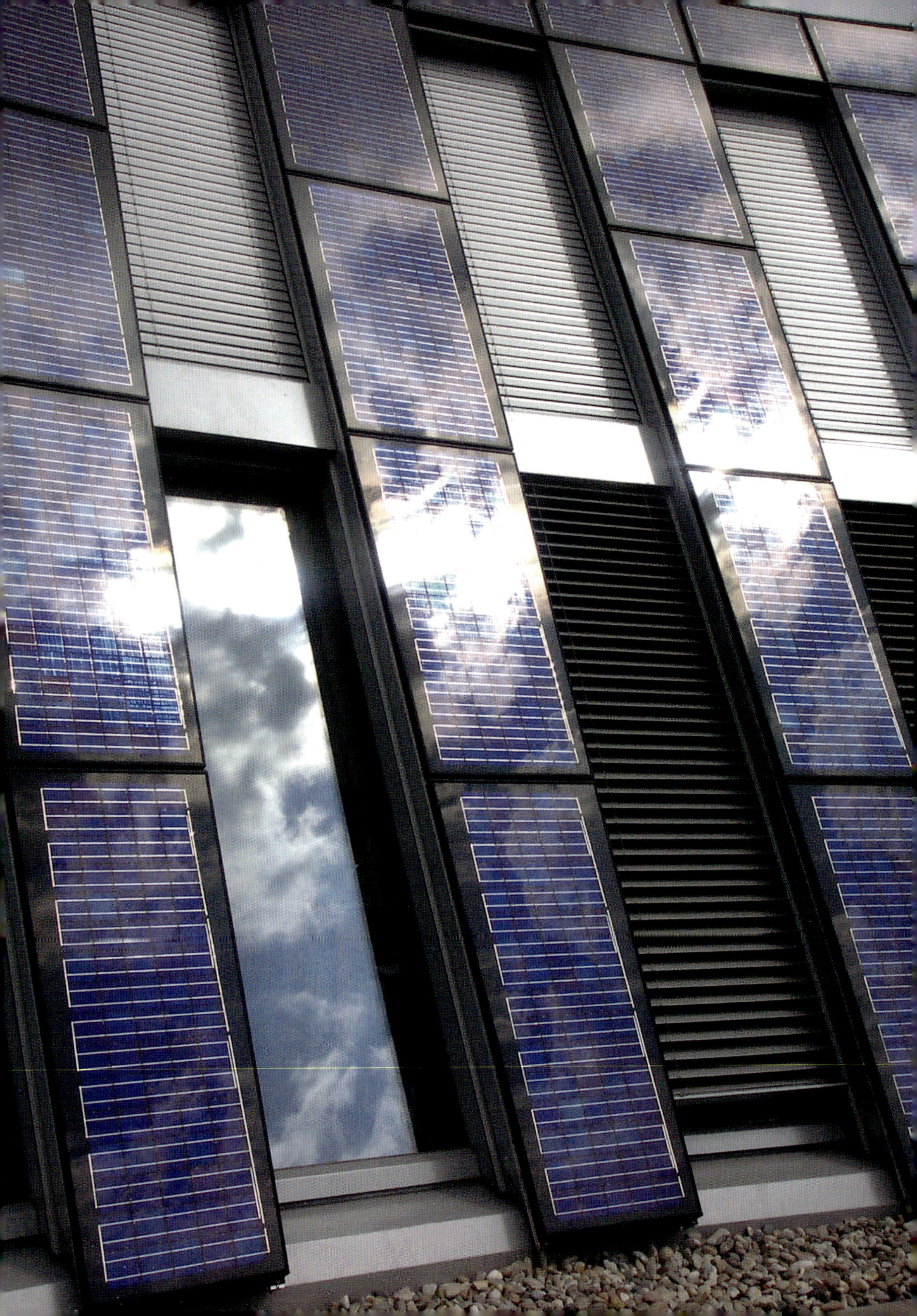

OEHLER FAIGLE ARCHKOM | BRETTEN
Office building JUWI
Bolanden, Pfalz, Germany | 2004

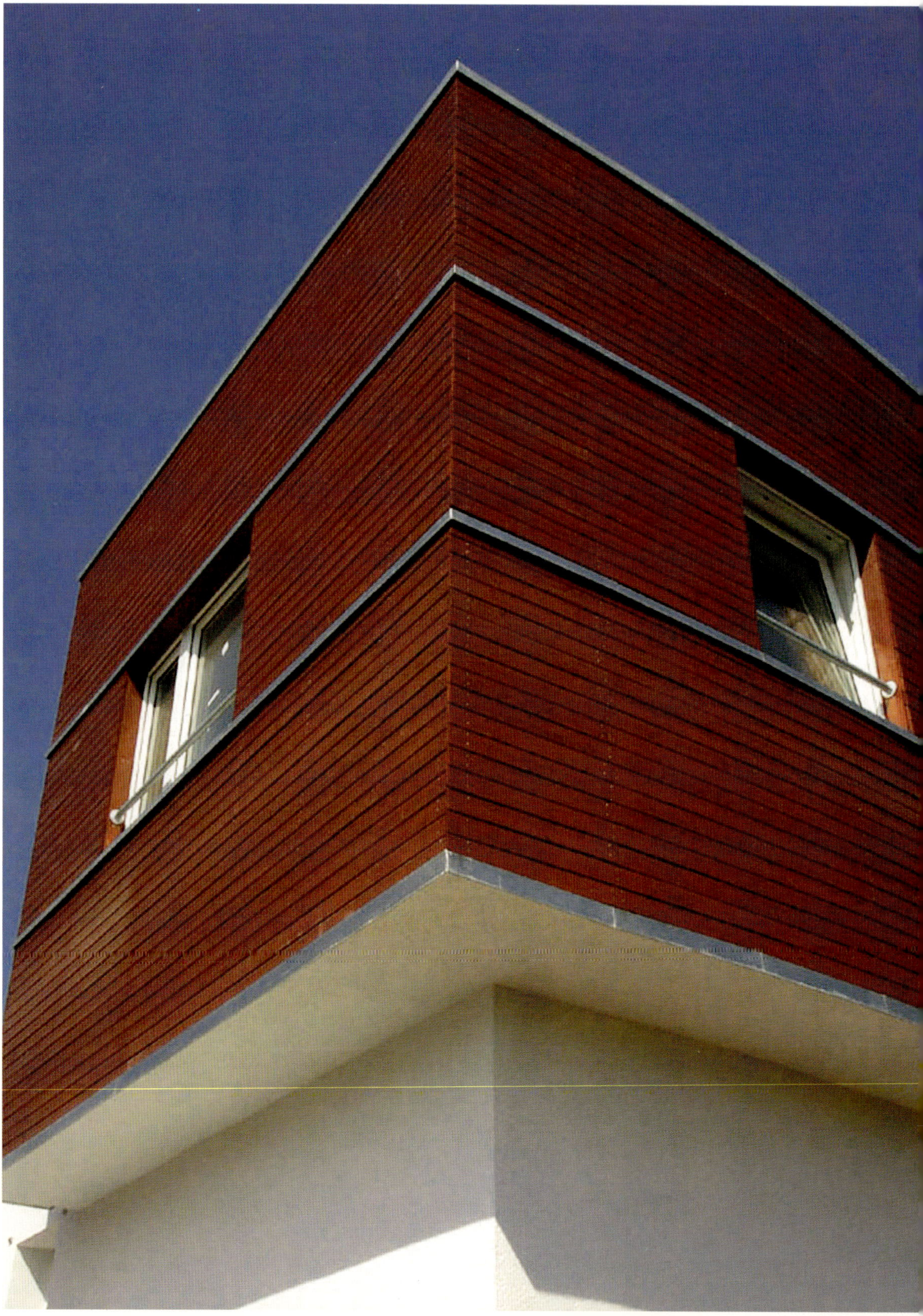

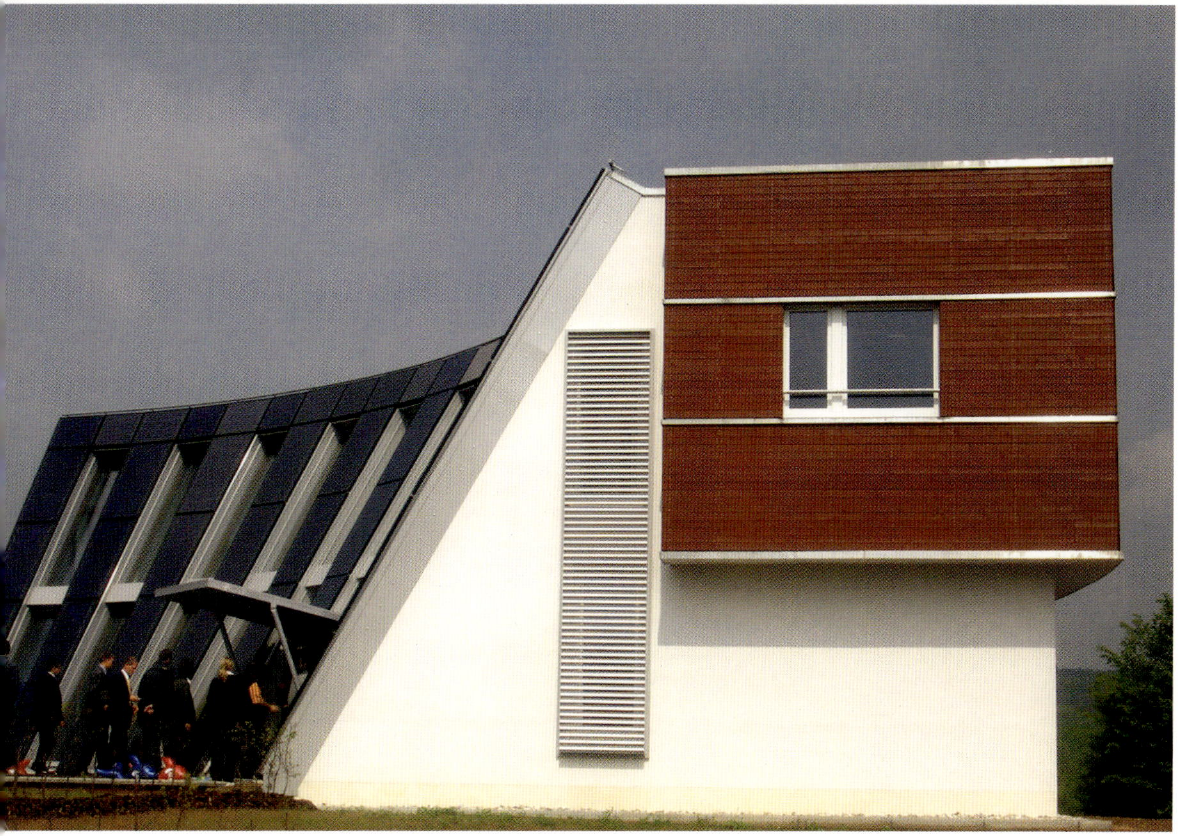

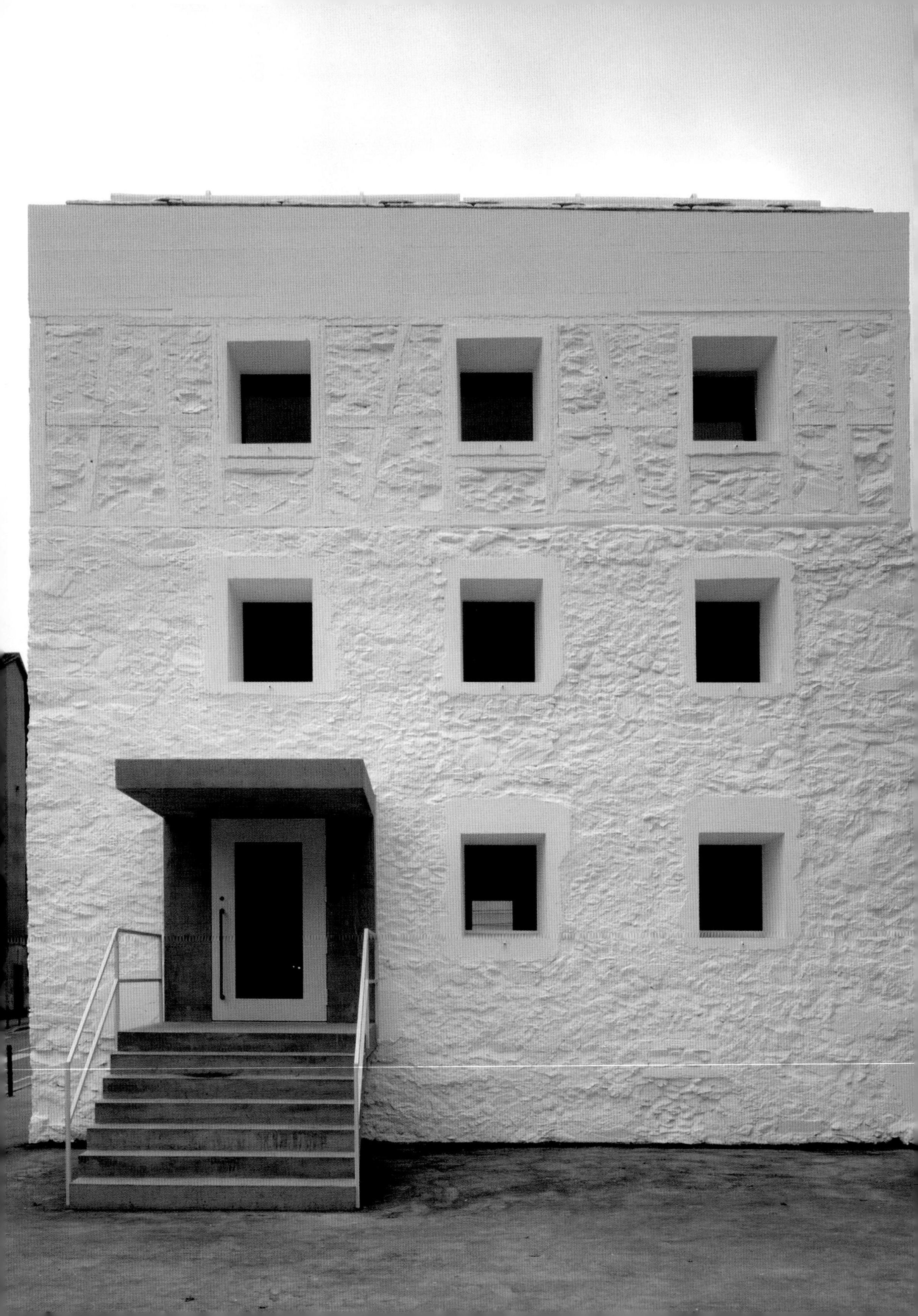

VALERIO OLGIATI | CHUR
Yellow House Museum
Flims, Switzerland | 1999

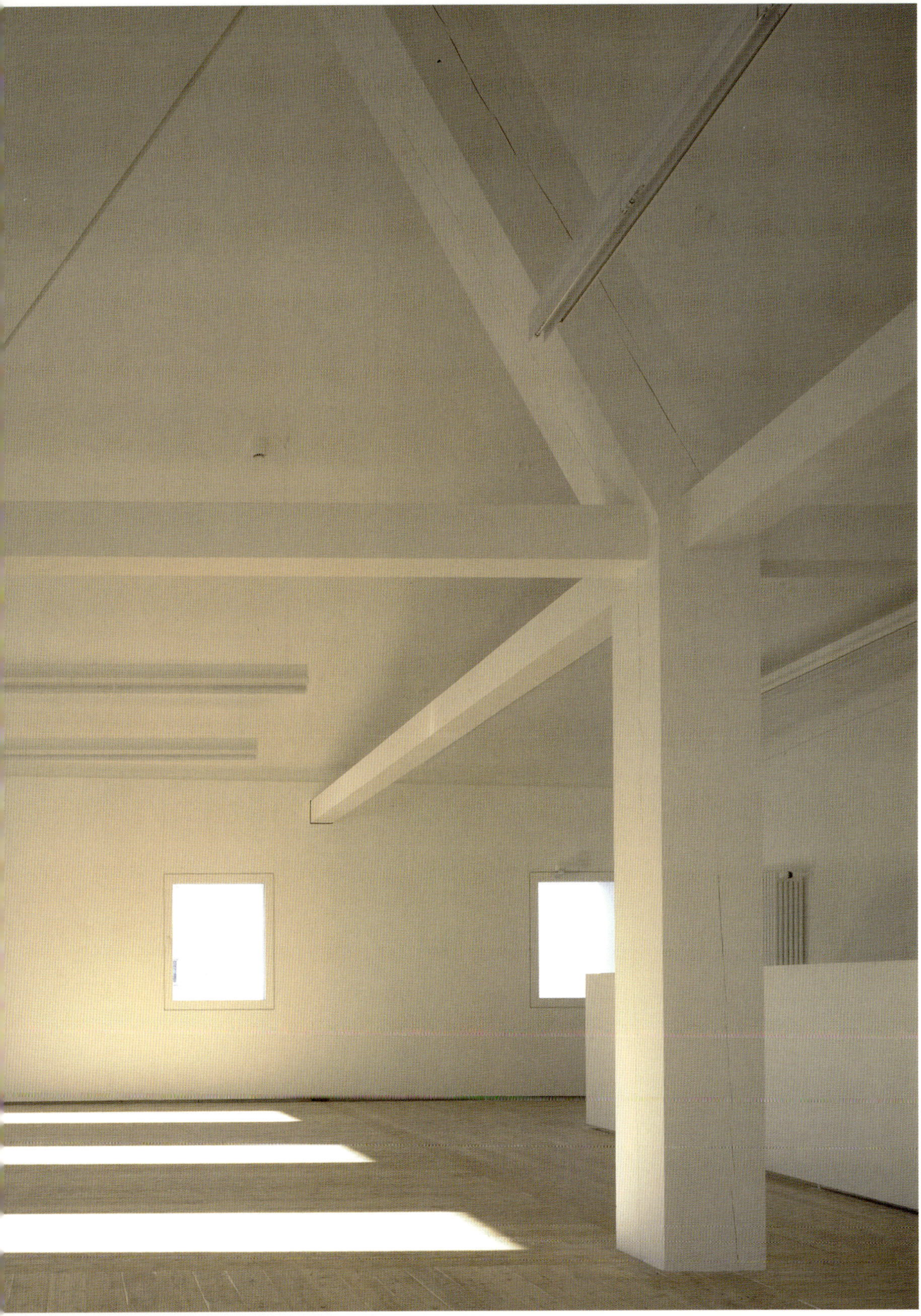

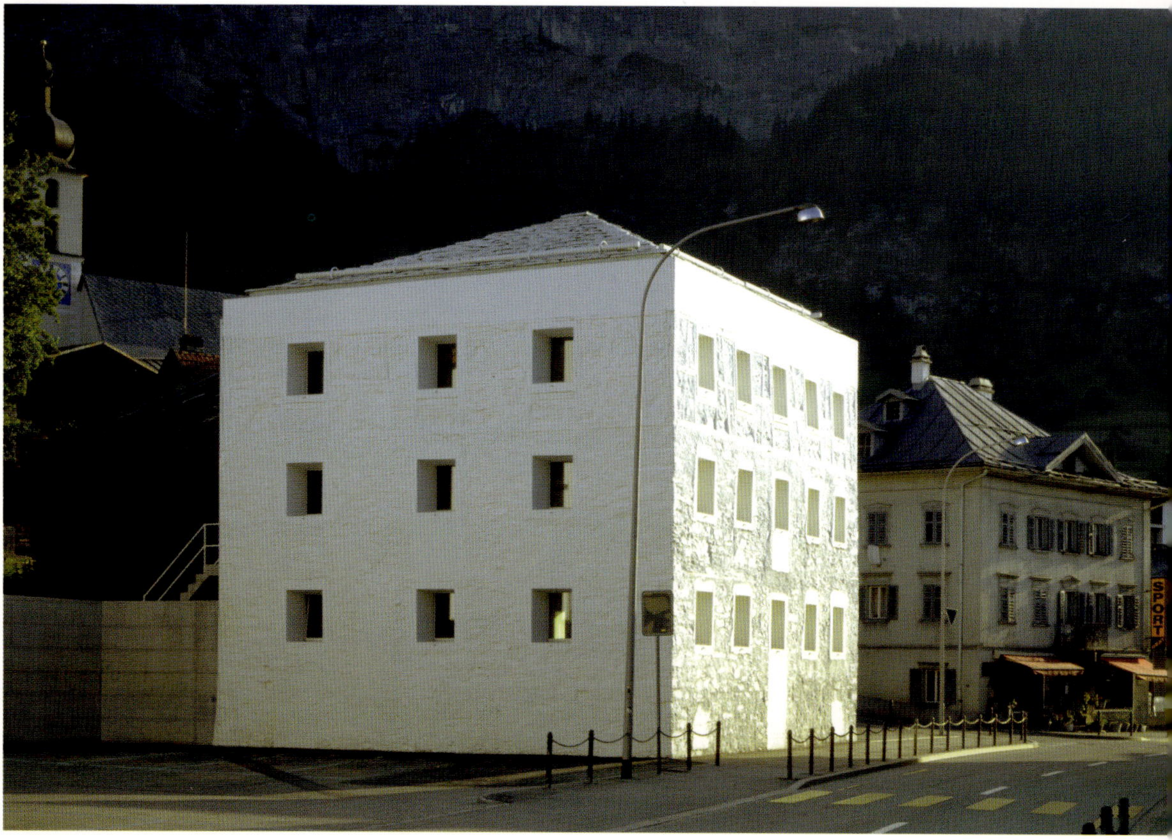
SPORT

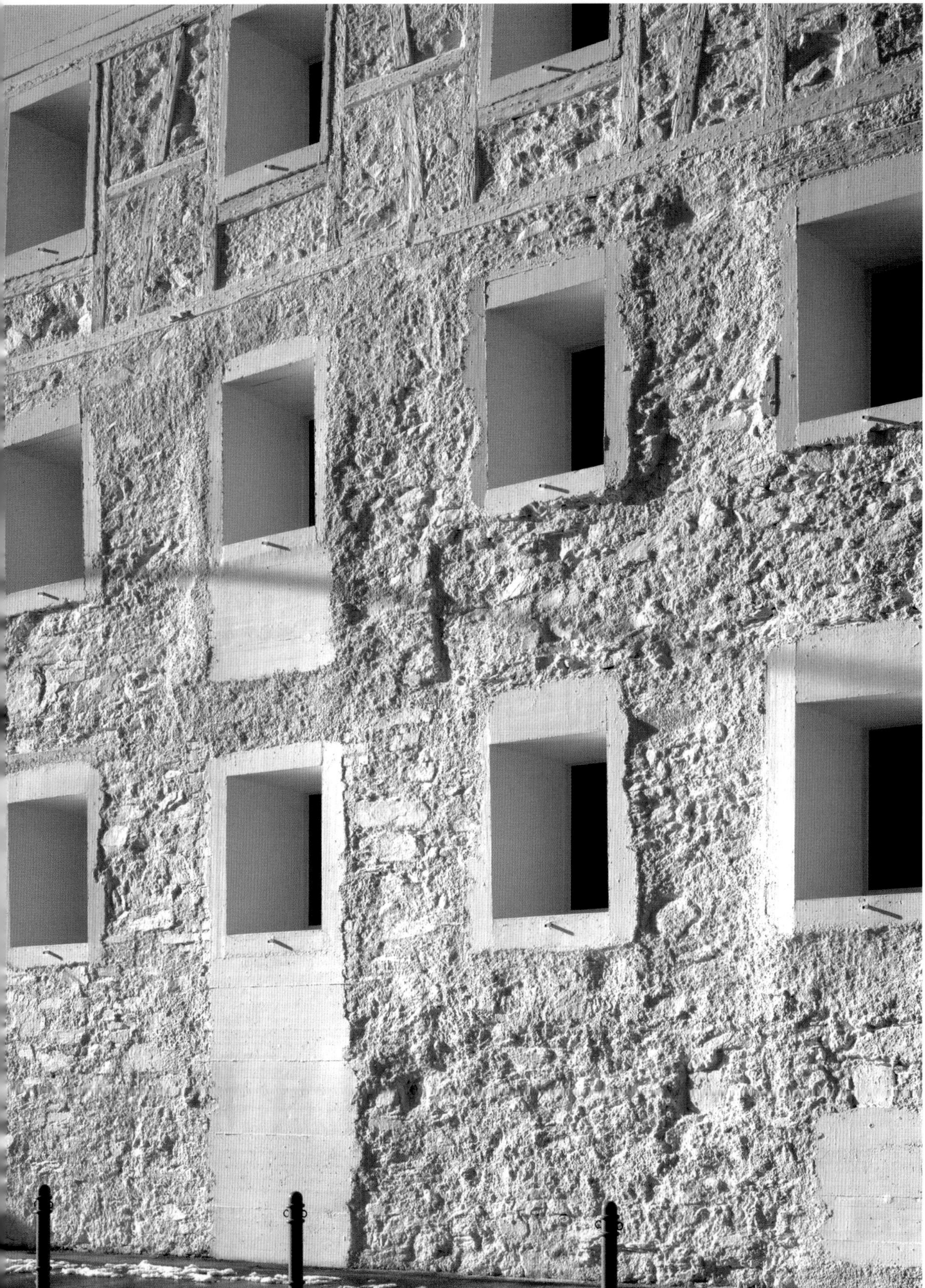

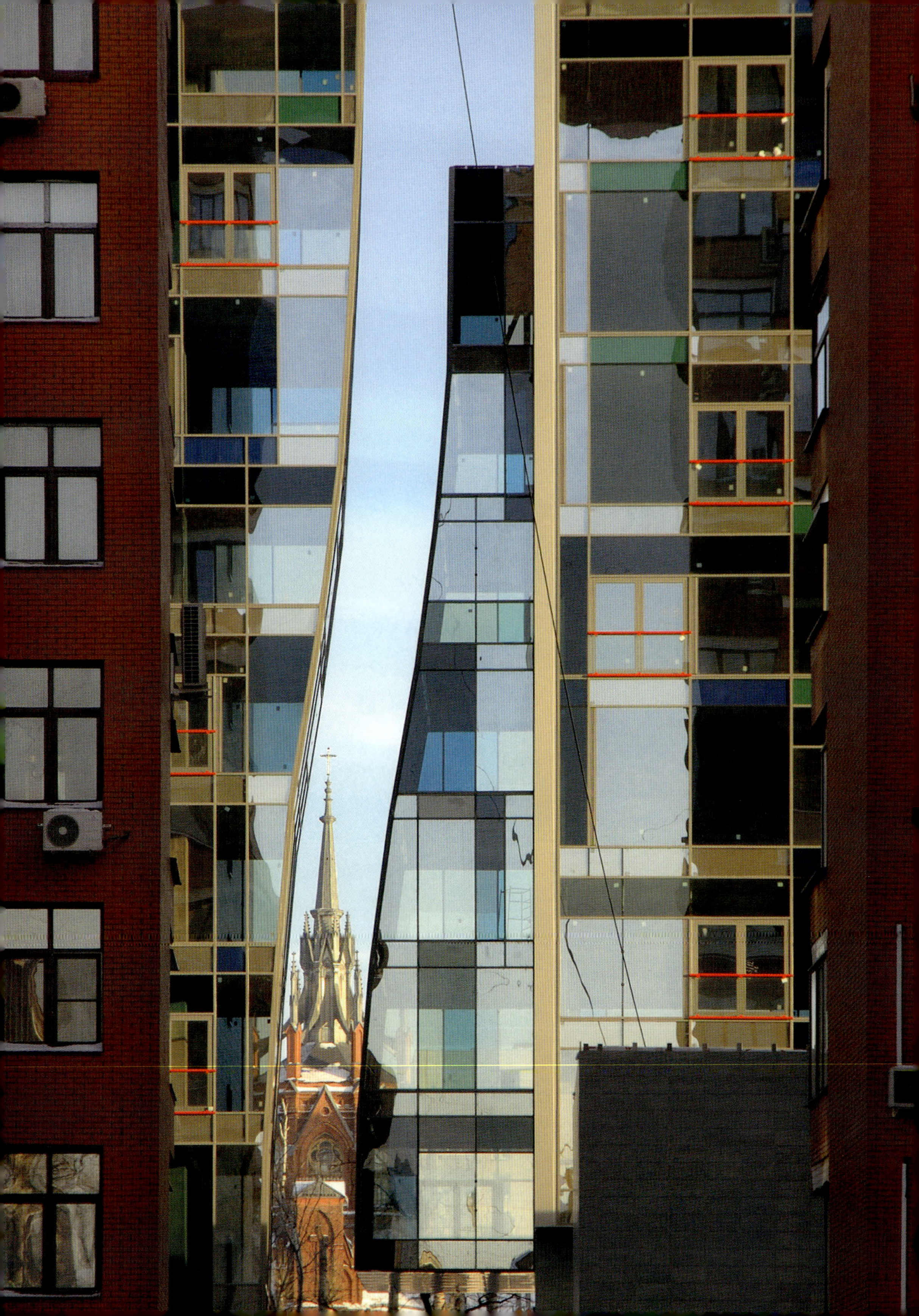

OSTOSHENKA ARCHITECTS | MOSCOW
Panorama House
Moscow, Russia | 2004

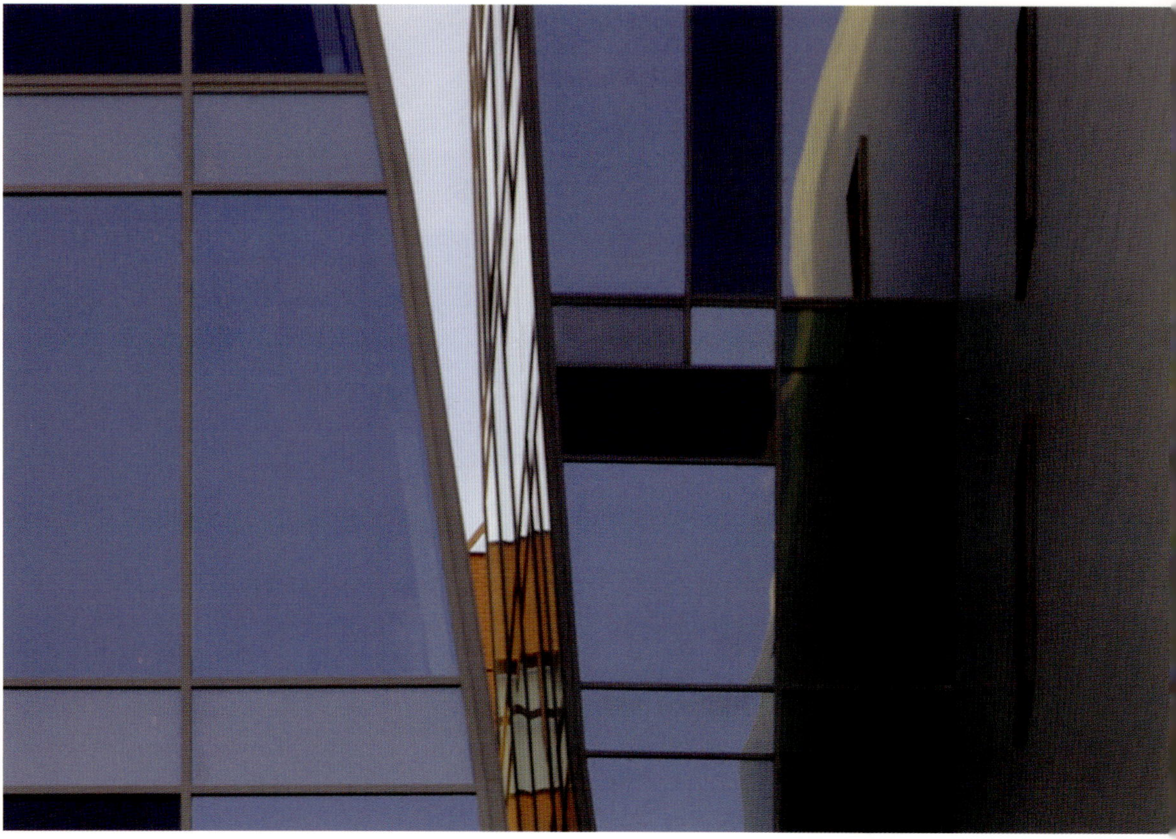

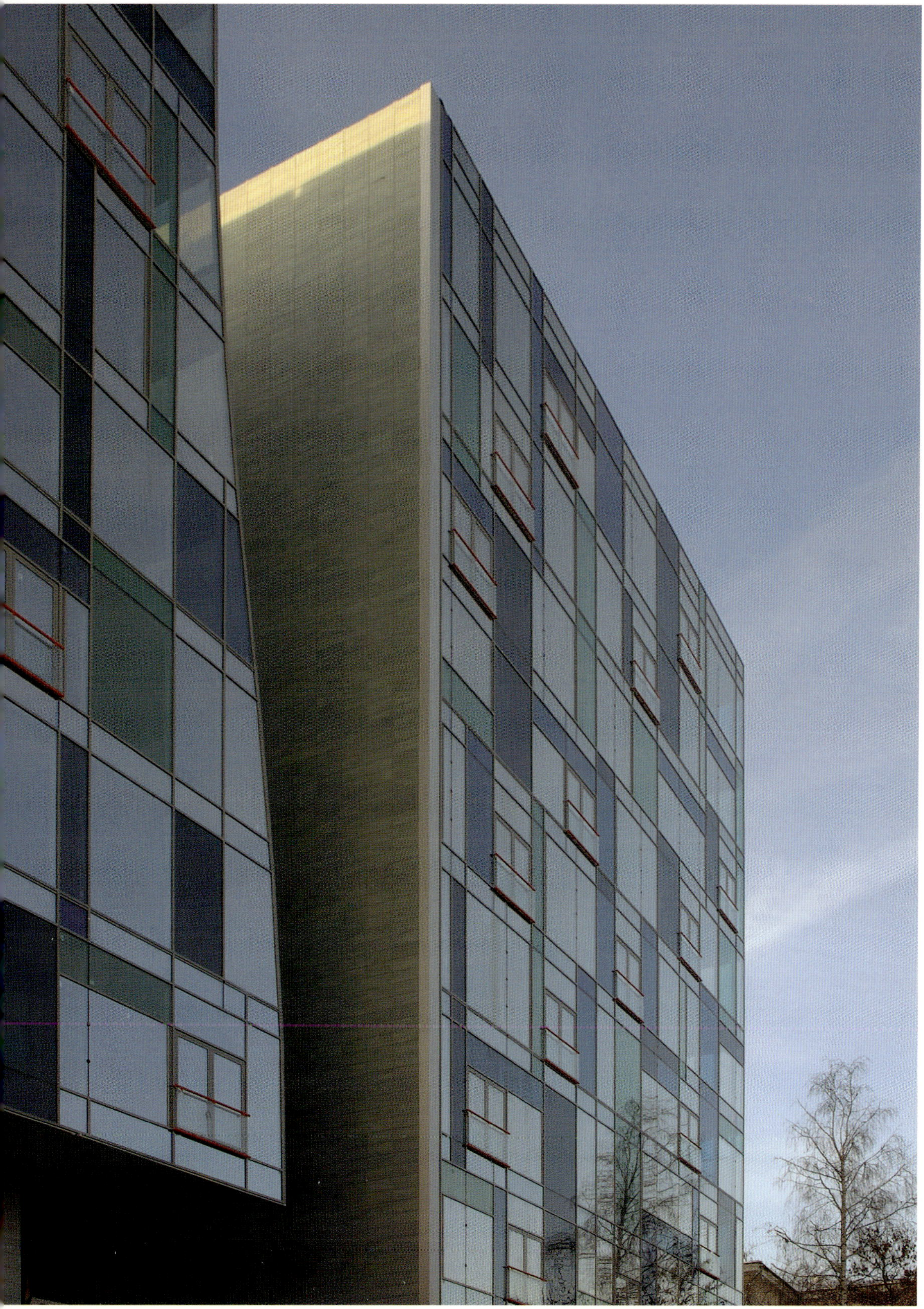

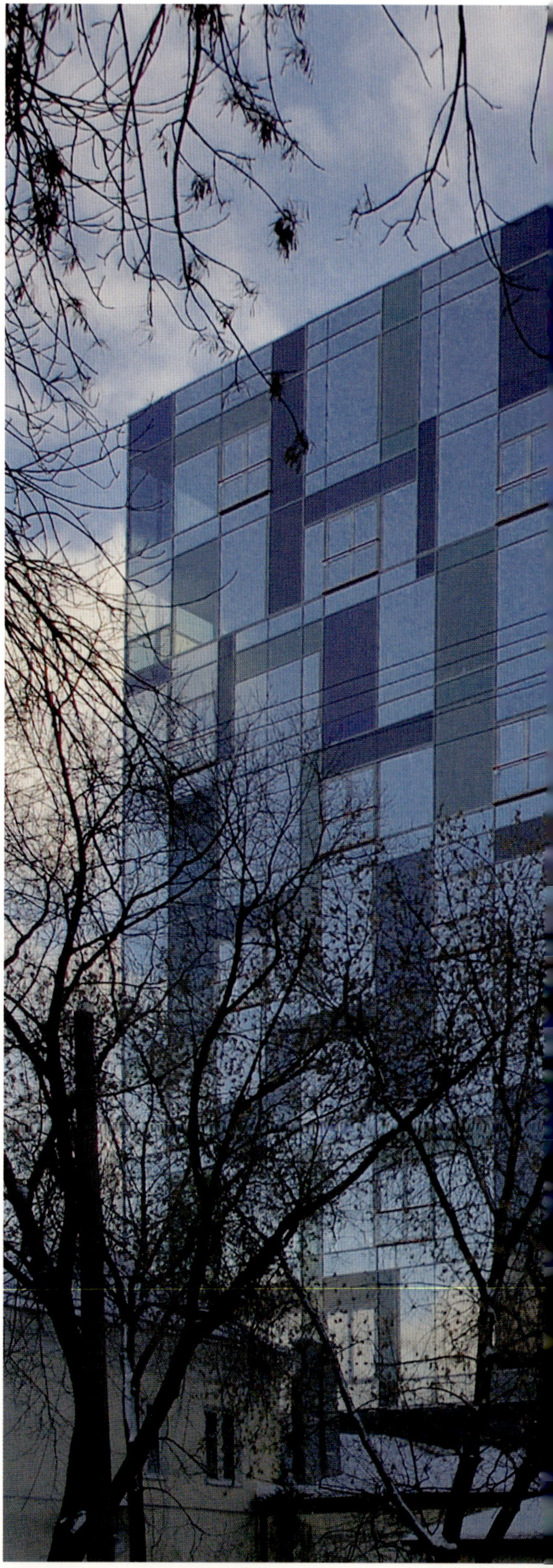

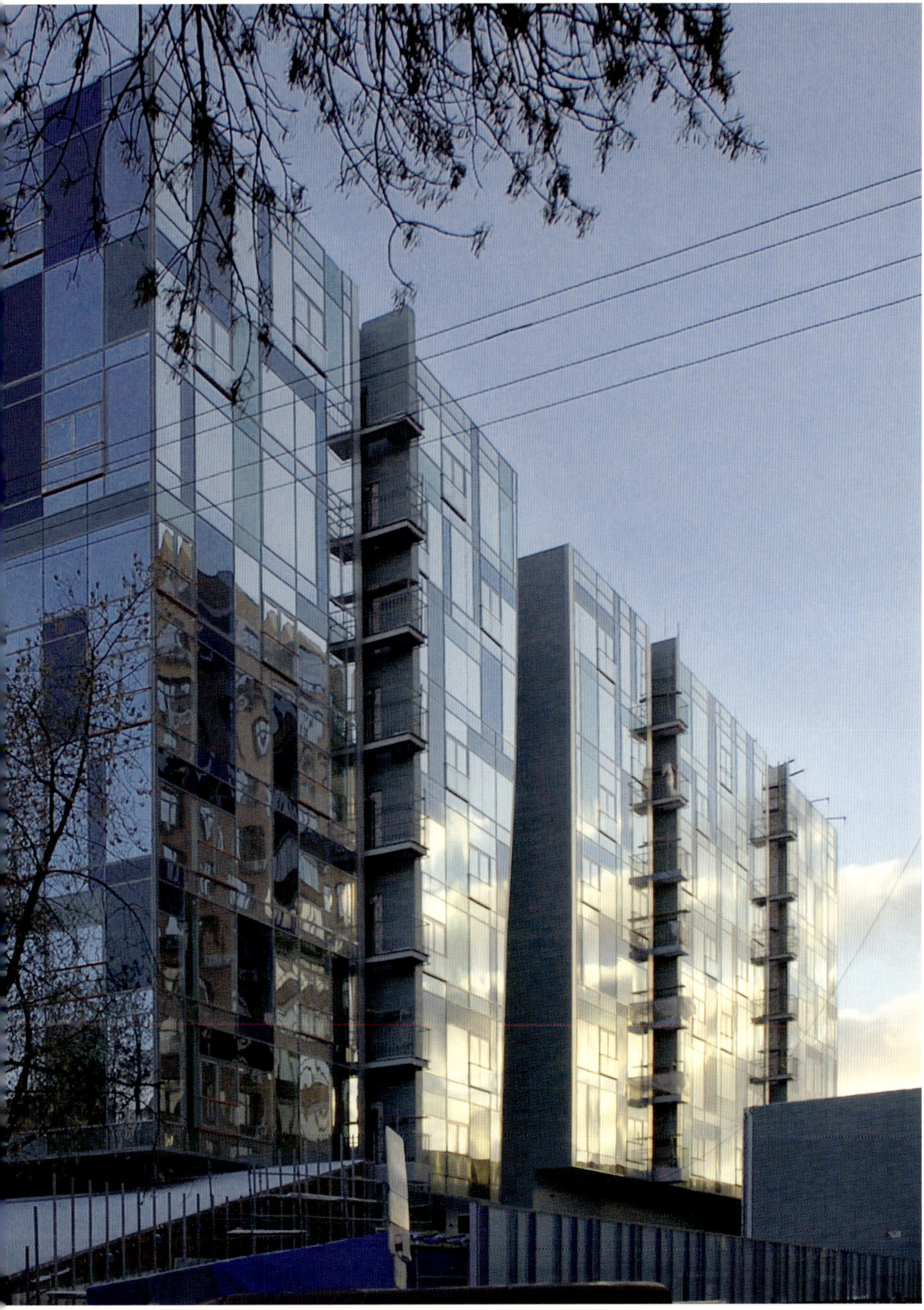

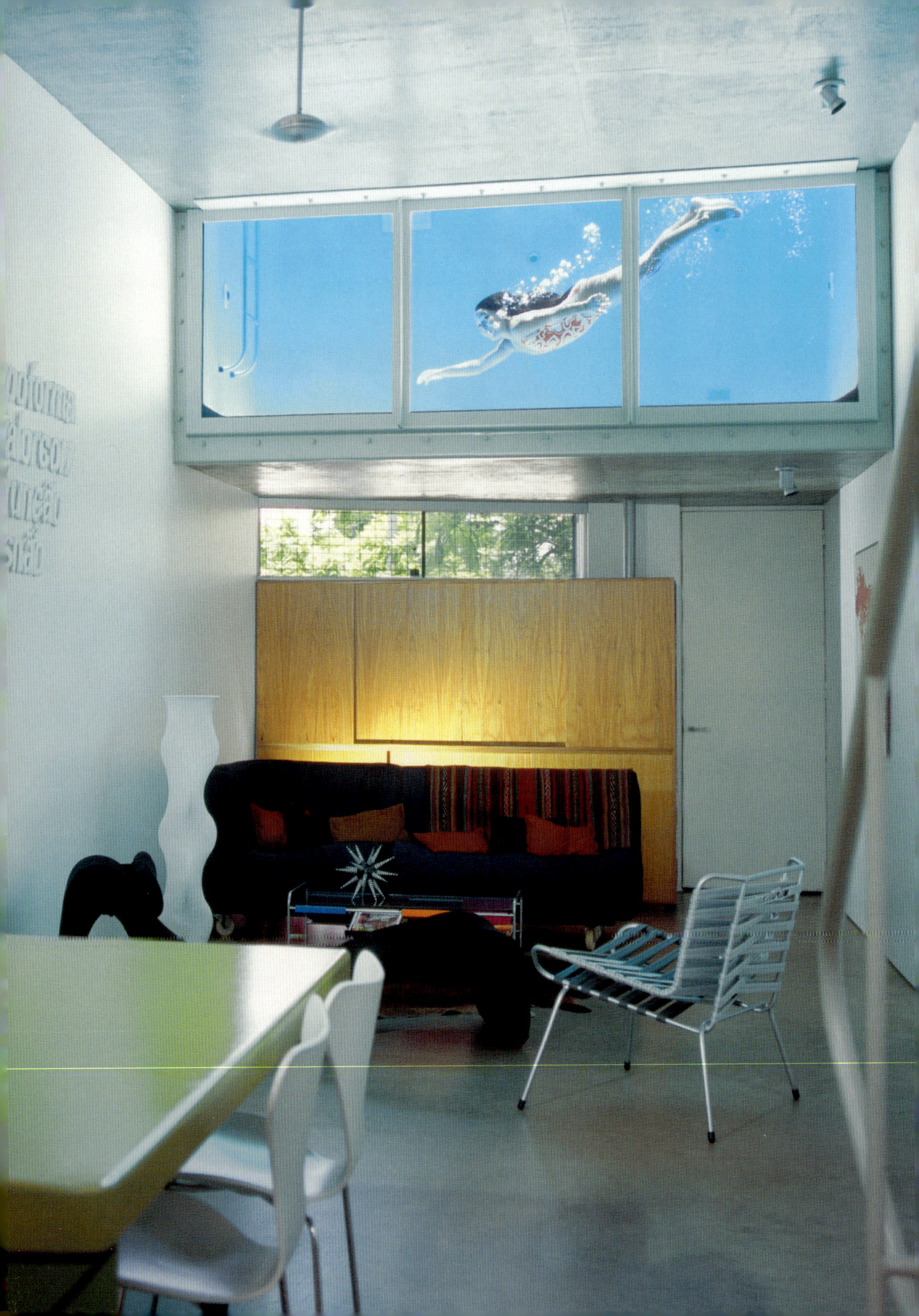

PROCTER:RIHL | LONDON
Slice House
Porto Alegre, Southern Brasil | 2004

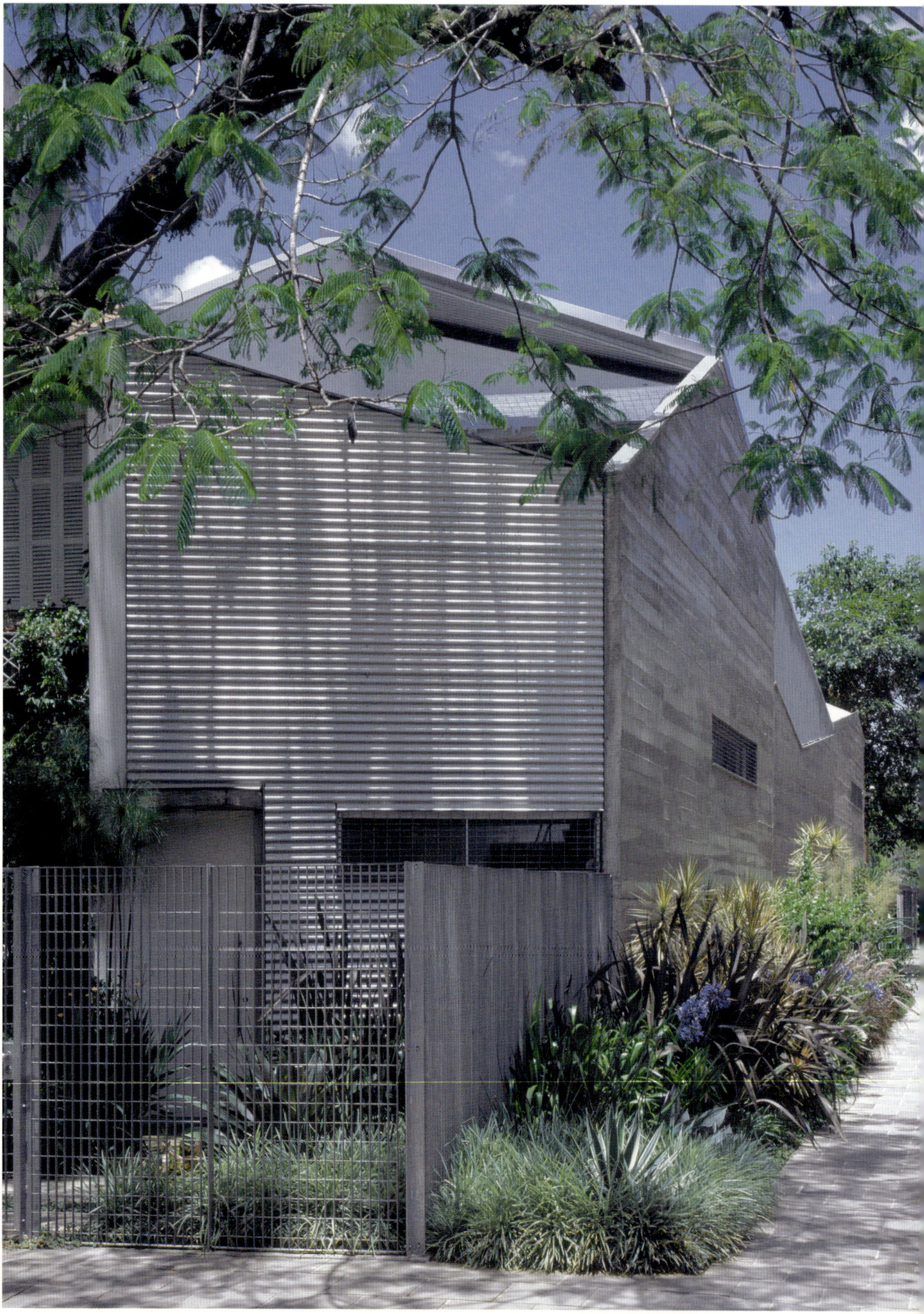

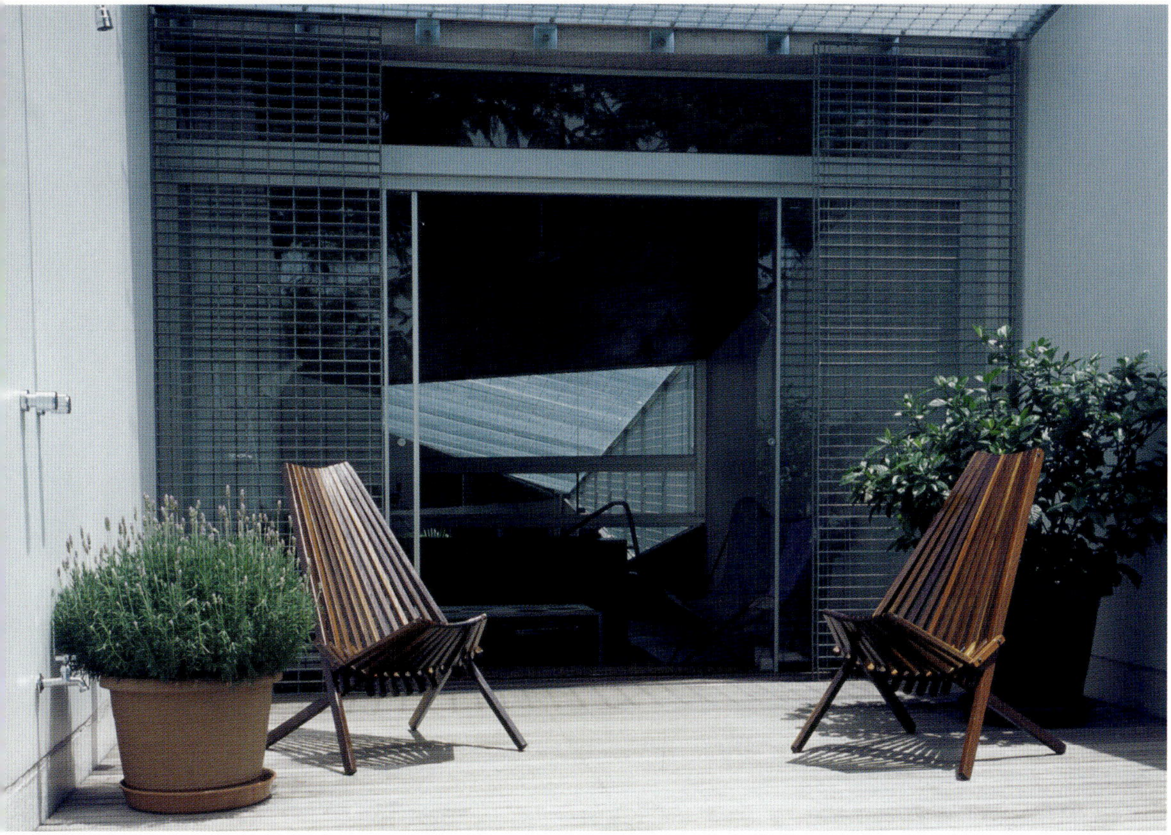

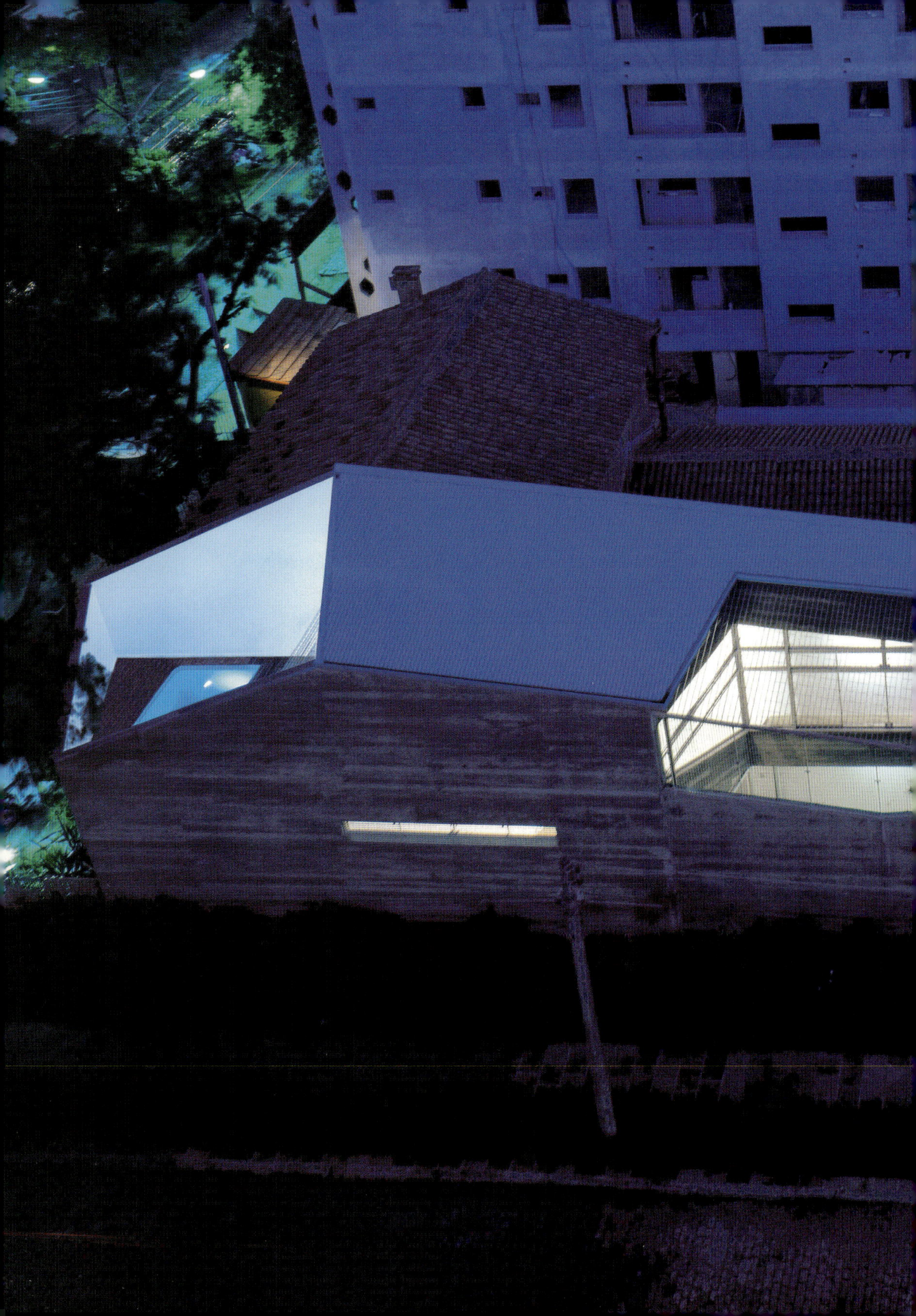

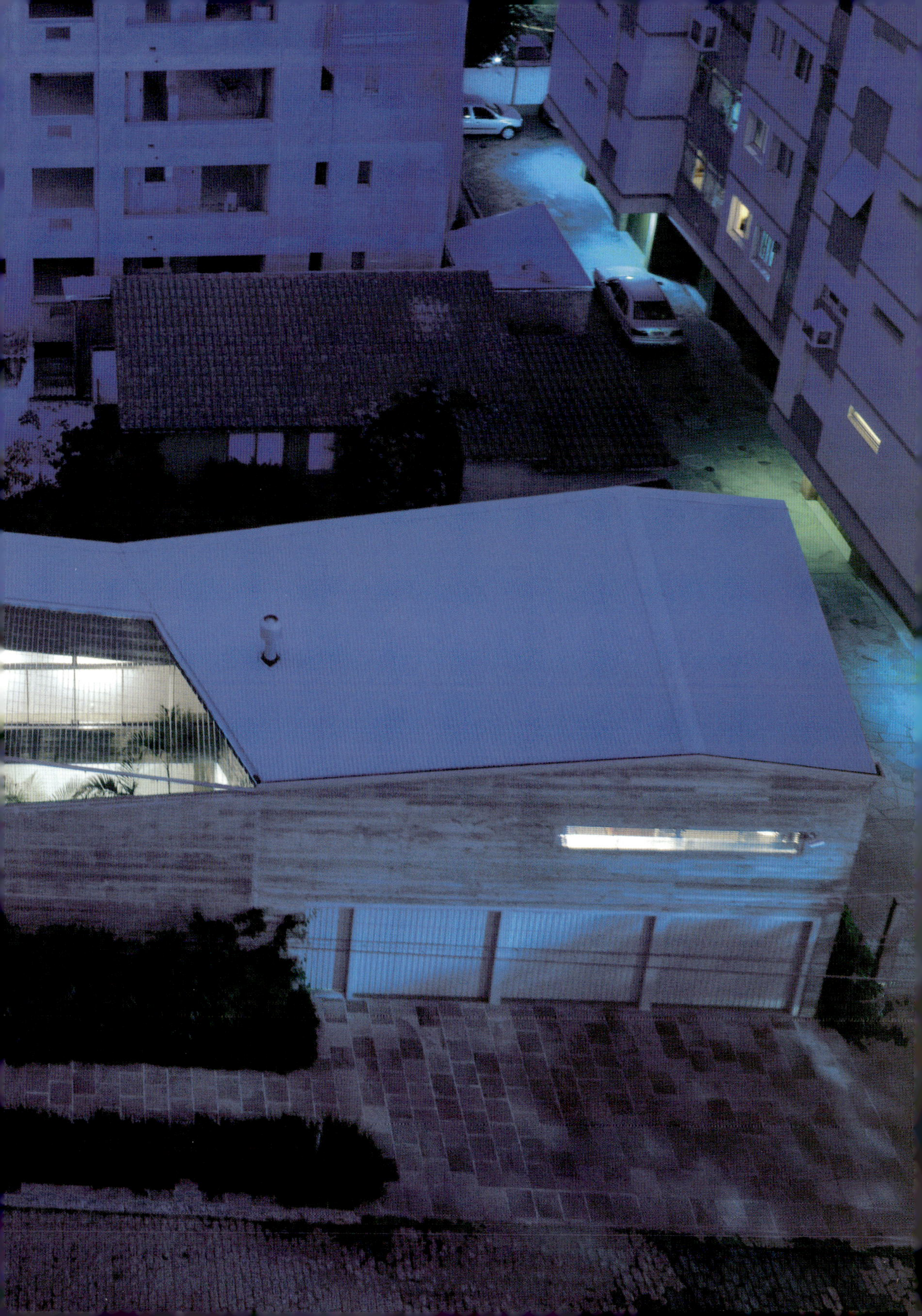

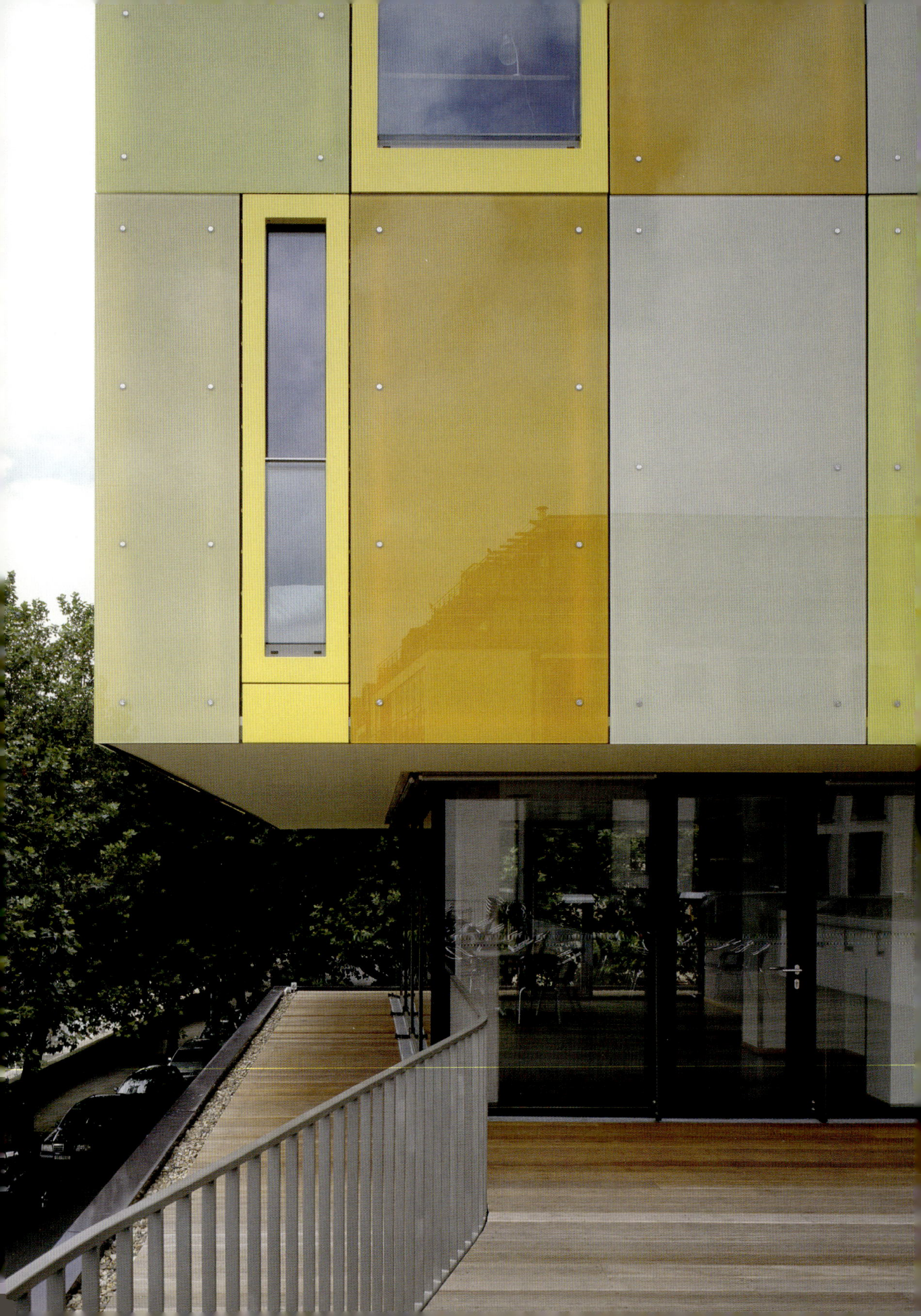

RAUMZEIT | BERLIN
Youth hostel Bremen
Bremen, Germany | 2005

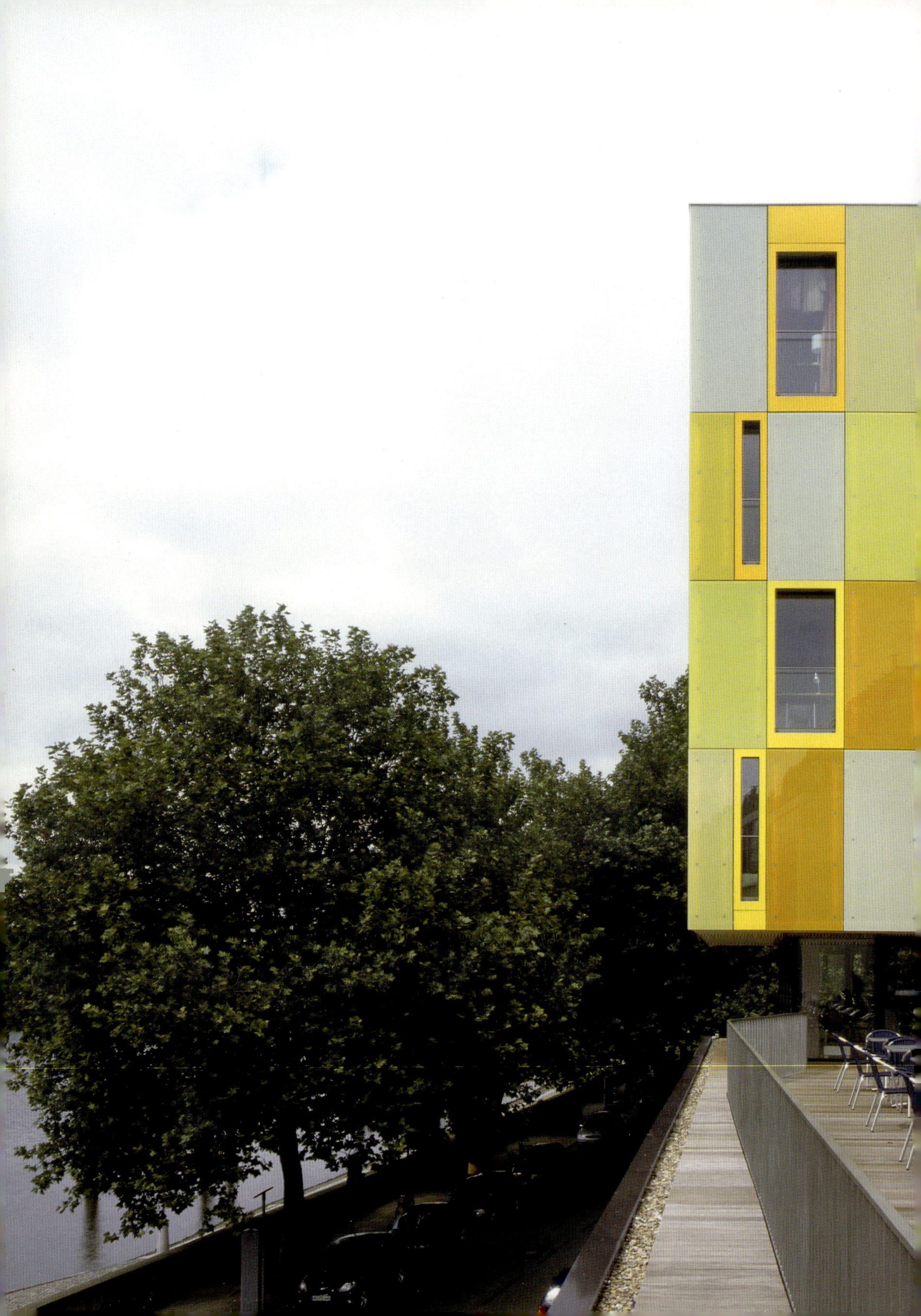

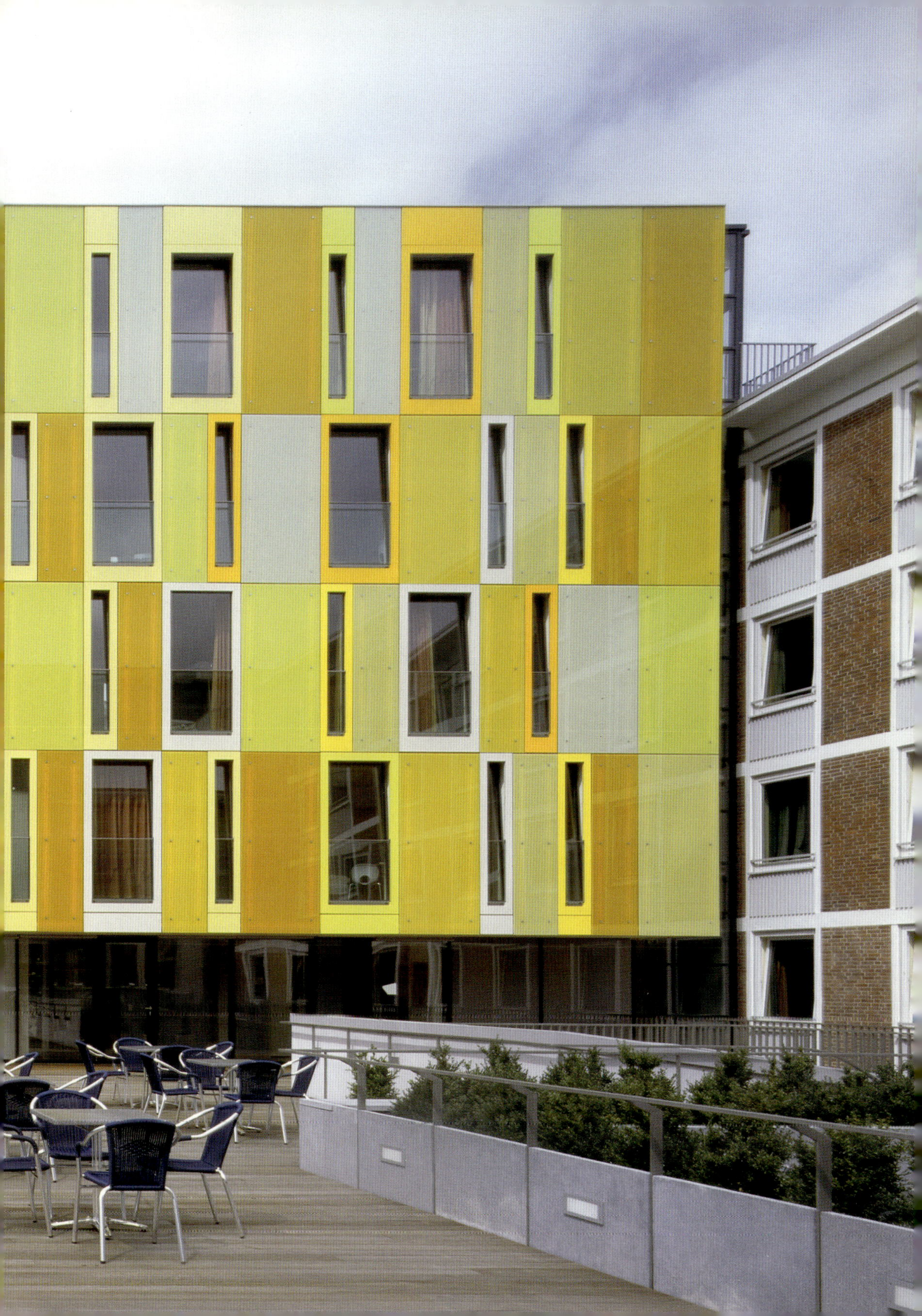

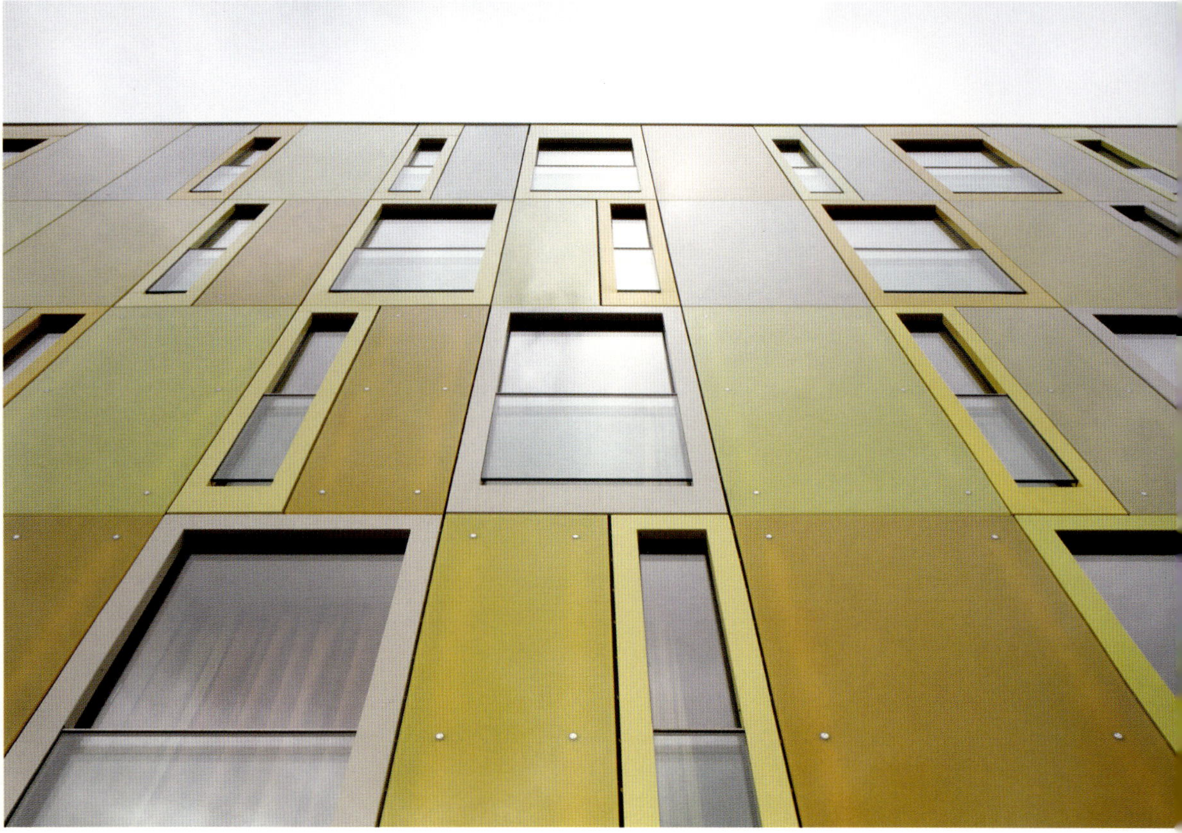

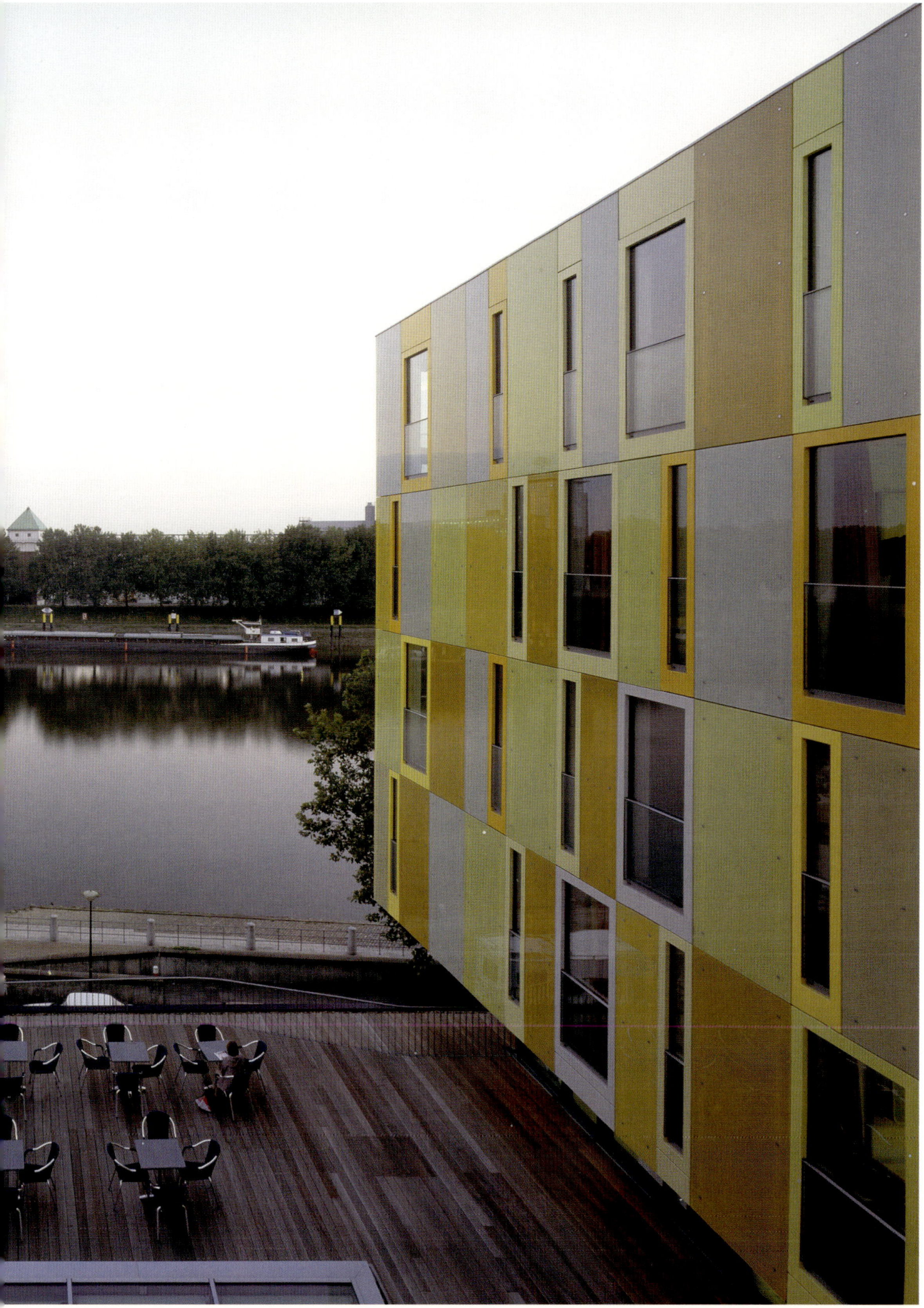

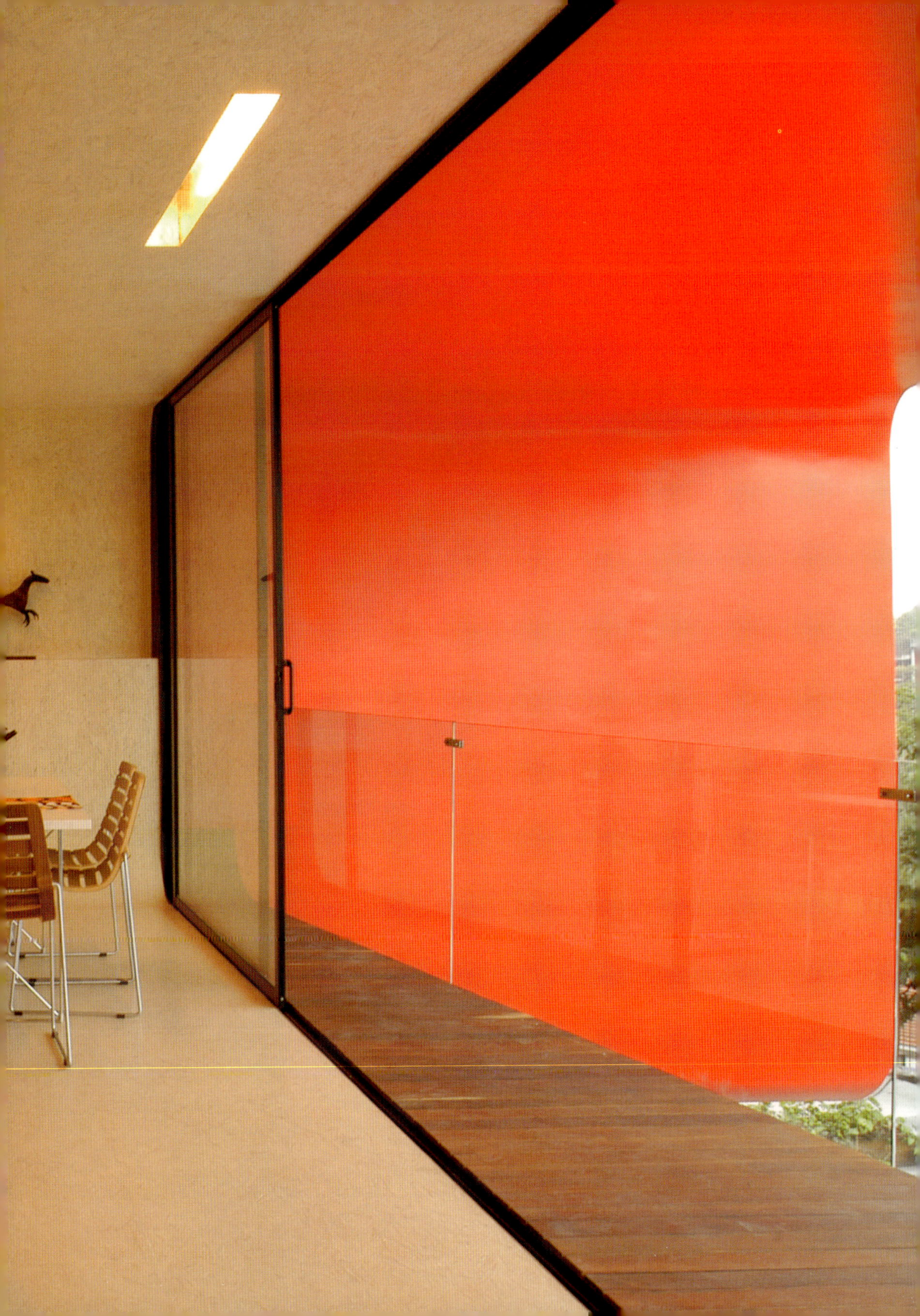

ROJKIND ARQUITECTOS | MEXICO CITY
PR34 House
Tecamachalco | 2003

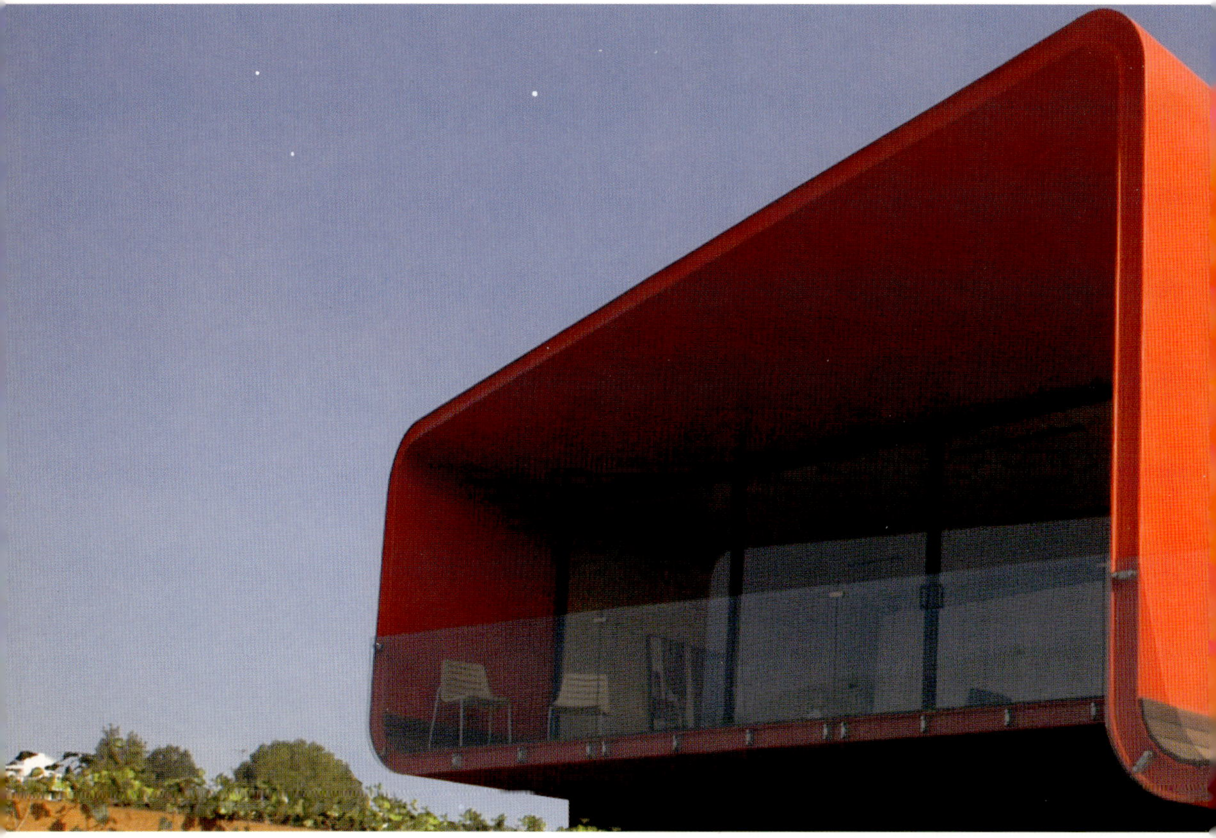

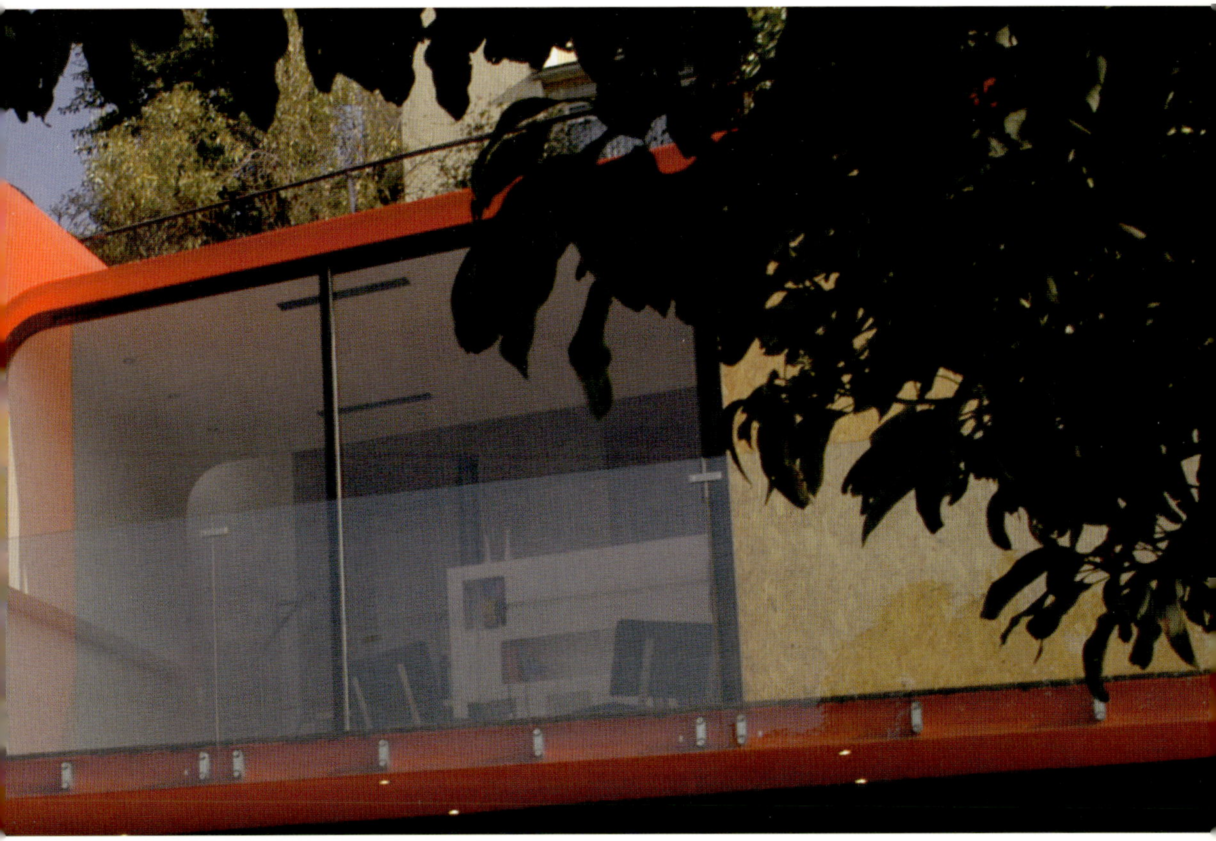

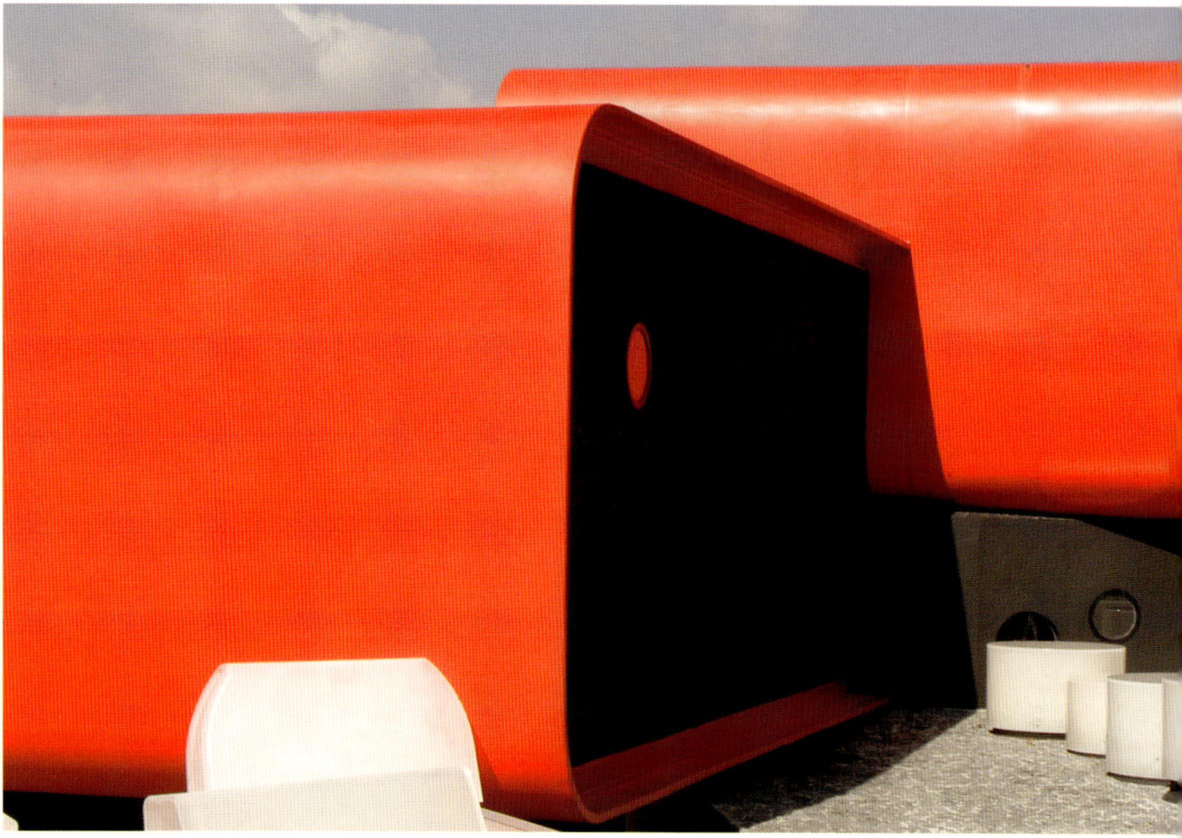

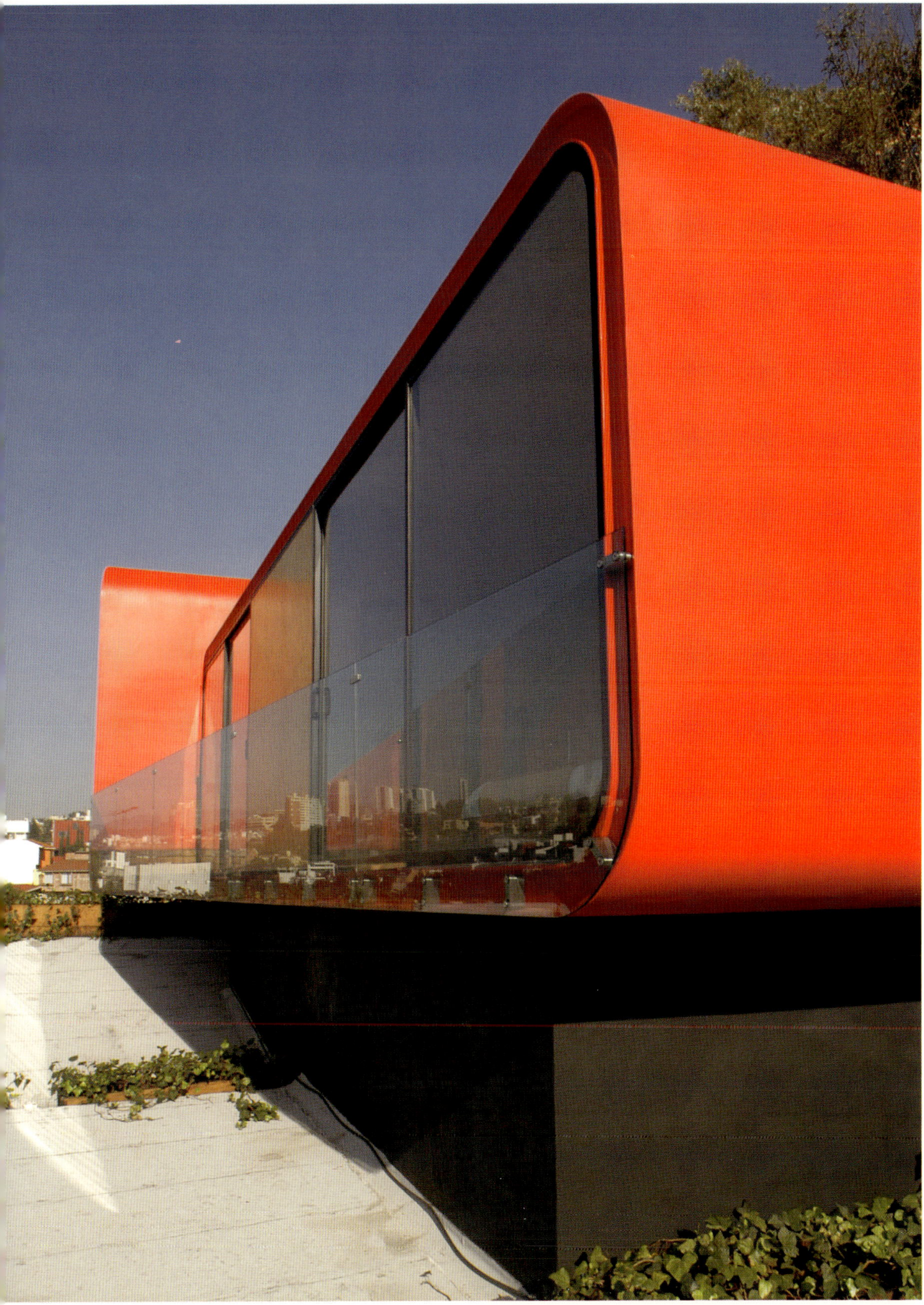

Charlottenstr.

SAUERBRUCH HUTTON ARCHITEKTEN | BERLIN
GSW Headquarters
Berlin, Germany | 1999

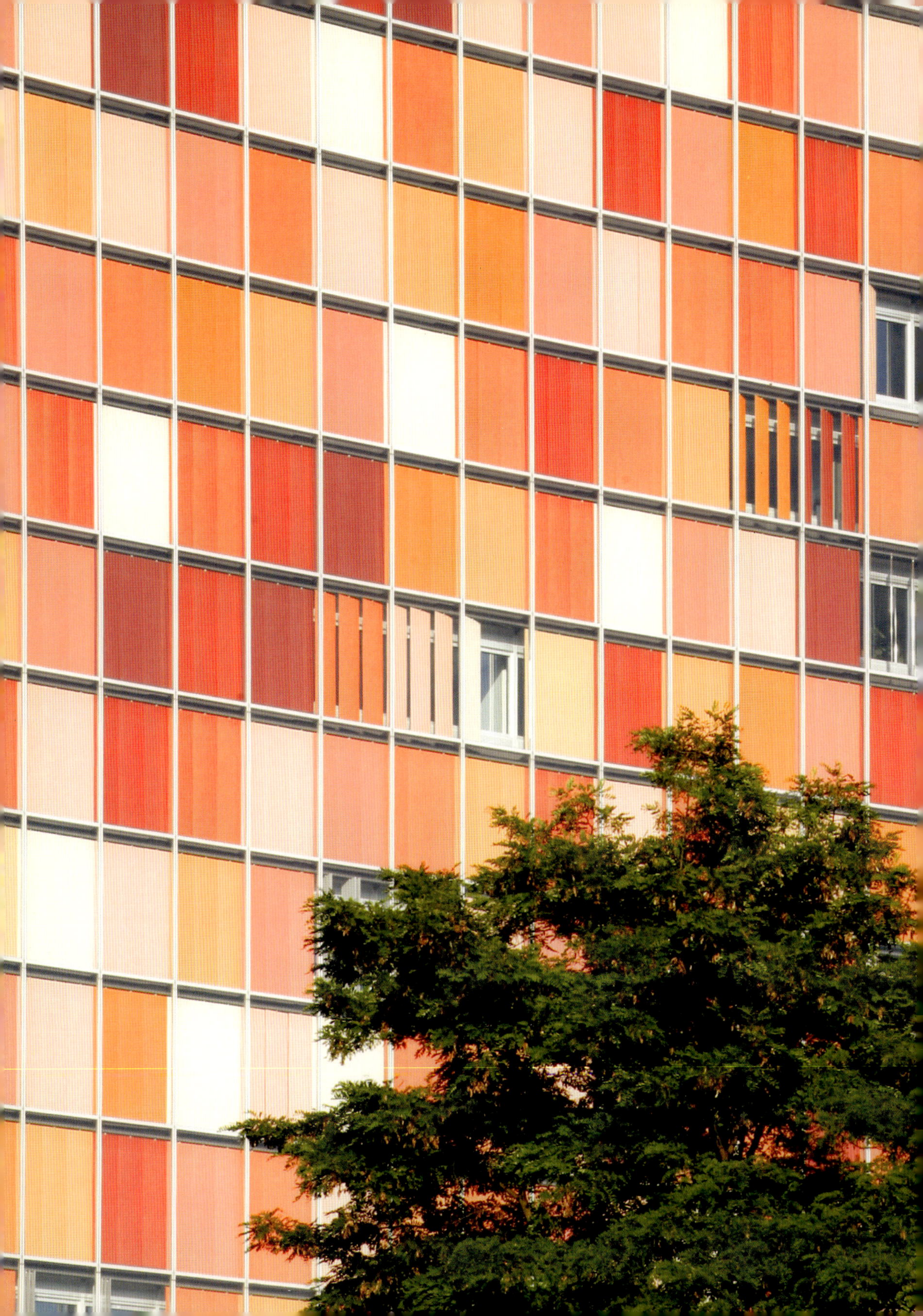

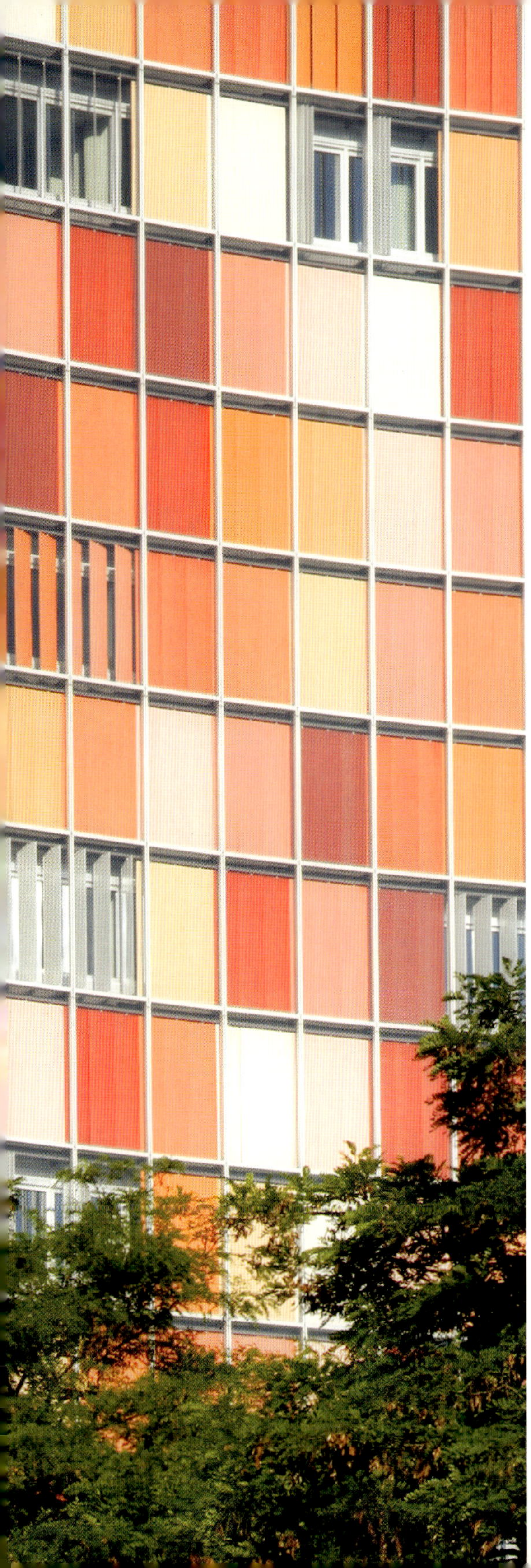

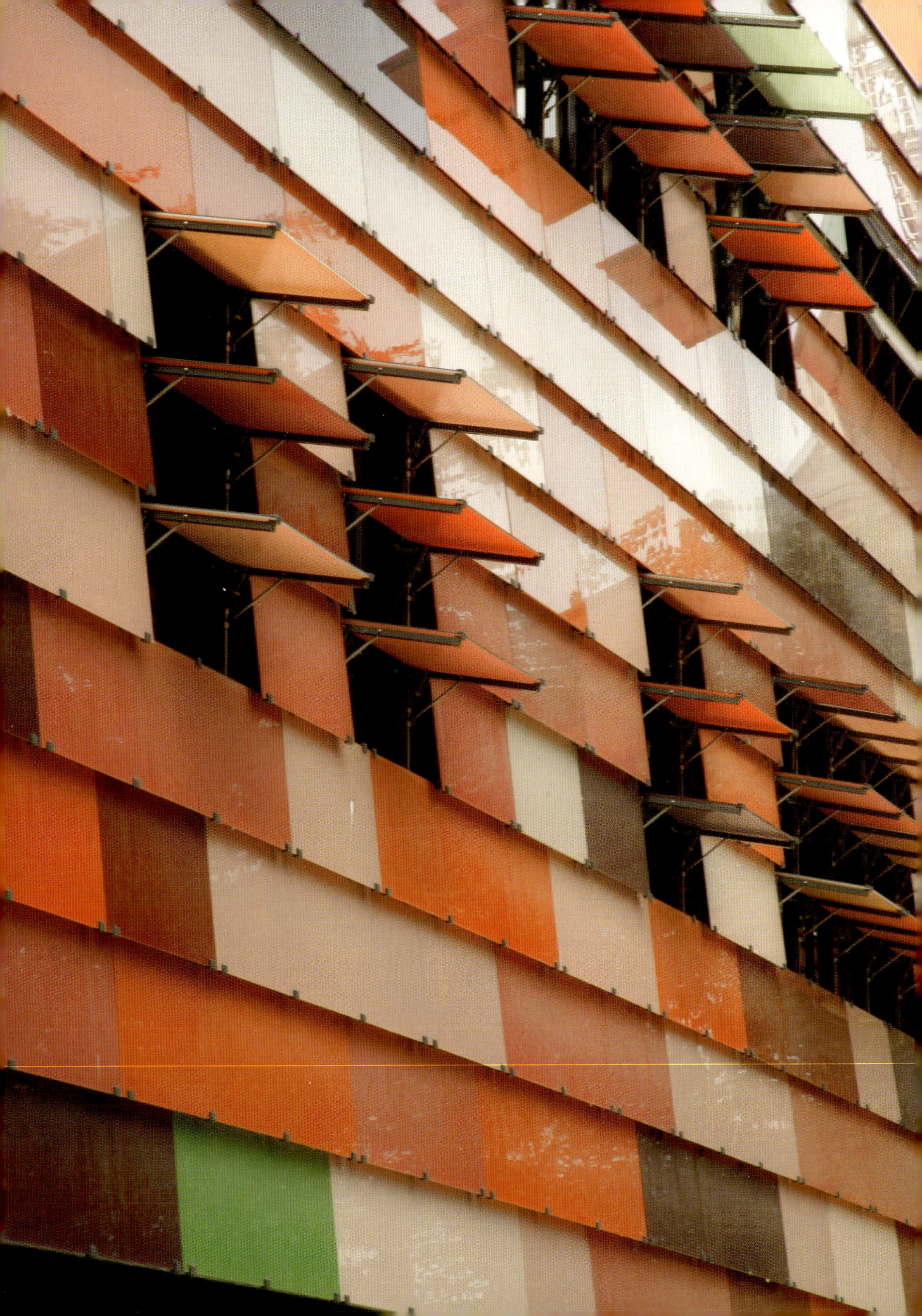

SAUERBRUCH HUTTON ARCHITEKTEN | BERLIN
Fire and Police Station for the Government District
Berlin, Germany | 2004

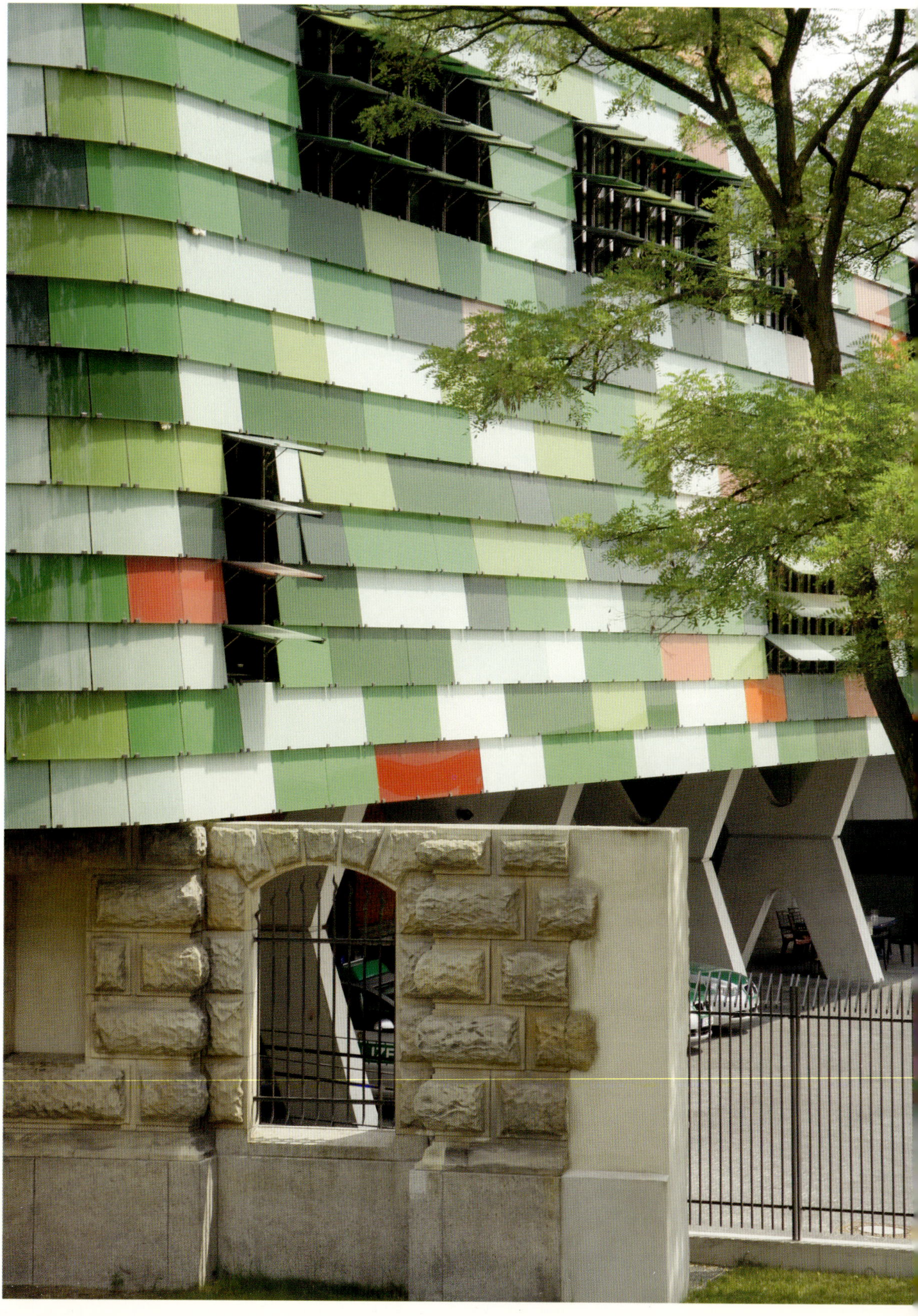

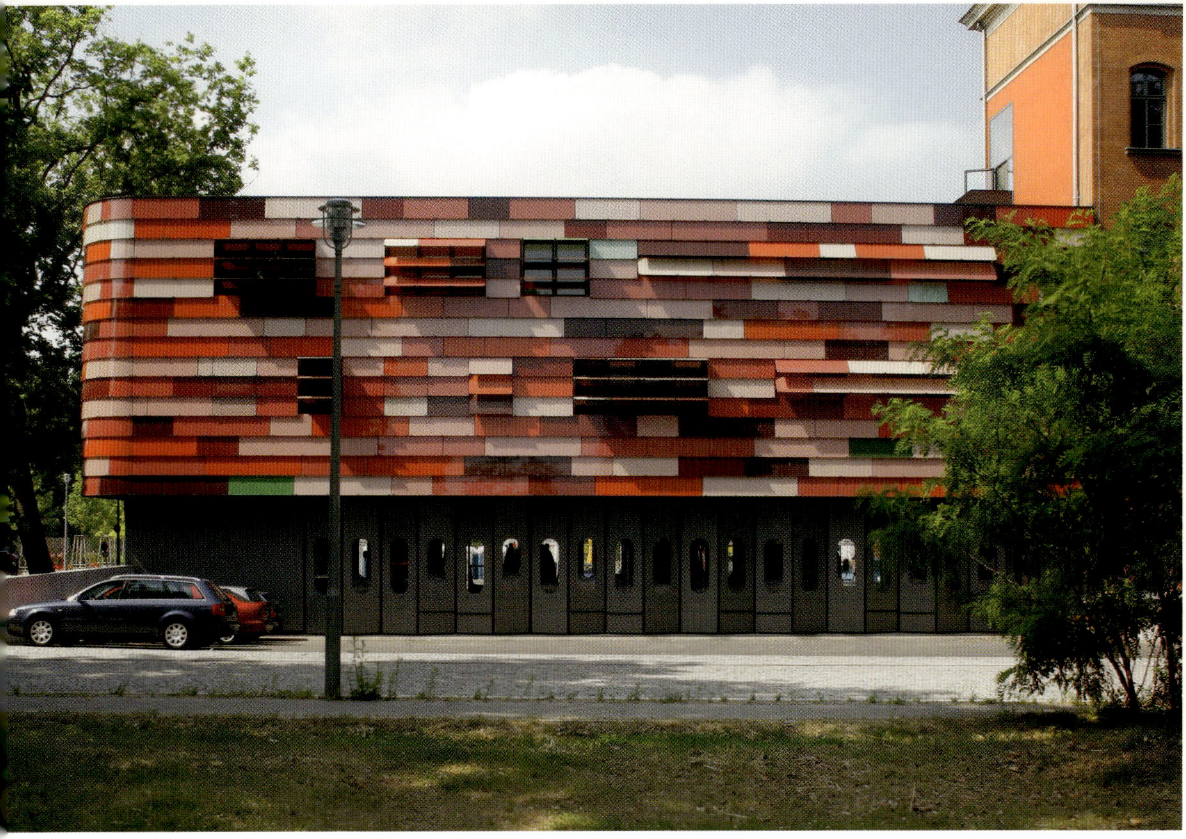

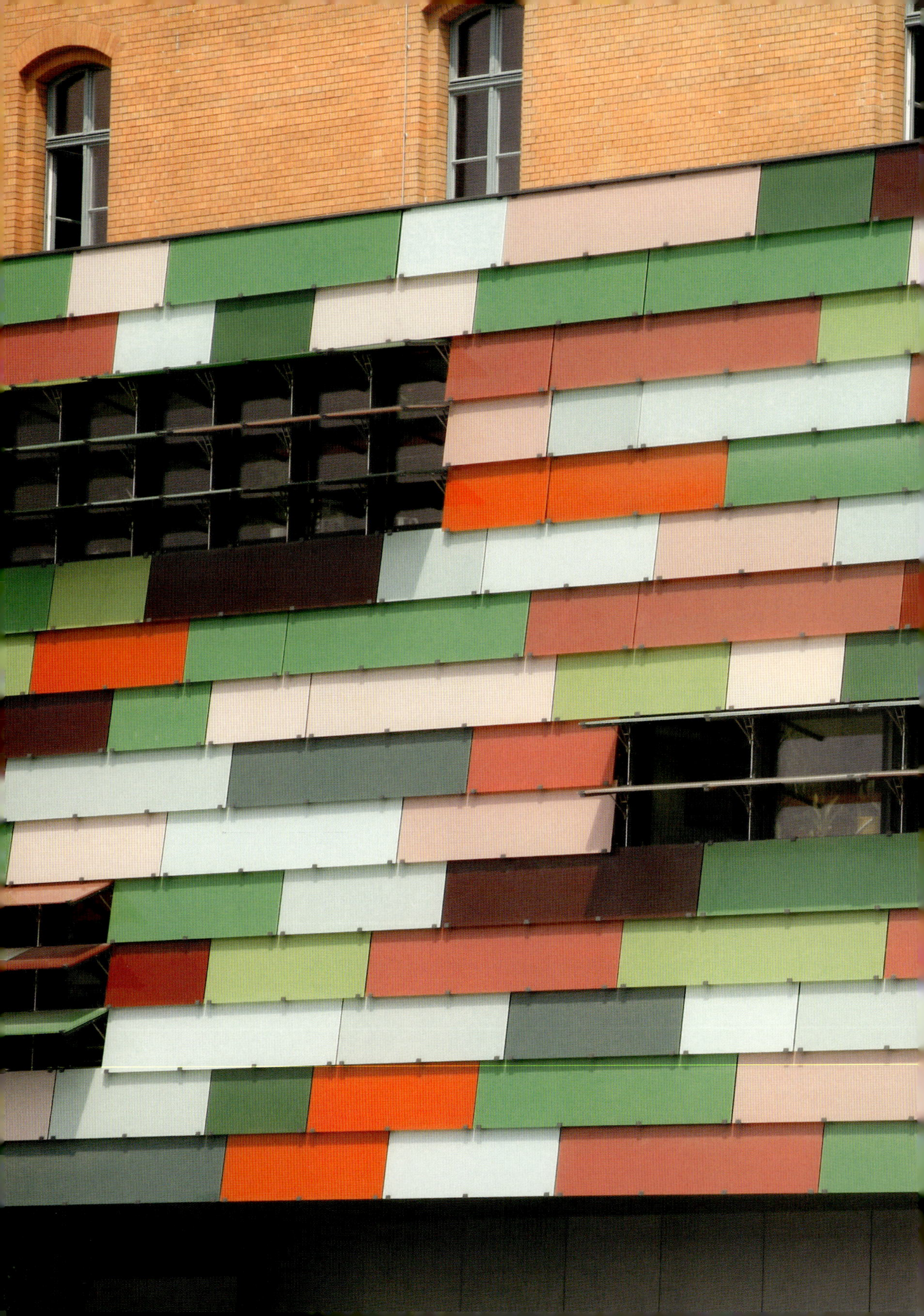

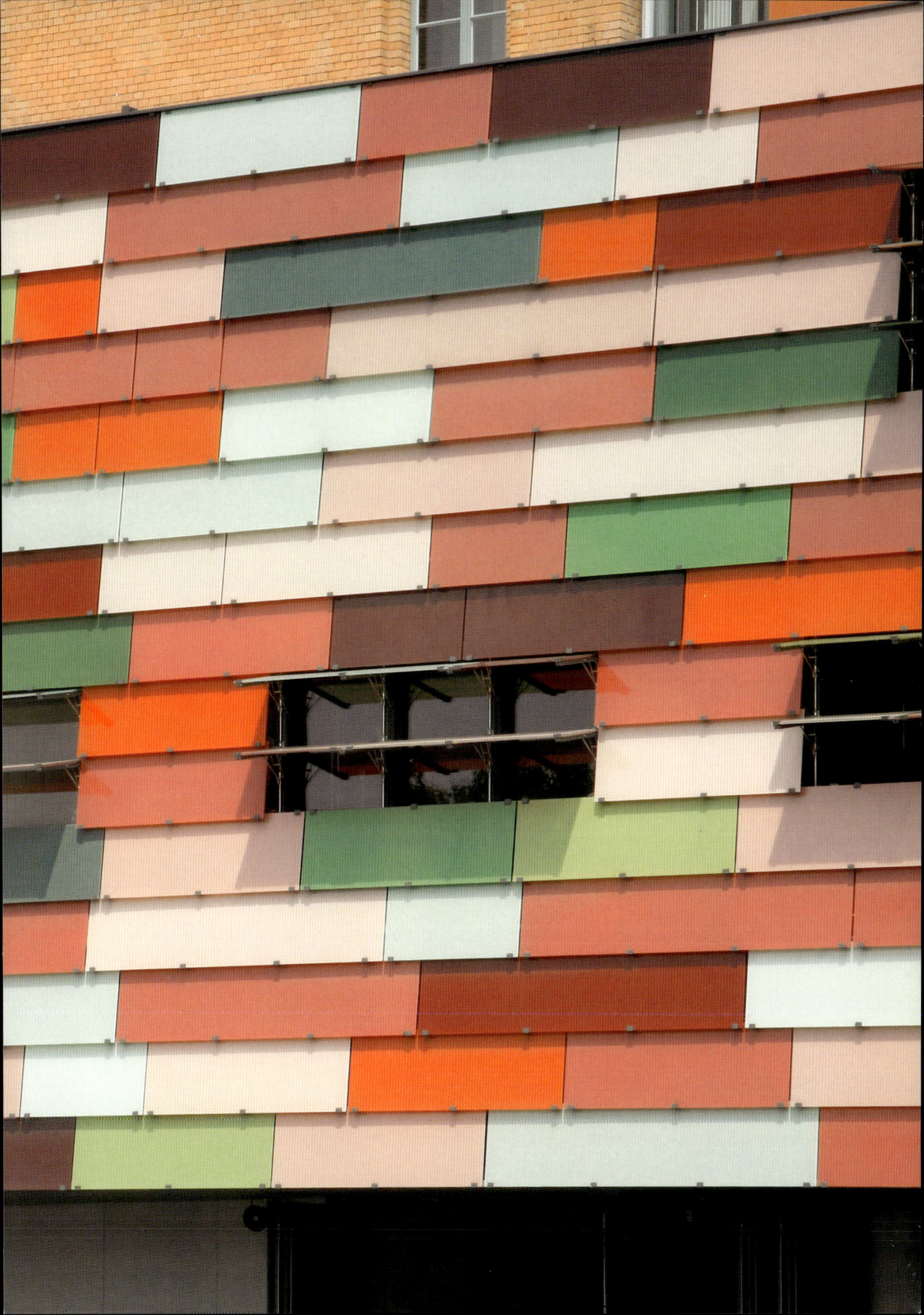

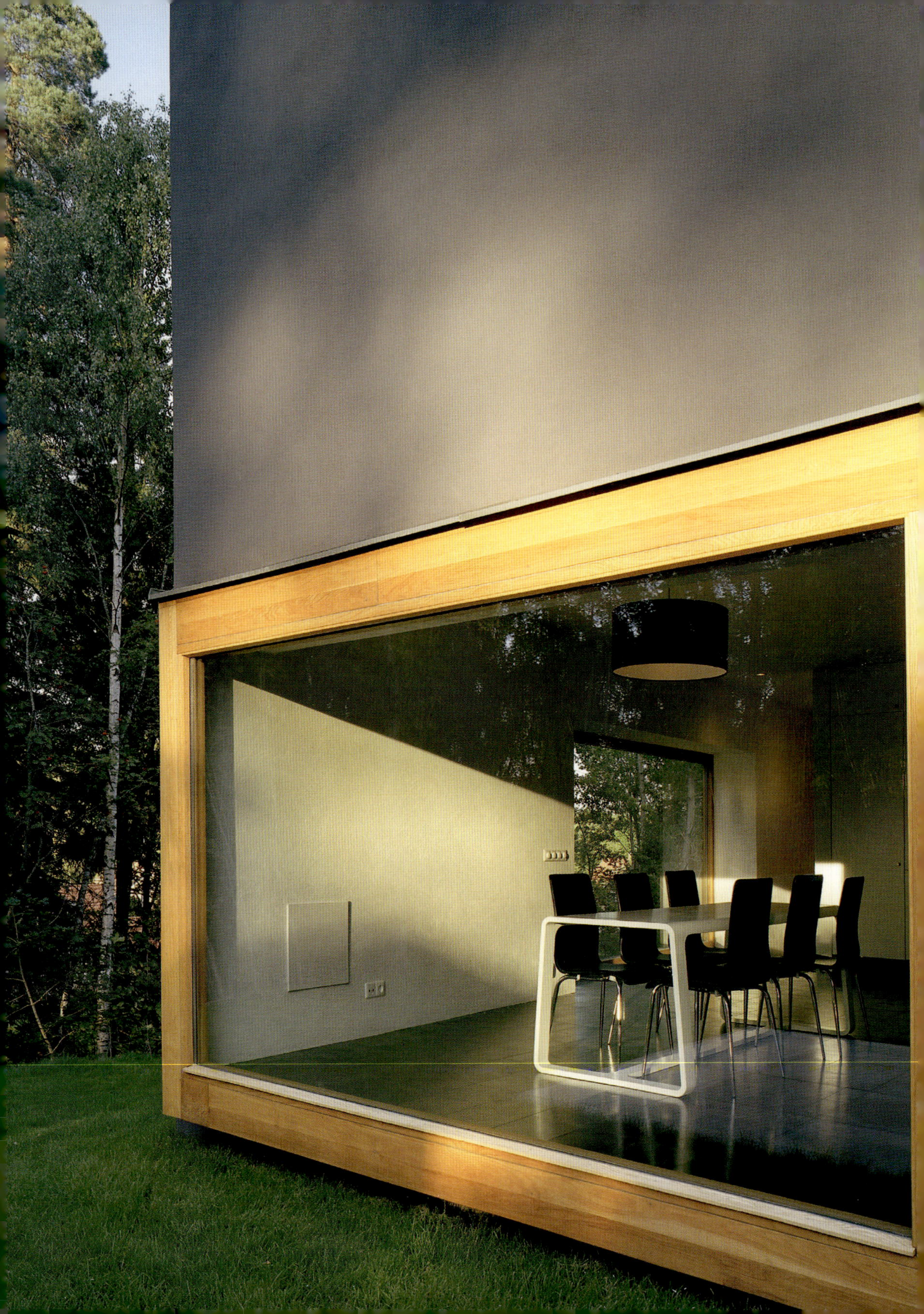

THAM & VIDEGÅRD HANSSON ARKITEKTER | STOCKHOLM
Two family house Kanoten
Danderyd, Sweden | 2005

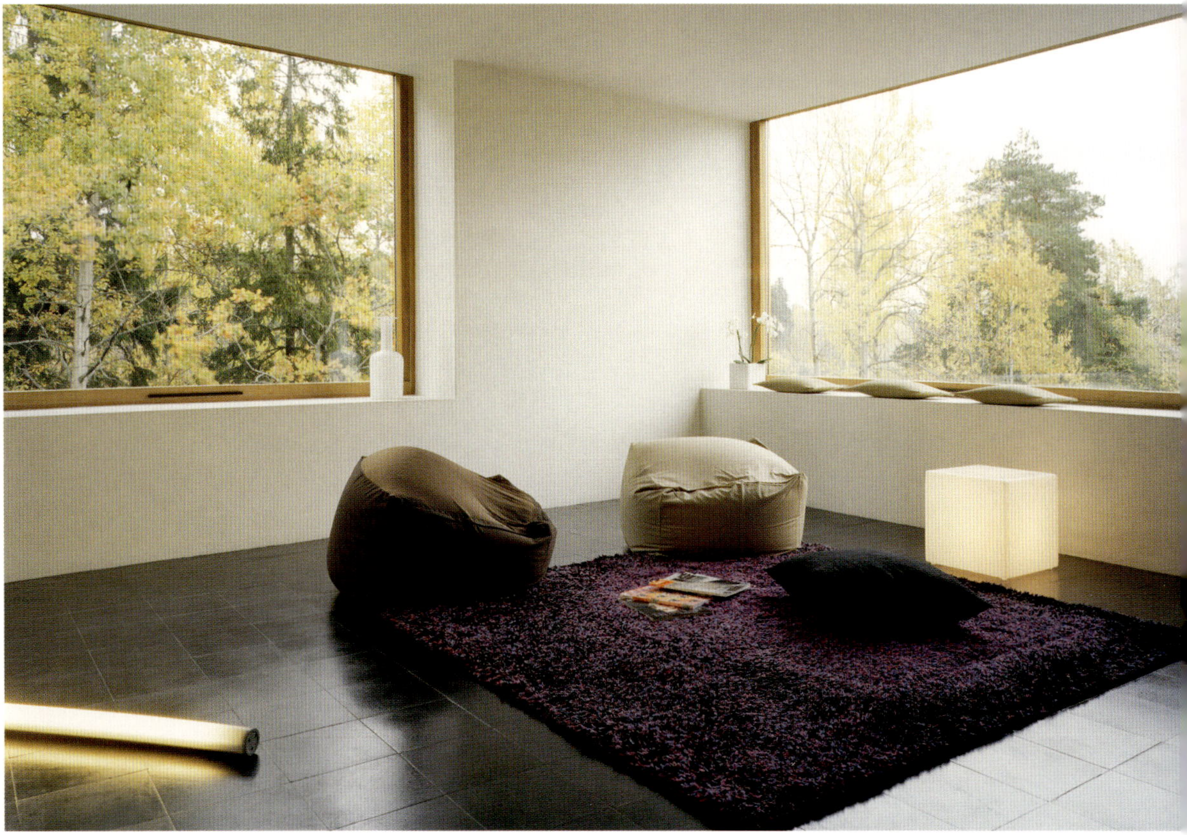

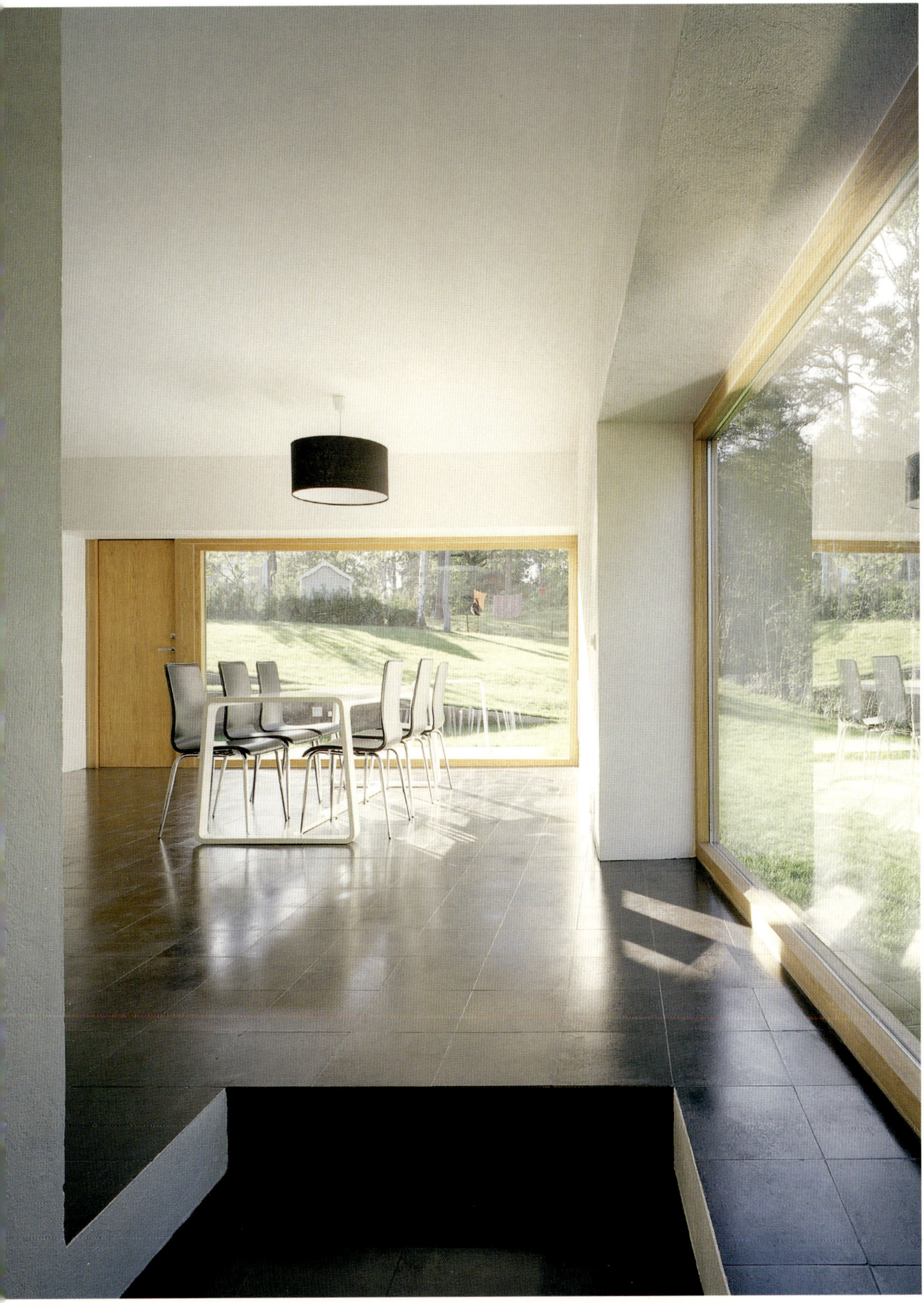

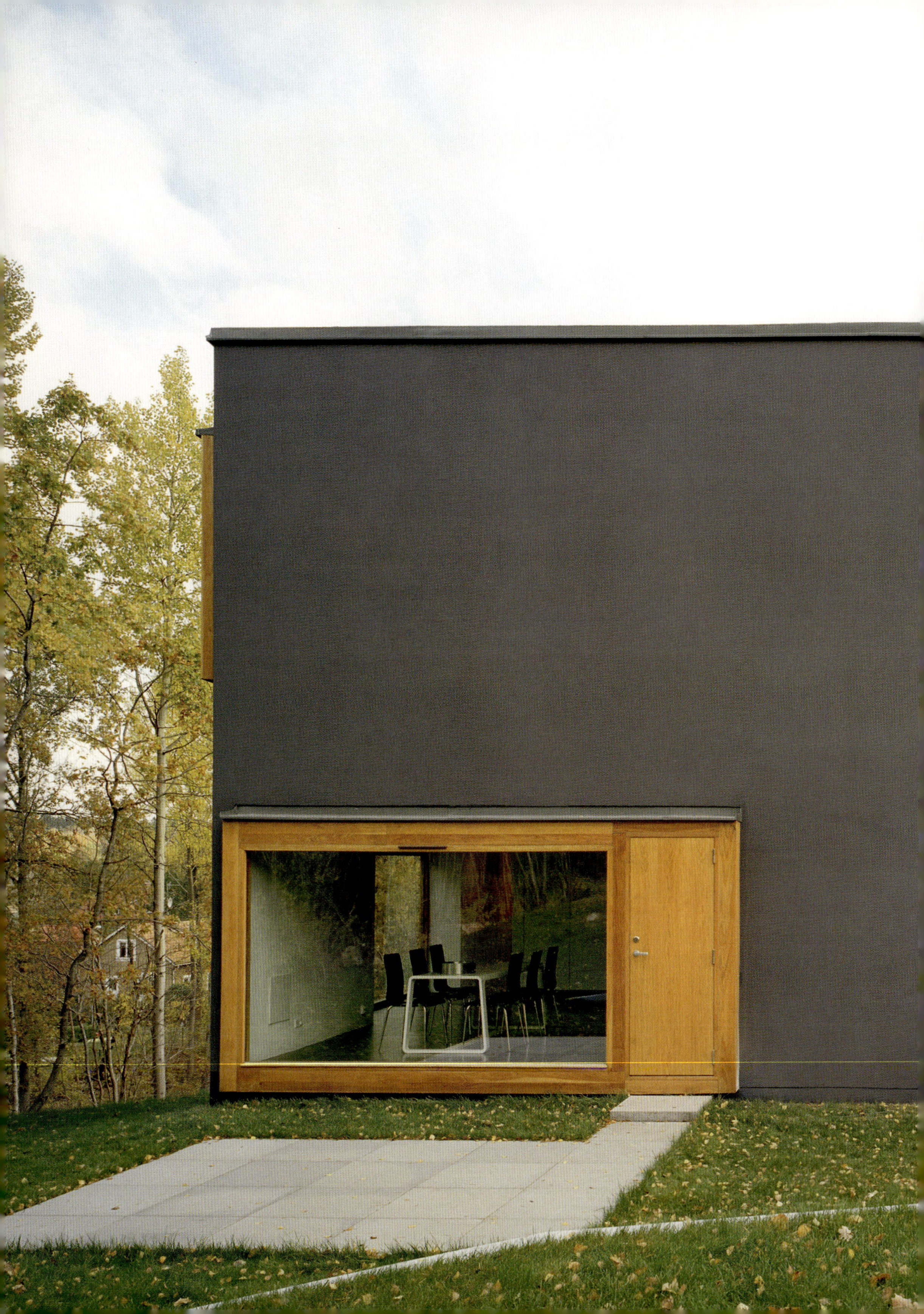

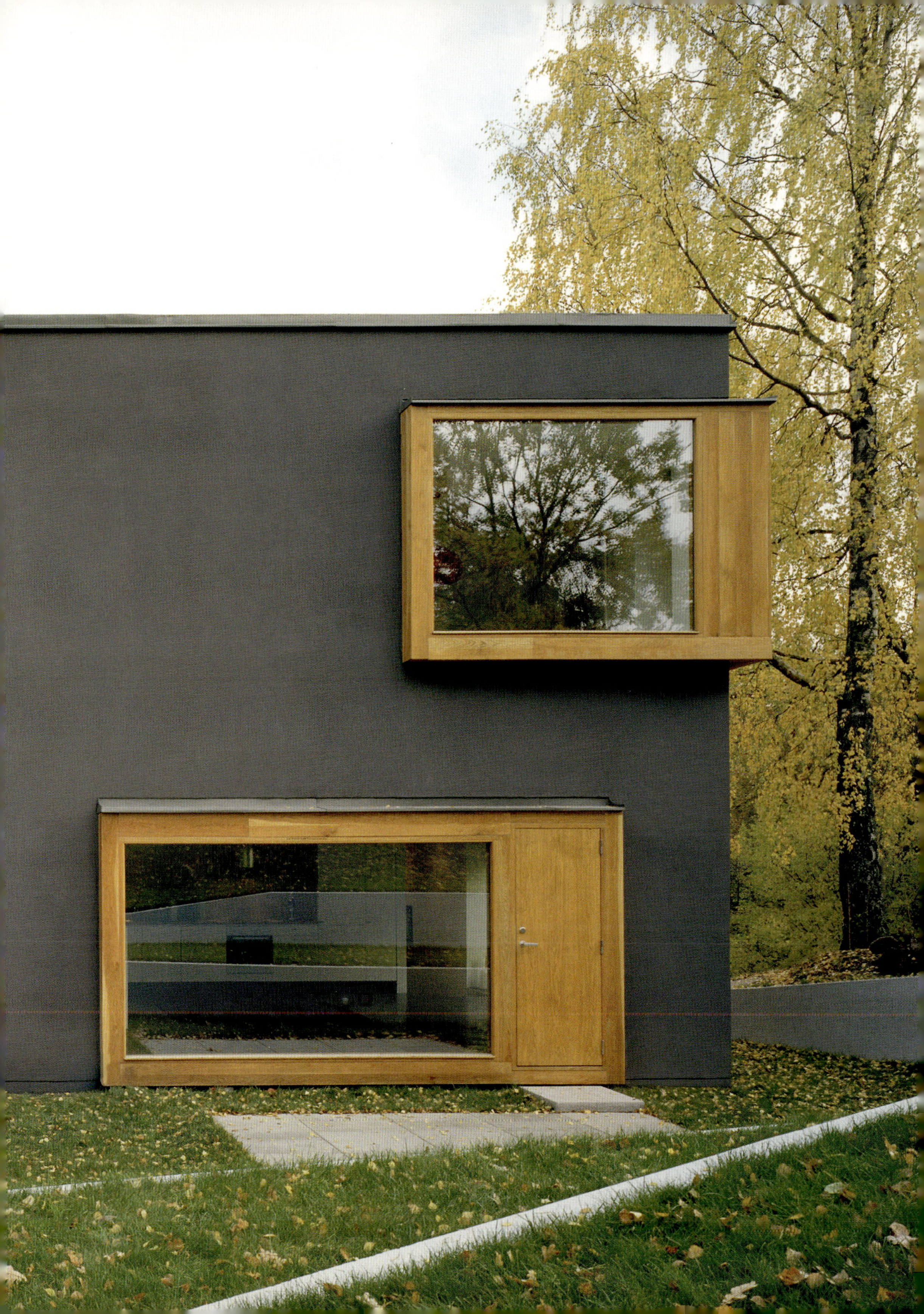

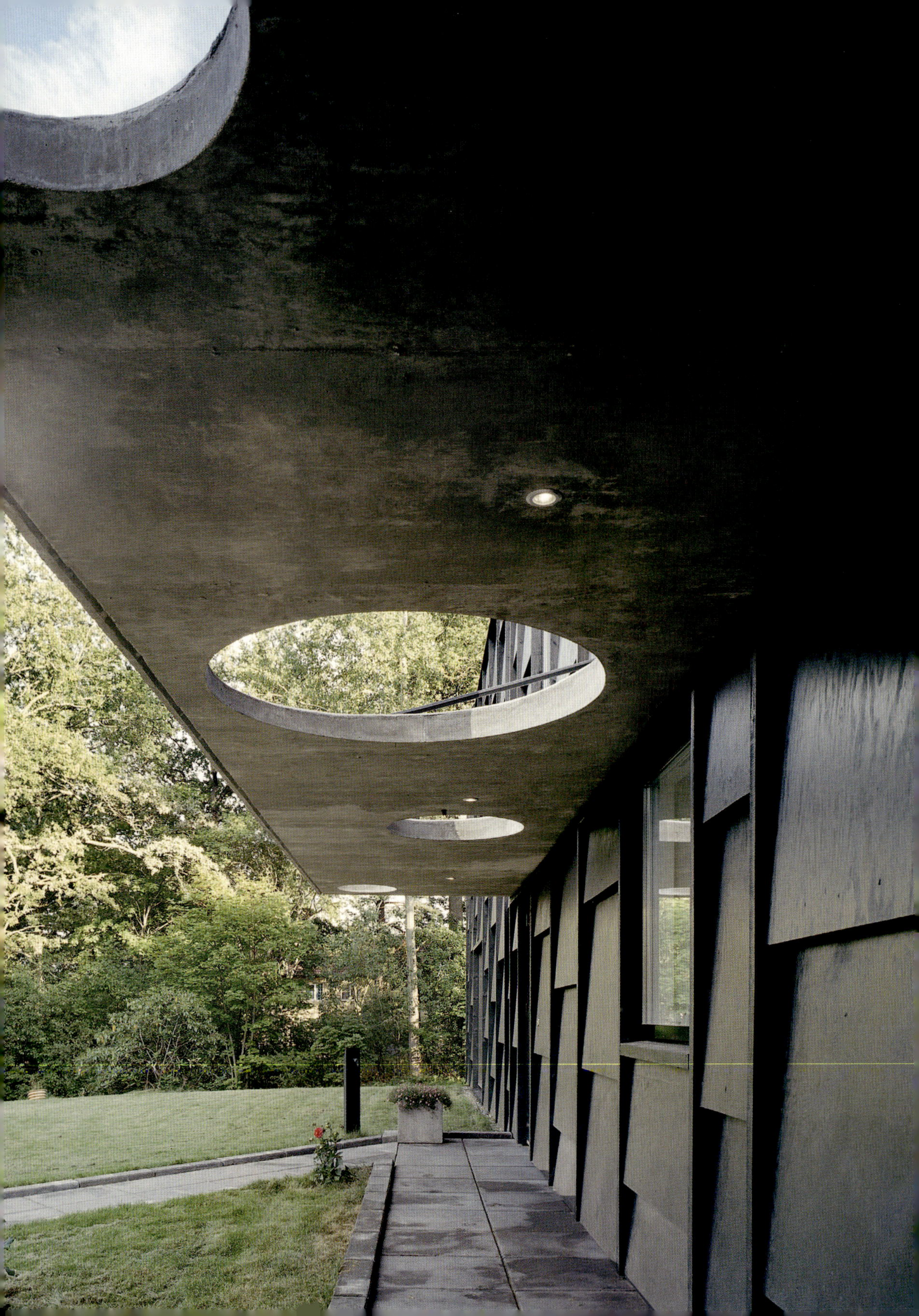

THAM & VIDEGÅRD HANSSON ARKITEKTER | STOCKHOLM
House K
Stocksund, Sweden | 2005

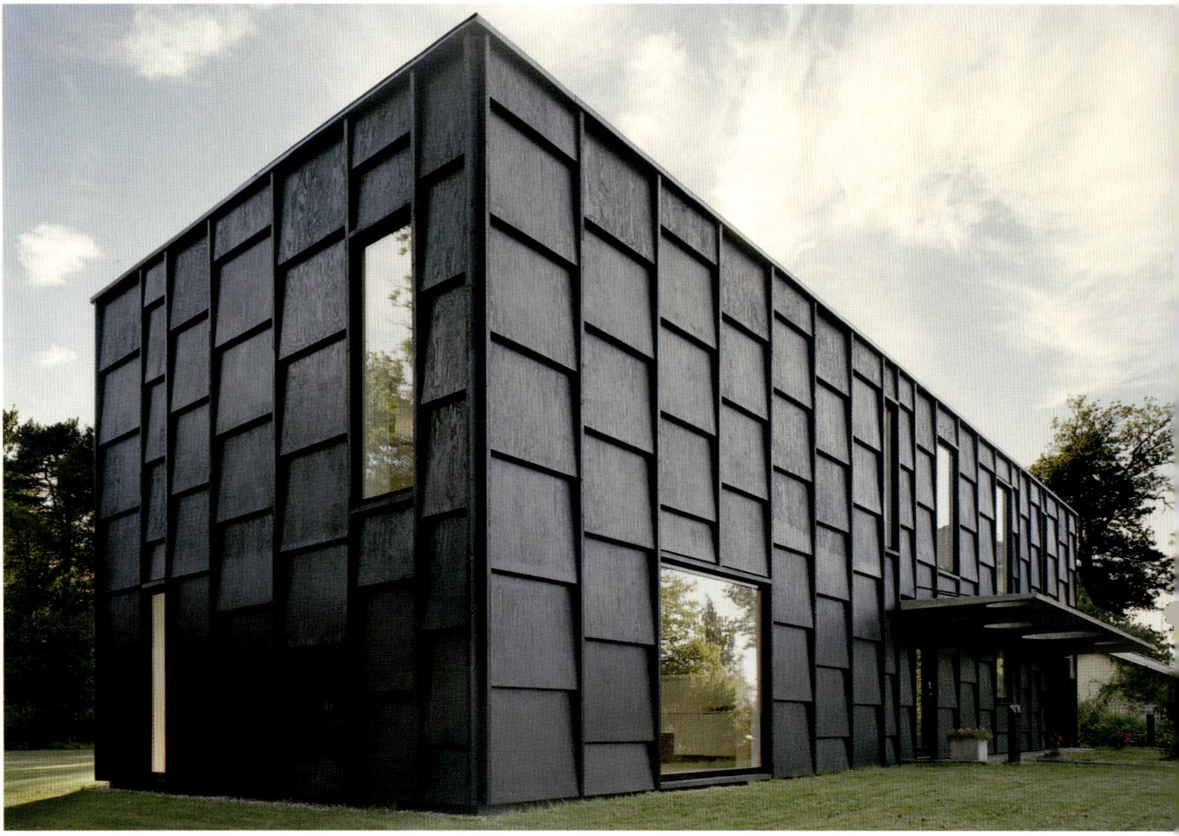

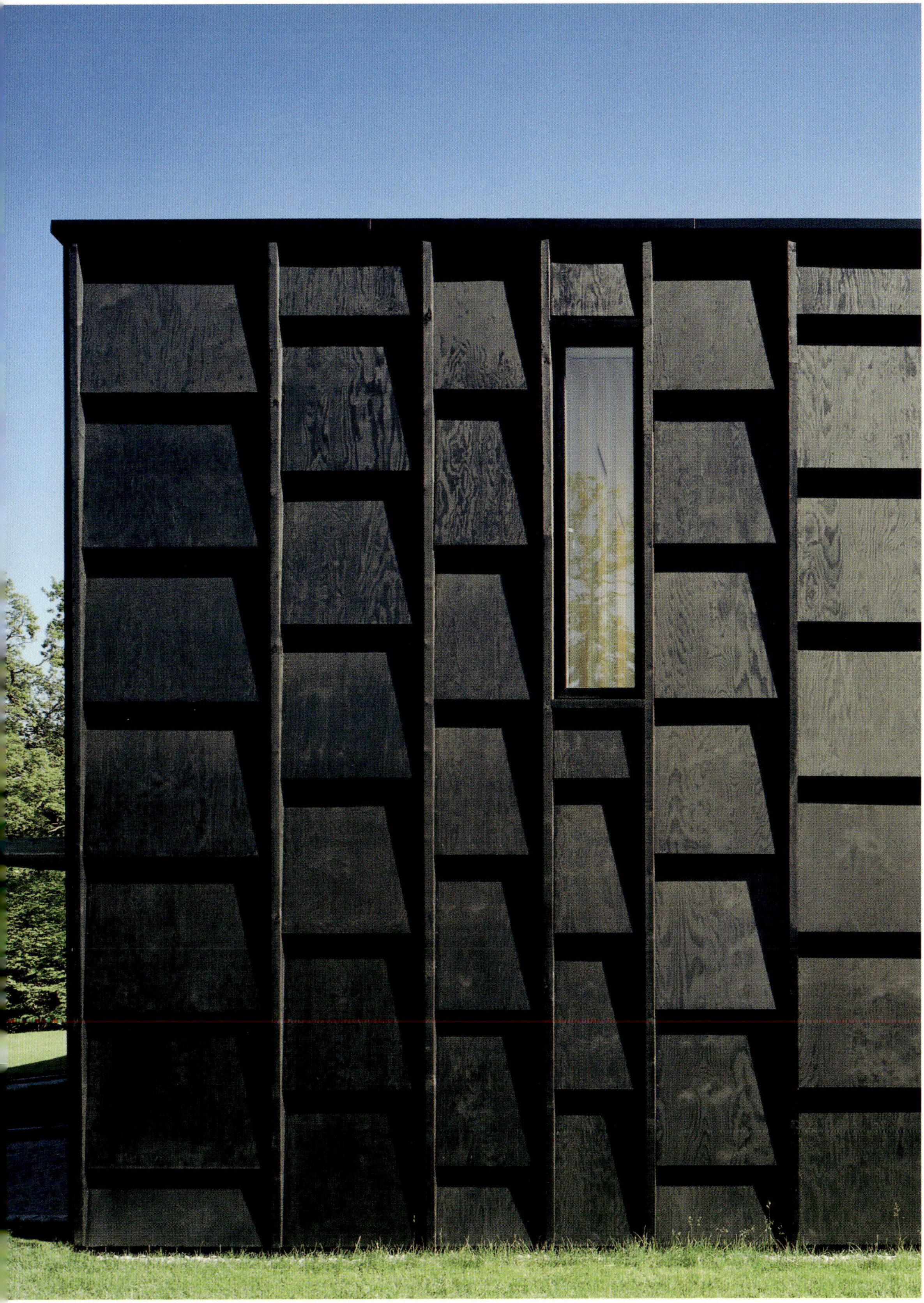

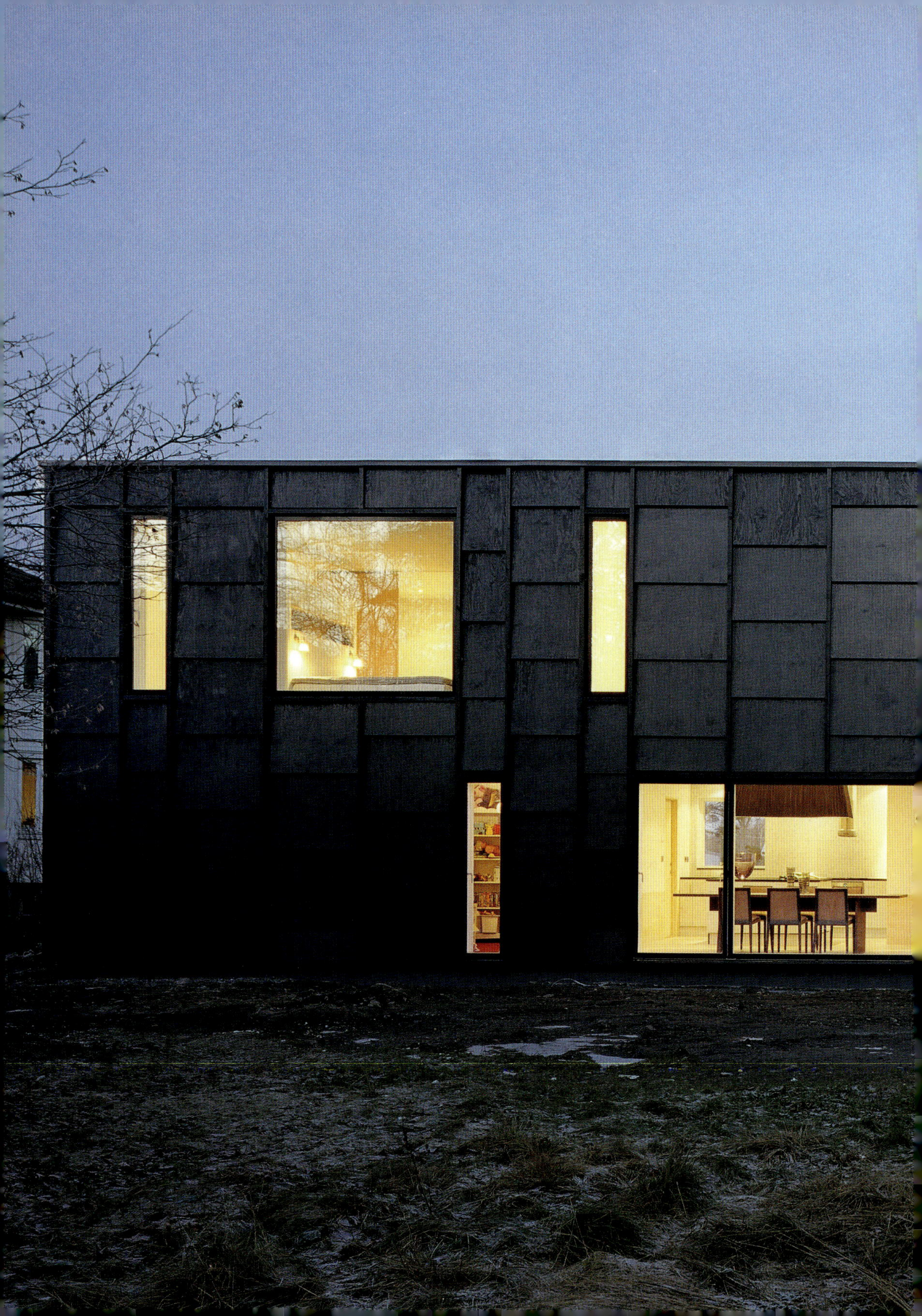

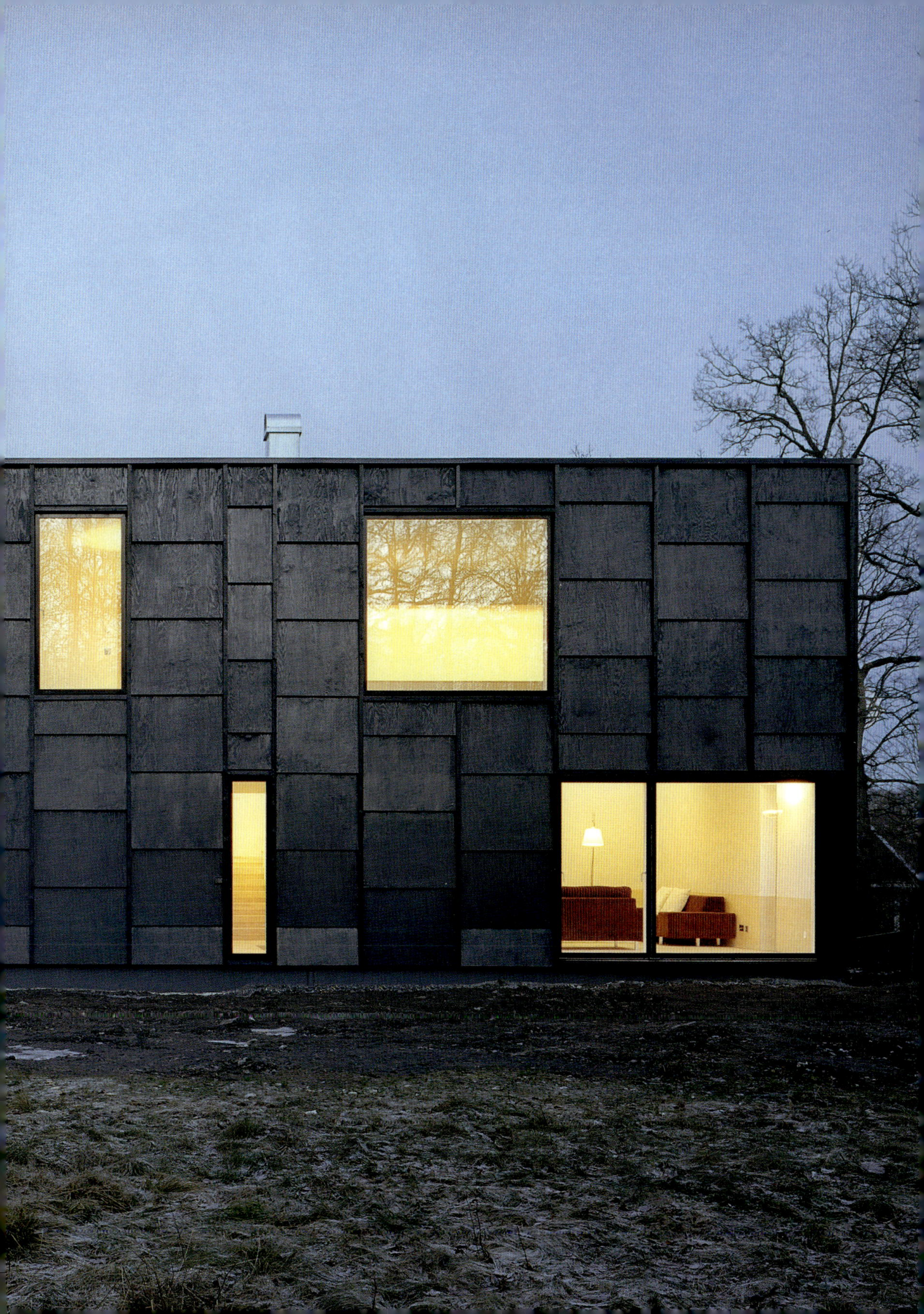

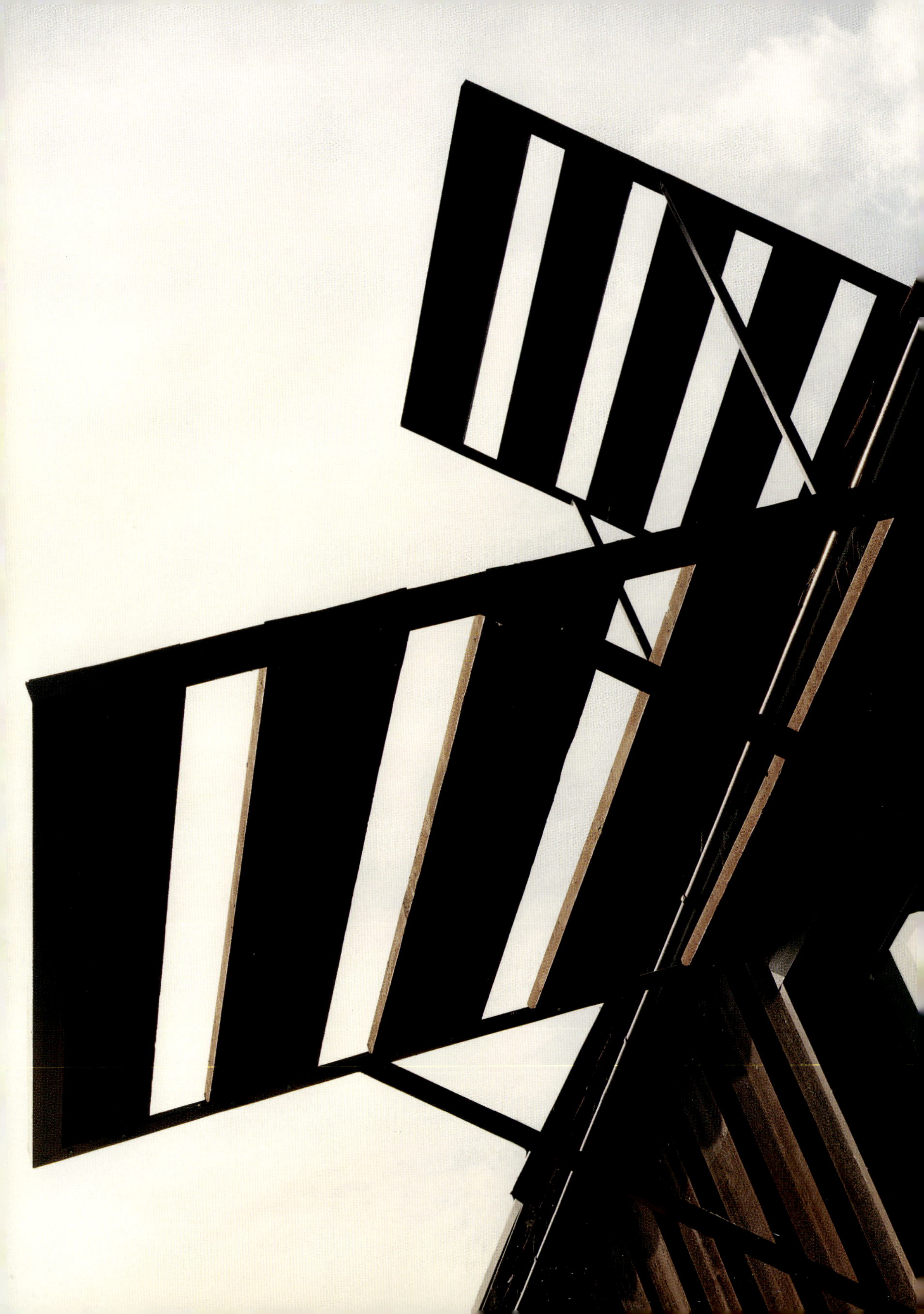

THAM & VIDEGÅRD HANSSON ARKITEKTER | STOCKHOLM
House Karlsson
Västerås, Sweden | 2002

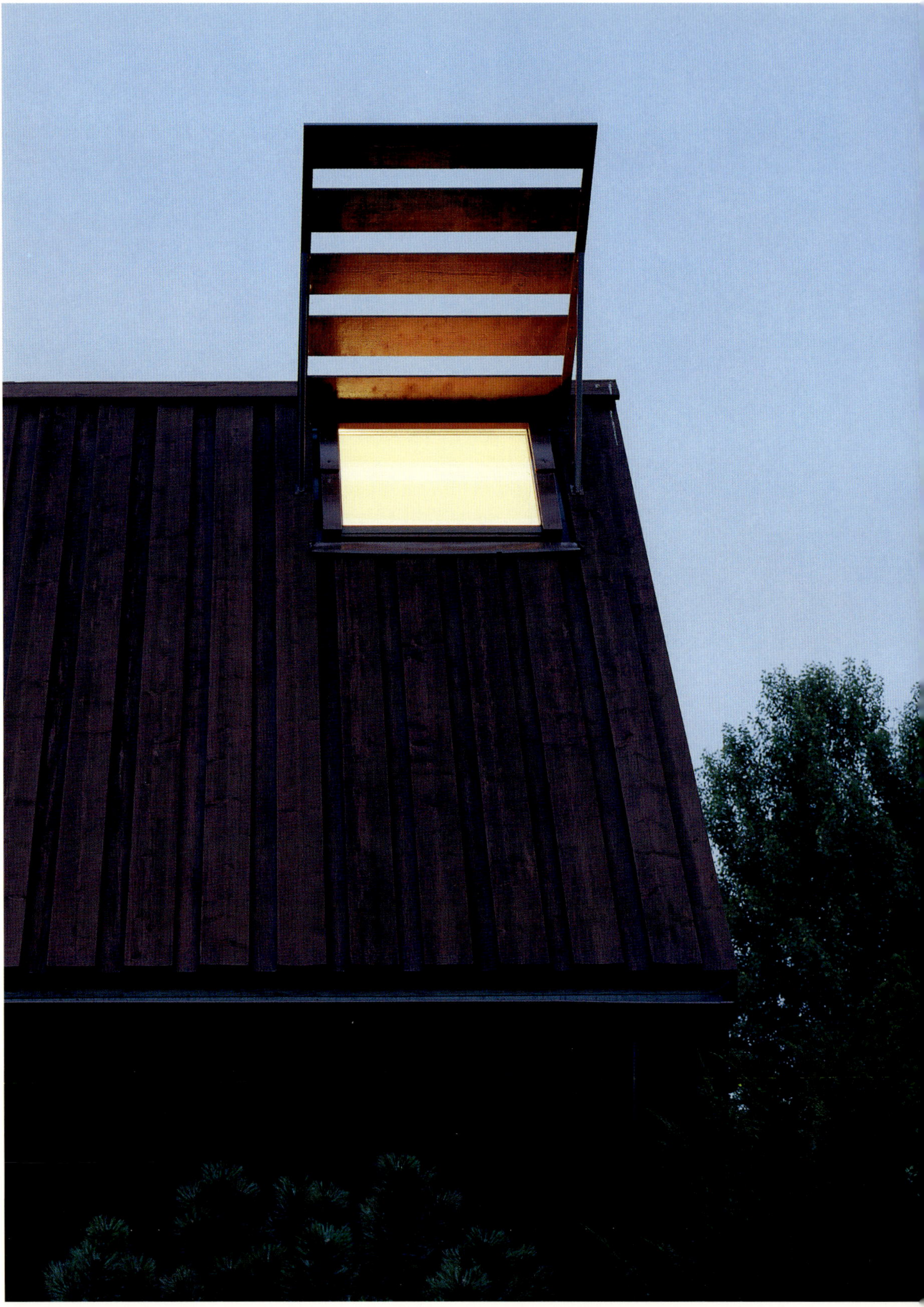

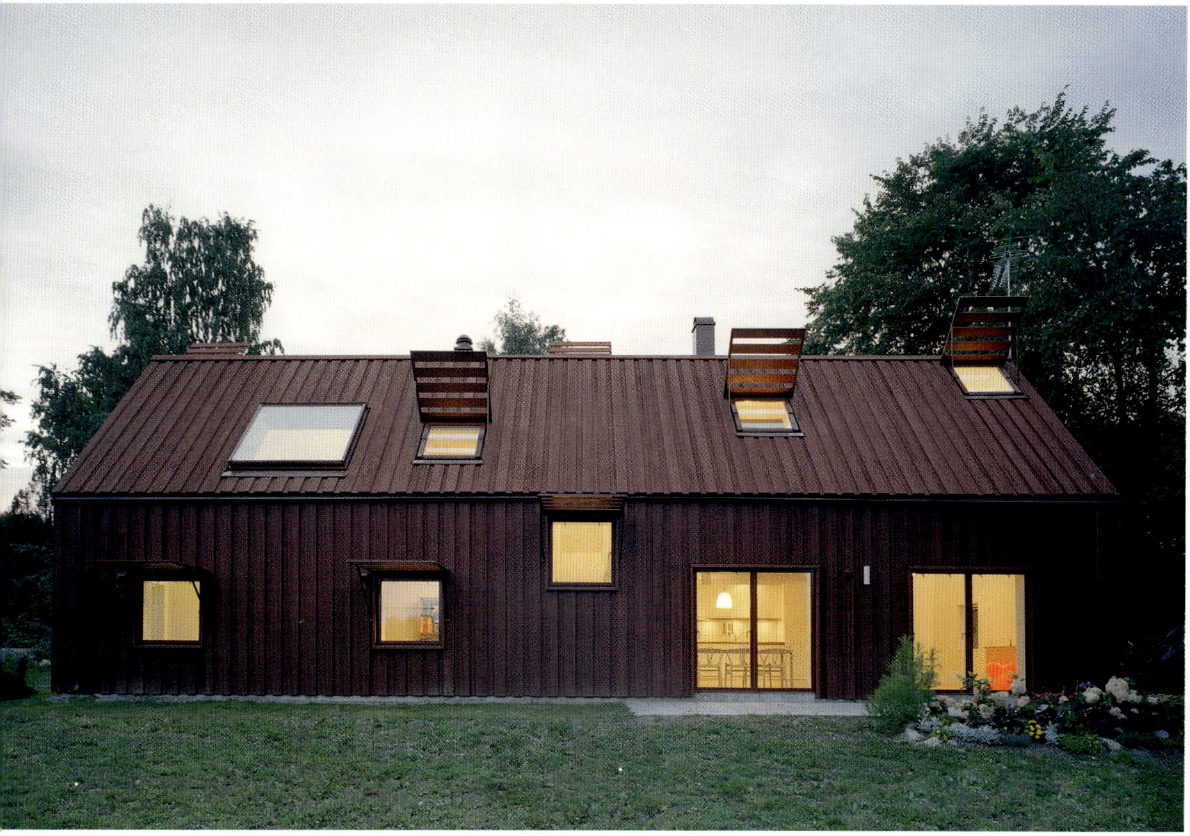

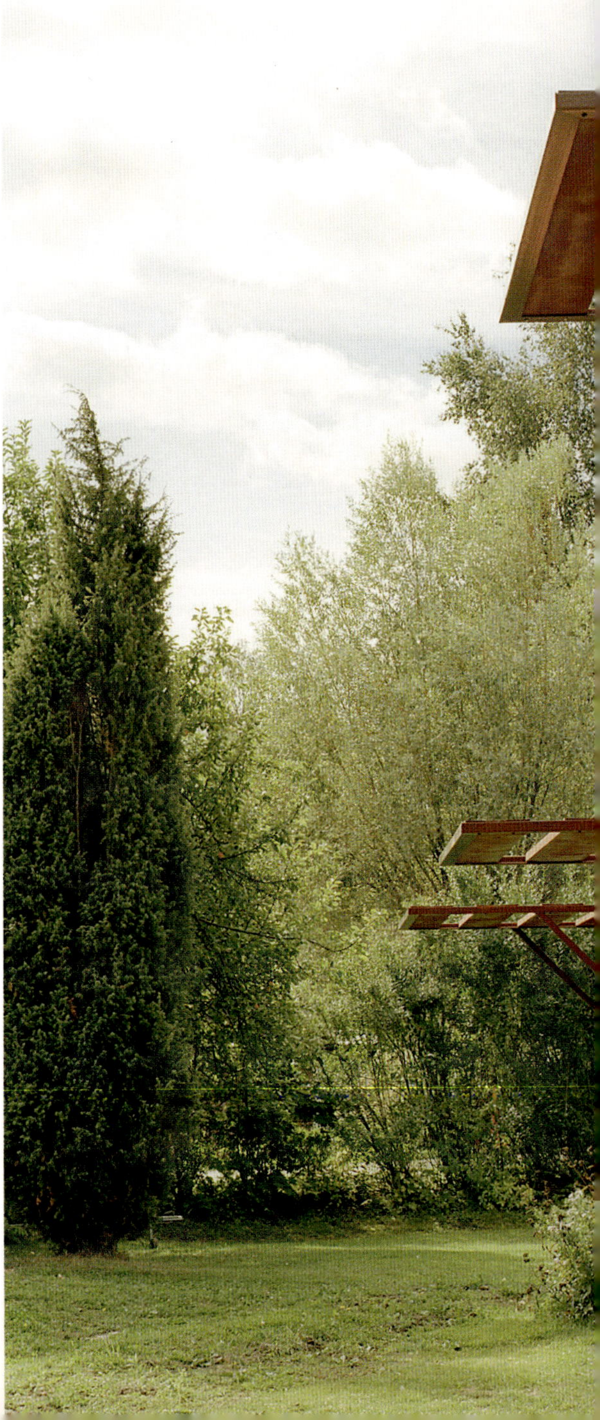

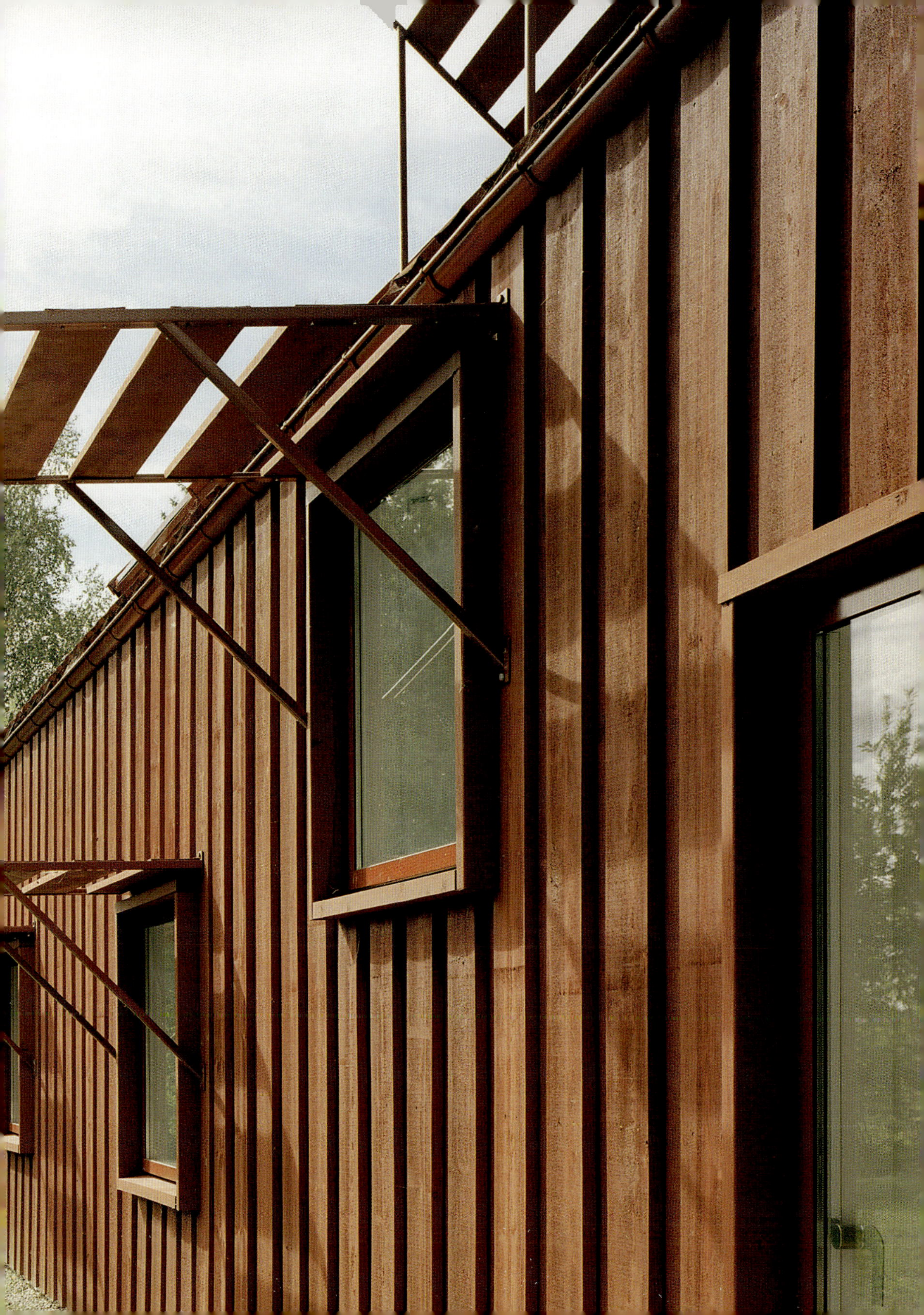

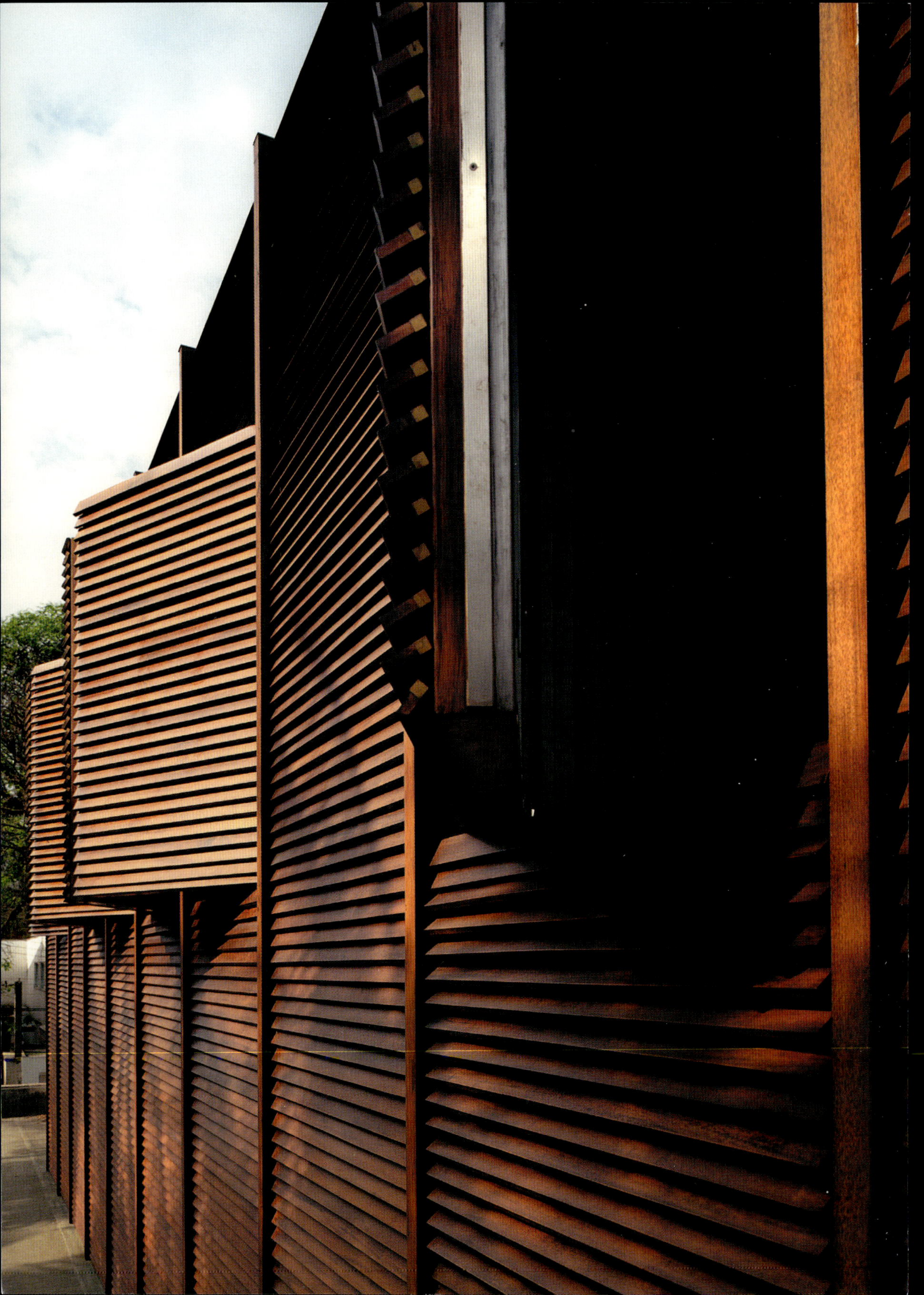

ISAY WEINFELD ARQUITETURA | SÃO PAULO
Casa Marrom
São Paulo, Brasil | 2004

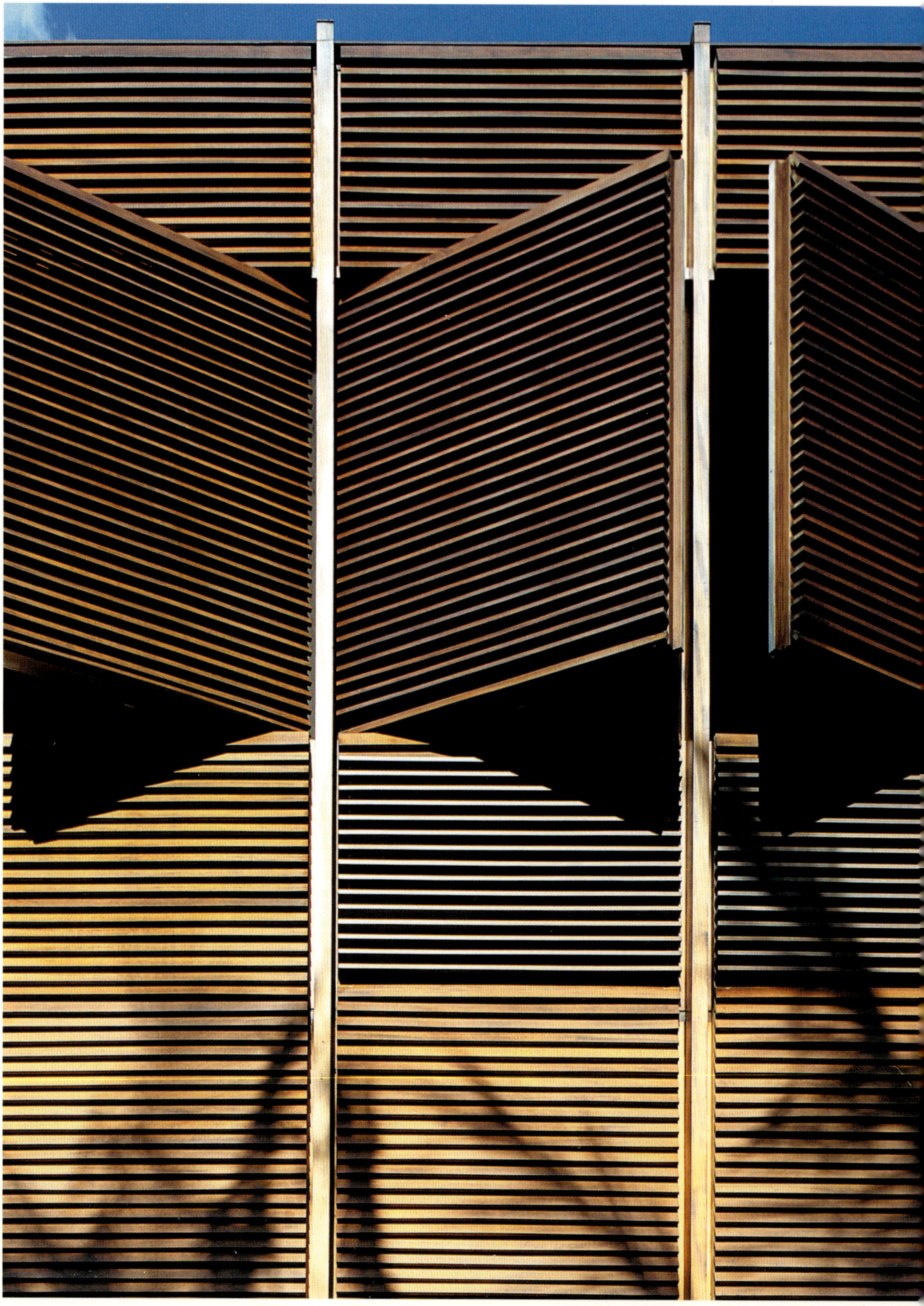

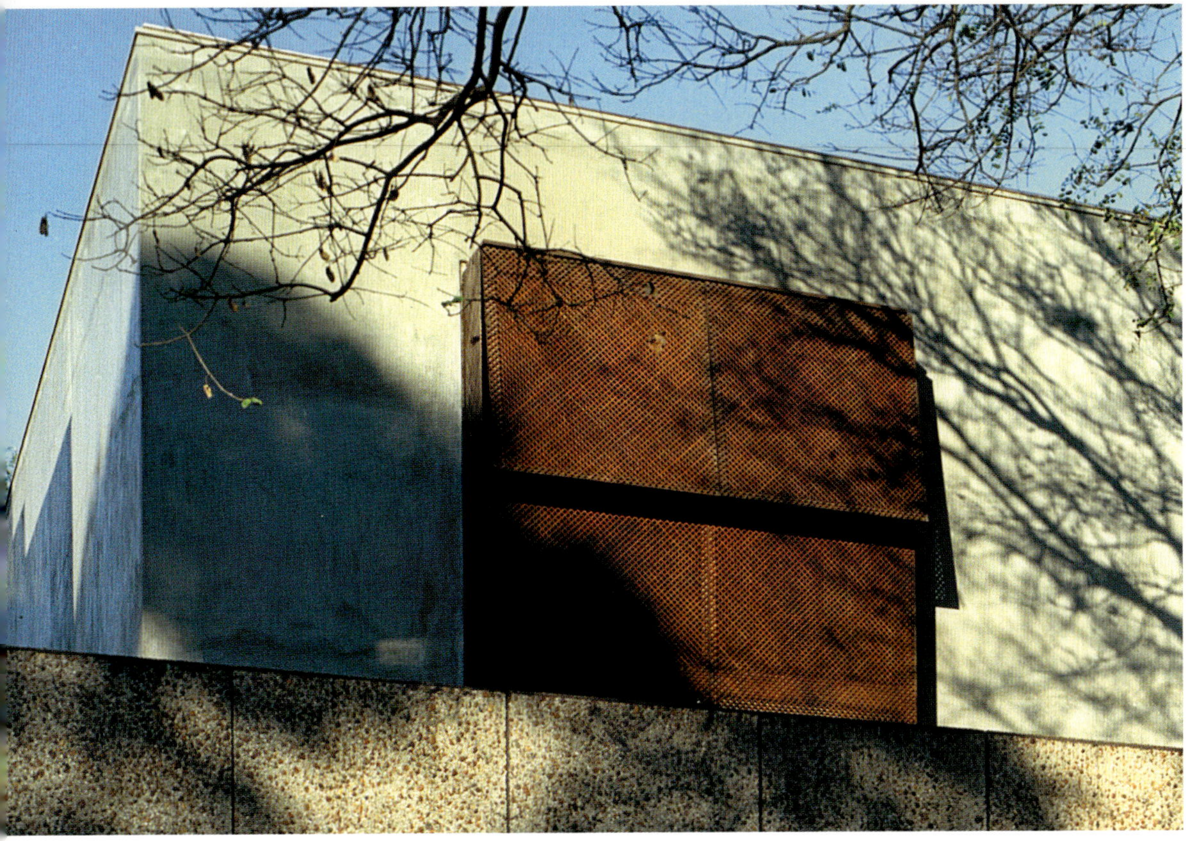

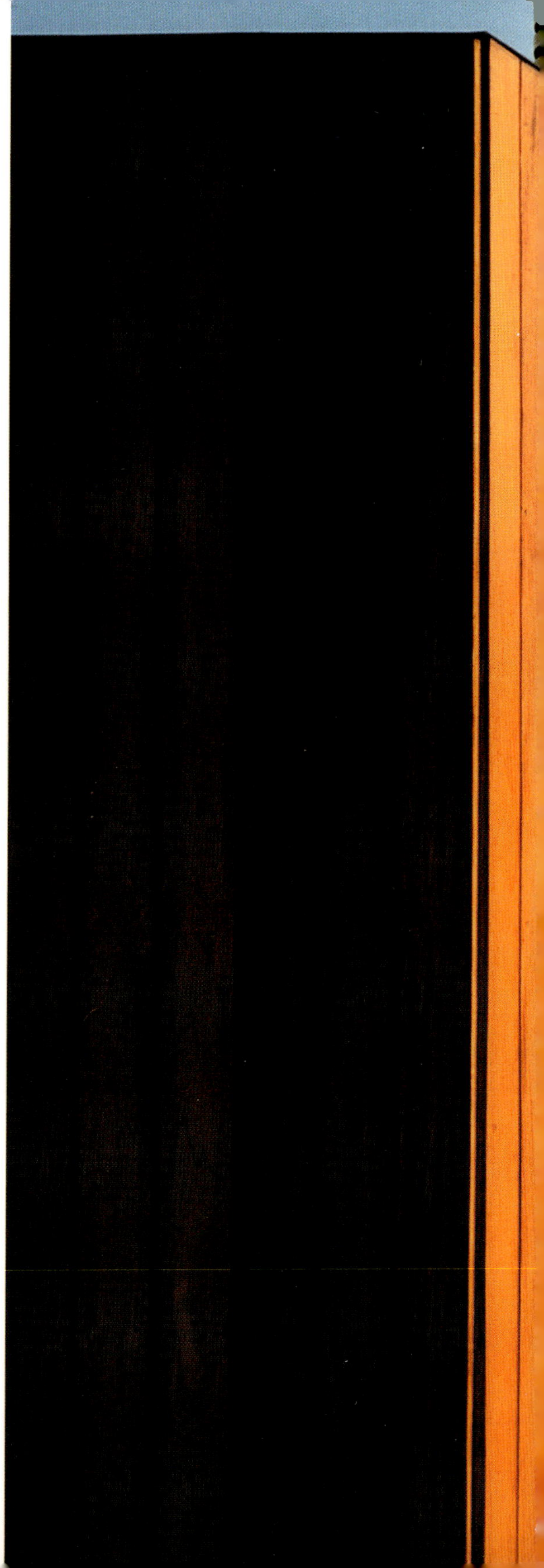

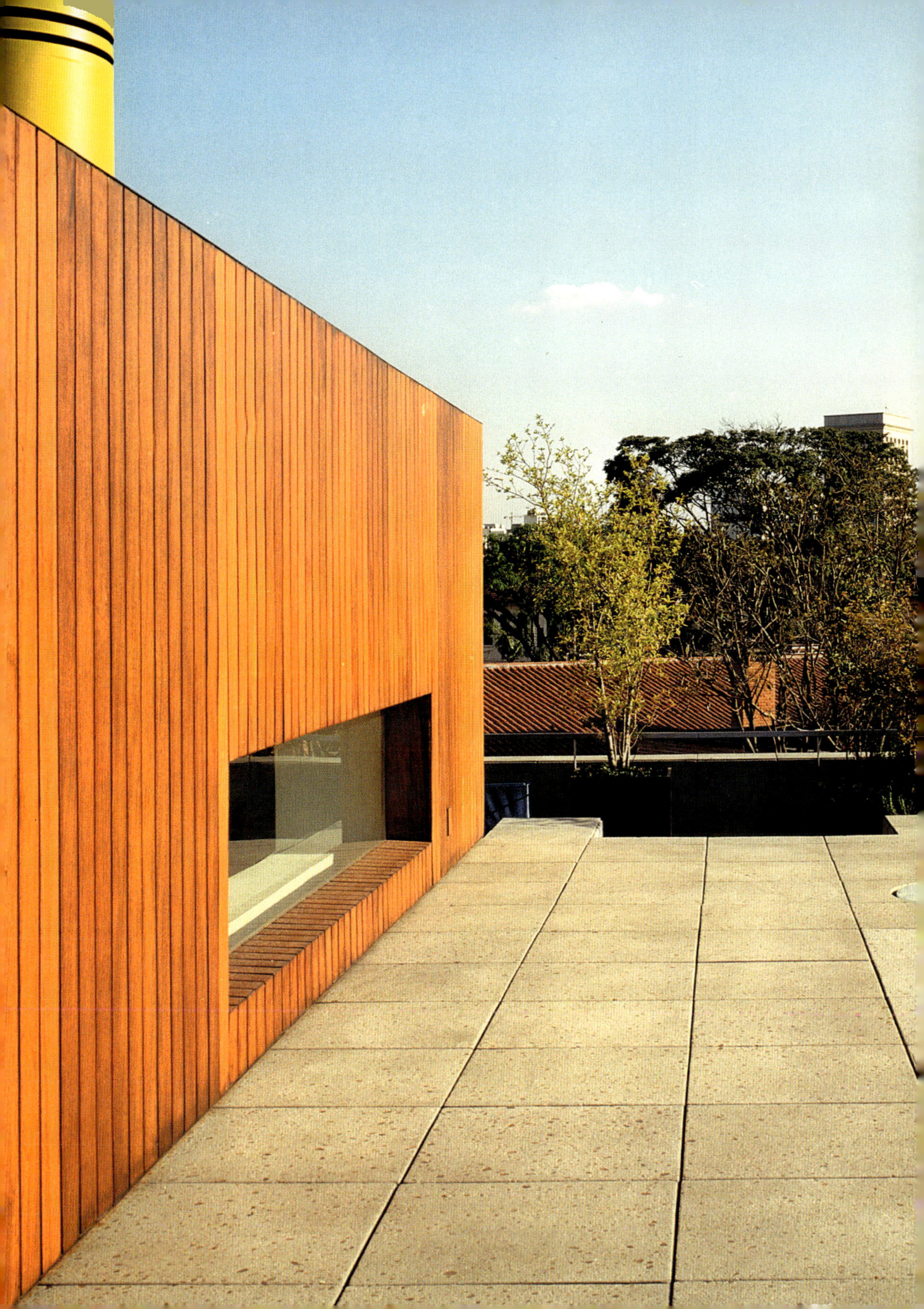

INDEX

A69 – Architects, Boris Redčenkov, Prokop Tomášek, Jaroslav Wertig | Cheb, Prague
www.a69.cz
Photos: Ester Havlová 16

Miquel Adria, Isaac Broid, Michel Rojkind | Mexico City
Photos: Luis Gordoa, Lourdes Grobet 22

Aldinger & Aldinger | Stuttgart
www.aldingerarchitekten.de
Photos: Katharina Feuer 26

arge Weingart Bauer Bracke Hoffmann Architekten | Erfurt
www.bauerarchitekten.de
Photos: Courtesy of arge w.b.b.h. architekten 32

Barclay & Crousse Architecture | Paris
www.barclaycrousse.com
Photos: Jean Pierre Crousse 38

Bearth + Deplazes Architekten | Chur, Zurich
www.bearth-deplazes.ch
Photos: Ralph Feiner 44

Behnisch & Partner | Stuttgart
www.behnisch.de
Photos: Christian Kandzia, Esslingen 50

Bernardo Bader | Dornbirn
www.bernardobader.com
Photos: Thomas Drexel, Friedberg/By 54

Bernd Kniess Architekten Stadtplaner | Cologne
www.berndkniess.net
Photos: Courtesy of campana, Michael Reisch, fvlr 60

Bevk Perovic Architects | Ljubljana
www.bevkperovic.com
Photos: Matevz Paternoster 68

Aldo Celoria | Balerna
Photos: Milo Keller 74

Central de Arquitectura | Mexico City
www.centraldearquitectura.com
Photos: Luis Gordoa 78

Moongyu Choi + ga.a architects | Seoul
www.gaa-arch.com
Photos: Courtesy of ga.a architects, Kim Yong Kwan 82, 88

Christoph Mäckler Architekten | Frankfurt
www.maeckler-architekten.de
All Photos: Christoph Lison 92, 98, 102, 108

Rafael de la Hoz | Madrid
www.rafaeldelahoz.com
Photos: Luis Asín 114

Degelo Architekten | Basel
www.degelo.net
Photos: Ruedi Walti 120

Dekleva Gregorič Arhitekti | Ljubljana
www.dekleva-gregoric.com
Photos: Matevz Paternoster 124

Dellekamp Arquitectos | Mexico City
www.dellekamparq.com
Photos: Courtesy of Dellekamp arquitectos 130

Max Dudler with Bernhard Meoller | Berlin
www.maxdudler.de
Photos: Stefan Müller 136

Max Dudler with Nina Barthélémy | Berlin
www.maxdudler.de
Photos: Stefan Müller 142

Enno Schneider Architekten | Berlin, Detmold
www.ennoschneider-architekten.de
Photos: Jochen Stüber 146

Feilden Clegg Bradley Architects LLP | London
www.feildenclegg.com
Photos: Courtesy of Feilden Clegg Bradley Architects 152

FKL architects | Dublin
www.fklarchitects.com
Photos: Paul Tierney 156

Franken Architekten | Frankfurt
www.franken-architekten.de
Photos: Die Photodesigner, Ken Schluchtmann 160

Andreas Fuhrimann, Gabrielle Hächler | Zurich
www.afgh.ch
Photos: Valentin Jeck 164
Photos: Courtesy of Fuhrimann & Hächler 172

glöggler prevosti architektur | Zug
www.gparchitektur.ch
Photos: Courtesy of glögger prevosti architektur 178
Hannes Henz Architekturfotograf, Zürich 184, 190

Peter Haimerl, studio für architektur | Munich
www.urbnet.de
Photos: Florian Holzherr 198

Hascher Jehle Architektur | Berlin
www.hascherjehle.de
Photos: Svenja Bockhop, Berlin; Sebastian Jehle, Berlin 204

HENN Architekten | Berlin, Munich
www.henn.com
Photos: Courtesy of Volkswagen 212

**Hofmann Keicher Ring Architekten
+ Reinhard May** | Würzburg
www.hofmann-keicher-ring.de
Photos: Gerhard Hagen, Bamberg 218

Ingenhoven Architekten | Düsseldorf
www.ingenhovenundpartner.de
Photos: H. G. Esch, Hennef, Holger Knauf/Düsseldorf 224

Johnston Marklee & Associates | LA, Venice
www.johnstonmarklee.com
Photos: Eric Staudenmaier Photography 232

Andreas Kanzian | Graz, Bochum
www.andreaskanzian.at
Photos: Walter Luttenberger 238

Ken Architekten | Baden, Zurich
www.ken-architekten.ch
Photos: Hannes Henz Architekturfotograf, Zürich 244

Kengo Kuma & Associates | Tokyo
www.kkaa.co.jp
Photos: Mitsumasa Futjisuka 250
Photos: Daici Ano 254

Marcio Kogan | Sao Paolo
www.marciokogan.com.br
Photos: Arnaldo Pappalardo 258

KSP Engel und Zimmermann | Frankfurt
www.ksp-architekten.de
Photos: Achim Reissner 262

Kuba, Pilař Architekti | Brno
www.arch.cz/kuba.pilar/
Photos: Courtesy of Kuba, Pilař Architekti 266

Lab Architecture Studio | Melbourne
www.labarchitecture.com
Photos: Sabina Marreiros,
Courtesy of Federation Square 270

Léon Wohlhage Wernik Architekten | Berlin
www.leonwohlhagewernik.de
Photos: Gavin Jackson 276

Mansilla Tuñón | Madrid
www.mansilla-tunon.com
Photos: Courtesy of Musac 282

Irie Masayuki | Tokyo
www.irie.arch.waseda.ac.jp
Photos: Kazuhiko Washio 286

**Jaime Varon, Abraham Metta, Alex Metta
Migdal Arquitectos** | Mexico City
www.migdal.com.mx
Photos: Paul Czitrom 290

Miyahara architect office | Tokyo
www.cam.hi-ho.ne.jp/y-ryutaro/arch/index_e.html
Photos: Teruo Miyahara 296

Neil M. Denari Architects, nmda | Los Angeles
www.nmda-inc.com
Photos: Courtesy of NMDA 300

Nike Fiedler Architekten | Stuttgart
Photos: Fredric Arnold 306

oehler faigle Archkom | Bretten
www.archkom.de
Photos: Courtesy of oehler faigle archkom 314

Valerio Olgiati | Chur
www.olgiati.net
Photos: Archive Olgiati 318

Ostoshenka Architects | Moscow
Photos: A. Naroditsky 324

Procter:Rihl | London
www.procter-rihl.com
Photos: Marcelo Nunes, Sue Barr/heathcotebarr.org 330

Raumzeit | Berlin
www.raumzeit.org
Photos: Werner Huthmacher 336

Rojkind Arquitectos | Mexico City
www.rojkindarquitectos.com
Photos: Jaime Navarro 342

Sauerbruch Hutton Architekten | Berlin
www.sauerbruchhutton.com
All Photos: Gavin Jackson 348, 352

Tham & Videgard Hansson Arkitekter | Stockholm
www.thamvidegardhansson.se
All Photos: Åke Eson Lindman 358, 364, 370

Isay Weinfeld Arquitetura | São Paulo
www.isayweinfeld.com
Photos: Christiano Mascaro 376

© 2007 daab
cologne   london   new york

published and distributed worldwide by
daab gmbh
friesenstr. 50
d - 50670 köln

p + 49 - 221 - 913 927 0
f + 49 - 221 - 913 927 20

mail@daab-online.com
www.daab-online.com

publisher ralf daab
rdaab@daab-online.com

creative director feyyaz
mail@feyyaz.com

editorial project by fusion publishing gmbh stuttgart . los angeles
© 2007 fusion publishing, www.fusion-publishing.com

editor jons messedat
editorial coordination katharina feuer

layout katharina feuer
imaging jan hausberg, martin herterich

photo credits
coverphoto christoph lison
introduction page 7 åke eson lindman, 9 archive olgiati, 11 svenja bockhop, berlin;
sebastian jehle, berlin, 13 christoph lison, 15 ralph feiner
text introduction jons messedat
translations by ade team übersetzungen/stuttgart, claudia ade
english translation claudia ade
french translation dominique santoro
spanish translation sara costa-sengera
italian translation jacqueline rizzo

printed in italy
www.zanardi.it

isbn 978 - 3 - 937718 - 69 - 9

all rights reserved.
no part of this publication may be reproduced in any manner.